C0-AZV-884

Volume 1

ACCOUNTANT'S ENCYCLOPEDIA, REVISED

Volume 1

ACCOUNTANT'S ENCYCLOPEDIA, REVISED

The Prentice-Hall Editorial Staff

Jerome K. Pescow, General Editor

Prentice-Hall, Inc. Englewood Cliffs, N.J.

Prentice-Hall International, Inc., *London*
Prentice-Hall of Australia, Pty. Ltd., *Sydney*
Prentice-Hall of Canada, Ltd., *Toronto*
Prentice-Hall of India Private Ltd., *New Delhi*
Prentice-Hall of Japan, Inc., *Tokyo*
Prentice-Hall of Southeast Asia Pte. Ltd., *Singapore*
Whitehall Books, Ltd., *Wellington, New Zealand*

This publication is designed to provide accurate and authoritative information in regard to the subject matter covered. It is sold with the understanding that the publisher is not engaged in rendering legal, accounting or other professional service. If legal advice or other expert assistance is required, the services of a competent professional person should be sought.

—From the Declaration of Principles jointly adopted by a Committee of the American Bar Association and a Committee of Publishers and Associations.

Library of Congress Cataloging in Publication Data

Prentice-Hall, Inc.
Accountant's encyclopedia, revised

Edition for 1962 published under title:
Accountant's encyclopedia.
Includes index.
1. Accounting—Addresses, essays, lectures.
I. Pescow, Jerome K. II. Title.
HF5635.P93 1981 657 80-11391
ISBN O-13-001305-6

Printed in the United States of America

Board of Contributors

The editor wishes to extend his sincere appreciation to the following who generously contributed to this and the prior edition of the ACCOUNTANT'S ENCYCLOPEDIA.

MARVIN BACHMAN, Certified Public Accountant; Assistant Professor of Accounting, Malloy College, Rockville Centre, New York

WILLIAM J. BADECKER, Certified Public Accountant; National Director of SEC Services, Main Hurdman & Cranstoun, New York

JAMES W. BAKER, Ph.D., Certified Public Accountant

NORTON M. BEDFORD, Ph.D., Certified Public Accountant; Arthur Young Distinguished Professor and Head of Department of Accountancy, University of Illinois

BERTRAND J. BELDA, Certified Public Accountant; Executive in Residence, John Carroll University School of Business, Ohio

LEOPOLD A. BERNSTEIN, Ph.D., Certified Public Accountant; Professor of Accounting, Baruch College, City University of New York

MAX BLOCK, Certified Public Accountant

HARRY G. BROWN, Certified Public Accountant

JAMES A. CASHIN, Certified Public Accountant; Professor Emeritus of Accounting, Hofstra University, New York

FRANCIS C. DYKEMAN, Certified Public Accountant

FREDERICK M. EISNER, Certified Public Accountant

FRANK J. FABOZZI, Ph.D., Chartered Financial Analyst; Associate Professor of Finance and Chairman of the Department of Banking and Finance, Hofstra University, New York

SAUL FELDMAN, Certified Public Accountant; Associate Professor of Accounting Emeritus, Hofstra University, New York

Melvin S. Ganskow

Hubert B. Hall, Certified Public Accountant

Robert E. Hammond, Certified Public Accountant; Partner, Ernst & Whinney, New York

Herbert Heaton, Ph.D., Certified Public Accountant; Comptroller, Rockefeller Foundation, New York; President, Support Services Alliance, Inc.

Charles B. Hellerson, Certified Public Accountant; Technical Advisor to the National Accounting and Auditing Director, Main Hurdman & Cranstoun, New York

J. H. Hennesy, Jr., Certified Public Accountant; Management Consultant, Ormond Beach, Florida

John H. Hindle, Ed.D.

Richard H. Homburger, J.D., Certified Public Accountant; Professor Emeritus of Accounting, Wichita State University, Wichita, Kansas

George E. Hunt, Jr., Certified Public Accountant; Clifton, Gunderson & Co., Champaign, Illinois

Bernard B. Isaacson, Certified Public Accountant

Miriam E. Katowitz, Certified Public Accountant; Vice President, Republic National Bank of New York

Robert L. Kelly, Certified Public Accountant; Deloitte, Haskins & Sells, New York

Thomas E. King, Ph.D.; Associate Professor of Accounting, Southern Illinois University at Edwardsville, Illinois

Robert A. Leitch, Ph.D., Certified Public Accountant; Associate Professor of Accounting & Business Law, University of Georgia

Valdean C. Lembke, Ph.D.; Associate Professor of Accounting, The University of Iowa

Henry T. Maschal, Certified Public Accountant

Joseph A. Mauriello, Ph.D., Certified Public Accountant; Professor of Accounting Graduate School of Business Administration, New York University

William N. McNairn, Certified Public Accountant

Shane Moriarity, Ph.D.; Assistant Professor of Business Administration, The University of Kansas

John W. Nuxall, Certified Public Accountant; Partner, Peat, Marwick, Mitchell & Co., New York

Jerome K. Pescow, Certified Public Accountant; Professor of Accounting, Hofstra University, New York; Partner, J. K. Pescow & Co., Roslyn Heights, New York

Robert W. Pivik, Certified Public Accountant; Deloitte, Haskins & Sells, New York

Arthur J. Radin, Certified Public Accountant; Partner, Rose, Feldman, Radin, Pavone & Skehan, New York

Joseph J. Schultz, Jr., Ph.D., Certified Public Accountant; Assistant Professor of Accounting, University of Illinois

Alvin M. Silver, Eng. Sc.D.; Professor of Management and Administrative Computer Systems, Hofstra University, New York; Partner, A. Silver Associates: Management Consultants, East Northport, New York

Milton Simon, Certified Public Accountant; Associate Professor of Accounting, School of Professional Accountancy, C. W. Post Center, Long Island University; Partner, Zwicker & Simon, Garden City, New York

William H. Speakman, 3rd, Certified Public Accountant; Main Hurdman & Cranstoun, Philadelphia, Pennsylvania

Howard Stettler, Certified Public Accountant; Professor of Business Administration, The University of Kansas

John F. Wagner, Certified Public Accountant; Partner, Ernst & Whinney, New York

Lawrence M. Walsh, Certified Public Accountant; Deloitte, Haskins & Sells, Miami, Florida

Robert A. Wofsey, Certified Public Accountant; Director, Arthur Young & Co., New York

L. Milton Woods, Ph.D., Certified Public Accountant; Briarcliff Manor, New York

Percy Yeargan, Ph.D., Certified Public Accountant; Professor of Accounting, University of Alabama in Birmingham

Contents

Volume 1

Volume 1

ACCOUNTANT'S ENCYCLOPEDIA, REVISED

1

Problem Areas of Financial Accounting

CONTENTS

1

Problem Areas of Financial Accounting

Norton M. Bedford, Ph.D., CPA, and Joseph J. Schultz, Jr.

The increase of the complexity and interrelatedness of economic activity in recent years has created both opportunities and problems for the accounting profession. Opportunities have arisen as the importance and need for reliable financial information has increased at an even greater rate. But the expansion has created new problems, sharpened old ones, and required answers that previously could be delayed. The major reason for these problems is the ever-increasing pace of technology—automation and the induced social value changes—though other factors are also involved.

What steps must the accountant take to stay abreast of these new developments? The answer to this question requires, first of all, an analysis of the problems of developing and applying the basic concepts underlying accounting—its assumptions, principles, rules, conventions and standards. With an understanding of these, at a conceptual level, the accountant will be better equipped to find solutions to the *practical problems* facing him and the profession.

Hence, this chapter first analyzes the conceptual problems. Then it introduces various currently vital practical problems such as accounting for price changes, forecasts, liquidity disclosure, leases, intangibles, foreign operations, and employee benefits. Finally, it suggests possible solutions for these and other pressing problems through the application of the concepts previously discussed.

With a background acquired from the discussion of these problems, the reader will be better able to evaluate and make use of the techniques, methods and approaches to the various areas of accounting discussed in later chapters of this encyclopedia. For example, the discussion of the problem of inventory pricing in this chapter will aid the reader in securing maximum comprehension of the INVENTORY AND INVENTORY VALUATION chapter. Similarly, the section on foreign operations and exchange is extremely valuable when read in conjunction with the BUSINESS COMBINATIONS AND CONSOLIDATED FINANCIAL STATEMENTS chapter.

► NOTE: This discussion will not consider non-technical problems, such as education for the profession, the structure of the profession, management of an office, developing employees and other issues. These areas are covered in other chapters of the book.

THE CONCEPTUAL PROBLEMS

Our discussion of the conceptual problems is broken down under:

1. Objectives and assumptions.
2. Principles and definitions.
3. Guidelines and rules.
4. Policies.
5. Standards.

ACCOUNTING ASSUMPTIONS

The general objective of accounting is to provide quantitative information for evaluating performance and decision making. To do so, various assumptions are necessary. An accounting assumption is that it represents a broad, basic proposition from which a series of logical conclusions may be derived. These conclusions should result in accounting principles and procedures which can be applied to specific situations.

The fundamental issue facing the accounting profession today is the need for a conceptual framework of the underlying concepts, objectives and assumptions upon which the entire accounting discipline rests. Concommitant with this is the need to develop guidelines to be used in reducing the conceptual framework and associated assumptions to specific principles and procedures. In recent years, these needs have received much attention from accountants and non-accountants at all levels. The Financial Accounting Standards Board (FASB) is gradually developing a conceptual framework for financial reporting from which it intends to derive various specific standards governing rules and procedures. The Securities and Exchange Commission (SEC), Congressional leaders, all types of accounting organizations and institutes, and governmental agencies have all directed their attention to the objectives and assumptions of accounting to provide general guidance to the function of accounting in society, and specific direction so the profession can pursue its objectives.

Disclosure assumptions. Since accounting is concerned with economic activity, disclosure assumptions in this group might relate to the accepted economic view of the nature of man and his motives and desires in carrying out economic activity. Obviously, it is difficult to analyze and develop such assumptions to a point where they can be applied to specific problems of the accounting profession.

► EXAMPLE: The proposition that man is motivated, subject to certain restrictions, to acquire maximum income, might well represent an assumption of accounting. If this assumption is accepted, it means that the accounting function should include reporting the income of a business entity. Such a report would reflect the effectiveness with which the business attained its income objective.

There is no reason to assume that all economic units are motivated solely by the income maximization objective. Some units may wish to maximize cash flow, alleviate risk, or contribute to social well-being. Also, the precise nature of the income that appears to motivate economic activity is not readily discernible. Further refinement on identifying the appropriate assumptions and their relationship is necessary. Some common assumptions are necessary in order for financial statements to be useful.

Operating assumptions. The primary objective of the accounting function is to (1) measure economic activity, and (2) communicate the results of this measurement to interested parties. Thus, the assumptions in this group underlie the measurement process and the communication process. These assumptions are practical in nature as they establish the framework used in financial statements. Even though some economic units may have different disclosure assumptions, each is considerably constrained in its financial accounting by these operating assumptions.

Measurement assumptions. Three assumptions are generally accepted in the measurement area. They appear to have been adopted by the profession as a result of certain practical problems that had to be answered. Hence they might be said to be expedient, rather than absolute, solutions.

These three measurement assumptions are:

1. Measuring unit.
2. Entity.
3. Going concern.

► NOTE: Some authorities would also include as assumptions such general principles as (a) the matching of costs and revenues, and (b) the requirement of objectivity before measurement is appropriate. Actually, these principles are more in the nature of general rules for measurement rather than underlying measurement assumptions.

1. *Measuring unit.* The first measurement assumption concerns the unit to be used in measuring the broad area of economic activity. Without a homogeneous measuring unit, it would be impossible, for example, to compare a company producing three thousand units of item "A" with a company producing three thousand units of item "B." The assumption that the appropriate

measuring unit is a monetary one does establish a universal measuring unit, thereby providing a basis for such value comparisons.

There is no conclusive evidence that the monetary unit assumption is the most appropriate one for this purpose. Some of its limitations, such as those discussed in the section on the unstable monetary unit, are well-known.

2. *Entity.* The problem of placing a boundary around the area for which accounting reports are to be rendered has resulted in the establishment of the concept of an entity distinct from the individuals who make it up. The entity assumption provides guidance to the accountant in deciding to whom the report is to be directed and in selecting the scope of the activities to be included in the accounting report.

There has never been a sufficiently clear statement of the nature of the entity assumption. While the legal business entity is typically assumed to be the accounting entity, development in the area of consolidated statements and divisional reporting have forced recognition of the fact that the accounting entity cannot be so circumscribed. Since attempts to delineate the nature of the accounting entity have not been entirely satisfactory, divergent practices arise. Additional work is needed on this assumption.

► EXAMPLE: Movement toward greater emphasis on segment reporting presents problems of deciding how segments should be separated. Often, there are no separate legal entities associated with the different segments and costs common to all segments are not readily allocable.

3. *Going concern.* The final measurement assumption assumes that the business entity is a going concern. Unless liquidation and dissolution are apparent, the business entity is treated as if it will continue in existence.

This assumption apparently has its origin in the need for periodic financial reports. If periodic reporting on a monthly, quarterly, or annual basis was not demanded by the readers of financial reports, the going concern assumption would be unnecessary. It is only when reports based on a period of life less than the full life of the entity are required that it becomes necessary to make some assumptions regarding the future of that entity. Depreciation, accruals, and a variety of other problems would not have to be considered if one report covering the entire life of the business were all that was required.

► COMMENT: The need for periodic reports has been referred to as a problem of periodicity. Some authorities claim that it is the cause of most of the accounting problems in the financial area. Certainly, realization of income requires some of the most subjective judgments an accountant must make or review.

Communication assumptions. The basic assumption in the area of communications is that accounting data may be communicated to the public by means of a balance sheet, income statement, and a statement of changes in financial position.

The adequacy of this assumption is subject to question. Evidence of the inadequacy of the assumption is provided by the extensive use of footnotes, by the endeavor of companies to arrange lease contracts and indulge in other activities that will not be reflected fully in the accounting statements, and by the demand for other special reports suitable for particular problems. Although such action may keep the account balances from reflecting the event, evidence indicates that the market is not misled if adequate footnote disclosures are made.

The communication assumptions are somewhat nebulous and have seldom been expressed in accounting literature. Support for the basic assumption that economic activity may be satisfactorily revealed by a balance sheet, income statement and statement of changes in financial position, is provided by the widespread distribution and reliance on financial statements.

Some authorities question the need for the formulation and enunciation of communication assumptions. But, the growing interest in public reporting of accounting data indicates that accountants should be aware of the assumptions underlying their activity in this area.

► EXAMPLE: To the extent that the accountant envisions a sophisticated user of his product, he may assume that complex footnote material will be correctly deciphered. Conversely, the accountant should expect a somewhat naive user to experience difficulty in interpreting complex footnotes and to rely more heavily on key numbers (e.g., earnings per share).

Fairness assumption. This alternative view of the problems states that the one and only assumption of accounting is fairness. It calls for fairness to all segments of the business community (management, labor, stockholders, creditors, customers, and the public), determined and measured in the light of the economic and political environment, and the modes of thought and customs of the entire business community.

This view perceives the underlying propositions as conditions rather than as assumptions. By suggesting that it is impossible to set forth all the premises assumed by the profession, it is possible to assert that the underlying accounting principles should be confined to those for which the profession is responsible.

In this manner, the fairness view excludes any general premises, such as the nature of man's motivations, from the area of accounting assumptions. After disposing of the disclosure assumptions, it then rejects the measurement and communication assumptions on the grounds that they inadequately reflect the practice of accounting. Fairness remains as the only guide for accounting practice.

Methods of establishing assumptions. Five approaches to the problem of developing assumptions underlying accounting principles and procedures are:

1. The axiomatic approach, suggested by Professor Richard Mattesich, is based on a few axioms and undefined terms from which theorems might be proved by mathematics and deductive logic.

2. The sociological approach extends concepts such as justice, truth and fairness into the accounting field.

3. The utilitarian approach considers the use to which accounting data is put as the best guide in determining the most useful data to develop.

4. The motivational approach attempts to use the underlying forces governing human behavior (as revealed by psychology, economics, and the behavioral sciences) to serve as a point for developing accounting principles.

5. The political approach selects and develops propositions useful as accounting assumptions by observing and studying the environment in which accounting operates.

► COMMENT: In recent years, several research efforts have been undertaken with the objective of establishing a "normative" theory of accounting— a theory resolving what accounting ought to do. In 1966, the American Accounting Association published *A Statement of Basic Accounting Theory* having normative overtones. In 1973, a study entitled *Objectives of Financial Statements* was published. This latter statement has served as the primary input to the FASB in its attempt to establish a conceptual framework for accounting. In 1979, the FASB issued its first *Statement of Financial Accounting Concepts.* While this statement represents a first step, no comprehensive list of accounting assumptions has been developed for the profession.

ACCOUNTING PRINCIPLES AND DEFINITIONS

The term "principles of accounting" has been used in a variety of ways. In general, however, there are three broad ideas involved in the concept of accounting principles.

1. Principles are the basic premises of accounting in the measurement and communication field of accounting.

2. Principles are generalized statements of several accounting rules and procedures. In this context, principles may be derived by observing accounting practice and formulating the underlying objectives and means of attaining these objectives into one or more general statements. The underlying objectives or ends of practice and means of attaining these ends are reflected by the variety of accounting procedures that are followed.

3. Principles are all rules, of whatever level, that may be used to guide practice. In this sense, principles are merely the rules and procedures of practice. When audit reports refer to "generally accepted accounting principles," the term "principles" is being used in this sense. Thus, this phrase in the auditor's report refers to the rules and procedures that would generally be used for reporting, taking into account the nature of the industry, the problems of the particular business, and the general economic environment.

Need for Accounting Principles. The problem is not that practice is impossible without these principles. Contemporary accounting practice is generally consistent in its application of accounting rules to practical problems. The growth of the practice of accounting, without a formal statement of principles, has been one of the most important developments of our economic society. However, principles are needed to (1) guide practice in areas where there are no rules or conflicting rules, (2) avoid inconsistent procedures, (3) aid practitioners in special problems, (4) guide practice when the complexities of economic society raise involved issues, and (5) explain to laymen why rules should be used.

The need for generalized statements to guide practice is most pressing in those areas where rules have not been developed or where conflicting rules have grown up. This need has become especially important in recent years because the rapid growth and changes in our economic society have created new problems in accounting practice. The resulting pressure for change in established accounting procedures has caused, in turn, the development of a number of alternative accounting procedures.

► EXAMPLE: The various methods of pricing inventory are typical of these alternate procedures. Generally accepted inventory procedures can be broadly grouped under such titles as Last-in, First-out (LIFO); Average; and First-in, First-out (FIFO). No guide, in the form of a principle, is available to indicate which of the variety of alternative procedures should be used for any one particular situation.

The need for generalized statements of the principles of accounting reports. Without these statements of principle to guide him, the layman can, at best, have only a general view of the meaning and content of accounting reports.

► EXAMPLE: Unless he knows the effect of accelerated depreciation on income, when it should be used, and when it has been used, reported income can have only limited significance to the layman.

Efforts by the profession to formulate principles. Statements issued by the American Accounting Association and the American Institute of Certified Public Accountants and, currently, the Financial Accounting Standards Board represent the best efforts in this direction to date. Also, the National Association of Accountants has established the Management Accounting Practices (MAP) Committee to address, among other issues, financial reporting problems. The Securities and Exchange Commission, in recent years, has begun to play a significant role in the formulation of accounting principles. Other groups, both within and outside the profession such as the Financial Executive Institute and individual accounting firms, have also contributed to the formulation of accounting principles.

► COMMENT: As there is a growing awareness of the urgent need for a set of principles, renewed efforts by all concerned parties, both in and out of the profession, can be expected. The existence of the FASB is a case in point. Research is being undertaken by many groups in an attempt to establish principles that will stand the test of time and enable the profession to cope with an ever-changing environment. The FASB is attacking both broad and specific accounting problems through the development of concepts and standards.

ACCOUNTING GUIDELINES AND RULES

Assumptions have been defined as the basic propositions upon which principles rest. Principles of accounting are general statements used to shape accounting procedures. Guidelines and rules differ from principles in that they provide more specific direction to accounting actions, whereas principles provide general direction.

In practice, there is no ready means of drawing a precise line between a statement representing a guideline or rule and one that represents a principle. The level of generalization that represents principles might be suggested by such statements as (1) fixed assets are valued at acquisition cost; (2) revenue is a realized amount; and (3) expense is the cost matched against realized revenue. Examples of rules, on the other hand, are: (1) freight-in should be included as part of acquisition cost; (2) interest revenue is realized as it accrued and not at the time the cash is received; and (3) product guarantee costs are an expense at the time the product is sold.

Uniformity of rules. The development of uniformity in accounting rules and in their application to diverse situations is the underlying objective for which assumptions and principles are formulated. To the extent that conflicting rules are enunciated or that rules are applied inappropriately to a variety of situations, the accounting profession faces a problem in communicating meaningful information to users of accounting reports.

Uniform rules do not imply a uniform system of accounting. An inflexible uniform system of accounting is undesirable because such a system prevents consideration of variations and changes in the underlying economic situation. Under a uniform accounting system, accounts and procedures might be procedurally similar but economically misleading.

► EXAMPLE: A uniform accounting system requirement that all entities use the same depreciation policy for similar assets would produce an image of economic similarity among all entities. In reality, the actual exhaustion of service potential of similar assets may vary greatly among entities due to differing usage patterns, differing intensity of usage and differing repair and maintenance policies. The guideline that the depreciation pattern adopted by an entity should be that pattern which systematically reflects the exhaustion of service potential permits an entity to approximate more closely economic reality by changing its depreciation policy when circumstances warrant.

The difficulty in trying to formulate guidelines or rules for all accounting actions stems from having to state the guideline or rule without establishing a rigid uniform accounting system. Yet, the guideline or rule must be stated in sufficient detail to allow it to be used to direct the application of accounting procedures to specific situations.

►COMMENT: In the absence of a framework to aid in selecting appropriate procedures for each situation, conflicting and diverse accounting procedures arise. There is, therefore, a need for guidance in applying procedures to situations and for minimizing the tendency to manufacture arbitrary procedures to meet the specific needs of an unanticipated situation.

ACCOUNTING POLICIES

Accounting policies can be thought of as:

1. Conventional procedures agreed upon by the profession.
2. General policy statements to guide or practice.
3. Specific policy statements of accounting rules used by the firm.

Conventional procedures agreed upon by the profession. This approach to establishing consistency in accounting procedures rests upon the belief that an organized profession of accountants may decide, by a consensus of its members, that a given rule is desirable. The profession may adopt the rule without relating it to some fundamental concept. Assumptions and principles arrived at in this manner are merely a set of conventions agreed upon by the profession. When the conventional way of thinking about accounting problems changes, these conventions should be subject to change too.

In general, the view that accounting assumptions, principles, and rules should be determined by conventional agreement of the profession without regard to the underlying purposes of the profession has not been especially successful. In another sense, it can be contended, that assumptions, principles and rules can have no greater validity than the extent to which they are accepted by the profession. In times of changing economic and social institutions, the validation of accounting methods by acceptance and use is too slow. There is need now for a more organized professional means of developing and disseminating procedures and rules to be used by the profession and to which the courts of the land could refer.

General policy statements to guide the profession. In another sense, the term convention is used to denote certain restraining considerations on accounting procedures. Possibly the best known of such conventions are:

1. *Conservatism.* In situations where there is no guide to indicate which procedure to use, select the one that will give a conservative result. Thus, when in doubt, accountants have preferred to understate rather than overstate income.

2. *Consistency.* A procedure adopted at one time should be used in subsequent time periods or similar situations. The purpose of consistency is to make possible the comparison of a company's statements from one year to the next and to prevent willful manipulation of income by a varying application of accounting principles.

3. *Full disclosure.* In making a decision as to the proper procedure to use, the general objective of fully disclosing all significant information should serve as a general guide. That is, all facts should be disclosed which, if not disclosed, would make the statements misleading.

4. *Materiality.* If the cost of applying the best accounting procedure is excessive, immaterial items may be treated by alternative procedures.

In this sense, conventions are general policy statements to guide practice. They are not principles or rules, but serve as general directives until assumptions, principles or rules are developed. As assumptions, principles, or rules are developed, conventions are expected to disappear. As practicing accountants follow principles governing procedures, there would be little reason to advocate conservatism, consistency, materiality or full disclosure.

Specific policy statements of accounting rules used by a firm. In 1972 the Accounting Principles Board (APB) issued an opinion requiring firms to include as an integral part of their financial statements a description of all significant accounting policies of the reporting entity. The Board decided the most useful method of disclosure would normally be in a summary of significant accounting policies set forth at the beginning of the footnotes to the financial statements.

► EXAMPLE: Where alternative procedures exist with respect to a certain item such as the flow assumption with respect to inventory, the reporting entity should disclose the policy which it follows. It should state that it uses LIFO, average, or FIFO and the specific form of the flow assumption.

ACCOUNTING STANDARDS

It is sometimes proposed that the profession does not need any formal list of assumptions, principles and rules. Other means may be used to establish objective standards against which any accounting procedure may be judged. This concept would then underlie the establishment of uniform accounting systems.

A rather strong case might also be made for having the government set appropriate standards to which accounting practitioners should adhere. This concept of an accounting standard has not been supported by our economic society.

Instead, another view has prevailed. It holds that if assumptions, principles and rules are properly developed by the profession, they will become the standards by which practice may be evaluated. There is some evidence to suggest that standards established by government decree or by conventional agreement are not adjusted to changing economic conditions as rapidly as standards established through private-sector development of assumptions, principles and rules.

In accounting, there are various types of standards.

1. *Standards of performance.* These standards require a certain level of human conduct or activity. In auditing, this type of standard refers to the adequacy of audit procedures such as the sampling of receivables or the checking of inventories.

2. *Standards of reporting.* These require a certain level of disclosure in the audit report.

3. *Standards of procedure.* These standards measure practice against the criterion of how well accounting measures economic activity.

4. *Standards enunciated by the FASB*. These standards are guidelines for the measurement and communication of financial accounting information. Some of these standards are fundamental and cut across all aspects of accounting, while others deal with rather narrow issues.

THE PRACTICAL PROBLEMS

The basic accounting concepts discussed in the first section of this chapter can be applied to help provide answers to the practical problems currently facing the profession. Some of the more fundamental practical problems that are currently of concern to most practitioners are discussed in the following pages. These are:

1. Unstable monetary unit.
2. Realization of income.
3. Inventory pricing.
4. Segment reporting.
5. Foreign operations and exchange.
6. Employee benefits.
7. Regulated industries.
8. Lease financing.
9. Intangible assets.
10. Materiality.
11. Forecasts.
12. Liquidity disclosure.

UNSTABLE MONETARY UNIT

Cause of the problem. Perhaps the most serious problem facing financial accounting is primarily attributable to a continuing inflationary trend. Intensified inflationary spirals in the mid and late 1970's resulted in the SEC requiring further disclosures of fixed asset cost, depreciation (or amortization), inventory valuation, and cost of goods sold on a current replacement cost basis. As inflation continues to increase at the quickened pace of the late 1970's, it seems inevitable that some more sweeping changes will necessarily be implemented for financial statement presentation. The FASB has recently issued an exposure draft on Financial Reporting and Changing Prices to provide for a more uniform treatment of this problem.

The basic problem involves the stability of the monetary unit measure employed in financial statements to gauge the progress of the entity. As inflation increases the difference between the real values of dollars in different years, it becomes increasingly questionable to combine the different years' dollars as if they were measures of the same worth. For example, it is clearly improper to assert that a one acre parcel of land bought in 1950 for $50 is worth one eightieth of an adjacent and similar acre of land bought in 1979 for $4,000. Such large shifts are uncommon but point out the basic problem in relying solely on a historical cost-based accounting system for financial statement presentation.

Virtually all serious theoretical inquiries since the American Accounting Association's study entitled *A Statement of Basic Accounting Theory* in 1966 have recognized the user in determining the primary obligation for financial reporting. A central problem in such a far-reaching conclusion is that there are many different financial statement users with varying objectives. An in-depth inquiry by A Study Group on Objectives of Financial Statements sponsored by the AICPA recognized this problem and conceded the need to use multiple valuation bases in certain circumstances to report on financial conditions and results of operations. Issues pertinent to the principal methods of dealing with the problem of an unstable measuring unit are now considered in this perspective.

General price level adjustments. The general price level adjustment procedure adopts the premise that historical cost prices can be brought up to date by applying measures of inflation in all goods and services in the economy to each item in the financial statement. It provides for the maintenance of the entity's position in an inflationary environment. For example, since cash is the epitome of current value, no adjustment of the current cash balance would ever be necessary. On the other hand, a building constructed in 1960 for $100,000 might be shown on the balance sheet at $250,000 if prices had generally risen by a factor or index of 2.5 since 1960. Supporters for the general price level adjustment procedure point to its favorable characteristics.

First, it is objective. The price index used would be determined outside the control of the entities that would use it. Furthermore, each firm would follow the same basic procedure in adjusting from the historical cost basis to the adjusted cost basis. This procedure would tend to preserve comparability between firms' performance in the same inflationary situation. Secondly, it offers simplicity in that it preserves the historical cost-based accounting system and simple modification is necessary only for financial statement preparation. Since the general price level adjusted method is historically based, the users should be able to understand this system easily. A third advantage cited by general price level proponents is that it provides for better analysis within the entity as changes attributable to inflationary shifts are eliminated. Finally, it is a comprehensive method. That is, it can be applied to each account balance and thereby eliminate the need for piecemeal remedies such as the LIFO inventory valuation method or current replacement cost estimates for selected accounts.

Opponents of general price level adjusted statements have cited numerous drawbacks of the method. First, the cost of preparing such statements is not offset by a commensurate benefit to the users. Particularly in evidence as a cost is the confusion that could result during the transition from historical cost-based statements and the general price level adjusted statements. In addition, the cost of constructing general price level adjusted statements is too great to justify allowing for only moderate increments in price level changes. Another major argument against general adjustment is that it implicitly assumes that all entities are equally affected by inflation. This is not the case. It could not reflect the real value of an asset either from the standpoint of what it would cost the entity at current prices or what the entity could sell it for at current prices. These points become clearer as the other methods are examined.

Current value accounting. This method differs significantly from the general price level adjusted statements in that it is not concerned with estimating the *general* effects of inflation—rather, it attempts to assess the specific ***current value*** of each asset and liability. In this regard, it is divorced entirely from the historical cost framework. It differs from the general price level adjusted method in that it employs an array of techniques for estimating various account balances.

Present value. This estimation technique relates to the future cash inflows or outflows or both associated with an asset or liability. Using an appropriate discount rate, the flows are discounted back to some current value to the entity. Due to the uncertainty and subjectivity associated with forecasting future cash inflows, this method has not enjoyed much practical support. Certain outflows are relatively fixed, however, and the technique has been useful in these instances. Examples include the amount determined in estimating the amount at which a lease should be capitalized and the appropriate valuation of a note when its lending terms are unusual.

Current replacement cost. This technique has gained considerable support in view of SEC requirements and the FASB position noted earlier. Essentially, it represents a capital maintenance approach to valuation. If an entity wishes to allow for replenishment of its existing assets and yield a reasonable return on its net assets, this method might be theoretically most appropriate. It contemplates replacement of existing assets and it is often referred to as an entry value technique. Limitations include the lack of available market prices for used standardized assets and unique assets (for example, self-constructed machinery or buildings). These limitations are often overcome by reference to specific price indices available for various industries. Such indices are applied to the historical cost of a particular asset to eliminate its specific current valuation. In a specific price index, a specific value change is estimated as opposed to a general value change due to inflation.

Net realizable value. This technique attempts to value assets at their disposal value in an orderly market (as opposed to a forced liquidation market). It is often referred to as an exit value approach. It has been commonly utilized in computing the market amount in lower of cost or market valuation methods for Inventories and Marketable Securities, and the net amount in accounts receivable. Its objective is not to provide the lowest valuation point, but to provide an estimate of the cash value an entity could expect should it convert its assets to cash. To a degree, it gives a measure of flexibility of being able to move from one asset combination to another. This method differs from the replacement cost method because the latter contemplates maintaining the current mix of assets.

Discussion. It is not necessary to choose between the two methods discussed. They can be combined. The essential differences between the two can be measured in terms of objectivity, relevance, and complexity. The general price level approach appears to be more objective, less relevant, and marginally less complex than the current value approach. Objectivity seems to be rather obvious in as much as management would normally have to make a number of estimates under the current valuation approach and virtually none under the general price level approach. For example, intangible fixed assets may be particularly troublesome under the former. The current value approach seems more relevant as it can react to economic forces other than inflation. It should possess a greater capacity to convey the "true" economic significance of reported information. Finally, the general price level approach is less complex because it can be applied directly to historical cost-based records. The information system demands seem less costly in terms of start up cost. It also offers one systematic approach where the current value approach is eclectic. On the other hand, the users may not interpret the monetary and non-monetary gains under the general price level approach as readily as they might under current value financial statements. Historical cost-based financial statements seem to have become so laden with footnotes that neither method may be as complex as the existing system of reporting.

Ultimately, social and economic forces may well lead to a dual-based system consisting of historical cost-based systems and some variant of the current value approach. This issue is pervasive to the user orientation of professions in the United States society. Already much experimentation has taken place, such as the SEC replacement cost disclosure requirements, and more is being advocated by the FASB.

REALIZATION OF INCOME

Typically, a manufacturing company generates income by (1) purchasing goods and services, (2) using them to manufacture a product, and (3) selling the product to its customers. Any income created or made must be the result of the performance of all three processes. It seems reasonable to assume that any income would be generated over the entire process. Accounting has not yet advanced to the stage where income can be recognized as it is created. Instead, accounting measures income as it is realized.

In attempting to report only income recognized as realized by most people, accountants tend to assume that no income is realized until goods are sold or when the earning process is effectively complete. One of these dates is normally used as the date for recognizing income, though there are exceptions to this general rule.

Alternative methods that delay or accelerate realization of income. A number of methods exist for recognizing the point or points in time at which income should be realized. Often the legal point of sale does not correspond to the economic point of sale. In franchise sales, for example, the sale may legally be effected at the time the contract is signed but the franchiser (the seller) should generally not recognize the income as realized until substantial performance has occurred. Real estate sales and retail land sales are often complex both legally and economically and thus special guidelines are provided to protect against too rapid recognition of income realization. Extra care must be exercised in these instances in order to guard against premature recognition of income realization. Percentage-of-completion type contract sales represent the opportunity for abuse of the realization principle as some entities may bias estimates to inflate income. On the other hand, cash sales, installment sales, and consignment sales arrangements may be utilized to delay timely recognition of income realization. Some managements may try to employ any of these to their advantage in either direction. Full exploration of the problems associated with income realization is clearly an involved matter well beyond the scope of this inquiry.

Seriousness of the problem. There are many points at which income may be realized and few objective standards are available to indicate when various dates should be used. This situation creates confusion in the minds of the readers of financial reports and represents a serious judgmental problem for the accountant. It is particularly in evidence with complex real estate and retail land sales. Evidence gathered from the SEC's 8-K reports indicates that disagreement over realization of income is the most frequently cited cause of disagreement between managements and auditors.

INVENTORY PRICING

There are two major problem areas facing the profession in determining the costs to be assigned to inventories. The first area involves the traditional questions associated with the amounts of historical costs to be allocated between cost of goods sold and inventory. The second is an outgrowth of current value acounting's apparent popularity with the SEC, which directly affects all public companies and indirectly affects private companies.

Traditional problems. The need for periodic reports has long made it necessary to allocate some portion of the cost incurred in one fiscal period to that period and some portion to future periods. Typically, accountants rely on the matching principle to guide them in this allocation. They attempt to correlate the expiration of the input effort with the realization of the output reward. Two special problems have continually plagued the accountant—flow assumptions and differentiating between period and product costs.

Flow assumptions. A seemingly ideal situation in this regard is the specific identity method whereby each item of inventory has a particular cost associated with it which can be readily expensed at the point of revenue recognition. Such a method is quite burdensome and inefficient in cases where there are large amounts of relatively small unit cost items. Such a method allows for income manipulation where there exists significant unit cost differences between standard products. Given a constant selling price, a salesman may elect the lower cost item in order to present a more favorable profit picture.

To overcome the problems associated with this method, accountants attempted to match the cost flow with the approximate physical flow of the inventory items. First-in, first-out (FIFO), average, and last-in, last-out (LIFO) methods were conceived. Although LIFO can offer considerable opportunity for income manipulation by adjusting year end stock levels, it does not seem to be a particularly compelling issue when compared to the product versus period cost controversy. Normally, the flow assumption is not important in income determination as long as one flow is used consistently.

Product versus period costs. To what extent should the cost of the environment under which a product is produced be included in the cost of the inventory? Managerial theorists have long argued against the usefulness of allocating a portion of fixed overhead to inventory. They have argued that variable cost is more relevant for decision making. They have pointed out that allocation is largely arbitrary and yields little information. Financial accountants have taken a quite different view. They contend any cost that is readily identifiable in preparing a product for sale should be expensed at the time of revenue realization. Such a policy is rooted in the matching principle.

An interesting and significant case may serve as an indicator of future developments. The case involves the costing of oil producers' inventory of crude oil yet to be mined. For many years management selected either the full costing method or the successful efforts method. The full costing method includes *all* exploration costs in the inventory cost of crude oil to be mined. The successful efforts method includes only the exploration and development costs associated with a producing well. All other exploration costs were treated as period costs and expensed. Acting under governmental directive to establish one method, the FASB elected the successful efforts method over the full costing method. This appears to reflect a change in FASB policy. It can be argued that the cost of non-producing wells held little potential for future benefit and thus their costs should be expensed. But it is virtually certain that no successful wells would be discovered if the environment of drilling were not present, as a relatively small percent of drillings result in a producing well. It also seems that the costs were significant and easily identifiable. One must conclude that the FASB may not have been so traditional in emphasizing cost allocation in this decision.

A more compelling issue in this case is the fact that the SEC effectively rejected the FASB's resolution and along with it the historical cost-based system. The SEC opted for a net realizable value method of reporting on the basis of "proven reserve" quantities. The SEC has emphasized that this situation represented a special case, but several things are noteworthy. It is the first time the SEC has publicly overriden the FASB. The net realizable value criterion is not unique to items such as oil which have an assured market value. Gold and certain grains also fall into this category. However, the range of "proven reserve" quantity estimates and the quite subjective assessment of recovery costs combine to give what appears to be an imprecise estimate.

► COMMENT: The SEC's decision may represent a message of discontent with the ability of the accounting profession to react quickly to problems the SEC sees as vital. The SEC had already indicated that more disclosure of current valuation was important in its earlier requirement regarding replacement costs associated with fixed asset and inventory accounting for large entities. A distinct trend seems to be toward more footnote disclosure which theoretically should allow for adjustment of the accounting bases used to generate account balances in financial statements.

SEGMENT REPORTING

During the 1960's a merger boom unrivaled in history occurred in the United States. The popularity of such diversified companies was, in part, due to their ability to utilize the pooling of interest method of accounting to enhance their earnings per share figure and increase their market strength. As their stock prices rose, they were able to achieve more favorable ratios in stock-for-stock exchanges of their merger targets. Although some of the stock price increase may have been superfluous, the fact that many companies effectively diversified their risk by holding varied asset groupings also increased their economic stability and strength. One aspect of their business might experience a very bad year while not significantly affecting the whole entity's performance picture. The trend toward diversification and merger has continued and seems likely to continue.

As a result of diversification, single figures for such important items as sales, operating profit and total assets largely obscured the results of individual lines of business in the entity. This condition made it impossible for users of financial statements to assess adequately the performance of the diversified company's segments in relation to other similar business segments. The SEC recognized this condition and introduced certain reporting requirements in the early 1970's. The Federal Trade Commission (FTC) entered the arena shortly thereafter when it became apparent to it that a segment of a diversified company may call on the economic strength of its fellow segments to compete unfairly against a single line business competitor. The FTC also contended it needed disaggregated data in order to establish national standards for various product lines. In 1977, the FASB addressed the problem of segment reporting along with a number of other special risk areas for reporting entities. These other areas include reporting certain information on major customers, foreign operations, and export sales. The major problem areas are the determination of the segment and appropriate disaggregation of financial data to the segment basis.

Determination of the segment. A number of diverse bases have been proposed for establishing segments. Some of these include using the nature of the product, the nature of the production process, markets and marketing methods, Standard Industrial Classification (SIC) codes, and existing profit centers. Since a major goal of segment reporting is to bring about comparability between segments engaged in the same business, need exists for greater specificity of criteria.

► EXAMPLE: Assume two different producers of a full line of electronic entertainment products; each makes a product called the home entertainment center, consisting of a radio, television, turntable, and stereo speakers. In one company, the final assembly is completed in the television assembly profit center, and, in the other, in the stereo assembly profit center. Each company logically includes it in different segments' operating results.

Disaggregation of financial data to the segment basis. Several potential problem areas arise in disaggregating data to the segment level. The major problem area lies in determining the segment's operating profit. Any diversified company is likely to have a considerable amount of costs common to all segments—most of which must be allocated to segments before arriving at operating profit. No uniform manner of allocating such costs exists, nor is the basis on which such costs are allocated a required disclosure. This condition may permit management to establish somewhat arbitrary methods of allocation, which could mislead the financial statement user.

FOREIGN OPERATIONS AND EXCHANGE

As with the surge of diversified companies, the proliferation of multinational companies has brought about numerous peculiar reporting problems. As with different product lines, major investments in, or sales dependence on, foreign governments is likely to create special risks that users of financial statements need to know in order to make informed investment decisions. Concomitant with the problem of increased evidence of multinational companies is the dramatic change in the international monetary market. Movement from the gold standard to the current dynamic international monetary system presents serious translation problems. Compounding the problem of an instant reacting exchange market is the shift away from the United States trade surplus to an ongoing trade deficit and its relatively high rate of inflation.

Foreign operations and export sales. Accepted procedure calls for reporting significant foreign operations by country or geographical region. Similarly, significant export sales are to be reported in this fashion. Problems arise in identifying the appropriate criteria for establishing a geographic region and for identifying the difference between foreign operations and export sales.

► EXAMPLE: A major portion of the construction of parts for a machine are accomplished domestically. Final assembly occurs in the foreign country to take advantage of certain import tax regulations. The major marketing effort is accomplished by the operation in the foreign company although costs related to this transaction are impossible to identify. Is the transaction properly assigned as a foreign operation or an export sale?

A related problem arises in classifying export sales made by foreign operations. Which country (foreign or domestic) bears the most relevant risk for the financial statement user? Clearly these rather arbitrary classification schemes leave open the possibility for manipulation.

Foreign exchange. Of the numerous problems in this area, the most serious for the financial statement user may lie in the area of conversion of fixed asset amounts. Where large shifts occur in exchange rates over a several year period, the historical exchange rate is likely to bear little relation to the current asset valuation. The problem is analogous to that discussed earlier under the "Unstable Monetary Unit" heading. In this instance the problem may be more severe.

► EXAMPLE: A building constructed in a foreign country three years ago cost $4,000,000 units of that country's currency, which was convertible to 1,000,000 dollars. Today the exchange rate is two to one. The same building would cost 2,000,000 dollars to construct but its valuation is at the old basis of $1,000,000.

EMPLOYEE BENEFITS

The supplementary benefits offered employees have grown and expanded substantially in recent years. The amount of non-wage benefits for which employees were formerly responsible now approaches 50 percent of basic salaries. The problem of providing for retirement, formerly an individual's responsibility, has been largely transferred to the employer and the government under pension plans now in existence. The same is true of health and welfare benefits. One compilation includes over 75 different benefits now available to employees by a variety of companies. These developments have created a number of problems for the accounting profession.

Pensions are the major employee benefit and they require payments to the employee long after the period in which the pension was earned. This problem represents a multidimensional accounting problem: (1) to acknowledge these employee benefit costs in a manner that will provide for future obligations; (2) to provide a reasonable determination of periodic income as the rights pass to the employees; and (3) to satisfy the diverse array of social, legal, tax, and political forces in this area.

Accounting for pension costs. Considerable diversity has existed in treating pension costs. Many entities treated it as a footnote item and followed a pay-as-you-go procedure for actually recording costs. Under this procedure, recording occurred only as retired employees received their pensions. This policy clearly failed to recognize the obligation in a timely manner and overstated current income by a significant margin.

Enactment of the Employee Retirement Income Security Act (ERISA) in 1974 established a number of mandatory guidelines. For private entities, it requires compulsory full funding of pension benefits earned currently by individual employees. In some cases, immediate and full vesting is mandated and in no case is the full vesting period greater than 15 years. It requires satisfying the company's pre-1974 pension obligations to the level for full funding over no more than a 40-year horizon. Although it may be asserted that such obligations are expenses of prior periods and should be recognized as reductions in retained earnings, most accountants have opted for spreading this recognition over the life of catch-up period.

REGULATED INDUSTRIES

A number of industries are regulated by federal and state agencies. These agencies may prescribe a uniform accounting system for the industry and require that financial statements be prepared in accordance with that system. These required statements are, at times, prepared in conflict with generally accepted accounting principles. Thus, the problem is how to comply with the requirements of the regulatory agencies and still conform to generally accepted accounting principles.

This problem occurs in many areas. Accounting practices prescribed by the Interstate Commerce Commission (ICC) allow replacement instead of depreciation accounting for certain items of railroad property. This departure from generally accepted accounting principles results in a materially different income being reported than if generally accepted principles were followed. The laws and regulations in the insurance field requiring insurance company statements to reflect more of a liquidation point of view than the going concern assumption, represent another material departure from generally accepted accounting principles.

Two viewpoints of the problem. Some authorities maintain that regulatory requirements represent the correct accounting procedures for each industry, even though these requirements vary from procedures used in other industries. In certifying to the correctness of such statements, the audit certificates often indicate that they were prepared in accordance with the principles and procedures prescribed by the regulatory agency.

Other accountants maintain that generally accepted accounting principles should be equally applicable to all types of industries, both regulated and unregulated. These take exception to public reports prepared in accordance with regulatory requirements where the departure from generally accepted accounting principles is material. (Chapter 28 treats both viewpoints of the problem from an audit report aspect.)

Possible solutions to the problem. One solution would be for regulatory agencies to adopt generally accepted accounting principles. Another would be to allow regulated industries to use generally accepted accounting principles in preparing their public reports. A third solution would have different accepted accounting principles developed for each industry, letting the already developed regulatory requirements serve as the accepted principles for regulated industries. While this last proposal may have merit, it is contrary to modern accounting thought.

LEASE FINANCING

As a result of price level increases after World War II, many companies found they held fixed assets purchased at prewar prices that were much lower than current valuations. Many felt that the annual charge for depreciation of these assets, based on low prewar costs, no longer represented realistic economic depreciation in terms of current replacement costs. Because only cost-based depreciation was allowed as a deduction for income tax purposes, the situation became doubly aggravated.

Some companies in this position discovered a method whereby they could upgrade their tax deduction and still retain use of their property. They could sell appreciated property to dummy corporations and then enter into lease arrangements giving them the use of the assets over their productive lives. In this manner, profits on the sale would be recognized at lower capital gain rates and periodic lease payments could be deducted as operating expense for income tax purposes—these periodic payments being roughly equal to depreciation at higher current values.

Shortly thereafter, a transition was made from the use of this method solely as a tax-saving device to a method of financing that enables companies to conserve their working capital. Lease financing is now being used in many forms. The sale and lease-back continues to be used, but the sale is now usually made to an independent rather than dummy corporation. Additionally, many leasing companies stand ready to purchase any specific equipment a potential lessee may wish to rent. Although there are many arguments regarding the advantages and disadvantages of this type of financing, this discussion will be confined to the accounting ramifications of lease financing.

Problems in accounting for leases. The problem of accounting for a long-term lease is to portray fairly the economic aspect of the lease transaction. In a sense, leasing of an asset is very similar to purchasing an asset on credit. In both cases, the intent is for the asset to provide service to an entity over a long period of time in exchange for periodic cash outflows. To provide similar asset and liability profiles for the two transactions, the accounting must be handled in a similar manner. This means that the value of the long-term lease must be capitalized as an asset and a corresponding liability.

The most fundamental problem in such treatment is twofold—first, establishing criteria governing capitalization of the lease as an asset and liability, and second, establishing the appropriate amount for capitalization. The first problem is precipitated by management's normal reluctance to laden their balance sheets with additional assets and liabilities. The attendant unfavorable changes in such numbers as the return on total assets and the debt to equity ratio apparently serve as motivation for such reluctance. Thus, rather objective criteria are necessary to permit the accountant to make a firm judgment. The second problem lies in determining the future cash outflows to the lessor and the appropriate rate at which these cash outflows should be discounted back to a present value (the capitalizable amount of the lease and the liability). Both aspects of the problem are accentuated by the facts that all relevant judgments are based on future occurrences and that leasing contracts tend to be complex. Thus, the desired simple and objective guidelines are often somewhat complex and subjective.

► COMMENT: Although experience with current guidelines should result in eventual refinements leading to greater objectivity, perhaps the best hope for accepting capitalization readily is convincing managements that full and fair disclosure in the balance sheet acounts is not significantly different from full and fair disclosure in the footnotes.

INTANGIBLE ASSETS

Intangible assets include such balance sheet items as goodwill, trademarks, patents, copyrights, and franchises. Their major characteristics include: (1) a high degree of uncertainty regarding future benefit to the enterprise; (2) a value related only to one particular entity; (3) a lack of sufficient evidence as to their real useful life; and (4) a high degree of sensitivity to environmental forces as their value is closely tied to competitive advantage. The major problems of accounting for intangibles can be grouped into two categories.

First, the profession needs some objective standard for determining the nature of an intangible asset and when it exists. On one extreme, a favorable government climate may represent an intangible asset available to American enterprises that may not be available to an entrepreneur in another country. Few would advocate recording such an asset. On the other hand, a patent purchased by a business for its exclusive use would be generally considered an intangible asset for book purposes. In between these two extremes are a host of situations in which items of value may or may not appropriately be considered intangible assets for accounting purposes.

The second aspect of accounting for intangible assets relates to their valuation. While there may be some agreement that a given right or value does represent an intangible asset, methods of measuring and valuing it may be so indefinite and so varied that any reported amount of an intangible asset would have limited meaning. Continuation of the above example related to patents emphasizes this situation. As noted, should the entity purchase a patent, then all costs would be capitalized as an asset and presumably the purchase price would approximate the market value of the patent at the time of the transaction. On the other hand, if the entity's own research and development efforts led to precisely the same patent, then current practice would dictate no asset recognition. That is, current practice treats such research and development costs for operating entities as period costs which should be expensed in the year in which they are incurred.

Clearly, this policy creates serious differences in economic profiles portrayed by the resulting accounting measures for the two entities even though the economic substances are identical.

Goodwill. Goodwill provides another good example of the problems associated with intangibles, and brings out the innate difficulty in identifying and evaluating intangibles generally. Essentially, goodwill is an entity's ability to earn an unusual rate of return on the available assets when each asset is assigned its individual market value. For example, a company with an established reputation for high quality products and service may be able to generate more earnings on the same amount of assets than a company without such a reputation. Theoretically, this goodwill should be recognized as an asset because it yields an economic return. A major drawback arises if the entity tries to sell the goodwill. It is inextricably linked to the asset package as a whole. With this rationale in mind, as well as some other issues, the profession has chosen not to recognize goodwill developed internally. Should the whole entity be purchased by another company, however, the purchasing company can recognize the goodwill as an asset. Much the same situation exists for goodwill as for patents.

A further problem arises in regard to treatment of goodwill once it is established as an asset. Should it be carried indefinitely or written off as an expense? For that matter, should it be incremented? For consistency, the latter question can be answered negatively. However, the former question has no theoretically standard answer. Some managements may argue that there is no reduction in purchased goodwill so it should remain intact. This position may be self-serving as reductions in goodwill will result in reduced incomes. At the same time, different goodwills—unlike different machines—do not have readily estimated lives. There is no truly objective and fair procedure for advocating the write-off of goodwill. Current practice has resolved the problem by not allowing the write-off of goodwill during the purchase period and simultaneously requiring that it be written off over a period not to exceed 40 years. Such arbitrary solutions point up the amorphous nature of the problem of intangibles generally and result in accounting differences between entities where no economic differences exist.

MATERIALITY

The concept of materiality is normally defined in terms of the financial statement user's decision model. If an amount or disclosure would cause an average prudent investor to alter his ultimate decision, then the amount or disclosure is material. An alternative view of defining the materiality of an amount or disclosure is the effect that it would have on the market price of the equity securities. An effect would indicate its materiality.

In an elemental sense, materiality is inextricably entwined with the purpose of financial statements. While financial statements are undoubtedly intended to provide investors with information concerning the entity's past performance and future prospects, many other factors enter into such evaluations of the entity. Among such factors are the macroeconomic environment (e.g., interest and inflation rates), industry environment (e.g., product stability and raw material cost stability), and the foreign political environment (especially for some multinational entities). While it may be assumed that these factors play no role in the accountant's decisions regarding what information should be contained in financial statements, as they are unlikely to constitute past transactions, such is not the case. These factors may play an important role in determining the future prospects of past transactions. For example, in a thinly capitalized entity in dire need of refinancing, a high interest rate coupled with a high inflation rate may cast a serious question as to its viability as a going concern. Raw material supply contracts at fixed future prices may have a favorable or unfavorable effect on an entity in an unstable market. A growing portion of a multinational situated in a politically tentative foreign environment may have an effect on the entity's prospects on the whole. While the financial statements may normally be expected to report these issues, the average *prudent* investor's reaction is likely to be nothing, as he is already aware of such conditions through more timely information sources. It seems likely that most accountants would view these events as generally material.

Perhaps the key issue in determining materiality is describing the ultimate user of the financial statements and his presumed information sources. If the user is indeed prudent and sophisticated, he may have the ability and sufficient interest to digest descriptions of the above events which are likely to be presented in news reports as well as in complex footnotes. At the same time, it is unlikely that he will absorb any useful information from the footnotes on which he will alter his decision to buy, sell, or hold securities. If the user is less than sophisticated, he too may not react to the information in the footnotes, as he may have neither sufficient ability nor interest to digest the material in the footnote. That is, too much disclosure (or too little summarization) may result in an information overload condition which frustrates rather than facilitates the flow of important information.

A major issue regarding materiality for both types of users is the clear presentation of information which the accountant has reason to believe would differ from their expectations. To the extent that some segregation of this information can be effected, the less likely either of the types of users will be misled. To achieve such a status the accountant must have some facility for assessing the status quo of the user's model. Guidelines for determining materiality (under consideration by the FASB at this writing) must provide the accountant with the ability to assess more accurately these user decision models in many diverse situations in order to achieve a higher level of consistency from one accountant to another.

FORECASTS

Throughout the 1970's, a movement for mandatory public forecasts in the United States gained impetus largely due to governmental bodies and especially due to the Securities and Exchange Commission (SEC). The central concern of the SEC is the fact that management's forecasts are selectively distributed, thus placing the recipients in a favored position to nonrecipients in making investment decisions. Repeated attempts to establish rather definitive mandatory guidelines for forecasts have met with such massive resistance that the SEC has currently settled for rather flexible, voluntary criteria for forecasts which are released to the public. From a conceptual standpoint the issue of public forecasts crystallizes on the information such forecasts could provide the user of financial statements.

Since it seems quite acceptable to assume that investments are made on the basis of anticipated results as opposed to past events, it may also seem acceptable to assume that public forecasts are useful. Such a linkage is not necessarily logical as investors (especially sophisticated investors) already make forecasts which influence the market prices of publicly available securities. Thus, while these forecasts may not be readily available to all investors, to a considerable degree the effect of the forecasters' beliefs tend to be reflected in the price of the security. Nevertheless, it can be argued that many investors, especially unsophisticated investors, would benefit by possessing more detailed knowledge of the bases for establishing the market price. Presumably, forecasts of such items as revenues, earnings, major cash sources and users would assist those investors. Indeed, such an argument seems cogent in helping many investors identify more clearly the risk associated with an investment. Uniform estimates based on stated assumptions would seemingly provide the smaller investor, who has limited resources for formulating his own forecasting model, with added relevant matter.

Such forecasts would not occur without creating some problems and potential costs. Many managers have expressed a reluctance to disclose the detailed assumptions on which their informal forecasts are formulated as they do not wish to provide information to their competitors. Some managers have argued that differential disclosure policies by nation may place domestic corporations at a particular disadvantage to foreign competitors in this regard. Many opponents of mandatory forecasting point out that uniform forecast may well imply a level of precision to future occurrences that simply does not exist. Managers, as well as some accountants, have voiced concern about legal liability problems associated with well-intentioned, but faulty forecasts. Even though the SEC has proposed a "safe harbor" rule for such forecasts, cases of this nature can still be litigated and thus prove costly to the forecasters. Some opponents of mandatory forecasts also feel that many managements will concentrate their efforts on achieving the forecast to the possible detriment of the entity. While this argument may not appear to be as compelling as some of the others cited, auditors have at times expressed the view that public statements regarding future earnings tend to place inordinate pressure on managers and may result in improper behavior.

With the above issues in mind, it seems clear that voluntary forecast disclosure can offer considerable wisdom on which the eventual decision regarding mandatory forecasting should be made. Even with such experience, a strong case either for or against mandatory forecasting is not apparent, due to the amorphous and imprecise nature of the attendant costs and benefits.

LIQUIDITY DISCLOSURE

The problem of decreasing liquidity intensified dramatically in the period following World War II until the present. In the quarter century beginning in 1950, the ratio of short term assets to short term liabilities decreased by more than 50 percent. To some extent such figures can be explained by more entities using LIFO valuation procedures for their inventories and the investment of current assets in longer run assets to realize better investment opportunities. The most important cause for concern was the erosion of debt to equity relationships which seem to have occurred primarily as an attempt to deal with inflation. That is, it seemed prudent to borrow funds to manage assets that appreciated in value due to inflation and yield an operating return as well. Such practices may indeed prove profitable if the entity retains sufficient flexibility to withstand periods of macroeconomic or industry slowdowns. Unfortunately, occurrences during such periods indicate that many entities overextended themselves, which resulted in bankruptcy. The users of financial statements then redressed accountants as well as auditors for the lack of information to serve as adequate warning signals for such failures.

The accounting issues. Accounting theoreticians and rule makers must accept some of the responsibility for the current state of affairs. Recent studies and proposals in both Europe and the United States have resulted in turning more emphasis in the financial statements to the measurements of liquidity and solvency. They point out the shift away from the concentration on solvency which existed before 1950 to the attention on earnings in the period following 1950. The accounting rules have, by implication, held out earnings streams to be indicative of solvency. Due principally to problems of refinancing debts or expanding financing during difficult macroeconomic times, such is not necessarily the case.

Perhaps, the most practical problem facing the profession is that generally accepted accounting principles focus on earnings as opposed to liquidity. Liquidity implies the ability to pay one's debts. The most relevant measures for assets and liabilities are the amounts of money that each item can command. Valuation for liquidity purposes is concerned with the monetary amount at which the asset or liability could exit the firm. Generally accepted accounting principles have traditionally been linked with the entry amount or historical cost of the asset or liability. While it is widely acknowledged that few prudent investors feel that fixed asset account valuations are representations of exit values, it should also be recognized that such assets compose the largest part of many entities' stock of assets and that little information is available in the financial statements regarding their exit values. Additionally, generally accepted accounting standards provide confusing treatments for estimating exit values. The example regarding self-developed, as opposed to purchased, patents presented under "Intangible Assets" provides a good example of the latter point. Until recently lease financing could be effected successfully without disturbing any asset-liability relationships in the financial statements. Nevertheless, the reduced flexibility with respect to liquidity is evident between an entity that leases most of its fixed assets and one that owns most of its fixed assets.

Possible solution. A possible solution would be to establish a financial statement directed at providing exit value information about assets and liabilities. Such a statement could highlight entities that are in imminent danger from lack of liquidity and could serve to reduce criticism of the profession. The statement would be no panacea because of the fact that user interpretation would still be necessary and because it would necessarily be directed to short term (that is, several years) assessments of liquidity positions. Nevertheless, it could prove to be a valuable tool in the face of an environment in which many firms seem to have increasingly unfavorable abilities to raise further capital via debt financing.

SUMMARY

The preceding description of the more pressing problems facing the profession of accounting today should be considered more in the nature of an illustration than an all-inclusive coverage of all the problems of the profession. In a very fundamental sense, the profession needs to eliminate the variety of alternative accounting procedures now available and to develop a systematic, organized body of knowledge to provide guides in selecting appropriate procedures for any given situation. While government decreed accounting procedures might be an expedient method for eliminating alternative procedures, this method would be inflexible and slow in adapting to changing economic conditions. Therefore, it seems appropriate that the profession direct its efforts to developing an organized systematic body of underlying knowledge that will provide the necessary flexibility to adapt to the needs of a great number of business situations and the constantly changing economic environment in which business operates.

2

General Rules for the Presentation of Financial Statements

CONTENTS

2

General Rules for the Presentation of Financial Statements

Arthur J. Radin, CPA and
Miriam E. Katowitz, CPA

The general presentation of financial statements used in the United States is governed by rules and traditions that have developed over the last one hundred years. These are usually referred to as *generally accepted accounting principles*. Today, no one particular source for generally accepted accounting principles (GAAP) exists. GAAP has different applicability depending on the purpose of the specific financial statements.

SOURCES OF ACCOUNTING PRINCIPLES

The various specific sources of generally accepted accounting principles are the following:

1. Statements and Interpretations of the Financial Accounting Standards Board (FASB) and the Opinions of its predecessors, The Accounting Principles Board (APB), and the Accounting Research Board (ARB)—These statements have been accepted by the American Institute of Certified Public Accountants (AICPA) and must be used in all financial statements issued in accordance with generally accepted accounting principles.

2. Accounting Series Releases (ASR) of The Securities and Exchange Commission (SEC). These releases cover the information required in statements filed with the SEC. Under the Securities Act of 1933 and the Securities Exchange Act of 1934, Congress gave the SEC responsibility to set accounting principles for all filing made with the SEC. In general, the SEC has delegated this responsibility for setting accounting principles to the FASB and its predecessors. The SEC guide entitled "Regulation S-X Form and Content of Financial Statements" contains the required financial statement rules and disclosures that the SEC rules go beyond the pronouncements of the FASB.

In cases where the SEC rules differ from the FASB pronouncements, the SEC rules do not apply to companies not required to file their financial statements with the SEC. Issuers of financial statements should be aware of the SEC requirements, as it may become necessary to justify why a disclosure made by the 10,000 largest companies was not necessary for a particular company.

3. Congress. Congress has become more interested in accounting principles as their impact has become more significant to the public. Congress periodically passes legislation to achieve a specific goal. For example, legislation was passed reinstating the investment tax credit which specifically stated that no one way of treating investment tax credit could be required by any Federal agency. The SEC has stated that there are two acceptable methods of treating investment tax credit:

1. Deferral and amortization over the life of the related asset or lease.
2. Reduction of the expense in the year utilized.

Congress has required that accounting rules must be created within a certain time span regarding accounting for oil exploration. As interest increases in accounting, more activity by Congress can be expected.

4. Industry Guides of the AICPA. These publications relate to particular industries or transactions and include the following titles: "Accounting for Real Estate Transactions," "Accounting for Motion Pictures," and "Accounting for Retail Land Sales." These publications have the same authority as the FASB pronouncements.

5. Tradition and analysis. Much of what is thought of as generally accepted accounting principles has grown up over the years without specific determination by any particular authoritative rule making body. Many of such principles were described in the Accounting Principles Board project "Inventory of Generally Accepted Accounting Principles." Accountants in the United States believed that accounting principles were generally accepted simply because they "are generally accepted," without a definition of what "generally accepted" really means. Further, many accounting problems are not covered by any of the pronouncements of the FASB and its predecessors. The treatment of these accounting problems must be deduced by analogy from pronouncements already made, or from what other companies are doing.

6. Statements of Position of the Accounting Standards Executive Committee of the AICPA (SOP). These statements are issued as suggestions to FASB, covering areas where FASB should issue rules. However, recently the FASB has not ruled on any of the areas suggested by the SOP's. While they do not have the force of the pronouncements of the FASB, they are preferred practice.

7. Statements of Auditing Standards (SAS). These statements, issued by a committee of the AICPA, generally cover auditing standards, not accounting principles. However, sometimes they cover accounting disclosures or principles. The most significant disclosures required by the SAS for related party transactions (SAS 6).

8. State and Municipal Financial Statements. Rules are issued by the Municipal Finance Officers Association.

9. International. An international committee is currently issuing general accounting and disclosure principles. While these are not effective in the United States, anyone dealing with international statements would be familiar with them.

10. Staff Accounting Bulletins (SAB). For many years, the staff of the SEC has informed accounting firms and other interested persons of internal policies followed by the staff of the Commission. These are policies which have not yet been included in Regulation S-X or in an ASR. While SAB's do not represent the official policy of the Commission, the SEC will generally object and issue a comment letter if a filing does not follow the rules issued in a SAB. As SAB's do not form an official part of GAAP, suggestions made in SAB's have not been included in this chapter.

11. Other. There are many financial statements that are not covered by generally accepted accounting principles. For example, financial statements conforming to the Internal Revenue Code, the requirements of other governments, or to different standards of accounting principles such as current value accounting. This chapter does not deal with financial statements covered by principles other than generally accepted accounting principles.

GENERAL CONCEPTS

There are general concepts that are used in financial statements irrespective of the principles employed. The following concepts arise more from logic than from any particular pronouncements:

1. Clarity
2. Comparability
3. Summarization
4. Completeness

Clarity. It is, of course, not possible to precisely define clarity. However, the preparer of a financial statement must realize that the statements will ultimately be read and used to make a financial decision by someone with less access than himself to the information used to prepare the statements. Accordingly, information should be as clear and as free from ambiguity as possible.

Comparability. A reader, in reading a financial statement, makes a basic assumption that the information has been compiled on a comparable basis except to the extent indicated. If a company changed its accounting principles at random, the usefulness of the statements would be greatly impaired. The APB issued Opinion 20 indicating that disclosure must be made whenever a principle is changed and that principles can only be changed when the new principle is preferable to the old principle.

Summarization. By definition, a financial statement is a summarization of the financial transactions that occurred. The appropriate level of summarization is a significant decision that must be made in the preparation of financial statements. Either too much detail or too little detail may result in the statements being misleading. As with clarity, no definitive summarization rules exist.

Completeness. The reader naturally makes the assumption that all information is given, which is necessary for the statements not to be misleading. If there is an essential piece of information, even if it is not required by any of the pronouncements, of course that information must be included in the financial statements.

One realizes that the concepts of clarity, completeness and summarization may in many circumstances be contradictory. It is for this reason that the preparation of financial statements is an art. The preparer of the financial statements has the responsibility to make them as clear, concise, and complete as possible.

Trueblood Report. In 1973, the AICPA established a Study Group headed by Mr. Robert M. Trueblood, to determine the needs of the users of financial statements. The final report, called "The Trueblood Report," detailed the objectives of financial statements. The report suggested sweeping changes in financial reporting and accounting principles, all of which are beyond the scope of this chapter. What is of significance to all preparers of financial statements, however, is the position taken in the report that all financial statements to be used outside of the company have the following characteristics in common:

1. They are to be used to help the reader make an economic decision related to the enterprise.
2. They are prepared for individuals who have limited access to information about the enterprise.
3. They are used to evaluate, predict, and compare future cash flows and earning power of the enterprise.

It may be helpful when a financial statement is drafted for the preparer to keep in mind the needs of potential users in order to make statements as useful as possible.

FINANCIAL STATEMENTS

Form. Financial statements present information at a point in time or the events over a period of time. Balance sheets and statements of owners present financial status at the former position, while income statements, statements of changes in financial position, and statements of changes of owners' equity report the events over a period of time. GAAP requires that if both a balance sheet and an income statement are given, then a statement of changes in financial position and the information normally contained in a statement of changes in owners' equity must also be given. However, there is no principle preventing the presentation of any one of the above statements individually.

The terminology used in this chapter is that required or suggested by the pronouncements or the most current usage. Most terminology is a matter of personal preference and other usages may also be appropriate. Certain usages are specifically proscribed by certain pronouncements, but these are relatively few.

General Information. There are infinite ways of presenting information in a financial statement. The rules generally require information to be given, but are not specific regarding the particular placement of the information. The following are disclosures and concepts related to disclosures which are generally required somewhere in all financial statements, but which do not necessarily lead to disclosure within any other caption:

1. *Form and identification of ownership*—The reader is entitled to know the form of ownership. This information is normally presented in the title of the statement (e.g., XYZ Corporation, ABC Partnership, etc). Frequently there is an identification of the ownership of the business, especially if there is a corporate owner. If the company has significant transactions with related parties, then the identification of ownership becomes more significant.

2. *Date of the statements and the period(s) covered.*

3. *Identification of the financial statements presented*—This identification is normally covered by the standard titles of balance sheet, income statement, etc.

4. *Accounting principles*—Under APB Opinion 22, all financial statements must indicate what accounting principles have been employed in the financial statements. Usually there is either an opening summary of the accounting principles or the principles are contained in the first footnote. These principles are usually stated without the specific amounts involved. The amounts are shown in later footnotes. Almost all financial statements have accounting principles notes on the following: (a) plant, property, and equipment, (b) depreciation, (c) inventory valuation, and (d) income tax accounting. Where applicable, one usually also sees footnotes on the following: (a) pension accounting, (b) consolidation accounting, (c) stock option accounting, (d) accounting for equity investment in subsidiaries, (e) lease accounting, etc. The significance of the accounting to each business shapes this disclosure. Most companies do not disclose their use of normal accrual accounting (e.g., the booking of sales on shipments or goods on receipt). However, if accrual accounting is not used in financial statements, then the basis that is employed, such as the cash basis, is always described.

5. *Other disclosures*—There is a general assumption in any presentation of financial statements that all information presented is that which is necessary to make the financial statements not misleading. Accordingly, the preparer of a financial statement must be confident that information taken at face value is not misleading. The most common example of such a disclosure is in related party transactions. A reader must have the information "Account receivable from related corporation" instead of a heading just called "Accounts Receivable." Further, as required by Statement of Auditing Standards No. 6, the amount of purchases from sales to or properties leased to or from related parties should be disclosed,

6. *Rounding*—While this subject sounds a bit mundane, the proper use of rounding can aid the preparer of a financial statement in expressing the proper view of the information being presented. Readers of financial statements have frequently complained that financial statements tend to exaggerate their degree of accuracy by showing amounts to the nearest dollar (or even to the penny) while the statements contain estimates, in significant areas. While no rules or guidelines exist in this area, a preparer of a financial statement may do well by rounding to the nearest thousand or possibly million.

7. *Pledged assets and secured debt*—As credit grantors are one of the important users of financial statements, a proper designation of assets that have been pledged as security against a debt is very important. A creditor reading a financial statement has the right to assume that all creditors share equally in all assets unless the financial statement indicates otherwise. Therefore, whereever a creditor has the right to receive a preference over any other, this preference should be disclosed. For example, the pledging of assets should be disclosed by reference to both the asset pledged and and the liability incurred.

8. *Materiality*—Materiality is one of the most difficult problems for any preparer of a financial statement. Everything could be designated as material, but the process of adjusting the financial statements and preparing the disclosures would be never ending. In order to make the financial statement reasonable and timely summaries of financial events, many matters must be deemed to be immaterial. There are few guidelines in the pronouncements of the FASB and its predecessors as to materiality. The SEC has defined "material" in Regulation S-X as follows: "The term 'material' when used to qualify a requirement for the furnishing of information as to any subject, limits the information required to those matters about which an average prudent investor ought reasonably to be informed."

The SEC further states in S-X many limits below which disclosure need not be made. The more important of these limits are noted in this chapter in the appropriate sections. It should be remembered that all disclosures suggested herein are assumed to be relating to material items only.

9. *Contingencies*—FASB 5 defines a contingency "as an existing condition, situation, or set of circumstances involving uncertainty as to possible gain or loss to an enterprise that will ultimately be resolved when one or more future events occur or fail to occur."

The proper treatment of contingencies is covered by FASB 5 and ARB 50. All material contingencies should be disclosed: (a) asset contingencies are recorded when there is reasonable assurance that they are collectible; (b) liability or loss contingencies are recorded when they are reasonably estimable and the loss probably will occur." FASB also defines when a contingent loss must be disclosed. A reader may reasonably assume that no contingencies exist unless there is disclosure to the contrary.

Approach of this chapter. The application of accounting principles has grown into a large and complex field. It is, of course, not possible to incorporate all the accounting principles that may affect an account into one chapter. This chapter is intended to present the more important disclosures that the preparer of a financial statement is likely to encounter. Further, this chapter is biased towards commercial profit-making organizations; however, almost all of the disclosure principles involved also apply to not-for-profit, governmental and other similar entities.

BALANCE SHEET PRESENTATION

The exact format of financial statements, including the balance sheet, is a matter of personal taste. The most common format is the standard two column balanced approach. Some companies utilize the step approach showing current assets, then current liabilities, then non-current assets and then non-current liabilities, with the remainder being equity.

The preparer has the choice of placing certain information on the balance sheet itself or in the footnotes. The only requirement as to placement is the SEC regulation requiring the aggregate preference on involuntary liquidation of a preferred stock to be on the face of the balance sheet itself.

Current assets and current liabilities are generally shown. Current assets are defined by ARB 43 as those "assets that may reasonably be expected to be realized in cash, sold or consumed within a year, or within the normal operating cycle of the business if the cycle exceeds one year." They are listed in general order of liquidity. There are, however, exceptions when current assets and liabilities are not felt to be significant. Examples are: leasing companies, real estate companies, insurance companies, and finance companies.

Cash. Accounting disclosures for cash are defined by Regulation S-X. Separate disclosure is required for the following:

1. Cash on hand and unrestricted demand deposits.
2. Deposits subject to restrictions such as compensation balance requirements.
3. Time deposits and certificates of deposits.
4. Funds subject to repayment on call from a lender or funds repayable immediately after balance sheet date.

All information pertinent to (2) and (4) should be disclosed. Questions often arise as to whether checks on hand at year end, but not yet deposited on a timely basis, or monies receivable at year end, but not received until later, should be included in cash. As a general rule, if the question "Can you draw a check on it?" can be answered affirmatively, then it is appropriate to include that amount in cash. Otherwise, a separate caption should be used.

The following are possible footnotes regarding cash:

	December 31,	
	19X2	*19X1*
a. Cash on hand and demand deposits	$1,225,000	$2,678,000
Deposits needed to support borrowings	4,000,000	3,000,000
Certificates of Deposits	3,000,000	2,000,000
	$8,225,000	$7,678,000

b. The cash balance included at December 31, 19X2, $4,000,000 ($3,000,000 in 19X1) of compensating balances needed to support borrowing arrangements and $3,000,000 ($2,000,000 in 19X1) certificates of deposits.

	December 31,	
	19X2	*19X3*
Cash, including restricted balances of $4,000,000-19X2 and $3,000,000-19X1	$5,225,000	$5,678,000
Certificates of Deposits	3,000,000	2,000,000
	$8,225,000	$7,678,000

c. Restricted cash shown on the balance sheet represents the portion of trusted cash accounts to be used for the payment of costs related to lease obligations.

Marketable securities. Marketable securities include investments which are either readily marketable or mature within a year. The following are types of securities which should *not* be included in current assets: securities intended to be used for non-working capital purposes, securities covered by sales restrictions, securities for which there does not exist a public market (unless maturing in one year), securities of affiliates, and securities pledged under long-term debt agreements. The carrying basis of the securities and the current market value should be given. The appropriate carrying values are prescribed by FASB 12.

The following are possible disclosures of marketable securities:

a. Temporary investments, at cost accumulated interest, which approximates market	$800,000
b. United States Treasury Notes, at cost (approximates market)	$800,000
c. Marketable equity securities, at market (cost $1,200,000)	$800,000

d. Marketable equity security portfolios are carried at the lower of aggregate cost or market value. Valuation allowances adjust aggregate cost to market value when market value is less than aggregate cost.

e. Marketable securities are valued at cost plus accrued interest which approximates market value. Marketable securities consist of the following at December 31:

U.S. Government securities	$100,000
State and municipal securities	200,000
Time deposits	100,000
Commercial paper	150,000
Industrial bonds and other	250,000

Accounts and notes receivable. This caption includes all amounts expected to be collected during one operating cycle (generally one year). The following amounts are normally shown as separate items:

a. Trade receivables from customers—If a few customers represent a major portion of the balance, this information should be disclosed.
b. Notes receivable amounts due from affiliates—Such amounts should be included only if the expectation is that the amounts will be collected within one operating cycle. This expectation should be supported by a review of the affiliates' financial statements or other objective evidence.
c. Amounts due from other related parties—such as stockholders, officers, employees, directors, etc.
d. Amounts due from companies the investment in which it is being carried on the equity method.
e. Receivables under long-term contracts recognized on the percentage of completion method including the extent to which they had not yet been billed.
f. Receivables generated from other sources—An appropriate description should be included.

To the extent that receivables are not expected to be collected within one operating cycle, the amount expected to be collected after one year and the interest being charged should be disclosed.

Allowances for doubtful accounts and returns. The allowance for doubtful accounts is the general allowance for uncollectible accounts. A known uncollectible balance should be written off.

The allowance for returns represents the estimated lost gross margin on returns on all sales made with the right of return privileges. The general approach to such an allowance is covered by the AICPA *Statement of Position on Accounting when the Right of Return Exists.* Wherever such a policy exists, the accounting for sales should be disclosed.

The following are examples of presentations of receivables and allowances:

a. Trade receivables	$13,000,000
Due from affiliated companies for sale of merchandise	1,289,000
Balance due on sale of property	890,000
	$15,179,000
Less: Allowance for uncollectible amounts	750,000
	$14,429,000

b. Receivables are stated net of an allowance for uncollectibles of $750,000 and include an amount from an affiliate of $1,289,000 and the balance due on the sale of property of $890,000.

c. The Company normally extends trade terms in excess of one year. Receivables expected to be collected after one year total $2,793,000.

d. Receivables include $3,526,000 under the long-term construction contract which includes revenues computed under the percentage of completion method. Of the total, $3,276,000 has not been billed.

e. Notes and accounts receivable less discounts and allowances: 19X2—$500,000; 19X1—$490,000.
The Company has sold certain receivables with recourse liability approximating $5,000,000 and $6,000,000 at December 31, 19X2 and 19X1.

f. Receivables include the following:

Trade receivables	$3,124,000
Installment notes	5,670,000
Retentions of long-term contracts	4,101,000
Due from nonconsolidated subsidiaries	2,284,000
Less: Allowance for doubtful accounts receivable	750,000
	$14,429,000

In accordance with generally recognized trade practices, all installment notes including those which mature subsequent to one year amounting to $3,541,000 at December 31, 19X2 and $3,210,000 at December 31, 19X1, have been included in current assets.

Retentions on long-term contracts include $3,000,000 at December 31, 19X2 and $3,100,000 at December 31, 19X1 which are collectible after one year.

Inventories. Inventories are stated separately for raw materials, work-in-process, finished goods, supplies, and unbilled costs on uncompleted contracts. The carrying basis for inventories, usually the lower of cost or market, must be stated along with the method of determining cost. Such methods include first-in, first-out (FIFO), last-in, first-out (LIFO), average cost, etc.

Additional disclosures should be made under the following circumstances:

1. If LIFO is used in excess of the current replacement cost or the current cost should be given.
2. Companies with long-term contracts using either the completed contracts method or the percentage of completion method should make the disclosures required by Regulation S-X or ARB 45, whichever applies.
3. Inventories of commodities are frequently carried at cost adjusted for hedging gains and losses.

4. If general and administrative expenses are included in inventories, Regulation S-X requires disclosures of the amount incurred during the year and the amount included in the year-end inventories.

Examples of the above additional disclosures are the following:

	19X2	*19X1*
a. Inventories at lower of cost (principally first-in, first-out) or market:		
Raw materials	$ 5,012,000	$ 3,521,000
Work in process	2,321,000	3,384,000
Finished goods	7,754,000	5,543,000
Costs recoverable under contract (net of progress billings of $1,984,000 and $2,101,000)	1,387,000	2,721,000
Fully and partially developed real estate	1,009,000	900,000
	$17,483,000	$14,429,000

b. Inventory amounts are based upon physical determinations during the year. The Company uses the LIFO method for determining costs for substantially all of its domestic inventories. All other inventories are stated at the lower of cost or market with cost prices determined by the FIFO method.

c. If the FIFO method of inventory accounting had been used, inventories would have been $5,291,000 and $4,986,000 higher than reported. In 19X2, as a result of a reduction in LIFO inventory, quantities which were accrued at lower costs prevailing in prior years, net earnings were increased by approximately $3,501,000 or $.50 per share.

d. Cocoa, grain, and meal are valued at market, adjusted for hedges and undelivered contracts. The policy of hedging grain and meal positions is followed in order to minimize the risk arising from market fluctuations. Feeds and poultry are valued at average processed cost (not in excess of market) and other items of inventory are valued principally at the lower of FIFO costs or market.

Inventories consist of the following:	
Cocoa, grain and meal	XXX
Feeds and poultry	XXX
Ingredients, containers and supplies	XXX

Prepaid expenses and other current assets. Prepaid expenses and other current assets should be stated separately, if significant.

Noncurrent receivables. Amounts due beyond one operating cycle should be stated by types similar to those used for current receivables. Disclosures should include general identification of the receivable, period over which payments are due, interest rate and any discount for interest required under APB Opinion 21. The following is a typical disclosure of the above:

> Noncurrent receivables arose from the sale of property in a prior year. The notes receivable carry an interest rate of 4%; they have been discounted ($46,000 at December 31, 19X2; $49,000 at December 31, 19X1) to the company's then normal borrowing rate for such receivables. The balance is collectible in equal payments over the next four years.

Investments in securities. Investments in securities, other than those carried on the equity method, should be stated with the carrying values prescribed by FASB 12. Disclosure examples are as follows:

a. Noncurrent marketable securities are held for future expansion. They are carried at cost. The market value of the securities is $3,849,000.

b. Noncurrent marketable securities are held for future expansion. They are carried at the market value of $2,849,000, which is $739,000 less than cost. The excess of cost over market is shown as a reduction of shareholders' equity.

c. Investments in securities are carried at the lower of the aggregate cost or market determined at the end of the year. The investment is classified as a non-current asset since the investment program is an on-going activity of the Company and does not represent a temporary investment of excess funds. Security transactions are accounted for on the date they are purchased or sold. Realized gains or losses are determined on the basis of specific identification of the securities sold. Dividend income is recorded on the ex-dividend date.

d. The cost of investment securities ($3,479,000 at December 31, 19X2 and 19X1) exceeds market value by $130,000 and $543,000 at December 19X2 and 19X1. The net unrealized loss on investment securities is recorded as a valuation allowance charged to stockholders' equity. At December 31, 19X2 there were no unrealized gains. The amounts of $320,000 and $453,000 have been credited and charged to stockholders' equity for the change in the net unrealized loss during 19X2 and 19X1 respectively.

Investments in, and advances to, companies carried on the equity method. Investments in companies are carried on the equity method as described in APB Opinion 18. If the assets or operations of such investees are material to the parent's statements, summary statements of the investee should also be given. Regulation S-X defines material as being more than 10% of sales, income or assets.

The following is a typical disclosure under the equity method:

a. Investments	$XXX
Associated companies at equity	XXX
Other, at cost	XXX
	$XXX

b. The equity method of accounting is used for all investments in companies in which the Company's investment is 20% or more. Under the equity method, the Company recognizes its share in the net earnings or losses of these companies as they occur rather than when dividends are received. Investments in companies in which the ownership interest is less than 20% are carried at cost.

Investment in joint ventures, at equity	$4,320,000
Investment in joint ventures, at cost	1,296,000
	$5,616,000

c. The consolidated financial statements include the accounts of the Company and all of its wholly-owned subsidiaries. Investments in significant unconsolidated affiliates owned 20% or more are recorded at cost plus equity in undistributed earnings since acquisition, except for one investment carried at cost plus equity in undistributed earnings.

d. The Company owned 50% of the following companies at December 19X2 and 19X1 which were accounted for on the equity method for the years then ended:

ABC
DEF
GHI

Plant, Property and Equipment and Related Depreciation. These assets include such captions as the following:

Land.
Building.
Machinery and equipment.
Leasehold improvements.
Leased assets.
Construction in progress.

For leasing companies, captions are used indicating revenue producing equipment or equipment leased to others. The carrying basis of these assets should be given, normally by stating "at cost."

Accumulated depreciation should be given. It is sometimes stated by asset caption. The accounting principle footnote should give the depreciation policy and in SEC filings the lives of the assets.

Assets not used in operations should be disclosed separately. Examples of such assets include assets held for sale, construction in progress or temporary excess capacity. Disclosure should be made to the extent that these or similar assets are not being depreciated.

Many companies have unusual policies regarding plant additions or depreciation. These include utilities, companies which manufacture products for their own use and include administrative costs and/or profits in plant, companies that capitalize interest, companies using group methods of depreciation, etc. Such policies should be disclosed.

The following are examples of footnotes:

a. Property, plant and equipment, at cost

Land and improvements	$ —	$ —
Buildings and equipment	5,124,000	5,124,000
Machinery and equipment	4,356,000	5,621,000
Leasehold improvements	8,185,000	5,227,000
Construction in progress	—	980,000
Less: accumulated depreciation and amortization	9,005,000	9,567,000
	$8,660,000	$5,425,000

b. Depreciation and amortization of plant and equipment are provided by the company and its subsidiaries, generally using the straight-line method, based on estimated useful lives of the assets. For Federal income tax purposes, most assets are depreciated using allowable accelerated methods.

c. Ranges of annual depreciation rates used by the company and its subsidiaries are as follows:

Land improvements	2-15%
Buildings and Equipment	2-15%
Machinery and equipment	5-33½ %
Leasehold improvements	Life of the Lease

Repair and maintenance costs are charged against earnings while renewals and betterments are capitalized by additions to the related asset accounts. The Company and its subsidiaries generally record retirements by removing the cost and accumulated depreciation from the asset and reserve accounts, reflecting any resulting gain or loss in earnings.

Goodwill and other Intangibles. Intangibles should be classified by type. The only material intangible tends to be goodwill. The proper accounting for goodwill acquired after November 30, 1970 is described in APB Opinions 16 and 17. The latter opinion requires the amortization of all intangibles over a life not to exceed 40 years. Normally intangibles are stated net of amortization. The accounting policy with respect to intangibles should be stated. If goodwill was acquired prior to November 30, 1970 and is therefore not being amortized, this fact should be stated. Further, a footnote should indicate that "in the opinion of management that there has been no diminution in value." Intangibles should be periodically revaluated to determine that the lives originally estimated are still clearly appropriate. This revaluation is particularly important for any intangible acquired before December 1, 1970 that are not being amortized.

The footnotes on goodwill normally read as follows:

a. Of the goodwill, $3,867,000 was acquired prior to December 1, 1970 and is not being amortized. In the opinion of management, there has been no diminution in the value of such goodwill. The balance was acquired after November 30, 1970 and is being amortized over 40 years from the dates of acquisition. Amortization expense was $60,000 and $45,000 for 19X2 and 19X1, respectively.

	19X2	*19X1*
b. Excess of cost over net assets of acquired companies less accumulated amortization of $1,201,000 in 19X2 and $986,000 in 19X1	4,256,000	4,321,000

The excess of purchase cost over the net assets of acquired companies includes $1,625,815 relating to an acquisition in 1971. Such excess is being amortized by charges to income on a straight-line basis over 40 years in accordance with accounting rules related to acquisitions subsequent to October 31, 1970. The excess of purchase cost over the net assets of companies acquired prior to November 1, 1970 is not being amortized since, in management's opinion, its value has not diminished.

c. Other Assets:

Excess of cost of net assets acquired over amounts assigned	$2,221,000
Patents, trademarks and other intangible assets at cost, net of amortization	976,000
	$3,197,000

Patents and trademarks of acquired companies are being amortized on a straight-line basis over 10 and 20 years, respectively.

d. Other Assets:

	19X2	*19X1*
Cash surrender value of insurance on lives of key employees	$ 120,000	$ 80,000
Deferred income taxes	600,000	100,000
Deposits and sundry	480,000	320,000
	$1,200,000	$500,000

Deferred charges. If significant (significant being defined as 5% of total assets by Regulation S-X) these should be stated separately.

Current liabilities. Current liabilities are defined by ARB 43 as "any liability whose liquidation is reasonably expected to require the use of existing resources properly classified as current assets." As no business uses an operation cycle of less than 12 months, all debts which come due within 12 months from the balance sheet date must be included in current liabilities.

The pronouncements of the FASB and its predecessors give little guidance as to what current liabilities should specifically be disclosed other than income taxes. However, most statements include the following:

- Due to banks and/or factors
- Notes payable
- Trade accounts payable
- Accrued expenses
- Current portion of long-term debt
- Due to affiliates
- Income taxes payable
- Other current liabilities
- Dividends declared

With the exception of the current portion of long-term debt, there is rarely a difficult problem of the classification of liabilities between long- and short-term. Debt problems are described below under "long-term debt."

Due to banks or other institutional lenders. For such amounts, disclosure should be made as to the interest rates, due dates and the general nature of the form of debt. Normally, such debt is covered by a formal agreement with the banks, the terms of which should be disclosed. The agreements usually contain provisions relating to assets pledged, provisions for extensions, compensating balances, restricted activities, etc. The more significant of these provisions should be disclosed. Under Regulation S-X, additional disclosures are required as to the average interest rates, average borrowings and maximum borrowings. Consideration should be given to similar disclosures in non-public companies where borrowings from banks are important. The extent of lines of credit should also be disclosed along with any related restrictions.

a. Borrowing Arrangements (in part)—The company had unused lines of credit amounting to $7,000,000 at December 31, 19X2. Bank balances of approximately $2,260,000 were maintained at the banks as compensating balances.

b. Notes Payable to Banks—The Company borrows funds from various banks on a short-term basis as required. During 19X2, the average balance of such borrowings was $5,298,000 at a weighted average interest rate of 8.43%. The highest month-end balance was $6,000,000 at February 29, 19X2. The average interest rate at December 31, 19X2 was 8.25%.

Trade accounts payable. No special disclosures are normally required as to these balances. However, consideration should be given to disclosing the extent that they are due to a limited number of creditors and to the extent amounts are past due. Amounts due to affiliates should not be included with other trade creditors.

Notes payable. The amounts of interest and due dates should be disclosed. Trade notes payable should be segregated from other payables.

Accrued expenses. Most balance sheets show this caption as one amount including the balance, a wide variety of unnamed liabilities. Regulation S-X requires a breakdown of accrued salaries, tax liability, interest and any other significant items. While it is difficult to state a general rule, no single items should be included in this caption where its separate disclosure would be significant to the reader.

Current portion of long-term debt. This amount is normally referenced to the footnote disclosure on long-term debt. (See below—long-term debt section.)

Due to affiliates. As with all balances between related parties, these must be shown separately and a description of the transactions included in the footnotes. It is normally not appropriate to include these balances with normal trade liabilities.

Income taxes payable. These, both the payable and the current deferred, are discussed under "Income Tax Disclosures" below.

Other current liabilities. Regulations S-X indicates separate disclosure should be made of any item in excess of 5% of current liabilities. If dividends have been declared but are unpaid, they should be separately disclosed. The following are typical of disclosures of current liabilities:

a. Current liabilities:

Notes payable—banks	$XXX
Notes payable—other	XXX
Accounts payable—trade	XXX
Accrued employee compensation benefits	XXX
Income taxes	XXX
Taxes other than income taxes	XXX
Other current liabilities	XXX
Total current liabilities	$XXX

b. Current liabilities

Notes payable to banks	$XXX
Accounts and trade acceptances payable	XXX
Income taxes	XXX
Estimated warranty costs	XXX
Commissions payable	XXX
Accrued expenses and other	XXX
Long-term debt due within one year	XXX
Total current liabilities	$XXX

c. Current Liabilities

Accounts payable	$XXX
Income taxes payable	XXX
Sundry liabilities and accrued expenses	XXX
Redemption requirement—preferred stock (200 shares)	XXX
Total current liabilities	$XXX

Long-term debt. Almost all companies raise some of their capital from borrowings, most of which contain a long-term segment. The proper treatment and disclosures relating to the debt have become more and more difficult as the instruments used for borrowings have become more and more complex and recent economic conditions have produced credit squeezes. Preparers of financial statements frequently have to obtain the counsel of attorneys in order to determine what the instruments mean and whether there have been any defaults.

There are no specific pronouncements on debt disclosures. Tradition and normal logic indicate that the following are the minimum disclosures:

1. Title of debt or the nature of the borrowing.
2. Interest rates.
3. Payment requirements and due dates.
4. General description of debt restrictions and defaults that have occurred.
5. Any assets pledged as collateral against the debt.
6. An indication of priority.
7. If convertible, the basis, terms and period.

Further, Regulation S-X requires the following additional disclosures which should be considered for non-public companies:

1. The aggregate maturities and payments for all debt for each of the next five years.
2. Amounts and terms of unused financing arrangements.

Disclosure of the title of the debt and the interest and payment terms rarely create problems. If the debt has a rate dependent on another rate, the most common example being the prime bank rate, then the terms should be stated with the appropriate rate at the end of the period. If this rate has changed significantly from the end of the year to the date that the preparer is issuing the statements, then the current rate should be indicated. Where there have been significant increases or decreases in the amount of debt recorded because of the use of an interest rate different from the stated rate, as required by APB Opinion 21, then the effect of the discounting or the accretion should be indicated with the new effective rate.

A general description of the most restrictive debt instrument is normally stated. This disclosure can be quite brief. If the availability of retained earnings for dividends are restricted under the loan agreements, the amount of the restriction should be indicated.

If the company is currently in default of any of the debt provisions at the balance sheet date which have not been waived, then the default must be described. The entire amount of the liability must be classified as current if the default causes the debt to become current. The liability should not be classified as current if the lender has waived the accelerated due date or agreed to a new due date more than a year from the balance sheet date. The provision waived by the lender and the waiver period should be described.

If the company is in default of some or all of the debt, or has a reasonable possibility of becoming in default, then the provisions should be described in some detail. Further, if the company's current projections indicate that it will be in default during the next 12 months, consideration should be given to classifying the debt as current, as it can be reasonably expected to require the use of current assets to satisfy the debt. Where the company has been in default during the year, but has obtained a waiver during the year as to one or more significant matters, consideration should be given to disclosing the defaults if the reader of the financial statements would be interested in that information.

Disclosures as to assets pledged, priority, and convertibility normally can be made routinely. Indications such as "mortgage payable" are frequently used to indicate that real property has been pledged. If the assets pledged are greater in number, then a footnote is normally used. Priority is normally indicated by the use of "subordinated" where appropriate.

Where there is current debt with agreements to refinance, FASB 15 should be consulted.

The capitalization of certain leasing arrangements is required under FASB 13. The debt portion of any capital leases requires disclosure as described above.

Due to the complexity and variety of long-term debt agreements no examples are presented here. The reader is referred to the current edition of *Accounting Trends & Techniques* published annually by the AICPA.

Deferred credits. The pronouncements of the FASB and its predecessors have produced a large number of deferred credit accounts. One may see in any financial statement, one or more of the following:

1. Deferred income tax investment credit
2. Deferred gain on sale and leaseback
3. Deferred income taxes
4. Deferred income on uncompleted sales arrangements
5. Excess of pension costs expensed over those funded
6. Deferred compensation

In each case, disclosure should be made describing the accounting policy creating the deferral and any other relevant information.

Equity account. This account states the composition of the excess (or deficiency) of assets over liabilities. Whether it is a corporation, partnership or proprietorship, a distinction is normally made between contributed capital and earned capital. There are many examples of varying ways of making this presentation. This section lists some of the lesser known disclosure areas relating to the equity section.

Difficulties sometimes arise in complex preferred stock issues. The following are disclosures which may apply to a preferred stock:

1. If callable, the price and date of possible call.
2. If convertible, the provisions of convertibility.
3. If on liquidation, voluntary or involuntary, the preference shares receive an amount in excess of the par or stated value, that information should be disclosed (in the aggregate on the face of the balance sheet for statements prepared in accordance with Regulation S-X).
4. If there is a dividend arrearage, the amount should be disclosed.

The issuance of FASB 12 in 1975, created a new caption in the equity section: "Reduction to market of portfolio securities with original carrying values in excess of cost." Whenever there are marketable securities not carried as a current asset and the aggregate market value of the securities is less than cost, FASB 12 requires that they be reduced to cost with the offsetting charges made to equity. This balance stays in equity until either the security's aggregate market value rises above cost or they are sold, in which case a charge is made to operations.

Regulation S-X requires that unpaid receivables from share subscriptions be treated as a reduction in the equity section.

Recent tax legislation created Employee Stock Ownership Plans (ESOP). Companies can, as part of an ESOP arrangement, guarantee the debts of a related ESOP. Wherever there is such a guarantee, the amount should be shown as a liability and an offsetting reduction to equity.

At January 1, 19X3, there were 55,000 shares of $500 par value non-cumulative 5% preferred stock issued and outstanding. The company is permitted to acquire all outstanding shares at any time and is required to provide sinking fund payments annually for mandatory redemption of the preferred shares of consolidated net income for the prior fiscal year. The July 19X3 requirement of $100,000 for redemption of 200 shares is reflected as a current liability in the accompanying balance sheet.

INCOME STATEMENT PRESENTATION

The interest in the financial community in the income statement has resulted in pronouncements by the FASB, its predecessors, and the SEC as to what should and should not be on the face of the income statement. The following represent such pronouncements:

1. Earnings per share must be stated (APB Opinion 15 partially suspended by FASB 21).
2. Per share effect of unusual and recurring changes and credits must be stated (APB Opinion 30).
3. Per share effect of unusual or recurring (but not both) must *not* be stated on the face of the income statement (APB Opinion 30).
4. The word "net" must be used only with the final "net income" and not with any preceding subtotal that could be confused with "net income" (APB Opinion 30).
5. The gain or loss and the reduction in sales, costs and expenses resulting from the disposition of a segment of a business must be disclosed on the face of the income statement.
6. The gain or loss and the reduction in sales, costs and expenses resulting from the disposition of a portion of a segment of a business must *not* be disclosed on the face of the income statement nor may the resultant earnings per share be shown (APB Opinion 30).
7. The amounts described in Item 5 above must be shown net of income taxes; the amounts in Item 6 above must *not* be shown net of income taxes.
8. Changes in accounting principles that result in cumulative adjustments to be shown on the face of the income statement (APB Opinion 20).
9. If interest is capitalized, in each year the amount of interest capitalized during the year and the amount of previously capitalized interest amortized must be disclosed in the income statement (Regulation S-X).

For Items (3) and (5), disclosure of the information forbidden in the income statement must be made in the footnotes.

Once past the specific "do's" and "don'ts," the income statement presentation is not complex. The accounting policy and related disclosures are covered elsewhere herein.

Sales. The amount of sales must be given. Generally sales taxes, freight charges and similiar items are not included in sales. Further, companies handling receipts for others, such as credit card companies, commissions merchants, etc., should state only their portion of the revenues although the total turnover may be included for information purposes. Regulation S-X requires disclosures if sales include more than 10% of other revenues and the majority of sales is tangible products.

Costs and expenses. There is no rule as to what information belongs here and what should be included in a footnote. Further, the use of subtotals is up to the preference of the preparer. Most companies show (a) cost of sales, (b) selling, general and administrative expenses, and (c) interest costs. After a subtotal, income taxes are deducted resulting in net income. However, this presentation should be changed as required.

If disclosures of discontinued operations or extraordinary items as required by APB Opinion 30 are made, then these must be included. Further, one frequently sees items such as pension costs, research and development, taxes other than income taxes, unusual or non-recurring charges or credits, depreciation, selling expenses or any significant item shown separately.

Certain industries have reporting formats developed by tradition or prescribed by accounting literature. For example, retailers traditionally have shown costs and expenses as follows:

—Costs and expenses other than those that follow
—Taxes, other than income taxes
—Depreciation
—Maintenance and repairs
—Interest

In SEC filings, they are required to include a footnote indicating cost of sales. The retail land companies have the format of their statements spelled out by the AICPA "Retail Land Sales Guide."

Earnings per share. In order to create uniformity in the reporting of earnings per share, APB Opinion 15 was issued. Earnings per share is a problem for accountants because it is not really an accounting matter. An accountant can, using the available tools, determine income; however, the shares outstanding in complex situations is a determination for an investment banker, not an accountant. The APB filled the gap with Opinion 15 which gives detailed explanations as to the computation of earnings per share and diluted earnings per share. Many accountants working with smaller companies objected to the disclosures believing them to be at best meaningless and possibly misleading. In April, 1978, the FASB with the issuance of FASB 21, suspended the requirement for such a disclosure on non-public companies. Earnings per share and similar disclosures are still required for all SEC reporting companies.

STATEMENT OF CHANGES IN FINANCIAL POSITION

APB Opinion 19 required the use of a statement of changes in financial position. The statement normally has two sections:

a. The presentation of sources and uses of working capital arriving at the net change in working capital, and
b. the tabulation of the changes in the individual current assets and current liabilities resulting in the same net change as shown in (a) above.

The APB required the use of a gross method of reporting. Under this method, all changes are to be included in the statement even though they do not affect working capital. For example, if convertible debt is converted into common stock, the issuance of stock should be shown as a source of funds and the reduction of debt as a use of funds.

The statement must start with earnings before extraordinary items, to which is added all non-cash charges to earnings (depreciation, amortization, undistributed loss of unconsolidated subsidiaries) and from which is subtracted non-cash credits to income (undistributed earnings of unconsolidated subsidiaries). The net total can be described as funds provided from (or used in) operations. However, the Opinion states that one cannot show this amount per share as that may reflect poorly on net earnings per share as the proper measure of an enterprise's earnings power.

STATEMENT OF CHANGES IN OWNERS' EQUITY

Various APB Opinions have required the presentation of information relating to changes in shareholders' equity whenever a full set of financial statements is presented. While the specific statement is not required, the changes in outstanding stock, treasury stock, paid-in capital accounts, and retained earnings are required. For the convenience of the reader, it is appropriate to present in one statement all of the equity accounts and details of the changes in these accounts.

Disclosures for certain areas. Certain areas require specialized disclosures beyond that required as a result of the asset, liability, and income statement captions. They are covered by rules which should be reviewed whenever the situation is encountered. They include the following:

—Income taxes
—Foreign currency translation
—Stock options and warrants
—Pension plans
—Segments of business disclosures
—Leases
—Contingencies

Income taxes. Income tax disclosures are described by APB Opinion 11 which provides for the deferred credit method of accounting. Under this method, as applied by Opinion 11, provisions are to be made for income taxes as if income tax returns were filed on the same basis that income is reported for financial reporting purposes. Accordingly, the income tax expense should be pre-tax income less permanent items multiplied by normal tax rates, less tax credits.

Permanent items are items such as non-deductible expenses, (e.g., life insurance premiums and goodwill amortization and non-reportable income such as proceeds of life insurance, etc.). More complex areas such as tax provisions on earnings and losses of equity investments and foreign earnings are covered by APB Opinions 23 and 24 and FASB 8 and 9.

As a result of the many differences in the timing of income and expenses for income tax purposes and financial reporting purposes, most financial statements reporting on GAAP show deferred tax liabilities or assets. Under APB Opinion 11, tax deferrals resulting from timing differences relating to current assets and current liabilities are to be shown as a current asset or a current liability. Timing differences relating to non-current assets and liabilities create non-current tax deferrals. The current items can be netted and the non-current items can be netted so that there is never a need for more than two deferred tax captions in any balance sheet.

APB Opinion 11 requires a general description of the reasons for timing differences and for any difference between tax provisions and normal tax rates. However, these explanations are not required to be detailed. The SEC in its ASR 149, required substantially more detail as follows:

1. Separate disclosure must be made of any timing difference which results in a deferral in excess of 5% of the statutory tax.
2. A reconciliation must be provided between the amount computed by multiplying reported income times the statutory tax rates and the amount shown for financial reporting purposes. Any differences in excess of 5% of the expected tax must be detailed.
3. If timing differences are expected to reverse in the next three years so as to create a cash outlay in excess of tax expense, this fact must be disclosed.

While the detailed information described in (a), (b) and (c) are only required in SEC filings, where there are unusual tax effects in other financial statements, consideration should be given to disclosures going beyond APB Opinion 11.

Net operating loss carry-forwards (NOL) create the following disclosures:

1. If they are utilized in any period, the reduction in taxes is to be shown as provision for taxes and an extraordinary credit;
2. If there are unsued NOL's at the date of the balance sheet, the amount and year of expiration are to be disclosed.

3. There are sometimes significant differences between the NOL's computed for financial reporting purposes and those shown on the tax return as a result of timing differences. If these are materially different, either as to amount or as to estimated period of expiration, then both should be disclosed.

In addition, any investment credit carry forwards, capital loss carry forwards or, charitable contribution carry forwards should be disclosed.

Examples of disclosures are as follows:

a. Deferred tax expense results from timing differences in the recognition of income for tax and financial statement purposes. The principal sources of these differences and their tax effects were as follows:
   Long-term contracts
   Depreciation
   Deferred compensation

b. The current liability for Federal income taxes includes $1,200,000 relating to the current portion of the timing differences.

c. The provisions for Federal income taxes were less than the U.S. Federal income tax rate of 48% of income before tax.

Investment tax credits	$498,000
Proceeds of insurance	280,000
Other	650,000

d. A reconciliation of the consolidated effect tax rate with the statutory 48% Federal income tax rate follows:

Consolidated effective tax rate	44.1%	45.6%
Investment tax credits	6.9	5.8
State income taxes, net of Federal income tax benefits	(2.9)	(3.1)
Other, net	48.0%	48.0%

Deferred Federal income taxes result from timing differences in the recognition of certain items for tax and financial reporting purposes. The deferred tax effect of the excess of tax reporting for depreciation over financial reporting for depreciation amounted to

Foreign translation. The appropriate method of translating foreign currency transactions, balances and contracts is remarkably difficult to present. Depending on the accounting used, there can be significantly different results, all quite logical. If money is borrowed in a different currency, it is equally logical to charge or credit current operations for a change in exchange rates as it is to amortize the effect of such changes over the term of the debt. Prior to the issuance of FASB 8 in October 1975, there was a substantial lack of consistency between different companies as to the policies to be followed for foreign currency translations.

Drafters of accounting principles always have problems as to whether to draft rigid rules giving no leeway, or flexible rules allowing the preparers of financial statements to decide what rule should be used. The first approach may force transactions into inappropriate results. Minor currency fluctuations may result in large earnings fluctuations, which management objects to as being misleading.

To counter the rigidness of the reporting rules of FASB 8, many companies have entered into currency transactions to minimize the effect of the fluctuations. Some commentators believe that corporate hedging to eliminate the unwanted effect of FASB 8 has produced both an unacceptable cost on American business and has added to the volatility of the foreign currency markets. The above is a very interesting example of the difficulty of creating accounting principles.

FASB 8 currently requires that accounts carried at prices in past exchanges be translated at historical rates and that accounts carried in current or future exchanges be translated at current rates. Forward exchange contracts gains and losses, both realized and unrealized, are included in income unless they are a "hedge of a foreign currency commitment" which is narrowly defined in the FASB. All other exchange gains and losses are also included in the income statement.

FASB 8 requires the following disclosures where foreign currency transactions are material:

1. The aggregate exchange gains and losses during a period.
2. The effects of rate changes on the reported operations to the extent not already covered by Item (1) above.
3. FASB 8 did not give specific requirements as to the disclosure of foreign operations, as its drafters expected that the Statement on Financial Reporting for Segments of a Business Enterprise (FASB 14) would cover such matters. It would appear that the applicable requirements from FASB 14 should be included where there are material foreign currency transactions even if FASB 14 remains suspended for the financial statement being prepared. The information required is the amounts of revenues, operating profit or loss, and identifiable assets of foreign operations. All of these items are carefully defined in FASB 14. Further, the geographic areas of operations are required to be presented.
4. It is frequently appropriate, although not specifically required, to give the currency in which debt is to be repaid if it is in a foreign currency.

Examples of footnotes are as follows:

a. Foreign currency cash and amounts receivable or payable are translated at current exchange rates. All other balance sheet accounts are translated at rates in effect at the time acquired (e.g., historical rate).

b. Revenue and expense transactions, except for depreciation and amortization, are translated at the average of exchange rates in effect during the period. Provisions for depreciation and amortization are translated at the same rates as the assets to which they apply.

   Resulting translation gains or losses are included in income for the year.

Foreign currency exchange adjustments charged or credited to income comprised:

Realized (gain)/loss on transactions during the year	XXX
Unrealized (gain)/loss on translation of assets and liabilities denominated in foreign currencies	XXX

c. In the consolidated statement of income realized gains or losses are included in divisional expenses. Unrealized gains or losses on translation are included in other income.

Stock options and warrants. Stock options and warrants create potential dilution of shareholders' equity and should be disclosed. Where there are stock options or warrants outstanding, the following should be disclosed:

1. The number of shares under option.
2. The portion currently exercisable.
3. The prices at which the options are exercisable.
4. Dates to which the options are exercisable.
5. Shares available for grant.
6. General description of the plan.
7. Accounting treatment of the plan and charges (or credits) required by APB Opinion 25.

For public companies, Regulation S-X requires additional tabulations which have not, by tradition, become part of the regular financial statements and therefore need not be included outside of SEC filings.

Examples of footnotes follow:

a. Options to purchase common shares of Company at market values on dates of grant have been granted to key employees under the Company's qualified stock option plans. The options exercisable over four years beginning one year from date of grant, are as follows:

	Shares
b. Under option at December 31, 19X1 ($10-$15 a share)	560,000
Exercised at $11.69 average a share	129,000
Cancelled	3,000
Under option at December 31, 19X2 ($15.46 to $10.26 a share)	428,000
Options exercisable at December 31, 19X2	306,000

Pension costs. Pensions have become a signficant cost to business. The APB wrote its Opinion Number 8 in order to obtain some consistency with the way companies were providing pension costs and disclosing the existence of pension responsibilities. The passage of the Employees' Retirement Income Security Act (ERISA) brought some consistency to plans but did not change any of the basic accounting. The disclosure requirements of this Opinion are as follows:

1. A statement that such plans exist, identifying or describing the employee groups covered.
2. A statement of the company's accounting and funding policies.
3. The provision for pension cost for the period.
4. The excess, if any, of the actuarially computed value of vested benefits over the total of the pension fund and any balance sheet pension accruals, less any pension prepayments or deferred charges.
5. Nature and effect of significant matters affecting comparability for all periods presented, such as changes in accounting methods (actuarial cost method, amortization of past and prior service cost, treatment of actuarial gains and losses, etc.), changes in circumstances (actuarial assumptions, etc.) or adoption or amendment of a plan.

An example of what the Board considered to be appropriate disclosure is as follows:

> The Company and its subsidiaries have several pension plans covering substantially all of their employees, including certain employees in foreign countries. The total pension expense for the year was $1,200,000 which includes, as to certain of the plans, amortization of prior service cost over periods ranging from 25 to 40 years. The Company's policy is to fund pension cost accrued. The actuarially computed value of vested benefits for all plans as of December 31, 19X2, exceeded the total of the pension fund and balance sheet accruals less pension prepayments and deferred charges by approximately $369,000. A change during the year in the actuarial cost method used in computing pension cost had the effect of reducing net income for the year by approximately $1,421,000.

Further, Regulation S-X requires the disclosure of unfunded past service costs. Also, since the passage of the Employee Retirement Income Security Act of 1974, most footnotes as to pension plans have indicated that the plans conform to the requirements of the Act and the regulations published under it.

Segments of a business enterprise. FASB 14 requires that in financial statements of public companies the following information as to each segment of business be present:

a. Types of products and services from which revenues are derived.
b. Revenue.
c. Profitability.
d. Identifiable assets.
e. Depreciation, depletion and amortizable expense.
f. Additions to plant, property and equipment.
g. Various other information specified in the Statement.

This statement was suspended in April 1978 for nonpublic companies. In general, these disclosures are being applied only to reports of public companies. However, it would seem appropriate to include in all reports Item (a) above in all statements being issued so that the reader of the financial statement knows in what business the company earns its revenues.

The statement contains many definitions as to rules of what is a segment and the nature of the information to be given. Whenever a financial statement to which FASB 14 applies is being issued, careful reference should be made to the statement.

Leases. FASB 13 gives the disclosure requirements for leases, both those treated as capitalized leases and those treated as operating leases.

Capital leases require the following disclosures:

1. The gross amount of assets recorded.
2. Future minimum lease payments in total and for each of the next five years.
3. Future sublease rentals to be received.
4. Total contingent rentals for each period for which an income statement is presented.

For operating leases, the following disclosures should be made:

1. Future rentals in total and for each of the next five years.
2. Future rentals to be received under subleases.
3. Rental expenses for each year for which an income statement is presented, separating minimum rentals, contingent rentals and sublease income.
4. A description of the leasing arrangement including such information as the basis for contingent rentals, renewal provisions, purchase options, escalation clauses, lease restrictions, etc.

Contingencies. The accounting and disclosure of contingencies is covered by FASB 5 which requires the following disclosures:

1. The nature and possibly the amount of a loss contingency for which an accrual has been made.
2. The nature and possible loss where no accrual has been made where there is a reasonable possibility that a loss has been incurred.
3. A post-balance sheet event which creates a reasonable possibility that a loss has been incurred.
4. An unasserted claim where it is considered probable that a claim will be asserted and that there is a reasonable possibility that there will be a loss.
5. Guarantees of the indebtedness of others or the repurchase of receivables.
6. Gain contingencies, although care should be taken to prevent misleading inferences of the likelihood of realization.

The terms used above have technical meanings. Where disclosure of a contingency is being considered, reference should be made to the statement itself.

ADDITIONAL SUGGESTIONS BEYOND GAAP

There are many ways of making financial statements useful to a reader beyond the specific rules of accounting principles. These depend on the circumstances and can be used as a preparer thinks best.

Analysis of the statements. For public companies in the past, there normally was some analysis of what had occurred. This analysis tended to support management. Recently the SEC has required "management's analysis of operations" to be included in annual reports. All changes over 10% must be discussed as well as certain other information. This analysis follows certain rules and tends to read like a footnote.

Another type of analysis is the description of that typically found in a president's letter in the annual report. These have been criticized as they tend to only indicate the positive even when it is almost impossible to find anything positive to say. Even so, it frequently is informative. Whatever type of analysis is used, it is almost always helpful to a reader to have some discussion of what has occurred.

Comparative information. Financial statements are much more useful when presented in a comparative format. All internal operating results are presented in some comparative format. For such statements, the format varies: this year to last year; this week to the same week last year and to last week; this month compared to plan and the same month last year. Most annual financial statements show a comparison of this year's statements to those of the preceding year. The SEC, understanding the necessity for comparative statements, requires two years' financial statements in annual reports and five years' statement of operations. Whenever comparative financial statements are used, the statements should be comparable unless a disclosure to the contrary is made.

Highlighting. Many readers do not have the interest to spend a significant amount of time analyzing financial statements. In most published annual reports, therefore, there is a page of financial highlights. On this page, the more significant financial items are stated. These items usually include sales, earnings, earnings per share, current ratios, shareholders' equity, and book value per share.

Computation of changes. Once financial statements are comparative, a reader has to make a mental (or written) calculation of the amount of the change in each caption. For the reader's convenience, some companies state the increase or decrease in a third column in the statements.

Use of Percentages. Most readers are comfortable with the use of percentages. Frequently, what is significant is not the amount of the change of an item, but rather the change in its relationship to another item. The statement of changes in financial position provides some, but not all, of such analysis for balance sheets.

Additional information. No matter how hard they try, those who write generally accepted accounting principles will never be able to define all information that might be useful to a reader. Such information may be tables, charts, verbiage, or additional data. The following are examples of additional data companies have provided:

—Sales by type of customer.
—Geographical breakdown of sales.
—Production by units rather than by dollars.
—Number of employees, by function and/or location.
—Production analysis between portion of products purchased and portion manufactured.

—Bad debt expense.
—Aging of receivables.
—Receivables by type of customer or type of sale.

Interim Financial Statements and Replacement Costs. For the aid of investors, the SEC has added to Regulation S-X the requirement that certain public companies include in a footnote the quarterly results for the year with an indication that they are unaudited. The major effect of this procedure is to obtain the level of auditors' review described in SAS 10.

For a limited number of large companies, the SEC has required disclosure of the replacement cost of plant and inventories. The rule for such amounts are described in Regulation S-X.

These disclosures have not been made by companies not covered by the specific regulations.

XYZ COMPANY

BALANCE SHEETS

AS OF DECEMBER 31, 19X2 AND 19X1

ASSETS

	19X2	*19X1*
Current assets:		
Cash	$ 8,225,000	$ 7,678,000
Marketable securities at market (Cost 19X2, $1,200,000; 19X1, $1,000,00)	800,000	850,000
Receivables:		
Trade accounts, less allowances of 19X2, $896,000; 19X1, $462,000	14,800,000	10,000,000
Due from officers	300,000	600,000
Other	1,200,000	—
Inventories, (lower of cost or market)	17,483,000	16,069,000
Prepaid expenses	700,000	679,000
Other current assets	200,000	500,000
Total current assets	43,708,000	36,376,000
Notes receivable	1,250,000	1,300,000
Investments and other assets	620,000	600,000
Investments and advances to 40% owned company carried on the equity method	900,000	—
Construction in progress	500,000	1,430,000
Property, plant and equipment, at cost less accumulated depreciation	9,160,000	7,835,000
Goodwill	4,256,000	4,321,000
Total assets	$60,394,000	$51,862,000

XYZ COMPANY

BALANCE SHEETS

AS OF DECEMBER 31, 19X2 AND 19X1

LIABILITIES AND OWNER'S EQUITY

CURRENT LIABILITIES	*19X2*	*19X1*
Notes payable to banks	$ 2,480,000	$ 2,248,000
Trade accounts payable	10,438,000	10,241,000
Trade notes payable	200,000	—
Accrued expenses	2,067,000	1,573,000
Due to related parties	890,000	—
Current portion of long term liabilities	1,221,000	1,119,000
Income taxes payable	2,442,000	2,629,000
Other current liabilities	936,000	925,000
Total current liabilities	20,674,000	18,735,000
LONG TERM LIABILITY		
Long term notes payable to banks and institutions	3,286,000	3,059,000
Subordinated convertible notes	1,250,000	1,300,000
Mortgages payable 5% to 12%, due 19X3, 19XX	4,445,000	3,206,000
Total long term liabilities	8,981,000	7,565,000
Deferred compensation	600,000	500,000
Deferred income taxes	1,200,000	995,000
OWNER'S EQUITY		
Preferred stock, 6% par value, $50 per share	250,000	250,000
Common stock, par value $1	3,000,000	3,000,000
Additional paid in capital	1,000,000	1,000,000
Retained earnings	25,394,000	19,612,000
Less treasury stock	1,225,000	1,225,000
Total owner's equity	32,999,000	26,582,000
Total liabilities and owner's equity	$62,654,000	$52,882,000

XYZ COMPANY

STATEMENTS OF INCOME

	19X2	*19X1*
NET SALES	$350,123,000	$306,997,000
Cost of sales	330,056,000	289,514,000
Selling, general and administrative expenses	10,946,000	9,835,000
	9,121,000	7,648,000
Proceeds of insurance	1,000,000	—
Interest income	382,000	350,000
Interest expense	(956,000)	(721,000)
Earnings before federal income taxes	9,547,000	7,277,000
Federal income taxes (including deferred taxes (credit) of 19X2 $1,110,000; 19X1 (200,000))	3,775,000	2,679,000
Net earnings	$ 5,772,000	$ 4,598,000
Net earnings per share	$1.93	$1.51

XYZ COMPANY

STATEMENTS OF OWNERS' EQUITY

	19X2	*19X1*
Balance at beginning of year	$22,367,000	$18,990,000
Net earnings	5,782,000	4,548,000
Deduct:		
Cash dividends	—	1,000,000
Preferred common stock	—	171,000
Balance at end of year	$28,149,000	$22,367,000

XYZ COMPANY
STATEMENTS OF CHANGES IN FINANCIAL POSITION

	19X2	*19X1*
Funds provided:		
Net earnings	$ 6,953,000	$4,598,000
Depreciation and amortization	809,000	784,000
Deferred federal income taxes	205,000	185,000
Deferred compensation	100,000	100,000
Funds provided from operations	8,067,000	5,617,000
Proceeds from issuance of long-term debt	2,637,000	—
Disposal of plant, property and equipment	523,000	—
Decrease (increase) in other noncurrent assets	50,000	75,000
Total funds provided	11,277,000	5,692,000
Funds used:		
Cash dividends	1,171,000	1,171,000
Reduction in long-term debt	1,221,000	1,119,000
Purchase of plant, property and equipment	2,572,000	1,394,000
Increase in investments	920,000	30,000
Total funds used	5,884,000	3,714,000
Increase in working capital	$ 5,393,000	$1,978,000
Changes in working capital:		
Increase (decrease) in current assets:		
Cash	$ 547,000	$ (30,000)
Marketable securities	(50,000)	100,000
Receivables	5,700,000	2,695,000
Inventories	1,414,000	2,492,000
Prepaid expenses	21,000	5,000
Other current assets	(300,000)	448,000
	7,932,000	5,710,000
Increase (decrease) in current liabilities:		
Notes payable to banks	232,000	(65,000)
Trade accounts payable	197,000	1,634,000
Trade notes payable	200,000	397,000
Accrued expenses	494,000	1,283,000
Due to related parties	890,000	100,000
Currtnt portion long-term liabilities	102,000	318,000
Income taxes payable	(187,000)	50,000
Other current liabilities	11,000	15,000
	1,939,000	3,732,000
	$ 5,393,000	$1,978,000

3

Business Combinations and Consolidated Financial Statements

CONTENTS

3

Business Combinations and Consolidated Financial Statements

Thomas E. King, Ph.D. and
Valdean C. Lembke, Ph.D.

Many companies have chosen to expand or diversify the scope of their activities by entering into some form of business combination in recent years. Along with this, the significance of intercorporate investments has increased, and the need for financial statements which reflect the operations of an economic entity composed of many related companies has grown. In fact, nearly all major corporations currently prepare consolidated financial statements. This chapter deals with the accounting for formal business combinations, the treatment of intercorporate investments, and the preparation of consolidated financial statements. Authoritative pronouncements of the American Institute of Certified Public Accountants and others are discussed where appropriate.

ACCOUNTING FOR BUSINESS COMBINATIONS

A business combination occurs when two or more separate companies join together under common ownership. This may take the form of one company obtaining a majority of the outstanding voting stock of another, with both companies maintaining their corporate existence, or one company may acquire the net assets of another, with the acquired company losing its separate identity and existence. A business combination may involve an exchange of assets, stock, notes, or any combination of the three, and would be accounted for as either a "purchase" or "pooling of interests."

Today the terms "purchase" and "pooling of interests" refer to methods of accounting for business combinations rather than to the nature of the combinations themselves. Accounting Principles Board Opinion No. 16, "Business Combinations," specifies the conditions under which a particular method of accounting for a business combination must be used and the way that each method should be applied. While APB Opinion No. 16 continues to allow both purchase and pooling of interests accounting, it does not permit the two methods to be used as alternatives to one another. The criteria for determining which of the methods must be used is specified by the Opinion in great detail.

The differences between the purchase and pooling of interests methods stem primarily from the view adopted under each method. The purchase method views the purchase of a business in the same way as the purchase of any other asset or group of assets. Thus, all assets (and liabilities) acquired are recorded at their fair values. Retained earnings, of course, can never be purchased.

Pooling of interest accounting, on the other hand, takes the view that the two (or more) companies joining together have always been together. Thus, the assets are maintained at their book values, and the retained earnings of the combining companies are carried forward. Comparative financial statements which include periods prior to the combination would give retroactive effect to the combination as if the companies had always been one.

Given the differences between the two methods, it is not surprising that prior to APB Opinion No. 16 most business combinations were accounted for as poolings of interests. If asset values of the acquired company exceed book values, as is often the case, the dollar value of reported assets will be higher using purchase treatment than if the pooling method were used in recording the business combination. Assuming those assets have limited lives, the purchase method income subsequent to the combinations will be less than the pooling method income due to the amortization of the higher asset values. In addition, goodwill is often recognized under purchase accounting, but should not be reported following a pooling unless it was already on the books of a combining company. The goodwill also would have to be amortized and would further reduce purchase method earnings. Worse still, the additional amortization recognized under the purchase method often is not tax deductible, depending upon the type of amortization involved and how the business combination was treated for tax purposes. Thus, net income and earnings per share after a business combination are often dramatically lower when the combination is treated as a purchase than if it had been accounted for as a pooling. Further, ratios such as return on total assets and return on stockholders' equity may receive a double blow under purchase accounting due to the lower earnings (numerator) and the higher asset or stock valuation (denominator).

POOLING OF INTERESTS TREATMENT

When to use pooling of interests accounting. APB Opinion No. 16 established a set of twelve conditions to be met to use the pooling method. If all twelve conditions are met, the business combination must be accounted for as a pooling of interests; if any one condition is not met, the combination must be treated as a purchase. Because of the difficulty of structuring business combinations to meet all 12 conditions, the number of business combinations treated as poolings was significantly reduced by APB Opinion No. 16, and now most combinations are treated as purchases.

Many of the twelve conditions established by APB Opinion No. 16 are extremely complex and will be dealt with only briefly here. In general, the conditions established by Opinion No. 16 attempt to insure that there is a continuity of (common stock) ownership in combinations treated as poolings. The basic idea of a pooling of interests is that the owners of the combining companies become the owners of the combined company. That is, the owners of the separate companies are putting together or "pooling" their interests so that they may all benefit as owners of a combined entity. Much of the complexity of APB Opinion No. 16 resulted from an attempt by the APB to plug "loopholes" in the Opinion which practitioners might use, as they did with Accounting Research Bulletin No. 48, to avoid accounting for business combinations as purchases. The twelve conditions set forth by APB Opinion No. 16 that must be met to treat a combination as a pooling of interests are summarized as follows:[1]

A. Attributes of the Combining Companies

1. Each of the combining companies must be autonomous in that it has not been a subsidiary or division of another corporation for at least two years prior to initiation of the plan of combination.

2. Each of the combining companies must be independent of the other combining companies in that, at the dates of initiation and consummaton of the plan of combination, the combining companies in total hold as intercorporate investments no more than 10% (excluding shares acquired pursuant to the combination plan) of the outstanding voting common stock of any combining company.

B. Manner of Combining Interests

3. The combination must be carried out in a single transaction (usually the result of an agreement between the managements of the combining companies) or be completed in accordance with a specific plan (usually resulting in a tender offer) within one year after the plan is initiated, unless delayed by litigation or governmental action. Alteration of the exchange terms of the plan would result in the initiation of a new plan unless the new terms were made retroactive; the initiation of a new plan would require applying the independence test (#2) once again.

4. A corporation must offer and issue its regular voting common stock for at least 90% of the voting common stock of the other

[1]These points have been summarized and paraphrased from APB Opinion No. 16, "Business Combinations," American Institute of Certified Public Accountants, 1970.

combining company or companies outstanding at the date the combination plan is consummated. Alternatively, the corporation may issue its voting common stock for the assets of the other combining company or companies as long as all of the assets are acquired (with the possible exception of a small amount of assets left to pay remaining liabilities). The application of this condition is extremely complex, and numerous detailed rules are set forth in APB Opinion No. 16 for applying the 90% criterion.

5. None of the combining companies may change the equity interest of the voting common stock in contemplation of the business combination for at least two years prior to initiation of the combination or between the initiation and consummation of the combination. In general, this means that during that period of time there may be no abnormal distributions, issuances, exchanges, or retirements of securities with respect to the common stock interest.
6. Each of the combining companies may reacquire shares of voting common stock only for purposes other than business combinations (e.g., stock option plans), and no combining company may reacquire more than a normal number of shares between the initiation and the consummation of the business combination.
7. The ratio of the interest of an individual common stockholder in a combining company to those of the other common stockholders in that same company may not change as a result of the exchange of stock to effect the business combination.
8. The voting rights of the common stockholders of the combined company may not be withheld or restricted for any period of time.
9. The combination must be resolved at the date of consummation of the business combination; that is, there may be no contingencies remaining related to any of the provisions of the plan of combination (e.g., additional shares to be issued based on future earnings).

C. Absence of Planned Transactions

10. The combined corporation may not agree in any way to retire or reacquire any of the common stock issued to effect the combination.
11. The combined corporation may not enter into any financial arrangement for the benefit of the former stockholders of a combining company that would have the effect of negating the exchange of common stock.
12. Except for normal disposals and the elimination of duplicate facilities and excess capacity, the combined corporation cannot intend or plan to dispose of a significant portion of the assets of the combining companies within two years of the combination.

How to account for a pooling of interests. If in a pooling of interest the assets and liabilities of one company are merged into the other company, the basic effect is that of simply combining the books of the two companies and adding together like accounts. Assuming existing book values are already stated in accordance with generally accepted accounting principles, those values will be maintained. The owner's equity of the combined company will be equal to the sum of the owners' equity totals for each of the combining companies. The sum of the retained earnings of the combining companies, in general, becomes the retained earnings of the combined company.

Because a pooling of interests must be effected through a transfer of common shares, the common stock of one company (issuing company) will replace that of the other combining company or companies. While the total stockholders' equity of the combined company must equal the total of the stockholders' equities for all of the combining companies (assuming only common stock is exchanged), the individual stockholders' equity accounts will not always represent a simple summation. If the total (not per share) par or stated value of the common stock issued in the pooling of interests is different from that of the stock of the combining company taken in exchange, the capital stock account of the combined company will be different than the summation of the capital stock accounts of the combining companies. Because total stockholders' equity will be the same regardless of the par or stated value of the stock issued, increases and decreases in the total par or stated value are offset by changes in additional paid-in capital and/or retained earnings. When the total par or stated value decreases, the excess will be credited to an additional paid-in capital account. When the total par or stated value increases, the difference will reduce the combined additional paid-in capital on common stock. If, in this second case, the difference exceeds the combined additional paid-in capital on common, the balance would be charged against combined retained earnings.

► EXAMPLE: Assume that Companies A and B agree to combine in a transaction which qualifies for pooling of interests treatment. At the date of combination their balance sheets appear as follows:

	A	*B*
Assets		
Cash	$ 1,000	$ 10,000
Inventory	10,000	90,000
Plant & Equipment	100,000	500,000
Accumulated Depreciation	(25,000)	(100,000)
Total Assets	$ 86,000	$500,000
Equities		
Liabilities	$20,000	$ 40,000
Common Stock A: $10 par	50,000	
B: $20 par		400,000
Premium on Common Stock	5,000	10,000
Retained Earnings	11,000	50,000
Total Equities	$ 86,000	$500,000

The combined balance sheet for Company AB appears below under each of the following assumptions:

Case 1: B issues 2,500 shares of its $20 par common stock for all 5,000 shares of A's $10 par common.

Case 2: B issues 2,000 shares of its $20 par common stock for all 5,000 shares of A's $10 par common.

Case 3: B issues 4,000 shares of its $20 par common stock for all 5,000 shares of A's $10 par common.

	Case 1	*Case 2*	*Case 3*
Assets			
Cash	$ 11,000	$ 11,000	$ 11,000
Inventory	100,000	100,000	100,000
Plant & Equipment	600,000	600,000	600,000
Accumulated Depreciation	(125,000)	(125,000)	(125,000)
Total Assets	$586,000	$586,000	$586,000
Equities			
Liabilities	$ 60,000	$ 60,000	$ 60,000
Common Stock ($10 par)	450,000	440,000	480,000
Premium on Common Stock	15,000	25,000	—
Retained Earnings	61,000	61,000	46,000
Total Equities	$586,000	$586,000	$586,000

In some cases, a company acquired in a business combination treated as a pooling of interests may retain its separate identity rather than being merged into the acquiring company. APB Opinion No. 16 (para. 49) states:

> Dissolution of a combining company is not a condition for applying the pooling of interests method of accounting for a business combination. One or more combining companies may be subsidiaries of the issuing corporation after the combination is consummated if the other conditions are met.

If the acquired company is to retain its separate identity, the parent (acquiring) company would record both the investment in the acquired company's stock and its own stock issued at the book value of the stock acquired. When financial statements are prepared, the subsidiary would be consolidated with the parent, if appropriate, or reported as an investment using the equity method.

Financial reporting after a pooling of interests. For financial reporting purposes, a pooling of interests is given retroactive application to reflect the assumption that the companies involved have always been a single company. That is, if financial statements prepared after a pooling include comparative statements for periods prior to the combination, those financial statements of prior periods must be restated as if the combination had occurred prior to the earliest period reported.

PURCHASE TREATMENT

When to use purchase accounting. A business combination would be accounted for as a purchase if one or more of the 12 criteria listed in APB Opinion No. 16 for a pooling of interests were not met. In general, business combinations treated as purchases involve those situations where there is not a continuity of ownership. This usually occurs when the acquiring company obtains a substantial portion of the common stock of the acquired company for cash, other assets, notes, or preferred stock, or where the amount of common stock to be issued by the acquiring company is contingent upon some future event.

How to account for a purchase. A purchase-type business combination in which the assets and liabilities of the acquired company are merged into the acquiring company is accounted for in the same manner as any other purchase of a group of assets. The total purchase price is allocated among the assets and liabilities acquired. All identifiable assets acquired, tangible and intangible, are valued at their fair values. Liabilities assumed also are recorded at their fair values, although the book values of liabilities assumed are often used as approximations of their fair values. If, as is often the case, the total purchase price exceeds the sum of the fair values of the net identifiable assets, the excess is considered to be a payment for the excess earning capacity of the acquired company and is capitalized as "Goodwill." The acquired assets and liabilities, once recorded at their fair values, are then accounted for just as any other assets and liabilities. Those tangible assets having limited lives are amortized over their remaining useful lives. Intangible assets, including goodwill, are amortized over their useful lives or 40 years, whichever is shorter, in accordance with APB Opinion No. 17.

Occasionally, the fair value of the net identifiable assets acquired in a business combination may exceed the purchase price. The value assigned to those assets, however, should not exceed the purchase price because assets are generally not recorded at more than cost. APB Opinion No. 16 (para. 91) states:

> An excess over cost should be allocated to reduce proportionately the values assigned to noncurrent assets (except long-term investments in marketable securities) in determining their fair values . . . If the allocation reduces the noncurrent assets to zero value, the remainder of the excess over cost should be classified as a deferred credit and should be amortized systematically to income over the period estimated to be benefitted but not in excess of forty years.

► EXAMPLE: To illustrate accounting for a business combination treated as a purchase, assume that Company B purchases all of the assets and liabilities of Company A for long-term notes payable of $120,000 face amount. Also assume the following values immediately before the combination:

	A Book Values	A Fair Values	B Book Values
Assets			
Cash	$ 1,000	$ 1,000	$ 10,000
Inventory	10,000	15,000	90,000
Plant & Equipment	100,000	90,000	500,000
Accumulated Depreciation	(25,000)		(100,000)
Total Assets	$ 86,000		$500,000
Equities			
Liabilities	$ 20,000	$20,000	$ 40,000
Common Stock	50,000		400,000
Premium on Common Stock	5,000		10,000
Retained Earnings	11,000		50,000
Total Equities	$ 86,000		$500,000

Immediately after the business combination, the balance sheet of Company AB would appear as follows:

		AB
Assets		
Cash		$ 11,000
Inventory		105,000
Plant & Equipment		590,000
Accumulated Depreciation		(100,000)
Goodwill		34,000*
Total Assets		$640,000
Equities		
Liabilities		$180,000
Common Stock		400,000
Premium on Common Stock		10,000
Retained Earnings		50,000
Total Equities		$640,000
*Purchase Price		$120,000
Fair Value of Assets Aquired	$106,000	
Fair Value of Liabilities Assumed	20,000	86,000
Purchased Goodwill		$ 34,000

► NOTE: When a business combination is treated as a purchase, the retained earnings of the acquired company is not recorded on the acquiring company's books. Past earnings cannot be purchased.

If the acquiring company purchases the common stock of the acquired company rather than its assets, and the acquired company is to retain its separate identity as a subsidiary of the acquiring company, the stock acquired would be valued at its cost to the acquiring company. When financial statements are prepared, the subsidiary would be consolidated with the parent, if appropriate, or reported as an investment using the equity method.

Financial reporting after a purchase. Financial statements prepared subsequent to a business combination treated as a purchase will give effect to the combination as of the date of combination, but financial statements of periods prior to the combination that are included for comparative purposes will appear as originally presented by the acquiring entity. For purchase-type business combinations, prior period financial statements are not restated to reflect the combinations retroactively as in the case of a pooling.

LEGAL CONSIDERATIONS

Anti-trust. Even those business combinations initiated as a means of reducing production or distribution costs or assisting in other corporate needs often have the potential of placing a greater concentration of economic power in the hands of a few individuals. The Federal Trade Commission and Department of Justice are empowered under the Sherman Act and Clayton Act to take action in those cases where a monoply may be created or competition substantially lessened. Over the past decades a number of proposed business mergers and acquisitions have been successfully challenged and, in some cases, subsequent divestiture of at least some parts of previously combined companies has been required. Increasing scrutiny of corporate actions by public interest and political action groups would appear to indicate that future business mergers and acquisitions will encounter increased review and examination, including actions by companies previously considered relatively moderate or small in size.

Securities and Exchange Commission. The Securities and Exchange Commission was given relatively broad powers by Congress to establish acceptable accounting procedures for those companies required to file financial statements with the SEC under the Securities Act of 1933 and the Securities Exchange Act of 1934. In the main, the SEC has permitted the private sector to establish standards for reporting business mergers and acquisitions. Significant indirect effects on financial reporting have been achieved by the SEC, however, through the initiation or suggestion of additional disclosure requirements, such as segmental reporting for diversified companies. The SEC now appears to be taking a more active posture in the determination of acceptable reporting standards and may well elect to take more directive action on business combinations, which have been a continuing problem.

More extensive powers to regulate intercorporate ownership and control have been given to the SEC in legislation covering specialized areas, such as the Public Utility Holding Company Act of 1935 and the Investment Company Act of 1940.

Internal Revenue Service. The decision as to whether a business combination will be classified as a taxable or nontaxable exchange may have a significant effect on the terms of the merger agreement. In a taxable combination, the shareholders of the acquired company are taxed on the value of any consideration in excess of the tax basis of the shares they give up. The assets received by the acquiring company in a taxable combination would be valued for tax purposes at their cost to the acquiring company, and any related amortization would be deductible. Amortization of goodwill arising from a taxable combination, however, is deductible only if it can be allocated to specific depreciable assets.

In a nontaxable combination, the sellers are not taxed on the disposition of their shares. The tax basis of the acquired assets will carry over from the acquired company to the acquiring company, which means that no additional depreciation or amortization will be deductible for tax purposes subsequent to the combination.

While the determination as to the tax status of a business combination is often complex, there are several general requirements that must be met for the combination to be nontaxable:

1. The combination must be according to a plan adopted in advance by each of the combining companies and filed with the tax return of each combining company.
2. The combination must have a business purpose other than the avoidance of taxes.
3. There must be a continuity of the ownership interests of all combining companies.
4. The combined company must continue in the general business (e.g., manufacturing, finance) of the combining companies.

In addition, a number of specific tests dealing with these points must be met for the combination to be classified as nontaxable, and expert tax advice is frequently required in determining the tax status of a given transaction.

CONSOLIDATED FINANCIAL STATEMENTS

Early use of consolidated statements. The National Lead Company began issuing consolidated financial statements in 1892, and the General Electric Company followed suit in 1894. The United States Steel Corporation issued its first consolidated balance sheet in 1902. These were the first consolidated financial statements issued in the United States, and they spurred the general adoption of this kind of reporting by other companies. In England, on the other hand, consolidated statements were not usually prepared for shareholders until required by the 1948 Companies Act.

Some of the early writers on consolidation topics display such an insight into the subject that one might think they were writing about today's consolidation problems. Sir Arthur Lowes Dickinson, a former senior partner of Price, Waterhouse and Co., who was instrumental in establishing the first precedents in the area of consolidated statements and paving the way for their wider use, was one of these early writers. His article in the April, 1906, *Journal of Accountancy* was the first extended discussion of this subject.

Importance of consolidated statements. The preparation of consolidated statements is often imperative if the financial statement reader is to be given a true picture of the magnitude of economic resources controlled by the reporting entity. A number of large conglomerate companies with as many as 100 or more subsidiaries have evolved as a result of the merger activity that occurred during the last few decades. Many smaller companies have also elected to create multiple legal entities through separately incorporating leasing or other operating subunits. The net result has been a substantial increase in the number of companies with subsidiaries that qualify for consolidation. In the annual survey of accounting practices followed by the 600 companies included in the 1977 Accounting Trends and Techniques, for example, 379 companies consolidated all subsidiaries, 215 consolidated at least one subsidiary and only 6 companies did not prepare consolidated financial statements. Similar statistics for 1957 indicated that 124 companies did not prepare consolidated statements.

NATURE OF CONSOLIDATED FINANCIAL STATEMENTS

Consolidated financial statements are based on the view that certain related companies often constitute a single economic entity. In preparing consolidated statements, the individual legal entities are ignored and, instead, a single set of financial statements is prepared from the viewpoint of the broader economic entity. Accounting Research Bulletin No. 51 (para. 1) states:

> The purpose of consolidated statements is to present, primarily for the benefit of the shareholders and creditors of the parent company, the results of operations and the financial position of a parent company and its subsidiaries essentially as if the group were a single company with one or more branches or divisions.

Consolidated statements are considered to be particularly useful in situations where a parent has a large number of subsidiaries. It may be very difficult and time consuming for statement users to analyze the statements of the individual subsidiaries and, even if they could, it may be difficult to discern the effect of each subsidiary on the overall company without additional information (e.g., intercompany transactions). For example, Gulf & Western Industries consolidates about 400 subsidiaries and related companies.

What statements are consolidated? Consolidated statements normally are prepared only when one of the companies in a group has a direct or indirect controlling financial interest in the other companies. The controlling company is said to be the "parent" and the controlled companies are referred to as "subsidiaries." The consolidation process involves combining the financial statements of a parent company with those of all subsidiaries that are considered to be part of the same economic entity, as discussed in a later section. The statements are combined in such a way as to reflect the group of companies as if they were actually a single company. If consolidation is appropriate, all of the basic financial statements (income statement, balance sheet, retained earnings statement, and statement of changes in financial position) are consolidated, along with any additional statements or schedules deemed to be appropriate. Information about certain individual companies might also be provided in addition to the consolidated data.

For whom are consolidated statements prepared? As indicated in ARB No. 51, consolidated statements are prepared primarily for the stockholder and creditors of the parent company. Consolidation represents the only means of attaining a clear picture of the economic resources actually controlled by the combined enterprise. As such, the statements could be useful to anyone with a long-run interest in the parent company. Transfers of funds and other assets between individual companies may make it very difficult to establish informed judgements about the riskiness and long-run profitability of the parent or major subsidiaries without the assistance of consolidated statements.

Short-term creditors of the parent generally would be more interested in the parent's separate financial statements than consolidated statements because of the short time period in which their claims need to be satisfied. While creditors of the parent do have an indirect claim on the assets of subsidiaries, short-term creditors generally prefer not to have to exercise this claim because to do so may involve considerable time delays. Such creditors look more towards the parent's separate position. Thus, the consolidated statements are primarily for the stockholders and long-term creditors of the parent, and perhaps others (e.g., regulators, labor unions) with a continuing interest in the parent.

Stockholders and creditors of subsidiaries generally are more interested in the separate statements of those subsidiaries than in consolidated statements. The subsidiaries normally have no claim upon the income or assets of the parent company because the parent is a separate legal entity. Thus, it is highly unlikely that the creditors of a subsidiary would be able to look to the assets of the parent to satisfy claims against the subsidiary. Of course, consolidated statements may be useful for stockholders and creditors of a subsidiary under certain conditions, such as when the parent guarantees the subsidiary's debt or if the parent is the subsidiary's major customer.

Limitations of consolidated financial statements. Although consolidated financial statements can be quite useful, several weaknesses must be recognized. These weaknesses stem from aggregating numerous companies, each company having its own individual characteristics, and include the following:

1. The separate operating results and financial position of individual companies are not disclosed. Thus, the unprofitable operations and poor financial position of some companies in the consolidation may be masked by the profitable operations and healthy position of others.

2. Some of the consolidated retained earnings may represent subsidiary earnings that have not been distributed to the parent. Thus, the balance in retained earnings may be even less of an indication of the parent's ability to pay dividends than is normally the case.

3. The financial ratios based upon the consolidated statements are merely

averages over all of the companies included and are not necessarily representative of any individual company, including the parent.

4. The accounts of the various companies that are combined in consolidated financial statements may not be entirely comparable. For example, the finished goods of one company may be the raw materials of another; or the maturities of the trade receivables of different companies may be considerably different.

5. Important information about individual companies may require voluminous footnotes.

In certain situations, it may be desirable to present separate financial statements for the parent, a particular subsidiary, or a group of subsidiaries in addition to the consolidated statements. When statements are prepared for a group of related companies, none of which controls the others, the statements are generally referred to as combined statements.

CRITERIA FOR INCLUSION OF SUBSIDIARIES

In deciding whether to prepare consolidated financial statements and in determining which subsidiaries to include in the consolidation, ARB No. 51 (para. 3) states that ". . . the aim should be to make the financial presentation which is most meaningful in the circumstances." Thus, there are no fixed rules, but rather judgment must be exercised in defining the consolidated entity. There are, however, several criteria for consolidation that were originally suggested by ARB No. 51 and have since evolved through practice. These criteria deal with the following areas:

1. Degree of ownership and control.
2. Similarity of operations.
3. Permanence of control.
4. Comparability of accounting methods and periods.

1. *Degree of ownership and control.* The usual condition for control is ownership of more than 50% of the outstanding voting stock of a company. However, APB Opinion No. 18 (para. 3c) points out that:

> . . . control may also exist with a lesser percentage of ownership, for example, by contract, lease, agreement with other stockholders or by court decree.

While control might be gained with less than a majority of the voting stock, practice generally dictates that only majority-owned companies be consolidated. If the minority interest (perhaps including preferred stock and debt) in a subsidiary is very large in relation to the parent's interest, separate statements for that subsidiary might prove more meaningful than a full consolidation.

Control might also be obtained indirectly, perhaps through affiliated companies or several layers of subsidiaries.

► EXAMPLE: Assume that Company P owns 90% of the common stock of Company A and 80% of the common stock of Company B. A and B each own 40% of the common stock of Company C. P would then control C because P controls both A and B. P's indirect interest in C would be calculated as:

$$(.90 \times .40) + (.80 \times .40) = 68\%$$

If control over the subsidiary is restricted, consolidation may be inappropriate. For example, control over a company in legal reorganization or bankruptcy does not rest with the majority shareholders; or a subsidiary in some foreign countries may have severe restrictions placed on the remittance of profits and assets to the parent. In either case, consolidation of the subsidiary would not be appropriate.

2. *Similarity of operations.* Consolidating companies with greatly heterogeneous operations may provide meaningless, or perhaps even misleading, financial reports. For example, the assets of a manufacturing firm (e.g., inventory, equipment) are considerably different from those of a bank (e.g., investments, loans receivable); likewise, the income statement items of the manufacturing firm (e.g., sales, cost of goods sold) differ from those of the bank (e.g., interest income, interest expense). Adding together the financial statements of two such different firms could provide a meaningless conglomeration.

While there are no specific rules that categorize firms for consolidation purposes, practice seems to have established the following classifications:

a. Manufacturing and trading.
b. Financial.
c. Real estate.
d. Leasing (other than to parent).
e. Other (e.g., service).

Subsidiaries whose principal activity is leasing assets to their parents must be consolidated.

3. *Permanence of control.* If control of a subsidiary is expected to be temporary, the subsidiary should be excluded from consolidation. This might occur, for instance, when a sale of the parent's investment in the subsidiary's stock is expected.

4. *Accounting methods and periods.* While a difference in accounting methods between the parent and a subsidiary generally will not preclude consolidation, there may be rare cases where the accounting methods are so dissimilar as to make consolidation meaningless.

A difference in the accounting periods of a parent and subsidiary should not preclude the consolidation of that subsidiary. Generally, the subsidiary would shift to the same fiscal period as the parent. However, both ARB No. 51 and the SEC permit consolidation of the subsidiary's statements without shifting fiscal periods if the difference in fiscal periods is no more than about three months and recognition is given to intervening events which materially affect financial position and the results of operations.

The consolidation policy adopted by a parent company must be disclosed as part of its accounting policies information.

► EXAMPLE: A typical footnote disclosing the consolidation policy of a manufacturing company might appear as follows:

> Consolidation Policy—The consolidated financial statements include, on a fully consolidated basis, all domestic and foreign subsidiaries except Fortress Savings and Loan Association, which is reflected on an equity basis due to the financial nature of its operations.

The Securities and Exchange Commission. The Securities and Exchange Commission has had a strong influence in many fields of accounting including consolidated financial statements. The Commission's *Accounting Series Releases* and Staff Accounting Bulletins, published irregularly, have dealt with many consolidation topics.

Regulation S-X, issued by the Commission, deals specifically with the form and content of consolidated statements. This regulation sets forth the requirements for all consolidated statements filed with the SEC, and includes a definition of all pertinent terms such as parent, subsidiary, majority-owned subsidiary, and the like. No accountant could hope to prepare a consolidated statement for submission to the SEC without complete familiarity with *Regulation S-X*. The pertinent features of the regulation may be summarized as follows:

1. Only majority-owned subsidiaries may be consolidated.
2. To be included in a consolidated statement, the subsidiary must have an accounting period that ends within 93 days of the parent's accounting period.
3. The effect of currency restrictions on foreign subsidiaries included in the consolidation should be disclosed.
4. Combined financial statements for groups of majority-owned subsidiaries not consolidated with the parent company are permitted and may, on occasion, be essential to proper disclosure.
5. The principles followed in consolidating subsidiaries, and any changes from the preceding year, must be described.
6. Differences between the investment in subsidiaries on the parent's books and the parent's equity in the net assets of the subsidiaries must be described for both consolidated and unconsolidated subsidiaries.
7. Differences between earnings of unconsolidated subsidiaries and dividends received from them must be reconciled.
8. Minority interests in capital, in retained earnings, and in profit or loss must be shown.
9. Intercompany items and transactions must be eliminated. If not eliminated, the treatment of such transactions must be explained and the reasons for nonelimination given.

Stock Exchange Requirements. Stock exchanges are naturally interested in providing stockholders of their listed corporations with as much financial information as possible. In its listing application, the New York Stock Exchange requires financial statements for the parent corporation and for each separate corporation in which it directly or indirectly holds a majority of the equity stock, ". . . or in lieu thereof, eliminating all intercompany transactions, a consolidated balance sheet of the Corporation and its subsidiaries as of the end of its last previous fiscal year, and a consolidated surplus statement and a consolidated income statement of the Corporation and its subsidiaries for such fiscal year." The exact form and content of financial statements to be filed by companies listed on the New York Stock Exchange, American Stock Exchange, or regional exchanges are commonly subject to requirements which may differ somewhat from those filed with the Securities and Exchange Commission. The NYSE, for example, requires a ten year summary of operations, while the SEC has required only five years. Similar differences exist in regard to comparative balance sheets, statement of changes in financial position, and statements of stockholders' equity. Therefore, care must be taken in preparing financial statements to be sure that such requirements have been met.

ACCOUNTING FOR UNCONSOLIDATED INTERCORPORATE INVESTMENTS

There are two main methods of accounting for investments in the common stock of another company: cost and equity. Under the cost method, the investment in common stock is recorded and carried at historical cost. Dividends on the stock are recognized as income by the investor when they are declared by the investee. However, dividends declared by the investee in excess of the investee's earnings since the date its stock was acquired by the investor are considered a return of capital to the investor and require a reduction in the carrying value of the investment.

Under the equity method, the carrying amount of the investment is adjusted periodically to reflect the investor's changing equity in the investee. The investor recognizes its share of the investee's income when the income is earned by the investee rather than when it is distributed as dividends. As income is recognized, the carrying amount of the investment is increased to reflect the increased equity of the investor. Losses reported by the investee are recognized proportionally by the investor as incurred, and the carrying amount of the investment is reduced accordingly. Dividends declared by the investee reduce the investor's equity in the net assets of the investee; hence, the investment carrying amount is reduced by the investor's share of investee dividends.

► EXAMPLE: Assume that Company A acquires 20% of Company B's common stock for $100,000 on January 1, and the following events occur during the year:

Event	*Cost Method*			*Equity Method*		
Jan. 1, A acquires 20% of B's stock for $100,000	Investment in B Cash		2,000 100,000	Investment in B Cash	100,000	 100,000
Jan. 2, B declares and pays a $10,000 dividend (earnings since A's acquisition equals $0)	Cash Investment in B	2,000	 2,000	Cash Investment in B	2,000	 2,000
Dec. 31, B reports net income of $50,000				Investment in B Investment Income	10,000	 10,000
Dec. 31, B declares and pays a $20,000 dividend	Cash Dividend Income	4,000	 4,000	Cash Investment in B	4,000	 4,000
Summary	Investment in B, 12/31 Dividend Income	98,000 4,000		Investment in B 12/31 Investment Income	104,000 10,000	

When to use the cost and equity method. APB Opinion No. 18 establishes the requirements as to when to use the cost and equity methods. The Opinion requires that investments in common stock be reported using the equity method in the following situations:

1. For investments in unconsolidated subsidiaries.
2. For investments in corporate joint ventures.
3. For all investments that give the investor the ability to significantly influence the operating and financial policies of the investee.

Whether the investor has the ability to significantly influence the policies of the investee is often a matter of judgment. Such a determination should consider factors such as representation on the board of directors, material intercompany transactions, technological dependence, and the extent of ownership in relation to concentration of other shareholdings. In order to achieve a reasonable degree of uniformity, APB Opinion No. 18 (para. 17) states:

> An investment (direct or indirect) of 20% or more of the voting stock of an investee should lead to a presumption that in the absence of evidence to the contrary an investor has the ability to exercise significant influence over an investee. Conversely, an investment of less than 20% of the voting stock of an investee should lead to a presumption that an investor does not have the ability to exercise significant influence unless such ability can be demonstrated.

Investments in common stock other than those listed above should be reported using the cost method. Whether an investment in common stock is reported using the cost or equity method, if a publicly reported price quotation is available for that stock, the stock is considered a marketable equity security and must meet the requirements of FASB Statement No. 12 as well as those of APB Opinion No. 18.

Applying the equity method under APB Opinion No. 18. The equity method, as described in APB Opinion No. 18, is viewed as a "one-line consolidation." The opinion indicates that the difference between full consolidation and the equity method lies only in the details reported in the financial statements. Therefore, the Opinion requires that an investor's income for the period and its total stockholders' equity at the end of the period be the same whether the investment is consolidated or accounted for using the equity method.

One adjustment required by APB Opinion No. 18 in applying the equity method is the elimination of any unrealized profit or loss on intercompany transactions. As in a full consolidation, profits and losses on intercompany transactions may not be recognized until confirmed by resale to outsiders. Thus, an entry is required on the investor's books to adjust the investor's net income and the investment account by the amount of the unrealized intercompany profit or loss.

► EXAMPLE: Assume that Company A owns 80% of the common stock of Company B and accounts for its investment in B using the equity method. Further assume that A sells to B for $5,000 inventory which had cost A $4,000; half of the inventory remained unsold by B at the end of the period. A would record a pro rata portion of B's net income for the period, and then would make the following entry to eliminate the unrealized intercompany profit on the unsold inventory:

Investment Income	500	
Investment in B		500

When the remaining inventory is sold and the intercompany profit is confirmed, the entry would be reversed.

If in this example the sale had been from the investee to the investor and the investor follows the practice of eliminating 100% of unrealized intercompany profits and losses against the majority interest, the adjusting entry would have been the same. On the other hand, if the investor follows the practice of eliminating the unrealized intercompany profits and losses proportionately against the majority and minority interests, the following adjusting entry would be made by the investor:

Investment Income	400	
Investment in B		400

A second type of adjustment is required in applying the equity method to amortize, when appropriate, the difference (differential) between the purchase price of the investment in common stock and the book value of the underlying net assets held by the investee at the date of acquisition. When one company purchases another's common stock and pays more than the net book value of that stock, the excess is usually due to either (1) unrecorded appreciation of some of the investee's assets or (2) the existence of goodwill.

If the excess applies to a limited life asset, that excess must be amortized against investment income over the remaining life of the asset. The amortization period may not exceed 40 years if the asset is intangible.

► EXAMPLE: Assume that Company P purchased 80% of the common stock of Company S for $100,000 when the underlying book value of the investment was $80,000. All of the excess is attributable to unrecorded goodwill of the investee with an estimated remaining life of 10 years. Company S reports net income of $60,000 for the period and declares no dividends. Company P would make the following entries to record investment income under the equity method:

Investment in S	48,000	
Investment Income		48,000
To record P's share (80%) of S's income.		
Investment Income	2,000	
Investment in S		2,000
To amortize over 10 years the excess cost of the investment over book value.		

If the differential is attributable solely to the increased value of a tangible asset with an unlimited life (e.g., land), no amortization is required. However, when an asset is disposed of, regardless of whether the asset is being amortized or not, any remaining differential relating to that asset must be eliminated as an adjustment to investment income for the period.

► EXAMPLE: Assume that Company P purchased 80% of the common stock of Company S at $20,000 more than the net book value of the investment and all of the differential was attributable to the increased value of S's land. After several years, S sells the land and reports net income of $70,000, including a gain on the sale of the land. Company P would record the following entries on its books to reflect its share of S's income for the period under the equity method:

Investment in S	56,000	
Investment Income		56,000
To record P's share (80%) of S's income.		
Investment Income	20,000	
Investment in S		20,000
To eliminate the differential related to the land of S that was sold.		

Interperiod income tax allocation. Another aspect of implementing the equity method involves the determination of tax expense in the books of the investor. When the equity method is used it is normally expected that the investor will accrue tax expense on all investment income recorded for the period. No particular difficulties should be associated with determining the appropriate expense accruals for those earnings actually remitted during the period. If the investee is not a subsidiary, APB Opinion No. 24 requires that tax expense also be accrued by the investor on its portion of the undistributed earnings of the investee. When evidence indicates that the earnings will ultimately be transferred in the form of dividends, the investor should record tax expense on the undistributed earnings at the applicable dividend rate as if all available deductions and credits were utilized. When evidence indicates that the undistributed earnings will ultimately be realized through disposition of the investment, the appropriate capital gains rate should be used. If, on the other hand, the investee is a subsidiary, APB Opinion No. 23 requires that tax expense be accrued on undistributed earnings of the subsidiary unless the parent can demonstrate that (1) those earnings have been invested indefinitely by the subsidiary or (2) that they will be remitted to the parent in a tax free transfer. No expense accrual on the unremitted earnings is required if one of these conditions is met.

CONSOLIDATED PRINCIPLES AND PROCEDURES

The consolidation process is primarily one of combining the financial statements of two or more related companies. Like items are summed across all firms in the consolidation. To reflect the group of firms as if they were actually a single company, certain items within the combined statements must be eliminated or adjusted because they would not appear, or would appear at different amounts, in the statements of a single firm.

In order to illustrate the preparation of a consolidated balance sheet, assume that Company A purchases 100% of the outstanding common stock of Company B for $600,000. Immediately after the acquisition, the balance sheets of the companies appear as follows:

		Company A	*Company B*
Assets			
	Current Assets	$1,300,000	$ 300,000
	Investment in B Stock	600,000	
	Other Assets	1,245,000	700,000
		$3,145,000	$1,000,000
Equities			
	Liabilities	$ 750,000	$ 400,000
	Common Stock	500,000	100,000
	Additional Paid-in Capital	1,000,000	300,000
	Retained Earnings	895,000	200,000
		$3,145,000	$1,000,000

A consolidation worksheet generally is prepared to facilitate the consolidation process. If a consolidated balance sheet were desired immediately after acquisition, the consolidation worksheet would appear as follows:

	Company A	Company B	Eliminations Dr.	Eliminations Cr.	Consolidated Balance Sheet
Assets					
Current Assets	$1,300,000	$ 300,000			$1,600,000
Investment in B Stock	600,000			$600,000	
Other Assets	1,245,000	700,000			1,945,000
	$3,145,000	$1,000,000			$3,545,000
Equities					
Liabilities	$ 750,000	$ 400,000			$1,150,000
Common Stock	500,000	100,000	$100,000		500,000
Additional Paid-in Capital	1,000,000	300,000	300,000		1,000,000
Retained Earnings	895,000	200,000	200,000		895,000
	$3,145,000	$1,000,000	$600,000	$600,000	$3,545,000

The consolidated balance sheet amounts appear in the last column and are obtained by adding each row across, taking into consideration the debit or credit effect of each elimination. In this example (and in every case), the investment in the subsidiary's stock must be eliminated because the consolidated statements reflect a single entity view and cannot include both the assets of the subsidiary and the parent's claim on those assets. The balance in B's common stock account and the balances of all accounts related to the common stock or accruing to the common stockholders are eliminated because the common stock is held entirely within the consolidated entity, by Company A.

A column has been added to the worksheet to reflect the 25% interest of the minority shareholders in B's net assets. As in the case of 100% ownership by the parent company, none of the balances of B's stockholders' equity accounts are carried over to the consolidated balance sheet. Seventy-five percent of each of B's stockholders' equity accounts is eliminated as A's investment account balance is eliminated, and the remaining 25% is assigned to the minority shareholders and carried to the minority interest column in the worksheet. The amount assigned to the minority interest generally is shown in the consolidated balance sheet either in the stockholders' equity section or between liabilities and stockholders' equity.

The consolidation worksheet also would include eliminations of any intercompany payable/receivables existing at the balance sheet date. For example, if B owed A $1,000 on a note, an entry would be made in the consolidation worksheet to eliminate both A's receivable and B's payable, as well as any accrued interest. As these are reciprocal accounts, the amounts will be equal.

► NOTE: The consolidation elimination and adjusting entries are made only in the consolidated working papers. These entries do not appear on the books of either the parent or subsidiary.

If, in the same example, Company A had acquired only 75% of B's outstanding common stock and had paid $450,000, the consolidation worksheet at the date of the acquisition would appear as follows:

	Company A	*Company B*	*Eliminations Dr.*	*Eliminations Cr.*	*Minority Interest*	*Consolidated Balance Sheet*
Assets						
Current Assets	$1,450,000	$ 300,000				$1,750,000
Investment in B Stock	450,000			$450,000		
Other Assets	1,245,000	700,000				1,945,000
	$3,145,000	$1,000,000				$3,695,000
Equities						
Liabilities	$ 750,000	$ 400,000				$1,150,000
Common Stock	500,000	100,000	$ 75,000		$25,000	500,000
Additional Paid-in Capital	1,000,000	300,000	225,000		75,000	1,000,000
Retained Earnings	895,000	200,000	150,000		50,000	895,000
					150,000	
Minority Interest					(150,000)	150,000
	$3,145,000	$1,000,000	$450,000	$450,000		$3,695,000

Excess of cost over book value. Many times a company's stock will be purchased at a price in excess of its underlying book value. There may be a number of reasons for paying an amount greater than book value for the stock of the acquired company, including perhaps the omission of some assets. If such is the case, the books of the acquired company should be corrected. Second, some specifically identifiable assets (tangible or intangible) of the acquired company could have fair values exceeding their book values. In this case, the excess purchase price, or differential, would be allocated to those specific assets. In those situations where the parent acquires full ownership of the subsidiary, the assets of the subsidiary may be revalued directly on the books of the subsidiary, thereby bringing into agreement the net book value of the subsidiary's assets with the balance in the parent's investment account. Often, however, the subsidiary's books are not changed to reflect the acquisition of its stock by the parent and, hence, the differential must be allocated to specific assets on the consolidation worksheet. Third, the differential could represent a payment for the excess earning power of the acquired company. In this case, the differential would be allocated to goodwill, usually in the consolidation worksheet.

Any time some or all of the differential is allocated to a limited-life tangible or intangible asset, the increment must be amortized over the remaining useful life of that asset, not to exceed 40 years for intangible assets (APB Opinion No. 17).

Excess of book value over cost. In a few cases, a company's stock might be purchased at a price less than its underlying book value. Again, there could be several reasons for a negative differential. First, there could be errors on the books of the acquired company and, if so, the books should be corrected. Second some of the assets of the acquired company might be over-valued. If so, those assets should be written down to their fair values, either on the books of the acquired company or in the consolidation worksheet, depending on the type of assets and whether a minority interest exists. Third, goodwill already on the books of the acquired company may no longer exist and should be written off the books. Finally, where all assets of the acquired company are properly valued, APB Opinion No. 16 (para. 91) requires the excess over cost to be treated as follows:

> An excess over cost should be allocated to reduce proportionately the values assigned to noncurrent assets (except long-term investments in marketable securities) in determining their fair values . . . If the allocation reduces the noncurrent assets to zero value, the remainder of the excess over cost should be classified as a deferred credit and should be amortized systematically to income over the period estimated to be benefited but not in excess of forty years.

Sometimes a single parent may acquire some subsidiaries at a cost in excess of book value and others at a cost less than book value. The proper treatment in such cases is to deal with each differential separately and to allocate them independently of one another. Many times in practice, however, positive and negative differentials are simply netted against one another.

Existence of preferred stock. If a subsidiary has outstanding preferred stock, the computation of the book value of the common stock must consider the effects of the preferred stock. The portion of the subsidiary's total stockholders' equity that should be allocated to preferred stock would equal the stated liquidation value (par or stated value if no liquidation value is explicitly stated) of the preferred stock plus any dividends in arrears if the preferred stock is cumulative. In addition, consideration would need to be given to the appropriate allocation of retained earnings under the preferred stock agreement if the preferred stock has participation rights.

Once the proper allocations to the preferred stock have been determined, the remaining stockholders' equity would be allocated to common.

CONSOLIDATION SUBSEQUENT TO ACQUISITION

Subsequent to acquisition, consolidated financial statements will include the results of operations of the consolidated entity as well as its financial position. Thus, the consolidated working papers need to be expanded to include income and retained earnings statement items in addition to the balance sheet items. The consolidated income statement and retained earnings statement are prepared by adding like items from all of the companies in the consolidated entity and eliminating those items that would not appear if the consolidated entity were actually a single company.

The minority interest share of income is calculated by applying the minority's percentage of the subsidiary's net income. This amount is usually treated as a deduction in the consolidated income statement to obtain consolidated net income. For example, assume that Company A owns 90% of Company B's common stock, Company A reports income from its own operations (excluding A's share of B's income) of $100,000, and Company B reports net income of $40,000. Then, consolidated net income and the minority interest's share of income are calculated as follows:

A's income	$100,000
B's income	40,000
	$140,000
Minority interest (10% of 40,000)	4,000
Consolidated net income	$136,000

Intercompany dividends. That portion of a subsidiary's dividends declared that relates to the parent's investment must be eliminated in preparing consolidated statements because it represents a transfer between related companies. The elimination entry is made in the consolidation worksheet, and, if the investment is carried by the parent using the equity method, the elimination of the dividends declared normally would be made when the balance of the investment account is eliminated.

Intercompany fees, rent, interest. If one company in the consolidated entity charges another company in the consolidated entity rent, interest, or fees for any type of service, the one company will recognize income while the other will recognize an expense for the same amount. Because both companies are viewed as being part of the same company in consolidated financial statements, the reciprocal income and expense accounts must be eliminated when the consolidated statements are prepared. For example, if Parent Company charged Subsidiary Company $10,000 during the period for consulting fees, the following elimination entry would have to be made in the consolidation worksheet at year-end:

Consulting Income	10,000	
Consulting Expense		10,000

Notice that this elimination entry reduces or eliminates two income statement items but has no net effect on consolidated net income. If this transaction gave rise to any intercompany receivable/payable that was unpaid at year-end, the receivable and payable also would have to be eliminated.

Unrealized intercompany profits. Some types of intercompany transactions give rise to profits which, from a consolidated viewpoint, must be considered unrealized until confirmed through transactions with outsiders. For example, a sale of inventory at an amount above cost or a fixed asset at an amount over book value from one company to another member of the same consolidated entity would give rise to unrealized intercompany profits. Such profits would have to be eliminated from consolidated income and from the reported book value of the transferred asset until the intercompany profit was deemed realized through the resale of the inventory or through the depreciation or resale of the fixed asset.

Accounting Research Bulletin No. 51 is clear in requiring 100% elimination of all unrealized intercompany profits when preparing consolidated financial statements. The Bulletin, however, seems to allow the profit elimination either to be allocated fully against the majority interest or to be allocated proportionally against both the majority interest and the minority interest if the unrealized profit has been recorded on the books of the subsidiary.

► EXAMPLE: Assume that Parent Company owns 80% of the common stock of Subsidiary Company. During the period, Subsidiary sells Parent 10 units of inventory for $30,000 which Subsidiary had purchased for $20,000. By the end of the period, Parent has resold 6 of the units to outsiders but is still holding 4. The amount of inventory reported on the consolidated balance sheet would have to be reduced by $4,000 (4 x $1,000), the unrealized intercompany profit included in the inventory. In addition, consolidated net income would have to be reduced by either of the following amounts:

1. If full allocation against the majority interest were chosen consolidated net income (majority interest) would be reduced by $4,000. The minority interest would be assigned a pro rata portion (20%) of Subsidiary Company's reported net income.
2. If proportional allocation were chosen, consolidated net income would be reduced by $3,200 (80% of $4,000) and the minority interest's share of subsidiary income would be reduced by $800 (20% of $4,000).

While both methods are acceptable, full allocation against the majority interest will be used here.

► NOTE: In eliminating intercompany profits, the related income taxes must be considered, if significant. When separate tax returns are filed, a tax is paid on the intercompany profits and the elimination, therefore, should be net of the tax effect. If the affiliated group elects to file a consolidated tax return, this problem does not arise.

Intercompany sales of inventory. When there is a sale of inventory between two companies in the same consolidated entity, not only must the unrealized intercompany profits be eliminated and the inventory balance adjusted, but the effect on sales and cost of goods sold must be eliminated whether or not the intercompany profit is actually realized during the period. In the example given earlier, Subsidiary Company sold 10 units of inventory, with an original cost of

$20,000, to Parent Company for $30,000; Parent resold 6 of the units during the period to outsiders (assume a sales price of $25,000) and was holding 4 of the units at year-end. With respect to the intercompany sale, the following computations would be made:

	Sales	*Cost of Good Sold*
Recorded by Subsidiary	$30,000	$20,000
Recorded by Parent	25,000	18,000
	$55,000	$38,000
Sales to Outsiders	25,000	
Original Cost (to Subsidiary) of Inventory sold to outsiders		12,000
Required Elimination	$30,000	$26,000

The following elimination entry would appear in the consolidation worksheet:

Sales	30,000	
Cost of Goods Sold		26,000
Inventory		4,000

As discussed earlier, if an investment in common stock is carried using the equity method, the parent's net income under the equity method must be adjusted to agree with consolidated net income. Thus, in this example, if the investment is carried using the equity method, the following entry would need to be made on the parent's book (prior to preparation of the consolidation worksheet) assuming all other appropriate equity-method entries had been made during the period with respect to this investment:

Income from Subsidiary	4,000	
Investment in Subsidiary Stock		4,000

If the remaining inventory was resold to outsiders the following year, consolidated cost of goods sold for that year would have to be reduced because of the unrealized intercompany profit included in the parent's beginning inventory. Because the investment account is carried on the parent's books using the equity method and has been reduced at the end of the first year to reflect the elimination of the unrealized intercompany profit, the investment elimination entry in the consolidation worksheet at the end of the second year would appear as follows (assuming no purchase differential):

Capital Stock-Subsidiary	XXX	
Retained Earnings-Subsidiary	XXX	
Income from Subsidiary	XXX	
Dividends Declared-Subsidiary		XXX
Investment in Subsidiary Stock		XXX
Cost of Good Sold		4,000

Recognition of an additional $4,000 in consolidated net income means the parent's equity-method income must also be increased by $4,000 (prior to preparation of the consolidation worksheet). This would be accomplished by the following entry on the parent's books:

Investment in Subsidiary	4,000	
Income from Subsidiary		4,000

Intercompany sales of fixed assets. An intercompany sale of a fixed asset at book value causes no problems. However, if the sale is at an amount other than book value, the gain or loss on the sale must be eliminated from consolidated net income and the new book value of the asset adjusted in the consolidation worksheet as if no sale had taken place. In addition, depreciation over the life of the asset, if that asset has a limited life, must be adjusted for consolidation purposes as if the intercompany sale had not been made.

► EXAMPLE: Company A sells a machine, with a remaining life of 5 years, to a subsidiary, Company B, for $25,000 at the beginning of the fiscal year. The machine originally cost A $28,000 when purchased 2 years ago. Company A previously recognized depreciation expense of $4,000 per year (28,000 ÷ 7). The following table shows the amounts that would appear on the separate books of A and B with respect to the machine and the amounts that would appear in the consolidated financial statements (the same amounts that would have appeared on A's books if there had been no sale):

	A's Books	B's Books			Consolidated Financial Statements			
	Gain	Depreciation Expense	Machine	Accumulated Depreciation	Gain	Depreciation Expense	Machine	Accumulated Depreciation
Year of Transfer	$5000	$5,000	$25,000	$ 5,000	0	$4,000	$28,000	$12,000
1st year after		5,000	25,000	10,000		4,000	28,000	16,000
2nd year after		5,000	25,000	15,000		4,000	28,000	20,000
3rd year after		5,000	25,000	20,000		4,000	28,000	24,000
4th year after		5,000	25,000	25,000		4,000	28,000	28,000

Intercompany bond transactions. If one company issues bonds that are purchased directly by another company in the consolidated entity, the effect for consolidation purposes is that of never having issued the bonds. The bonds payable and any related discount or premium would be eliminated against the investment in bonds in the consolidation worksheet. Also, the bond interest expense and interest income, including amortization of discount or premium, would be eliminated against one another.

Occasionally, one member of the consolidated group may acquire the bonds of another member of the group in the open market. For consolidation purposes, the effect is the same as if the issuer reacquired and retired the bonds. A gain or loss would be recognized for the difference between the purchase price of the bonds and the carrying amount on the issuer's books. Again, the investment in bonds, the bonds payable, and all related accounts would have to be eliminated. This case is somewhat more complicated because the bonds payable (including discount or premium) and investment in bonds are not equal unless the bonds were repurchased at their book value.

► EXAMPLE: Company Y purchases in the open market $100,000 face amount of bonds payable originally issued at par by Y's subsidiary, Company Z. Company Y purchased the bonds for $106,000 at the end of the year. The following eliminating entry would be made in the consolidation worksheet:

Bonds Payable	100,000	
Loss on Retirement on Bonds	6,000	
Investment in Bonds of B		106,000

Stock dividends. A stock dividend declared by a subsidiary on its common stock (payable in the same class of stock) does not affect relative ownership interests, and, hence, requires only a memo entry on the parent's books. In the consolidation process, however, consideration must be given to the fact that a portion of the subsidiary's retained earnings has been shifted to the common stock account. Thus, in the year of the stock dividend, the investment elimination entry would include a proportionate elimination of the stock dividends declared account, just as for cash dividends, and a proportionate elimination of the new larger balance of common stock. Eliminations in subsequent years would be made as if the stock dividend had occurred prior to acquisition.

ILLUSTRATIVE PROBLEM

To illustrate the application of the consolidation procedures, assume that you are to prepare consolidated financial statements for Companies P and S as of December 31, 1981. The pre-closing adjusted trial balances for the two companies at December 31, 1981, appear as follows:

Trial Balances
December 31, 1981

	Company P	*Company S*
Debits		
Cash	$ 89,500	$ 48,700
Receivables	502,600	79,100
Inventories	1,193,200	308,600
Investment in Company S Bonds	196,400	—
Investment in Company S Stock	542,100	—
Plant & Equipment	8,651,200	960,200
Other Assets	100,900	31,400
Discount on Bonds Payable	—	9,000
Cost of Goods Sold	3,702,500	1,013,400
Depreciation Expense	486,600	52,300
Interest Expense	163,900	41,700
Other Expenses	282,000	164,200
Income Tax Expense	570,800	160,800
Dividends Declared	400,000	100,000
Total Debits	$16,881,700	$2,969,400

Credits	*Company P*	*Company S*
Allowance for Uncollectibles	$ 15,100	$ 1,200
Accumulated Depreciation	2,153,100	142,600
Short-term Liabilities	632,700	96,200
Bonds Payable	2,000,000	500,000
Capital Stock	1,000,000	100,000
Additional Paid-in Capital	3,212,000	300,000
Retained Earnings 1/1/81	1,965,300	175,000
Sales	5,625,300	1,621,500
Other Income	142,600	32,900
Income from Subsidiary	135,600	—
Total Credits	$16,881,700	$2,969,400

The following information is also available about the two companies:

1. Company P purchased 80% of the outstanding common stock of Company S on June 30, 1978 for $417,400. The investment was recorded by P at cost and is carried on P's books using the equity method.
2. The purchase price of the investment ($417,400) exceeded the book value of the underlying assets of S by $55,000. Of that amount, $15,000 was attributable to the increased fair value of equipment owned by S with a remaining useful life (from June 30, 1978) of 5 years. The other $40,000 was allocated to goodwill with an expected life of 10 years.
3. The accumulated depreciation on S's books at June 30, 1978, was $32,900. None of S's depreciable assets have been sold or retired since that date.
4. The retained earnings of S on June 30, 1978, was $53,000. From June 30, 1978, through December 31, 1980, S reported a total net income of $372,000, and declared total dividends of $250,000. In each case, P recognized its proportionate (80%) share.
5. For 1981, S reported net income of $222,000 and declared dividends of $100,000. At December 31, 1981, $25,000 of the dividends were not yet paid.
6. During 1981, S sold inventory to P for $145,000. The inventory had cost S $87,000 to manufacture. P resold 3/4 of the inventory during the year but 1/4 remained unsold at year-end. During the previous year, S had sold inventory that cost $52,000 to P for $85,000. P held 1/3 of that inventory on December 31, 1980, but sold all of the remaining amount during 1981.
7. On January 2, 1980, S issued $500,000 of 20-year, 8% bonds at 98. P purchased $200,000 face amount of those bonds directly from S. Bond interest is paid on January 1 and July 1.
8. On January 2, 1981, P sold a piece of equipment to S for $95,000. The equipment had been constructed by P at a cost of $60,000 and had an expected life of 10 years with no salvage value.

To facilitate the preparation of consolidated financial statements, a consolidation worksheet would be prepared, as illustrated on page 98. Following are the adjustment and elimination entries that appear in the consolidation worksheet with explanations and letters keying them to the worksheet:

Company P and Subsidiary Company S
Consolidation Worksheet
For the Year Ended December 31, 1981

	P Company	S Company
Income Statement		
Sales	$5,625,300	$1,621,500
Other Income	142,600	32,900
Income from Subsidiary	135,600	-----
Total Credits	$5,903,500	$1,654,400
Cost of Goods Sold	3,702,500	1,013,400
Depreciation Expense	486,600	52,300
Interest Expense	163,900	41,700
Other Expenses	282,000	164,200
Income Tax Expense	570,800	160,800
Total Debits	$5,205,800	$1,432,400
	697,700	222,000
Minority Interest in Net Income		
Net Income-forward	$ 697,700	$ 222,000
Retained Earnings Statement		
Retained Earnings 1/1	$1,965,300	$ 175,000
→ Net Income-brought forward	697,700	222,000
Dividends Declared	400,000	100,000
Retained Earnings 12/31-forward	$2,263,000	$ 297,000
Balance Sheet, 12/31/81		
Cash	$ 89,500	$ 48,700
Receivables	502,600	79,100
Inventories	1,193,200	308,600
Investment in S Co. Bonds	196,400	------
Investment in S Co. Stock	542,100	------
Plant & Equipment	8,651,200	960,200
Other Assets	100,900	31,400
Discount on Bonds Payable	-----	9,000
Differential		
Goodwill		
Total Debits	$11,275,900	$ 1,437,000
Allowance for Uncollectibles	$ 15,100	$ 1,200
Accumulated Depreciation	2,153,100	142,600
Short-term liabilities	632,700	96,200
Bonds Payable	2,000,000	500,000
Capital Stock	1,000,000	100,000
Additional Paid-in Capital	3,212,000	300,000
→ Retained Earnings-brought forward	2,263,000	297,000
Minority Interest		
Total Credits	$11,275,900	$1,437,000

Eliminations Dr.	Eliminations Cr.	Minority Interest	Consolidated
(f)$145,000			$7,101,800
(h) 16,200			124,300
(j) 35,000			
(a) 135,600			-----
			$7,226,100
	(a)$ 11,000		4,574,400
	(f) 130,500		
(c) 3,000	(k) 3,500		538,400
	(h) 16,200		189,400
(c) 4,000			450,200
			731,600
			$6,484,000
			742,100
		$44,400	(44,400)
$338,800	$161,200	$44,400	$ 697,700
(a)$140,000		$35,000	$1,965,300
338,800	$161,200	44,400	697,700
	(a) 80,000	(20,000)	(400,000)
$478,800	$241,200	$59,400	$2,263,000
			$ 138,200
	(d)$ 20,000		553,700
	(i) 8,000		
	(f) 14,500		1,487,300
	(g) 196,400		-----
	(a) 542,100		-----
(b) 15,000	(e) 32,900		9,558,500
	(j) 35,000		
			132,300
	(g) 3,600		5,400
(a) 37,500	(b) 37,500		------
(b) 30,000	(c) 4,000		26,000
			$11,901,400
			$ 16,300
(e)$ 32,900	(b)$ 7,500		2,269,800
(k) 3,500	(c) 3,000		
(d) 20,000			700,900
(i) 8,000			
(g) 200,000			2,300,000
(a) 80,000		$20,000	1,000,000
(a) 240,000		60,000	3,212,000
478,800	241,200	59,400	2,263,000
		139,400	139,400M
$1,145,700	$1,145,700		$11,901,400

(a)

Capital Stock—Company S	80,000	
Additional Paid-in Capital—Company S	240,000	
Retained Earnings—Company S	140,000	
Income from Subsidiary (1)	135,600	
Differential (2)	37,500	
Dividends Declared		80,000
Investment in Company S Stock (3)		542,100
Cost of Goods Sold (4)		11,000

To eliminate the investment account, the income from S, a proportionate share of S's owners' equity accounts, and a proportionate share of the dividends declared by S. Also to adjust cost of goods sold for the unrealized intercompany profits included in beginning inventory.

(1) Income from Subsidiary, 1981:

80% of S's net income	$177,600
Amortization of goodwill	(4,000)
Amortization of equipment increment	(3,000)
1980 intercompany inventory profit realized	11,000
1981 unrealized intercompany inventory profit	(14,500)
1981 unrealized gain on intercompany sale of equipment	(35,000)
1981 portion of gain on intercompany sale of equipment realized	3,500
	$135,600

(2) Amount of Differential Remaining Prior to 1981 Amortization:

Equipment:	$15,000	
less 2½ years amortization at $3,000/year	7,500	
		$ 7,500
Goodwill:	$40,000	
less 2½ years amortization at $4,000/year	10,000	
		30,000
		$37,500

(3) Investment in S Company Stock 12/31/81:

Original cost, 6/30/78		$417,400
Income from S, 6/30/78-12/31/80 (.80 x 372,000)	$297,600	
Less unrealized intercompany inventory profit, 12/31/80	11,000	286,600
Dividends from S, 6/30/78-12/31/80 (.80 x 250,000)		(200,000)
Amortization of differential, 6/30/78-12/31/80 from (a) (2)		(17,500)
Income from S, 1981, from (a) (1)		135,600
Dividends from S, 1981		(80,000)
		$542,100

(4) Unrealized Intercompany Inventory Profit, 12/31/80:

1/3 ($85,000 − $52,000) = $11,000

(b)

Plant & Equipment	15,000	
Goodwill	30,000	
Accumulated Depreciation		7,500
Differential		37,500

To allocate the differential, less the prior years' amortization—see (a) (2).

(c)

Depreciation Expense	3,000	
Other Expenses	4,000	
Accumulated Depreciation		3,000
Goodwill		4,000

To record the 1981 amortization of the differential.

(d)

Short-term Liabilities	20,000	
Receivables		20,000

To eliminate P's share of the dividends owed by S.

(e)

Accumulated Depreciation	32,900	
Plant & Equipment		32,900

To eliminate the accumulated depreciation of S existing at the date of acquisition.

(f)

Sales	145,000	
Cost of Goods Sold (1)		130,500
Inventories (2)		14,500

To eliminate the intercompany sales (145,000) made by S to P during 1981 and to adjust cost of goods sold and inventories as follows:

(1) Cost of goods sold, with respect to intercompany sales:

Recognized by S	$ 87,000
Recognized by P when resold ¾ x 145,000	108,750
Total cost of goods sold recognized	$195,750
Cost to S of goods resold by P to outsiders, ¾ x 87,000	65,250
Adjustment to consolidated cost of goods sold	$130,500

(2) Unrealized intercompany profit in ending inventory:

¼ ($145,000 − $87,000) = $14,500

(g)

Bonds Payable	200,000	
Discount on Bonds Payable		3,600
Investment in Company S Bonds		196,400

To eliminate the intercompany bonds held by P ($200,000 out of $500,000) and the related discount (40%) against P's investment in bonds.

(h)

Other Income	16,200	
Interest Expense		16,200

To eliminate the interest expense and interest income on the intercompany bonds, as follows:

Cash interest = .08 x $200,000 =	$16,000
Amortization of discount = 1/20 x $4,000 =	200
Total interest	$16,200

(i)

Short-term Liabilities	8,000	
Receivables		8,000

To eliminate the accrued interest on S's bonds held by P.

(j)

Other Income	35,000	
Plant & Equipment		35,000

To eliminate the gain recognized by P on the sale of equipment to S and to adjust the equipment to its original cost to P.

(k)

Accumulated Depreciation	3,500	
Depreciation Expense		3,500

To eliminate the depreciation on the intercompany gain included in the cost of S's equipment, as follows:

Depreciation recognized by S, 1/10 x $95,000	$9,500
Depreciation based upon original cost to P, 1/10 x $60,000	6,000
Depreciation reduction	$3,500

CONSOLIDATION AFTER A POOLING OF INTERESTS

The previous discussion of consolidated financial statements assumed that the acquisition of the intercorporate investment in common stock was accounted for as a purchase. Thus, the stock acquired by the parent was recorded at the cost to the parent, and, for consolidation purposes, assets of the acquired subsidiary were revalued to their fair values at the date of combination.

In business combinations that result in a parent-subsidiary relationship and that are accounted for as poolings of interests, the common stock acquired by the parent is recorded at its book value rather than at the purchase price or fair value. The cost or equity method, as appropriate, would then be applied in the normal manner. If such a subsidiary were not consolidated, it generally should be reflected in the financial statements using the equity method because qualifying for pooling of interests treatment almost always assures that the "significant influence" criterion from APB Opinion No. 18 is met.

If the subsidiary is consolidated, the assets of the subsidiary are not revalued at the date of combination. Instead, the book values of the subsidiary's assets are reflected in the consolidated financial statements. All consolidation procedures are applied in the normal manner. Because the investment in the subsidiary's stock is recorded originally by the parent at an amount equal to the book value of the subsidiary's net assets, no differential arises upon consolidation.

COMBINED FINANCIAL STATEMENTS

As discussed previously, ARB No. 51 indicates that the preparation of consolidated financial statements is appropriate only when one company in the group controls and has a dominant financial interest in the other companies in the group. Under certain circumstances, however, it may be desirable to prepare financial statements for a group of related corporations as if they were a single company, even though none of the companies has control over or a dominant financial interest in the other companies. These financial statements are referred to as "combined" rather than consolidated financial statements. They may be appropriate, for example, for a group of subsidiaries having operations similar to one another but different in nature from those of the parent, or for companies under common management, or for a group of corporations owned by the same individual.

The procedures to be followed in the preparation of combined financial statements are, according to ARB No. 51, the same as those used in the preparation of consolidated financial statements, including the elimination of intercompany transactions and unrealized intercompany gains and losses. However, there normally would be no investment elimination against related companies' stockholders' equity unless there were intercompany stockholdings within the combined group.

TAXATION ON A CONSOLIDATED BASIS

The Federal tax law, by permitting the filing of consolidated income tax returns, recognizes that several legal entities may, in fact, constitute one business entity. The Supreme Court, in the case of Handy and Harman vs. Burnet, stated the purpose of permitting such returns as follows:

> The purpose of section 240 was, by means of consolidated returns, to require taxes to be levied according to the true net income and invested capital resulting from and employed in a single business enterprise, even though it was conducted by means of more than one corporation.

The filing of consolidated tax returns was first permitted in 1917. Under the present Internal Revenue Code, corporations have the option of filing a consolidated tax return with affiliated corporations. An affiliated group of corporations eligible to file a consolidated tax return exists if (1) at least 89% of all classes of each (other than the common parent) includible corporation's voting stock and at least 80% of each class of nonvoting stock is owned directly by one or more of the other includible corporations, and (2) the common parent owns directly at least 80% of all classes of voting stock and at least 80% of each class of nonvoting stock of at least one of the other includible corporations. The term "stock" excludes nonvoting preferred stock and employer securities held under a qualified employee stock ownership plan.

To file a consolidated tax return, all corporations that were part of the affiliated group at any time during the tax year must consent to it before the last day to file the return. Once a consolidated return is filed, the group must continue to file consolidated returns as long as the common parent and at least one subsidiary remain, unless permission is received from the IRS to discontinue the consolidated returns.

Before the provisions of the 1969 Tax Reform Act became effective, affiliated groups could receive one surtax exemption and one accumulated earnings credit for each affiliated corporation if separate returns were filed. Now, only a single surtax exemption and a single accumulated earnings credit are allowed for the affiliated group whether a consolidated return or separate returns are filed. Following are some current advantages and disadvantages of filing consolidated tax returns:

Advantages

1. One company's loss may be used to offset another's profits in the current tax year. Otherwise the loss would have to be carried back or forward to reduce taxes of some other year, and the benefit could be lost completely if the company had no taxable income during the carryover period.
2. Capital losses of one company may be used to offset another's capital gains in the current tax year. Otherwise, the loss would have to be carried back or forward and could be lost.
3. The tax on intercompany dividends is avoided. Normally, 15% of the dividends from other (domestic) corporations would be taxable.
4. There is no tax on intercompany profits until such profits are confirmed by transactions with outsiders.
5. Some deductions and credits are calculated in a more favorable way in a consolidated return.
6. Accounting and tax concepts of income are similar with regard to consolidation.
7. Filing on a consolidated basis may permit better centralized tax planning.

Disadvantages

1. Some of the corporations in the affiliated group may have to change their accounting periods and methods to achieve uniformity.
2. Filing a consolidated return in one year may bind the group to file consolidated returns in future years.
3. Intercompany sales of fixed assets may require burdensome bookkeeping because of the deferred gains or losses.

ACCOUNTING FOR FOREIGN INVESTMENTS

Many of the accounting procedures used by companies in accounting for foreign investments were altered by FASB Statement No. 8, issued in 1975. The procedures now in effect generally require that when the equity method (one line consolidation) or full consolidation is to be used, the financial statements of the foreign company are first restated to comply with U. S. generally accepted accounting principles but stated in terms of the local currency. Individual components of the financial statements are then translated into dollars using procedures comparable to those used by domestic companies in reporting foreign currency transactions. The resulting contribution to parent company or consolidated income may be very different from the dollar amount that would be computed by having the parent simply pick up a pro rata portion of the reported net income of the subsidiary (in local currency) and translating that amount into dollars.

Rates used in translating individual asset and liability accounts are presented in Table 1. In effect, the temporal method of translation has been adopted, with income statement recognition of exchange gains and losses for the full impact of currency rate fluctuations on monetary assets and liabilities held by foreign subsidiaries. Prior to Statement No. 8 some companies had deferred recognition of such gains and losses or amortized them over a number of years rather than including the full effect in current period income. The current exchange rate is considered to be the exchange rate in effect at the balance sheet date and the historical rate represents the rate in effect at the date a specific event or transaction occurred.

The method used in acquiring ownership of a foreign subsidiary will affect the rates used in translating its assets and liabilities held at the date of acquisition. If a business combination is treated as a purchase, the historical rate to be used in translating those assets and liabilities will be the rate in effect at the date of acquisition. If, on the other hand, pooling of interest treatment is used, the historical rate would be the rate in effect at the date the asset was acquired or the liability incurred by the foreign subsidiary.

A parent company may encounter difficulties in determining the appropriate exchange rate to be used in those countries where the official exchange rate and free exchange rate differ or where other forms of multiple exchange rates exist.

Under the requirements established in Statement No. 8, the rate applicable to dividend remittance should normally be used in translating foreign currency statements into dollars.

Preferred stock and common stock are normally translated at historical rates. However, if preferred stock is carried at liquidation price or redemption price in the foreign subsidiary's balance sheet, and liquidation or redemption appears imminent, it should be translated at the current rate. Other specific requirements relating to the translation of deferred taxes, inventory, and marketable securities should be carefully examined before an attempt is made to prepare consolidated financial statements. As in the case of any consolidated statements, all unrealized profits on intercorporate transactions must be eliminated in preparing the consolidated statements and in accruing investment income under the equity method.

Disclosure requirements. As in the case of domestic corporations, the basis for exclusion of majority-owned nondomestic subsidiaries must be presented in the footnotes to the financial statements. Careful consideration obviously must be given to the parent's ability to control the subsidiary and its ability to repatriate funds. Where the subsidiary is not consolidated, consideration should be given to providing separate financial statements or some form of summary data regarding operating results and financial position of unconsolidated foreign subsidiaries. It also may be desirable to provide separate parent company statements or supplemental consolidated statements for domestic operations when a significant portion of the primary consolidated financial statements are from foreign investments.

The bases used in computing exchange rate effects included in the financial statements should be disclosed in the footnotes to the financial statement. When rate changes have occurred after the date of the financial statements, the financial statements should not be adjusted; however, disclosure of the rate change and its effects, if significant, should be given.

TABLE 1

RATES USED TO TRANSLATE ASSETS AND LIABILITIES

	Translation Rates	
	Current	*Historical*
Assets		
Cash on hand and demand and time deposits	X	
Marketable equity securities:		
Carried at cost		X
Carried at current market price	X	
Accounts and notes receivable and related unearned discount	X	
Allowance for doubtful accounts and notes receivable	X	
Inventories:		
Carried at cost		X
Carried at current replacement price of current selling price	X	
Carried at net realizable value	X	
Carried at contract price (produced under fixed price contracts)	X	
Prepaid insurance, advertising, and rent		X
Refundable deposits	X	
Advances to unconsolidated subsidiaries	X	
Property, plant, and equipment		X
Accumulated depreciation of property, plant, and equipment		X
Cash surrender value of life insurance	X	
Patents, trademarks, licenses & formulas		X
Goodwill		X
Other intangible assets		X
Liabilities		
Accounts and notes payable and overdrafts	X	
Accrued expenses payable	X	
Accrued losses on firm purchase commitments	X	
Refundable deposits	X	
Deferred income		X
Bonds payable or other long-term debts	X	
Unamortized premium or discount on bonds or notes payable	X	
Convertible bonds payable	X	
Accrued pension obligations	X	
Obligations under warranties	X	

Source: FASB Statement No. 8

4

Partnership Accounts

CONTENTS

4

Partnership Accounts

Richard H. Homburger, J.D., CPA

The partnership form of business organization occupies somewhat of a middle position between the proprietorship and the corporation. It combines the flexibility peculiar to the proprietorship with the advantages of consolidating resources that are characteristic of the corporation. Because of its particular characteristics, the partnership form is most suitable for small and medium-sized business enterprises. Consequently, there are more partnerships than corporations in the U.S., although those businesses organized as corporations employ a considerably larger amount of capital.

This chapter first discusses those factors that distinguish the partnership from other forms of business enterprise. Next, various aspects of partnership accounting are explained both textually and through the use of examples. The accounting situations that are covered include opening the books of a new partnership, dividing profits and losses between partners, adding new partners, realizing and liquidating a partnership, as well as other partnership matters.

This chapter also covers various auditing and tax problems of partnerships including the taxable years of partners and partnerships, the tax basis of contributed property, and the tax basis of a partner's interest in the partnership. The chapter concludes with a discussion of the procedures involved in incorporating a partnership.

► NOTE: A form of business organization, sometimes treated as a partnership, is the joint venture (see Chapter 5).

THE PARTNERSHIP FORM OF BUSINESS

Special characteristics of partnerships. The legal, financial, and operational characteristics of partnerships have a bearing on accounting procedures for partnerships, on the presentation and valuation of items in the accounts, and on their financial statements. Among the special characteristics that influence accounting for partnerships are the following:

1. Operation by agreement—articles of co-partnership.
2. Partners' liability for business debts—general and limited partnerships.
3. Financial and operational flexibility.

1. *Operation by agreement—articles of co-partnership.* The relationship between individual partners and the partnership depends largely on agreement among the partners, although the Uniform Partnership Act has established some subsidiary rules of interpretation where an agreement is not apparent. The obligations of partners to contribute capital and services; their rights with regard to the sharing of profits, the withdrawal of capital, and retirement from the partnership depend on such an agreement. To avoid later difficulties a formal agreement should be drawn at the outset and revised whenever a need for change arises. These articles of co-partnership should contain at least the following:

The names and addresses of partners.
The name and address of the partnership business.
The nature of business or the purpose of the partnership.
The date and duration of the partnership agreement.
Provisions concerning capital contributions and withdrawals.
Provisions concerning the sharing of profits and losses.
Other rights and duties of partners during the operation of the partnership.
The rights and duties of partners in case of liquidation.
Provisions concerning retirement from the partnership.

2. *Partners' liability for business debts—general and limited partnerships.* Partners are jointly and severally liable for all partnership debts. This legal characteristic of a partnership constitutes one of its disadavantages from the viewpoint of an individual partner. For, if a partnership is unable to meet its obligations, an individual partner can be held liable for all partnership debts, regardless of his capital contribution.

By using the limited partnership form, it is possible to limit a partner's personal liability to the amount of his capital contribution to the partnership. Under such an agreement, however, at least one of the partners must be a general partner and, therefore, fully liable.

► WARNING: Limited partners who wish to avoid full liability must communicate their limited status. If they deal with third persons who have no knowledge of the limitation of their liability, they may be held fully liable.

The limited partnership form is usually preferred by persons who wish to invest in an enterprise without taking an active role in its operations and who desire to limit their capital risk. The limited partnership is widely used in the theatrical field for these reasons.

In the financial statements of limited partnerships, the names of limited partners should be disclosed on, or in connection with, the partnership balance sheet. Where partners are numerous, it is quite common to state the total partnership capital in a single amount on the balance sheet, and to attach a list of general and limited partners. Where individual partners' capital balances are shown on the balance sheet itself, those with limited liability should be identified through annotation or the use of footnotes.

3. *Financial and operational flexibility.* Flexibility and informality of financing are salient characteristics of the partnership. Because of the relative informality of the conduct of partnership affairs, any one partner may be given the power to act for the partnership in a certain area of business activity. Even extraordinary business decisions, which would require stockholders' consent in a corporation, can be quickly made in a partnership by agreement of the partners. While the corporation has the ability to amass large capital resources from the general public, the partnership can obtain needed funds more quickly, within the limits of the financial strength of its members.

On the other hand, the partnership lacks the organizational stability and continuity characteristic of the corporation. Withdrawal or death of a partner may pose not only a serious financial problem, but may jeopardize the very existence of the partnership business.

BASIC ACCOUNTING PROCEDURES FOR THE PARTNERSHIP

Opening the books for a new partnership. The first accounting procedures to be considered are those connected with the formation of a new partnership. Opening the books may involve the following accounting problems:

1. Valuing contributed assets.
2. Valuing purchased assets.
3. Recognition of intangibles.

1. *Valuing contributed assets.* In opening the books for a new partnership, the various assets accounts are debited, and the individual partners' capital accounts are credited, at the fair market value of the assets contributed. Each partner's contribution should be shown by a separate journal entry. Separate memoranda records should be kept showing the Federal tax basis of assets contributed by the partners.

Sometimes, a sole proprietor admits a partner to his business in return for a cash contribution. If it is desired to use the old set of books, any asset adjustments from book value to current market value may be carried directly to the proprietor's capital account, or to a market value adjustment account, the latter to be closed into his capital account.

► EXAMPLE: A's books show the following asset values: cash $4,000; merchandise, $10,000 equipment (net), $15,000. He admits partner B at a time when the value of the merchandise is $8,000 and the value of the equipment is $18,000. In using his old set of books, he will adjust the accounts as follows:

Equipment (net)	3,000	
Merchandise		2,000
Market valuation adjustment		1,000
Market valuation adjustment	1,000	
A, capital		1,000

After A's capital account has been adjusted in this manner, B's fair cash contribution can be determined, depending on the share in the business he is to acquire.

2. *Valuing purchased assets.* Assets purchased from a partner ordinarily are recorded at their cost to the partnership, in the same manner as assets acquired from outsiders. In cases where the consideration paid to a newly admitted partner is substantially above market cost, it may be more realistic to charge the excess to the old partners' capital accounts.

3. *Recognition of intangibles.* Goodwill may be allowed to a partner contributing a going business to a newly formed partnership. The amount of goodwill allowed should not be more than an outsider would pay for such goodwill. Similarly, the fair market value of a covenant not to compete may also be recognized on the books of the partnership, using the same criterion as for goodwill.

Dividing profits and losses among partners. Partners are free to agree on how profits or losses are to be distributed. To be satisfactory to all partners, such an agreement must take into consideration the various factors determining the value of each partner's contribution to the partnership, such as capital provided, services rendered, skill, experience, reputation, and the like. The agreement must also be flexible enough to yield reasonably satisfactory results should profits be substantially higher or lower than anticipated, or should unexpected losses occur. The boiling down of all the determining factors to a simple arithmetic distribution ratio has the advantage of simplicity of computation. Yet it may possibly work a hardship on the preferred partners in case of a loss, as such a loss is usually distributed in the profit ratio. As an alternative, advance credits for differences in services or capital contributions may be allowed. Such advance credits reduce any residuary gain, or, as the case may be, add to any residuary loss. The balance of any gain or loss remaining after such credits have been taken into account is usually distributed equally.

Advance credits to compensate partners for their superior contribution in work or skill are commonly called salaries. However, rather than having these salaries reflect the actual value of their services, partners' salaries are usually employed merely as a device for dividing profit among the partners. Therefore, nominal salaries are arbitrarily established for only the preferred partners. This procedure is flexible enough to adjust to any particular situation and to meet the wishes of all the partners concerned. Sometimes, instead of a fixed amount of salary, a bonus of a certain percent of profits may be allowed to one or several partners. Another use of advance credits is to compensate partners for differences in their capital contributions. These credits are usually computed at an arbitrary annual rate of interest on capital balances. Where partners have some freedom to change the amount of their capital investment, such interest is best computed on average capital balances maintained, rather than on balances at the beginning of the year. Credits for salaries and for interest on capital balances may be combined. Another method for allowing interest on capital balances is to share profits in the ratio of capital balances, beginning or average. While this method is simpler, it is more crude in that it penalizes the partner with the larger capital when applied in case of losses.

In the foregoing, the relative advantages and disadvantages of various common methods of profit or loss distribution among partners have been presented. The following will illustrate the procedures involved in computing the distributive shares of profit or loss by each of three methods:

1. Average capital ratio.
2. Allowance for interest on capital balances.
3. Allowance for salaries and interest on capital balances.

1. *Average capital ratio.* Assume that in the newly formed ABC partnership, A invested $50,000, B $30,000, and C $20,000 at the beginning of the calendar year. On April 1, A added $10,000 to his capital investment, and on November 1 he withdrew $5,000; B withdrew $4,000 on July 1, but re-invested $2,000 on December 1; C added $5,000 to his investment on July 1. The average capital contribution of each partner for the calendar year is obtained by multiplying each amount of capital held without change by the number of months it was so held, and then dividing the total amount of dollar-months so obtained for each partner by 12.

SCHEDULE 1

COMPUTATION OF AVERAGE CAPITAL

A			*B*			*C*		
Capital/Months		*Dollar Months*	*Capital/Months*		*Dollar Months*	*Capital/Months*		*Dollar Months*
$50,000	3	$150,000	$30,000	6	$180,000	$20,000	6	$120,000
60,000	7	420,000	26,000	5	130,000	25,000	6	150,000
55,000	2	110,000	28,000	1	28,000			
	12	$680,000		12	$338,000		12	$270,000

The average capital invested by each partner is 1/12 of the total amount of dollar-months for that partner, or $56,667 for A, $28,167 for B, and $22,500 for C. This is equivalent to a ratio of 52.8% for A, 26.2% for B, and 21% for C. An assumed profit of $20,000 would, therefore, be distributed as follows: $10,560 to A, $5,240 to B, and $4,200 to C.

► SUGGESTION: To find the ratio of average capitals, it is not necessary to divide the dollar-months by twelve to obtain the average capitals. The ratio of the totals of dollar-months for each partner serves the same purpose and saves one step in the computation. Also, where changes in partners' capitals occur only at the beginning or end of quarters, the use of dollar-quarters rather than dollar-months simplifies the computation.

2. *Allowance for interest on capital balances.* Assume that the partners agree to allow each partner an advance credit at the rate of 6% per annum of capital funds invested, instead of sharing the profit in the ratio of their average capitals. The interest allowed each partner is shown in Schedule 2.

SCHEDULE 2

COMPUTATION OF INTEREST ON CAPITALS

A			*B*			*C*		
Capital	*/Months*	*/Interest*	*Capital*	*/Months*	*/Interest*	*Capital*	*/Months*	*/Interest*
$50,000	3	$ 750	$30,000	6	$ 900	$20,000	6	$ 600
60,000	7	2,100	26,000	5	650	25,000	6	750
55,000	2	550	28,000	1	140			
	12	$3,400		12	$1.690		12	$1,350

The distribution of a $20,000 profit under such an agreement is shown in Schedule 3.

SCHEDULE 3

DISTRIBUTION OF ANNUAL PROFIT OF $20,000

	A	*B*	*C*	*Total*
Credit for Interest	$3,400	$1,690	$1,350	$ 6,440
Residuary Share	4,520	4,520	4,520	13,560
Total Share	$7,920	$6,210	$5,870	$20,000

By comparing the distribution of the $20,000 profit in Schedule 3 with the distribution obtained on the basis of average capitals ($10,560 to A, $5,240 to B, and $4,200 to C), one can see that the setting of an interest rate lower than the rate of profit on total capital will tend to reduce the difference between the individual partners' shares in the profit. In our example, the rate of profit on average capital is 18.6%, while the interest rate used in Schedule 3 is only 6%.

3. *Allowance for salaries and interest on capital balances.* Assume that advance credits for nominal salaries of $3,000 each for B and C were agreed upon, in addition to the 6% per year interest allowance on capital balances maintained by each partner. The following schedules will illustrate the computation of the partners' distributive shares in case of a $20,000 profit, an $11,000 profit, and a $10,000 loss respectively. (Parenthesized amounts indicate charges to partners.)

SCHEDULE 4

DISTRIBUTION OF ANNUAL PROFIT OF $20,000

	A	*B*	*C*	*Total*
Credit for salary	$ ——	$3,000	$3,000	$ 6,000
Credit for interest	3,400	1,690	1,350	6,440
Residuary share	2,520	2,520	2,520	7,560
Total share	$5,920	$7,210	$6,870	$20,000

SCHEDULE 5

DISTRIBUTION OF ANNUAL PROFIT OF $11,000

	A	*B*	*C*	*Total*
Credit for salary	$ ——	$3,000	$3,000	$ 6,000
Credit for interest	3,400	1,690	1,350	6,440
Residuary share	(480)	(480)	(480)	(1,440)
Total share	$2,920	$4,210	$3,870	$11,000

SCHEDULE 6

DISTRIBUTION OF ANNUAL LOSS OF $10,000

	A	*B*	*C*	*Total*
Credit for salary	$ ——	$3,000	$3,000	$ 6,000
Credit for interest	3,400	1,690	1,350	6,440
Residuary share	(7,480)	(7,480)	(7,480)	(22,440)
Total share	($4,080)	($2,790)	($3,130)	($10,000)

These distributive shares of profits or losses are ordinarily closed into the partners' personal accounts at the end of each accounting period. For example, assuming the same data as in Schedule 5, the closing entry is journalized as follows:

Profit and loss summary	11,000	
A—Personal account		2,920
B—Personal account		4,210
C—Personal account		3,870

A summary showing the distribution of profit or loss among partners is usually presented at the bottom of the profit and loss statement for the period.

Distributive shares of salaries and/or interest may be credited to partners' accounts currently. The journal entries to record partners' salaries and interest for the month of January, again assuming the data in Schedule 5, would be:

Partners' salaries	500	
B—Personal account		250
C—Personal account		250
Interest on partners' capitals	500	
A—Personal account		250
B—Personal account		150
C—Personal account		100

At the year-end closing, the accounts for partners' salaries and interest on partners' capitals are closed to the profit and loss summary account. The residuary loss of $1,440 is charged to the partners' personal accounts, thereby closing the profit and loss summary account.

Partners' drawing and loan accounts. The drawing, or personal, accounts are credited for profit shares, and debited for losses, other charges, and withdrawals. Whether or not the balances of these accounts are closed into partners' capital accounts as part of the routine closing procedure depends on the partnership agreement. Where capital balances are fixed by agreement and cannot be increased arbitrarily, drawing account balances should be carried over from one period to the next.

Partners' loans, from and to the partnership, are recorded in special partners' loans receivable or payable accounts. On the balance sheet of a going partnership, such loans are properly shown among the business assets or liabilities, though separate from other types of loans. In liquidation they rank behind outside creditors and are in the nature of capital adjustments, even though, among partners, loans from partners are given preference before partners' claims on capital balances.

ADMISSION OF A NEW PARTNER TO A PARTNERSHIP

General. The admission of a new partner to an existing partnership is possible only with the consent of all partners concerned; legally, it dissolves the old partnership agreement, replacing it with a new agreement. How the rights and obligations of a new partner are defined is entirely up to the partners, and is ordinarily the result of bargaining between the new and the old partners. A new partner may be admitted to the partnership without any capital contribution, and simply share in profits or losses as agreed. This situation does not pose any particular accounting problem. Most often, however, a new partner contributes some capital. A partner's capital credit on the books of the partnership forms the basis of his share in liquidation. Therefore, the new partner ordinarily expects to receive a capital credit either equal to, or possibly higher than, the cost of his share in the partnership; although, under certain conditions, he may accept a smaller capital credit.

Where a partner acquires an interest in a partnership by contributing funds or properties to the partnership business, thereby increasing its total invested capital, the net market value of the assets contributed ordinarily determines the amount of his capital credit. There is usually a desire, however, to determine beforehand the size of the capital share, as related to total partnership capital, that the new partner is to receive for his contribution. All of these circumstances raise a variety of financial and accounting problems. Some typical situations of this type, and the accounting procedures for each of them are discussed and illustrated below.

Purchase of an interest. A new partner may negotiate with one of the old partners to buy his share in the partnership, or a fraction of it. The purchase price agreed upon between the new and the selling partner may be more or less than the value of the share as shown on the partnership books. As the agreed price is simply the settlement paid to the old by the new partner, it does not affect the capital invested in the partnership. No adjustment in the book value of partnership capital accounts need be made.

► EXAMPLE: C's $20,000 share in the ABC partnership is sold to a new partner, D, for $23,000 cash. A and B agree to the sale. The only entry to be made on the partnership book is:

C—Capital	20,000	
D—Capital		20,000

Investment matching book value of share acquired. Assume that C negotiates to be admitted as a third partner to the AB partnership. A's capital account balance is $40,000, B's $30,000. The partners share profits and losses equally. It is agreed that C should acquire a capital interest equal to that of B. C owns merchandise purchased for $15,000 and now valued at $17,000; this merchandise is part of his contribution to the partnership. To match B's share, C must contribute $13,000 in cash.

Investment in excess of book value of share acquired. Assume, in this case, that C is to be admitted to a capital share equal to that of B's $30,000, but it is also agreed that present conditions justify a contribution of $37,500 from C. The proper accounting procedures for C's investment depend on the financial factors that cause a higher price to be placed on the share to be acquired by C. These factors, which will be discussed in turn, may be due to any of the following:

1. Undervaluation of assets.
2. Bonus paid to old partners.
3. Partnership's unrecorded goodwill.

1. *Undervaluation of assets.* A payment by C, exceeding the book value of his acquired share, could reflect undervaluation of existing partnership assets. The entries to record C's admission are:

Various asset accounts	15,000	
A—Capital account		7,500
B—Capital account		7,500
Cash (or property accounts)	37,500	
C—Capital		37,500

2. *Bonus paid to old partners.* In those situations where there is no evidence of either an undervaluation of partnership assets or the existence of unrecorded goodwill, the admission of a partner whose investment exceeds the book value of his acquired share is best treated as a bonus paid by the new partner to the old partners for the privilege of admission to the partnership. This method is conservative, but has the disadvantage of giving the new partner

a capital credit lower than the amount of his contribution to the partnership. If such a bonus is treated as a gain, and consequently shared by the old partners in their profit ratio, the following entry will, in our example, achieve the desired result:

Cash (or property accounts)	37,500	
A—Capital account		2,500
B—Capital account		2,500
C—Capital account		32,500

► NOTE: In order to equalize B's and C's capital account balances, as required by the partner's agreement, the $7,500 excess over book value paid by C must be distributed equally among all three partners, including C.

3. *Partnership unrecorded goodwill.* In the past, if the individual assets were properly valued on the books of the partnership, the excess in C's investment over the book value of his acquired share has often been interpreted as a pro rata payment by the new partner for the existing partnership's unrecorded goodwill, which has led to the following entries:

Goodwill	15,000	
A—Capital account		7,500
B—Capital account		7,500
Cash (or property accounts)	37,500	
C—Capital account		37,500

This method of disposing of the excess paid by the new partner over the book value of his acquired share, generally identified as the goodwill method, is not in accord with the wording or the spirit of AICPA Principles Board Opinion 17 of August 1970. While not referring to partnerships in particular, this Opinion, in paragraph 24, approves the recording of goodwill on a company's books only if acquired from other enterprises or individuals. ("Company", according to paragraph 5 of the Opinion, refers to both corporate and unincorporated enterprises.) The Opinion further stipulates that costs which are inherent in a continuing business and related to an enterprise as a whole—such as goodwill—should be deducted from income when incurred. The only way to comply with this provision is to record, in effect, a new partner's payment for unrecorded goodwill as a bonus to the old partners, as was illustrated under 2. above.

Investment of less than book value of share acquired. Assume that in the example used previously, C is admitted to a share equal to B's for an investment of only $20,000. Recording his admission again depends on the circumstances and on the partners' agreement. The following possible circumstances will be separately treated:

1. Overvaluation of assets.
2. Goodwill to new partner.
3. Bonus to new partner.

1. *Overvaluation of assets.* In this circumstance the required entry to reduce the asset overvaluation is:

A—Capital account	10,000	
B—Capital account	10,000	
Various asset accounts		20,000

2. *Goodwill to new partner.* To record C's admission, allowing him a credit for goodwill as well as cash or tangible property contributed, the entry is:

Cash (or property account)	20,000	
Goodwill	10,000	
C—Capital account		30,000

This method of recording is justified only if C contributes a business of his own that includes goodwill that would be realizable if the business were sold. Intangible personal qualifications, such as skill or experience, should not be recorded on the books as goodwill when admitting a partner for less than the book value of his share.

3. *Bonus to new partner.* Where asset values are not in need of adjustment, C's admission for less than book value is best recorded as a bonus paid to him by the old partners, as follows:

Cash (or property account)	20,000	
C—Capital account		20,000
A—Capital account	3,334	
B—Capital account	3,333	
C—Capital account		6,667

Or, if recorded to maintain the old capital ratio:

A—Capital account	4,000	
B—Capital account	3,000	
C—Capital account		7,000

WITHDRAWAL OF A PARTNER

General. When a partner ceases to be a member of a partnership due to retirement or death, a financial settlement with the retiring partner or the estate of the deceased is necessary. The funds for such a settlement may be provided by one or more of the remaining partners buying the share of the withdrawing partner with their own funds. In this case, the capital invested in the partnership remains unimpaired by the withdrawal, and the same accounting procedure is followed as the one outlined for the purchase of an interest. If partnership invested capital is used for the settlement, the capital accounts are reduced and accounting problems involving the adjustment of capital accounts arise. The general accounting problems that apply to all situations of total capital withdrawal from the partnership will be discussed first and special problems arising from the death of a partner later.

Factors involved in retirement from a partnership. In order to determine the amount to pay the retiring partner, the book value of his share must first be determined. If a partner retires at any time other than the end of an accounting period, this determination of book value may involve the accrual of profit or loss from the last closing date to the date of his retirement. It may also involve a revaluation of partnership assets.

The book value of the retiring partner's share is determined by closing the income and expense accounts as of the date of retirement and distributing the profit or loss to that date in the profit ratio. This may be inequitable where seasonal factors are involved. As an alternative, settlement with the retiring partner may be delayed until the close of the accounting year. Then, a fraction of the profit or loss for the year may be allocated to the retired partner for the portion of the year when he was a member in the partnership.

► EXAMPLE: A, B, and C share profits in the ratio of 2:2:1. The partnership books are kept on a calendar year basis. C withdraws on September 30. At the closing on December 31, a net profit of $20,000 is distributed as follows:

Profit to:	*Total*	*A*	*B*	*C*
January 1 to September 30 (9/12 × $20,000)	$15,000	$6,000	$6,000	$3,000
October 1 to December 31 (3/12 × $20,000)	5,000	2,500	2,500	—
	$20,000	$8,500	$8,500	$3,000

As in the case of admission of a new partner, it may be necessary to make adjustments for over- or undervalued assets to determine the book value of the retiring partner's share. The accounting procedure is the same as previously illustrated in revaluing assets upon the admission of a new partner.

Retirement at book value. The partnership may provide that, under certain conditions, a partner who retires may receive cash or other partnership assets equal to the book value of his share, or an agreement to that effect may be made at the time of retirement. The partnership agreement may also provide this type of settlement in case of the death of a partner. Under any of these conditions, the entry for the withdrawal and settlement will be a debit to the withdrawing partner's capital account and a credit to cash or other assets.

Retirement for a consideration higher than book value. Assume that C, a member of the ABC partnership, is to retire and withdraw his capital. The book value of his share at retirement is determined to be $20,000. It is agreed among the partners, however, that C should receive $25,000 as his settlement. C's retirement is recorded on the partnership books as follows:

Bonus to the retiring partner. The $5,000 excess over book value that C is to receive may be looked upon as a bonus paid to C by the remaining partners. If this bonus is to come out of partnership capital, and assuming equal capital and profit ratios among A and B, the entry to record C's retirement is:

C—Capital account	20,000	
A—Capital account	2,500	
B—Capital account	2,500	
Cash or Other Assets		25,000

If A and B's capital and profit ratios differ, both would have to agree on whether to charge the $5,000 bonus to their respective capital accounts in the ratio of capitals or of profits and losses. An acceptable alternative is to pay only the amount of the book value ($20,000) out of partnership funds. The remaining partners could then pay the bonus out of their personal funds.

Recognition of unrecorded goodwill by the partnership. The excess of $5,000 over book value paid to C has sometimes been viewed as payment for C's share in the unrecorded goodwill of the partnership and has thus been recorded as a debit to goodwill upon C's retirement. Such a procedure is not in accordance with AICPA Principles Board Opinion 17. The bonus method, explained above, should therefore, be applied in all cases of this type.

Retirement for a consideration less than book value. If, in the example being used, C were to receive only $16,000 for his $20,000 share, the method of accounting would again depend on whether the difference was due to a bonus paid to the remaining partners or a reduction in existing goodwill.

Bonus paid to remaining partners. Ordinarily, C's sacrifice of $4,000 would be viewed as a bonus paid by C to the remaining partners (or to the continuing partnership) in consideration for the privilege of withdrawing. The following entry gives effect to this view:

C—Capital account	20,000	
Cash (or other assets)		16,000
A—Capital account		2,000
B—Capital account		2,000

Reduction in existing goodwill. If goodwill has been brought on the partnership books previously, it may be assumed that partnership goodwill is being reduced proportionately by C's retirement. There may be an agreement that C is entitled only to an amount representing his share in the tangible assets of the partnership. In this case, the entry to show the withdrawal would be:

C—Capital account	20,000	
Cash (or other assets)		16,000
Goodwill		4,000

Withdrawal by reason of death. *Contractual payments to estate or survivor.* In the event of a partner's death, the partnership agreement frequently determines how the amount due the decedent's estate is to be computed. Where such a provision is lacking, the book value of the decedent's share, adjusted to market value at the date of death, normally provides the basis for settlement.

If life insurance on the deceased partner is owned by the partnership, proceeds from the policy may totally or partially cover the amount needed for settlement. This will allow the surviving partners to retain part of all of the deceased partner's capital investment in the partnership. Such amounts can then be transferred to the capital accounts of the surviving partners.

Agreements to continue sharing profits after death. Agreements are also possible to continue a profit-sharing arrangement with the decedent's estate or his heirs for a certain period of time. This requires the decedent's capital investment to be retained in the partnership enterprise for that period. If this is done, the decedent's capital account balance is transferred to a properly designated capital account representing the continuing investment of the estate or the heirs of the decedent.

SALE OR LIQUIDATION OF THE PARTNERSHIP BUSINESS

Sale of the business as a unit. *Recording the profit or loss.* If the partnership business is sold for a lump sum, the nominal accounts are closed as of the date of sale to allow distribution of operating profits or loss to the partners. The customary year-end closing procedure is used to determine the operating profit or loss. In addition, to record the gain or loss on the sale, a special income account, *Gain or loss on sale of business,* is opened. This account is credited with the contract price for the sale and the remaining asset and liability accounts are closed into this same account. A credit balance remaining in this account represents a gain on the sale; a debit balance would indicate a loss.

Selling among partners and closing the books. The gain or loss on the sale is distributed among the partners in their customary gain or loss ratio, crediting their capital accounts with any gain or charging them with any loss, and thereby closing the special income account. The last entry is for the distribution of cash, crediting the cash account for the distribution and charging each capital account with its distributive share.

Complete realization of assets before distribution. If a partnership business is liquidated rather than sold, the ultimate gain or loss in the liquidation cannot be known until all assets have been sold and all liabilities paid. Only then can the final share of each partner be determined. It is, therefore, safer and simpler to delay any distribution until that time. The following procedures apply:

1. *Paying the liabilities.* Any proceeds from assets sold are first applied to the payment of outstanding liabilities. Book gains or losses on individual assets sold are recorded in a special income account, *Gain or loss in liquidation.*
2. *Adjusting partners' capital accounts.* The net gain or loss in liquidation, as ultimately determined, is distributed to the capital accounts in the gain or loss ratio. The credit balance remaining in each partner's capital account indicates his share in the ultimate distribution.
3. *Capital deficiencies and insolvency of a partner.* In the event that a partner's share in the liquidating loss exceeds the balance in his capital account, charging the loss to his account produces a debit balance. The partner is legally

liable to the other partners for the amount of such debit balance and must pay this amount into the partnership treasury, thereby allowing the balancing of his account. If he is unable to do so, this amount is considered as an additional loss of the partnership to be charged to the capital accounts of those partners who still have credit balances in their capital accounts. This charge to eliminate a debit balance is made in the usual gain or loss ratio prior to any final distributions. The charging of an insolvent partner's debit balance may cause one or more of the remaining partners to have debit balances in their accounts. In such case, the same procedure applies as in the case of the first deficiency.

4. *Insolvency of the partnership.* In liquidating a partnership business, it may be that the proceeds from the sale of all the assets are not sufficient to pay all the liabilities of the partnership. If this occurs, the individual partners are jointly and severally liable to partnership creditors for the amount of the deficiency. Any partner can be held liable by any partnership creditor for the full amount of the partnership debt. After all book losses from sales have been charged, each partner's liability to the other partners for the payment of partnership debts is determined by the debit balance in his capital account. As a practical matter, however, a partner may be compelled by partnership creditors to pay more than his share in the partnership debt.

In an insolvent partnership, the proper accounting procedure is necessary to reveal the rights and obligations of partners. As a partner pays any of the partnership debts, an entry is made debiting the creditor's account, and crediting the paying partner's capital account. After all liabilities have been paid by individual partners, the remaining debit or credit balances in the partners' accounts will indicate the extent of their respective claims or obligations under the partnership agreement.

Liquidation by installments. Frequently partners do not wish to wait until the final outcome of the liquidation of all assets before making a distribution of proceeds. In cases where the capital balances of partners before a distribution bear the same ratio to each other as the profit or loss sharing ratio, any partial distribution is made in such a ratio.

► EXAMPLE: A, B, and C show capital balances of $50,000, $30,000, and $20,000 respectively and share gains and losses in that ratio. A preliminary distribution of $12,000 can be made as follows: $6,000 to A, $3,600 to B, and $2,400 to C. Any future distribution may be made in the same ratio, as any final loss will have to be shared in that ratio.

Where capital ratios before any liquidating distribution differ from the partners' gain or loss distribution ratios, the procedure is to regard any book balances remaining undistributed at the time of each distribution as a total loss and to charge this loss to partners' capitals in their loss ratio. The following two examples illustrate this procedure.

► EXAMPLE 1: A, B, and C have capital balances of $50,000, $30,000, and $20,000 respectively. They share profits and losses equally, however. As part of the liquidation proceedings, after paying all liabilities, a first installment of $40,000 is to be distributed. Their distributive shares are determined by charging the entire potential loss of $60,000 equally to their capital accounts. This leaves A with a $30,000 credit, B with a $10,000 credit, and C with no balance. Therefore, A receives $30,000, and B $10,000.

► EXAMPLE 2: Assume that the first distribution is only $25,000. After charging a $75,000 book loss equally, C's account is left with a $5,000 debit balance. This debit balance must be further distributed as a charge to A's and B's account. After this is done, A's account is left with a balance of $22,500 and B's with a balance of $2,500. These are their shares in the first distribution.

The amounts received by the partners in a distribution are charged to their respective capital accounts. Then, for each subsequent distribution, a similar computation must be carried out up to the point where, as a consequence of capital adjustments for distributions received, the partners' capital accounts have been brought into the ratio of their shares in profits and losses. After this point has been reached, any subsequent distributions are made in profit and loss ratios.

► NOTE: To simplify computations of the type described above, partners' loan accounts should be merged with their capital accounts to determine their shares in a liquidating distribution. The results obtained are the same as if the loans are treated separately.

OTHER PARTNERSHIP PROBLEMS

The partnership form of organization entails other problems of an accounting nature. Certain audit procedures are unique to partnerships and certain of their tax-accounting problems are unique. In addition, partners frequently decide to incorporate their business. Each of these problems will be discussed in turn.

Auditing procedures peculiar to partnerships. Partners' proprietory accounts represent the main aspect of audit procedures that are peculiar to partnerships. In this respect, Howard F. Stettler writes:[1]

> In the examination of a partnership the auditor should satisfy himself that the provisions of the partnership agreement have been carried out as they pertain to the distribution of net income and the maintenance of partners' capital and drawing accounts. Points likely to be covered in the agreement would include the basis of distributing profits, including any provisions for salaries or interest, maximum drawings permitted during the year, minimum capital balances to be maintained, additional capital to be contributed, and the treatment of loans by the partnership to and from the partners.

[1]Stettler, Howard F., Systems Based Independent Audits, 2nd Edition, p. 434, Englewood Cliffs, N.J., Prentice Hall, Inc. 1974.

In certifying the financial statements of the usual partnership, the auditor should include in his report a statement to the effect that no provision has been made in the financial statements for the partners' individual income tax liabilities on their distributive shares of partnership profits, and that the extent to which partnership assets may be used for this purpose has not been determined. As an alternative, in the interest of full disclosure, footnotes to that effect may be included as part of the statements.

The practice of including a provision for the partners' tax liability on partnership profits among the partnership expenses and liabilities cannot be condoned as it violates the *entity concept* (see Chapter 1). Whether other liabilities of individual partners that have a direct bearing on partnership funds—such as loans incurred for capital investment—should be disclosed in the auditor's report, has to depend on the information available and on the auditor's judgment. As a rule, an auditor is not obliged to examine an individual partner's affairs in connection with the audit of a partnership.

Tax accounting problems of partnerships. Under Federal income tax laws, the partnership is not a separate taxable entity. Instead, the individual partners are taxed on their share of the taxable income of the partnership. However, an information return, Form 1065, must be filed for the partnership. The discussion of tax accounting problems will include:

1. Accounting aspects of Form 1065.
2. Taxable years of partners and partnerships.
3. Tax basis of contributed property.
4. Tax basis of partner's interest in the partnership.
5. Limited partnership tax shelter.
6. Election to exclude application of Subchapter K.

1. *Accounting aspects of Form 1065.* This form provides not only for a detailed statement of partnership income and deductions, but also for comparative balance sheets as of the beginning and end of the taxable year (Schedule L), for distribution of partners' shares of net taxable income and of special items of income and deductions (Schedule K), and for a reconciliation of individual partners' capital accounts at the beginning and end of the year (Schedule M). Multi-column work sheets are helpful in assembling this data. One type of work sheet that may be useful in providing data for the schedules mentioned is shown in Figure 1.

Income And Expense Per Books	Excluded For Tax Purposes	Allocated To Individual Partners (Schedule K)	Income And Expenses Per Tax Return (Page 1, Form 1065)

Fig. 1. Work Sheet for Preparing Form 1065, the Partnership Information Return.

2. *Taxable years of partners and partnerships.* A partnership may have a taxable year different from one or several of its partners, but the taxable year adopted may not be different from that of all its principal partners without prior approval. (A principal partner is one who has an interest of 5% or more in the partnership's profits or capital.) In the case of different taxable years, a partner must include his distributive share of partnership income in his return for the tax year within which the partnership tax year ends. No particular accounting problems of allocation are posed under this rather simple rule.

3. *Tax basis of contributed property.* The contribution of property by partners to a partnership is not viewed as giving rise to taxable gain or loss. The partnership credits the contributing partner's capital account with the fair market value of the property. The tax basis for the partnership, however, remains the same as the basis of the property in the hands of the contributing partner. Because of this difference between book value and tax basis, subsidiary records showing tax bases and adjustments for contributed property items should be maintained by the partnership.

4. *Tax basis of partner's interest in the partnership.* The tax basis of a partner's interest is ordinarily equal to the total bases of all properties contributed by him, properly adjusted for profit accumulations, capital distributions and withdrawals. This basis does not agree with the book value of a partner's capital account that is based on market values at the time of contribution. Because of this difference in book value and tax basis, memorandum subsidiary records showing the tax basis of contributed property will aid in determining the tax basis of a partner's interest. Where such an interest is acquired by purchase rather than contribution, cost to the buying partner is his basis for tax purposes.

5. *Limited partnership tax shelter.* As was mentioned earlier, the limited partnership offers the limited partner the advantages of participation in an enterprise with reduced risk. Under certain conditions it may also be availed of as a tax shelter, taking advantage of the "conduit" effect of partnership expenses as income tax deductions on the individual partner's return. A person with high current income may invest, as a limited partner, in an enterprise which produces currently high start-up expenses with income delayed to future years. Enterprises fitting this description are generally those engaged in real estate development operations and in the exploration of natural resources. While normally a partner may deduct losses to the extent of his basis including his share of partnership liabilities, the Internal Revenue Code has been amended to exclude from taxable basis, in most instances, nonrecourse liabilities. Real estate ventures are excluded from those "at risk" provisions. Caution is advised in this area because of rapidly evolving tax legislation and Internal Revenue practice.

► Warning: Most tax shelter limited partnerships are organized with corporate general partners. The Internal Revenue Service has very specific regulations which must be carefully followed to prevent the limited partnership from being treated for tax purposes as a corporation, thus forfeiting the pass through of partnership losses to the limited partners.

6. *Election to exclude application of Subchapter K.* Under IRC Section 761 partners who are either co-owners of investment property and do not themselves actively engage in business, or are participants in the joint production, extraction or use of property but do not jointly sell services or the property produced or extracted, may exercise an election to exclude application of all or part of Subchapter K of Chapter 1 of the Internal Revenue Code, i.e., the provisions dealing with the tax treatment of partnership income.

► NOTE: The election formerly available to certain types of partnerships to be taxed as corporations under Section 1361 was repealed on April 14, 1966.

Incorporation of a partnership. Having decided on incorporation, it is necessary for the partners to file a certificate of incorporation with the office of the secretary of state and to obtain a charter authorizing the issuance of stock. Provision may be made in the certificate for the issuance of shares to outsiders, in addition to the shares that are to be issued to the partners in exchange for the capital interests they transfer to the newly formed corporation. After the charter has been obtained, the following types of entries for the transfer may be made.

1. *Revaluation of assets and recognition of goodwill.* Partners' capital accounts must first be adjusted to the date of transfer. This involves the usual closing of income and expense accounts and a possible revaluation of asset accounts to reflect market values at the time of incorporation. It may also involve a recognition of goodwill if such goodwill is reflected in the going market value of the partnership business. The accounting procedure applied is similar to the procedure for the admission of a new partner to a going business.

2. *Closing the partnership books.* In formally closing the partnership books, an account with the newly formed corporation is opened on the books of the partnership. This account is charged with the adjusted book values of all the partnership assets transferred, credited with the face amount of all liabilities assumed, and credited with the partners' capital balances to indicate the partners' receipt of shares or cash in exchange for their capital interest. After these entries have been made, this new account should be in balance, and all partnership asset, liability, and capital accounts closed out.

3. *Opening the corporation books.* On the books of the new corporation, all partnership assets and liabilities transferred are entered at their book value adjusted to the date of the transfer, and a capital stock account—or accounts, if more than one class of stock is issued—is credited for the par or stated value of shares issued to partners. If such par or stated value is less than the recorded value of net assets transferred, a *Premium on capital stock* account is credited for the difference.

4. *Using the old set of books.* The old partnership books may be used by the corporation, especially if shares in the new corporation are issued only to partners. In this instance, after all the entries to adjust asset and capital accounts have been made, all that is needed is an entry to close the partners' capital acounts and to open the corporate proprietorship accounts by debiting the former and crediting the latter.

5

Joint Venture Accounting

CONTENTS

5

Joint Venture Accounting

L. Milton Woods, Ph.D., CPA

In this chapter, the origins and historical uses of the joint venture are explored, as are the reasons for the growing popularity of this form of business organization. Its modern use and advantages are described in fields ranging from the entertainment industry to oil and gas ventures.

Various methods and procedures involved in accounting for joint ventures are explained, along with illustrative journal entries for representative transactions under the two alternative methods of accounting most commonly employed. A third method is also briefly described.

The tax and legal problems inherent in the use of ventures are analyzed, and specific accounting and auditing problems of ventures are explained in detail. An extract from standard procedures developed by the *Petroleum Accountants' Society is* presented in the appendix to illustrate some typical accounting procedures that have been developed for one widely-used form of joint venture—the oil and gas venture.

HOW THE JOINT VENTURE DEVELOPED

Ancient forms. Although the true beginnings of the joint venture are lost in antiquity, we can discover one of its ancestors in the Babylonian "partnership." This partnership consisted of a loan of money granted by one partner to one or more other partners for a single commercial transaction. The party advancing the money was repaid, together with his pro-rata share of profits.

Later, during the Middle Ages, a type of maritime joint venture arose in which one or more associates provided the capital while remaining in the home port, and the others traded goods overseas. This type of business organization became very common, and during this period was perhaps the dominant form of business organization.

In England, the East India Company, chartered in 1600, really operated as a joint venture until 1613, since each member contributed varying amounts of capital for each voyage. Every voyage was a complete transaction, after which there was an accounting. These arrangements were known by various names in England and on the continent; it is not until the nineteenth century that we find "joint venture" (or "joint adventure" as it was then called) being used as a term of art (in Scotland).

The modern venture defined. A joint venture is generally defined as an association of persons (which may include corporations) to engage in and carry out a single business adventure for joint profit. It is neither a partnership nor a corporation, although it is treated as a partnership in some jurisdictions, as well as for Federal tax purposes.

Closely related to the joint venture is the joint enterprise. A joint enterprise is an association of persons who jointly undertake something for the mutual benefit or pleasure of the parties. The distinction between them is the lack of joint profit motive in the join enterprise.

► EXAMPLE: Two corporations may pool all or a part of their manufacturing operations as a means of reducing costs. If they retain separation of the selling function, the concept of a joint profit motive is thereby eliminated. The pooled manufacturing, therefore, would constitute a joint enterprise rather than a joint venture.

Most of the examples in the chapter will deal with joint ventures, although one important form of joint enterprise, the oil and gas venture, will also be considered.

COMPARISONS WITH OTHER FORMS OF BUSINESS ORGANIZATION

Because of the broad nature of its definition, the joint venture is sometimes difficult to identify. The mere joint ownership of property does not constitute a joint venture. There must be something more—an actual carrying on of business. The joint venture is simple to distinguish from a corporation because the venture is an unincorporated organization, and also because the centralized management of the corporation is lacking in the joint venture. The coadventurers *jointly* carry on the business. This, of course, does not imply that there cannot be some measure of delegation to one of the coadventurers as "operator," as we shall see later.

By the same token, a trust can generally be distinguished by its specialized form, and by the centralization of management in trustees who serve in a fiduciary capacity.

A single venture is easily identified as a simplified form of the joint venture. The single venture is conducted by one individual or business as sole owner.

The greatest difficulties arise in distinguishing the joint venture from a partnership. In some jurisdictions, no distinction is recognized. In those jurisdictions that do recognize the separate form of the joint venture, the following comparisons and distinctions can be noted. Both joint ventures and partnerships may be formed by simple contract agreements. Venturers assume unlimited liability for the debts of the venture, as is the case with general partners. On the other hand the joint venture, in one sense, has somewhat more permanence than the general partnership. Although a member cannot withdraw without the consent of all the venturers, his withdrawal does not dissolve the joint venture. Similarly the bankruptcy or death of a member does not necessarily dissolve the joint venture. Furthermore, unlike a partnership a member of a joint venture cannot bind the other members by his acts, although a manager usually is given, by contract, wide powers to act for the other members. The primary difference, however, is in the intention of the members of the joint venture to be liable only for transactions arising from the one venture. While a venture may last only a short time, or extend for many years, it is a *single* business venture in either case.

USES OF THE JOINT VENTURE

The great diversity of the joint venture can be illustrated by the following examples of its uses in different fields of business:

1. Real estate syndicates.
2. Entertainment ventures.
3. Securities underwriting ventures.
4. Ranching.
5. Oil and gas ventures.
6. International ventures.

Real estate syndicates. One of the forms that a real estate syndicate may take is the joint venture. A typical venture could arise as follows. The promoter obtains an option on the property to be acquired. He then transfers this option to the venture, in return for either a cash payment or a share of the venture capital. The other members of the venture are, of course, the investors, who provide the capital to purchase or develop the property. In this type of venture, there may be an agreement between the coadventurers for a special allocation of depreciation expense, so that the investors may receive the tax deductions related to their tax basis in the syndicate.

Entertainment ventures. Although the form of organization for most theatrical productions today is the limited partnership, at least one well-known stage play has been produced by a joint venture.

The production of motion pictures is an area that makes extensive use of the joint venture. An independent production company will provide the actors, writers, producers, directors and the script, while a distributor will supply part of the financing (so-called "second money"), the studio, and other facilities. The venture commonly secures financing of 60% to 70% of the budget from banks, which lend on the basis of commitments or contracts covering the story, star, director, studio and distributor. The second money provided by the distributor will be perhaps 15% of the budget, and the balance will be in the form of deferrals of salary for the actor, producer, director and writer. The typical agreement specifies the priorities of any payments to be made from earnings of the picture.

Securities underwriting ventures. An investment banking firm organizes a syndicate of underwriters to purchase and distribute a new security issue. The firm acquires the role of managing underwriter by reason of its being the organizer of the group that makes the low bid in the case of an issue awarded by competitive bidding, or by being the originating underwriter in the case of a negotiated issue. The terms of the offering are delineated in the agreement between issuer and manager, and syndicate operating rules are formalized in the agreement between manager and members. Generally, the agreement among the underwriters gives the manager wide authority to negotiate the purchase and direct the distribution of the security issue.

Ranching. Although there are numerous examples of the joint venture's use in farming and ranching operations, cattle fattening will be used to illustrate its application in this area. In ventures of this type an investor purchases cattle to be fattened for subsequent sale. Ordinarily, the investor will have no facilities for handling the cattle. In order to provide feed and physical facilities for the cattle, he will form a joint venture with a farmer or rancher who has facilities for caring for the cattle. The cattle are sold at the end of the venture and the profits divided. This type of venture seldom lasts more than a few months.

Oil and gas ventures. The number of forms that the joint venture may take in the oil and gas field are very diverse. Unlike many of the ventures previously described, the relationships of the parties in these ventures will often be spelled out to the minutest detail in formal documents. Also, unlike many other ventures, the oil and gas venture may last many years if successful. The most striking peculiarity of the oil and gas venture is that it is usually not a joint venture at all, but merely a form of joint enterprise.

The venture may arise before the discovery of oil or gas, or subsequent thereto. If it arises before discovery, the venture may include preliminary exploration and activity to determine the geology and geophysics of an area, in addition to the drilling of the discovery well, and possibly other wells. After commercial production is established, the venture may furnish and operate the production facilities. The venture is commonly formed by lessees of contiguous parcels of land that have attractive geologic characteristics. The exploration and production activities on the land will be covered by an operating agreement designating one of the lessees as operator, usually the holder of the largest interest. The operator arranges for all necessary materials and services and charges the "joint account" for them. The operator may arrange for the disposition of the production from the property and pay the proceeds to the co-owners.

However, each co-owner will usually have the right to take physical possession of his share of production. Technically this prevents this relationship from being characterized as a true joint venture—the option to physically possess a share of production means that there is no joint profit motive.

In accord with the absence of a joint profit motive, the operator usually bills each co-owner for his share of expenses, and issues a check for the co-owner's full share of any proceeds, without offsetting the expenses. There are important tax and legal reasons for conducting the venture in this manner.

The operating agreements for this type of venture generally provide for the accounting requirements of the venture in some detail, including the manner of charging and crediting the point account for the usual transactions. Other matters relating to auditing and the taking of inventories are also likely to be quite detailed in the operating agreements.

International ventures. All of the ventures that have been discussed so far are representative of ventures in a particular industry or business. The international venture, however, cannot be identified with any particular business. Instead it is best characterized by the diverse nationalities of its participants. The international venture may be formed to sell American products abroad, to participate in foreign construction projects, or to engage in the extraction of minerals, to name only a few of the many possibilities. The international venture will be seriously affected by, and must consider carefully the operation of foreign laws, and the interaction of the tax laws of the various tax jurisdictions.

REASONS FOR FORMING THE JOINT VENTURE

The joint venture form may be chosen for any of a number of reasons. The chief reasons for the selection of the joint venture are likely to be the following:

1. Minimizing of risk.
2. Pooling of capital.
3. Tax savings.
4. Pooling of knowledge.
5. Saving of expense.
6. Legal advantages.

Minimizing of risk. The desire to minimize individual risk is today, just as it was in the time of the ancient maritime ventures, the primary reason for the formation of many joint ventures, particularly those dealing with natural resource. Exploration for oil and gas is so costly and carries with it such high risk of loss that many individual participants do not wish to undertake the risk by themselves. By investing in several ventures, an individual is able to spread his risk, thus effectively lessening it.

Pooling of capital. Although the corporation is normally thought of as the vehicle to achieve the pooling of capital, the joint venture can be effectively utilized in those cases in which the corporate form is not suitable. A prime reason for the formation of some of the very large ventures today is the substantial amounts of capital required to be raised. The construction of nuclear power plants could be cited as an example of projects having large capital requirements that are suitable for joint ventures. The highly speculative venture is another example of capital accumulation through use of a joint venture, but for a different reason. The amount of capital required in this case may not be excessive, but the speculative nature of the venture will preclude borrowing from the usual commercial sources. Participating investors may be the only available source of capital.

Tax savings. The use of the corporate form for single transactions has been seriously limited by legislation penalizing the so-called "collapsible" corporation. Also, closely-held corporations of the investment type often run the risk of being subjected to the very high personal holding company rates. In addition, the corporation will often insulate its stockholders from tax deductions in the early years of the venture, when losses may be incurred. This is particularly important in regard to oil and gas ventures, where the tax deduction for intangible drilling costs may cause the venture to show large tax losses in the early years. For these and other tax reasons, the joint venture has become a favored device for participating in single transactions.

There are certain tax dangers in the use of the joint venture. A poorly-drawn agreement may be construed for tax purposes as an "association" taxable as a corporation, with all of the tax disadvantages of that form of organization, and none of its legal and business advantages. Also, the use of the joint venture will expose an individual participant to income at the steeply graduated individual rates, whether or not the income is distributed to him.

However, some of these dangers can be avoided by an election to be taxed as a partnership (see Chapter 8, *Other Techniques of Financial Accounting).* This may be of value in eliminating the insulation from losses in the early years previously referred to, since the income of such corporation will be taxed, in a proper case, to the stockholders in much the same manner as if they were partners.

Because the joint venture is treated as a partnership for income tax purposes, it must file partnership information returns, and the tax on venture income is paid by the participants.

Pooling of knowledge. Many joint ventures are being formed by non-competing firms in situations where the technology of one firm complements that of the other. This is particularly true of ventures formed to construct specialized facilities. Besides the obvious advantage of profit sharing by all participants, this type of joint venture can furnish an effective foundation for diversification by single-line companies into other fields. Also, substantial savings may be obtained by eliminating duplicate research efforts in specialized areas.

Saving of expense. Joint ventures are often undertaken in order to mininize expenses in connection with a specific project. Nearly every type of expense may be affected, direct expense as well as indirect expense. If the venture is not unusually large, the operator of the venture may provide supervision for a nominal sum, charging only for his incremental costs. Even when separate staffing must be maintained, substantial savings may still be possible from the pooling of operations. Thus the use of the venture may permit patented processes belonging to one of the participants to be used at a reduced royalty without triggering the so-called "equal treatment" clauses commonly used in patent licensing agreements.

► EXAMPLE: A grants a license to B for the use of A's patent at a royalty of $10,000 per year. The agreement contains an equal treatment clause. Normally, if A were to grant a similar license to C for $5,000 royalty per year, B would also be entitled to pay royalty at the reduced rate. But it the patent is used by a joint venure in which A is a participant, the equal treatment clause may not be triggered.

Legal advantages. The joint venture is frequently used to avoid legal pitfalls or stumbling blocks inherent in other forms of business organization. For example, in those jurisdictions where a partnership form cannot be used when one or more of the participants is a corporation, the joint venture may be a suitable alternative.

Another legal advantage of the joint venture is the ease with which it can often be set up in foreign countries, especially when one of the participants is a national of the foreign country. Corporations and partnerships often face serious difficulties in obtaining permission to do business in foreign countries. The venture, on the other hand, may be much more welcome because of the limited scope of its operations.

ACCOUNTING FOR THE VENTURE

Why venture accounting is different. As we have noted, the joint venture is a creature of shadowy definition. Its legal existence borders closely on the partnership, and it is sometimes indistinguishable from a partnership. In fact, some joint ventures have ended in partnerships. Why, then, is accounting for the venture treated as a separate subject? The very informality of many ventures fully justifies separating the subject of joint venture accounting from partnership accounting. Because of the limited scope of the venture, the usual concept of balance sheet and income statement reporting is generally not applicable to the venture. If one were to try to characterize joint venture reporting in a general way, it might best be compared to a statement of application of funds, or to fiduciary's charge and discharge statement. The parties interested in these statements, like the participants in a joint venture, are not so much interested in the balance sheet as they are in the flow of funds.

Another reason for a separate treatment of joint venture accounting is the widespread use of specialized forms of the venture in certain industries. These ventures often have highly developed accounting requirements that are very different from conventional partnership accounting.

This is not to imply that some ventures do not require the preparation of conventional balance sheets and income statements on an orderly periodic basis, but such ventures have progressed far on the road towards partnership accounting, and do not need separate treatment in this chapter.

It is apparent from the great diversity of forms that the joint venture may take that the agreements underlying the venture have a profound effect upon the accounting for the venture. Unfortunately, since these agreements are commonly drawn without the assistance of accounting personnel, they often contain unreasonable requirements. A common failing is the requirement of periodic settlements that does not take into account the time required to close the books. Another costly failing is the frequent requirement that all transactions be listed in detail on periodic statements. Many ventures have been operating for a number of years under such agreements. Their monthly statements contain a laboriously prepared listing that shows in detail for every invoice: the item purchased, the unit price, discount, tax, etc., without regard for the materiality of the items involved.

Regardless of its failings, the joint venture agreement forms the basis for accounting between the parties, and must be strictly observed. Nevertheless, the accountant should bring any undesirable features of the agreement to the attention of his client so that he has an opportunity to eliminate these wasteful practices by amending the agreement. The features of a joint venture agreement that are of particular importance to an accountant are likely to be: the settlement and statement requirements, the basis of accounting (cash, accrual, or a combination of both), any special priorities for payments that may influence the statement format, the allocation of profits (including the allocation of any special deductions), and the auditing provisions.

METHODS OF ACCOUNTING

Three methods of accounting for the joint venture are commonly used. These methods may be classified as follows:

1. A separate set of books for the joint venture.
2. No separate set of books for the joint venture.
3. Combination methods.

► NOTE: Accounting for a single venture is not discussed in this chapter because it offers few problems. One account may be opened for the single venture, the final balance in this account being the gain or loss on the venture.

A separate set of books for the joint venture. Under this method all of the venture transactions are kept in the joint venture books. Each participant records in his own books only those transactions to which he is a party.

No separate set of books for the joint venture. For ventures of limited duration, it is common practice not to maintain a separate set of books for the venture, but rather for each of the participants to record all entries in detail.

This is quite satisfactory when the venture is a simple one involving only a few entries. However, if the venture is to involve many entries and extend over more than one year, the task of keeping the venture "books" in agreement may prove a formidable one. Therefore, there has evolved a modification born of the necessity to cope with this problem. This modified method is frequently used in practice and is a combination of the first two methods.

Combination method. Under this method, a separate set of books will be maintained for the venture, but detailed entries of transactions will be made by the participants. This method may be used when there is a divergence of accounting methods between the participants as, for example, in inventory costing methods. It is particularly appropriate when participants are using different methods of depreciating property. The statements prepared from the venture's separate books form the basis for determining that the requirements of the venture agreement have been satisfied, each participant's own entries are then made to conform to his individual accounting system. Aside from the implementation of the individual accounting policies of the participants, this method is further justified by the ease of auditing provided by the separate venture books.

Examples of entries. For the purpose of showing journal entries that illustrate the different methods of accounting for the joint venture, the following set of facts will be assumed:

Coadventurer A is manager of the venture, and is to receive a fee for his services.

A and B are to contribute money, or inventory of equivalent value.

B is to loan the necessary equipment at an agreed value, will keep the equipment in repair at his own expense, and will repossess the equipment at the end of the venture at an agreed salvage value.

Profits are to be shared equally, after charging the venture with the results of the above transactions.

Based on these facts, wherever they are applicable, nine transactions are illustrated as they would appear on the books of the venture and the ventures' participants under the first two methods of accounting:

(a) A contributes $10,000.
(b) B contributes equipment having an agreed value of $1,000 and inventory having an agreed value of $10,000. The equipment has a net book value on B's books of $800, and the inventory is recorded at $9,800 on B's books.
(c) Inventory is purchased for $10,000.
(d) The management fee for services rendered by A is accrued at the agreed sum of $100.
(e) The entire inventory is sold for $24,000.
(f) Depreciation of $100 is recorded on the equipment.
(g) The equipment is returned to B, at the agreed salvage value of $750.
(h) The venture accounts are closed.
(i) The final settlements are made with participants.

It should be noted that there may be variations in the above entries. In entry (b) under the first method, since the net book value of the equipment is $800 on B's books, the excess of the transfer price over the net book value is credited to a deferred income account. The *Equipment loaned to venture* account is used to maintain a separation of fixed assets included in the joint venture accounts, and for statement purposes the account is substracted from the account, *Joint venture.* This will leave the loaned equipment in the regular fixed

METHOD I—SEPARATE

	A's Books			*B's Books*		
(a)	Dr.—Joint venture	10,000		—No entry—		
	Cr.—Cash		10,000			
(b)	—No entry—			Dr.—Joint venture	11,000	
				Cr.—Inventory		9,800
				Cr.—Equipment loaned to venture		800
				Cr.—Sales—		200
				Cr.—Deferred income—equipment usage		200
(c)	—No entry—			—No entry—		
(d)	Dr.—Joint venture	100		—No entry—		
	Cr.—General and administrative expense		100			
(e)	—No entry—			—No entry—		
(f)	—No entry—			Dr.—Depreciation expense	100	
				Dr.—Equipment loaned to venture	100	
				Cr.—Allowance for depreciation		100
				Cr.—Deferred income—equipment usage		100
(g)	—No entry—			Dr.—Equipment loaned to venture	700	
				Dr.—Deferred income—equipment usage	300	
				Cr.—Joint venture		750
				Cr.—Equipment usage income		250
(h)	Dr.—Joint venture	1,825		Dr.—Joint venture	1,825	
	Cr.—Income from venture		1,825	Cr.—Income from venture		1,825
(i)	Dr.—Cash	11,925		Dr.—Cash	12,075	
	Cr.—Joint venture		11,925	Cr.—Joint venture		12,075

asset accounts. This treatment is used because B retains title to the equipment and is obligated to take it back at the conclusion of the venture. If A had become a co-owner of the equipment upon its transfer to the venture, B would treat A's interest in the equipment as a sale, and the gain or loss on this transaction would be taken into the income accounts.

BOOKS FOR VENTURE

Venture Books

(a)	Dr.—Cash	10,000	
	Cr.—A		10,000
(b)	Dr.—Equipment	1,000	
	Dr.—Inventory	10,000	
	Cr.—B		11,000
(c)	Dr.—Inventory	10,000	
	Cr.—Cash		10,000
(d)	Dr.—Management fee	100	
	Cr.—A		100
(e)	Dr.—Cash	24,000	
	Cr.—Sales		24,000
(f)	—No entry—		
(g)	Dr.—Equipment usage expense	250	
	Dr.—B	750	
	Cr.—Equipment		1,000
(h)	Dr.—Sales	24,000	
	Cr.—Management fee		100
	Cr.—Inventory		20,000
	Cr.—Equipment usage		250
	Cr.—A		1,825
	Cr.—B		1,825
(i)	Dr.—A	11,925	
	Dr.—B	12,075	
	Cr.—Cash		24,000

The venture books do not contain depreciation accounts, since recovery of the cost of fixed assets is achieved through the charge for equipment usage. Because joint ventures utilize cash basis accounting, no effort is made to currently match costs with revenue through periodic depreciation charges. On B's books an entry is made to increase the deferred income account by the amount of the depreciation, so that the *Equipment loaned to venture* account will con-

METHOD II—NO SEPARATE BOOKS FOR VENTURE

	A's Books			*B's Books*		
(a)	No entry, assuming no separate bank account for the venture			Dr.—Joint venture	10,000	
				Cr.—A		10,000
(b)	Dr.—Joint venture	11,000		Dr.—Joint venture	11,000	
	Cr.—B		11,000	Cr.—Inventory		9,800
				Cr.—Equipment loaned to venture		800
				Cr.—Sales		200
				Cr.—Deferred income—equipment usage		200
(c)	Dr.—Joint venture	10,000		—No entry—		
	Cr.—Cash		10,000			
(d)	Dr.—Joint venture	100		Dr.—Joint venture	100	
	Cr.—General and administrative		100	Cr.—A		100
(e)	Dr.—Cash	24,000		Dr.—A	24,000	
	Cr.—Joint venture		24,000	Cr.—Joint venture		24,000
(f)	—No entry—			Dr.—Depreciation expense	100	
				Dr.—Equipment loaned to venture	100	
				Cr.—Allowance for depreciation		100
				Cr.—Deferred income—equipment usage		100
(g)	Dr.—B	750		Dr.—Equipment loaned to venture	700	
	Cr.—Joint venture		750	Dr.—Deferred income—equipment usage	300	
				Cr.—Joint venture		750
				Cr.—Income—equipment usage		250
(h)	Dr.—Joint venture	3,650		Dr—Joint venture	3,650	
	Cr.—B		1,825	Cr.—A		1,825
	Cr.—Income from venture		1,825	Cr.—Income from venture		1,825
(i)	Dr.—B	12,075		Dr.—Cash	12,075	
	Cr.—Cash		12,075	Cr.—A		12,075

tinue to be in balance with the net of the related fixed asset and depreciation accounts.

Combination system. It is not necessary to use journal entries to illustrate the combination system. Under this system, the participants record in detail in their own books those venture transactions that are applicable to themselves.

These detailed entries are made when the participants receive their monthly statements listing the venture transactions. In the combination system, the participants make their detailed entries in accordance with their own accounting methods, and there can be considerable variation in the different accounting methods. The greatest amount of variation is probably encountered in the policies regarding capitalization vs. expense, and in depreciation rates and methods.

SPECIFIC ACCOUNTING PROBLEMS OF THE VENTURE

Accounting variations between venture and participants. There are often variations between the accounting system prescribed by the venture agreement and the individual accounting systems of the participants. In an oil and gas venture, for example, a standard list of "controllable" material replaces the usual concept of the difference between capital expenditures and expense items. This may result in some of the participants capitalizing and depreciating items that are treated as operating charges on the venture statement, and vice versa. The emphasis in the oil and gas venture is upon the controllable concept, so that intangible costs may not be detailed although the participants will usually capitalize intangible charges incurred in connection with the installation of fixed assets. Intangible costs are those items incurred in the drilling of the oil well or installation of equipment, such as labor, fuel, etc., as distinguished from tangible costs such as casing and tubing.

Another variation commonly found is the difference in fiscal periods between the venture and its participants. If the venture agreement provides for monthly statements, the "month" of the venture will frequently be closed on the twentieth or twenty-fifth of the month to permit the participants to enter the venture transactions in their own books of account before their closing.

By far the most important variation, however, is the result of maintaining the venture accounts on a cash basis, whereas the participants' accounts are generally maintained on the accrual basis. For example, if a three-year insurance policy is purchased, the participants are immediately charged with the entire cost of the policy. In order to more nearly match the expense with revenues, the participants may segregate this charge and carry the unexpired portion of it in a prepaid expense account. The same treatment may be accorded fixed assets purchased by the venture. It is in this area that participants find it most necessary to reclassify the venture accounts according to their usual accounting treatment.

Valuing property transferred to and from members of venture. When a venture extends over a long period of time, problems often arise in connection with the valuation of property transferred to, or removed from, the venture. In the venture, property is often valued at an agreed amount, without regard for the cost to the contributing member. A common provision in some venture agreements requires new property to be priced at 100% of current replacement market, and used (but still usable) material to be priced at 75% of current replacement market. When such a system is used during a period of inflation, it is possible to remove used material at a greater value than had been charged to the joint venture. In order to meet this problem, some agreements provide that the venture be credited for equipment removed at a price that leaves a net charge commensurate with usage. This, however, is only a partial solution, since any removal price that is less than a reasonable market value permits the equipment owner to obtain a bargain at the expense of the other participants. On the other hand, if used property is transferred to the venture at the contributing participant's net book value, the other participants will have the benefit of the use of the property at less than the current market value. Since all participants usually have the right to supply property to the venture, the transfer price obviously must be uniform for all similar property. Also, the use of participant's cost gives rise to serious auditing problems in order to support the cost, whereas the current replacement market is readily determinable by all participants.

If new equipment is purchased by the venture from joint cash, no problems arise; but if new property is transferred from the warehouse of one of the participants, the cost on the contributing participant's books may be different than the transfer price, even if the transfer is made at replacement market and there has been no price change. This is primarily because such items as quantity discounts may not be passed on to the joint venture under the agreement. Also, the transfer price to the venture may be based upon carload shipments, so that if small shipments are made by the contributing participant, the difference in shipping costs will not be chargeable to the venture.

Valuing services to venture. When one or more of the participants render services to the venture, another problem of valuation arises. Many venture agreements provide for the use of commercial rates for this purpose. Obviously, commercial rates may permit the participant supplying the service to make a profit from the venture, apart from the usual distributing of profits. This may not be consistent with the intent of the agreement, particularly when the services rendered entail little, if any, incremental cost to perform. Commercial rates do, of course, have the advantage of ease in auditing. Nevertheless, some agreements provide for the recovery by the participant supplying the service of only the incremental costs associated with the service. This incremental cost may be difficult to determine and often will require negotiation between the parties. Also, since the service is provided by the participant's existing organization, there may be a natural reluctance to permit a full audit determination of the cost. Where depreciation is an important factor in cost determination, difficulties arising from the many methods of depreciation accounting will face the accountant.

Allocation of indirect expense. The preceding discussion was concerned with services rendered directly to the venture by one or more of the members. (At the end of this chapter is an extract from an agreement that spells out in detail the basis on which different types of charges are made to a joint oil and gas venture.)

A difficult problem of allocation sometimes arises when indirect expenses are charged to the venture, particularly when the venture's participants are from noncompeting industries that have dissimilar overhead structures. In these cases the allocation of indirect expenses should be covered in detail by the venture agreements to avoid subsequent auditing difficulties. When the venture has its own supervisory staff, the problem is narrowed to the general office services (accounting, legal, etc.), which are usually provided by the manager's staff. In such cases, it is common to provide a negotiated fee to cover all of such services. This fee may be in the form of a lump sum, or a percentage of direct labor, total costs, or even of gross profit. The securities underwriting venture, for example, compensates the manager at a percentage of the "spread" of a competitive bid offering.

Profit allocation. Because of the great importance that income taxes have assumed in the formation of a joint venture, the allocation of profits is no longer a simple matter of applying the participation percentages to the net profits.

In the real estate syndicate, it is often desirable to allocate the depreciation deductions exclusively to the investing members, rather than allocate them pro rata to all members. Otherwise the promoter, who usually has little or no tax basis in his share of the venture, may receive a portion of the return of venture capital through depreciation.

Also, it is often desired to allocate capital gains on a special basis in some ventures. In the oil and gas ventures, for example, the agreements are drawn with great care to provide tax deductions to the member who provides the capital investment.

In the entertainment ventures, the priorities of payment are particularly important. The deferred salaries of the star, director, and producer will enjoy a priority over payments to the writer for his script, although all of these items are in reality a form of profits distribution. Of course, all these priorities must be strictly observed.

Accounting reports and statements. The accounting reports prepared for joint ventures cannot be characterized generally. Since the primary objectives of these reports are to satisfy the members that the agreements have been observed, and to provide sufficient information for individual entries by the participants, the form and content of such reports must generally be improvised. Most of these statements account for the cash flow of the venture's operations. If settlement is made periodically, a statement of participant's accounts will be included. If the venture has a prolonged existence, the statements will most likely be cumulative. The amount of detail in the reports will depend to a large degree upon the agreements. There may be specific requirements for detailing entries affecting certain types of equipment. The concept of controllable equipment in the oil and gas venture is illustrative of this sort of requirement. This requirement is primarily for the purpose of providing information to permit the members to properly classify the venture transactions. Beyond this, the members will not be likely to insist upon detailed reports if adequate provision is made for the audit of the venture accounts.

AUDITING OF THE JOINT VENTURE

The auditing of joint ventures poses some unique auditing problems. Among these problems are:

1. The right to audit.
2. Access to information.
3. Inventories.
4. Cost of the audit.

The right to audit. It is, of course, desirable to have the subject of audits adequately covered in the agreements. In the absence of such provision, there may be some uncertainty as to the right of the members to demand an audit of the manager's accounts. If the venture is treated as a partnership under local law, the right to an accounting exists. If it is treated as a mere co-tenancy, there may not be a right of accounting. When ventures involve foreign operations, the members should have a firm understanding as to the right of audit, since auditing is not so readily accepted as a usual business practice in some countries. Even when the right to audit is specified, the American participant may be surprised to learn that political considerations and customs in the foreign country often render this right meaningless. Audits are commonly performed by the internal audit staff of the nonmanaging participants, although large ventures are likely to require the services of an independent public accountant.

Access to information. Perhaps the most important problem facing the accountant when setting up the books of the venture is to provide a system that can be audited. If the venture is formed by competing firms, the manager will wish to provide sufficient safeguards so that competitive information will not be divulged in the course of auditing. If audits are performed by the internal audit staffs of the members, the problem of safeguarding competitive information is considerably increased. The direct charges to the venture for services and materials can often be made through a separate series of journal vouchers, removing the necessity for auditors to be directly involved in the manager's accounting system. The supporting documents for these vouchers can be readily segregated and made available to the auditors.

Allocated expenses present a somewhat more difficult problem. If supervisory payrolls are allocated to the venture, the manager may be especially reluctant to make this information available to the auditors. This factor sometimes leads to setting an agreed sum for supervision rather than allowing the manager to be reimbursed through an allocation of actual expenses.

When replacement market prices form the basis for charges and credits to the venture, much of the auditing can be performed away from the manager's offices, if competent pricing assistance is available.

Inventories. Audits of physical inventories may be provided for, either periodically, or at the conclusion of the venture. The auditor should be present at the taking of the inventory. When the venture involves firms with technologies that complement each other, the observation of the inventory may present certain problems of identification. If the venture is conducted near to other similar operations of the manager, there may be difficulty in maintaining segregation of all of the venture property. In these circumstances, overages and shortages of inventory may be artificially created. This raises the question as to how the overages and shortages will be borne. It is commonly provided that overages and shortages that do not result from the manager's negligence shall be borne jointly.

► NOTE: Inventories for construction projects are particularly troublesome. Much of the equipment may be inaccessible for inspection, causing the inventory taking to be incomplete. Several inventories at various stages of completion may be necessary in such cases to insure complete coverage.

Cost of the audit. It is commonly provided that reasonable cost of the audit shall be borne jointly. In the absence of such provision, the manager may be reluctant to bear any part of the cost of auditing the venture accounts. The actual amount to be charged will ordinarily be negotiated between the members, and may be either a per diem or actual cost charge.

Extract from "Accounting Procedure (Unit and Joint Lease Operations)" Form PASO-T-1955-2 (For Use in Oil and Gas Ventures)

III. BASIS OF CHARGES TO JOINT ACCOUNT

1. *Purchases*

   Material and equipment purchased and service procured shall be charged at price paid by Operator after deduction of all discounts actually received.

2. *Material Furnished by Operator*

   Material required for operations shall be purchased for direct charge to joint account whenever practicable, except that Operator may furnish such material from Operator's stocks under the following conditions:

   A. New Material (Condition "A")

   (1) New material transferred from Operator's warehouse or other properties shall be priced f.o.b. the nearest reputable supply store or railway receiving point, where such material is available, at current replacement cost of the same kind of material. This will include material such as tanks, pumping units, sucker rods, engines, and other major equipment. Tubular goods, two-inch (2″) and over, shall be priced on carload basis effective at date of transfer and f.o.b. railway receiving point nearest the joint account operation, regardless of quantity transferred.

   (2) Other material shall be priced on basis of a reputable supply company's preferential price list effective at date of transfer

and f.o.b. the store or railway receiving point nearest the joint account operation where such material is available.

(3) Cash discount shall not be allowed.

B. Used Material (Condition "B" and "C")

(1) Material which is in sound and serviceable condition and is suitable for reuse without reconditioning shall be classed as Condition "B" and priced at seventy-five per cent (75%) of the new price.

(2) Material which cannot be classified as Condition "B" but which,

(a) After reconditioning will be further serviceable for original function as good secondhand material (Condition "B"), or

(b) Is serviceable for original function but substantially not suitable for reconditioning,

shall be classed as Condition "C" and priced at fifty per cent (50%) of new price.

(3) Material which cannot be classified as Condition "B" or condition "C" shall be priced at a value commensurate with its use.

(4) Tanks, building, and other equipment involving erection cost shall be charged at applicable percentage of knocked-down new price.

3. *Premium Prices*

Whenever materials and equipment are not readily obtainable at the customary supply point and at prices specified in Paragraphs 1 and 2 of this Section III because of national emergencies, strikes or other unusual causes over which the Operator has no control, the Operator may charge the joint account for the required materials on the basis of the Operator's direct cost and expense incurred in procuring such materials, in making it suitable for use, and in moving it to the location, provided, however, that notice in writing is furnished to Non-Operator of the proposed charge prior to billing the Non-Operator for the material and/or equipment acquired pursuant to this provision, whereupon Non-Operator shall have the right, by so electing and notifying Operator within 10 days after receiving notice from the Operator, to furnish in kind, or in tonnage as the parties may agree, at the location, nearest railway receiving point, or Operator's storage point within a comparable distance, all or part of his share of material and/or equipment suitable for use and acceptable to the Operator. Transportation costs on any such material furnished by Non-Operator, at any point other than at the location, shall be borne by such Non-Operator. If, pursuant to the provisions of this paragraph, any Non-Operator furnishes material and/or equipment in kind, the Operator shall make appropriate credits therefor to the account of said Non-Operator.

4. *Warranty of Material Furnished by Operator*

Operator does not warrant the material furnished beyond or back of the dealer's or manufacturer's guaranty; and in case of defective material, credit shall not be passed until adjustment has been received by Operator from the manufacturers or their agents.

5. *Operator's Exclusively Owned Facilities*

The following rates shall apply to service rendered to the joint account by facilities owned exclusively by Operator:

A. Water, fuel, power, compressor and other auxiliary services at rates commensurate with cost of providing and furnishing such service to the joint account but not exceeding rates currently prevailing in the field where the joint property is located.

B. Automotive equipment at rates commensurate with cost of ownership and operation. Such rates should generally be in line with the schedule of rates adopted by the Petroleum Motor Transport Association, or some other recognized organization, as recommended uniform charges against joint account operations and revised from time to time. Automotive rates shall include cost of oil, gas, repairs, insurance, and other operating expense and depreciation; and charges shall be based on use in actual service on, or in connection with, the joint account operations. Truck and tractor rates may include wages and expenses of driver.

C. A fair rate shall be charged for the use of drilling and cleaning-out tools and any other items of Operator's fully owned machinery or equipment which shall be ample to cover maintenance, repairs, depreciation, and the service furnished the joint property; provided that such charges shall not exceed those currently prevailing in the field where the joint property is located. Pulling units shall be charged at hourly rates commensurate with the cost of ownership and operation, which shall include repairs and maintenance, operating supplies, insurance, depreciation, and taxes. Pulling unit rates may include wages and expenses of the Operator.

D. A fair rate shall be charged for laboratory services performed by Operator for the benefit of the joint account, such as gas, water, core, and any other analyses and tests; provided such charges shall not exceed those currently prevailing if performed by outside service laboratories.

E. Whenever requested, Operator shall inform Non-Operator in advance of the rates it proposes to charge.

F. Rates shall be revised and adjusted from time to time when found to be either excessive or insufficient.

(By permission of the Petroleum Accountants' Society of Oklahoma.)

6

Depreciation, Depletion, and Fixed Asset Valuation

CONTENTS

6

Depreciation, Depletion, and Fixed Asset Valuation

Joseph A. Mauriello, Ph.D., CPA

After briefly describing the nature of the subject matter, this chapter provides a point-by-point discussion of the accounting for fixed assets. This discussion embraces the following areas:

1. Determination of the acquisition value of the asset.
2. Treatment of expenditures made subsequent to acquisition.
3. Allocation of the acquisition value over related service-life (depreciation).
4. Treatment of asset retirements.
5. Treatment of asset appreciation, based on independent appraisal.
6. Treatment of value-declines.
7. Treatment of assets subject to depletion.

DEFINING OUR ITEMS

To clarify the areas covered by this chapter, we must first briefly describe the nature of (1) fixed assets, (2) tangible and intangible fixed assets, and (3) depreciation, amortization, and depletion.

Fixed assets. Fixed assets are assets of relatively long life acquired by an enterprise for use rather than for conversion through sale. These assets are reflected on the books and financial statements at cost, or the equivalent of cost. Since fixed assets have value because of the future income and benefits they will produce, the cost of each asset is allocated over its service life.

Tangible and intangible fixed assets. Fixed assets are classified as tangible and intangible. *Tangible fixed assets* include land, buildings, machinery and equipment, tools and dies not readily expended, motor vehicles, office equipment, and furniture and fixtures.

Intangible fixed assets fall into two categories: (1) those of limited or determinate life, and (2) those of unlimited or indefinite life.

1. *Limited or determinate life.* Assets having limited or determinate life include leasehold improvements, patents, and franchises and distributorships whose lives are specified by agreement.
2. *Unlimited or indefinite life.* Items in this classification include goodwill, trademarks which are legally renewable indefinitely at 30 year intervals), franchises and distributorships whose existence are based on mutually satisfactory relations between licensor and licensee, and organization costs.
3. *Indeterminate life.* Items in this category are not capable of measurement as to life, and fall under either of the first two classifications, but are separately stated because of the inability to measure their lives. Examples are product experimentation costs, machinery rearrangement costs, and research and development costs.

Depreciation, amortization and depletion. Through the process of *depreciation,* the cost of tangible fixed assets, excluding land, is allocated over the service lives of the assets. Similiarly, the cost of all intangible fixed assets, irrespective of their classification, is allocated over their definite lives or over arbitrarily selected periods through the process of *amortization.* For items of indeterminate, unlimited, or indefinite life acquired after October 31, 1970, Accounting Principles Board Opinion No. 17—Intangible Assets requires that they must be amortized over a period not exceeding 40 years after acquisition. An exception is the cost of research and development, which, in accordance with a pronouncement of the Financial Accounting Standards Board, must be treated as expense at the time of incurrence.

The conversion of a natural resource type of fixed asset, often referred to as a "wasting asset," into inventory is termed *depletion.* As the natural resource is extracted from the ground and processed for sale as merchandise, an applicable portion of the capitalized cost of the resource is prorated to cost of goods.

DETERMINING ACQUISITION VALUE

Acquisition through purchase. The acquisition value of a purchased asset consists of all the expenditures necessary to acquire title to the asset, to place it in the form or condition to fulfill its intended use, to bring it to its place of use, and to install it. Accordingly, the cost of the asset includes (1) purchase price per invoice or bill of sale, (2) brokerage and purchase commission, (3) duties, transportation, insurance and other items incident to getting the asset to the enterprise, and (4) alteration, installation, clearing, moving, removal, and all costs of placing the asset in a form or condition for use.

Form of payment. Where an asset is acquired for cash, acquisition value is equal to the cash disbursed. Where payment is in notes, bonds or the corporation's stock, the valuation of the asset is based on the value of the consideration given or the value of the asset itself, whichever is the more determinable.

Asset cost is equal to the amount of money that would have been paid if the contract had called for payment on delivery. Accordingly, in the case of bonds and stock, the cost of the asset is measured by the fair market value of the securities. Any discount on bonds should be set up as unamortized discount to be amortized over the life of the bonds. It should not be reflected as a cost of the asset subject to depreciation. Any premium on bonds should likewise be amortized over the life of the bonds, and should not be treated as a reduction of asset cost. Assessment values may not be representative for the reason that they may not be changed by the tax jurisdiction for protracted periods of time.

In the case of notes used to finance the purchase of assets, the common practice is to include the interest for the life of the notes in the face value of the notes. Such interest should be excluded from the cost of the asset and separately set up to be written off over the life of the note.

In those cases where the cash value of notes, bonds, or stock cannot be accurately determined, the property should be appraised and the fair market value used as the measure of both the total cost of the asset and the value of the consideration given.

If several assets are purchased for a lump sum price, such price should be allocated, over the assets on the basis of (1) relative market values (best determined by appraisal), or (2) assessment values, or (3) any other reliable criterion of value. Assessment values may not be representative for the reason that they may not be changed by the tax jurisdiction for protracted periods of time.

Rental-purchases. Agreements for the rental of fixed assets coupled with an option to buy must be analyzed in order to determine whether they are not in fact purchases in the inception. Examples of purchases include the following: (1) when the option price is nominal and the option is to be exercised toward the end of the service life of the asset; (2) when the rentals exceed the rentals which would be payable in the absence of an option to buy; (3) when the rental period is coterminous with the life of the asset; and (4) when the circumstances indicate that the rental arrangement is basically a technique of financing a purchase. If the rental arrangement is in fact a purchase, the asset is set up at the price payable on a cash basis, or, in the absence of such an objective price, at the discounted value of the rentals, using an appropriate interest rate. Depreciation is computed on such reduced amount. The present value of the rentals is shown as a liability, and the portion pertaining to the following year is classified as current. Interest is reflected as expense on the declining carrying amount of the asset.

Cash discounts. Irrespective of the mode of payment, any cash discount on the purchase of the asset is a reduction of the asset cost. This conforms to two theories: (1) that discounts represent price concessions resulting from the buyer's converting a possible credit transaction to a cash transaction, and (2) that gain does not result from a purchase. Alternately, if an available discount is not taken, it represents a form of loss. This treatment is consistent with the handling of discounts on material and merchandise purchases.

Other expenditures. Expenditures to protect or perfect title to assets (such as patents) constitute asset cost. These expenditures can occur at the time of acquisition or later. Expenditures that add to the cash or utility value of the asset are also proper components of asset cost.

Land and land improvements. Land is recorded at its purchase cost. Even though land is not subject to depreciation, reduction from cost value is required in cases of decline in economic value of a material amount, relatively permanent in character, and measurable with reasonable accuracy. This point is covered later in the chapter.

Land may be improved by the construction of sidewalks, the installation of drainage systems, the planting of shrubbery, the establishing of lawns, and paving for parking and traffic circulation. These expenditures have to be analyzed individually to determine whether they are subject to depreciation. Thus, the cost of initial shrubbery and lawn is classified as a nondepreciable asset. In contrast, subsequent expenditures for shrubbery and lawn replacement constitute expenses. Sidewalks, drainage pipe, and surface paving are depreciable, and the respective costs should be allocated over the applicable service lives.

Acquisition through donation. Assets acquired by gift should be reflected at their fair market value measured by the cash price that would have been paid if the asset had been purchased. A separate donated capital account should be opened and treated as a part of the stockholders' equity. If the assets involved are depreciable, they should be depreciated in the same manner as assets purchased. This mode of accounting places responsibility on management for efficient administration of the donated asset, placing it in the same category as a purchased asset. Gain or loss on sale is computed by reference to the fair market value adjusted downward by depreciation, if any.

Acquisition by combination. Two or more corporations may be grouped to form a single new corporation, termed a *consolidation,* or one or more corporations may become components of another existing corporation, termed a *merger.* In both cases, the same question arises: at what values will the assets of the constituent predecessor corporation or corporations appear on the records and financial statements of the successor corporation?

At issue here is the difference between a *pooling of interests* and a *purchase,* described and treated in accounting principles Board Opinion No. 16—Business Combinations. In a pooling of interests, two or more companies exchange voting common stock and combine resources without adding to or subtracting from the net assets (i.e., stockholders' equity, existing just before the combinations). The groups of stockholders merely combine their resources, activities, and enterprises, and mutually exchange risks and benefits. In a purchase, a corporation distributes cash or other assets, or incurs liabilities, or issues stock other than voting common stock, so that a group of stockholders ceases to exist or, in the case of their receipt of stock other than voting stock, the group incurs risks different from those to which other groups of stockholders are subject.

In a pooling of interests, the carrying amounts of assets on the books of the constituent companies are combined on the records of the successor corporation, adjustment being restricted to making the values and accounting concepts uniform for the two or more companies involved. In a purchase, the assets of the predecessor companies are reflected at fair market values.

Retention of book values under a pooling of interests presumes that the retained earnings of the predecessor companies will continue as retained earnings of the acquiring corporation. Conversely, in the case of a purchase, retained earnings of the predecessor corporations will constitute additional paid-in capital to the acquiring corporation, as will adjustments of the original book values to the new fair market values.

Acquisition through self-construction. The cost of a fixed asset constructed by the company includes, of course, the out-of-pocket costs caused directly by the construction. However, the question of whether to include the following items as part of the cost of a constructed asset is subject to debate:

1. Normal overhead.
2. Interest and discount during period of construction.
3. Savings attributable to construction.

Normal overhead. Opinions differ as to whether the "normal" overhead of the company, which is incurred whether or not the asset is constructed, should be allocated to the cost of the constructed asset. Since overhead is not increased by the construction, those opposed to the inclusion of overhead in the cost of constructed assets maintain that overhead should be handled just as though there were no construction. They point out that the very fact that normal overhead does not increase may be the motivation for self-construction.

Furthermore, this group also claims that where self-construction is infrequent, the allocation of normal overhead to construction increases the profit of the period of the construction and depresses the profit of subsequent periods. This is the result of increased current depreciation charges that are applicable to facilities previously constructed and the lack of subsequent construction to help shift overhead from current-period cost accounts to fixed asset accounts.

While the foregoing arguments are potent, the prevailing theory and practice are based on the opposing view that overhead should be allocated on the basis of the activities, objects, or services that benefit a particular fiscal period. According to this view, overhead should be allocated to asset construction for the following reasons:

1. If efficiency in regular manufacturing is impaired by the construction, logic requires relieving manufacturing cost of the overhead equitably allocable to the asset under construction.

2. If efficiency in manufacturing is not impaired, personnel and facilities are being utilized more intensively in manufacture, implying reduction in manufacturing cost.

3. If construction were done by an outside contractor, his bid price would include overhead.

Interest and discount during period of construction. Debt financing may be used to finance all or part of the purchase or construction cost of an asset. As indicated previously, the interest cost of financing a purchased asset, adjusted by related discount or premium, should be excluded from the cost of the asset. Because interest is an expense of maintaining the investment in the plant already acquired, it constitutes a current expense that should offset the increased revenues from the use of the plant. Similarly, interest incurred *after* the completion of a constructed asset should also be treated as a period expense.

A problem arises, however, as to the treatment of interest and discount during the period that an asset is under construction. Assuming that the borrowing is justified and that the ratio of debt to stockholder capital is balanced, the interest during the period of construction should be capitalized as cost of the asset. This treatment is based on the fact that management construes the interest as an unavoidable cost of acquiring plant and expects to recover such interest from revenues derived from the use of the completed asset. The only way in which interest cost can be offset against future revenues is by capitalizing the interest as part of the cost of the asset. In this way, future depreciation will include a charge for interest and discount during the period of construction.

Real Estate taxes during period of construction. The theory and treatment relating to interest and discount during the period of construction also applies to real estate taxes. Together, interest and real estate taxes constitute carrying costs (e.g., costs to maintain ownership and investment in property, whether productive or not). Logically, both types of items are subject to identical treatment.

► COMMENT: Interest and real estate taxes for the period of construction are generally deductible as current expense for income tax purposes. The sole exception has reference to interest and real estate taxes applicable to new realty, which, under the Tax Reform Act of 1976, are partially deductible in different percentages depending on the type of realty, with the balance capitalized and deducted over a specified number of future years. Eventually, interest and taxes during the period of construction of all types of realty will be required to be capitalized and amortized over ten years.

Savings attributable to construction. Frequently, the question arises as to how to treat savings resulting from the lower cost of self-construction as compared to purchasing from third parties. Since income cannot result from one's dealing with himself, such savings do not represent income. The lower construction cost is reflected in the lower total cost of the asset. This, in turn, results in lower future depreciation and, therefore, higher future net income. Accordingly, the asset is recorded at cost and the savings are ignored in the accounts.

Carrying costs on property held for future use or sale. Land, and less often buildings, are many times purchased for long-term holding, either for future use or sale. In order to retain title to and physically maintain these properties, the company must unavoidably incur *carrying costs* such as mortgage interest, real estate taxes, watchman's salary, repairs and maintenance, and insurance.

If the property produces current income, these carrying costs would represent current benefit-producing expense. If the property had been in use but is now idle, the lack of benefit requires that the carrying costs be treated as a loss for the period. In the case of property purchased for future use, the carrying costs during the period management estimates must elapse before the asset is pressed into service should be treated as part of the cost of the asset. After such period, carrying costs during periods of idleness represent loss.

The reason for this latter treatment is clear. The asset is expected to produce revenue and is capable of doing so; failure to utilize such opportunity entails a loss to the extent that costs are being incurred. Since there is no future benefit, such loss cannot be deferred.

TREATMENT OF EXPENDITURES MADE SUBSEQUENT TO ACQUISITION

Original asset costs are modified by the following types of expenditures made subsequent to acquisition:

1. Additions.
2. Renewals.
3. Replacements.

Additions. An addition is an attachment or extension made to an original part or asset. An addition adds value to the asset. If the addition is detachable from the asset, the cost of the addition is allocated over its life. On the other hand, if the addition is not detachable, its cost is allocated over the remaining life of the asset as a whole. Even though the life of the addition may be longer than that of the asset, because it is not detachable, its useful life is no longer than the life of the asset it is attached to.

Renewals. A renewal is an extraordinary overhaul, reconditioning, or repair that prolongs the economic usefulness of a major part or asset beyond its originally estimated life. The cost of a renewal is either shown as an increase in the asset account or as a reduction of the allowance for the depreciation account that reflects the depreciation accumulated to the date of the renewal. While the first procedure is more common in practice, the second procedure is preferable, theoretically, because the renewal helps "make good" past depreciation.

Replacements. A replacement is a substitution of an asset or part for a former asset or part performing a similar or related function. The term *betterment* or *improvement* is used to denote the excess of the cost of the new major part or asset over the book value of the part or asset that it replaced. It implies an increase in the quality rather than quantity of an asset.

A major replacement is the replacement of an entire asset or a major part of an asset. The cost of a major replacement is added to the asset account. The cost of the asset, or part replaced, and related depreciation are removed from the accounts. Any gain or loss (book value less disposal proceeds) should be shown separately. As in the case of additions, a detachable replacement is depreciated over its life, while the cost of a part that is not detachable is spread over the remaining life of the asset.

Minor replacements are expenditures for small parts or items of small value that are readily expendable and, hence, require frequent replacement. Minor replacements are treated as ordinary repairs and charged to expense accounts as expenditures are made.

► OBSERVATION: In order to help expedite record keeping, it is wise to set a definite boundary, say $100, under which all expenditures are charged to expense rather than asset accounts.

Trade-ins. In the case of replacement of an entire asset, the old asset is often traded in for the new. Proper accounting treatment involves:

1. Debiting the new asset account for the cash payment plus the trade-in value of the old.
2. Relieving the asset and allowance for depreciation accounts of the cost of the old asset and accumulated depreciation, respectively.
3. Recording gain or loss on the trade-in. Gain or loss is measured by the difference between trade-in value and book value of the old asset.

► EXAMPLE: A trade-in allowance of $2,700 is given for Machine A to be applied on the purchase of Machine B costing $7,000. Machine A originally cost $6,000; its allowance for depreciation is $4,000. The entry summarizing this transaction is:

Machinery—Asset B	7,000	
Allowance for depreciation—Asset A	4,000	
Machinery—Asset A		6,000
Profit on trade-in machinery—Asset A		700
Cash		4,300

The foregoing treatment is modified when the trade-in allowance is artificially raised to include a concession in the price of the new asset. In such case, the cost of the new asset is reduced by the discount and the gain or loss on trade-in is adjusted accordingly.

► EXAMPLE: In the last example, if the fair market value of Asset A were only $2,200, the cost of the new asset and profit on trade-in would have to be reduced by $500 ($2,700 — $2,200). This amount represents a reduction from the list price of the asset. The revised entry follows:

Machinery—Asset B	6,500	
Allowance for depreciation—Asset A	4,000	
Machinery—Asset A		6,000
Profit on trade-in of machinery—Asset A		200
Cash		4,300

For Federal income tax purposes, gains or losses on trade-ins are not recognized. Instead, the cost of the new asset is adjusted by the amount of the unrecognized gain or loss on trade-in. A gain reduces the cost basis of the new asset, and a loss adds to the cost basis. The effect, of course, is to postpone the recognition of the gain or loss, by affecting subsequent depreciation and gain or loss on sale.

► EXAMPLE: Using either set of facts, the entry for tax purposes remains the same. The summary entry for income tax purposes is:

Machinery—Asset B	6,300	
Allowance for depreciation—Asset A	4,000	
Machinery—Asset A		6,000
Cash		4,300

When the gains or losses on trade-ins are small, the accounting practice is to follow the tax treatment and recognize no gain or loss on the trade-in, but instead adjust the recorded cost of the new asset by the gain or loss.

DEPRECIATION

The subject of depreciation is discussed under the following headings:

1. Concepts of depreciation.
2. Depreciation techniques.
3. Classification of property for depreciation purposes.
4. Tax and accounting depreciation.
5. Depreciation and changing price levels.

Concepts of depreciation. The Committee on Terminology of the American Institute of Certified Public Accountants, in *Accounting Research Bulletin No. 20*, defines depreciation as follows:

> *Depreciation* accounting is a system of accounting that aims to distribute the cost or other basic value of tangible capital assets over the estimated useful life of the unit (which may be a group of assets) in a systematic and rational manner. It is a process of allocation, not of valuation.
>
> Depreciation for the year is the portion of the total charge under such a system that is allocated to the year.

The concept that depreciation is an allocation of the cost of an asset over its service life is an application of the principle of matching costs against revenues. Each period that obtains the beneficial use of an asset is charged with an equitable share of its total cost less salvage value.

This concept of depreciation differs greatly from the engineering view. Engineers view depreciation as an expense representing the decline in market value of an asset. Engineers would impute heavy depreciation immediately after the acquisition of an asset because of the substantial drop in market value of a "used" asset. Accountants might also reflect heavy depreciation during the early years of asset life, but they would do so because of the greater economic usefulness of a new asset.

Depreciation techniques. The allocation of the cost of a fixed tangible asset involves:

1. An estimate of total service life.
2. A method of determining the portion of total cost assignable to each fiscal year of an asset's service life.

1. Estimate of total service life. The useful life of an asset, over which the cost of an asset is allocated, is estimated by referring to the following factors:

(a) *Physical deterioration,* because of wear and tear, action of the elements, and natural decay.

(b) *Inadequacy,* due to increased demands resulting from higher production volume and other contingencies.

(c) *Normal obsolescence,* because of the development of new superior assets or methods of production.

(d) *Maintenance,* in that a systematic and orderly repair and maintenance program will tend to prolong the life of an asset.

(e) *Intensity of use,* in that the more hours or shifts an asset is used, the higher the rate of depreciation.

Service life is invariably measured in time or in units. Because time is easier to estimate, it is far more common to measure service life in terms of years than in units. Additionally, a depreciation charge based on units requires production or sales as a prerequisite to the allocation of expense. Although a charge based on number of units produced or sold produces a cost that conforms with the principle of *benefit,* the low or nominal depreciation assigned to a period of little use overlooks the factors of obsolescence and natural decay affecting depreciation.

2. Depreciation methods. Depreciation methods may be classified as follows:

(a) Methods producing a uniform charge each fiscal year.
  (1) Straight-line method.
  (2) Annuity method.
(b) Methods producing a decreasing charge each fiscal year (accelerated methods).
  (1) Fixed percentage on declining balance—scientific method.
  (2) Fixed percentage on declining balance—unscientific method (income tax method).
  (3) Sum-of-the-years'-digits or reducing fraction method.

(c) Methods producing an increasing charge each fiscal year.
   (1) Sinking fund method.

(d) Methods producing a fluctuating charge each fiscal year.
   (1) Unit of production method.
   (2) Working hours method.
   (3) Inventory or revaluation method.

► NOTE: Since the annuity and sinking fund methods, both based on the compound interest concept, are complex and, therefore, rarely used, they will be discussed last.

Straight-line method. This method derives its name from the fact that a graph of the annual depreciation charges or depreciated book values computed under this method takes the form of a straight line.

The cost of the asset less net salvage value (disposal value less costs of dismantling and removal at time of retirement) is divided by the estimated life of the asset to arrive at the uniform depreciation charge for each year.

► EXAMPLE: Assuming an asset cost of \$8,400, a scrap value of \$400 and a ten-year life, the computation would be:

$$\frac{\$8{,}400 - \$400}{10} = \$800 \text{ yearly depreciation}$$

The straight-line method is realistic in that it avoids refining a computation that is basically an estimate. It is also simple and easy to apply. However, there are two objectionable features to this computation. First, since repairs increase with the age of the asset, the combined depreciation and repairs charge is too low in the early years and too high in later years. Secondly, when the use of an asset fluctuates in great degree, costs are not properly matched with revenues. Thus, the same depreciation is charged in a period of extraordinary use as in a period of sub-normal use.

Fixed percentage on declining balance method—scientific. A constant rate is applied to a declining book value to produce the depreciation charge for each succeeding year.

The following formula is used to determine the rate:

$$\text{Rate} = 1 - \sqrt[n]{\frac{s}{c}}$$

n = years of service life.
s = scrap value (if no scrap value, \$1 is used).
c = cost.

► EXAMPLE: Using the same figures as the last example, asset cost of \$8,400, scrap value of \$400, and ten-year life, the formula reads:

$$\text{Rate} = 1 - \sqrt[10]{\frac{400}{8400}} = 26.247\%$$

The rate of 26.247%, found through the use of logarithms, is applied initially to cost and then to each succeeding declining value. The following table of depreciation results:

Year	*Book Value at Beginning of Year*	*Depreciation (26.247% times Book Value)*
1	$8,400.00	$2,204.75
2	6,195.25	1,626.07
3	4,569.18	1,199.27
4	3,369.91	884.50
5	2,485.41	652.35
6	1,833.06	481.12
7	1,351.94	354.84
8	997.10	261.71
9	735.39	193.02
10	542.37	142.37
	Total Depreciation	$8,000.00

The declining balance method and other methods producing a decreasing depreciation charge are especially appropriate for use with assets having their maximum economic usefulness immediately after acquisition, or for assets whose repairs increase substantially in the later years of use. These methods are ideal for companies getting an early start in a new industry, such as the manufacture of teaching machines, or companies whose revenues are greatest during the early life of the asset, such as motion picture companies that necessarily derive the bulk of their earnings from early showings of films produced.

This method also has the advantage of being conservative in that assets are quickly written down. However, a prime objection to the scientific declining balance method is its mathematical complexity, a particularly acute point in those cases where asset changes are frequent. This disadvantage is somewhat overcome if the unscientific declining balance (income tax method) or the sum-of-the-years'-digits method is used. These will be described next.

Fixed percentage on declining balance method—unscientific (income tax method). The Internal Revenue Code permits the use of a constant rate of 1.25, 1.50, or 2.00 times the straight-line rate, depending on the type of asset and whether it is new or used, to depreciate assets acquired after December 31, 1953, and having a life of at least three years.

The constant rate is applied to the declining book value of the asset, and depreciation ceases when the asset is depreciated to its salvage value.

The method is unscientific because the accumulated depreciation at the expiration of service life will not, except as a coincidence, measure the cost less salvage value. It was developed for income tax purposes for the sole purpose of avoiding the mathematical complications of the scientific fixed percentage on declining balance method.

The fact that this method will never fully depreciate the asset can be seen in the following tabulation using the previously assumed asset cost of $8,400, 10 year life, and depreciation rate of 20%, or 2 times the straight-line rate of 10%:

Year	*Book Value at Beginning of Year*	*Depreciation (20% times Book Value)*
1	$8,400.00	$1,680.00
2	6,720.00	1,344.00
3	5,376.00	1,075.20
4	4,300.80	860.16
5	3,440.64	688.13
6	2,752.51	550.50
7	2,202.01	440.40
8	1,761.61	352.32
9	1,409.29	281.86
10	1,127.43	225.49

The book value of the asset at the end of the tenth year is $901.94, as compared with an assumed salvage value of $400. If the salvage value had been, say $1,000, the tenth year depreciation would have been limited to $127.43 ($1,127.43—$1,000), instead of $225.49.

Because of the "tail" inherent in this method, the Internal Revenue Service permits the taxpayer to shift to the straight-line method at any point, and to depreciate the remaining book value, reduced by estimated salvage value, over the remaining life.

Although inaccurate, the unscientific method is widely used because of its acceptability for income tax purposes and because of its simplicity of application.

Sum-of-the-years'-digits method. This method produces a decreasing depreciation charge by applying diminishing percentages to the cost of the asset less salvage value. These percentages are usually expressed as fractions. The denominator, which remains constant, measures the sum of the digit or numbers representing the years of life. The numerators, representing the same digits or numbers taken in inverse order, are variable.

► EXAMPLE: Once again using the illustration of an asset costing $8,400, having a scrap value of $400, and a 10-year life, the depreciable cost of $8,000 is multiplied by a series of fractions developed as follows:

Denominator for each year = 55 (1 + 2 + 3 + 4 + 5 + 6 + 7 + 8 + 9 + 10 = 55)

Numerator for each year = 10 for 1st year; 9 for 2nd year; 8 for 3rd year; etc.

The resulting depreciation amounts follow:

Year	*Fraction*	*Depreciation (Fraction × $8,000)*
1	10/55	$1,454.55
2	9/55	1,309.09
3	8/55	1,163.64
4	7/55	1,018.18
5	6/55	872.72
6	5/55	727.28
7	4/55	581.82
8	3/55	436.36
9	2/55	290.90
10	1/55	145.46
	Total	$8,000.00

As compared with the fixed percentage on declining balance methods, the sum-of-the-years'-digits method produces smaller depreciation charges in the early years of life. By the same token, it decreases at a slower rate and results in a lesser spread between years.

This method is as accurate as the scientific fixed percentages on declining balance method without the complexity of the latter. In addition, it achieves simplicity without incurring the inaccuracy of the unscientific fixed percentage on declining balance method.

The sum-of-the-years'-digits method is allowable for income tax purposes, computed in the manner described, but solely with respect to new personal property and new residential rental realty.

Unit of production and working hours methods. The unit of production and working hours methods measure service life in units and working hours, respectively. These methods are called "activity" methods. Activity may be measured by units of production, machine hours, man hours, flying hours and mileage.

A rate per unit or per hour is computed by dividing the cost of the asset (less salvage value) by the estimated total unit or hour life of the asset. The depreciation for the period is then calculated by multiplying actual units produced or hours worked by the rate per unit or per hour.

The advantages of using an activity method, regardless of the measure of activity employed, are its simplicity and the fact that it causes depreciation to vary with use, and thus with benefit.

The disadvantages, on the other hand, are also twofold and somewhat outweigh the advantages. First, the theory behind these methods assumes *use* as the sole factor in determining depreciation, thus ignoring the other factors of obsolescence and physical deterioration caused by time. If an asset is not being used, for example, the use of one of these measures will produce the untenable result of zero depreciation.

Secondly, these methods require a very difficult estimate of the activity of an asset in very small units of measure.

Inventory or revaluation method. The inventory method is a variation of the activity methods just described. Under this method, the value of the asset at the beginning of the year or project is compared with the value at the end; the difference in values is the use-cost or depreciation.

The method is ideal for special utility assets purchased for use on a specific project and whose utility at the end of the project is problematical. The cost of the asset, diminished by its utility or market value at the end of the project, equals the depreciation chargeable to the project. Depreciation is thus measured in terms of decreased utility value.

The inventory method is also applied to fixed assets of small value, such as small machine and hand tools, that are rapidly consumed in factory operations. Depreciation for the period is determined by adding purchases for the period to the beginning inventory and substracting the ending inventory. Both beginning and ending inventories are valued at estimated depreciated cost.

Annuity and sinking fund methods. Both these methods are based on the assumption that income should be earned on the capital invested in an asset. The cost of the asset is viewed as the present value of services to be rendered over the asset life. Because these methods are complicated and impractical, especially in the case of frequent asset changes, they are rarely, if ever used.

In addition to the practical objections to these methods, there are also theoretical drawbacks. For example, the uniform depreciation charge characterizing the annuity method, and the increasing charge produced by the sinking fund method, penalize the later years of asset life when repairs usually prove heaviest. Furthermore, the hypothetical interest in the depreciation charge under the annuity method is indictable on two counts. First, because it is set forth as depreciation instead of interest, and, second, because it overstates inventories by including interest that never was expended by the firm. Again, the sinking fund method can be criticized because it erroneously views depreciation as a fund to replace an asset. Thus, this method confuses the financial problem of asset replacement with the accounting problem of asset allocation.

Because of these serious practical and theoretical defects of the annuity and sinking fund methods and their rare use, these methods are described only briefly, primarily to furnish the reader a complete perspective of the available depreciation methods.

1. *Annuity method.* Application of this method requires (1) a determination of the present value of the estimated salvage value of the asset, and (2) the present value of an ordinary annuity that will recover the cost of the asset (less present value of the salvage value) over the life of the asset, with a provision for interest.

The depreciation is uniform. However, the offsetting credits consist of the following elements:

(a) Imputed income earned on the asset. This is at decreasing annual amounts to conform to the declining book value of the asset. Income is generally presumed to be at the going interest rate, and is credited to the Interest Income account.

(b) A reduction in the cost of the asset, at increasing annual amounts to counterbalance the decreasing income amounts. This amount is credited to the Allowance for Depreciation account.

► EXAMPLE: Using the figures developed for the previous problems and an interest rate of 8%, the computations and entries for the first two years are as follows:

First year:

Cost of asset	$8,400.00
Deduct-Present value of estimated salvage value: salvage value $400 times Present value of $1, 10 years hence, at 8%, $.3855	154.20
Depreciable cost of asset	$8,245.80
Present value of ordinary annuity of $1 for 10 years, at 8%	$6.710
Depreciation for first year ($8,245.80 ÷ $6,7101)	1,228.86
Interest income—$8,400 x 8%	672.00
Reduction of fixed asset—$1,228.86 less $672.00	556.86
Entry:	
Depreciation Expense 1,228.86	
Allowance for Depreciation	556.86
Interest Income	672.00

Second Year:

Depreciation—same as year 1	1,228.86
Interest income—$8,400 less 556.86 times 8%	627.45
Reduction of fixed asset—$1,228.86 less $627.45	600.41
Entry:	
Depreciation Expense 1,228.86	
Allowance for Depreciation	600.41
Interest Income	627.45

2. *Sinking fund method.* The sinking fund method views depreciation as a fund to replace the asset at the end of its service life. Yearly uniform amounts are presumed to accumulate at a predetermined interest rate. The annual depreciation expense is the sum of the constant annual amount plus the interest earned on the accumulated principal. Since, because of the increase of accumulated principal, the interest element increases each year, the annual depreciation also increases. This annual depreciation amount, debited to Depreciation Expense and credited to Allowance for Depreciation, is exactly equal to the increasing annual credits to the Allowance for Depreciation under the annuity method.

► EXAMPLE: The entries for the first two years under the sinking fund method are:

First Year

Depreciation expense	556.86	
Allowance for depreciation		556.86

Second Year

Depreciation expense	600.41	
Allowance for depreciation		600.41

Classification of property for depreciation purposes. Depreciable properties are classified in the following ways for the purpose of simplifying the computation of depreciation:

1. Item accounts.
2. Group accounts.
3. Classified accounts.
4. Composite accounts.

Item accounts. Each asset item is stated separately and depreciated as an individual unit. Individual items may appear separately on memorandum schedules, or on card records showing such particulars as cost, acquisition date, salvage value, estimated life, depreciation rate, depreciation for the current period, cumulative depreciation, etc.

Item accounts are desirable for several reasons. These individual records help in avoiding the possibility of depreciating an asset for more than its cost less salvage value. By showing the book value of each asset, an accurate determination for tax purposes may be made of gain or loss on disposal. Additionally, item accounts are valuable in supporting insurance claims for casualty or theft losses. Finally, they are a distinct aid in accurately estimating the service lives of items subsequently acquired.

Group accounts. Assets similar in kind or use and having approximately the same useful lives are grouped together and depreciated as a group. Acquisitions are recorded by years. Each year's acquisitions are depreciated over the particular group life. A record must be kept of the cost of each item and date of acquisition. This information coupled with the group depreciation rate and holding period is used to establish the book value, gain or loss on disposal, or loss from theft or casualty of any specific asset.

Classified accounts. Assets similar in kind or use are grouped together without regard to their useful lives. Typical classifications are machinery, furniture and fixtures, and transportation equipment. An average or blanket rate of depreciation is used for each classification. Because assets are not grouped by service lives, depreciation rates computed under this type of classification are not as accurate as those computed for *group accounts.*

Composite accounts. Assets are included in the same account regardless of kind, or useful lives. In the extreme, all the assets of the enterprise are reflected in a single account. An asset-wide or blanket rate is used for all assets. The rate is developed by correlating the total depreciation for all assets with the total cost of all such assets less salvage value.

Tax and accounting depreciation. Accounting must be subservient to tax law. Depreciation methods for reporting and book purposes should be chosen on the basis of which method best reflects proper income for the period, not merely to conform to tax statutes or to secure tax benefits. Accordingly, it is common for depreciation to be computed under the declining balance or sum-of-the-years'-digits method for income tax purposes and under the straight-line method for reporting purposes.

The effect of this disparate treatment is that in the early years of asset life the actual income tax liability is less than would be called for by book net income. Conversely, in the later years of asset life, the tax returns will show a higher tax than that based on book net income.

Accounting treatment. The difference between the actual tax to be paid and the tax computed on book income is handled under the *deferred method.* The operation of this method is relatively easy.

Assuming that accelerated depreciation is used for tax purposes and straight-line depreciation for book purposes, income tax expense computed on the basis of book income will be higher than the actual tax in the early years of asset life. The reverse will be true in later years. Therefore, in order to correctly match costs and revenues, in each of the early years, the difference between the lower actual tax liability on the books and the higher tax computed on book income is accrued by using the statutory tax rate or rates, federal and state combined, for the year involved. Such rate or rates are those at the margin (e.g., are applicable to the taxable income inclusive of, and exclusive of, the difference in depreciation).

The tax currently unpaid, and hence deferred, is reflected as a deferral tax credit. Since the deferred tax credit relates to a noncurrent asset, it is classified as a noncurrent liability. In later years, the higher tax payable per return is adjusted to the lower tax based on book net income by reducing the noncurrent liability. The title of the noncurrent liability account is either *Deferred Income Taxes* or *Deferred Tax Credits.*

► EXAMPLE: Given a constant book net income of $300,000 before depreciation and taxes, a book depreciation of $5,000 for 20 years as compared with a tax depreciation of $20,000 for five years, and a 50% tax rate for the current year and each subsequent year, the following entries for income tax result:

Entry for each of the first five years:

Provision for Federal income tax (per return)	140,000	
Provision for deferred income tax	7,500	
Federal income taxes payable—current		140,000
Deferred income taxes		7,500

Explanation:

1. The two debits combined measure the tax at 50% of the book net income of $295,000.

2. The first credit represents the tax currently payable at 50% of the taxable income of $280,000.

3. The second credit represents the amount of tax saved each year for the first five years, or 50% of the $15,000 difference in the two annual depreciation amounts.

Entry for each of the next fifteen years:

Provision for Federal income tax	147,000	
Deferred income taxes	2,500	
Federal income taxes payable—current		150,000

Explanation:

1. The first debit measures the tax at 50% of the constant book net income of $295,000.

2. The second debit represents the conversion of the deferred tax liability into a current tax liability at the rate of $2,500 a year. This amount will accumulate over the remaining 15 years of asset life and will amount to the $37,500 tax saving effected in the first five years.

3. The credit measures the tax of 50% on the taxable income of $300,000, shown on the tax return and payable currently.

The presentation of Federal income tax expense and payable amounts on the income statement and balance sheet, respectively, are illustrated in Chapter 2.

AICPA Accounting Research Bulletin No. 44. The Committee on Accounting Procedure of the American Institute of Certified Public Accountants, in *Accounting Research Bulletin No. 44 (Revised),* expressed the opinion that deferred tax accounting should be applied to:

> . . . a single asset or to a group of assets which are expected to be retired from service at about the same time; in this case an excess of depreciation taken from income-tax purposes during the earlier years would be followed by the opposite condition in later years, and there would be a tax deferment for a definite period. It applies also to a group of assets consisting of numerous units which may be of different lengths of life and which are expected to be continually replaced; in this case an excess of depreciation taken for income-tax purposes during the earlier years would be followed in later years by substantial equality between the annual depreciation for income-tax purposes and that for accounting purposes, and a tax deferment would be built up during the earlier years which would tend to remain relatively constant thereafter. It applies further to a gradual expanding plant; in this case an excess of depreciation taken for income-tax purposes may exist each year during the period of expansion in which event there would be a tax deferment which might increase as long as the period of expansion continued.

The treatment of deferred tax credits described above is prescribed in Accounting Principles Board Opinion No. 11, issued in 1967.

Depreciation and changing price levels. Considerable discussion has taken place since World War II regarding the depreciation charge on the income statement. There is being strongly revived, at the time of this writing, the argument that depreciation should be computed with reference to the replacement cost of the asset, thereby taking into account the current purchasing power of the dollar, instead of the traditional computation based on the number of dollars expended at the date of acquisition. The following reasons have been advanced in favor of this thesis:

1. Other expense elements, such as labor and inventories costed under LIFO, are shown in the income statement at the current price level. A computation of depreciation on replacement cost, or, less preferably, on historical cost adjusted to the current price level, will result in a determination of all expense elements in terms of a uniform current dollar. The income statement will thus be prepared by means of a simple monetary yardstick that will properly measure operating performance for the period, unobscured by the use of unlike dollars.
2. The capital invested in fixed assets should be retained intact. Accordingly, depreciation, as a medium for recovering capital investment, should fluctuate with the number of dollars required to replace the asset.
3. Use of replacement cost as a basis for depreciation will result in depreciation charges that are more comparable in the industry.

The foregoing arguments have been rejected up to now for the following reasons:

1. Other expense elements are based on actual expirations of asset cost, rather than on hypothetical replacement costs reflecting changing price levels.
2. At law, for Federal income tax purposes, and in business relationships, recognition is given to number of dollars, instead of to their purchasing power. Accounting should therefore be governed accordingly.
3. The replacement of an asset is an element of financial policy, rather than a criterion for financial reporting.

The Committee on Accounting Procedure of the American Institute of Certified Public Accountants, summarized the public accounting profession's position on the problem, as follows:

1. In the case of substantial differences between replacement cost and book value, it is proper for management to make annual appropriations of retained earnings in contemplation of replacement at higher price levels.
2. The generally accepted concept of depreciation on cost should be adhered to until the dollar is stabilized at some level, at which time it would be practicable for business as a whole to recognize current prices in computing depreciation.

3. The effect of changing replacement cost and price-level can be reflected through supplementary financial schedules, explanations or footnotes, that would also serve to support a policy of retention of earnings.

The Securities and Exchange Commission now requires that corporations with plant and inventory in excess of $100 million and constituting more than 10% of total assets, include the replacement cost of fixed assets and depreciation on such replacement cost in their annual filings with the Commission.

If replacement costs of fixed assets were to be expressed in the body of the financial statements, the accounting required would parallel that for appreciation, discussed later in this chapter. The significant difference between the two situations is that in replacement cost accounting changing replacement costs are recognized each year, whereas in appreciation accounting fair market values based on appraisals are recognized only in the infrequent case of a quasi-reorganization or reorganization.

ASSET RETIREMENTS

It was pointed out earlier that gain or loss on trade-in is measured by the difference between the trade-in allowance and the book value of the asset. Where the trade-in allowance is arbitrarily high and reflects a price discount on the new assets, the profit or loss is adjusted accordingly.

Similarly, a general rule on a sale or scrapping of an asset is that the gain or loss on disposal is equal to the difference between the disposal price and the book value of the asset. However, this general rule must be qualified, depending on which classification of property accounts is being used.

Retirements—item and group accounts. The rule applies without modification, to item and group accounts. When either of these classifications is used, the book value of the asset at the time of disposal can be determined with absolute accuracy. Since the disposal price is also definite, the gain or loss on disposal will be correct.

In the case of item accounts, the book value can be determined from the separate record for the item. If group accounts are used, the cost and acquisition date of the asset are known. Depreciation up to the date of disposal can be computed by applying the group rate separately to the cost of the asset for the period it was held.

The entry is as follows:

	Dr.	*Cr.*
Cash or miscellaneous receivables	*Sales price*	
Allowance for depreciation—asset	*Accumulated depreciation to date of disposal*	
Asset		*Cost*
Profit or loss on asset disposal	*Loss*	*Gain*

The gains or losses on disposal are, in some degree, a correction of prior-period depreciation. However, since this element cannot be isolated, the full difference between disposal price and book value is treated as gain or loss for the period of retirement. Accounting Principles Board Opinion No. 30 requires that the gain or loss be shown on the income statement as a separate item incident to determining net operating income. The gain or loss may not be shown as an extraordinary item.

Retirements—classified and composite accounts. In the case of classified and composite accounts, the gains or losses cannot be absolutely established. The reason for this is that an average rate of depreciation is applied to assets of varying lives. Accordingly, some assets will be retired before the expiration of the average life; others will be retired after the expiration of the average life. Therefore, gains and losses on retirement should be recorded in the Allowance for Depreciation account, rather than in income or expense accounts.

In the exceptional case, where the enterprise uses a group rate based on the asset or asset class having the longest life, retirements create gains and losses which should be reflected in determining net operating income. This treatment is based on the fact that a rate based on the longest-lived asset is understated for all items except for such asset. Accordingly, the book value on items other than the item of longest life tends to be overstated, maximizing retirement losses and minimizing retirement gains. Since these gains will not be offset by later losses, nor losses offset by later gains, gains or losses on disposal should be recorded.

APPRECIATION OF FIXED ASSETS

Conditions under which recognition appreciation is proper. Occasionally, assets may be written up above their book value (based on cost). This kind of write-up, termed "appreciation," represents a departure from the cost principle. Appreciation of assets is the exception rather than the rule, and may be reorganized only in connection with quasi-reorganizations or reorganizations, as expressed in Accounting Principles Board Opinion No. 6.

Recording and reporting appreciation. The write-up of assets may be effected indirectly through footnotes to the balance sheet. However, this method of disclosure may not be satisfactory to management. The company may insist on reflecting the appreciation in the books and financial statements.

Whether appreciation is recognized by footnote or by entry in the books, the public accountant will require an independent, responsible appraisal to support the written-up values, and a resolution by the board of directors authorizing the write-up.

Assuming that the appreciation is to appear in the accounts and the body of the financial statements, the accountant is required to observe the following principles:

1. The appreciation must be recorded as an *adjustment* of the accounts already recorded and being depreciated on a cost basis. Stated another way, the appreciated values should not be treated as a substitute for, or a replacement of, book values based on cost. Instead, cost amounts should be adjusted only for the appreciation, and otherwise remain unaffected. The appreciated values, as such, do not appear on the books and the financial statements. They are reflected only as the sum of the book value based on cost and appreciation.

2. Any difference in estimated remaining life, as between that appearing in the appraisal report and that on the books, must be resolved in favor of the appraisal report. Accordingly, before the appreciation is determined and recorded, the Allowance for Depreciation account, based on cost, must be adjusted to conform to the revised remaining life per the appraisal report.

3. Appreciation serves to increase the stockholders' equity. It should be segregated in a separate capital account so as not to be confused with capital contributed by stockholders and the realized earnings retained by the corporation. Such appreciation represents unrealized increment in the value of the asset, and should be so described in the capital section of the balance sheet.

4. Depreciation expense subsequent to the appraisal should be based on the higher appreciated value. It is illogical and inconsistent to allege a higher value on the balance sheet and then to deny such value in computing depreciation on the income statement. Accordingly, depreciation expense on the income statement should consist of the sum of the depreciation on the cost portion of the assets plus the depreciation on the appreciation. In order to conform to the principle that the recognition of appreciation must not obscure cost reporting, the cost and appreciation components of the depreciation charge should be shown separately.

5. Profit or loss on the sale of the asset must be computed with reference to the appreciated value—under the same reasoning governing the computation of depreciation.

6. The separate capital account for the appreciation, Unrealized Increment, is treated in different ways, depending on the circumstances:

(a) If the write-up takes the form of a quasi-reorganization, as in the case of a new financing or new management, the increment is construed as part of the permanent capital structure of the company. The account itself may either be left intact or, by means of a stock dividend, transferred permanently to the Capital Stock account.

(b) If the write-up is motivated by other reasons than cited in (a), it is acceptable to transfer the amount of depreciation on appreciation for the year from the Unrealized Increment account to the Retained Earnings account. This transfer recognizes that unrealized increment is gradually realized through the use of the asset. Any balances in the Unrealized Increment account at the time the asset is sold or otherwise disposed of is also transferred to the Retained Earnings account.

▶ EXAMPLE: The foregoing principles are illustrated in the following example:

Data. Equipment costing $100,000 has accumulated $16,000 depreciation to date. The equipment is now appraised at a replacement cost (new) of $150,000, on which the accumulated depreciation is estimated to be $30,000 or 20%. This compares with 16% ($16,000/$100,000) depreciation now reflected on the books. The estimated remaining life of the equipment is eight years. One year after appraisal the equipment is sold for $107,500.

Journal entries. Assuming that it is the company's policy to transfer annually an amount equal to the depreciation on appreciation from the Unrealized Increment account to the Retained Earnings account, the entries to record these transactions are:

1. Adjustment of depreciation from 16% of cost ($16,000) to 20% of cost ($20,000), to conform to the appraisal report.

Profit and loss—adjustment of prior profits	4,000	
Allowance for depreciation—machinery		4,000

2. Reflection of appreciation.

Machinery appreciation	50,000	
Allowance for depreciation—machinery appreciation		10,000
Unrealized increment in machinery		40,000

3. Depreciation for the following year.

Depreciation—machinery cost ($80,000 ÷ 8 years)	10,000	
Depreciation—machinery appreciation ($40,000 ÷ 8 years)	5,000	
Allowance for depreciation—machinery cost		10,000
Allowance for depreciation—machinery appreciation		5,000

4. Transfer of $5,000 depreciation on appreciation from Unrealized Increment account to Retained Earnings account.

Unrealized increment on machinery	5,000	
Retained earnings		5,000

5. Sale of machinery.

Cash	107,500	
Allowance for depreciation—machinery cost	30,000	
Allowance for depreciation—machinery appreciation	15,000	
Machinery cost		100,000
Machinery appreciation		50,000
Profit on sale of machinery		2,500

6. Transfer of balance in Unrealized Increment account to Retained Earnings account.

Unrealized increment on machinery	35,000	
Retained earnings		35,000

Balance sheet presentation. The balance sheet presentation as of the appraisal date appears as follows:

FIXED ASSETS:		
Equipment, at current value based on appraisal by the X Appraisal Company as of January 1, 19—:		
Cost	$100,000	
Less—Allowance for Depreciation	20,000	
Cost, less Depreciation on Cost	$ 80,000	
Add—Appreciation, based on Appraisal	40,000	
Current Value		$120,000

VALUE DECLINES IN FIXED ASSETS

Although the basic objective of fixed asset accounting is the allocation of cost over service life, accepted accounting principles require that the decline in the utility value of an asset be currently recognized. The impairment in utility value may be attributable to sudden obsolescence caused by new equipment on the market; reduced demand for machinery because of product changes and discontinuances; reduced use of buildings because of a decline in value of the location due to higher labor costs, taxes, or lessened accessibility to materials or labor supply, etc. In view of the expected reduced benefits that will be derived from the asset in the future, failure to record these declines as current loss results in excessive allocations being made to future periods.

Accordingly, the principle has been developed that a significant shrinkage in fixed asset value, expected to be of relatively permanent duration and capable of being measured with reasonable accuracy, should be recorded as a current loss. The loss should be reflected incident to the determination of the net operating income for the current year.

DEPLETION

Nature of depletion. Depletion is the physical disappearance of a natural resource through extraction and conversion into salable product. Thus, what was formerly oil tract is replaced by barrels of oil, timberland by board feet of lumber, and mineral deposits by tons of iron ore. Since the natural resources physically disappear when embodied in the finished product, they are referred to as diminishing or wasting assets.

Depletion is like depreciation in that both constitute methods of allocating asset cost. They differ in that depletion is invariably charged to the product extracted on the basis of units, whereas depreciation is most commonly computed on the basis of elapsed time.

Recording depletion. The depletion rate per unit is determined by dividing the total cost of the natural resource, less the estimated salvage value of the land surface by the total number of units that the resource is expected to yield during its useful life. This rate per unit is multiplied by the number of units extracted during the year to arrive at the depletion charge. This amount is debited to Provision for Depletion and credited to Allowance for Depletion.

The debit to the Provision for Depletion account measures the addition to the cost value of the product extracted, whereas the credit to the Allowance for Depletion account measures the portion of the wasting asset that is allocated to the current period. The accumulated amount in the credit account is subtracted from the cost of the depletable asset on the balance sheet in the same way that the Allowance for Depreciation account is deducted from the related depreciable asset.

Since the capacity of the natural resource is difficult to determine, the balance in the Allowance for Depletion account is continually in error. Any revision in the estimate of the remaining deposits is itself subject to later revision. Accordingly, the practice is to divide the book value of the asset at the end of each current period by the estimated remaining number of units to be extracted at the beginning of the period.

Often, it is suggested that depletion not be recorded until the extracted units are sold. This procedure is erroneous in that it overstates the wasting asset and understates finished goods and work in process inventories. Since earnings are immune to depletion until the units are sold, net income is unaffected.

Depletion and dividend policy. If the enterprise is to be dissolved after the natural resources are extracted, the cash provided through the recovery of depletion expense in the sales price of units sold is not needed to replace the wasting asset. Management may, therefore, distribute this cash to stockholders. To the extent that the cash distribution is provided by depletion, it is a liquidating dividend returning a part of their original investment to the stockholders. The liquidating portion of the dividend is chargeable to a Capital Distributions to Stockholders account and is shown as a reduction of capital on the balance sheet.

Amortization of development costs. Cost of initial investigation, land-clearing and surface-stripping, drilling, sinking of shafts, etc. are chargeable to the Development Costs account. This account is amortized over the estimated units of the entire deposit or the restricted section of the deposit to which such costs relate.

The balance in the Development Costs account at the end of the year is divided by the expected total unit yield of the development, estimated at the beginning of the year, to arrive at a rate that is then applied to the actual units extracted during the year.

Because of the speculative nature of preliminary development costs, the Internal Revenue Code permits the taxpayer either to capitalize these costs and amortize them in the future, or to treat the costs as an expense as soon as expended.

Depreciable assets at the site of wasting assets. The remaining life of the wasting asset limits the utility and service life of depreciable buildings and equipment at the site of the natural resource. Also, the costs of removing these depreciable assets are usually prohibitive. Therefore, they are generally abandoned after the natural resource is extracted. Accordingly, such fixed assets should be depreciated over their life or the remaining life of the natural resource, whichever is shorter. Equipment items that have future utility and that will be moved after cessation of operations should be depreciated over their separate lives. Depreciation charges should usually be computed on the basis of units extracted.

Discovery value. Often, land acquired at a relatively nominal cost is found to contain resources of substantial value. Equally common are instances in which a purchase price that was originally presumed to measure the value of known deposits is later found to be extremely low in relation to the value of subsequently discovered deposits.

For the purpose of showing a realistic asset valuation and computing a meaningful depletion charge in these cases, the book value of the asset should be increased by the "discovery value." Correspondingly, the corporate capital should be increased by an entry to the account entitled Unrealized Increment Based on Discovery Value. Recording of the increment and balance sheet presentation are the same as for the appreciation of assets, discussed previously.

Depletion and income tax. Some of the reasons for special treatment of depletion for Federal income tax purposes are the public value of natural resources, the speculative character of resources explorations and development, and the substantial capital required to be invested. Therefore, the taxpayer is allowed an income tax deduction for depletion that is equal to the higher amount computed under either the cost or percentage method.

Cost method. The cost method applies to all types of property subject to depletion. Cost is deemed to be the adjusted basis for determining gain or sale. As an alternative to cost, value as of March 1, 1913 is used for property acquired prior to March 1, 1913 at a lower cost. Value as of date of death (or six months after) is used where property is transmitted at death.

The depletion rate is arrived at by dividing the cost basis by the total estimated remaining units. This rate is, in turn, multiplied by the number of units sold during the year in order to arrive at the depletion deduction.

Percentage method. The percentage method, giving rise to percentage depletion, is statutory in origin. It now applies to about 100 minerals. Depletion is computed by multiplying the income derived from a mineral by a designated rate for the specific mineral. The deduction is not to exceed 50% of the taxable net income from the property, computed without reference to the depletion deduction; nor may it exceed 65% of taxable income from all sources, computed without reference to the depletion deduction and to any net operating loss carryback and capital loss carryback to the taxable year. The rates on gross income include 22% for sulphur and uranium; 15% for gold, silver, copper, and iron ore; 10% for coal; 7½% for clay and shale; and 5% for gravel, peat, peat moss, and sand. Percentage depletion rates for oil and gas have been repealed, except in two basic cases with respect to which the rate of 22% applies. While the rates on gross income vary, the factors of 50% of taxable income on mineral property and 65% of taxable income generally, apply to all resources.

7

Inventory and Inventory Valuation

CONTENTS

7

Inventory and Inventory Valuation

Saul Feldman, CPA

Inventory valuation is one of the most difficult areas of accounting. The accountant meets and must resolve many perplexing theoretical and practical problems in this area. He must determine the kind and amount of costs that are properly chargeable to inventory. He must choose one of many methods of assigning costs to inventory (LIFO, FIFO, etc.). He must develop methods to apply these costs expeditiously. Finally, he must find ways to revalue inventory when market declines occur.

It is the purpose of this chapter to outline and evaluate the various methods of valuation and to clarify their underlying concepts. To accomplish this, the subject of inventory and inventory valuation will be treated in the following sections:

1. Nature of inventory and inventory costs.
2. Methods of assigning costs to units of inventory.
3. Cost or market, whichever is lower.
4. The retail method.
5. Other inventory problems.
6. Absorption costing vs. direct costing.
7. Special cost problems.

NATURE OF INVENTORY AND INVENTORY COSTS

The ending inventories of manufacturers are made up of two main types of cost: (1) all materials used in the creation of the finished product valued at a cost determined by one of several cost determination methods (LIFO, FIFO, Specific Identification, etc.) and (2) all other costs of production allocated between the units that were sold and those still on hand at the end of the period.

With the above as a basis, the overall inventory valuation procedure may be expressed in simple terms, despite the many practical and theoretical problems involved. The combination of (1) and (2) results in a valuation of the ending inventory at cost. This cost figure is used as the value of the ending inventory except in the special circumstance of the market value of the inventory being lower than cost. If this occurs, the lower market valuation is used within certain limits that are explained in the section *Cost or Market Whichever is Lower.*

While this overall view of inventory valuation is valid, it overlooks many practical problems, alternatives, and questions of judgment that the accountant meets in carrying out the procedure.

This section will define and discuss the following key concepts connected with inventory valuation:

1. What is inventory?
2. Title to goods.
3. What is cost?

What is inventory? Actually there are almost as many kinds of inventories as there are business firms. Inventories consist of those goods:

1. Awaiting sale in the ordinary course of business.
2. Being worked on for the purpose of eventual sale.
3. Waiting to be consumed in the production of other goods or services.

This definition implies the following kinds of inventories with which most accountants are familiar:

1. Merchandise.
2. Raw materials.
3. Supplies.
4. Work in process.
5. Finished goods.

The fact that inventories are classified into the above types does not enable an accountant to automatically pigeonhole a specific item. Classification is less dependent on the item itself than on the use of the item in a specific business.

► EXAMPLE: An ordinary length of board may be classified in any of the following ways, depending on its use:

1. If used in a factory for minor repairs—supplies.
2. In a woodworking factory—raw materials.
3. In a lumber yard held for sale—merchandise.
4. The end product in a saw mill—finished goods.
5. In production in a furniture factory—work in process.

Title to goods. Whether or not an item should be included in inventory is often more of a legal question than anything else. Simply stated, the rule is that only goods to which the company has title should be included in inventory. The date on an invoice is not necessarily conclusive as to title. Title is considered to pass, in most cases, when goods are set aside in accordance with the contract between the buyer and the seller. Thus, an item need not be physically present to be included in inventory. Goods may belong in inventory and yet be in transit, out on consignment, or stored in a public warehouse. In most states the Uniform Sales Act embodies the definitive provisions determining when title has passed. As a practical means of insuring that the inventory includes only goods that are owned as of the inventory date, a cut-off of merchandise shipments and receipts must be effected.

The cut-off date. To effect a cut-off of outgoing shipments, a note should be made of the invoice or charge ticket number of the last goods billed before the cut-off date. Any goods billed on later invoices are included in the inventory. It is also helpful to stamp all receiving reports either "Include in Inventory" or "Exclude from Inventory," depending on when the goods are received.

Although the effect of overlooking the cut-off date is minimal when an invoice for goods that are not owned is entered as a purchase and the goods are included in the inventory, in other cases large distortions can occur.

► EXAMPLE: A $5,000 invoice for raw materials is entered in the purchase journal prior to the inventory date. The goods, not being on the premises, are omitted from the inventory count. The reported profit would be decreased by $5,000, current assets would be understated by $5,000, and the current ratio would be unfavorably affected.

Distortions may also occur when the cut-off dates for sales invoices and goods sold are not properly coordinated.

Although the general rule—*only goods to which the company has title should be included in inventory*—is easy to state, precautions must be taken to see that it is observed.

What is cost? The concept of cost as a basis of inventory valuation is probably as old as accounting itself. As applied to inventories, cost means in principle the sum of the applicable expenditures and charges directly or indirectly incurred in bringing an article to its existing condition and location.

The meaning is plain. Inventories are to be priced at cost in conformity with the cost principle used in accounting for other types of assets. Furthermore, selling costs, and general and administrative overhead, are not proper valuation costs since these types of expenditures are not "directly or indirectly incurred in bringing an article to its existing location and condition."

Inventoriable costs. In practice, the costs that are "incurred in bringing an inventory to its specific location and condition" are not always easy to determine. The starting point is the invoice price of materials. (The related question of purchase discounts is discussed under the next heading.) Other items, such as transportation charges, duties, and labor, are proper additions to invoice costs.

Even the apparent truism that the invoice price of raw materials is the starting point of inventoriable cost is not always accepted without controversy.

► EXAMPLE: A manufacturing company may suddenly find that it is on the point of running out of a particular item that is badly needed in the manufacturing process. To retain a customer's goodwill by completing his order in the scheduled time, the company may purchase the material in short supply at a much higher than normal price. If the inventory is taken in the interim, how is this particular lot to be valued?

Under a strict interpretation of the first-in, first-out method, some accountants would price any of these raw materials still in inventory at their actual cost. Others would argue, perhaps a bit more realistically, that the premium paid for these materials is not an inventoriable cost. From this point of view, those who would price these materials at their actual cost appear to be *capitalizing* management's mistakes.

Using absorption costing, fixed and variable overheads are also added to the cost of inventory. Under direct costing, only variable costs of production—direct labor, direct materials, and the variable portion of other manufacturing expenses—are used to value inventories. Direct costing is not as yet an approved method for external reporting. Nevertheless, this method has value for internal management purposes (see Chapters 9 and 13). Both direct and absorption costing will be further explained and evaluated in the section, *Absorption costing vs. direct costing.*

It is important to understand that the decision as to whether transportation, labor, and other costs are part of inventory costs is not based merely on the fact that these costs were incurred. Rather, these costs are carried forward to the next accounting period because they have added some value (utility) to the inventory. Conversely, if these or other costs have not added to the value of an inventory, they should not be carried forward. Examples of costs not properly inventoriable are costs of strikes, fires, and poorly-timed deliveries. Costs that may be spoken of as "beyond the factory door" are another example of costs that should not be carried forward.

Depreciation, although an estimate, is properly allocated between the goods that have been sold and those still in inventory. Even costs that are intangible, in the sense that do they not effect a physical change in the units produced, may be proper costs for inventory valuation purposes. Inspection costs and certain types of engineering costs are examples of such intangible costs.

Basically, there is no set rule that is applicable in every circumstance for determining which of these costs should be charged to operations in the period and which should be allocated between the goods that have been sold and the goods in inventory. The basic aim is to match revenues with the costs incurred to produce the revenues and to defer all other costs to the next period by capitalizing them in inventory.

Purchase discounts. The accounting profession is divided on the question of how to treat purchase discounts in determining the costs of raw materials. Some hold that the taking of purchase discounts is, in effect, the earning of money through the use of money. Therefore, purchase discounts represent earnings not at all connected with the sales function.

Other accountants argue that the "cost" principle of accounting demands that purchase discounts be treated as any other item. If inward freight is added to the cost of raw materials, purchase discounts should be deducted from the cost. In fact, they say, invoices should be recorded net of discounts to give proper expression to the cost concept.

These opposing viewpoints of how to treat purchase discounts are illustrated in the following example.

► EXAMPLE: Assume that a company has purchased 100 pounds of raw materials at a unit cost of $2 per pound. A discount of 1% is allowed for payment within 10 days. If the theory that purchase discounts are merely the result of the use of money is followed, the journal entries for the recording and payment of the invoice would be as follows:

Raw materials purchases (or inventory)	200	
Accounts payable		200
Accounts payable	200	
Purchase discounts taken		2
Cash		198

Under the cost concept, the journal entries would be as follows:

Raw materials	198	
Accounts payable		198
Accounts payable	198	
Cash		198

Or, if the invoice is not paid on time under this method, the following entry would be required:

Accounts payable	198	
Discounts lost	2	
Cash		200

If a significant amount of discounts were lost, would consistency, under the cost method, require that these discounts be added back to the cost of raw materials? "Not at all," say the proponents of this method. Lost discounts are a sign that the managers of the enterprise have not planned properly in terms of available working capital funds, and serve to call attention to management's shortcomings in this area.

METHODS OF ASSIGNING COSTS TO UNITS OF INVENTORY

The previous section discussed the specific costs that enter into the valuation of inventories and the theory under which costs are, or are not, proper additions to the value of an inventory.

Now we must determine how costs are applied to units in the inventory, particularly in the case of raw materials. The following five methods will be outlined and evaluated:

1. Specific identification.
2. Average cost.
3. First-in, first-out (FIFO).
4. Last-in, first-out (LIFO).
5. Base stock.

Specific identification. The essential element of this method of pricing is the correlation of a specific item of inventory with a specific cost.

The correlation may be with a particular invoice that can be referred to, or with a cost record of the manufacturing process. The general frame of reference is to one unit that is readily identifiable as having been either purchased or manufactured at some specific point in time.

The application of this method of specific identification presupposes that the unit of inventory has some distinguishable characteristic that sets it apart from all other units of a similar nature. For example, a machinery dealer with a stock of lathes can identify each machine by serial number, as can the piano or refrigerator dealer. It is apparent that this type of record keeping will be maintained only for units that are expensive enough to warrant this type of inventory control. The three indispensable elements of the method of specific identification are:

1. A serial number, or other means of identification correlated with
2. The source from which the item was obtained, and
3. The cost of the item.

► NOTE: The subsequent methods of assigning costs to inventory that will be covered in this section are "flow pricing" methods. An evaluation of how the method of specific identification contrasts with flow pricing methods is given in Chapter 1.

Average cost. The term *average cost,* in and of itself, is rather meaningless for pricing purposes since it means different things to different people. There are three distinct types of average costs: the simple average, the weighted average, and the moving average. Each type of average cost will be illustrated, based on the following data:

XYZ CORPORATION

Record of Purchases and Sales
Material Y

Purchases

	Unit Cost	*Quantity*	*Total*
Inventory, January 1	$1.00	100	$ 100
March 10	1.05	500	525
June 18	.95	600	570
August 15	1.20	400	480
October 22	1.10	800	880
Total		2,400	$2,555

Sales	
February 11	50
April 2	200
May 5	300
June 20	300
July 9	200
August 2	100
September 19	300
October 10	100
November 14	600
Total sales	2,150
Inventory, December 31, 19—	250

Simple average. The simple average figure used in pricing the final inventory is computed by adding together the unit cost of each purchase during the period, including the unit cost of the beginning inventory (if any), and dividing by the total number of purchases. Based on the illustrative material, the computation is as follows:

$$\frac{\$1.00 + 1.05 + .95 + 1.20 + 1.10}{5} = \frac{5.30}{5} = \$1.06$$

Final inventory valuation: 250 units $\times$ \$1.06 = \$265.00

The chief advantage of this method is its simplicity. It produces valid results if unit prices are stable during the period. If unit prices are not stable, or are affected by the level of purchases, illogical results are obtained since both large and small purchases would be given the same weight.

Weighted average. One way of avoiding the disadvantages of the simple average method is to weight the unit prices by the quantity purchased (including any beginning inventory), and to divide by the total quantity available during the period. This computation, based on the same data used in determining the simple average cost, follows:

$$\frac{\text{Total cost of available inventory}}{\text{Total units available}} = \frac{\$2,555}{2,400} = \$1.065$$

Value of ending inventory: 250 $\times$ \$1.065 = \$266.25

The assumption implicit in this method is that the cost of sales is derived proportionately from all purchases during the period. It is also assumed that the inventories always contain a part of the earliest acquisitions of the item. From the point of view of the *flow of goods,* this may be an entirely illogical concept. On the other hand, from the point of view of the *flow of costs,* this concept may be just as logical, under certain circumstances, as the LIFO concept.

It must also be borne in mind that an inventory valuation based on a weighted average is, in essence, a composite of the entire range of costs during a given period. Therefore, when price levels are falling, weighted average costs will be in excess of current costs. When price levels are rising, weighted average costs will be less than current costs.

Moving average. Although, strictly speaking, this method is not a moving average as statisticians know the term, it has come to be known as such by accountants. The chief feature of this "average" method is the fact that new unit average costs are computed after every purchase. Using the same illustrative material, the calculation of the inventory valuation figure based on the moving average method is shown in Figure 1.

The theoretical objections to the moving average method are essentially the same as those presented for the other average methods, except that the lag between current market price and inventory valuation has been shortened somewhat by the introduction of the moving average.

For comparative purposes, the valuation figures for the final inventories under each of the three average methods are as follows:

Method	*Value per Unit*	*Total Valuation for 250 units*
Simple average	$1.06	$265.00
Weighted average	1.065	266.25
Moving average	1.104	276.10

First-in, first-out (FIFO). In most industries and retail and wholesale establishments, it is considered good practice to dispose of the oldest items in the inventory first, although in some situations (coal pits, silos, etc.) it may be a physical impossibility to do so. Carried to its logical conclusion, the inventory remaining on hand is considered to consist of the last purchases made.

In valuing the in and out movements under the FIFO concept of the flow of costs, the unit prices simply follow the same flow as the inventory. To illustrate this method, Figure 2 shows a perpetual inventory card kept on the FIFO basis. The data in the illustration are the same as were used to illustrate the average cost methods.

It is not necessary to maintain a perpetual inventory system in order to use this method. The carrying value of the 250 units on hand at the end of the period could easily be determined by just referring to the October 22nd purchase invoice.

Last-in, first-out (LIFO). The concept of LIFO cost can be clarified by a simple example.

► EXAMPLE: Assume that an enterprising young man, age nine, desires to enter into the business of selling razor blades. He purchases a razor blade for 5¢ and promptly sells it (to his father, presumably) for 10¢. Upon going back to his supplier, he finds that the cost of the same razor blade is now 10¢. He buys the blade and sells it for 20¢. Over the course of a certain period of time his purchases and sales show the following relationship (only one razor blade is involved at each step):

	Purchases	*Sales*
	5¢	10¢
	10¢	20¢
	15¢	25¢
	25¢	
Total	55¢	55¢

XYZ CORPORATION

PERPETUAL INVENTORY CARD—MATERIAL Y

Date	*Purchases*			*Sales*			*Balance*		
Inventory	*Quantity*	*Unit Cost*	*Total*	*Quantity*	*Unit Cost*	*Cost of Sales*	*Quantity*	*Unit Cost*	*Total*
Jan. 1, 19—	100	$1.00	$100.00				100	$1.00	$100.00
February 11				50	$1.00	$ 50.00	50	1.00	50.00
March 10	500	1.05	525.00				550	1.045	575.00
April 2				200	1.045	209.00	350	1.045	366.00
May 5				300	1.045	313.50	50	1.045	52.50
June 8	600	.95	570.00				650	.958	622.50
June 20				300	.958	287.40	350	.958	335.10
July 9				200	.958	191.60	150	.958	143.50
Aug. 2				100	.958	95.80	50	.958	47.70
Aug. 15	400	1.20	480.00				450	1.173	527.70
Sept. 19				300	1.173	351.90	150	1.173	175.80
Oct. 10				100	1.173	117.30	50	1.173	58.50
Oct. 22	800	1.10	880.00				850	1.104	938.50
Nov. 14				600	1.104	662.40	250	1.104	276.10[1]

Fig. 1. Inventory Valuation Using the Moving Average Method.

[1]Had the moving average unit cost figure been carried out to more decimal places, the result would have been more accurate. The final inventory figure would have been as follows:

250 × $1.04	276.00
As shown	276.10
Difference	.10

XYZ CORPORATION

PERPETUAL INVENTORY CARD—MATERIAL Y

Date	*Purchases*			*Sales*			*Balance*		
Inventory	*Quantity*	*Unit Cost*	*Total*	*Quantity*	*Unit Cost*	*Cost of Sales*	*Quantity*	*Unit Cost*	*Total*
January 1	100	$1.00	$100.00				100	$1.00	$100.00
February 11				50	$1.00	$ 50.00	50	1.00	50.00
March 10	500	1.05	525.00				50	1.00	50.00
							500	1.05	525.00
April 2				50	1.00	50.00			
				150	1.05	157.50	350	1.05	367.50
May 5				300	1.05	315.00	50	1.05	52.50
							50	1.05	52.50
June 18	600	.95	570.00				600	.95	570.00
June 20				50	1.05	52.50			
				250	.95	237.50	350	.95	332.50
July 9				200	.95	190.00	150	.95	142.50
Aug. 2				100	.95	95.00	50	.95	47.50
Aug. 15	400	1.20	480.00				50	.95	47.50
							400	1.20	480.00
Sept. 19				50	.95	47.50			
				250	1.20	300.00	150	1.20	180.00
Oct. 10				100	1.20	120.00	50	1.20	60.00
Oct. 22	800	1.10	880.00				50	1.20	60.00
							800	1.10	880.00
Nov. 14				50	1.20	60.00			
				550	1.10	605.00	250	1.10	275.00

Fig. 2. Perpetual Inventory Card on the First-In, First-Out Basis.

He now has an inventory consisting of one razor blade for which he has paid 25¢, and he also has his original capital of 5¢ with which he began the venture. The young man knows, of course, that he has made money because, in addition to his original capital, he now has a razor blade. But the question in his mind is how much has he made.

It is possible to give two answers to the young man, both of which are acceptable to the accounting profession and to the tax authorities. If the young entrepreneur adopts the FIFO concept, the razor blade in his possession will be valued at 25¢, and that will be his gross profit. If he adopts the LIFO method of inventory valuation, the razor blade will be valued at 5¢, the value of the first blade he purchased, and that will be his gross profit.

The implications of this example begin to take shape. The young man was only slightly better off at the end of the period than at the beginning. Try as he might, he could only keep replacing his stock-in-trade. He could not expand because he had been caught in an inflationary spiral over which he had no control. His inventory contained the same number of units at the end of the period as it did at the beginning. In fact, if he now wanted to buy another razor blade in order to expand his business, he would have to invest five times as much money as when he started.

One thing, at least, seems clear. The concept of LIFO is *not* one of a movement of goods; it is one of a movement of costs. It is an attempt to equate current prices of goods sold with the most recent acquisition costs of the same goods. Some accountants even go so far as to say that the use of LIFO automatically values the cost of goods sold in a way that is truly expressive of the concept of accrual accounting—the matching of sales revenues with proper costs.

The technical aspects of pricing an inventory on a LIFO basis revolve about two matters. First, a reference point must be established against which to measure "normal" prices. The second matter involves the prices to be used if the level of inventory is raised sometime in the future.

In the following illustration it is assumed that a company desires to establish its inventory pricing on a LIFO basis as of the end of year 2. Its inventory of a particular commodity at the end of year 1 is assumed to consist of 2,000 units priced on a FIFO basis as follows:

INVENTORY PRICED ON FIFO BASIS

DECEMBER 31, YEAR 1

1,000 units Commodity A	@ 2.05	$2,050
500 " " "	@ 1.90	950
500 " " "	@ 2.20	1,100
2,000 " " "		$4,100

The first step in the conversion to a LIFO inventory is the establishment of the "normal" price. In this situation, a normal price is established by merely converting the total cost of the inventory, $4,100.00, to an average unit cost, which in this case amounts to $2.05. Having established this reference point, the accountant is now faced with the question of pricing any units added to the inventory base. Figure 3 illustrates the pricing of 200 units that have been added to the base of 2,000 units.

XYZ CORPORATION

WORK SHEET FOR PRICING COMMODITY A
December 31, Year 2

Inventory: Commodity A as of December 31, Year 2—2,200 units

Purchase record Commodity A for Year 2:

Date	*Quantity*	*Unit Cost*
Feb. 10	600	$2.10
March 15	1,000	2.15
April 20	1,500	2.25
May 30	2,000	2.30
Aug. 15	2,000	2.32
Oct. 12	2,000	2.40
Dec. 5	1,500	2.50

The final inventory on a LIFO basis is priced as follows:

	Number of Units	*Unit Cost*	*Total*
	2,000	$2.05	$4,100.00
	200	2.10	420.00
Total	2,200		$4,520.00

On a FIFO basis the inventory would be priced as follows:

	1,500	$2.50	$3,750.00
	700	2.40	1,680.00
Total	2,200		$5,430.00

Fig. 3. Converting to a LIFO Basis.

In addition to the pricing problem at the end of the first year of operation, the question of pricing the inventory in successive years of operation also exists. While there may be increases in the inventory level at the end of some years, there will be decreases at the end of others. Figure 4 illustrates the techniques employed to solve these pricing problems for Commodity A in years subsequent to year 2.

XYZ CORPORATION

WORK SHEETS FOR PRICING COMMODITY A
FOR YEAR 1, 2, 3, AND 4

Units in inventory of Commodity A:

December 31, Year 1	2,500
December 31, Year 2	2,400
December 31, Year 3	2,100
December 31, Year 4	1,000

Purchase record—Commodity A: Jan. 1, Year 1—December 31, Year 4

	Date	*Quantity*	*Unit Cost*
Year 1	April 5	2,000	2.75
	July 14	1,500	2.80
	Oct. 10	3,000	2.90
		6,500	
Year 2	Feb. 14	2,500	3.00
	May 9	2,000	3.00
	Nov. 5	3,000	3.10
		7,500	
Year 3	March 12	3,000	3.50
	June 16	2,500	3.60
	Nov. 14	3,000	3.75
		8,500	
Year 4	Jan. 22	2,000	3.80
	May 13	4,000	3.85
	Sept. 15	4,000	4.00
	Dec. 11	2,000	4.10
		12,000	

Pricing of final inventory—LIFO basis

	Quantity	*Unit Cost*	*Total*
Year 1	2,000	$2.05	$4,100
	200	2.10	420
	300	2.75	825
	2,500		$5,345
Year 2	2,000	$2.05	$4,100
	200	2.10	420
	200	2.75	550
	2,400		$5,070
Year 3	2,000	$2.05	$4,100
	100	2.10	210
	2,100		$4,310
Year 4	1,000	$2.05	$2,050

Fig. 4. Work Sheet for Pricing Commodity A.

In the event that the inventory of Commodity A at the end of year 5 increases by 500 units to a total unit inventory of 1,500, the additional 500 units would be priced at LIFO costs.

As with other inventory pricing methods, there are disadvantages as well as advantages in the use of LIFO. The disadvantages are revealed by questions that have not been answered to this day by proponents of LIFO. For example, although the emphasis on the matching of current selling prices with current costs makes for a more meaningful profit and loss statement, what is the effect on the balance sheet of an inventory priced at the earliest costs of acquisition? Most proponents answer that a footnote giving the current costs of the inventory is adequate. In effect, the reader of the balance sheet must make his own adjustments (mental or otherwise), if he is so inclined. Furthermore, it is entirely possible that because of long-term price level increases, comparisons of working capital ratios will become almost a meaningless exercise.

Another weakness in the use of LIFO arises from the application of the trite maxim that "whatever goes up, must come down." Cyclical fluctuations may cause prices of certain commodities to fall below LIFO costs, particularly if a company has adopted this method near the peak of the price level. Under a rather strict interpretation of the doctrine of consistency, the company faced with this situation would have to revalue its inventory on a LIFO basis. Not to do this would disturb the matching of current revenues with current costs. Here, of course, the accountant can call upon another doctrine—the doctrine of conservatism—to help him out of his dilemma (see Chapter 1). The weakness of the method still exists, but need not be fatal.

Of far greater importance is the possible distortion of the income statement if the inventory level falls below the "normal" amount. If current sales prices are responsive to current costs of production, and the inventory quantity falls below normal after a large rise in prices, a strict application of the LIFO method could result in the matching of low inventory values with high sales prices. This situation will be illustrated using the same data for the year 3 and year 4 inventories and purchases that appeared in Figure 4.

XYZ CORPORATION

Profit and Loss Worksheet
December 31, Year 4

SALES OF COMMODITY A

Units in inventory, beginning	2,100
Purchases for year	12,000
Total units available	14,100
Units in inventory, Ending	1,000
Units sold	13,100
Total sales at $8 per unit	$104,800

DETERMINATION OF COST OF GOODS SOLD IN LIFO BASIS

Purchases for Year	*Quantity*	*Unit Cost*	*Total*
Jan. 22	2,000	$3.80	$ 7,600
May 13	4,000	3.85	15,400
Sept. 15	4,000	4.00	16,000
Dec. 11	2,000	4.10	8,200
Totals	12,000		$47,200
SOLD FROM BASE INVENTORY	100	2.10	210
	1,000	2.05	2,050
	13,100		$49,460

The results of operations for the period would show the following:

Sales revenue	$104,800
Cost of goods sold	49,460
Gross profit	$ 55,340

If a FIFO basis were substituted for LIFO, the gross profit would amount to $53,340. To do this, however, the opening inventory would have to be put on a FIFO basis. The computations would be as follows:

Inventory beginning on a FIFO basis (2,100 units @ 3.75)	$ 7,875
Purchases	47,200
Total cost of goods available for sale	$55,075
Inventory, ending on a FIFO basis (1,000 units @ 4.10)	4,100
Cost of goods sold	$50,975

After this conversion, the results of operations would be as follows:

Sales	$104,800
Cost of goods sold	50,975
Gross profit	$ 53,825

It should be pointed out that the conversion of the opening inventory from a LIFO to a FIFO basis created an additional book profit of $3,565 measured as follows:

Value of opening inventory on a FIFO basis	$7,875
Value of opening inventory on a LIFO basis	4,310
Book profit	$3,565

This discussion of LIFO has concentrated thus far on a physical inventory to which unit costs were applied in order to state the final inventory on a LIFO basis. Not all inventories, however, are expressed in units. The inventories of department stores, for example, are usually expressed in terms of gross selling prices. The various departmental mark-on percentages are applied to the total selling prices to reduce the inventories to some consistently expressed cost basis.

Even for inventories expressed in terms of dollars instead of units, it is possible to approximate the LIFO basis of valuation. The techniques and assumptions required to do this will be discussed in the section dealing with the retail method.

Base stock method. The underlying assumption of the base stock method of inventory valuation is that operating management has made a decision to maintain inventories at a certain level, and that a reduction below this level would interfere unduly with the "normal" activities of the enterprise. In actual operation, this type of decision is reflected by a stock clerk automatically ordering a part when his stock card, or his physical count, tells him that the inventory level has fallen to some designated minimum point.

The decision to maintain a "normal" inventory means more than the maintenance of physical quantities. It also means that the base stock is always priced so that no increase in replacement cost is regarded as realized income. The effect, therefore, is to cost out sales at current prices. In this respect the base stock method closely approximates the LIFO method.

Unlike LIFO, however, if the final inventory quantity exceeds the base stock, the excess is priced at current costs. Similarly, if the final inventory quantity is less than the base stock, this deficiency is priced at current costs and subtracted from the base stock. An illustration will be used to clarify these principles.

In Figure 4, the physical inventory at December 31, year 3 amounted to 2,100 units. If the company were using the base stock method, the inventory would be priced as follows:

2,000 units @ 2.05	$4,100
100 units @ 3.75 (current cost)	375
Total value	$4,475

If the inventory at year-end had been 1,900 units instead of 2,100, the valuation would be computed as follows:

2,000 units @ 2.05	$4,100
Less: 100 units @ 3.75	375
	$3,725

Unlike the LIFO method, the costs used to express the base are ordinarily the lowest costs experienced. If market prices (current costs) are less than those normally used, the current prices automatically replace the latter, thus effectively establishing a new base.

COST OR MARKET, WHICHEVER IS LOWER

As was pointed out previously, inventory values are based primarily on cost. Since different methods that can be used to determine cost have been explained, no further discussion would be required if the cost concept was absolute. However, it is possible for goods to lose their "utility." If a loss of utility occurs, the cost basis of inventory valuation is modified to the extent of using a lower "market" value. The concept of utility, therefore, is an important part of inventory valuation.

The utility concept. Utility does not mean usefulness in terms of quality or the specific uses to which the inventory may be put. Rather, the utility of goods refers to their ability to command a selling price that will provide a normal profit.

The concept of utility is not always easy to apply since it involves measuring future sales, and this can be done only by predicting the price level in the future. Neither management nor accountants can claim to be omniscient about predicting future price levels. And yet, within the limitations of their knowledge, a decision must be made. The profession is faced with the thought that in this area, as in others, the judgment of the accountant is an essential feature of the financial recording process. His judgments cannot always be right even though they are based on all the available evidence—it must be recognized that some mistakes are bound to occur.

A departure from the cost basis of pricing the inventory is required when the utility of the goods is no longer as great as its cost. Where there is evidence that the utility of goods, in their disposal in the ordinary course of business, will be less than cost, whether due to physical deterioration, obsolescence, changes in price levels, or other causes, the difference should be recognized as a loss of the current period. This is generally accomplished by stating such goods at a lower level commonly designated as *market.*

As used in the phrase *lower of cost or market* the term *market* means current replacement cost (by purchase or by reproduction, as the case may be) except that:

(1) Market should not exceed the net realizable value (that is, estimated selling price in the ordinary course of business less reasonably predictable costs of completion and disposal); and

(2) Market should not be less than net realizable value reduced by an allowance for an approximately normal profit margin.

The effect of this is to limit the term *market* to a "ceiling" measured by the net realizable value, and a "floor" measured by net realizable value less a normal profit margin. The following tabulation will be used to illustrate how these concepts operate in determining the inventory price of a commodity.

	Commodity		
	A	*B*	*C*
1. Cost	$1.00	$1.00	$1.00
2. Replacement cost (market)	.90	.90	.90
3. Net realizable value (ceiling)	1.20	1.20	.80
4. Net realizable value less a normal profit margin (floor)	.85	.98	.70

It seems clear, first of all, that if cost is equal to or less than 2, 3, or 4, no adjustment is made to the inventory valuation at cost. Such a situation poses no problem. However, where replacement cost is less than actual cost, replacement cost is to be used unless it fails to meet the conditions imposed by the "ceiling" and the "floor" of the definition. If replacement cost is used, therefore, it must lie between the ceiling and the floor.

Commodity A in the tabulation offers a clear-cut situation. Since replacement cost is less than actual cost and lies between the ceiling and the floor, it will be the inventory valuation figure. For Commodity B, replacement cost is below the floor. The commodity will be valued at $.98, at which figure the firm will still be making a "normal" profit margin. Commodity C does not lend itself readily to a determination of this type as replacement cost is higher than both the floor and ceiling. In theory, perhaps, the goods should be priced at $.70, since at the valuation the firm would be making a normal profit margin, whereas at $.80, the firm will only be recovering its actual cash outlay.

In the business world each of these examples finds its counterpart in the movement of costs and prices. The example of Commodity A clearly illustrates a situation where the goods can be replaced (either by manufacture or purchase) at a price below the actual cost of the goods on hand. The net realizable value of Commodity A, $1.20, will yield the firm a profit of $.30, based upon replacement cost. Pricing the inventory, therefore, at $.90 is satisfactory, even though at that price the full potential profit of $.35 will not be realized. In the case of Commodity B, the company is saying, in effect, that even though the items in the inventory can be replaced for $.90, a normal profit can be realized at a valuation figure of $.98. Obviously, as far as this item is concerned, the company expects to make a larger than normal profit as these goods are replaced.

The case of Commodity C illustrates a situation frequently encountered—manufacturers or retailers being left at the end of a season with goods that are not readily disposable. Although Commodity C can be replaced for less than it originally cost, the company cannot realize even the replacement cost of $.80.

"Normal profit margin." One of the difficulties that accountants face in applying the cost or market rule is the question of what constitutes a "normal profit margin." More often than not, selling prices are the result of market conditions outside the control of the individual firm. Furthermore, the costs of raw materials and labor may often be beyond the control of the individual company, particularly in the case of small manufacturing establishments.

Even in situations where the firm can exercise some control over its selling price and/or costs, the question of what is a "normal" profit margin still remains to be answered. The one-product firm can have one profit margin when selling just a few items, and another profit margin when selling to quantity purchasers. The multi-product firm has the problem of determining a normal profit for the company as a whole as well as for each product. In this case, the question of the product mix becomes important. If each product has its own gross margin percentage, the overall percentage will reflect, and be weighted by, the absolute dollar figures of sales and costs of each product. Any change in these relationships will affect overall company results so that "normal profit" for one period may, in fact, be meaningless when compared with the same dollar figure for another period.

Determination of periodic net income. The concept of "cost or market" rests, of course, upon the possibility that the firm's products may have suffered a loss of utility. To measure this loss, the accountant must make a determination of how much value has been lost. Presumably, if there had been an increase in utility, the doctrine of conservation would prevent the accountant from writing up the value of the inventory. This is attested to by vast amounts of literature enjoining the profession from formally recognizing any contingent profits in this and other areas. Therefore, while the profession may, and does, recognize contingent losses due to changes in price levels, it will not recognize contingent gains. The effect of recognizing contingent losses is to shift profits from one period to another.

► EXAMPLE: If the price level for a particular item shows evidences of rising within the next operating cycle, inventories of this item will still be priced at cost even though these units command a higher utility in terms of selling price. This increased utility will be reflected in a higher profit margin in the next operating cycle. In the reverse situation, Commodity C of the last example, the present period will absorb the loss of \$.20 (\$1.00 less \$.80), and the subsequent period will reflect a normal profit margin. In both cases profits have been shifted from one period to another.

It appears that the use of cost or market cannot be adequately defended either on the basis of consistency or conservatism. There is nothing consistent about an inventory valuation method that can yield one value this year and another value the following year. Nor can there be anything really conservative about the shifting of income between periods, no matter how one tries to rationalize in this area. If the basis of accounting is the completed transaction that gives rise to a right or an obligation, and to a profit or a loss, then cost or market as an inventory valuation method cannot be defended in principle.

Methods of compiling "lower of cost or market." One of the fundamental disagreements among accountants today is whether the lower of cost or market concept is to be applied to individual items, to inventory divisions, or to grand totals. It would seem that a strict application of the cost or market rule would require applying it to each item in the inventory. On the other hand, some accountants feel that the determination of cost or market either by inventory divisions or by grand totals is sufficient to meet the requirements in this area.

Figure 5 indicates the various alternatives. The method used is the side-by-side valuation of each item on both the cost and the cost or market bases.

Inventory write-downs and valuation accounts. There are two methods of accomplishing a reduction in inventory from cost to market. The first method is to price the inventory at the lower market figure and to use the resulting valuation to arrive at the cost of goods sold. The second method is to price the inventory at cost and to reduce it by an allowance sufficient to bring the final valuation to market.

The advantage of the first method is that no inventory valuation account need be created. It is direct. On the other hand, the cost of goods sold figure — and, therefore, the gross profit on sales—may be so distorted by fluctuations in market values as to make these figures almost worthless for purposes of comparison with other years. In addition, if perpetual inventory cards are kept, all unit prices affected must be changed.

The second method, since it prices the inventory at cost, does not allow for any distortion of the gross profit margin (everything else being equal) and, therefore, permits a more accurate and meaningful comparison of the gross profit with that of other years. Under this method, the write-down is accomplished through the creation of a nominal account and an inventory valuation allowance

ABC CORPORATION
DETERMINATION OF LOWER OF COST OR MARKET
December 31, 19__

	Quantity		Unit Price Cost	Unit Price Market	Total Cost	Total Market	Lower of Cost or Market
Sporting goods							
Baseballs	500		.75	.65	375.00	325.00	325.00
Fishing rods	100		2.50	2.75	250.00	275.00	250.00
Tennis balls	250		.50	.40	125.00	100.00	100.00
Golf balls	1,000		1.00	.95	1,000.00	950.00	950.00
					1,750.00	1,650.00	1,625.00
Men's wear							
Athletic shirts	12 doz.		7.50 doz.	8.50 doz.	90.00	102.00	90.00
Sweat shirts	6 doz.		15.00 doz.	18.00 doz.	90.00	108.00	90.00
Sport jackets	50		20.00	17.50	1,000.00	875.00	875.00
					1,180.00	1,085.00	1,055.00
Footwear							
Rubbers	100 pair		2.25 pair	2.50 pair	225.00	250.00	225.00
Galoshes	75 pair		4.00 pair	3.90 pair	300.00	292.50	292.50
Sneakers	200 pair		3.00 pair	3.50 pair	600.00	700.00	600.00
					1,125.00	1,242.50	1,117.50
Grand totals					4,055.00	3,977.50	3,797.50
Inventory valuation							
Item-by-item method		$3,797.50					
Inventory division method							
Sporting goods	$1,650.00						
Men's wear	1,085.00						
Footwear	1,125.00						
Total		$3,860.00					
Grand total method		$3,977.50					

Fig. 5. Alternative Methods of Compiling Lower of Cost or Market.

account. The former is charged to operations of the period and the latter serves to reduce the balance-sheet inventory to the lower of cost or market.

How to write down the inventory. Writing down an inventory is obviously not required when the inventory itself is priced at a lower market figure. But, if an allowance account is used to reduce an inventory to market, a journal entry such as the following is made:

Loss on reduction of inventory to market	5,000	
Allowance for the reduction of inventory to market		5,000

The debit portion of this entry is handled in the income statement as follows:

Sales		$100,000
Less cost of goods sold:		
Purchases	$75,000	
Less Dec. 31 inventory at cost	25,000	
Cost of goods sold		50,000
Gross profit on sales		$ 50,000
Less loss on reduction of inventory to market		5,000
Gross profit on sales after inventory loss		$ 45,000

For balance sheet purposes, the allowance account is treated in the same manner as any other valuation reserve—as a deduction from the asset.

Merchandise inventory Dec. 31, 19—, at cost	$25,000
Less allowance for the reduction of inventory to market	5,000
Merchandise inventory at the lower of cost or market	$20,000

The following year may not require an inventory reduction to a lower market price or it may require a reduction but not of the same amount. If the allowance of $5,000 must be increased to $7,500 the following year, a nominal account would be charged with the $2,500 and the allowance account credited. On the other hand, if the allowance were no longer needed or had to be reduced, the valuation reserve would be charged and the offsetting credit would appear in the income statement as an addition to gross profit on sales. When this method is used, the opening and closing inventories are always stated at cost regardless of the adjustments made for market prices.

The advantages of this approach to the question of inventory valuation at the lower of cost or market are obvious. Since cost of sales and gross profit are stated on a cost basis, the results are comparable (all else being equal) with those of any other year. Secondly, the effect of market changes during the year are shown separately, something greatly to be desired from the point of view of full disclosure. And last, but not least, if the company uses perpetual inventory methods, unit prices need not be changed; only parenthetical notations need be made of market prices.

Reserves for possible future market declines. In essence, the creation of a Reserve for Possible Future Market Decline can be justified, at best, only by making a great many assumptions. Therefore, a reserve of this nature should be created only by a charge to the retained earnings account. To do otherwise would mean a charge against earnings based on mere conjecture. Consequently, in effect, the reserve account merely becomes another portion of appropriated earnings. As soon as the necessity for it has gone, the reserve account should be returned to retained earnings.

THE RETAIL METHOD

The retail method of inventory is dealt with separately because it has unique aspects and is built on some of the concepts previously explained. This method, in particular the LIFO method of pricing as applied to the retail method, is becoming increasingly popular. It can be understood best only by appreciating the problems connected with merchandise inventories of department and chain stores. Because the retail method evolved as a result of these problems, it is only by understanding them that one can appreciate the final results.

Inventory problems of department and chain stores. As stores grew larger, their managers found the quick determination of profitable and unprofitable lines of merchandise becoming more important as well as more difficult. Also, managerial control over operations had to be maintained as a means of maximizing profit within the physical limitations of the store's selling area. In addition, and just as important, was the proper functioning of the merchandising budget that assigned to each department its share of contribution to the overall store profit for the period.

In order for these objectives to be realized, management had to have pertinent information readily available. The taking of a physical inventory at the end of each week, or month, or any other period of time, was too cumbersome and costly an operation. By the time the inventory could be taken, priced, summarized, and the results shown in the traditional profit and loss statement, the figures were quite old and comparatively useless. Modern department stores, for instance, take a maximum of two physical inventories during any 52 or 53 week period.

The introduction of inventory controls utilizing selling prices enabled store management to accomplish several things at once. First, inventory could be estimated with a great deal of accuracy because of the relationship between cost and selling price. The application of this relationship to the total inventory at retail automatically reduced the figure to cost, and enabled overall and departmental profit and loss statements to be prepared quite rapidly. Management could then evaluate the performance of specific merchandise lines in time for this analysis to influence current operations.

Second, departmental merchandise budgets became more flexible as the daily reporting of inventory levels at retail became more common. The merchandising manager could plan his purchasing by watching the results of operations by departments. Departments that showed rising inventory levels could be stopped from buying heavily (except for "fill-in" items), whereas those that showed declining inventory levels in relation to sales could be spurred by making funds available to them. In addition, timely promotional sales and advertising campaigns could be undertaken for those departments showing rising inventory levels. Department store management found in the retail inventory method a partial answer to the bugaboo of all retailing—the fear of being left with merchandise that doesn't move.

Thus, out of the problems of managerial control, a method of inventory valuation evolved that has become quite popular with department stores and all types of chain retail operations. This method, the retail method of inventory cost valuation, can, moreover, be made to yield results that are consistent with those obtained by a strict application of any of the bases previously discussed. In fact, the retail method is actually more than an inventory valuation device—it is part and parcel of the control function. It is not too much to say that what the standard cost system has accomplished for the manufacturing organization, the retail method has done for the department and chain store.

Important aspects of the retail method. The two most important aspects of the retail method are these:

1. The planned grouping of articles for sale into departments and subdepartments. The intent is to bring together not only whole families of related items (ladies' dresses), but also to subdivide the basic department into smaller units (evening gowns, better street dresses, etc.) for control purposes. To facilitate the conversion of the inventory from selling price to cost, this grouping also brings together items having a similar gross profit percentage. Obviously, if all ladies' dresses were indiscriminately mixed in one department, the final cost ratio would be a mixture of heterogeneous relationships less clearly reflecting the results of operations for the period.

2. The establishment of the original retail price. Since everything under the retail method is expressed in terms of the ultimate selling price to the consumer, it is understandable why so much importance is attached to this figure. The original retail price serves these purposes:

   a. It is a rough guide to the departmental buyer as to how much he can spend for a certain item and still maintain his gross margin percentage.
   b. The comparison of interim gross margin percentages enables management to evaluate the performance of the various departments. It is thus a control tool. Unless changes in original selling price are handled properly, however, the cost ratio may become distorted and not serve this purpose.

3. The original selling price of the article is the focal point around which the technical accounting aspects of the retail method revolve.

The retail terminology. Department stores were the first to develop a terminology in connection with the retail inventory method, and other retailers have since adopted this terminology. The following terms are in general use and will be used in accordance with the definitions stated below:

Original retail. The price at which the goods are initially offered for sale.

Mark-ups. Additions to the selling price of the item that raise it above original retail.

Mark-up cancellations. Deductions in selling price that do not decrease the price below original retail.

Mark-downs. Deductions that reduce the price below original retail.

Mark-downs cancellations. Additions to the retail price that do not increase it above original retail.

Net mark-ups. Mark-ups less mark-up cancellations.

Net mark-downs. Mark-downs less mark-down cancellations.

Mark-on. The difference between cost and original retail plus net mark-ups.

► COMMENT: The practitioner must know not only the meaning of these terms, but also how their underlying concepts are applied in practice. The following example of determining the ending inventory by the retail method illustrates the apparent simplicity of the method and the related computation. Note, however, that in determining the cost ratio (60%), net mark-ups enter into the computation but net mark-downs do not. The reasoning behind this is shown in the next section.

	Cost	*Retail*
Inventory at beginning	$ 50,000	$ 80,000
Purchases for the period	100,000	160,000
Net mark-ups		10,000
Totals	$150,000	$250,000
Net mark-downs		25,000
Goods available for sale at retail		$225,000
Sales		175,000
Inventory at end of period at retail		$ 50,000
Inventory at end of period at cost (50,000 × 60%)	$ 30,000	

Calculation of cost ratio:

$$\frac{150,000}{250,000} = 60\%$$

Using the retail method. The prime objective of the retail method in terms of inventory valuation is the reduction of the inventory to the lower of cost or market. This is properly effected when the sale of the inventory at prevailing prices will yield a gross profit percentage approximating the prevailing one. In order to illustrate the possible methods of achieving this result, and to compare the results of each method, the following facts are assumed:

1. Opening inventory at cost and at retail—None
2. Purchases:
   - at cost— $60,000
   - at retail— $100,000
3. Net mark-ups— $5,000
4. Net mark-downs— $10,000
5. Ending inventory at retail— $20,000

There are four possible methods of determining the gross profit percentage. These are:

1. Using both mark-ups and mark-downs.
2. Using mark-ups but not mark-downs.
3. Using mark-downs but not mark-ups.
4. Using neither mark-ups nor mark-downs.

The gross profit percentage, computed under each of the above methods, yields the following results when applied to the ending inventory of $20,000 at retail.

Method	*Cost Ratio*	*Final Inventory at cost*
1. Using both mark-ups and mark-downs.	63.16%	$12,632
2. Using mark-ups but not mark-downs.	57.14%	$11,428
3. Using mark-downs but not mark-ups.	66.67%	$13,334
4. Using neither mark-ups nor mark-downs.	60.00%	$12,000

The second method yields the lowest inventory valuation. This method presumably conforms most closely to the "lower-of-cost-or-market" rule for inventory valuation. Since mark-downs reflect a loss in utility caused by decreases in the retail price level due to general economic conditions, or for any similar reason, they are omitted from the determination of the gross profit percentage. Mark-ups of retail prices, on the other hand, are generally associated with upward price movements at the wholesale level. Including mark-ups in the determination of the gross profit percentage, therefore, serves to reduce the ending inventory to cost.

The retail inventory method and FIFO. Although the retail method is generally used to reduce the current inventory to the lower of cost or market, this method need not be limited to that particular concept of valuation. The retail method can also be used to obtain close approximations of average cost and FIFO cost. This discussion will be confined to the latter cost concept.

The basic feaure of FIFO valuation is that the inventory at the end is deemed to have come from the latest purchases made. Applying this to an inventory stated at retail prices requires that the traditional retail method be modified so that (1) the cost ratio applied to the inventory at retail will yield a figure closely approximating cost, and (2) the cost ratio so applied will be as close as possible to the actual cost ratio prevailing at the close of a period.

The first requirement can be accomplished by using both mark-ups and mark-downs in computing the cost ratio. If an opening inventory is involved, it too must be brought to a cost basis.

The second requirement means that the cost ratio must be so constructed as to be indicative of current trends between costs and selling prices. This can be accomplished by securing cost relationships at frequent intervals during the period and eliminating the opening inventory at both cost and retail from the computation of these relationships. Since department stores usually draw financial reports for management on the basis of a four week period, this requirement can be fulfilled rather easily. See Figure 6.

	Period 1		Period 2		Period 3		Period 4		Total	
	Cost	*Retail*	*Cost*	*Retail*	*Cost*	*Retail*	*Cost*	*Retail*	*Cost*	*Retail*
Purchases	$36,000	$60,000	$52,500	$ 75,000	$49,000	$ 70,000	$60,000	$ 90,000	$197,500	$295,000
Net mark-ups		15,000		5,000		10,000		15,000		45,000
Net mark-downs		(3,000)		0				(5,000)		(8,000)
Total	36,000	72,000	52,500	80,000	49,000	80,000	60,000	100,000	197,500	332,000
Inventory, beginning of period	0	0	10,000	20,000	19,686	30,000	12,250	20,000	0	0
Total value of goods available	36,000	72,000	62,500	100,000	68,686	110,000	72,250	120,000	197,500	332,000
Sales		52,000		70,000		90,000		80,000		292,000
Inventory end of period at retail		20,000		30,000		20,000		40,000		40,000
Cost ratio *	50%		65.62%		61.25%		60%		59.49%	
Inventory end of period at cost	10,000		19,686		12,250		24,000		23,796	

* Cost ratio computations:

$\frac{\text{Total cost}}{\text{Total retail}}$ $\frac{36,000}{72,000} = 50\%$ $\frac{52,500}{80,000} = 65.62\%$ $\frac{49,000}{80,000} = 61.25\%$ $\frac{60,000}{100,000} = 60\%$ $\frac{197,500}{332,000} = 59.49\%$

Fig. 6. Approximation of FIFO Basis by Retail Inventory Method.

The results obtained in Figure 6 show a small difference between the value of the ending inventory at the end of the fourth period and the same value computed on an overall basis for the entire period. This stems from calculating separate cost ratios for each period.

The retail method and LIFO. Our earlier discussion of LIFO centered about the pricing of individual items in the inventory. It was noted that records had to be kept of the LIFO cost of each item in the base year inventory so that the current inventory could be priced at the same unit cost. If subsequent inventories contained more units than the base year, these increases had to be related to LIFO costs in the year of acquisition.

In the retail method, however, specific items tend to lose their identity. Although physical inventories are taken, they are stated at retail prices. The question is how to reduce such an inventory stated at selling prices to a cost figure stated at LIFO.

To achieve this objective, three things must first be accomplished. These objectives are listed below, followed by a discussion of how they may be attained.

1. The ordinary use of the retail inventory method produces a valuation closely approximating the lower of cost or market. Since LIFO is a cost method, some means must be found of modifying the traditional retail method to produce results based on costs.

2. The opening inventory of the year chosen as the base must be reduced to a cost basis.

3. A procedure is required to eliminate the influence of rising prices from the inventory at retail. This should allow the inventory at adjusted retail to be reduced to a LIFO basis by the application of the proper cost percentage.

Modification of the retail method. The retail method can be modified to produce a valuation based on approximate cost by using mark-downs as well as mark-ups in determining the cost ratio. The rationale for this was covered in the section, *Using the retail method.*

Restatement of the base year inventory at cost. To illustrate how this is accomplished, assume that the XYZ Department Store, Inc. wishes to convert to a LIFO basis for the year 19X2 and thereafter. Their opening inventory, therefore, as of January 1, 19X2 must be stated on a cost basis. The following example indicates the methodology involved in accomplishing this:

XYZ DEPARTMENT STORE, INC.
REVISION OF INVENTORY AT DECEMBER 31, 19X1
Restatement of Final Inventory on Cost Basis

(Original Computation)

	Cost	*Retail*	*Cost Ratio*
Inventory, January 1	$ 90,000	$150,000	60%
Purchases—19X1	210,000	300,000	70%
Mark-ups		20,000	
Total	$300,000	$470,000	63.83%

	Cost	*Retail*
Mark-downs		40,000
Total value of goods available		$430,000
Sales		320,000
Ending Inventory December 31, 19X1 at retail		$110,000
Ending Inventory December 31, 19X1 at cost	$ 70,213	

The final inventory of $70,213 corresponds to a valuation approximating the lower of cost or market. In order to put the valuation on a cost basis the computation must be modified as follows:

	Cost	*Retail*	*Cost Ratio*
Purchases	$210,000	$300,000	
Net mark-ups		20,000	
Net mark-downs		(40,000)	
Final inventory December 31, 19X1	$210,000	$280,000	75%
at cost	$ 82,500	$110,000	

This example indicates that for the opening inventory to be stated at cost, the cost ratio has to be modified by taking into account mark-downs as well as mark-ups. In addition, since the opening inventory at January 1, 19X1 is presumed to be stated at the lower of cost or market, it is also necessary to remove that figure from the computation. The net result is that the base inventory is restated at cost without being influenced by any other method of inventory valuation. Since increments in the final inventory are priced at a cost deemed to have been incurred in the years in which they arose, the omission of the opening inventory in calculating the cost ratio for any one year is a characteristic feature of this method as well as the FIFO method.

Changes in price levels. The previous discussion of LIFO illustrated the general method to be followed in pricing increments to the inventory in subsequent periods. Generally speaking, this involved no special difficulties provided that adequate records were kept by years of the costs of particular items. The key point was that by using *incremental units,* the inventory could always be valued on a LIFO basis.

The reduction of department store inventories stated at retail to a LIFO basis, however, cannot be done on the basis of incremental units. This objective can only be achieved through the application of *incremental dollars.* However, it must be understood that selling prices (dollars) are the result of the general price level and, as such, are influenced by many factors in our free enterprise economy. To reduce an inventory stated at retail to a cost figure by the application of a cost ratio, as has been illustrated, is not enough for our purpose. We must first reduce this inventory at retail to the base period level by eliminating the effects of general price increases.

The general method of accomplishing this is through the use of an index that measures the relative price change in a particular commodity (price index) with a given period used as a base.

► NOTE: Although the construction and use of index numbers is beyond the scope of this chapter, the necessary competence for making index numbers can be secured by reading any good book on business statistics.

The technique for making use of index numbers is quite simple. The ending inventory at retail is first reduced by the application of the appropriate index number. The resulting figure represents the retail value of the present inventory stated at base year prices. If the value thus derived is greater than the base inventory, the value of the base is removed from the total inventory. The balance, at retail, represents the incremental amount stated at base year prices. These are reconverted to current year retail prices by again applying the index number. To this is applied the cost percentage for the current year.

Figure 7 is an illustration of this technique. The data used to illustrate the revision of inventory of the XYZ Department Store, Inc. at December 31, Year 1 are continued through Year 5.

	Year 2	*Year 3*	*Year 4*	*Year 5*
Index number (Year 1 = 100)	104	107	110	114
Opening inventory at retail	110,000	130,000	144,450	159,500
Opening inventory at lifo cost	70,213	80,743	87,698	95,260.50
Cost ratio (purchases, mark-ups & mark-downs)	67.5%	65%	68.75%	70%
Final inventory at retail	130,000	144,450	159,500	136,800
Final inventory at lifo cost	80,743	87,698	95,260.50	77,168

REDUCTION OF FINAL INVENTORY TO LIFO COST

	Cost	*Retail*
Year 2		
Year 2 retail inventory at Year 1 prices (130,000 ÷ 104)		125,000
Year 1 base inventory	70,213	110,000
Year 2 increment at Year 1 prices		15,000
Year 2 increment at Year 2 prices (15,000 × 1.04)		15,600
Year 2 increment at lifo cost (15,600 × .675)	10,530	
Year 2 inventory at lifo cost	80,743	
Year 3		
Year 3 inventory at Year 1 prices (144,450 ÷ 107)		135,000
Year 1 base inventory	70,213	110,000
Increment		25,000
Year 2 increment	10,530	15,000
Year 3 increment at Year 1 prices		10,000
Year 3 increment at Year 3 prices (10,000 × 1.07)		10,700
Year 3 increment at lifo cost (10,700 × .65)	6,955	
Year 3 total inventory at lifo cost	87,698	

Fig. 7. Reduction of Final Inventories at Retail to LIFO Basis.

Year 4

Year 4 retail inventory at Year 1 prices (159,500 ÷ 110)		145,000
Year 1 base inventory	70,213	110,000
Total increment		35,000
Year 2 increment	10,530	15,000
		20,000
Year 3 increment	6,955	10,000
Year 4 increment at Year 1 prices		10,000
Year 4 increment at Year 4 prices (10,000 × 1.10)		11,000
Year 4 increment at lifo cost (11,000 × 68.75%)	7,562.50	
Total lifo cost	95,260.50	

Year 5

Year 5 retail inventory at Year 1 prices (136,800 ÷ 114)		120,000
Year 1 base inventory	70,213	110,000
Total increment at Year 1 retail prices. Increment deemed to have arisen in Year 2		10,000
Year 2 increment at Year 2 retail prices (10,000 × 1.04)		10,400
Year 2 increment at Year 2 lifo cost (10,400 × 65%)	6,760	
Total Year 5 inventory at lifo cost	76,973	

Fig. 7. Reduction of Final Inventories at Retail to LIFO Basis. (Continued.)

OTHER INVENTORY PROBLEMS

The following special problems connected with inventory and inventory valuation will be discussed in this section:

1. The gross profit method of inventory valuation.
2. Long-term construction contracts.
3. The valuation of consigned goods.
4. Computing unit costs of equivalent units.

The gross profit method. The essence of the gross profit method is that it utilizes past percentage relationships between the cost of goods sold and sales to estimate the value of a current inventory. The precision of this technique is enhanced if the percentage relationships have been built up over a long period of time and if they have been reasonably stable.

Assuming that a particular company has consistently maintained a gross profit percentage of 35%, the ending inventory can be estimated if the following additional information is available:

1. Inventory at the beginning of the period.
2. Purchases for the period plus any inventoriable costs, such as freight in.
3. Sales for the period.

For illustrative purposes, assume that these items amount to $30,000, $100,000, and $150,000, respectively. Based on this information, the estimated value of the ending inventory would be $32,500, computed as follows:

Inventory, beginning of period		$ 30,000
Cost of purchases for period		100,000
Total cost of goods available for sale		$130,000
Sales for period	$150,000	
Gross profit at 35%	52,500	
Estimated cost of goods sold		97,500
Estimated value of inventory on hand at end of period		$ 32,500

This method of estimating the value of the ending inventory is more complicated if the company sells more than one product, and these products have differing gross profit relationships. In such a case, the past gross profit percentages, the beginning inventories, and the purchases and sales for the period would be required for each product or group of products. Although a composite gross profit rate for the company as a whole is sometimes feasible, the reliability of such a rate would be dependent on the steadiness of the "product mix." It is safer not to use composite rates if other information is available.

The gross profit method of inventory valuation can be used to verify an existing inventory or to estimate a nonexistent inventory. For instance, an insurance claim for merchandise destroyed by fire can be prepared from information contained in the general ledger. Even if the company sells more than one product, a reasonable estimate of the value of the destroyed merchandise can be arrived at by means of a statistical sampling of both sales and costs to determine a composite gross profit rate.

Another common use of the gross profit method is to verify the reasonableness of an ending inventory. For example, suppose the physical inventory submitted by the company to its auditor (in the illustrative example) amounted to $40,000, instead of $32,500 as estimated by the gross profit method. This may indicate several things to the auditor. There might be mistakes in the inventory or else the company is actually working on a 40% gross profit ratio. In either case, the auditor would certainly investigate further.

Long-term construction contracts. Organizations engaged in constructing bridges, buildings, etc., whose completion will take place in subsequent periods, have the problem of what to do with the costs of incomplete projects at the end of any fiscal period. In general, accounting theory recognizes two methods of handling these costs—(1) the completed-contract method in which no income is taken up until the contract is completed; (2) the percentage-of-completion method in which income is taken up as the work progresses.

The completed-contract method. In this method, the accumulated construction costs are shown as a current asset, and progress billings are deducted therefrom. The classification of these costs as "current" is based on the theory that the "normal" operating cycle of this type of organization is greater than one year. This approach is similar to that allowed installment dealers, who are permitted to classify their installment receivables as "current," despite the fact that a large percentage of their receivables have a maturity date extending beyond the usual one year period for classification as a current asset.

In addition to inventorying actual construction costs in the balance sheet, some accounting writers feel that, in this case, it might be proper to inventory administrative overhead. They theorize that, by so doing, a better matching of income and expenses would occur, especially for those years in which no contracts were completed. But, by reasoning on this basis, a very good case could be made for inventorying not only administrative overhead but also selling costs, particularly for new organizations. The argument is that not to do so would cause a mismatching of costs and revenues in future years and, also, that the doctrine of consistency would require future inventories to include these costs.

The percentage-of-completion method. If this method is adopted, the current asset section of the balance sheet will show not only accumulated construction costs, but also a portion of the anticipated profit on the contract. The amount of profit capitalized in inventory is based upon the ratio of incurred costs to total anticipated costs this ratio being applied to the entire anticipated profit. The following computation illustrates these principles:

Contract price of project	$250,000
Less: Estimated total cost	200,000
Anticipated profit on contract	$ 50,000
Costs incurred to date	$150,000
Portion of estimated profit earned to date: 150,000/200,000 of $50,000	$ 37,500

Actual costs may prove to be higher than the original cost estimate. This can result in the profit either being turned into a loss or, at best, being lower than was anticipated. If this occurs, the reported income of prior periods will prove to have been distorted.

In another case, unexpected costs may arise so that it is known that not only will there be no profit, but that a loss will occur. In this case, current provisions can and should be made for the full amount of the loss.

► WARNING: Under the percentage-of-completion method, profits should be accrued only if:

1. Costs at each stage are within estimates, and
2. Construction progress is according to the planned schedule.

Cost-plus contracts. Cost-plus contracts are of the same general nature as long-term construction contracts. In fact, some construction contracts are based on the principles of cost-plus, particularly where costs cannot be estimated with any degree of reasonableness because of the nature of the service or work. In general, therefore, this type of contract should be treated as merely one type of long-term construction contract.

The main distinction between cost-plus and other long-term construction contracts lies in the fact that under the former an assured amount of income is earned by the contractor. There is usually no risk in reporting this income as a job progresses. The contractor can expect to be reimbursed for all his costs (provided they are reasonable and comply with the contract) and, in addition, he can accrue his profit based on the contract.

Consigned merchandise. Merchandise consigned for sale is always the property of the consignor. The problem of valuing consigned merchandise, one frequently mentioned in textbooks, centers about what costs to include. Some writers feel that it is quite proper to include any applicable expenses along with the cost of goods. Freight charges paid on consigned goods, for example, are considered properly capitalizable to the extent of the remaining goods in the possession of the consignee. Advertising costs, on the other hand, are not considered to be costs that are properly capitalizable in inventory even though incurred on the same goods.

In general, the same principles of valuation apply to consigned goods as to other merchandise. If a considerable amount of inventory is on consignment, it should usually be shown in the balance sheet as a separate item. The reason for this is that such goods are likely to be realized more slowly than goods on hand.

Equivalent units. In order to value work in process, the total costs of production have to be allocated between completed units and units in the ending inventory of work in process. In process cost systems, this allocation may be easiest to make when the entire production (units transferred to the next process or finished goods, and units being worked on at the end of the period) is stated in terms or equivalent finished units.

One of the factors to be considered in computing unit costs for equivalent units is that direct materials are often added to the product at the start of a manufacturing process instead of uniformly throughout the process. In such case, the question of equivalencies may have to be handled separately for direct materials, direct labor, and manufacturing overhead. Figure 8 is an illustration of the use of equivalent finished units to value an ending inventory.

ABSORPTION COSTING VS. DIRECT COSTING

In order to deal properly with absorption costing and direct costing as cost bases for inventory valuation, it is important that they be discussed jointly. Only by doing so can their essential differences be highlighted.

The way in which factory overhead is defined and applied in manufacturing industries has a significant effect on inventory valuation. Since the use of direct or absorption costing involves a different treatment of cost classifications involving overhead, these costs and cost classifications will be analyzed.

The nature of production costs. Accountants have long been familiar with the fact that production costs have a hybrid nature. Costs such as direct material

THE XYZ MANUFACTURING CO., INC.
FOR THE YEAR ENDED DECEMBER 31, 19__

PRODUCTION AND INVENTORY STATISTICS

Work in process units:	
Beginning of period	0
End of period:	
100% complete as to material and	
50% complete as to labor and overhead	200
Finished goods units:	
Beginning inventory	0
Ending inventory	400
Transferred from work in process	2,300
Costs:	
Material	$ 5,000
Labor	7,200
Overhead	4,800
Total manufacturing costs	$17,000

CALCULATION OF UNIT COSTS

Quantity:	
Units started in production	2,500
Completed and transferred	2,300
Remaining in process (100% material, 50% labor and expenses)	200

Costs charged to production:

	Equivalent Units	*Total Cost*	*Unit Cost*
Material	2,500	$ 5,000	$ 2
Labor	2,400	7,200	3
Overhead	2,400	4,800	2
Total cost to be accounted for		$17,000	$ 7

Fig. 8. Using Equivalent Units for Purposes of Inventory Valuation.

and direct labor seem to vary in total with the level of production, while others do not vary at all but remain fixed over almost the entire range of output. Other production costs fall between these extremes. While they change according to the output level, they do not appear to do so according to any regular or predetermined pattern. These three types of costs are called "variable," "fixed," and "semi-variable," respectively.

The usefulness of this classification of production costs is not the subject of this chapter. The reader who desires further information on this subject can find it in Chapter 9 of this volume entitled, *Production Cost Accounting.*

THE XYZ MANUFACTURING CO., INC.—(Continued)
FOR THE YEAR ENDED DECEMBER 31, 19__

COSTS ACCOUNTED FOR AS FOLLOWS		
Completed and transferred (2,300 units × $7)		$16,100
In process inventory at end of period:		
Materials (200 units × $2)	$ 400	
Labor (200 × ½ × $3)	300	
Mfg. Expenses (200 × ½ × $2)	200	
Value of work in process inventory		900
Total costs accounted for		$17,000
VALUE OF FINAL INVENTORIES AT DECEMBER 31, 19__		
Work in process (as above)		$ 900
Finished goods (400 units × $7)		2,800
Total		$ 3,700

Fig. 8. Using Equivalent Units for Purposes of Inventory Valuation. (Continued.)

Here, it is only intended to show how this classification is used in absorption and direct costing for inventory valuation purposes.

Absorption costing. The concept of absorption costing is a relatively simple one: all production costs—no matter how they behave—are allocated to the units produced during the period.

In a job order system the allocation of all material and labor to the job is made directly. Manufacturing overhead is generally allocated to each job on some predetermined basis.

In a process cost system all costs, including manufacturing overhead, are charged to the departments incurring them. To obtain a unit cost for valuation purposes, all that is required is to divide the total costs of production for the period by the number of units produced during that period, and to apply the unit cost so derived to the remaining inventory.

In both these systems, the emphasis on the inclusion of all manufacturing costs sometimes leads to curious results. For illustrative purposes, assume the following facts:

Variable costs per unit:		
Material	$ 4.00	
Direct labor	10.00	
Manufacturing overhead	2.00	
Total variable costs per unit		$ 16.00
Fixed manufacturing overhead per period		$10,000.00
Units in inventory at end of period		500

Under absorption costing, the valuation of the 500 units remaining in inventory at the end of the period varies with the level of production as follows:

	Output level		
Cost incurred:	*2000 units*	*3000 units*	*4000 units*
Material	$ 8,000	$12,000	$16,000
Labor	20,000	30,000	40,000
Manufacturing overhead:			
Variable	4,000	6,000	8,000
Fixed	10,000	10,000	10,000
Total cost of production	$42,000	$58,000	$74,000
Unit cost of production	$ 21.00	$ 19.33	$ 18.50
Units in ending inventory	500	500	500
Value of ending inventory	$10,500	$ 9,665	$ 9,250

In attempting to answer the inevitable question, "Which of those inventory computations is right?" one must also ask, "Are any of them right?" These questions cannot be answered in terms of a mechanical computation. The answer must be a value judgment to be made by the individual accountant on the basis of all available evidence.

Critics of absorption costing claim that since profits ultimately depend on sales made during the period, a company cannot recover any costs until goods have been sold. It follows that the results achieved by absorption costing are unrealistic since period costs (fixed) of production are capitalized as inventory values.

Another example of this is illustrated by the following facts:

	Periods			
	(1)	*(2)*	*(3)*	*(4)*
Units produced	2,000	4,000	1,000	2,000
Units sold	1,500	1,500	3,000	3,000
Inventory—beginning of period	0	500	3,000	1,000
Inventory—end of period	500	3,000	1,000	0
Units normally produced	2,000	2,000	2,000	2,000
Variable standard cost of production per unit	$10	$10	$10	$10
Fixed standard cost of production per unit (based on 2,000 units per period [$4,000])	$ 2	$ 2	$ 2	$ 2

In addition to the above facts, assume a selling price of $20 per unit, and selling and general administrative costs of $2,000 per period. On the basis of these facts, the traditional profit and loss statement would show the following:

	Periods			
	(1)	*(2)*	*(3)*	*(4)*
Sales	$30,000	$30,000	$60,000	$60,000
Cost of goods sold:				
Inventory—beginning of period at standard costs	$ 0	$ 6,000	$36,000	$12,000
Standard cost of good manufactured	24,000	48,000	12,000	24,000
Total	$24,000	$54,000	$48,000	$36,000
Less: Ending inventory at standard	6,000	36,000	12,000	0
Standard cost of goods sold	$18,000	$18,000	$36,000	$36,000

Gross profit at standard	$12,000	$12,000	$24,000	$24,000
Deductions: Variances from standard	$ 0	$(4,000)	$ 2,000	$ 0
Operating expenses	2,000	2,000	2,000	2,000
Total deductions	$ 2,000	$(2,000)	$ 4,000	$ 2,000
Net Profit	$10,000	$14,000	$20,000	$22,000

During periods 1 and 2, sales were the same yet profit increased by $4,000. Between period 2 and 3, sales doubled yet profit went up to only $6,000. Finally, sales were at the same level between periods 3 and 4, but profit increased by $2,000.

It appears, therefore, that absorption costing should be approached with care, and that it reflects proper costs best in those industries that are characterized by a high degree of productive stability or where the investment in plant and equipment is relatively low as compared to the output.

Direct costing. The discussion of absorption costing indicates that as production falls the unit cost of the item increases. Conversely, as production increases the unit cost of the item decreases. The underlying reason for this is that certain costs of production continue whether the company is producing at maximum or minimum capacity.

The concept of direct costing in its simplest form is that the fixed costs of production are not treated as inventory values to be assigned to the units remaining at the end of the period. Rather, these fixed costs are completely written off to operations in the period in which they are incurred. The distinction is between "period costs" and "product costs," or, as some writers say, between "sales-made costs" and "management-made costs." For purposes of inventory valuation, the costs that are inventoried are those that vary in total with the number of units produced. This would include, therefore, only the cost of direct materials and direct labor, plus any variable portion of manufacturing overhead. All others (management-made costs) would be charged off to operations in the period incurred (period costs).

Under the concept of direct costing, the $4,000 of fixed manufacturing overhead per period of the XYZ Manufacturing Co., Inc. would be written off to operations during the period instead of being capitalized in inventory. The inventory at the end of any period, therefore, would be valued at $10.00 per unit representing the variable standard cost of production. As a result the profit and loss statement for the four periods shows results that are based on the level of sales achieved and not on the level of production.

To arrive at a "direct unit cost of production," all production costs are separated into fixed and variable categories. When these categories are extended to cover all operating expenses, relationships are derived that are useful to management. Data derived from such relationships have their greatest value when used in making cost-volume-profit studies for decision-making and managerial control. The same information also contributes to the use of break-even analysis and flexible budgeting.

XYZ MANUFACTURING CO., INC.

Direct Costing Profit and Loss Statement[1]

	Periods			
	(1)	*(2)*	*(3)*	*(4)*
Sales	$30,000	$30,000	$60,000	$60,000
Variable cost of goods sold:				
Inventory at beginning at standard	$ 0	$ 5,000	$30,000	$10,000
Variable costs of production at standard	20,000	40,000	10,000	20,000
Total	$20,000	$45,000	$40,000	$30,000
Inventory at end of period at standard	5,000	30,000	10,000	0
Variable standard cost of goods sold	$15,000	$15,000	$30,000	$30,000
Marginal income	$15,000	$15,000	$30,000	$30,000
Fixed Expenses				
Manufacturing overhead	$ 4,000	$ 4,000	$ 4,000	$ 4,000
Selling and administrative expenses	2,000	2,000	2,000	2,000
Total fixed expenses	$ 6,000	$ 6,000	$ 6,000	$ 6,000
Net Profit	$ 9,000	$ 9,000	$24,000	$24,000

[1]It is assumed that there are no variances for either labor, materials, or variable manufacturing overhead.

It is obvious that a prime requisite in utilizing direct costing is some knowledge of the behavior of production costs so that a breakdown can be made of those costs that actually do vary with the level of production. Direct labor and direct material costs are not much of a problem, although these costs are not always as "direct" as theory would have them. The chief problem lies with the breakdown of production overhead into fixed and variable classifications.

If all production costs are analyzed over their entire range, it may be observed that almost no costs are precisely uniform. Still, for direct costing purposes, a subjective analysis is made as a result of which all expenses are segregated into the fixed or variable category. In making this kind of separation into categories, direct cost adherents are really making estimates, just as much as absorption cost adherents make estimates.

Demonstrably, certain fixed expenses can be charged against a particular order instead of against the period; for example, the purchase of a special machine to manufacture a unique product for a customer would apply to a particular order. In addition, there are fixed expenses that are readily identifiable with product lines, even though they may not be chargeable to a specific customer's order—a manufacturing facility devoted solely to the manufacture of air conditioners can certainly be identified costwise with the end product.

But the chief objection to direct costing from the viewpoint of the accounting profession is that this concept of inventory valuation ignores an important fact. In our modern economy, it is precisely those assets that make possible the satisfaction of consumer wants, namely plant and equipment, that are omitted from the inventory valuation of such goods. Plant and equipment are facilities that are used to create values, not to reduce profits.

The direct cost adherents, in effect, deny the full implications of the accrual concept of income so laboriously developed over the past century to properly match income and expense. The fact that a proper matching of cost is difficult to accomplish is no reason to abandon it entirely. The profession has met and solved challenging problems before this. If some methods of handling overhead costs result in high unit costs in periods of low output, and low unit costs in periods of high output, then some method of cost "normalization" seems to be called for. Or, it could mean that a year is not a long enough period over which to determine the burden rate.

Furthermore, the industrial scene is a rapidly changing one, and what is considered good accounting theory today may have little or no applicability tomorrow. Production in the future may be carried on by machines, not men. Automation appears to be the key to our industrial future. Automation means *high fixed* costs for plant and equipment, not only in terms of depreciation rates, but also in terms of obsolescence. It means less and less direct labor as the character of the work force changes from machine operators to machine tenders. With automation, the need for more preventive maintenance programs to avert machine breakdowns will create larger maintenance departments. Our only variable in the future may be the cost of the material itself. If the direct cost concept is applied under these conditions, all other costs would become period costs to be written off during the period and not as the goods are sold.

Finally, direct costing is most inapplicable for interim statements of seasonal industries where production is spread out in order to avoid the headaches and increased costs of last minute bottlenecks. Although these enterprises generally produce for stock over a long period of time, their selling season may actually be concentrated over a period of not more than two months during the year. Under direct costing, interim statements of these businesses would be penalized in a period when production is high and sales are low. During the relatively short selling period, such businesses would reap a real windfall.

It should be repeated, however, in all fairness to the advocates of direct costing, that the concept has value in the uses to which it can be put for internal management purposes.

SPECIAL COST PROBLEMS

Although all business enterprises that deal with goods, as distinguished from services, have inventory valuation problems, these problems are not the same in any two industries, or even in any two companies. The special cost problems of some industries will be discussed in this section. Also, the use of standard costs as a method of pricing inventories will be explained. (This section should be read in conjunction with Chapter 9, *Production Cost Accounting.*)

Wholesale and retail establishments. Wholesale and retail establishments are primarily concerned with the movement of goods after they have been manufactured. For this reason, the problems of inventory valuation confronting the accountant are considerably reduced. The generally accepted valuation principle is that goods are valued at cost plus the expense incurred in bringing them into the establishment. This statement implies that the goods will be sold in the same condition as they were received.

There are distributors, however, and sometimes even retailers, who further process the goods before offering them for sale. To the extent that this is done in any establishment, an additional amount has been added to the cost of these goods.

► EXAMPLE: A distributor may purchase yarns and knitting needles from various sources, and put them into a kit for sale to housewives. The cost of this kit consists of (1) the cost of the components, (2) the cost of the package, and (3) labor and overhead cost incidental to the packaging.

This example holds true for any retailer who engages in a similar operation. In this type of activity, the components of these kits are "raw materials" that require further processing before they can be marketed.

For the most part, however, the problems of inventory valuation for distributing and retail establishments are rather simple. The basis of valuation is generally cost or market, which ever is lower. As the size of these establishments increase, a greater number of them are adopting the LIFO method of pricing as applied to the retail method, which has been explained.

Natural resource industries. The extractive industries have a peculiar inventory valuation problem in that most of them are dealing with a wasting asset. If the mine, the well, or the forest, are exhausted, the activities of the company must be terminated, at least in this area. Conventional theory dictates that the depletion allowance be handled in the same way as the depreciation allowance is used for valuing inventories in the case of a manufacturing company. (See Chapter 6 for a detailed discussion of depletion.) This is not an entirely satisfactory method because the amount of ore that can be extracted from a mine, or the barrels of oil from a well, are not always subject to precise measurement. Therefore, accounting theory permits an alternative practice in this area—inventory may be valued on the basis of selling price less any additional expenses incurred in subsequent processing or marketing, and less a reasonable profit margin. This use of selling price is particularly sanctioned for precious metals that have a fixed monetary value and immediate marketability at that value.

The same principle is used, or can be used, to place a valuation on the inventory of crops in the hands of farmers. Climatic conditions play such an important part in the amount of crops that a farmer may secure from his land that, were the cost basis to be strictly applied, this method might actually result in distorting income from one year to the next.

The manufacturing industry. The very nature of the manufacturing process itself—the conversion of raw material into finished goods through the application of labor, machines, etc.—automatically creates the distinct inventory categories of raw materials, work in process, and finished goods.

Valuing work in process. The chief characteristic of work in process inventory is that there are items in various stages of production throughout the premises (unless, of course, all work in process has been completed prior to the physical inventory). At this intermediate point in the production cycle, other costs have been added to the cost of raw materials. These added costs include direct labor, and manufacturing overhead allocated to the individual items on some predetermined or historical basis, depending on the stage of completion of the individual units. By its very nature, the valuation of work in process inventories offers more complications than the valuation of either raw materials or finished goods inventories.

It might appear that the most fundamental requisite in the pricing of work in process is a good cost accounting system tied in with the general books of account, or, at the very least, maintained outside them on some sound and consistent basis. (For a detailed discussion of cost accounting principles and practices the reader is referred to Chapter 9, *Production Cost Accounting.*) Practically speaking, the problem of valuing inventories is compounded when there are not even the rudiments of a cost system in existence. Therefore, the problems encountered in valuing work in process in a manufacturing industry are different:

1. Without a cost system.
2. With a cost system.

1. *Without a cost system.* Without a cost system the accountant must rely chiefly upon the owners of a business to tell him not only the price of work in process but also their stage of completion. The most that the accountant can do in such a situation is to make as careful an evaluation as he can of the information given him by management. His ingenuity in devising tests of the inventories will play an important part in his evaluation of them. While this is not theoretically acceptable, it is sometimes the best that an accountant can do.

► EXAMPLE: Many firms in the radio and television industry do not maintain cost records as part of their regular accounting system or outside of it. Nevertheless, the valuation of work in process of such firms can be tested. The cost of materials for each chassis model can be determined by making use of the production bill of materials that lists the order in which these materials or component parts are wired into the set. Materials used in subassemblies are usually also listed separately. From these production bills of material it is possible to know the material costs for each position on the assembly line.

The direct labor in the work in process inventory can also be easily determined by comparing management's production figures for each assembly line with payroll records that show the actual labor costs for employees on that line. Computing the average labor time required to move one set through the production process is, then, just a matter of simple arithmetic.

The chief point of this example is that the lack of a good cost accounting system is not an insurmountable obstacle if the problem is approached with a little ingenuity and the application of common sense. The basic requirements for valuation of work in process inventories without a cost system are that the accountant have a thorough grasp of the flow of costs through the manufacturing process, that he decide which elements enter into the costs of production, and that he investigate all possible sources of information to achieve his objective.

2. *With a cost system.* The problem of pricing a work in process inventory is obviously simplified if the cost records disclose the necessary information. In a company that maintains a job order cost-system, direct material and labor will normally be allocated to each job in the usual recording process. All that remains, theoretically, is for the accountant to apply the burden or overhead percentage. If the accountant has satisfied himself that these jobs are actually in process, the valuation process should be complete. Practically speaking, however, this does not quite finish the accountant's job.

Keeping in mind the concept of ultimate utility, in terms of realizing a normal profit on the sale of the goods being manufactured, it is apparent that the job order must also be examined from this point of view. This can be done by equating the projected cost of the product with its anticipated selling price.

Suppose it is found, for example, that costs that will never be realized have been charged into the job. In such a case, the full cost of the job is meaningless for valuation purposes, or even as a basis of comparison with production jobs for the same item in the future. What can the accountant do when confronted with such a situation? The best that he can do is to insist that management remove these extraordinary charges from the cost records and charge them off to current operations.

This situation illustrates the necessity for the accountant to exercise his independent judgment. Even with an excellent cost system, the judgment of the accountant cannot often be bypassed in favor of some mechanical means of arriving at a valuation.

Valuing finished goods. The problems involved in inventory valuation of finished goods in manufacturing concerns are essentially the same as those that confront the accountant in pricing work in process. The same common-sense approach used in valuing the latter will generally serve as a good basis for valuing the former. Again, a good cost accounting system is not a prerequisite for pricing purposes. If it were, it is obvious that many accountants would not be able to function properly in this area.

The moment management commits raw materials, labor, and production overhead to the manufacturing process, it is gambling that the finished article will be sold; moreover, that it will be sold at a price that yields a predetermined profit margin, in most cases. If the goods must be sold considerably below that price, then the utility of those inventory items has been lost. Having lost the gamble, management must suffer the consequences of its past decision. The inventory must now be written down to the point where the usual profit margin will be realized.

It would seem from the viewpoint of flexibility that the most valuable portion of an inventory in the hands of manufacturers is the raw materials inventory. Raw materials by their very nature can be made into a variety of goods, and if one item does not sell, the others may. This is generally true, and credit grantors are particularly interested in a breakdown of the total inventory for this very reason.

Standard costs. Although the subject of standard costs is covered in Chapter 10, it will be mentioned briefly here insofar as it pertains to inventory valuation. Since predetermined standards can be prepared for any or all costs, they may be employed in either an absorption cost system or a direct cost system.

The use of predetermined standards as a method of pricing inventories is subject to the qualification that the standards be adjusted at reasonable intervals to reflect actual current costs for work in process and finished goods. In the case of raw materials, the prevailing practice is to price this portion of the inventory at actual costs determined on the FIFO, LIFO, or some other basis.

The main problem in pricing inventories at standard concerns the disposition of the variance accounts. Some accountants believe that variances should be allocated between the standard costs of goods sold and the various inventories. Others, however, feel that such allowances should be charged to production in the period they occur.

If variances are written off to operations in the period in which they occur, we are valuing inventories at their standard costs. If variances are prorated to their respective inventories, we are, in effect, using pure absorption costing. It is obvious that in this area, as in others, the chief ingredient is still the personal judgment of the accountant. There are no hard and fast rules, only guides to the theory to be followed.

The use of standard costs for inventory pricing purposes has one marked advantage over other pricing methods. It automatically eliminates excessive costs due to low volume or unusually low costs due to an unexpectedly high volume.

SUMMARY

Like a thread weaving in and out of this chapter has been the thought that the judgment of the accountant facing an inventory valuation problem is of paramount importance. To him and on him falls the burden of making the decision as to which of the alternative methods presented herein he shall use for a particular client. It is his burden to defend that decision, if need be, with a well-reasoned and logical presentation of the peculiar circumstances that cause him to select one method above all others. Only in one other area of accounting theory, fixed assets and depreciation accounting, is the practitioner called upon to exercise as much judgment as in inventory valuation. As has been pointed out before, there are no hard and fast rules in inventory valuation; there are only guideposts.

8

Other Techniques of Financial Accounting

CONTENTS

8

Other Techniques of Financial Accounting

P-H Editorial Staff,
J. K. Pescow, CPA, Editor

The following subjects are considered in this chapter:

1. Home office and branch accounting.
2. Consignments.
3. Installment sales.
4. Principles of amortization—bond discount, expense, premium.
5. Choosing the form of business organization.
6. The Professional Corporation
7. Choosing a business year.
8. Financial statement analysis.

HOME OFFICE AND BRANCH ACCOUNTING

It is fairly common for companies to extend their sales organization into territories far removed from the home office. This is normally accomplished through the establishment of either branches or agencies. The operational set-up of the selling units—that is, whether they are under a branch system or an agency system—will dictate the basic accounting procedures to be followed. Thus, a branch that carries merchandise, makes its own collections, and pays its own expenses, must keep a complete set of books. On the other hand, an agency that carries a line of samples and operates by means of a working fund provided by the home office, needs only a cash book.

Therefore, accounting under an agency system is a relatively simple matter —the agency records the amounts it receives from the home office and the disbursements it makes. Usually, the disbursement record is kept in duplicate, so that one copy can be sent to the home office as a basis for a request to replenish the working fund. The home office records sales and expenses for the agency; if desired, the cost of agency sales is determined so that agency net income may be segregated.

Under a true branch system, where a complete set of books must be maintained by the branch, the accounting procedures are naturally more complex. We will discuss these procedures, under the following headings:

1. Methods of billing.
2. Combining the accounts.
3. Accounting for freight.
4. Recording fixed assets.

► OBSERVATION: Apart from the true branch, there are various modifications, depending on the degree of control exercised by the home office. Basically, the question is whether control is centralized or decentralized. In the former instance, the branch might operate under what is almost an agency system, except that more detailed and more frequent reports would be required by the home office; sometimes, however, the branch will keep certain subsidiary records while the home office maintains the principal records. When control is decentralized, a complete set of books is kept by the branch, as described in the following discussion.

Methods of billing. The method of billing by the home office for shipments to the branch influences the entries on the home office books. In any case, the branch will debit Shipments from Home Office and credit Home Office Current for the amount at which it is billed by the home office. If the home office bills at cost, the entry on the home office books will be a debit to Branch Current and a credit to Shipments to Branch. However, when the home office bills at either the selling price or a value between cost and selling price, the total amount is debited to Branch Current with the contra entry broken down between Shipments to Branch—Cost, and Shipments to Branch—Loading.

► EXAMPLE: Assume that the home office: (1) bills a shipment to its branch at $750, which represents the cost of the merchandise; (2) bills a shipment costing the same amount at $800, which could represent either the selling price of the merchandise or a value between cost and selling price. The entries would be:

(1)	*Branch books:*	Shipments from Home Office	750	
		Home Office Current		750
	Home office books:	Branch Current	750	
		Shipments to Branch		750
(2)	*Branch books:*	Shipments from Home Office	800	
		Home Office Current		800
	Home office books:	Branch Current	800	
		Shipments to Branch—Cost		750
		Shipments to Branch—Loading		50

Obviously, billing at cost results in the easiest accounting method. But, if the home office bills at selling price, a perpetual inventory at selling price will automatically be carried on the branch books, furnishing a constant control on branch operations. This is basically the *retail method of inventory pricing,* described in Chapter 7.

The home office might bill at some value between cost and selling price for either of two reasons. In some cases, the value may be arbitrary, intended only to keep the branch manager "in the dark" concerning actual branch profit and loss. In other cases, it may be a carefully worked out value designed so that the branch books will present a picture of a self-contained operation. Thus, the branch would be billed at an amount comparable to what it would have to pay an outside source for the same sort of merchandise. The logic of this procedure is evident. The branch performs a selling function and can be best judged on the performance of this function if the picture of its operations is not colored by the effect of the company's ability as a producer.

Combining the accounts. The preparation of a combined statement for the home office and its branch or branches is a relatively simple procedure. The reciprocal accounts—that is, Branch Current against Home Office Current—should be eliminated. Of course, in practice these accounts will not always balance on the books because of cash or merchandise in transit, bookkeeping errors, or lack of information on the part of either the branch or the home office. Therefore, the accounts must be reconciled and the necessary adjustments made.

► NOTE: When there is more than one branch, there is a chance that merchandise will be shipped from one branch to another. However, interbranch accounts should not be carried. All interbranch transactions should be handled through the branches' Home Office Current accounts, and the home office should make the appropriate entries in the respective Branch Current accounts.

The accounts Shipments to Branch, and Shipments from Home Office should also be eliminated. When the home office bills at cost, there is no problem—the procedure is the same as for any ordinary reciprocal accounts. But if the branch is billed at selling price, or at an arbitrary value between cost and selling price, there is the question not only of eliminating Shipments to Branch—Cost, and Shipments to Branch—Loading, against Shipments from Home Office, but it is also necessary to adjust the inventory figure carried on the branch books, since it will include loading. Therefore, the cost of sales must be decreased by the amount of loading in the beginning inventory and increased by the amount of loading in the ending inventory; and the ending inventory on the balance sheet must also be adjusted to reflect cost. On the home office books, an account called Loading in Branch Inventory is set up, which is eliminated against Cost of Sales (Beginning Inventory) when the accounts are combined.

Accounting for freight. If goods are shipped directly from the home office to the branch, any freight may be recorded by the branch in the same manner as freight-in is normally recorded—that is, it may be included in inventory. But when the shipment is made from one branch to another, only the amount of freight that would have been paid if the goods had been sent directly from the home office should be included in the inventory of the branch receiving the goods. If there is any additional freight, it should be recorded as an expense on the home office books through the Interbranch Excess Freight account.

Recording fixed assets. Branch fixed assets are normally recorded on the home office books. If the home office purchases the fixed assets for the branch, no entry will appear on the branch books. If the branch purchases the fixed assets, the branch will debit Home Office Current and credit Cash, while the home office will pick up the fixed assets with a contra entry to Branch Current.

When branch fixed assets are recorded by the home office, the depreciation on these assets will be reflected on the home office books. Therefore, after taking up the branch net income as per the branch books, the home office should debit Branch Net Income or Loss, and credit Depreciation Expense for the depreciation applicable to branch fixed assets.

► COMMENT: Any other branch expenses carried on the home office books should be handled in the same manner as depreciation expense.

CONSIGNMENTS

Legally, a consignment is a mutual benefit bailment in which the bailor (consignor) authorizes the bailee (consignee) to sell merchandise and deduct a commission and expenses from the sales price. Since it is a mutual benefit bailment, the loss from destruction of consigned merchandise falls on the bailor, provided, of course, that reasonable care has been exercised by the bailee.

Accounting for consignments is governed by the legal relationships set forth above. Thus:

1. Unsold goods on consignment are included, at all times, in the inventory of the consignor.
2. Cash or accounts receivable from sales of consigned goods belong to the consignor, subject to the consignee's rights to his commission and reimbursement of expenses.

The key document in accounting for consignment is an *account sales*. This is a report, by the consignee, of his sales of the consignor's goods, and an accounting of his expenses and commission in connection with such sales. A typical account sales is shown below. (The data contained in Smith Company's account sales will also be used to illustrate entries on the books of the consignee and consignor.)

ACCOUNT SALES OF SMITH COMPANY

Consignor: Johnson Co.		Consigned goods: 20 bookcases
Sale of 20 bookcases		$1,000
Deductions:		
Freight	$150	
Commission—20%	200	350
Check for net proceeds		$ 650

Consignee's books. The account sales is prepared from the books of the consignee. The first entry a consignee makes is usually a memorandum entry upon receiving the consigned merchandise. Other entries, in journal entry form, follow:

(1)		
Consignment in—Johnson Co.	150	
Cash (or expense accounts)		150
To record freight on consigned merchandise.		
(2)		
Cash	1,000	
Consignment in—Johnson Co.		1,000
To record sale of 20 bookcases.		
(3)		
Consignment in—Johnson Co.	200	
Commissions earned		200
20% of selling price.		
(4)		
Consignment in—Johnson Co.	650	
Cash		650
Check in final settlement.		

When these entries have been posted, the consignment in account appears as follows:

Consignment in—Johnson Co.

Received 20 bookcases		Sales—20 bookcases	1,000
Freight	150		
Commission	200		
Final settlement	650		
	1,000		1,000

Consignor's books. In a similar manner, the consignor keeps a separate account for each consignment. Prior to receiving an account sales from the consignee, the consignor has recorded this data in connection with the consignment to Smith Co.

(1)		
Consignment out—Smith Co.	500	
Inventory (or consigned shipments)		500
To record shipment of 20 bookcase.		
(2)		
Consignment out—Smith Co.	40	
Cash (or expense accounts)		40
Trucking expense to railroad		
(3)		
Consignment out—Smith Co.	36	
Shipping department expense		36
Allocation of shipping department expense, per schedule		

When the consignor receives the account sales for the entire transaction, he records the additional data. The form of the entry depends on whether profits on consignments are kept separate from profits on regular sales. If management decides that bookkeeping separation of consignment profits and regular profits has no significance, the following entry is made:

Shipping department expense	36	
Cash	650	
Freight	190	
Selling commission	200	
Cost of sales (or consigned shipments)	500	
Consignment out—Smith Co.		576
Sales		1,000

If it is desired to keep consignment profits separate from profits on other sales, the following entry would be made in place of the preceding entry:

Cash	650	
Consignment out—Smith Co.		576
Consignment profits		74

When profits are kept separate there is a possibility that the cost of sales applicable to regular sales may be overstated. The following entry may, therefore, be required:

Consigned shipments	500	
Cost of sales		500

Account sales for portions of the consigned goods. A consignee frequently sends the consignor a remittance accompanied by his account sales for only a portion of the goods that have been consigned to him. From this sale of less than all the goods consigned to him, he may deduct expenses attributable to the entire shipment, not including his selling commission, of course. The consignor may treat these expenses as part of the inventory cost of goods on consignment.

INSTALLMENT SALES

An installment sale is basically an ordinary sale for longer than usual credit terms. Installment sales typically involve a small down payment and collection of the balance by a series of payments over a period of time.

Some companies treat installment sales in the same manner as ordinary sales by recording the full amount of revenue when the sale is made. The entire profit is thus considered to be realized in the same period as the sale. Installment payments that become uncollectible—a major problem due to the long credit terms—are taken care of by the usual method of providing for bad debt losses.

When the installment method of accounting is used, income is reported proportionately as installment payments are received. While this method is considered more conservative, its use is largely confined to situations where a clear tax advantage is apparent.

Accounting for installment sales. The accounting method for installment sales involves these special procedures:

1. Installment sales are recorded separately from other sales.
2. The gross profit on installment sales must be separately discernible from the gross profit on other sales.
3. The cash collected on installment accounts is segregated by the years in which the sales were made.
4. The deferred gross profit on each year's sales is set up separately. Each year's cash collections are separated into the years in which the original sales were made. The gross profit percentage of the year of sale is used to separate the cash collected for that year into amounts designated as return of cost and realized gross profit. The net amount of deferred gross profit remaining is carried over to each succeeding year until all of the installments receivable for a particular year have been collected.

In order to illustrate the accounting method for installment sales, assume the following:

A retailer sells appliances on terms of 5% down, the balance payable in installments. His gross profit on installment sales for the first two years of operation are as follows:

	1st Year	*2nd Year*
Installment sales	$10,000	$16,000
Cost	7,000	11,000
Gross profit	$ 3,000	$ 5,000

Cash collections of installments receivable for the two years are as follows:

1st year	$4,000
2nd year:	
On 1st year's sales	$5,000
On 2nd year's sales	$6,000

General entries in summary form to record this information are as follows:

1st Year

(1)

Installment accounts receivable	10,000	
Inventory		7,000
Deferred gross profit		3,000
To record the sale of appliances.		

(2)

Cash	500	
Installment accounts receivable		500
To record the cash down payments received.		

(3)

Cash	4,000	
Installment accounts receivable		4,000
To record cash collections other than down payments.		

(4)

Deferred gross profit	1,350	
Gross profit on installment sales		1,350
To record realized gross profit on total cash receipts of $4,500 @ 30%.		

2nd Year

(1)

Installment accounts receivable	16,000	
Inventory		11,000
Deferred gross profit		5,000
To record the sale of appliances.		

(2)

Cash	800	
Installment accounts receivable		800
To record the cash down payments received.		

(3)

Cash	11,000	
Installment accounts receivable (current year)		6,000
Installment accounts receivable (previous year)		5,000
To record cash collections other than down payments.		

(4)

Deferred gross profit (current year)	2,125	
Deferred gross profit (previous year)	1,500	
Gross profit on installment sales (current year)		2,125
Gross profit on installment sales (previous year)		1,500
31.25% of current year's cash collections of $6,800; 30% of previous year's cash collections of $5,000.		

It is assumed that the appliance dealer uses a perpetual inventory system. The entries would be slightly different under a system of periodic inventories.

There are many ways of presenting this information in financial statements. Assuming that sales are made for cash as well as on installments, one form of the income statement at the end of the second year is as follows:

STATEMENT OF INCOME
END OF YEAR 2

Sales—other than installment sales	$40,000
Less cost of merchandise	25,000
Gross profit	$15,000
Realized gross profit on installment sales:	
1st year sales	1,500
2nd year sales	2,125
Total realized gross profit	$18,625

Alternatively, the gross profit realized could be shown in one amount. In either case, a schedule of realized gross profits by years of sale is helpful. This schedule, based on the information in the illustration, would appear as follows:

SCHEDULE OF REALIZED GROSS PROFITS ON INSTALLMENT SALES

	Year 1	*Year 2*
Installment sales	$10,000	$16,000
Cost of goods sold	7,000	11,000
Gross profit	$ 3,000	$ 5,000
Rate of gross profit	30%	31.25%
Collections in Year 2	$ 5,000	$ 6,800
Gross profit realized	$ 1,500	$ 2,125

The balance sheet. The balance sheet presentation of installment accounts receivable does not depend on the due dates of the various installments. According to the position of the Committee on Accounting Procedure of the American Institute of Certified Public Accountants, installment accounts receivable may be classified as a current asset even though some installments are not due for a year or longer, if such a period of time is in accordance with normal trade practices and within the concept of an operating cycle. The balance sheet is improved if installments receivable are classified by the years in which they mature, and if past due installments are disclosed, parenthetically or otherwise.

Although valid arguments can be made for locating deferred gross profit on installments sales in the proprietary section, or as a deduction from the related receivable, most balance sheets carry the item in the liability section under a deferred income or deferred credits caption.

The essence of the installment method—the proportionate recognition of income and cost as cash is collected—prohibits any charge against income for anticipated bad debts. Still, the probability of bad debts and the certainty of incurring expenses in the handling of sales made in prior years are information that may be desirably incorporated in the balance sheet. If a deferred gross profit of $40,000 is expected to result in bad debts of $1,800 and collection expenses of $300, this information might be presented in the balance sheet as follows:

Allowance for bad debts (Deducted from installment accounts receivable)	$ 1,800
Deferred gross profit on installment sales, against which estimated future expenses of $300 will be applied	$38,200

► NOTE: It should be reiterated that estimated bad debts and collection expenses are not charges against income. The breakdown shown above is for balance sheet purposes only. Under this method, bad debts and collection costs are charged to income only as they occur.

Bad debts. The default of a buyer in the payment of his installments, and the probability that no future payment will be made, usually results in the seller repossessing the merchandise. Whether this results in a gain or loss to the seller depends on the amount of the unpaid installments and the value of the repossessed merchandise. In any case, however, the balance in the customer's account and the deferred gross profit contained in that balance should be written off.

There are several methods of making such write-off. The method that will be illustrated is the most common one, probably because it is acceptable for income tax purposes.

► EXAMPLE: On 6-15-X1, Ross, a dealer who reports on the installment basis, sold for $100 an article that costs him $60, receiving $20 down, the balance being payable in 16 monthly installments of $5 each. After paying 9 of these installments (6 in 19X1 and 3 in 19X2), the buyer defaulted. Under the agreement, Ross took back the article, which at the time of repossession was worth $25. Gain on the repossesion is figured as follows:

Value of property at time of repossession		$25
Basis of obligations surrendered (7 unpaid installments):		
Face value (7 × $5)	$35	
Less: Unrealized profit (40%)	14	21
Taxable gain on repossession in 19X2		$ 4
Profit to be reported on 3 installments paid in 19X2 (40% of $15)		6
Income in 19X2		$10

A journal entry to record the above information follows:

Repossessed merchandise	25	
Deferred gross profit on installment sales	14	
Installment accounts receivable		35
Gain on repossession		4

The repossessed article is, of course, put into inventory at a cost of $25. If the repossessed merchandise has no value, as often occurs, a loss on repossession would have resulted. In such a case, the following journal entry would be used in place of the preceding journal entry.

Deferred gross profit on installment sales	14	
Loss on repossesssion	21	
Installment accounts receivable		35

PRINCIPLES OF AMORTIZATION — BOND DISCOUNT, EXPENSE, PREMIUM

Bond discount and expense are usually written off over the life of the bond issue to which they apply, preferably as a charge to interest. But when a bond issue is refunded before reaching maturity, the remaining unamortized discount and expense may be:

1. Written off in full in the year of refunding.
2. Amortized over the remainder of the original life of the retired issue. If the life of the new issue is shorter than the remainder of the original life of

the retired issue, then the amortization should be over the life of the new issue.

3. Amortized over some shorter period than the alternatives in (2) above.

Clearly, there is no one accepted practice in this area. Many accountants have the problem of choosing from alternative practices the one that best fits a particular situation. Those who have an understanding of basic theory will be better able to select a method that best fits the actual situation.

Terms defined. *Bond discount* is the amount by which the selling price of a bond is lower than its face value. A $100,000 issue sold for $90,000 results in a bond discount of $10,000.

Bond premium is the amount by which the selling price of a bond is higher than its face or par value as, for example, a $100,000 issue sold for $110,000.

Related expenses may include such items as legal, accounting, appraisal, and engineering fees, and the costs of registration and printing. These are sometimes absorbed as expenses when incurred, or combined and set up as a deferred charge, or set off against bond premium.

The nature of bond premium and discount. Bond premium or discount arises as a result of market pressure on interest rates. The face or par value of a bond is adjusted to compensate for the bond interest rate being too high or low in the eyes of the financial market. It is, therefore, a reasonable assumption that bond premium or discount is a measure of the difference between the stated interest rate of a bond and the going interest rate for a similar long-term investment. Extending this assumption, the amount of the actual discount or premium should be the present value of the series of interest payments presumptively contained in the difference between the bond rate and the going market rate. Whether or not this is valid as a practical matter, the important point is that bond premium or discount is, in effect, an adjustment of the interest rate that a bond carries. When this interest adjustment is properly amortized, the bond account (together with the premium, discount, and related expenses) will approach closer and closer to the redemption value of the bond as its maturity date nears.

Setting up premium or discount in the accounts. *The bond purchaser.* When bonds are required, the purchaser has the choice of carrying his investment at cost, or of debiting the bond investment account with the par value of the bonds and setting up a bond premium or discount account. The first method is commonly used and subsequent adjustments for amortization of premium or discount are made directly to this account.

The bond issuer. Conventional recording practice for bonds *issued* above or below par value is contrary to preferred practice in the case of bonds *purchased* for other than par value. The bond issuer usually credits the account for bonds payable with par value and sets up premium or discount in a deferred charge or credit account.

There is a body of accountants who feel that bonds issued should be carried at the amount actually received, and that amortization adjustments should be made directly to the bond liability account. This practice would result in showing bonds on the balance sheet at their present value, instead of at their face value.

Related expenses in the accounts. Commissions paid to a broker are usually regarded as deductions in determining net proceeds, and, therefore, do not find their way into the accounts. Related expenses are not considered in the illustrations that follow since they do not affect the basic principles of amortization whichever way they are handled.

Amortization of bond premium and discount. Amortization methods for bond premium and discount fall into two major categories: straight-line methods and scientific (effective-interest-rate) methods.

Straight-line amortization. The straight-line method has the advantage of simplicity and is, therefore, used most often. Inasmuch as amortization principles are the same for bonds purchased at a discount or at a premium, only amortization of premium on a straight-line basis will be illustrated.

► EXAMPLE: Assume that $10,000 par value of bonds are purchased for $10,800 and accrued interest on Feb. 1, 19X2. The bonds bear 10% interest, payable January 1 and July 1, and are scheduled to be redeemed December 31, 19X5. Entries made for the purchase of the bonds, the accrual at June 30, and the receipt of the interest payment on July 1st follow.

Feb. 1, 19X2		
Bond investment	10,800.00	
Interest income	83.33	
Cash		10,833.33
June 30, 19X2		
Accrued interest receivable	500.00	
Bond investment		85.10
Interest income		414.90
July 1, 19X2		
Cash	500.00	
Accrued interest receivable		500.00

Since the bonds mature three years and eleven months from the purchase date, the monthly amortization of premium is $17.02 ($800÷47), or $102.13 every six months. The scheduling of interest and amortization of premium over the life of the bonds is shown in the following table.

SCHEDULE OF AMORTIZATION

Date	*Amount of Premium*	*Interest Income*	*Bond Investment Account*
2-1-X2			$10,800.00
7-1-X2	$ 85.10	$ 331.57	10,714.90
1-1-X3	102.13	397.87	10,612.77
7-1-X3	102.13	397.87	10,510.64
1-1-X4	102.13	397.87	10,408.51
7-1-X4	102.13	397.87	10,306.38
1-1-X5	102.13	397.87	10,204.25
7-1-X5	102.13	397.87	10,102.12
12-31-X5	102.12	397.88	10,000.00
	$800.00	$3,116.67	

If, instead of being held to maturity, these bonds were sold on March 1, 19X4 for $10,500 including accrued interest, a computation such as the following would have to be made to determine all of the elements involved in the sale.

Selling price		10,500.00
Accrued interest for 2 months @ 10%		166.67
Price received for bonds		$10,333.33
Value of bonds when sold:		
Bond account Jan. 1, 19X4	$10,408.51	
Less 2 months amortization, 1/3 of $102.13	34.04	10,374.47
Loss on sale		$ 41.14

The journal entry to record the sale would be:

Cash	10,500.00	
Loss on sale	41.14	
Interest income ($166.67—$34.04)		132.63
Bond investment		10,408.51

Scientific methods. The distinguishing feature of the scientific methods is that an effective-interest rate is determined and applied to the carrying value of the bond account at the beginning of each accounting period. The periodic amortization is determined by comparing the effective yield with the nominal interest rate. This process results in a uniform *rate of yield.* It contrasts with the straight-line method that results in a uniform *amount of yield.*

Using the data from the previous example, assume that the same bonds yielding 10% were purchased by an investor who desired a return of no less than 8%. He would, therefore, be willing to pay as large a premium for the bonds as would still enable him to earn 8% on his investment. Using appropriate tables, it can be determined that such an investor might pay $10,673.27 for these bonds, since at that price the investor's actual yield will be 8%. If the bonds are purchased at January 1, 19X2, the following schedule would form the basis for the amortization and interest entries.

SCHEDULE OF AMORTIZATION

Date	*Cash Debit*	*Interest Credit*	*Bond Credit*	*Bond Investment Account*
1-1-X2				$10,673.27
7-1-X2	$ 500	$ 426.93	$ 73.07	10,600.20
1-1-X3	500	424.01	75.99	10,524.21
7-1-X3	500	420.97	79.03	10,445.18
1-1-X4	500	417.81	82.19	10,362.99
7-1-X4	500	414.52	85.48	10,277.51
1-1-X5	500	411.10	88.90	10,188.61
7-1-X5	500	407.54	92.46	10,096.15
12-31-X5	500	403.85	96.15	10,000.00
	$4,000	$3,326.73	$673.27	

Bonds-outstanding method. Although the straight-line and scientific methods of amortization have been illustrated from the viewpoint of the bond purchaser, these methods may also be used by the bond issuer. No additional problems are created thereby.

Likewise, when an issuer sells bonds that mature at various dates, the discount or premium on these serial bonds can be amortized on the straight-line or on the effective-interest-rate basis. When the straight-line basis is used in connection with the amortization of serial bonds, it is referred to as the bonds-outstanding method. Under this method, a changing fraction is applied to the total premium or discount to determine the annual amortization. The numerator of this fraction is the total par value of bonds outstanding during the year; the denominator is the total for each year of the par value of bonds outstanding that year, added to similar totals for all other years of the bond issuer's life.

► **EXAMPLE:** Assume that 3% bonds with a par value of $100,000 are issued January 1 for $110,000, and that $25,000 of these bonds mature at the end of each year. The annual amortization of premium by the bonds outstanding method is illustrated in the following table:

End of Year	*Bonds Outstanding*	*Fraction*	*Premium Amortization*
1	$100,000	10/25	$ 4,000
2	75,000	7.5/25	3,000
3	50,000	5/25	2,000
4	25,000	2.5/25	1,000
	$250,000		$10,000

Other considerations. Bonds are often subject to the issuer's right to redeem them prior to maturity at a call premium. The same bonds may be subject to call at two or more dates with a different call premium at each date. Usually, the call premium is highest when closest to the issue date. Bonds purchased at a premium and subject to call at a premium should be so amortized that the bond investment will never be carried at a higher amount than would be received in the event the bonds were called prior to maturity.

If bonds subject to early call are purchased at a discount, the discount should be amortized in the usual way—raising the bond investment to par at maturity.

Tax treatment. The sale, exchange, or retirement of bonds have different tax consequences for the bondholder and debtor.

Corporate bonds issued before 5-28-69 and government bonds. The tax treatment of corporate bonds issued before 5-28-69 (or under a contract binding before that date) and certain government bonds continues to apply as before the changes made by the 1969 Tax Reform Act. If at the time of original issue, there was no intention to call the bond or other evidence of indebtedness before maturity, the discount is apportioned over the entire period to the maturity of the bond. If the bond is sold before maturity, only a pro rata portion of the discount is treated as ordinary income. Any gain in excess of that amount is long-term capital gain (if the bond is a capital asset).

Corporate bonds issued after 5-27-69. Owners of original issue discount bonds issued after 5-27-69 must include discounts in their gross incomes on a ratable basis over the bonds' life.

If you sell or exchange an original issue discount bond issued after 5-27-69 before maturity or if you redeem it, you treat an amount over your adjusted basis as capital gain. You increase the basis of your bond by the discounts included in income. However, as with bonds issued before 5-28-69 and certain government bonds, if the issuing corporation intended at the time of original issue to call the bond before maturity, any realized gain is ordinary income to the extent of the original issue discount less any amounts previously included in income.

Bond premium. The holder of a bond acquired at a premium is either permitted or required to amortize the premium, depending on the type of bond. The owner of a fully taxable bond may elect to amortize bond premium or not, as he pleases. If he does elect to amortize, he is allowed a yearly deduction for the bond premium so amortized and his basis for the bond is correspondingly reduced.

The owner of a fully tax-exempt bond must amortize a portion of the bond premium each year and reduce his basis by that amount, but he is not allowed a deduction.

If bonds are issued at a premium, the amount of the premium is considered to be income to the issuer to be prorated over the life of the bonds.

CHOOSING THE FORM OF BUSINESS ORGANIZATION

The most frequent forms in which businesses are organized are the proprietorship, the partnership, and the corporation. Joint ventures, which are popular in some fields, are fully discussed in Chapter 5.

The major factors to be considered in choosing a form of business organization can be classified under (1) the tax aspects, and (2) the general and legal considerations.

► NOTE: Often, all the other tax, and general and legal characteristics of the various forms of business organizations take second place to the one factor of *limited liability*—partially obtainable through the use of the limited partnership, but fully utilized only through the adoption of the corporate form or organization.

Tax aspects. Individual proprietorships and partnerships do not pay Federal income taxes as business entities. The sole owner of a business pays an income tax on the entire taxable income of his business. This is true whether profits are withdrawn from or left in the business. In a partnership, each owner pays a tax on his share of any profits, also regardless of whether such profits are withdrawn from or left in the business.

The corporation, however, is taxed as a business unit. While the corporation receives a tax deduction for salaries that it pays to its owner-stockholders—and the owners are taxed on these salaries—dividends declared by the corporation are not deductible from corporate income. In addition, dividends are also taxed to the recipients. Thus, corporate earnings are first taxed as income to the corporation and then to the owners when received as dividends. Taxwise, this is the primary disadavantage of the corporate form of doing business. This disadvantage may be overcome, to some extent, by the leeway that corporate owners have, particularly in closely held corporations, in determining (within reasonable limits) the amounts of their compensation, and by the fringe benefits, such as pension and profit-sharing plans, insurance, death benefit payments, medical payment, wage continuation plans, etc., allowed as deductions from corporate profits.

The following table shows some of the important tax differences between corporations, and proprietorships and partnerships. Proprietorships and partnerships are grouped together since, in many respects, the tax situations of both are similar.

PROPRIETORSHIPS AND PARTNERSHIP	CORPORATIONS
	Tax Status
Not a separate taxable entity.	A separate taxable entity.
	Returns
Schedule C for proprietorships. Individual information return, Form 1065, for each partnership.	Tax return
	Tax Rates
No tax on proprietorship or partnership itself.	17% of first \$25,000. 20% of excess over \$25,000 up to \$50,000; 30% over \$50,000 up to \$75,000; 40% over \$75,000 up to \$100,000; 46% over that.
	Distributions
Sole owners or partners are taxed on their share of income, whether or not distributed.	Stockholders are taxed on dividends distributed. \$100 excluded from taxable income.
	Salaries
Owner or partners are not employees.	Employee-stockholder salaries are deductible by corporation.
	Profits
Taxed to partners or sole owner in full.	Taxed to corporation.
	Losses
Passed through to partners or owner.	Not normally available to shareholders.

Social Security

Not paid on compensation from firm. Owner or partners pay self-employment tax.	Compensation of stockholder-employees is subject to tax.

Stock Options

Not applicable.	Available as possible source of capital gains to owners, although limited.

Pension and Profit-Sharing Plans

Keogh and IRA plans.	IRA and corporate plans—usually allowing greater contributions and greater flexibility.

Capital Gains and Losses

Partners taxed on their proportionate shares of gain and loss.	Alternative computation may be used. Unlike individuals, there is no deduction of 60% of net long-term gain, and losses are deductible only as they offset capital gain.

Charitable Contributions

Proportionate shares of partnership contributions are added to partner's personal contribution.	Contributions are deductible only by the corporation making them and only to the extent of 5% of taxable income.

Taxable Year

Generally same as owners.	Can elect any fiscal year at time of incorporation.

From the foregoing, it is apparent that, in normal circumstances, the corporate form of organization is valuable to owners-stockholders of close corporations who are in the higher tax brackets. In a corporation, high individual tax rates can be somewhat lessened by the judicious mixing of owner's salaries, dividends, fringe benefits, and income retained within the business.

Multiple corporations. For tax years starting after 1978, members of a controlled group of corporations are limited to a total of $25,000 in each of the graduated tax rate brackets below 46% which is divided equally among them or shared as they elect. Members of a controlled group of corporations are limited to one accumulated earnings credit totaling $150,000 which must be divided equally among the component members.

Personal holding company tax. The ability to use the corporation as a tax shelter (i.e., to pay the corporate rate) and postpone the higher rates that apply to individuals, is not available to holding or investment companies. These companies are generally those with the bulk of their income dividends, interest, gains from the sales of securities, rents and royalties. Personal holding companies pay a tax of 70% of their undistributed personal holding income. In brief, these companies pay the ordinary income tax on their entire income and a surtax or retained earnings. However, if gross income from either rents or royalties equals or exceeds 50% of the adjusted ordinary gross income from the business, the tax does not apply.

Corporation taxed as a partnership. Subchapter S corporations can elect to be taxed as partnerships. Under these rules instead of the corporation being taxed as such, the taxable income of the corporation is passed through to the stockholders, each of whom pays an individual tax on the portion of the income allocable to him. If a corporation can qualify for this election, numerous advantages are possible. The following examples show the nature of the advantages of this method:

1. When the individual stockholders' rates are lower than the corporation's rates, and the corporate earnings are to remain in the corporation, it may be preferable for the individual to pay the tax rather than the corporation.
2. Where the individual stockholders have profits and the corporation has losses, they can offset the corporation's losses against their personal profits.
3. Even though a successful partnership may desire to participate in corporate fringe benefits, the unwillingness to become subject to double taxation may keep them from incorporating. By making use of this election, the partners can incorporate, receive the fringe benefits available to corporations, and still be taxed as a partnership. (Pension benefits are limited, however, to similar amounts allowed by Keogh plans.)

Only a "small business corporation" may elect partnership type taxation. Although this is the statutory term, it may be somewhat misleading since there is no limit on corporate net worth or volume of business. Generally a small business corporation is one that meets the following requirements:

1. It must be a domestic corporation, not a member of an affiliated group eligible to file a consolidated return with another corporation.
2. It must not have more than 15 shareholders.
3. All shareholders must be individuals, estates and certain trusts.
4. No nonresident alien may be a shareholder.
5. The corporation may not have more than one class of stock.

Other general and legal considerations. While the tax factors are sometimes decisive in determining the form of a new business, other general and legal considerations may play an important part as well. The following table highlights the main differences between a partnership and corporation. In most of the differences illustrated, the sole proprietorship is in the same position as the partnership.

Partnership	Corporation
Formation	
Comparatively simple, usually by having the interested parties sign a partnership agreement.	More formal, strict compliance with the laws of the state where organized required.

	Duration
Unstable, terminated by death or withdrawal of any partner.	Stable, corporation continues even though its owners change.
	Legal Entity
Not a separate entity apart from the partners.	Separate entity apart from its stockholders. Can sue or be sued, and hold or sell property in its own name.
	Owner's Liability
Each general partner can be individually liable for all partnership obligations; special or limited partners are usually liable for the amount of their contributions.	A stockholder has no individual liability beyond his capital contribution.
	Sources of Capital
Capital can be raised only from its own members or by outside loans.	Stocks, bonds, or other securities can be sold to the general public to raise capital.
	Changes of Ownership
A change in owners creates a new partnership. All partners must consent to a change.	Stock can be sold or otherwise transferred at will, but public offerings subject to S.E.C. regulations.
	Policy Decisions
Unanimous agreement of partners are usually required.	Made by a majority vote of the Board of Directors.
	Credit Standing
Depends on credit of individual partners.	Corporation has credit potential apart from that of the individual stockholders.
	Management
General partners are responsible for management.	Employees responsible for management of corporation, may or may not be stockholders.
	Doing Business in Other States
Can do business in any state with the same privileges and immunities of citizens of that state.	Corporations must comply with the specific requirements of each state in which they do business.
	Governing Law
The Uniform Partnership Law is in effect in most states.	Corporations governed by state statutes that vary from state to state.

THE PROFESSIONAL CORPORATION

The Treasury Department had fought for many years to prevent members of licensed professions from securing the benefits of incorporation. The key battles of this campaign were the *Morrissy* case in 1935 and *Kintner* in 1954. It was decided in both cases that an unincorporated enterprise could be treated for tax purposes as a corporation if it evidenced enough characteristics of a corporation.

Since the states have enacted professional corporation statutes, this problem has become virtually moot. I say virtually moot because the IRS did successfully attack a professional in *Roubik* on the grounds that the incorporated group continued to operate as individual practitioners.

Generally, professional corporations differ from ordinary corporations in the following ways:

1. Method of incorporation.
2. Scope of powers and stock ownership.
3. Liability.
4. Tax strategy.

Method of Incorporation. The process of incorporating a professional practice is similar to that of an ordinary corporation with some notable exceptions. First, each shareholder must offer proof that he or she is licensed by the state to practice that particular profession. Ordinarily, officers and directors must also be licensed members of the profession. To expedite matters in a one-person professional corporation, some states will allow one officer and director to be unlicensed, while others may allow an unlicensed corporate secretary. The latter will most likely turn out to be the physician's spouse.

The corporate name should be followed with the identification *P.C.*, or *Professional Corporation,* or *P.A.*, or *Professional Association.*

Scope of powers and stock ownership. The professional corporation can only engage in activities for which the state licenses its shareholders. Similarly, each shareholder must be so licensed by the state for that area. This means that a certified public accountant and a physician usually cannot form a professional corporation to practice jointly. It also means that all partners must be licensed to practice that particular profession in that particular state—an impediment more likely to affect CPA's who practice nationally than medical practitioners. One possible solution to this problem is to form separate professional corporations in each state in which a partner is licensed to practice and then to practice as a partnership of professional corporations.

The licensing requirement makes a buy-sell agreement and/or stock redemption plan most important. In some states, even an estate cannot be a member of the corporation, while in others it may do so for a short time after the death of the licensed shareholder.

In addition to rendering professional services, the state may or may not allow the corporation to invest in stocks, bonds, real estate, or in other medically oriented ventures.

Liability. Although shareholders of professional corporations are *not* granted limited liability to the same extent as those of ordinary corporations, in most states, the liability for malpractice will not be extended past the shareholder committing the tort. Here again, this feature may be more valuable to a group of surgeons, in which it is clear which member of the corporation is providing the service than for a group of CPA's in which a firm signs financial reports. It may also be of value in a speculative professionally oriented undertaking.

Tax strategy. First of all, because of the specter of Roubik — the professional corporation that was upset by the IRS because of operating as individual practitioners — it is necessary to make sure that the professional corporation runs "by the numbers."

Secondly, although the Internal Revenue Code doesn't distinguish between an ordinary and professional corporation, the state in which the professional corporation is domiciled may treat it differently for state tax purposes. For example, New York State requires certain fringe benefits received by the stockholder-employees to be included in the stockholder-employees' personal tax returns.

Particular attention should be paid to planning and selecting options in connection with choosing a tax year, Subchapter S election, cash versus accrual basis, and setting up pension and fringe benefits.

CHOOSING A BUSINESS YEAR

The natural business year. The natural business year is that point in the twelve-month cycle where business activities have reached their lowest point. For a seasonal business, this usually takes place shortly after the close of the season. The natural business year concept has obvious value over the traditional calendar year closings that may come at a time when business activities are at a peak, the client's office staff is busy with year-end payroll taxes and other matters, and the accountant is at the yearly peak of his activity.

The following concrete advantages can be obtained by a firm on a natural business year:

1. Inventory is usually taken at its lowest ebb and at a time when the employees are least busy.
2. The year-end balance sheet will show the company's most liquid position, thus helping to obtain bank credit.
3. The income statement will show results of operations during a complete business cycle—rather than a mixture of the end of one cycle and the beginning of another.
4. Financial statements will be available earlier in the inception of a new cycle, and thus be a greater aid in planning for the new cycle.
5. Disputable items on tax returns, such as inventories and accounts receivable, will be at their lowest point, thus reducing the area of possible conflict with the Government.

► NOTE: A partnership cannot adopt or change to a tax year that is different from all of its principal partners unless it can show that a good business reason exists for the proposed taxable year. The natural business year is often, by itself, such a valid business purpose.

19—	Production		Raw Materials		Goods in Process		Finished Goods		Sales		Accounts Receivable		Accounts Payable		Notes Payable	
			Inventories at Close of Month													
	$	%	$	%	$	%	$	%	$	%	$	%	$	%	$	%
Jan.																
Feb.																
March																
April																
May																
June																
July																
Aug.																
Sept.																
Oct.																
Nov.																
Dec.																
		100		100		100		100		100		100		100		100

Fig. 1. Chart to Use in Determining Natural Business Year.
(Prepared by the National Business Year Committee of the American Institute of Certified Public Accounts.)

FINANCIAL STATEMENT ANALYSIS

Illustrative statements. The following statements of the mythical Michaels Inc. for the year 19X4 will be used for illustrative purposes. A set of 19X3 statements are also furnished for comparative purposes.

Although the relationships shown in the following pages compare statements of two successive years of the same company, similar analyses can be made using internal standards set up within the company itself, statements of other companies in the same industry or in different industries, or standard ratios for the industry.

► OBSERVATION: Standard ratios are built up from financial statements submitted by a large number of companies in the same line of business and sufficiently similar in size, nature of business, and other factors to make the group homogeneous. The building of standard ratios is done by such organizations as Dun and Bradstreet, Inc., Robert Morris Associates (the National Association of Bank Loan Officers and Credit Men), agencies of the Federal Government, trade associations, universities, and private organizations such as banks and accounting firms.

The tools of analysis to be discussed in this section are.

1. Horizontal analysis.
2. Vertical analysis.
3. Ratios and other useful analytical tools.

MICHAELS INC.
Balance Sheet
December 31, 19X4

Assets

Current Assets:			
Cash		$ 4,500	
Accounts receivable—customers	$35,095		
Less provision for doubtful accounts	1,400	33,695	
Merchandise inventory		31,200	
Prepaid expenses		750	
Total Current Assets			$ 70,145
Fixed Assets:			
Land		$15,000	
Buildings, machinery and equipment	$74,500		
Less allowance for depreciation	15,000	59,500	
Total Fixed Assets			74,500
Deferred Charges:			
Organization expense			1,200
Total Assets			$145,845

Liabilities and Net Worth

Current Liabilities:			
Accounts payable	$15,700		
Notes payable to banks	3,000		
Accrued taxes, wages, and other expenses	12,440		
Total Current Liabilities		$31,140	
Long-Term Liabilities:			
First Mortgage Bonds Payable		10,000	
Total Liabilities			$ 41,140
Net Worth:			
Capital stock—par $10		$90,000	
Retained earnings—Exhibit C		14,705	
Total Net Worth			104,705
Total Liabilities and Net Worth			$145,845

Fig. 2. Balance Sheet as at December 31, 19X4.

MICHAELS INC.
Income Statement
For the Year Ended December 31, 19X4

Gross sales	$294,500	
Returned sales and allowances	4,500	
Net sales		$290,000
Cost of goods sold		157,475
Gross profit		$132,525
Operating expenses:		
Selling expenses	$ 57,000	
General and administrative expenses	35,000	
Total operating expenses		92,000
Net income from operations		$ 40,525
Other income		3,000
Net income before interest and Federal income tax		$ 43,525
Interest expense		1,000
Net income before Federal income tax		$ 42,525
Federal income tax		22,113
Net income		$ 20,412

Fig. 3. Income Statement for the Year Ended December 31, 19X4.

MICHAELS INC.
Statement of Retained Earnings
For the Year Ended December 31, 19X4

Balance, January 1, 19X4	$ 7,195
Add: Net income for the year	20,412
	$27,607
Less: Dividend declared during the year	12,902
Balance, December 31, 19X4	$14,705

Fig. 4. Statement of Retained Earnings for the Year Ended December 31, 19X4.

MICHAELS INC.
Balance Sheet
December 31, 19X3

Assets

Current Assets:			
Cash		$11,000	
Accounts receivable—customers	$22,475		
Less provision for doubtful accounts	900	21,575	
Merchandise inventory		35,500	
Prepaid expenses		500	
Total Current Assets			$ 68,575
Fixed Assets:			
Land		$10,000	
Building, machinery, and equipment	$67,400		
Less allowance for depreciation	11,500	55,900	
Total Fixed Assets			65,900
Deferred Charges:			
Organization expense			1,500
Total Assets			$135,975

Liabilities and Net Worth

Current Liabilities:			
Accounts payable	$12,100		
Notes payable to banks	2,500		
Accrued taxes, wages, and other expenses	9,180		
Total Current Liabilities		$23,780	
Long-Term Liabilities:			
First-Mortgage Bonds Payable		15,000	
Total Liabilities			$ 38,780
Net Worth:			
Capital stock—par $10		$90,000	
Retained earnings—Exhibit C		7,195	
Total Net Worth			97,195
Total Liabilities and Net Worth			$135,975

Fig. 5. Balance Sheet as at December 31, 19X3.

MICHAELS INC.
Income Statement
For the Year Ended December 31, 19X3

Gross sales	$211,000	
Returned sales and allowances	2,500	
Net sales		$208,500
Cost of goods sold		104,250
Gross profit		$104,250

Operating expenses:		
Selling expenses	$ 35,000	
General and administrative expenses	30,000	
Total Operating expenses		65,000
Net income from operations		$ 39,250
Other income		2,700
Net income before interest and Federal income tax		$ 41,950
Interest expense		1,200
Net income before Federal income tax		$ 40,750
Federal income tax		21,190
Net income		$ 19,560

Fig. 6. Income Statement for the Year Ended December 31, 19X3.

MICHAELS INC.
Statement of Retained Earnings
For the Year Ended December 31, 19X3

Balance, January 1, 19X3	$(3,365)
Add: Net income for the year	19,560
	$16,195
Less: Dividend declared during the year	9,000
Balance, December 31, 19X3	$ 7,195

Fig. 7. Statement of Retained Earnings for the Year Ended December 31, 19X3.

Horizontal analysis. A horizontal analysis of two statements measures changes in statement items from year to year. This is done by comparing income statements for the two years, then listing the change from year to year in each item. This change can be shown in dollars or as a percentage increase or decrease. Thus, since its purpose and effect is to show change from year to year, horizontal analysis is primarily a trend analysis.

Comparing income statement items. Analyzed horizontally, the comparative income statements of the Michaels Inc. (Figure 8) show that gross sales for 19X4 had increased over 19X3 by $83,500, or 39.57%. However, cost of goods had also increased by $53,225, or 51.06%, and operating expenses were also up $27,000, or 41.54%, thus nullfying most of the sales increase. Hence only $852 of the $83,500 additional sales were brought down to net income.

Through this horizontal analysis of the income statements of the Michaels Inc., the reader begins to see a picture of a company that is on a treadmill; one that has to drastically increase its sales merely to stay even. At this point, an analyst would begin making notes of questions to raise to enable him to ferret out the reasons for this phenomenon.

MICHAELS INC.
Comparative Income Statements
For the Years Ended 19X4 and 19X3

	19X4	*19X3*	*Increase-(Decrease) Amount*	*%*
Gross sales	$294,500	$211,000	$83,500	39.57
Returned sales and allowances	4,500	2,500	2,000	80.00
Net sales	$290,000	$208,500	$81,500	39.09
Cost of goods sold	157,475	104,250	53,225	51.06
Gross profit	$132,525	$104,250	$28,275	27.12
Operating expenses:				
Selling expenses	$ 57,000	$ 35,000	$22,000	62.86
General and administrative expenses	35,000	30,000	5,000	16.67
Total Operating expenses	$ 92,000	$ 65,000	$27,000	41.54
Net income from operations	$ 40,525	$ 39,250	$ 1,275	3.25
Other income	3,000	2,700	300	11.11
Net income before interest and Federal income tax	$ 43,525	$ 41,950	$ 1,575	3.75
Interest expense	1,000	1,200	(200)	(16.67)
Net income before Federal income tax	$ 42,525	$ 40,750	$ 1,775	4.38
Federal income tax	22,113	21,190	923	4.36
Net income	$ 20,412	$ 19,560	$ 852	4.36

Fig. 8. Horizontal Analysis of Income Statements for 19X4 and 19X3.

MICHAELS INC.
Comparative Balance Sheets
December 31, 19X4 and 19X3

	19X4	*19X3*	*Increase-(Decrease) Amount*	*%*
Assets				
Current Assets:				
Cash	$ 4,500	$ 11,000	$(6,500)	(59.09)
Accounts receivable (net)	33,695	21,575	12,120	56.18
Merchandise inventory	31,200	35,500	(4,300)	(12.11)
Prepaid expenses	750	500	250	50.00
Total Current Assets	$ 70,145	$ 68,575	$ 1,570	2.29
Fixed Assets:				
Land	$ 15,000	$ 10,000	$ 5,000	50.00
Buildings, machinery & equipment (net)	59,500	55,900	3,600	6.44
Total Fixed Assets	$ 74,500	$ 65,900	$ 8,600	13.05
Deferred Charges:				
Organization expense	$ 1,200	$ 1,500	$ (300)	(20.00)
Total Assets	$145,845	$135,975	$ 9,870	7.26

Liabilities and Net Worth				
Current Liabilities:				
Accounts payable	$ 15,700	$ 12,100	$ 3,600	29.75
Notes payable to banks	3,000	2,500	500	20.00
Accrued taxes, wages, and other expenses	12,440	9,180	3,260	35.51
Total Current Liabilities	$ 31,140	$ 23,780	$ 7,360	30.95
Long-Term Liabilities:				
First Mortgage Bond Payable	$ 10,000	$ 15,000	$(5,000)	33.33
Total Liabilities	$ 41,140	$ 38,780	$ 2,360	6.09
Net Worth:				
Capital stock—par $100	$ 90,000	$ 90,000	$ —	—
Retained earnings	14,705	7,195	7,510	104.38
Total Net Worth	$104,705	$ 97,195	$ 7,510	7.73
Total Liabilities and Net Worth	$145,845	$135,975	$ 9,870	7.26

Fig. 9. Horizontal Analysis of Balance Sheet for 19X4 and 19X3.

Comparing balance sheet items. A look at comparative balance sheets for 19X4 and 19X3 shows that cash and inventory decreased, but accounts receivable and the company's investment in land and equipment increased. Short-term debt (accounts payable and accrued expenses) increased, but long-term debt was reduced.

Comparing other statement items. Horizontal analysis can be used in more ways than have been illustrated here. Since horizontal analysis is a trend analysis, the trend of many different statement items can be described. One way to do this is in chart form. For example, a business' net income can be charted over the course of its life, trend lines drawn, and the future course of the business estimated. Another form of trend analysis would involve charting percentage increases in an income or expense item and possibly comparing it to a similar trend of the industry, or the economy.

MICHAELS INC.
Comparative Income Statements
For the Years Ended 19X4 and 19X3

	19X4		*19X3*	
	Amount	*% of Net Sales*	*Amount*	*% of Net Sales*
Gross sales	$294,500	101.55%	$211,000	101.20%
Returned sales and allowances	4,500	1.55	2,500	1.20
Net sales	$290,000	100.00%	$208,500	100.00%
Cost of goods sold	157,475	54.30	104.250	50.00
Gross profit	$132,525	45.70%	$104,250	50.00%

Operating expenses:				
Selling expenses	$ 57,000	19.66%	$ 35,000	16.79%
General and administrative expenses	35,000	12.07	30,000	14.39
Total Operating expenses	$ 92,000	31.73%	$ 65,000	31.18%
Net income from operations	$ 40,525	13.97%	$ 39,250	18.82%
Other income	3,000	1.03	2,700	1.29
Net income before interest and Federal income tax	$ 43,525	15.00%	$ 41,950	20.11%
Interest expense	1,000	.34	1,200	.57
Net income before Federal income tax	$ 42,525	14.66%	$ 40,750	19.54%
Federal income tax	22,113	7.62	21,190	10.16
Net income	$ 20,412	7.04%	$ 19,560	9.38%

Fig. 10. Vertical Analysis of Income Statements for 19X4 and 19X3.

Vertical analysis. It is not enough to merely describe trends. For example, the horizontal analysis of the income statements of the Michaels Inc. showed that sales rose, but so did expenses. However, it obviously costs more (both in product and selling expenses) to sell more of a product; thus the unresolved question is whether expenses have gone up in proportion to the increase in sales.

A vertical analysis of the income statements can provide an answer to the last question. It converts each income statement amount into a percentage of net sales (net sales: 100%). This comparison is shown below.

The vertical analysis shows that although gross profit on sales in 19X4 increased $28,275 in dollar value, there was a proportionate (to net sales) decrease of 4.30%. Similarly general and administrative expenses increased $5,000 on an absolute basis, but decreased 2.32% proportionately to sales. And finally, there was a dollar increase in net income of $852, but a percentage decrease of 2.34%.

By converting statement amounts to percentage relationships, statements are reduced to a common base. This makes it possible to compare statements of large and small business, of companies in the same industry, of companies in different industries, and so forth. For example, in the case of the Michaels Inc., its 19X4 income statement could thus be compared with the composite for the industry. Such a comparison might show that its gross profit percentage of 45% is 5% higher than the industry average, and that its net income percentage of 7.04% is just about average for the industry.

Fixed-variable analysis. A vertical analysis can be somewhat misleading when applied to income statement amounts. The reason for this is that some expenses tend to increase and decrease as sales and production rise and fall, while others tend to remain more or less constant. Expenses that tend to vary with sales are called *variable,* or *semi-variable,* while those that barely vary with sales are termed *fixed expenses.* The effect of this behavior of costs will be demonstrated by reference to the general and administrative expenses of the Michaels Inc.

To recap our previous findings, in 19X4 general and administrative expenses had *increased* $5,000, but in relation to the increase in sales, this was a *decrease* of 2.32%. A breakdown of general and administrative expenses for 19X4 and 19X3 is shown in Figure 11.

If we analyze these expenses one by one, we find that officers' salaries is a fixed expense that does not vary with an increase or decrease in sales or production. The next item, office salaries is a semi-variable expense; $8,000 of this expense is necessary at a minimum level of sales, while the remainder varies with the increase or decrease in sales. By continuing in this manner down the expenses in this schedule, the following analysis (Figure 12) can be constructed.

This analysis shows that the variable portion of general and administrative expenses increased in direct proportion to the increase in sales (2.62% to 2.63%). The fixed portion of these expenses (the expenses that shouldn't have gone up because of an increase in sales) increased $2,875 ($27,400-$24,525). Thus, this analysis presents a very much different picture of the behavior of expenses than either the horizontal analysis, which showed that general and administrative expenses rose $5,000, or the vertical analysis, which showed a percentage decrease of 2.32%. This situation calls for further inquiry into the reasons for the rise in fixed expenses.

MICHAELS INC.
Schedule of General and Administrative Expenses
For the Years Ended December 31, 19X4 and 19X3

	19X4	19X3
Officers' salaries	$11,000	$ 8,500
Office salaries	10,050	9,000
Office rent	2,000	2,000
Stationery and supplies	1,500	1,000
Telegraph and telephone	1,700	1,575
Legal and audit	2,500	2,000
Postage	800	1,150
Bad Debts	4,200	3,400
Miscellaneous	1,250	1,375
	$35,000	$30,000

Fig. 11. Schedule of General and Administrative Expenses.

MICHAELS INC.
Fixed-Variable Analysis of General and Administrative Expenses
For the Years Ended December 31, 19X4 and 19X3

	19X4			19X3		
	Total	*Fixed*	*Variable*	*Total*	*Fixed*	*Variable*
Officers' salaries	$11,000	$11,000	$	$ 8,500	$ 8,500	$
Office salaries	10,050	8,000	2,050	9,000	8,000	1,000
Office rent	2,000	2,000		2,000	2,000	
Stationery and supplies	1,500	750	750	1,000	750	250
Telegraph and telephone	1,700	1,200	500	1,575	1,200	375
Legal and audit	2,500	2,500		2,000	2,000	
Postage	800	700	100	1,150	700	450
Bad debts	4,200		4,200	3,400		3,400
Miscellaneous	1,250	1,250		1,375	1,375	
	$35,000	$27,400	$7,600	$30,000	$24,525	$5,475
Variable Costs as a Percentage of Sales			2.62%			2.63%

Fig. 12. Fixed-Variable Analysis of General and Administrative Expenses.

Ratio analyses and other useful analytical tools. As we have seen in the last section, horizontal analysis is a left-to-right comparison (year-to-year, industry-to-industry, etc.) of statement items; and vertical analysis is a top-to-bottom analysis of financial statements, showing the inter-relationships of the statement items. Vertical analysis can be expanded to include a left-to-right comparison of these relationships.

Additional analytical tools have been developed to supplement horizontal and vertical analyses. Most of these tools use variations of the methods used in making horizontal and vertical analyses. For example, each of the percentages used in the illustrated vertical analysis (Figure 10) is a ratio, showing the relation of one statement item to another. Such test ratios are among the most useful analytical tools available.

Some of these additional analytical tools, including test ratios, will be described, and their use illustrated, in the remaining section of this chapter.

Working capital. Working capital is the life's blood of a firm, often determining its capacity for survival and growth. The sufficiency of available working capital can be analyzed by assessing current ratios and using acid test ratios, horizontal or vertical analyses, and the like.

> Current ratio. The current ratio is the ratio of current assets to current liabilities. This ratio measures the ability of the company to pay its current obligations as they come due and to finance its current operations. As a rule of thumb, an acceptable minimal current ratio runs about two to one (two dollars of current assets for every dollar of current liabilities). The current ratios for the Michaels Inc. are computed as follows:

$$\textit{Current ratio} = \frac{\textit{Current assets}}{\textit{Current liabilities}}$$

	19X4	*19X3*
Current assets	$70,145	$68,575
Current liabilities	$31,140	$23,780
Current ratio	2.25	2.88

Acid test ratio. The acid test ratio is an even more rigorous test of the company's ability to meet obligations than the current ratio. It is a measure of the ratio of the so-called quick assets—cash, accounts and notes receivable, and marketable securities—to current liabilities. At least a one-to-one ratio is considered desirable.

The computation of the acid test ratio for the illustrative problem is as follows:

$$\textit{Acid test ratio} = \frac{\textit{Quick assets}}{\textit{Current liabilities}}$$

	19X4	*19X3*
Quick assets:		
Cash	$ 4,500	$11,000
Accounts receivable (net)	33,695	21,575
Total quick assets	$38,195	$32,575
Current liabilities	$31,140	$23.780
Acid test ratio	1.23	1.37

Horizontal analysis of working capital. The working capital position of a company can also be analyzed horizontally, in the same manner as the balance sheet and income statement. This analysis is shown in Figure 13.

Vertical analysis of working capital. A vertical analysis of working capital, showing the percentage relationships of each of the current assets to total current assets, and of each of the current liabilities to total current liabilities, helps pin down shifts in the distribution of current assets and liabilities. This is shown in Figure 14.

This analysis points out that the distribution of current liabilities hardly changed at all, but that there was a shift in current assets from cash and inventory to accounts receivable.

Source and application of working capital. This statement shows the sources of working capital and its disposition. The difference between the amount of working capital provided and that applied accounts for the increase or decrease in the amount of working capital during the year.

MICHAELS INC.
Working Capital Analysis
December 31, 19X4 and 19X3

Current Assets:	*19X4*	*19X3*	*Increase-(Decrease)*
Cash	$ 4,500	$11,000	$(6,500)
Accounts receivable—customers (net)	33,695	21,575	12,120
Merchandise inventory	31,200	35,500	(4,300)
Prepaid expenses	750	500	250
Total Current Assets	$70,145	$68,575	$ 1,570

Current Liabilities:			
Accounts payable	$15,700	$12,100	$ 3,600
Notes payable to banks	3,000	2,500	500
Accrued taxes, wages, and other expenses	12,440	9,180	3,260
Total Current Liabilities	$31,140	$23,780	$ 7,360
Working Capital	$39,005	$44,795	$(5,790)

Fig. 13. Horizontal Analysis of Working Capital.

MICHAELS INC.

Working Capital Analysis

December 31, 19X4 and 19X3

	19X4		*19X3*	
Current Assets:	*Amount*	*%*	*Amount*	*%*
Cash	$ 4,500	6.41	$11,000	16.05
Accounts receivable—customers (net)	33,695	48.04	21,575	31.46
Merchandise inventory	31,200	44.48	35,500	51.77
Prepaid expenses	750	1.07	500	0.72
Total Current Assets	$70,145	100.00%	$68,575	100.00%
Current Liabilities:				
Accounts payable	$15,700	50.42	$12,100	50.88
Notes payable to bank	3,000	9.63	2,500	10.51
Accrued taxes, wages, and other expenses	12,440	39.95	9,180	38.61
Total Current Liabilities	$31,140	100.00%	$23,780	100.00%

Fig. 14. Vertical Analysis of Working Capital.

MICHAELS INC.

Statement of Changes in Financial Position

For the Year Ended December 31, 19X4

Source of Funds:			
Net income		$20,412	
Add expenses not requiring expenditures of working capital:			
Depreciation of building, machinery and equipment	$3,500		
Organization expense	300	3,800	
Total			$24,212

Application of Funds:		
Dividends on capital stock	$12,902	
Purchase of land	5,000	
Purchase of building, machinery and equipment	7,100	
Retirement of First Mortgage Bonds	5,000	
Total		30,002
Decrease in Working Capital		$ 5,790

Changes in Components of Working Capital	
Cash	(6,500)
Accounts receivable	12,120
Merchandise inventory	(4,300)
Prepaid Expenses	250
Accounts payable	(3,600)
Notes payable to banks	(500)
Accrued taxes, wages and other expenses	(3,260)
Decrease in Working Capital	(5,790)

Fig. 15. Statement of Source and Application of Working Capital.

Analyzing accounts receivable. To determine the quality of the accounts receivable and to check if the provision for bad debts is adequate, obtain from the company a schedule showing the age of its accounts receivable outstanding. Compare this aging with the company's credit terms and estimate the possible valuation of the accounts (based on their age and past record of the debtors involved). The table below shows such an estimate.

	December 31, 19X3		
	Amount	*% estimated collectible*	*Amount estimated collectible*
Less than 30 days old	$50,000	100%	$50,000
31 to 60 days old	20,000	90%	18,000
61 to 90 days old	12,000	75	9,000
91 to 120 days old	6,000	50	3,000
Over 120 days old	2,000	0	....
	$90,000		$80,000

The above is the preferable method of analyzing a company's accounts receivable. However, if a schedule of the age of the company's accounts receivable outstanding cannot be obtained, the average age of such receivables can be estimated as follows:

Let: D = Average age of receivables (in days)
A = Net accounts receivable at end of period (from company's balance sheet for that date)
S = Net sales for period (from company's income statement for period)
P = Period for which average is being estimated (in days)

Then:

$$D = \frac{A \times P}{S}$$

Thus, for the Michaels Inc., the computation for 19X3 and 19X4 would be as follows:

For 19X3: $D = \dfrac{21{,}575 \times 365}{208{,}500} = 37.77$ days

For 19X4: $D = \dfrac{33{,}695 \times 365}{290{,}000} = 42.41$ days

A meaningful comparison can then be made between the average age of the company's receivables and its credit terms. In the case of the Michaels Inc. this indicator shows that the average age of the receivables at the end of 19X4 is about five days more than at the end of 19X3. If the company's credit terms were considerably less than this average age, it would indicate that many of its receivables are probably uncollectible, and that the situation is worsening.

► NOTE: Care should be exercised in using this average because the ending balance in accounts receivable may not be representative. For example, if the company reports on a natural business year, accounts receivable would be abnormally low.

Inventory. Inventory turnover ratio. The ratio of inventory turnover measures the number of times during the year that the average inventory is turned into sales and must be replaced. The more times the inventory turns over during the period, the greater the utilization of capital and the greater the profit potential.

An inventory turnover ratio that is lower than the average for the particular industry indicates a too large investment in inventory (sometimes caused by speculation in inventories), a large amount of unsaleable goods included in inventory, poor merchandising, or undervaluation of inventories. On the other hand, a high inventory turnover ratio may indicate efficient inventory and merchandising practice, but may also indicate an overvaluation of inventories.

Here again, extraneous factors can distort the computation, lessening the value of this indicator. These factors include the use of LIFO in valuing inventories, and abnormally small inventories on hand at the beginning and end of the company's fiscal period. Since LIFO valuation usually results in lower than actual inventory valuation, this problem may be partially resolved by using estimates of inventory worth. The problem of abnormally small inventories at the end of the fiscal year can be resolved by using an average of monthly inventory balances.

The computation of inventory turnover ratio is made as follows:

$$\textit{Inventory turnover ratio} = \frac{\textit{Cost of goods sold}}{\textit{Average inventory}}$$

	19X4	19X3
Cost of goods sold	$157,475	$104,250
Average inventory		
Inventory on 1/1	$ 35,500	$ 33,400
Inventory on 12/31	31,200	35,500
Total	$ 66,700	68,900
Average inventory (1/2 of Total)	$ 33,350	$ 34,450
Inventory turnover ratio	4.72	3.03

Average number of days for turnover. Using the turnover ratio just computed, the average number of days per turnover can be easily computed, as below:

$$\textit{Average number of days per turnover} = \frac{365}{\textit{Inventory turnover ratio}}$$

Thus, in 19X4 the average number of days the inventory turned over is 77, and in 19X3, 120 days. These two statistics would seem to indicate that one of the contributing factors to the rise in sales in 19X4 was the increased efficiency in the use of inventories.

► NOTE: If the company whose statements are being analyzed has both raw material and finished goods inventory, the turnover rate should be computed separately for each type of inventory.

Financial condition. Ratios of liabilities to net worth. The two ratios liabilities to net worth help supply the information necessary to evaluate the financial condition of a business in terms of what it owes and what it owns. The ratio of *current* liabilities to net worth is valuable for the short-term view, while the ratio of *total* liabilities to net worth is necessary for the long-term picture.

1. $\textit{Ratio of current liabilities to net worth} = \frac{\textit{Current liabilities}}{\textit{Net worth}}$

	19X4	19X3
Current liabilities	$ 31,140	$23,780
Net worth	$104,705	$97,195
Ratio of total current liabilities to net worth	29.74%	24.47%

2. $\textit{Ratio of total liabilities to net worth} = \frac{\textit{Total liabilities}}{\textit{Net worth}}$

	19X4	19X3
Total liabilities	$ 41,140	$38,780
Net worth	$104,705	$97,195
Ratio of total liabilities to net worth	39.48%	39.90%

The foregoing computations show that in 19X4 for every dollar of financing, short-term creditors have contributed roughly 30 cents, long-term creditors 9½ cents, and stockholders 60½ cents. This relationship indicates a fairly strong financial condition. In fact, from the stockholders' point of view, it might be advantageous for the company to increase its long term financing in order to obtain more leverage.

► OBSERVATION: Some analysts prefer to substitute tangible net worth for total net worth. They base their preference on the theory that intangible assets cannot be properly measured in the case of a going concern and are worth little to the firm that is being forced out of business. Tangible net worth is computed by subtracting intangible assets from net worth. In any of the ratios in which net worth or assets are considered, the intangible element may be omitted from consideration merely by performing this subtraction.

Fixed assets to net worth. This ratio gauges the relationship between investment in fixed assets and equity—helping to determine whether there is an overinvestment in fixed assets. A larger ratio is of course expected in the case of manufacturing businesses than in non-manufacturing companies.

$$\textit{Ratio of fixed assets to net wosth} = \frac{\textit{Fixed assets (net book value)}}{\textit{Net worth}}$$

	19X4	19X3
Fixed assets	$ 74,500	$65,900
Net worth	$104,705	$97,195
Ratio of fixed assets to net worth	71.15%	67.77%

Number of times bond interest is earned. In industries having heavy bond financing, such as utility and transportation, the number of times that bond interest is earned is a vital indicator of a company's financial condition. A company can omit dividends on preferred and common stock without serious consequences, but a default on its bond interest can lead to receivership. This ratio is computed by dividing net income before deducting interest and federal income taxes by the amount of bond interest. Since bond interest is a negligible factor in the illustrative example, the ratio is an astronomical 43.53 in 19X4, and 34.96 in 19X3. Prospective investors in a company's preferred or common stock can make a similar computation to gauge how well dividends are protected.

Turnover of net worth. By dividing net worth (or tangible net worth) into net sales, a ratio is developed that measures the capitalization of the business and the efficient employment of capital. While a high ratio of net worth turnover tends to indicate an efficient employment of capital, it can also indicate a dangerous undercapitalization.

$$\textit{Turnover of net worth} = \frac{\textit{Net sales}}{\textit{Net worth}}$$

	19X4	19X3
Net sales	$290,000	$208,500
Net worth	$104,705	$ 97,195
Turnover of net worth	2.77	2.15

Other indicators. Other indicators of financial condition include ratios of funded debt to net working captial, funded debt to total capitalization, fixed assets to funded debt, net worth to total assets, etc.

Profitability analysis. The vertical analysis of the income statement on page 259 yielded ratios that can be compared to past years, to standards within the company, to averages for the industry, and to other businesses. The results of the analysis can be used to determine, among other things, if the company is in a good competitive position and if it has a good profit potentiality. The ratios of gross profit to net sales, and net income to net sales are of particular value.

Gross profit percentage. The gross profit percentage indicates the margin the business works on. For example, if it costs seventy cents to manufacture a product and it sells for one dollar, the percentage of gross profit is 30%. Thus, the firm retains thirty cents of each sales dollar, which must pay for general and administrative expenses, selling expenses, taxes, other non-manufacturing expenses, and must provide a profit for its owners. If most of the companies in the same industry show a higher gross profit percentage, this fact indicates that the company's operation may be inefficient, that their competitive position may be poor forcing them to sell at lower prices than their competitors, or that their product mix features the lower priced, lower profit items. On the other hand, management may have decided that there is more to be gained from emphasizing volume rather than high gross profit margins.

Using the gross profit percentage to estimate inventories. In addition to being used as a measure of profitability, the gross profit percentage can also be used to estimate and check inventories. For example, given sales, opening inventory, direct material purchases, direct labor, and indirect expenses, the amount of ending inventory may be estimated as follows:

Data

Net Sales		$100,000
Opening inventory	$25,000	
Direct material purchases	40,000	
Direct labor	20,000	
Indirect expenses	20,000	
Total		$105,000
Estimated gross profit percentage (Last year's percentage adjusted for increased labor costs.)		30%

Computation

Net sales ×*Est. gross profit* =*Est. gross profit*
$100,000 ×30% =$30,000

Net Sales —*Est. gross profit* =*Est. cost of goods sold*
$100,000 —$30,000 =$70,000

Total costs—*Est. cost of goods sold*=*Est. ending inventory*
$105,000 —$70,000 =$35,000

MICHAELS INC.

Statement Accounting for Variation in Net Income

For the Years Ended December 31, 19X4 and 19X3

Items Increasing Net Income			
Increase in Gross profit caused by increase in volume:			
Net Sales 19X4		$290,000	
Net Sales 19X3		208,500	
Total increase		$ 81,500	
Gross profit at 19X4 rate (50%)			$40,750
Increase in other income:			
19X4		$ 3,000	
19X3		2,700	300
Decrease in interest expense:			
19X4		$ 1,200	
19X3		1,000	200
Total Items Increasing Net Income			$41,250
Items Decreasing Net Income			
Decrease in gross profit caused by decrease in rate of gross profit:			
19X3	50.00%		
19X4	45.70		
	4.30%		
4.30% x $290,000		$ 12,475	
Increase in selling expenses:			
19X3	$57,000		
19X4	35,000	22,000	
Increase in general and administrative expenses:			
19X4	$35,000		
19X3	30,000	5,000	
Increase in Federal Income tax:			
19X4	$22,113		
19X3	21,190	923	
Total Items Decreasing Net Income			40,398
Increase in Net income			$ 852

Fig. 16. Analysis of Variation in Net Income.

Net income percentage. The net income percentage indicates how much of each sales dollar remains after production, selling, administrative, taxes, and other expenses of running a business are paid out.

Analysis of variation in net income. The horizontal analysis of the income statement showed that net income increased $852 in 19X4. The statement (Figure 16) analyzes this variation in net income. Note how the decrease in the rate of gross profit eats up $12,475 of the $40,750 increase in net sales.

It is possible to go one step further and analyze in a similar manner the reasons accounting for the variation in gross profit. This analysis would be made in terms of increased or decreased units sold, price increases and decreases, and increased and decreased cost of units sold.

Rate of return on capital invested. This ratio is one of the most widely used measures of profitability and efficient use of capital. The simplest use of this measure is made by the prospective investor who calculates his expected yield, or rate of returns as follows:

$$\textit{Expected rate of return} = \frac{\textit{Expected dividends}}{\textit{Market price}}$$

$$= \frac{\$1.20 \textit{ per share}}{\$30 \textit{ per share}} = 4\%$$

The most complicated use of this measure is made by management when evaluating alternate investment opportunities, new equipment, product lines, and the like. This computation will not be further explored because of its complexity and because it does not depend primarily on information presented in financial statements.

Another use of the ratio of return on capital invested is made by both investors and management. Investors and prospective investors use this version of the ratio to evaluate the company and the overall management, while top management uses it to evalute the performance of their plant and divisional managers using the capital and assets entrusted to them. The overall rate of return computation on stockholders' capital investment for the Michaels Inc., for 19X4 and 19X3 is:

$$\textit{Rate of returns on stockholder's capital investment} = \frac{\textit{Net income}}{\textit{Average stockholders' capital investment}}$$

	19X4	19X3
Net income (after taxes)	$ 20,412	$ 19,560
Stockholders' capital investment (capital + retained earnings) at:		
beginning of year	$ 97,195	$ 86,635
ending of the year	104,705	97,195
total	$201,900	$183,830
Average stockholders' capital investment during year (½ of total)	$100,950	$ 91,915
Rate of return on stockholders' capital investment	20.22%	21.28%

A similar computation could have been made using either total average tangible assets entrusted to management, or all average long-term capital available (stockholders' equity + long-term liabilities) in place of the average stockholders' capital investment. These variations of the rate of return ratio provide a more accurate picture of the efficiency with which management put to use the gross actual capital assets it had available.

Assuming that the rate of return on total capital invested in the illustrative example is around 15% and that additional capital can be put to equally good use, additional capital acquired by loan at 6% interest should net the company 9% profit (15%-6%).

Earnings per share. Earnings per share is probably the most popular measure used by investors in evaluating and comparing securities. When there are only common shares outstanding, the computation is made by simply dividing net income after taxes by the number of common shares outstanding. But if there are also preferred shares outstanding, the current dividends attributable to the preferred shares are first deducted from net income before computing the amount of earning attributable to each common share. The computation for the mythical Michaels Inc. follows:

$$\textit{Earnings per share} = \frac{\textit{Net income}}{\textit{Common shares outstanding}}$$

	19X4	19X3
Net income (after taxes)	$20,412	$19,560
Common shares outstanding	9,000	9,000
Earnings per share (net income ÷ common shares o/s)	$2.27	$2.17

► NOTE: If a valid comparison is to be made between years, net income should be the result of operations and not contain large non-recurring items such as profits from sale of plant and equipment.

Cash flow earnings per share. Cash flow earnings per share is a variation of the earnings per share measure. It is computed by using the earnings per share ratio formula, but adding back to net income major non-cash expenditures such as depreciation and depletion. When not misused, this measure affords some valuable comparisons with past years' figures.

For example, a comparison of cash flow earnings and reported earnings of corporations for ten years showed that while corporate reported earnings had not increased substantially, cash flow earnings per share rose about 50%. One explanation for this phenomenon pointed up by this analysis is that most corporations took advantage of the liberalized depreciation provisions in the 1954 Income Tax Code and switched to accelerated depreciation methods. The resulting increase in depreciation charges obscured a 50% increase in earnings.

If, on the other hand, the increase in depreciation in this analysis had resulted from increases in fixed asset investments rather than from a change in depreciation methods, the adding back of depreciation expenses to net income would result in a misleading statistic. This is especially true since the computation of cash flow earnings per share takes into account only one-half the cash flow in connection with fixed assets. The deduction from net income is made for the cash outflow when an asset is acquired but no deduction is allowed for the depreciation of the asset each year of its useful life. In the vernacular, this is known as having your cake and eating it too.

Valuation of a company's worth. Of course every ratio and indicator discussed in the previous pages enters into the valuation of the worth of a company. Nevertheless, there are some specific rules of thumb and guides used in the area of valuation. Some of these follow.

Price earnings ratio. The price earnings ratio is calculated by dividing the market price of shares of a publicly owned company by the per share earnings, as follows:

$$\textit{Price earnings ratio} = \frac{\textit{Market price per share}}{\textit{Per share earning}} = \frac{\$30 \textit{ per share}}{\$3 \textit{ per share}} = \underline{\underline{10}}$$

The price earnings ratio can be turned around to help value the securities of a close corporation. This is done by computing the price earnings ratio of one or group of publicly owned companies in the same industry and roughly in similar financial positions. By multiplying the yearly per share earnings of the company by the price earnings ratio, it is possible to compute an approximate market price of the company's securities. This computation is of little use, however, in assessing the market value of shares in new companies with potential, but with little or no history of earnings, or in other companies with past histories of deficits. (Even a bankrupt company is usually worth something.)

The price earnings ratio is also a useful comparative measure. If the average ratio for the industry is higher than for the company being evaluated, it may indicate that the company's stock is undervalued and consequently a good buy, or on the other hand, that the company is not as highly regarded as others possibly because of old inefficient equipment, or a record of earnings and dividend instability, or poor management.

Book value per share. Book value per share indicates how much of net assets (asset less liabilities) is attributable to each share of stock. It is computed by dividing net worth by the number of common shares outstanding. However, any special preference rights of preferred stockholders must be considered. Where these exist, the portion of the net worth applicable to the preferred stock must first be deducted before the book value of the common stock is computed. This is done by deducting from net worth the par value or liquidating value of the preferred stock, plus any cumulative dividends in arrears.

In recent years many have come to realize that book value provides little guide to a company's worth. One reason for this de-emphasis of a formerly highly regarded ratio is that it is now generally realized that asset values shown on the balance sheet do not represent market values, or cost of replacement of these assets. Secondly, even if the balance sheet amounts were converted to market value, book value would only be important upon liquidation. If a company continues in operation, the market value of its assets is less important than the future earning capacity of the company.

Gross income measures. By trade custom, many types of businesses are valued at a multiple of gross income for a given period. For example, an office building is valued at from 8 to 12 times yearly rent roll, or an accounting practice at from 1 to 2 times yearly gross fees. Most retail businesses will sell at a multiple of gross earnings, plus an agreed upon valuation of the inventory, say 80 cents on the dollar, and an agreed upon amount for the fixtures and other fixed assets.

The valuation multiple for any particular business can be determined by consulting the appropriate trade association or a business broker. If the range of the multiple varies from say 2 to 5 times yearly gross earnings, the specific figure to be used must be estimated by taking into consideration the relative attractiveness and specific circumstances of the business being considered.

Additional statements. There are many additional statements that can be constructed or acquired that can aid the analyst in evaluating a business. Three that will be briefly discussed here are:

1. Pro forma statements.
2. Cash flow projections.
3. Breakeven statements.

Pro forma statements. Pro forma statements are made up to show approximately how the financial statement will look upon successful completion of the proposed transaction. In the case of a bank loan, a pro forma balance sheet will show the projected financial position of the company after the additional monies are acquired and expended in accordance with the terms of the loan agreement. For example, if the terms of the loan agreement specify that $10,000 would be expended for additional equipment and $5,000 would be for additional working capital, the pro forma balance sheet would reflect the changes in working capital and equipment on the asset side of the balance sheet and the corresponding $15,000 due to bank on the liability side of the statement. If a merger is proposed, the pro forma statement would show approximately how the statements of merged corporation would appear.

Pro forma statements should be analyzed in the same way as ordinary statements to find out whether the consummation of the proposed transaction will result in a strengthening of existing financial relationships.

► EXAMPLE: The Allan Corporation requests a $20,000 loan from the Second National Bank. The stated reason for the loan is to provide additional working capital funds. When the credit department of the bank analyzes the pro forma balance sheet, it finds that even with the addition of $20,000 to working capital, the company's current ratio is still less than 2:1 and its acid test ratio is less than 1:1. What's more, the $20,000 addition to liabilities increases the ratio of liabilites to net worth to a point that for every dollar of financing the creditors will have supplied, the stockholders will have provided only 25 cents. Under the circumstances, the loan officer of the bank will reject the application and recommend that the owners of the Allan Corporation seek additional equity financing through the issuance and sale of stock, before renewing their loan request.

Cash flow projections. The working capital analysis evaluates a company's liquidity on an average basis. A good average working capital position, however, does not assure that the company has funds available to meet specific obligations and needs as they occur. To fill this information void, cash flow projections can be made up showing the expected in and out flow of cash on a weekly or monthly basis.

► EXAMPLE: Although the current ratio of the Fullman Company (on a pro forma basis) is a healthy 3:1, cash flow projections indicate that during the company's busy season there will not be sufficient funds to pay the second installment on the proposed loan. Forewarned, the management of the Fullman Company arranges with a factor for short-term accounts receivable financing during this period.

Break-even statements. Previously, in the section covering fixed-variable analysis, a distinction was made between fixed and variable costs. Fixed costs, it was said, remain relatively stable as volume fluctuates, while variable costs change almost directly in proportion to volume changes. Using this knowledge of cost behavior, a break-even statement may be constructed showing the minimum volume necessary to neither lose or make money. We know that the break-even sales volume has to equal the fixed costs plus the variable costs, or B=F+V. We also know that the variable costs (V) vary in almost direct proportion to sales volume (S). To find this proportion (for most practical purposes) take a situation where V and S are known, and divide V by S. This fraction, V/S, can then be used to find V for any other sales volume by multiplying the sales volume by this fraction. Thus, we find that our first formula, B=F+V, becomes (after various algebraic computations) $B = \frac{F}{1 - V/S}$ or:

Break-even sales = Fixed costs

$$\textit{divided by} \left(1 - \frac{\textit{Variable costs}}{\textit{Given sales volume}}\right)$$

► EXAMPLE: The A & J Company has sales of \$500,000, fixed costs of \$120,000, and variable costs of \$200,000. Break-even sales volume would be computed as follows:

$$B = \frac{\$120{,}000}{1 - \frac{\$200{,}000}{\$500{,}000}} = \$200{,}000$$

If sales in this example are made at two dollars a unit, break-even sales represent 100,000 units, while current sales of \$500,000 represent sales of 250,000 units. Thus, there is a safety margin of 150,000 units, or \$300,000.

Summarizing the ratios. The following chart summarizes many of the ratios and percentages we have already computed, and compares them with those of competitors in the same line and with the industry average.

	MICHAELS INC.		COMPETITORS				INDUSTRY AVERAGE
	19X4	19X3	Alex, Inc.	Bacon Co.	Clemons Corp.	Dean Ltd.	
Financial Condition							
Current ratio	2.25	2.88					
Acid test	1.23	1.37					
Current liabilities to net worth	29.74%	24.47%					
Total liabilities to net worth	39.48%	39.90%					
Fixed assets to net worth	71.15%	67.77%					
Turnover of net worth	2.77	2.15					
A/C Receivable Collections							
Aver. no. of days a/c's are o/s	41.91 days	36.80 days					
Inventory Turnover							
Turnover ratio	4.72	3.03					
Aver. no. of days per turnover	77 days	120 days					
Profitability and Valuation							
Rate of return on stockholder's capital invested	20.22%	21.28%					
Earnings per share of common stock	2.27	2.17					
Price earnings ratio	15.27	14.39					
Income Statement Relationships (to sales)							
Gross profit	45.70%	50.00%					
Selling expenses	19.66%	16.79%					
General and administrative	12.07%	14.39%					
Net income after taxes	7.04%	9.38%					

Fig. 17. Suggested Chart for Summarizing and Comparing Analyses of Financial Statements of Clients and Competitors.

9

Production Cost Accounting

CONTENTS

9

Production Cost Accounting

Robert L. Kelly, CPA

Cost accounting is the general term that describes the process used to account for costs—costs of a product, of a service, or of an operation or procedure.

Cost accounting is an extension of general accounting, and production cost accounting is the most highly developed form of cost accounting. The rapid industrialization of the United States in the twentieth century and the increased application of scientific methods to management fostered the development of production cost accounting systems.

The work of the cost accounting pioneers at the beginning of the century was devoted almost entirely to gaining an understanding of the costs of production so that they might be able to price their products competitively and profitably. This is still one of the basic purposes of a cost accounting system. There has been little change from the cost principles identified at the turn of the century to those in use today. Most of the changes are refinements in procedural techniques rather than in cost accounting principles.

Starting with its passage in 1913, the income tax law has resulted in a constantly increasing need for acceptable determination of production costs. Taxable income rises or falls considerably as certain production costs are included in, or excluded from, inventory valuation. And inventory valuation still is, and has always been, a basic purpose of a cost accounting system.

After World War I, when the question of contract renegotiation arose, it became apparent that those manufacturers with good cost systems were in a much better position to obtain satisfactory settlements from the responsible authorities. There had developed by this time an awareness of the desirability of controlling costs by comparisons with predetermined standards. This led to the formation, in 1919, of the National Association of Cost Accountants, which has since been renamed the National Association of Accountants. This organization greatly encouraged the development of cost accounting in the United States into an effective planning and control mechanism.

The Federal government's interest in and influence on cost accounting and procedures continues. The government has uniform cost principles for grants and contracts with State and local governments and with educational institutions. Public Law 91-379 enacted in 1970 established a Cost Accounting Standards Board (CASB). The CASB publishes cost accounting standards that are followed by many manufacturers selling to the Federal government. Cost standards which are required in accounting for the cost of sales to the government may sometimes be adopted by manufacturers for all their production.

It is, however, factors in the private sector that have given cost accounting its greatest impetus. The application of industrial engineering techniques has developed standards which have been incorporated in cost accounting leading to an improved basis for exercising cost control. The growth in use of profit planning and budgeting systems has provided both the incentive to and opportunity for development of production cost accounting techniques.

PRODUCTION COST ACCOUNTING SYSTEM

The basic purposes of a production cost accounting system are to:

1. Determine units costs (as a guide to setting sales prices).
2. Value inventories.
3. Assist efforts to control costs.
4. Assist efforts to plan for the future.

Any well-conceived cost accounting system can achieve or provide the basis for achieving all of these purposes. As developed later in the chapter, a cost accounting system may be characterized as standard or actual, job or process, direct or allocated. In this chapter, illustrative material will reflect actual cost systems. Further, the illustrative material is presented largely as a manual system. The particular method of implementation has little effect on the underlying principles and concepts. Proper consideration of the special matters relating to computerized implementation, which is certainly widespread, is beyond the scope of this chapter.

Additional insights into the characteristics of direct and allocated cost systems can be gained from study of Chapter 7 on "Inventory and Inventory Valuation."

How advantages outweigh additional expenses. When a company installs a production cost accounting system for the first time, some additional expense is incurred not only in its design, but also in its maintenance. There are, however, many advantages to be considered. The Company may be better able to adjust prices to meet competition and to move swiftly to take advantage of special situations. The Company will be able to prepare financial statements at regular periods, such as each calendar month, without the necessity of taking a physical inventory. The company will be better able to review its past performance and take corrective action when necessary. It will have a much better knowledge of its manufacturing costs and will thus be in a position to exert more control over these costs. Moreover, by using the knowledge it gains from past operations, the company will be in a position to plan future actions more effectively.

► COMMENT: There is a tendency for some areas in cost accounting systems to become so complicated that the cost of operating the cost system cuts appreciably into the benefits to be derived. Cost accounting is, by its nature, a rather complex subject, but a cost accounting system should be as simple as possible to fulfill its purpose. There are degrees of complexity that can be fitted to apply only to particular situations. *A cost accounting system should be a means to an end and not an end in itself.*

Production cost accounting defined. Production cost accounting can be described as the classification, collection, and analysis of production costs in such a way as to determine the unit cost of each product manufactured. It is an integral part of the general accounting system. Production costs, as developed by the cost accountant, are used to determine the cost of goods manufactured, to price inventories, to determine the cost of goods sold, and consequently to determine profits, all of which are important elements of the financial statements.

This is accomplished by classifying the various expenditures that are considered to be production costs in such a way that the elements of cost, such as material, labor, and overhead, may be properly attributed, or applied, to the products manufactured.

The various principles involved in classification and application, together with the related procedures, form the body of what is generally known as production cost accounting. The extension of these principles and procedures into the area of cost control and future planning is usually desirable, but is not essential to the general accounting function. The term cost accounting is sometimes loosely applied to cost control efforts of industrial engineers that are not related to accounting data, and to analytical studies for pricing or equipment replacement purposes that may or may not be based on accounting data. Those efforts may more properly be referred to as cost analysis. The term cost accounting should be restricted to a system operated as a part of the general accounting records that embodies the double entry principles of debit and credit, and that records original entries at the proper time by appropriate journal entries in the general ledger.

Objectives and functions of a cost accountant. The principal objectives and functions of a cost accountant should be the following:

1. Preparing period cost reports.
2. Determining product costs.
3. Making cost analyses.
4. Assisting in cost control.

Preparing period costs reports. One of the basic advantages of a good cost accounting system is that reliable financial statements can be prepared without the necessity of taking physical inventories. In those industries where the taking of physical inventories is a sizable undertaking, this means that management can obtain statements monthly, or at some other desired frequency, instead of having to wait for semiannual or annual physical inventories and closings. The preparation of such periodic statements is related to the maintenance of the necessary perpetual inventory records. These records together with the production data and unit cost data are needed to determine the cost of sales for the period. To be effective, managers must have reliable profit figures more than once or twice a year. This requirement makes a cost accounting system a prime requisite for good management.

Determining product costs. Before period or monthly financial statements can be prepared, as well as for other purposes, it is necessary to determine product costs. A major function of the cost accountant is to classify the various production costs, and to apply them to the products in such a way as to ascertain the unit costs of manufacturing the different products. This is a highly skilled function that requires a knowledge and understanding of various cost accounting principles and procedures.

Making cost analyses. Another major function of the cost accountant is to prepare such cost analyses as may be required by management. Unit cost information is required in connection with equipment replacement studies. In addition, special analyses may be made for the purpose of setting selling prices or for planning future operations. If, in making these analyses, the cost accountants gives some thought to the results (in addition to compiling the information), the opportunity is created to be of more than routine assistance to company management.

Assisting in cost control. Yet another major function of the cost accountant is to assist in controlling costs. Effectiveness in this area may be accomplished in many ways.

The performance of individual operations, or departments, can be measured by comparing unit costs to similar costs of prior periods, or to pre-determined standards, and this information can be brought to the attention of the responsible individuals.

The cost accountant can analyze costs in such a way as to assist in the reduction of the production costs. Excessive material usage, due to poor yields or wastage, may be avoided by better planning. Material prices may be reduced by larger purchases or by competitive bidding. Labor may be used more efficiently following analysis of downtime or other delays. Departmental supervisors may control their production costs more carefully if responsibility reports are prepared for their use. Finally, costs may be reduced by simplifying the work process, or by standardizing the processing operations involved.

In the area of cost control, the cost accountant works closely with the industrial engineer and production management. Industrial engineers often get involved in cost accounting to achieve their own objectives, but it is usually more effective to have the cost accountant perform the cost accounting function.

RELATIONSHIP OF COST ACCOUNTING TO GENERAL ACCOUNTING

Advantages of integrating with general accounting system. It is important to keep in mind the relationship of the cost accounting system to general accounting. To be most useful, cost accounting should be an integral part of the general accounting system and subject to accounting principles. Where it is not, it loses much of its value. This is not always clearly understood, particularly by non-accountants.

There are certain areas where a need exists for close liaison between the cost accountant and the general accountant. In these areas, both will have less difficulty if they adhere to the same accounting principles. These areas, where the advantages of integration can be clearly seen, are:

1. Reporting period to be used.
2. The timing of costs.
3. Classification into production or selling costs.
4. Inventory accounts.
5. Budgetary control.

Reporting period to be used. One of the more important matters that should be resolved before proceeding too far with the cost accounting system is the reporting period to be used. Most manufacturing payrolls are on a weekly basis and it is quite desirable, therefore, to prepare certain cost reports on a weekly basis or in multiples thereof. It is awkward, however, to have cost reports prepared on a weekly basis when the financial reports are prepared on a monthly basis because of the difficulty of summarizing the weekly reports and reconciling them to the monthly statement. Of course, this can be, and is, accomplished through the use of proper accruals.

► SUGGESTION: Many companies have solved this problem by using periods of even weeks for their financial statements. A fiscal year would thus be composed of either 13 periods of four weeks each, or four quarters, each consisting of two four-week periods and one five-week period.

Consideration should also be given to the nature and content of the reports to be presented to the various levels of operating management. The closer to the operating level, the more quickly the reports should be prepared and disseminated to the supervisors. Appearance and decimal point accuracy may well be sacrificed to get the reports more quickly to where they can do the most good.

The timing of costs. A second area of common interest is the determination of when costs should be applied against income. In one aspect, this deals with whether an expenditure should be considered as resulting in a capitalizable asset or as a production cost. The question of whether a particular expenditure is to be considered a capital or an expense item is governed not only by accounting principles, but also by tax considerations and materiality. Certain expenditures are clearly additions to capital and some are clearly operating expense, but other expenditures may reflect elements of both. The accounting principles relating to repairs, replacements, alterations, and improvements are generally understood, but it is sometimes difficult to determine whether a particular expenditure may have created value extending beyond the year of expenditure. Where an expenditure prolongs the life of a depreciable asset, such as in rebuilding certain types of production equipment, the extension beyond the original projected life would have to be determined. Court rulings and governmental regulations, sometimes conflicting, on many of these matters somewhat limit the area of decision.

Depreciable assets will, of course, be charged to expense eventually, but in this area there are questions of policy as to whether expenses should be charged to operations for financial statement purposes in the same amounts as charged for tax purposes. The effect of accelerated depreciation on product costs should be carefully examined. Many attachments and components used in a manufacturing plant may have average lives of less than a year. It is generally considered reasonable to charge these to production expense in the year of acquisition, even though they may not all be consumed in one fiscal year. Similar treatment is often accorded purchases of capital items of a low unit value in order to avoid inventory records and other accounting details associated with capitalized expenditures. Items in common usage, such as nuts, bolts, screws, and washers, will often be charged to expense when purchased rather than when used.

Another aspect of the timing of costs relates to items which are clearly expense, but whose incurrence is time related to a given period (e.g., a fiscal year) rather than production volume related. Although definitions identifying which of these expenses should be considered as production costs are not precise, the following comments will provide some useful guidelines. Certain expenses are only applicable to the period in which they are incurred, while other costs of the period will be determined to be costs of the product and should be charged against income only when the products are sold. Those costs that are considered to be not particularly related to the product should be charged against income during the current period. For example, the cost of moving equipment from one location to another could, under certain circumstances, be charged to expense as a period cost. This might be preferable to capitalizing all or part of the cost and, through depreciation, charging it to inventory as part of the cost of the product.

► SUGGESTION: Items of an annual nature (e.g., depreciation, insurance, taxes) or of a seasonal nature (e.g., light, heat) may best be controlled by a budget or schedule of charges. A reserve can be set up for the actual expenses expected to be incurred by charging operating expenses of each period with the amount budgeted for that period. This procedure also helps to relieve operating personnel of the responsibility for expenses over which they may have very little control.

Classification into production or selling costs. The cost accountant is concerned with the costs of production, which are the costs up to the time when the product has been manufactured and is ready to be sold. Other expenses, such as sales commissions, advertising, warehousing, freight out, and other administrative costs are typically considered as period costs, to be absorbed by the income of the period, whereas the manufacturing costs are considered part of the product costs, and are only charged to income as the goods are sold. Variations in the classification of costs as period and product costs result from a number of practical reasons, and also because of different attitudes regarding the nature of production costs.

The cost accountant and the general accountant, therefore, have a common interest in a broad classification of costs as between production costs and those period costs which are generally known as selling and administrative costs. The cost accountant is usually assigned the responsibility of maintaining detailed records on production costs, commonly assembled in a manufacturing or factory ledger. He would also be responsible for preparing the manufacturing section of the profit and loss statement, and determining the cost of goods sold. He usually prepares the necessary journal entries to transfer this information to the general ledger.

Inventory accounts. The fourth area of common interest between the cost and general accountant is in maintaining inventory records. The inventory records are of interest to the general accountant for they constitute an important segment of the financial statements. The inventory accounts are usually considered to be a part of the factory ledger and to be the responsibility of the cost accountant. As raw materials are purchased, put into production, and manufactured into finished goods, the cost accountant accumulates the necessary data, from cost and production records, to enable him to make the necessary journal entries at the end of the period. Where perpetual inventory records are maintained, it is his responsibility to maintain these records in agreement with the control accounts in the general ledger.

Budgetary control. The final area of common interest is that of budgetary control. Performance reports of organizational units give executive management an opportunity to practice management by exception, that is, by placing emphasis on those areas where their control and experience appear to be most needed. Budgetary control involves more than the mere preparation of annual budgets. Control is not achieved until each responsible individual is given some means of checking his performance toward the desired goal and acts on the information provided.

This requires, if it does not already exist, the development of a responsibility accounting system, so that the actual expenses may be collected not only according to the nature of the expenses, but also by organizational units. The same would be true for sales and income accounts for those organizational units where such responsibility exists. This permits the preparation of monthly statements relating the actual income and expenses to the budgeted amounts and showing the variances from budgeted performance.

It is obvious, therefore, that the cost accounting system would be part of the responsibility accounting system and that the organizational units must coincide. Similarly, the budgets that are prepared for the production department have to coincide with those used in the cost accounting system. The cost centers used for budgeting production costs and determining the costs of individual operations may be considerably smaller than the organizational units recognized for budgetary control purposes. As is developed in Chapter 10, the use of standard costs is an advanced form of budgetary control.

Nature of production costs. Production costs are those generally associated with making a product ready for the market. This includes labor and materials directly associated with the manufacture of the product, and generally indirect charges and certain administrative costs closely allied to production.

The terms *cost* and *expense* are often used interchangeably, and at times they may be so used without confusion, but the term *cost,* as used in *cost of goods sold* or *cost of goods manufactured,* is an inclusive term composed of various cost elements. Costs clearly associated with the product, such as direct material and direct labor, are rarely referred to as expense, whereas production overhead includes a wide variety of items that are properly termed expenses. In the manufacturing expense section of the factory ledger, items such as heat, light, and power are properly referred to as expenses at the time they are incurred, and they are usually charged to natural expense accounts with appropriate titles. These natural expense accounts may be distributed over a wide variety of departmental overhead accounts, from where they may eventually be incorporated into the product costs. Before discussing production cost accounting any further, it may be well to clarify some additional cost terms that will be used later in this chapter.

Cost elements. There are three generally accepted cost elements: material, labor, and overhead. As a refinement for specific purposes, overhead is often classified into labor overhead and material overhead. In some cases, it is useful to take this into account in the classification of the natural expense accounts.

Direct charges. The principal direct charges are the direct material used in the product, and the direct labor expended in its production. There may be, in certain instances, other expenses that can also be classed as direct expenses applicable to the product, but, generally, all other expenses are included in the overhead cost element.

Indirect charges. In most situations there will be indirect material, indirect labor, and a considerable amount of indirect expense incurred in the manufacture of a product. Inefficiency factors, such as rework and idle time, as well as idle capacity, quite often enter into the overhead calculation.

Prime cost, cost to make, and cost to sell. Direct material and direct labor together are often referred to as prime cost. The prime cost, together with the associated overhead, is variously referred to as the product cost, the cost to make, or the cost of manufacture. When selling costs and administrative costs are added to the cost of manufacture, the resulting total is generally referred to as the cost to sell.

Types of cost accounting systems. Accounting for product costs may be accomplished in a large variety of ways. While reference is made to actual or standard cost systems, to job order cost or process cost systems, and to direct or allocated cost system, very few of the accounting systems in use today fall completely into one category or another. Most of these involve variations and combinations of the classic cost accounting systems. These variations tend to occur in the following areas:

1. Use of actual or standard data.
2. Methods of finding product costs.
3. Bases for applying costs to product.

In evaluating an existing installation, or in planning a new installation, the cost accounting system should be considered from the various aspects listed above.

Use of actual or standard data. The earlier cost accounting systems were historical in nature. Direct labor and direct material costs were accumulated and little attention was paid to any indirect items of manufacturing expense. If any consideration was given to these costs, it was generally in the nature of a percentage added to the prime cost. There are cost accounting systems in existence today that follow these early procedures.

Early in the history of cost accounting, it became apparent to the more astute observers that some products did not incur indirect manufacturing expenses in a fixed relationship to their prime cost. Furthermore, some of these products might not incur certain of these expenses at all. This led to the departmentalization of such overhead expenses and to their application on more precise bases than the prime cost. It became customary to distribute the actual expenses to various departmental overhead accounts in order to facilitate further distribution to the products. This required a considerable amount of clerical detail.

There are many accountants who contend that only actual costs should be used in the financial statements, and this is a defensible viewpoint. It does not necessarily require, however, that specific actual costs be applied to each product to arrive at a cost of goods sold that in all material aspects represents actual costs. Costs cannot always be determined exactly, and even the cost accountant who uses actual costs often applies these costs on an average basis, on a first-in, first-out basis, or on a last-in, first-out basis, without regard to the particular cost incurred when the material actually used was purchased. Cost accounting necessarily involves judgmental factors and many short cuts have been developed over the years that provide a satisfactory result in every material respect and, at the same time, avoid excessive clerical detail.

An early departure from actual costs—an approach that is still used, for example, in the garment industry—is an estimated cost system. It is quite effective where a large number of items of a reasonably similar type are to be manufactured. The material content and the amount of labor required is estimated, and an additional amount added to cover the overhead expense. Actual production costs are accumulated only in total, as manufacturing progresses. At the end of the production period, the total quantity produced is multiplied by the estimated cost and compared to the accumulated total of actual production costs. Minor differences are ignored and the estimated cost is used as the cost of goods produced whether they are inventory or sold. Major differences would call for a revision of the estimated costs.

A further refinement is to accumulate the actual production costs by the elements of material, labor, and overhead, and to compare these individual totals with the material, labor, and overhead elements of the estimated costs, each multiplied by the same total production. An estimated cost system of this nature is sometimes confused with a standard cost system.

A standard cost system normally involves more precise measurement of production costs than is found in an estimated cost system. Where product costs are predetermined on a reasonably scientific basis, either on past performance or engineered standards, a company is able to predict its production costs. Through comparison, a company can investigate unpredicted departures from the expected costs. Thus, a standard cost system provides an excellent basis for cost control.

In addition, a standard cost system serves to eliminate excessive detail in determining costs. In any manufacturing operation in which some products are consumed in the manufacture of other products, the use of a standard cost system greatly facilitates the cost accounting process. When a standard cost system is used, all transfers can be made at standard. When an actual cost system is used, the transfers at actual cost can only be made by developing such costs for transfer in the sequence of the production operations.

Methods of finding product costs. The earliest approach to finding the cost of goods manufactured, an approach that can hardly be called a cost accounting system, is the use of a manufacturing account into which all the production costs are closed at the end of a period. This method may still be used advantageously in certain situations. It requires physical inventories to be taken both at the beginning and at the end of the period. This manufacturing account, plus or minus the changes in raw material and work in process inventories, represents the cost of the products transferred to finished goods during that period. These costs, plus or minus the change in finished goods inventories, represent the cost of goods sold. The physical inventories should be valued at actual costs if they are determinable, but estimated costs may sometimes be used with satisfactory results.

Where a reasonable effort is made to find reliable product costs, and it must be remembered that this is not an exact science, the methods usually employed are either a *job order cost system* or a process cost system. Each has its particular advantage, depending on the nature of the products manufactured. The two systems could be combined in one plant.

Job order systems are commonly found in automobile repair shops, sheet metal plants, and other places where the items produced differ considerably from other items produced in the same place. A work order is prepared for each item or group of items to be manufactured, and costs are accumulated by that particular work order number. Material used to produce the goods is charged by requisition to the work order, and labor charges are similarly applied thereto. The total costs, as they accumulate on individual work orders, constitute the total carried in the work in process account. Manufacturing overhead may be added currently if it is a percentage of some factor included in the prime cost. Alternatively, it is often added at the completion of the work order. As each work order is completed, the total costs so accumulated are transferred from work in process to finished goods, or sometimes directly to cost of sales.

Through the use of work orders and move tickets, a job cost system provides a reasonable indication of how orders are moving through a plant, but the accumulation of costs by job, rather than by organizational responsibility, tends to aggravate the problem of controlling costs.

A *process cost system* is one that accumulates costs as the product travels from one cost center to another. A product unit is defined as a uniform quantity which will bear the same cost as any other product unit if subjected to the same treatment in the same cost centers. Cost records are not maintained by individual units, but only on total production and total costs in each cost center. Unit costs are determined progressively and cumulatively in each successive cost center by dividing total production costs by total production of like or equivalent units. Industries that are likely to employ process cost systems include food processing, paint, foundries, chemical, petroleum, steel, and paper processing.

In process costing, expenses are charged to the various cost centers where they are incurred. Raw materials are charged to the first and other processes as they are consumed, with other materials being charged to various processes as they are utilized. Direct labor costs are charged to the cost centers to which the employees are assigned. Indirect labor may also be applied to various cost centers, to the extent possible. The remaining overhead may be charged to the various cost centers where incurred, to the extent that this is feasible, and any residual cost may be allocated on some reasonable basis.

At the end of the cost period, the production in the first department is determined, together with the total costs. Where the units of production are not similar, or absorb varying treatment, a relationship will need to be established so that total production may be resolved into equivalent units of production. Once equivalent units of production are ascertained, the unit cost at the end of the first operation is determined by dividing the total production into the total costs. The quantities transferred to the next operation within the period are transferred at the unit cost so ascertained. This unit cost is considered as direct material cost for the next operation, even though it includes labor and overhead from the first operation.

The same procedure is repeated until the products have passed through all of the various cost centers and are transferred to finished goods. The work in process inventories at the various stages is valued at the unit costs at that stage and is absorbed into the costs of that cost center for the next period.

The application of standards permits the foregoing steps to be accomplished in any convenient order rather than in the production-determined sequence only.

Bases for applying cost to product. The third way in which cost systems may vary is in the bases for applying costs to the products. Regardless of which type of cost system is used, the charges for direct material and direct labor represent no particular problem. The more charges that can be made directly to jobs or processes, the more accurate the final product costs will be. It is almost invariably in the overhead area that improper bases may be used and that errors are likely to occur.

If specific charges cannot be made by lot, job, or product, it is possible that charges may be made to operations based on some other measurement such as weight. In a lumber mill, costs may be applied on the basis of board feet, and in a foundry on the basis of tons produced.

For the application of indirect expense, productive hour charges are probably more widely used than any other basis. These charges may be based on labor hours or machine hours, and may be used to apply labor costs, machine costs, overhead costs, or a combination of any or all of them.

In addition to variations in the bases for allocation of indirect expense, there are differences in the degree to which general expense is allocated to products. The range is from direct costing with little or no allocation and correspondingly high "contribution to overhead or profit," to complete absorption or full allocation of all expenses on some basis or another, and correspondingly lower reported product profit margins.

► COMMENT: A cost accounting system can be an actual or standard cost system. It can also be a job order or process cost system, or a direct or allocated cost system. Within the framework of whatever system is used, different bases can be used for applying costs to the product. The only real criterion possible is that a cost system must meet the needs of the particular company for which it is designed. These needs may arise internally or, particularly in government contracts, from customer insistence. The CASB strongly supports full allocation for negotiated contracts.

In certain industries, trade associations have developed uniform cost accounting systems so that each member of the industry can prepare cost information in the same way. This has the advantage of permitting comparisons of unit costs to be made between various companies. Sometimes, each company compares its own costs to the average costs that are computed by the trade association or a third party. A uniform cost system usually prescribes the various cost centers to be recognized, the way in which products are to be classified, the bases used to apply costs, and a chart of accounts to provide uniform classification of the various production costs.

In much the same way, government, through such agencies as the Interstate Commerce Commission and the Federal Power Commission, has provided accounting guidance for industries that come under regulation. Defense procurement, however, does not relate to any single industry and the history of government's role here has been different.

A long-standing goal of the Congress has been eliminate "war profiteering" from government procurement. Among the approaches tried have been excess profits taxes, cost-plus contracts, "incentive" contracts, renegotiation of contracts, and renegotiation of profits. The establishment of the CASB represents an approach to this goal primarily by concentrating on the task of the procurement officer. In this case, the underlying rationale is to attempt to assure satisfactory outcomes while procurement is still being negotiated, by minimizing the uncertainties that could lead to windfall or unintended profits. The Board operates on the premise that costs are easier to negotiate and monitor than prices or profits, especially under two provisions: that pre-agreed cost-finding methods are used, and that full allocation principles are adopted.

In furtherance of the latter, the Board normally rejects the criticism that the bases for full allocations are frequently quite arbitrary. While this criticism may often be valid, the CASB indicates that its requirements of uniformity and consistency in application are, in its view, a good defense against the charge of arbitrariness on its part. Additionally, under a given pricing situation, such an approach results in lower product margins when compared to less fully allocated procedures. This approach also puts the government in the position of stating that it is prepared to recognize and recompense any relevant cost.

For contractors there are two classes of unsatisfactory aspects, however. First, costs disallowed because not deemed relevant to government contracts may be regarded as fully allocable to nongovernment business. With comparable pricing, the effect of this is to make the profit margin on government business appear larger, which may induce the negotiator for the procurement agency to request a lower price. (Promotion, credit, and collection expenses are examples of expenses that may be treated this way.) The second class involves costs that are allocable but not allowable, such as material spoilage above an agreed-upon allowance. The Board's rules require that indirect costs related to nonallowable allocable costs must be identified and reported as equally nonallowable.

ELEMENTS OF PRODUCTION COST

Over the years a technical vocabulary has developed in the industrial accounting field to the point where certain terms in common use have a generally accepted meaning. This meaning may not always be clearly understood by other parties, such as production or sales people, who may be interested in the development of a cost accounting system. It may be desirable, therefore, to provide a glossary of the more important technical terms to be used.

While these terms were acquiring generally accepted meanings, a respectable body of cost accounting principles was being developed through the individual and joint efforts of accounting professors, industrial accountants, and the accounting profession. The glossary of technical terms and the cost accounting principles will be discussed under the following general areas in which they fall:

1. Material cost principles.
2. Labor cost principles.
3. Overhead cost principles.
4. Overhead cost allocation.
5. Service department cost principles.

Material cost principles. A few generally accepted definitions of the terms commonly used in connection with material costs are set forth below:

Raw material is a material purchased or otherwise acquired for incorporation in manufactured products. It may be either a natural material or the finished product of another manufacturer. As a class, raw materials are a subclass of direct materials.

Direct material is material that can be definitely measured and specifically charged to the product. It is usually, but not necessarily, identifiable in the finished product.

Indirect material is material that cannot conveniently be measured and charged to the product; indirect materials are often referred to as factory supplies.

Supplies are materials used in various operating and service departments that cannot, or should not, be measured and charged to the product.

Waste is the part of a basic raw material that is lost in processing and has no recovery value.

Scrap is the incidental residue from certain types of manufacturing. It is usually of small amount and low value, and recoverable without further processing.

Spoilage is the defective portion of regular production, having a value recoverable only through reprocessing.

There are many factors that need to be considered carefully in arriving at a reasonably accurate material cost. The determination of material costs is dependent on at least one, and often more, of the following:

1. Basis of price.
2. Costs included or excluded.
3. Bases of allocation.
4. Quantity used or allowed.
5. Wastage and yield.

Basis of price. There are at least twelve important bases of pricing that are used in charging direct material costs to the product. These bases are:

1. Specific costs.
2. First-in, first-out (FIFO).
3. Last-in, first-out (LIFO).
4. Standard costs.
5. Base stock.
6. Retail inventory method.
7. Simple average.
8. Weighted average.
9. Moving average.
10. Periodic average.
11. Replacement cost.
12. Cost or market, whichever is lower.

Different bases of pricing may produce different material costs. For example, assume 200 units of Part X are used in production during the month of July out of 750 available in stock. From the inventory records we find the following:

	Received	*Cost*	
Month	*Quantity*	*Total*	*Per Unit*
April	150	$ 285.00	$1.90
May	350	700.00	2.00
June	250	545.00	2.18
	750	$1,530.00	

Basis	*Material Cost*
Weighted average	$408
First-in, first-out	385
Last-in, first-out	436

Chapter 7, "Inventory and Inventory Valuation," contains a complete discussion of inventory pricing.

Costs included or excluded. While practice varies from one company to another, it is generally considered permissible to include the following costs:

1. Invoice price.
2. Cash discount.
3. Transportation charges.
4. Costs of purchasing, receiving, handling, and storing.

The last two are often grouped together and treated as material overhead, or as a material handling cost that is applied as a percentage of material costs.

► SUGGESTION: Develop a standard unit cost for such items for each kind of material. This unit cost can be added to, or included in, the material unit cost at the time requisitions are priced.

Bases of allocation. Appropriate bases are required for distributing these included costs to specific materials. The following are frequently used:

Cost	*Basis of allocation*
Freight-in.	Charges from FOB points.
Purchasing.	Purchase dollars or requisitions.
Receiving.	Quantity or weight.
Handling.	Quantity or weight.
Storing.	Volume or square feet occupied.

Joint products and by-products. One of the more interesting phases of accounting for raw material is the allocation of costs to *joint products, by-products, graded products,* and *seconds.*

A *joint product* is the product of an operation in which several products are produced, such as ham, bacon, and lard from hogs, in such proportions that no single one can be designated as a major product. *Joint products* are often encountered in process industries as exemplified by oil refinery operations or the electrolysis of salt to produce caustic soda and chlorine. A *by-product* is a product incidentally recoverable in the course of production of a major product, such as hides and tallows in the production of dressed beef, where the material value needs to be considered at the time of severance from the main product. *By-products* are frequently encountered in chemical operations. A *graded product* is a product obtained from raw material, such as lumber, which is purchased in bulk and subsequently graded for quality. A *second* is a product obtained from certain types of manufacturing, such as nylon hosiery, wherein defective processing causes a lower value to be placed upon the product.

Although general patterns have been established for the accounting for raw materials in the above circumstances, quite often one of the general patterns is not adequate to determine costs in specific instances, so another must be developed. An accepted principle is that these material costs should be determined and allocated to the separate products at that point of the process at which the products gain their separate identity. Failure to do this may result in one product absorbing the subsequently applied costs of another product. Depending on the particular stage of the process at which the separation is made, certain other costs are perhaps added to the raw material costs. If so, these other costs have to be considered as part of the costs to be allocated.

Where the profit margins on the major products are satisfactory, where the other products have little value, and where there is no clear basis for cost separation, it may not be necessary to make a cost allocation, but as competition narrows the margin of profit, more concerns desire and need an equitable allocation of cost. There is, of course, the possibility that processing is being applied to a by-product whose sales value is less than the additional processing cost. In such a case, it might be less costly to dispose of the material. In a period of high concern for the environment, however, disposal can, in itself, be costly. Therefore, at times, processing for sale even at a cost in excess of sales value might prove to be the most economical alternative.

Industries with special concerns in this area are: agricultural product industries, such as meat packers, dairies, canners, millers, and sugar refineries; extractive industries, such as metal and coal mining, oil refining, logging, and lumber; and chemical processors, such as manufacturers of dyes, solvents, preservatives, fertilizers, and explosives.

Commonly used bases of allocation for joint products are weight, market value, and purity tests. Costs are not normally allocated to by-products. The income from by-products is either treated as other income, added to total sales, subtracted from total costs for the main and by-product(s), or the total costs are reduced by the market value or expected revenue.

Quantity used or allowed. The determination of quantities used introduces the problem of inventories. Accurate cost accounting requires either perpetual inventories or physical inventories at the end of each cost period. If perpetual inventories are used, the amount of material put into production during any cost period is determined by summarizing the requisitions, or bills of material, that have been issued during the period. Where physical inventories are taken at the end of each cost period, it is normally assumed that all materials unaccounted for in the closing inventory were used in production during that period. Errors made in taking the physical inventory cause offsetting differences in the material costs from one period to another.

Wastage and yield. Standard bills of material quite often provide for a normal wastage allowance, so that unused material should be returned to the stockroom and properly accounted for. Excessive wastage may be determined by the need for additional requisitions to complete the work order. Spoilage should also be accounted for and should be part of a definite program of quality control.

Where, in a process, material is converted from one basis of measurement to another, the question of yield must be taken into consideration. Paper or wire, for instance, that is usually purchased by weight and used by length, may not exactly meet the prescribed basic weight or tolerance, so that other than a normal yield may result. Although many factories have highly developed systems of waste control, it is difficult to measure the dollar effect of wastage without using standard costs. By measuring actual wastage against the standard allowances for wastage, it is possible to use accounting techniques to monitor performance in respect to wastage and yield, providing a basis for exercising control.

Other aspects of material costs. Satisfactory material control is rarely obtained unless locked storerooms are provided, and unless adequate control is set up to see that all material purchased enters the stockroom and that no material leaves without a requisition. This also tends to insure agreement between perpetual inventory records and physical inventories, as perpetual inventories merely parallel physical situations in the stockroom, by recording the additions to, and withdrawals from, the stock. For items not susceptible to storeroom control, for example bulk solids or liquids and the like, equivalent controls should be provided to the degree possible. Meters, scales and in some cases locked bins or locked valves are indicated. In any case the basic criterion is the same, that is, practicable, physical security of the material against unauthorized or unrecorded withdrawal from stock.

► SUGGESTION: It is a good practice to arrange for cyclical counting of the physical inventory and reconciliation to the perpetual records. In this way such differences as may develop will be found progressively over the year rather than all at one time.

There are certain types of material, such as nuts, bolts, washers, or other items of low cost, where it often does not seem advisable to maintain perpetual records, but rather to determine usage by periods. These items are usually expensed as purchased, and used by production workers as required. As long as these purchases are made fairly evenly throughout the year, no particular distortion appears in the cost records or reports. In the event of an unusually heavy purchase, however, due to anticipation of a strike or some similar cause, it may be more suitable to allocate the cost over the normal purchase period to avoid distorting the cost reports.

A requisition should be prepared for all material that leaves the stockroom. An example of a form suitable for this purpose is shown in Figure 1. Where applicable, either a job number or product identification number would also be shown.

MATERIAL REQUISITION	Stock Room	DEPARTMENT		REQUISITION NO. 13579	1
DELIVER TO:	CHARGE ACCOUNT NO.			DATE	
DESCRIPTION OF MATERIAL	QUANTITY	PRICE		TOTAL AMOUNT	
REQUISITIONED BY:		RECEIVED BY:			

Fig. 1. Material Requisition Form.

If a stock clerk is not on duty on all shifts, someone, such as a foreman, empowered to remove material from the stockroom or other storage must also see to it that a requisition is prepared. A copy of the requisition is normally used for pricing material issues. A prepriced bill of materials can be used to advantage in those situations where the material requirements of work orders can be calculated in advance.

From an internal control standpoint, it is desirable that access to storerooms and other storage be limited to those individuals responsible for safeguarding the stock, and that someone other than the stock clerk should prepare the requisitions. If requisitions are prepared by the stock clerk, they should be approved by the foreman or supervisor.

Unusual material costs sometimes arise because of price declines or material becoming obsolete. These cases sometimes require special treatment. They are sometimes treated as costs of the period in which they occur or are recognized, rather than as product costs.

Labor cost principles. In some manufacturing operations, labor costs form so large a part of the total cost that efficient use of labor is required for any effective control of production costs. Labor costs are usually spoken of in terms of direct and indirect labor cost. Direct labor is defined as labor used in the actual production of a product, or specifically identifiable with the product. Indirect labor includes supervisory and clerical help, cleaners, and service department personnel. There are many borderline cases where certain types of labor could be classified in either category. These are more apt to occur under actual job cost systems where, as a matter of convenience, certain operations, such as the plating of parts, may be classified as indirect labor. This reduces the problem of keeping numerous time records for small job orders. Generally speaking, the more labor that can be charged directly to the product, the tighter the control of labor costs can be.

Certain costs, such as overtime premium, shift premium, vacation pay, holiday pay, payroll taxes, insurance, and pension costs, can quite properly be included in manufacturing overhead, but it may be desirable to segregate these as labor overhead and add them to the direct labor through use of a percentage. It is not uncommon for these additional costs to amount to as much as 25% or more of the direct labor costs. To include them with the direct labor costs tends to force them into their proper perspective and helps insure their getting adequate consideration and review. Whichever policies are followed should be clearly set out in writing so that the proper expense classifications will be made.

Timekeeping and payroll accounting. In order to obtain an adequate payroll distribution, it is often necessary to set up a timekeeping department to account for all time paid for, and to distribute the costs properly. Where the amount of work involved is not too great, this work can usually be performed by the foreman. Where individuals are employed exclusively for timekeeping, it is important that the controller supervise their activities. Whether the plant manager or the controller has the organizational responsibility is a matter to be determined according to the facts of a given situation, but the methods and the procedures used should be initiated by the controller and should be subject to his audit.

A practical approach to labor distribution is shown in Figure 2. The Daily Operations Report shown in Figure 2 is prepared for each employee. It illustrates entries required to report the four activities in which employee John Smith worked during one day.

The Daily Operations Reports for all employees are shingled, or overlapped, so that the hours charged to each function may be cross-footed and recorded on a monthly summary sheet in the column for that day. At the end of each month these daily hours are summarized by cross-footing to obtain totals for each type of work. This is illustrated in Figure 3.

If the functions served by these hand records are adapted to computer service, the records would also be redesigned to promote keypunching (or other data-entry method) accuracy. This would also require the assignment of codes to the various operations.

It should also be evident that in certain cost systems the operations outlined in Figure 2 would be replaced by cost center designations.

Labor cost accounting. An adequate classification of labor costs is essential for control of labor costs. The treatment accorded to certain labor costs can affect the costs of the jobs or products. For instance, overtime premium is only

DAILY OPERATIONS REPORT Grants Pass YARD DATE Jan. 2 196

NOTE: If work starts before 7 A.M. or stops after 5 P.M. enter the time in these spaces

INDICATE: START ✓ STOP X

Operation	7	8	9	10	11	12	1	2	3	4	5	HOURS WORKED
Receiving	Crane											3½
Loading Out												2½
Shaving												2½
Machine Framing												
Hand Framing												1½
Hand Peeling												
Reshaving												
Disposition of Culls												
Taking Inventory												
Work Orders												
Work for Others Intra-Co.												
Work for Others Outside Co.												
Work Outside Yard												
Supervision												
Office Work												
Other Work (Explain)												
Maintenance Work*												
Handl'g Treated Stock*												
Handl'g Cedar Stock*												
Boom Truck*												
Vacation Pay												

(Each hour column is subdivided 15 | 30 | 45; the 5 o'clock column shows 30.)

* The detail of these operations on reverse side must also be marked for time worked

TOTAL HOURS 9½

REMARKS:

O/T HRS. IN TOTAL 1½

MACHINE HOURS WORKED

OPERATION	GILLY #1	GILLY #2	HIGH LINE #1	HIGH LINE #2	HIGH LINE #3	CRANE	FORK LIFT #1	FORK LIFT #2	STRDL TRUCK	TRACTOR #1	TRACTOR #2	SHAVER
Receiving												
Loading Out												
Shaving												
Framing												
Other:												

EMPLOYEES

CLOCK NO.	NAME	HOURLY RATE	HOURS WORKED
12	J. Smith		

FOREMAN J. Doe SUPT. Unto

FORM 142 – PROD.

Fig. 2. Daily Operations Report.

MONTHLY SUMMARY OF MAN-HOURS WORKED — Grants Pass YARD — MONTH OF January 19__

HDLG. & MFG.	Jan. 2	3	Jan 29	January 30	31
Receiving	20	10	6		
Loading Out	30	30	8		
Shaving	40	30	20		
Machine Framing					
Hand Framing		20	7½		
Hand Peeling					
Reshaving					
Disposition of Culls	4	4			
Taking Inventory					
Work Orders					
Work for Others Intra-Co.					
Work for Others Outside Co.					
Work Outside Yard					
Supervision					
Office Work					
Other Work (Explain)					
Maintenance Work*	2	4	2½		
Handl'g Treated Stock*					
Handl'g Cedar Stock*					
Boom Truck*					
Vacation Pay					
TOTAL HOURS	96	98	44		
O. T. HRS. IN TOTAL	—	2	4		
MTCE. DETAIL					
Crane	2				
Gilly #1					
Gilly #2					
Trackage					
Straddle Truck					
Fork Lift #1					
Fork Lift #2					
High Line #1		2			
High Line #2		2			
High Line #3					

DAILY OPERATIONS — Jan 29 19__

NOTE: co…

INDICATE START ✓ STOP X (time grid 7, 8, 9 … 4, 5 in 15, 30, 45 minute intervals)

Operation	Start	Stop	Hours Worked	Hours Worked	Hours Worked	Hours Worked	Hours Worked
Receiving	✓ 8:00		2	1	1		2
Loading Out	✓ 4:00	X 5:30	2		2	2	2
Shaving		X 4:00	4	4	4	4	4
Machine Framing							
Hand Framing				2½	2½	2½	
Hand Peeling							
Reshaving							
Disposition of Culls							
Taking Inventory							
Work Orders							
Work for Others Intra-Co.							
Work for Others Outside Co.							
Work Outside Yard							
Supervision							
Office Work							
Other Work (Explain)							
Maintenance Work*	✓ 7:45	X 8:00	1	1½			
Handl'g Treated Stock*							
Handl'g Cedar Stock*							
Boom Truck*							
Vacation Pay							
TOTAL HOURS			9	9	9½	8½	8
O. T. HRS. IN TOTAL			1	1	1½	½	—

* The detail of these operations on reverse side m…

REMARKS

MACHINE HOURS W…ES

OPERATION	Gilly #1	Gilly #2	High Line #1	High Line #2	High Line #3	C…	Hourly Rate	Hours Worked	Hours Worked	Hours Worked	Hours Worked	Hours Worked
Receiving						Smith		9	9	9½	8½	8
Loading Out												
Shaving												
Framing												
Other:												
…T.												

FORM 142 – PROD.

Fig. 3. Illustration of the Shingling of Daily Operations Reports.

that portion of a person's wages paid to him in excess of the value of the actual hours worked at straight time rates. Such a payment may be made for one of the following reasons:

1. Unavailability of facilities for straight-time work.
2. Existence of an emergency or immateriality of the overtime hours.
3. Unavailability of a worker of comparable skill.
4. Increasing compensation without adjusting base pay.
5. Avoidance of hiring added personnel.

If a particular job or product is clearly and uniquely the cause of the overtime, charging the premium directly to that job or product would reflect this. In most cases, however, overtime is required because of the overall situation and not because of any one job. Therefore, the overtime premium would usually be charged to production overhead and spread over all production. The premium for regularly scheduled overtime, which may occur when six or seven days' coverage is needed, or when the production cycle is longer than eight hours, should likewise be spread over all production. This kind of overtime premium is labor overhead and may, accordingly, be distributed as a percentage of direct labor costs.

Shift premium. It is common practice to pay premiums for night or late shifts. When these shifts on which premiums are paid are regularly scheduled, the premiums are spread over all production. If night shifts are added only occasionally to meet production peaks, such premiums might be included in the general overhead rate.

Vacation pay. The actual vacation pay of hourly workers should be excluded from the cost distribution to departments. The most satisfactory method is to set up a vacation reserve, based on direct labor hours, against which vacation pay can be charged. In this way the costs of vacation pay can be included as overhead applicable to direct labor. This method recognizes the cost of vacations as a cost incurred while the individual is working, and not during the time that he doesn't work.

Holiday pay. In general, the treatment of holidays is no different from that of vacations. In certain industries it is usual practice to pay for work on holidays at double time. In this case, provided that the double time payment represents total compensation for the worked holiday, one half of the pay should be charged against the reserve.

Payroll taxes and fringe benefits. Certain payroll costs, such as Federal old age benefit taxes, unemployment insurance, temporary disability insurance, compensation insurance, group insurance, pension plans, etc., are either based on a percentage of payroll, or are easily expressed in such a way that they can be applied as a percentage of payroll.

As more and more taxes and fringe benefits are imposed on employers, it becomes increasingly obvious that such payroll costs are as much a part of the direct labor costs as the money actually paid to the worker for time worked. These are costs that would be eliminated or reduced, if an operation were mechanized completely or in part.

Setup time. Setup time in the broad sense varies from a few minutes for only a slight change in the machine setup to several weeks, as exemplified by a model changeover in the automobile industry. Setups are normally classified as direct labor and applied to products on the basis of either actual or estimated production resulting from the setup. When setups are costly, and the resultant production is carried on over a long period of time, part of the cost may be carried in inventory to be absorbed by production over the entire period. Normally, however, it is possible to disregard, as a matter of accounting convenience, the fact that allowances need to be made for setups in prior periods or that some setups are made for production in later periods.

Idle time. Certain types of productive operations require a considerable amount of waiting or idle time. Where this is characteristic of the operation, such idle time is part of the labor cost and should be included in the direct labor or direct labor overhead. Not to do so results in labor costs that are not charged directly to the product.

If waiting or idle time is due to inefficient supervision or poor planning, it should be so identified. Depending on the type of cost system employed, such idle time should be charged to an overhead or variance account.

Special allowances. Other time paid for but not worked is a category that represents such things as time allowed for union meetings, company meetings, service on juries, etc. It is desirable to classify it separately, wherever feasible, to obtain a better knowledge of operating costs, and it is often absorbed as part of departmental or cost center overhead.

Trainees. Although the costs of apprentices, helpers, and trainees are usually not considered as a direct labor cost, when such costs are incurred year in and year out, they are considered as normal expenses. It would be proper in such cases to include these costs in the product overhead. Should they, however, be unusual expenses, it is more logical to consider them as period expenses and charge them entirely to current operations than to treat them as product costs.

Average hourly rates. Labor distribution can be facilitated, in many instances, by using average rates for job classifications or departments. Where direct labor is paid on an hourly basis, this average rate would be a weighted departmental (or classification) hourly rate. In most cases, the use of individual rates would not appreciably improve the accuracy of the resultant costs and would require significantly greater accounting effort.

Labor overhead may also be taken into consideration in determining this average hourly rate. Overtime premium, shift premium, vacation pay, holiday pay, payroll taxes, compensation insurance, group insurance, and pension costs are a few of the more important costs that might be included with the direct labor cost for distribution on a departmental hourly rate basis.

Figure 4 illustrates the computation of labor cost distribution using an average hourly rate. In an actual cost system, the monthly summary of man-hours worked would be extended by the average hourly rate to obtain the labor cost distribution.

MONTHLY SUMMARY OF MAN-HOURS WORKED GRANTS PASS YARD MONTH OF JANUARY

HDLG. & MFG.	2	5	6	7	28	29	30	31	TOTAL HOURS FOR MONTH	LABOR COST DISTRIBUTION
Receiving	20	30	10	22¼	32	26¾	24¾		646¾	$ 1,723
Loading Out	30	26	36	30¾	22	20¼	29¼		281	749
Shaving	40	40	40	36	40	40	32		431¼	1,149
Machine Framing										
Hand Framing										
Hand Peeling										
Gen. Yard Operations	4	2			2			6	14	37
Work Orders										
Work for Others										
Work Outside Yard										
Supervision										
Office Work										
Other (Explain)										
Vacation Pay										
Maintce. (Detail Rev. Side)										
Boom Truck Hauling										
Handl'g Treated Stock										
Handl'g Cedar Stock										
TOTAL HOURS	96	98	96	96	96	90	88	6	2,092½	$ 5,574
O/T IN TOTAL		2				2		6	10	
MTCE. DETAIL										
Crane	2						2		4	11
Jillies						3			3	8
Trackage										
S										

Labor Payroll for Month	$ 5,038.33	
Payroll Tax	$ 210.84	
Compensation Insurance	$ 325.31	
Total Labor Cost		$ 5,574.48
Divided by - - Total Hours for Month		2,092½
Equals - - - - Average Hourly Rate		$ 2.6643

Fig. 4. Illustration of the Month-End Distribution of Labor Cost.

Incentive systems. A large number of factories have piecework incentive systems or some modification, such as bonus for production over a fixed quota, or a guaranteed daily wage if the quota is not met. If there is no variation from a straight piecework rate, the unit labor cost is the piecework rate, and distributions are made on the basis of the number of pieces produced. Where a bonus is paid for production over a certain quota, the bonus should be treated as a direct labor cost. The effect of such treatment on labor cost per unit of production is, of course, a function of the bonus system. The treatment itself, however, does not necessarily imply an increase in the unit cost.

Overhead cost principles. Production overhead, or manufacturing expense, consists of all charges other than those directly identified with the product. Charges directly identified with the product include direct material, direct labor, and such other charges as constitute specific costs of product units. There is always a residue of costs representing those activities in support of the direct production costs that cannot be charged directly to product units. This residue of costs falls into the overhead category. Overhead is in reality a composite of costs that are incurred for varying reasons and that relate to the direct costs in many different ways.

Control of these costs, as well as accurate costing of the product, requires that overhead be broken down into elements that are reasonably homogenous. Where this is not done, and unlike costs are lumped together, many essential facts are obscured. Depending on whether the additional expense is justifiable, these costs can be controlled by budgets, requisitions, work orders and other similar control devices.

It has long been recognized that while some products pass through a few departments, others pass through many departments, and that even within productive departments the amount of effort spent on various products is not necessarily uniform.

Cost center rates. Provided the cost of maintaining the system can be justified, cost center rates are more accurate than departmental rates, and departmental rates are more accurate than blanket rates covering several departments or an entire plant. There is less likelihood with cost center rates that certain products will bear a disproportionate share of the overhead costs. Separate cost center rates are essential to take care of products requiring high capital investment, on which the overhead is high, when other products going through the same department are made with simple hand tools, on which the overhead is low. (Later in this chapter is a discussion of what constitutes a cost center.)

Defining responsibility for costs. Because of the complex nature of overhead costs, control over various items of overhead rests with different individuals in the organization. For example, foremen in productive departments may be able to control usage of indirect labor; superintendents may be able to control factory clerical expenses; and heads of service departments may be able to control costs of supplying heat, cleaning, and plant transportation. As a result, it is important to define carefully the responsibility for costs.

Variable and fixed costs. Some overhead costs vary rather directly with changes in production volume, whereas others remain essentially unchanged in total regardless of changes in rates of activity. Costs that vary with volume are ordinarily called variable costs, and those costs that do not vary with volume are called fixed costs. The terms variable and fixed apply to the totals of overhead costs rather than to product unit costs. Fixed production costs include those costs that represent the capacity to do business, such as depreciation of buildings, machinery and equipment and the cost of an administrative organization. Variable production overhead costs are the costs of goods and services (other than direct labor and material) that are incurred in an amount closely related to the level of production. Therefore, variable overhead can be treated in a manner similar to direct material and direct labor.

In classifying costs as to whether they are fixed or variable, it is important to study the physical reality of the manufacturing process and not be led astray by a conventional accounting treatment or concept. While depreciation is normally classified as a fixed cost for accounting purposes, it may be found that the life of an asset is highly dependent on the amount of use it gets and that it depreciates, therefore, primarily through wear and tear. In such a case, it would be logical to use a unit of production method of depreciation. This would have the effect of making depreciation a variable cost.

Major repairs occurring irregularly can cause violent fluctuations in maintenance charges. It may be desirable to stabilize these charges over a full year or some naturally recurring interval of production by anticipating the repairs that will be made over this time and allocating such costs to each cost period. This, in effect, identifies the planned maintenance as a fixed charge over the interval.

As items of manufacturing expense are incurred or paid, they are usually charged to natural expense accounts in the expense ledger. These quite commonly are grouped so as to maintain a distinction between fixed and variable costs. When such expense items are entered, or at some later time, these manufacturing expenses are distributed to departments and cost centers. Where it is feasible, they are charged directly to the departments or cost centers where the cost is incurred. In other cases, they may be allocated on some reasonable basis. In an actual cost system, costs which are distributed to nonproductive departments, in the primary distribution, are redistributed subsequently to the productive departments, in relation to the service received. The accumulated overhead costs for each productive cost center are normally absorbed by the goods produced in that cost center.

Direct costing. There are many cost accountants who advocate omitting all fixed costs from product costs and treating these fixed costs solely as period costs. This is known as direct costing and differs sharply from complete absorption costing in the treatment of fixed overhead costs. In some versions of direct costing, unit costs are determined by adding direct labor and direct material costs together with those overhead costs that vary with volume. These costs are used as product costs in the determination of the cost of goods sold, and the resulting gross profit is reduced by the total fixed costs for the period.

The following condensed income statement, prepared in a simplified form, shows an essential difference between the two approaches of complete absorption costing and direct costing:

	Complete Absorption Costing Basis	*Direct Costing Basis*
Sales	$305,026	$305,026
Cost of Sales:		
Material	$ 86,431	$ 86,431
Labor	75,026	75,026
Variable overhead absorbed	27,394	27,394
Fixed overhead costs absorbed	31,271	
Total Cost of Sales	$220,122	$188,851
Gross Profit	$ 84,904	$116,175
Less:		
Selling expense	$ 25,921	$ 25,921
Administrative expense	17,763	17,763
Fixed overhead costs		39,127
	$ 43,684	$ 82,811
Net Income	$ 41,220	$ 33,364

As can be seen readily, the fixed overhead costs absorbed in the cost of sales on the complete absorption basis are less than the fixed overhead costs deducted from gross profit on the direct costing basis. This difference of $7,856 occurs because units sold in the period were at a lower level than the units produced. Consequently, some of the goods manufactured remained in inventory. Under the complete absorption costing basis, the portion of fixed overhead costs associated with those goods remained in the inventory valuation. Under the direct costing basis the fixed overhead costs are considered period costs and are recorded in the period incurred.

Note that the reverse can also occur. When sales exceed production, the amount of fixed overhead costs included in cost of goods sold under the complete absorption costing basis can be greater than the fixed overhead costs attributed to the period under the direct costing basis.

Overhead cost allocation. The mechanics of allocating overhead costs to product units consist of setting overhead rates and applying these rates to the product. Each step in this process will be discussed separately.

Setting overhead rates. It is possible to distribute all overhead expenses to departments or cost centers and, after making the distribution, to determine overhead rates in relation to direct labor, prime cost, or other factors. This means, however, that the overhead cannot be applied to work in process or to finished work until these percentages have been determined. In actual practice, therefore, it is much more common to find that a company is using an estimated rate that is expected to absorb the overhead of the various departments or cost centers over the entire fiscal year. These rates may be adjusted annually, or even more often if a material over- or under-absorption of expenses is occurring.

One of the more satisfactory methods of doing this is to prepare overhead budgets by cost centers. This process usually begins with a description of current practices, which is then modified to reflect such changes as are expected to occur in the periods for which the budgets are being prepared.

The use of predetermined overhead rates would require consideration of plant capacity. The level chosen would be the one at which it is expected that 100% of the overhead costs would be absorbed by the products. Where a standard cost system is utilized, the selection of the capacity level might be quite different.

Applying rates to product. The general theory underlying the application of overhead costs to a product is that the overhead costs of a cost center benefit the production passing through that cost center. Where the products passing through a cost center are equal in size and receive similar treatment, there is no problem in computing relative benefits received by each product. Where products of a different size pass through a cost center, or products receive different treatment in the same cost center, it may be possible to relate these products to each other in terms of equivalent units and to continue to apply overhead on the basis of a cost per equivalent unit of product. Similarly, where production is measured in tons or board feet or the like, it may be possible to use such units as a basis for applying overhead. As the production in a particular cost center grows more complex, new relationships are required for determining the benefit from overhead costs received by each product unit.

An assumption is necessarily made that the overhead costs of a cost center have a proportional relationship to some basis such as labor hours, machine hours, or productive hours. The basis for applying overhead is usually referred to as the cost unit. The unit that is used to measure production in a department or cost center is normally called the product unit. If, for example, a labor hour is used as the cost unit and a ton is used as the product unit, a conversion factor is required to convert from the cost unit to the product unit, and vice versa. The conversion factor in this case, of course, is tons produced per labor hour.

It is doubtful if any basis for applying overhead can ever be considered as completely satisfactory. More precise application of costs is usually gained only with greater expenditure of time and effort. The factor of materiality should regulate the application of overhead. The basis to be used should be one that gives reasonably accurate product costs at an expenditure of time and effort that is not unreasonable. Although the final product cost is arrived at through the addition of a number of different processing costs in various cost centers, it is not necessary to use the same basis in each cost center. The basis used should be that which most clearly reflects the productive process in the particular cost center. (Where warranted, multiple bases can be used within a cost center.)

A rate per machine hour or productive hour may be used where machines are the main productive element. Where only one product is manufactured, or where the products can be related to each other in equivalent product units, the overhead may be applied as a cost per unit of product.

In small shops, where labor may be the main productive element, overhead may be applied as a percentage of direct labor dollars or as a rate per direct labor hour. Generally speaking, the labor-hour approach is preferable to the labor-dollar basis, as many items of expense, such as depreciation, insurance, and taxes are functions of time.

There is a tendency, at least in large manufacturing plants, toward the use of departmental or cost center cost rates that include both direct labor costs and overhead. This procedure considerably simplifies the process of calculating the unit costs of various products.

Consideration must also be given to the information required from various departments in order to make the cost accounting system function effectively. Information on production in various locations must be obtained and summarized, usually on a daily basis. The need for accuracy in these reports will not always be readily understood by those responsible for their preparation. Hence certain controls and safeguards are needed to provide for the necessary accuracy.

Service department cost principles. Service departments, such as repair shops, power plants, and print shops are support activities for the producing departments. They differ from the producing departments in that the primary control over expenditures is in the productive departments. The cost principles of service departments will be discussed in terms of:

1. Relationship to production departments.
2. Bases of distributing costs.
3. Methods of distributing costs.

Relationship to production departments. Costs are first accumulated by these various service departments or service cost centers, and secondly, distributed to productive cost centers on some reasonable basis for each service cost center. Preferably, charges to the productive departments should be stated in such a way that managers of the productive departments can measure the value of the services received. It is difficult to control service department costs unless there is some way of measuring their performance.

The service cost center principle is often extended to such costs as employee fringe benefits that can be collected in a cost center set up to collect these costs and to provide for subsequent distribution. Similarly, costs of handling materials might be collected in a material handling cost center, although no such organizational units actually exist. It is interesting to note that fixed costs in the service department are added to other service department costs and become variable costs in the production departments, if the usage of the service department is controllable by the production department.

Bases of distributing costs. In considering bases for distributing service department costs, the question often arises of the treatment to be accorded to costs of those departments that, while ready to serve at all times, may not be used during certain periods. This might be handled by making an appropriate demand charge to the various productive departments involved, in much the same way that an electric company makes a fixed charge for the highest anticipated demand for electric service.

In most cases, however, more satisfactory results are obtained by using a basis related to requests for service. In the case of a building operation, this would probably be square feet occupied, and in repair shops it would normally be on the basis of work orders. The cost of a purchasing department might be distributed on the basis of the number of purchase requisitions, and the cost of storekeeping on the number of material requisitions. Timekeeping costs might be distributed on the basis of time cards or job tickets, and supervisory costs on the basis of direct labor hours or dollars. Employee fringe benefits costs could be distributed as a percentage of payroll cost, and material handling costs as a percentage of material cost.

Methods of distributing costs. The complete distribution of service department costs is rather difficult to achieve in practice. This is because many of the service department costs are first distributed to other service departments. It thus becomes difficult to distribute the cost of a service department without knowing what other costs may be distributed to that department subsequently. Where data processing equipment is utilized, a precise distribution may be achieved through a formula utilizing simultaneous equations.

A satisfactory approximate result, however, may be obtained on a trial and error basis. It is important to set up the cost of distribution worksheet in such a way that the costs of those service cost centers involving larger amounts of money and more numerous distributions to other service cost centers are the first to be distributed. A reasonable estimate of the amounts to be received from subsequent distributions can be included in the total of the earlier service center costs to be distributed. The resultant differences can be either ignored on the basis of materiality, or a second attempt at distribution could be made using the experience gained in the first distribution to make more precise allocations. The second attempt usually produces an acceptable distribution.

If this distribution is made once a year on a budgeted basis, standard rates can be developed for distributing the service department costs during each cost period. This permits service department costs to be distributed more easily, and any unabsorbed costs or overabsorbed costs may be regarded as a variance. Such variances may be attributed to product cost but this, in itself, can require relatively complex allocation procedures. Therefore, it may be preferable to treat them as period costs and possibly without product identification.

INSTALLING A COST ACCOUNTING SYSTEM

As stated before, a cost accounting system should be tailored to fit the company's requirements. While there are some cases in which a cost accounting system is developed and installed where one did not exist before, in most cases a new system modifies or replaces an existing system. Certain basic records may already be in effect, and procedures for material control and labor control are probably already developed. These controls may be adequate, or they may require some modification. The following problems associated with installing a cost accounting system will be dealt with:

1. Determining company requirements.
2. Structuring the cost accounting system.
3. Developing a chart of accounts.
4. Developing procedures and controls.
5. Forms and records.
6. Journal entries required.

Determining company requirements. A good first step is to make a physical review of the manufacturing facilities. This can begin with the receiving department and follow the various processes through to final completion and shipping. Work orders, time reports, material requisitions, and other paper work in connection with the plant operations should be collected during this tour for study at a later time. Office procedures concerned with perpetual inventories, invoicing, and sales analysis should also be reviewed at an early date.

Organization charts are most helpful in determining the adequacy of existing cost centers, or the need for new ones. Blueprints of the plant are useful in becoming acquainted with the physical movement of goods throughout the plant and for determining the boundaries of departments and cost centers. Procedure flow charts are also helpful in following paper work through the plant and in determining sources of information for the cost accounting system. Procedural manuals, if available, will aid in determining the existing procedures and the requirements for improvement to meet the needs of the new cost system. Special requirements arising from government contract work should be given consideration as appropriate.

Structuring the cost accounting system. The structure of the cost accounting system should be compatible with the units of the corporate organization. Although this is normally achieved by adaptation of the cost system to the organization, it is sometimes necessary to redefine some organizational responsibilities. While such redefinition is the prerogative of management, the cost accountant must also be familiar with the organization structure so that he can properly assess it as it relates to the objective of the cost system.

The structure of the cost accounting system is the framework devised for the accounts to provide the necessary data in the most direct and economical manner. A proper structure should provide for the following points, preferably in the order listed:

1. Division according to responsibility.
2. Subdivision of departments into cost centers.
3. General framework of the chart of accounts.
4. Cost of sales analysis.
5. Inventory accounts.
6. Cost of goods manufactured.
7. Manufacturing cost ledger.
8. Service department costs.
9. Overhead variances.

Cost centers are organization units within a department, or natural groupings of machines or processes. The operations should be sufficiently similar that it is reasonable to apply the same productive overhead rate. Cost centers can usually be determined by following the natural flow of work through the departments. Cost centers are not always required, however, where an organizational unit exists, and they may be required where no organizational unit is recognized. Separate cost centers are normally required where the following situations exist:

1. Products require different overhead rates.
2. Intermediate inventories are recognized.
3. Different products receive different treatments.
4. Different products receive different amounts of a particular treatment.

Developing a chart of accounts. The development of a satisfactory chart of accounts is a key factor in the installation of a cost system. It is the medium by which the various costs are collected, classified, and distributed to the various accounts, product costs, inventory, and finally to the cost of sales. It is an unusual situation to find an existing chart of accounts that is adequate for fulfilling the requirements developed for a revised cost accounting system. In developing a chart of accounts, considerable thought should be given to both the basic structure and the coding system.

Basic structure. An essential characteristic of a cost accounting system is the classification of operating income and expense, not only by natural account, but also by responsibility and by product. This normally constitutes the minimum requirement. It is often considered necessary to classify the material and labor elements of product costs further into direct and indirect costs, and the overhead cost element is usually analyzed into variable and fixed components. Additional classifications, such as territorial, geographical, or functional, may be required for other analytical purposes, and regulated companies may need an additional type of classification to meet regulatory requirements.

The principle usually followed in accounting for production costs is to classify the expenses in two dimensions—by natural expense account and by the cost center or service center incurring that expense. The same principle may be applied to income.

In constructing a chart of accounts it is well to think in terms of a columnar spread sheet, with the natural expense accounts listed on the left and the various cost centers spread across the top of the sheet. Theoretically, any expense can be incurred in any cost center, but in usual practice certain expenses occur only in certain cost centers.

Coding system. Each item of expense, then, needs to be classified in two ways. This is normally accomplished by applying two codes, one for the cost center or organizational unit and one for the natural expense account, at the time the expenses are paid or approved.

Costs that cannot be classified in a primary distribution may be classified in a secondary distribution, using the same procedure.

In developing a coding system, the capability of accumulating costs at the most discrete level required for analysis and control should be provided. However, consideration should also be given to facilitating the summarization of such discrete entries for reporting and control at higher levels. To illustrate, cost center numbers may be assigned in the same sequence as the production process. Where several departments are involved, each department may be assigned a block of numbers, such as 31-39, so that the lead digit can be used to distinguished cost centers in that department from cost centers in other departments. Cost center 34, for example, might be the milling cost center in the machining department. Similarly, where a company is made up of several plants, a three digit code might be useful in separating the departments and cost centers of one plant from those of another. This is particularly advantageous where data processing equipment is used. Summary statements can be prepared by department, by plant, and by company, through use of the respective digits representing these groups.

In a like manner, the numbers assigned to expense accounts can be assigned in a way that reflects significant groupings of expense, such as direct material, indirect material, direct labor, indirect labor, variable overhead, fixed overhead, and redistribution of service department costs.

Generally, developing a chart of accounts for production cost accounting purposes involves changing the chart of accounts for the company as a whole. Various broad groupings of accounts are usually recognized, such as assets, liabilities, income, production expense, selling expense, distribution expense, and administrative expense, by assigning blocks of numbers to these broad groups. The proper assignment of these blocks of numbers can assist in the quick and easy preparation of summary and detailed financial statements. An expense account number could quite usefully consist of at least three numbers, such as 521. The 5 could denote that it was in the 500 group consisting of production expenses; the 2 might indicate that it was a direct labor cost and the 1 could represent the natural expense account of wages.

In actual use, the expense account number is preceded or followed by the cost center number, for example 34-521. The order is immaterial as long as it is consistently followed. To avoid confusion, it is well to have a different number of digits in the cost center code than in the expense account code. In this way, should the order be reversed, it would be apparent to anyone handling the data subsequently.

Developing procedures and controls. Information is required on which to base the distributions of production costs to products, so that the products carried in inventory include these production costs, and these costs are eventually distributed to the cost of sales. Various procedures and controls must be instituted to collect this required information. In developing these procedures and controls, it is usually quite effective to first determine the end result or desired objective of the procedure or control, and then develop the details required to achieve such ends.

Cost of sales analysis. Arriving at a satisfactory cost of goods sold figure requires an accurate count of the quantities sold by individual products. If sales invoices show the items sold in the same classification (e.g., product codes) as those used for unit costs, the information can be obtained using such invoices. If this is not the case, or if classification from this source is too burdensome, perpetual inventories can be used, physical inventories may be taken, or still other approaches may have to be developed.

Where cost differences between products and product groups, or between colors, sizes, etc. of the same products, are not material, percentages may be applied to determine the respective costs to be credited to the inventory accounts in total. Although this procedure may sometimes be satisfactory, the possibility of unreliable results should be investigated before such a procedure is adopted.

Many companies use data processing equipment to obtain a satisfactory analysis of sales, and to compute the cost of sales. Where this is done daily, using sales invoices for individual product data, such useful information can be developed as gross profits by customer, by salesmen, by territory, and by daily or weekly time periods.

Inventory accounts. To obtain reliable costs, it is essential that accurate inventory records be maintained. The nature of the product and the manufacturing process partially determine how the inventory values are obtained.

In certain process cost systems, it is convenient to take physical inventories of work in process at the end of each cost period. An alternate procedure is to charge the cost center with all material put into production and credit it with the production sent to the next cost center. Physical inventories should be taken at specified intervals to verify the balances shown in the perpetual records.

In job cost systems, the work in process is usually derived from the total of the costs accumulated on the various jobs. The reasonableness of the accumulated charges against individual jobs is difficult to determine until the job is completed, unless additional investigation is made specifically for this purpose.

Unless the quantities on hand are quite small, it is unlikely that physical inventories of raw materials or finished goods are taken completely at the end of each weekly or monthly cost period. Raw materials are normally issued on requisitions, and these would constitute the basis of the charge to the work in process. Receiving reports would constitute the source of information on incoming receipts of raw materials. Production reports normally form the basis for transferring from work-in-process inventories to finished goods inventories. Relief of the finished goods inventories would be based on the cost of goods sold and other incidental adjustments for returned merchandise, employee purchases, sample goods, and the like.

If cost reports are not based on satisfactory physical inventories, other controls should be instituted to insure against the possibility of a major error. The perpetual records should be reconciled with the control account in the general ledger periodically. The existence of physical quantities corresponding to the inventory detail should also be verified, on a planned periodic basis, to guard against unexplained losses or pilferage.

In some systems, for convenience, the work-in-process inventories may be part of the factory ledger. In this case, the sum of the detail cost records should be agreed to the control account in the factory ledger.

Cost of goods manufactured. The work in process at the beginning of the period normally becomes part of the cost of goods manufactured during the period, particularly where the manufacturing cycle is short. The work in process at the end of the period is normally part of the manufacturing costs that are deferred until the next period. Stated another way, the cost of goods manufactured can be represented by the sum of the work in process at the beginning, plus manufacturing costs for the period, minus the work in process at the end of the period.

While, as in the case of the inventory accounts, there is a considerable amount of detail supporting the control account in the general ledger, all the manufacturing costs are normally represented in one general ledger account, or in one factory ledger control account, as the case may be. Detailed entries made during the cost period are usually summarized in journal entries and posted to the control accounts at the end of each cost period.

Labor and material accounts are sometimes included with the expense accounts in the manufacturing cost control. Alternatively, they may appear in the general ledger or factory ledger as separate controls. Either approach is permissible, and the method chosen should depend upon accounting convenience.

It is common practice to offset these control accounts with cost absorbed accounts, rather than to credit control accounts directly for costs transferred to finished goods or work-in-process accounts. At the end of any given cost period, the amounts charged to the manufacturing cost control(s) would be offset in total by contra amounts credited to the manufacturing costs absorbed account(s). The charges would arise from payments for labor, materials, and expenses, plus charges for depreciation, deferred expenses, and other general expenses. The credits would arise from transfers to finished goods, work in process, or variance accounts, and should equal the total manufacturing charges.

When the appropriate journal entries are made each month to the control accounts, the manufacturing cost control accounts will have a zero balance. If the inventory control accounts are in the general ledger, a balance sheet and earnings statement can be produced readily. For this reason, it seems desirable to include inventory control accounts, manufacturing cost accounts, and costs absorbed accounts in the general ledger. This is particularly true in designing charts of accounts for computerized general accounting and cost accounting systems.

Manufacturing cost ledger. The manufacturing cost ledger contains the detail of the manufacturing cost control account. It is often referred to as the expense ledger, or, collectively with the inventory accounts, as the factory ledger. This should represent, after the various original entries have been made, the production costs of the period. In a job cost system, these costs are transferred to job order cards that represent the work in process. Labor and material are posted as incurred and the overhead is applied on a suitable basis. Journal entries are used to transfer the totals to work in process.

In a process cost system, these costs are accumulated progressively by cost center, usually on a work sheet. These costs are then divided between the work in process remaining in a cost center and the production recorded as going through to the next process. This procedure is continued until all of the costs have been assigned either to finished goods or to work in process. The work sheets form the basis for the journal entries required to distribute the manufacturing cost control account balances.

The manufacturing cost ledger can be maintained in a variety of ways—in bound books, on columnar spread sheets, with key sort cards, on a loose leaf ledger basis, on punched cards, and on magnetic tape or in a computer. The choice depends partly on the volume of detail and partly on the availability of certain types of equipment. In spite of the widespread use of computers today, many effective cost accounting systems are still based on manually posted ledgers.

When the use of more sophisticated data processing equipment can be justified, it does create greater flexibility, particularly in the preparation of reports from these basic records. Reports can be prepared for various levels of management from the cost center to the department, to the plant or division, and to the company as a whole. At the same time, the detail by natural expense accounts can be presented in summary form for executive management and in correspondingly greater detail for each lower level of management.

Service department costs. Production service department costs can be construed as part of the manufacturing costs. Expenses can be coded initially to these service centers in much the way that productive costs are charged to productive cost centers. Before the productive cost center indirect costs are charged to products, the service department costs need to be allocated on one basis or another to the productive cost centers. As the activity of these service departments varies from period to period, or is influenced by seasonal conditions, it is not always reasonable to arrive at a zero balance in each service center after this secondary distribution has been made each period. It is usually considered satisfactory if the cumulative annual result approximates zero, at which time any residual balances are normally charged to profit or loss.

► WARNING: Care should be exercised to see that these residual balances at the end of any period are not building up excessively. They may reach the point where they represent unrecorded losses instead of costs that will be absorbed in later periods.

Overhead variances. While it is possible to determine and apply overhead to products on the basis of actual overhead costs, such a process cannot be started until the manufacturing cost ledger is completely posted and the overhead rates applicable in each department have been determined. This tends to delay the application of overhead to the product and, consequently, to delay the determination of the cost of goods sold. To counteract this, many cost accounting systems that have material and labor distributed on an actual cost basis distribute the departmental overhead on a standard percentage or a standard rate.

This results in a certain amount of under- or over-absorbed overhead each period that must eventually be transferred to profit and loss. A journal entry is required for this amount to be cleared from the manufacturing cost control and charged or credited to profit and loss. Sometimes, these amounts are divided between inventory and profit and loss, in the same ratio as manufactured goods unsold to those sold, thus including the full amount of actual overhead in the cost of products. In instances where the volume by period fluctuates widely from the norm, these overhead variances may be quite material, but they should balance out against similar variances in later periods as a result of volume fluctuations in the opposite direction. Large cumulative over- or under-absorption that will not be balanced out indicates that the absorption rate should be adjusted.

Forms and records. Cost accounting forms and records are of two types: those used to initiate a step in the productive process and those used to record the various transactions that take place. Most of these forms are of simple design and numerous standard forms are available that are often adequate for the purpose.

Job order form. In a job order cost system, the job order is the basic form used to start the productive process. This form normally contains the following information:

Date.
Part or product.
Quantity to be manufactured.
Delivery date or date required.
Operations to be performed.
Tools required.
Raw material requirements.
Serial number.

These forms are usually numbered consecutively and this number serves as an identifying number to which all the various labor and material charges can be made. An example of a job order form used in a machine shop is shown in Figure 5.

JOB NO.	PIECES REQ.	ISSUED	REQUIRED	DEL. TO	CHARGE TO	MAT'L QUAN.	PART NO.	STOCK ISSUED	DATE	FOREMAN	SHEET
29117	1	12-16-	12/22	ST	146	1	G-1-1280				1 OF 2

OPER.	10	20	30	40	50	60	70			
MACH.	E. LTH.	E. LTH.	INSP.	O.P.	INSP.	HAND	ST			
HRS.	.3	.167	—	—	—	.167	—			
SCHED.										
OPER.										
MACH.										
HRS.										
SCHED.										

CLOCK NO.	3 STOP
PIECES	3 START
CLOCK NO.	2 STOP
PIECES	2 START
CLOCK NO.	1 STOP
PIECES	1 START
PIECES	TOTAL HRS.

SPECIAL INSTRUCTIONS

PART NAME	NEXT ASSEMBLY	CUSTOMER
NOZZLE	G-1-1279	BOILER

RAW MATERIAL	UNIT QUAN.	DATE FINISH	MATERIAL COST & PRO-CUREMENT	DATE DUE	P.O. NO.	TOTAL COST	UNIT COST
G-1-1216 BLANK							

FIRST PART RUN ON EACH OPERATION MUST BE CHECKED & APPROVED BY INSPECTOR BEFORE PROCEEDING WITH MORE PARTS.

MACHINING ORDER

OPER. NO.	OPERATION INSTRUCTIONS	FIXTURE TOOLING GAGES	STANDARD METHOD: MACHINE	STANDARD METHOD: FEED	STANDARD METHOD: SPEED	ALLOWED HRS.: SET-UP	ALLOWED HRS.: MFG.
10	Chuck on 1-3/8 dia. & turn .377–.373 dia x .030 dim.		E. lathe				20 min.
	Drill .257–.260 dia. x 9/16 deep.						
	Bore 15° taper x .310–.314 dia. (Note: Turn sharp corners)						
	TURN 30° CHAMFER X .500 DIM.						
20	Reverse part & locate from 1" dia. thread.	Lathe holder	E. lathe				10 min.
	Drill 7/32 dia. drill thru						
	Form drill 7° bore to .562 dia. (Grind 7° taper on 9/16 dia. drill to .234–.240 dia. on small end.)	Form drill 7° Taper					
30	Inspect.		Insp.				
40	Ht. per drawing.		O.P.				
50	Inspect.		Insp.				

Fig. 5. Job Order Form Used in a Machine Shop.

Material requisitions and vouchers. Material requisitions are used for recording the quantity of materials to be charged to each job order. The quantities withdrawn from the storeroom are charged to work in process and any unused material is returned to the storeroom for credit. A material requisition normally contains the following information:

Date of issue.
Quantity issued.
Item or product number.
Unit price.
Extension.
Job order number to be charged.
Signature of individual making the withdrawal.
Serial number.

Where predictable quantities of a product are normally put into production, it may be feasible to use a prepriced bill of materials on which quantities normally required would be extended at current prices and totaled. Material not required, or material required in excess of the bill of materials, would be handled separately.

Material that has been ordered solely for a certain job may be charged directly to a job number from the voucher register or in the expense distribution process, thereby avoiding a transfer into stores and requisitioning out again.

In a process cost system, a batch ticket normally takes the place of both a job order form and a material requisition.

Production reports. In a job order system, production reports or move tickets are desirable at the various stages of production, and in a process cost system, production reports at the various stages are essential. These reports are usually quite simple, listing the date, the quantities, and the products manufactured. In some cases a copy of the job order may be returned to production control to indicate that a particular job order has completed a particular stage of production.

In a process cost system, these reports are tallied to determine the final production in each department. The unit costs are determined on the basis of these production reports.

Cost detail records. In a job cost system, the cost detail records consist of ledger cards for posting the various labor and material charges. A job cost ledger form is shown in Figure 6.

In some cases an envelope is used instead of a ledger card. The various charges are posted to the outside of the envelope and the supporting papers are then deposited in the envelope for subsequent reference. A job cost envelope used for that purpose is shown in Figure 7. The ledger card or envelope is normally prepared at the time the job order is prepared, and may be an extra copy of the job order form printed on heavy stock.

Job time tickets, indicating the name or number of the operator and the time required, may be prepared for each operation. These time cards are

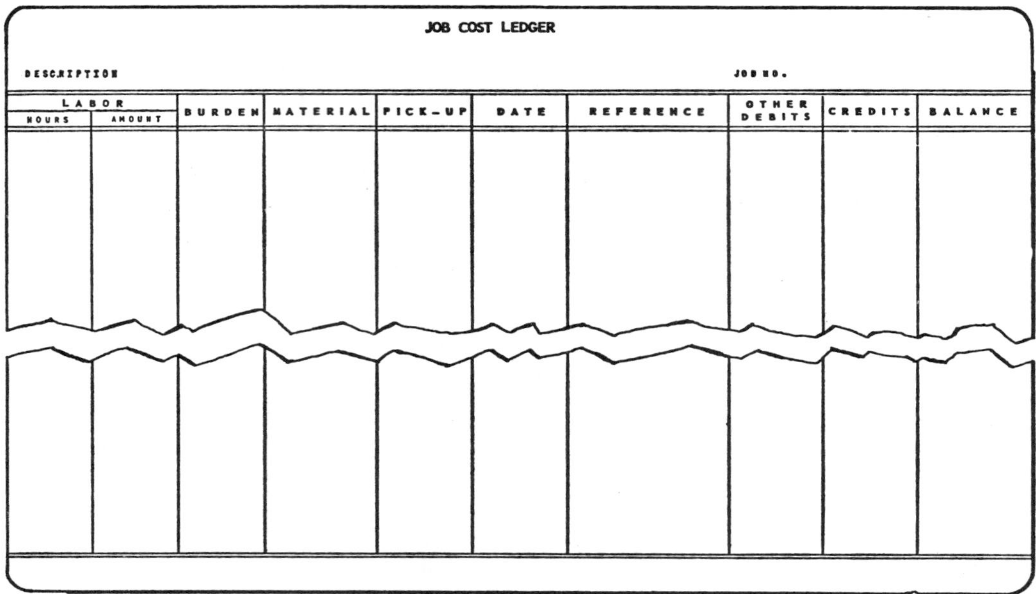
JOB COST LEDGER

DESCRIPTION JOB NO.

LABOR		BURDEN	MATERIAL	PICK-UP	DATE	REFERENCE	OTHER DEBITS	CREDITS	BALANCE
HOURS	AMOUNT								

Fig. 6. Job Cost Ledger Form.

posted subsequently to the ledger record. In some cases, the posting is made directly to the job envelope by the individual performing the work. Overhead may be applied to each job in the form of an inclusive rate for labor and overhead, or overhead may be applied at the end of each cost period based on the hours of work during the period or as a percentage of labor cost. If material handling charges are made separately, they are also made at the end of each cost period, and the total of all amounts posted to the detail records is charged to work in process and credited to overhead costs absorbed.

Cost reports. Useful and informative cost reports are a logical result of a well developed cost accounting system. Such reports may be used as a basis to exercise control of operations. While control efforts are greatly facilitated by use of standard cost systems (see Chapter 10), a considerable amount of control over production costs is possible through reports prepared intelligently from an actual cost system. An example of such a report is shown in Figure 8.

Good control reports are tailored to the user. A foreman or first-line supervisor may find reports showing labor hours or tons of material more useful than those showing dollar costs. Unit costs per ton produced may be helpful when compared to estimates or similar costs incurred last week or a year ago. Executive management may prefer brief written explanations of the more significant matters disclosed by analysis of the cost reports and financial statements.

Cost reports must be prepared on a timely basis if they are to be useful to operating supervisors. At times, some degree of precision may well be forgone in favor of more timely reporting. Standard forms help in preparing such reports quickly.

JOB COST ENVELOPE

PART NO.	DATE ISSUED	DATE NEEDED	DATE COMPLETED	JOB NO.

QUANTITY | DESCRIPTION:

DELIVER FINISHED WORK TO: | FOR: | CHARGE:

OUTSIDE WORK ☐

COST

DATE	REFERENCE	HOURS	LABOR	BURDEN	MATERIAL & OTHER	CUM. TOT.	WRITE-OFF	REF.

FINISHED WORK DELIVERED			
DATE	QNTY.	UNIT COST	POSTED

TIME PER UNIT				
				TOTAL

COSTED BY: DATE

POSTED BY: DATE

Fig. 7. Job Cost Envelope Used as Ledger Card.

MONTH **PRODUCTION YARD COST STATEMENT** MONTH

LABOR AMOUNT	CODE NO.	______ YARD LABOR COST DISTRIBUTION	QUANTITIES HANDLED PIECES	CUBATURE	LIN. FT.	L. F. COST EST'D	ACTUAL
$	11	Receiving					
	15	Loading Out					
	21	Shaving					
	24	Machine Framing					
	26	Hand Framing					
	31	Hand Peeling					
	32	Reshaving					
	33	Disposition of Culls					
	51	Taking Inventory					
	91	Work Orders*					
	92	Work for Others – Intra-Co.*					
	93	Work for Others – Outside Co.*					
	94	Work Outside Yard – (Explain below)					
	95-1	Supervision					
	95-2	Office Work					
	98	Other Work – (Explain)					
	-	Maintenance & Optg. Supplies		(Detail Below)			
	-	Handling Treated Stock*		(Unit costs on separate report)			
	-	Handling Cedar Stock*		(Unit costs on separate report)			
	-	Boom Truck – Hauling & Mtce.*					
	99	Vacation Pay					
		TOTAL LABOR AMOUNT		*Detail on Labor Transfer Report			

Explanations:

LABOR AMT.	8151-	MAINTENANCE DETAIL	TOTAL COST	ESTIMATE	OVER	UNDER
$	-4111	Crane	$	$	$	$.
	-4114	Gilly				
	-4114	Gilly				
	-4115	Trackage				
	-4116	Straddle Truck				
	-4117	Fork Lift				
	-4117	Fork Lift				
	-4121-66	High Line #1				
	-4121-67	High Line #2				
	-4121-68	High Line #3				
	-4122	Stiff Leg Derrick				
	-4138	Storage Skids, Bins & Boom				
	-4371-71	Shaver & Incinerator				
	-4372	Hand Framing Tools				
	-4373	Machine Framing Tools				
	-4711	Yard Buildings				
	-4712	Roads & Grades				
	-4713	Sewer, Water, Fire Lines				
	-4714	Yard Electric Lines				
	-4715	Fuel Storage, Tanks & Lines				
	-4716	General Yard Tools				
	-4717	Yard Vehicles				
	-4718	Tractors				
	-4721	Housekeeping				
		TOTAL MAINTENANCE				
	8161-	OPERATING SUPPLIES				
	-4875	Loading Out Supplies				
	-4876	" " " Trsfrd. Out				
		NET COST OPERATING SUPPLIES				
	8165-	FUEL & UTILITIES				
	-4993	Gasoline				
	-4994	Diesel Fuel				
	-4995	L.P.G. Fuel				
	-4998	Water				
	-4999	Light & Power				
		TOTAL FUEL & UTILITIES				

Remarks:

Fig. 8. Cost Report Form Used in Actual Cost System.

RAW MATERIAL INVENTORY

Date	Ref.	In	Out	Balance	Date	Ref.	In	Out	Balance	Date	Ref.	In	Out	Balance

	Number	Article	Unit	Min.	Max.	Sec.	Sle.

Fig. 9. Raw Material Inventory Card.

The cost accountant should become familiar with the productive processes. In this way he can bring his imagination to bear so as to provide all levels of management with useful reports and analyses.

Inventory records. Inventory records of raw materials are quite often carried in a loose-leaf ledger. A single sheet may be used for each part or material showing quantity on hand, quantity ordered, quantity issued, balance on hand, and sometimes, unit and total cost. A similar record often suffices for finished goods. Figure 9 is an example of a card form that can be used for this purpose.

A work in process inventory is either carried as a single total in the general ledger or divided into the various cost elements of labor, material and overhead. This latter division may be useful in reconciling a detail ledger with the general ledger control in a job order cost system. This is rarely required in a well designed system. In a process cost system this separation of the work in process inventory by elements is not normally required, as the inventories are computed on a work sheet basis and the journal entries are prepared from this work sheet.

In a job order cost system, the detail of the work-in-process account is represented by the job order ledger cards to which the various entries affecting the control accounts have been posted in detail.

Journal entries required. A review of, and understanding of representative cost accounting journal entries provides further understanding of a cost accounting system and its relationship to the determination of profit for the cost accounting period. Key journal entries required for both a job order cost system and a process cost system are illustrated in the following two subsections. In both cases, it is assumed that journal entries for the purchase of raw materials, for the payment of labor, and for the payment or accrual of other production expenses have already been made from sources such as the payroll register or voucher system.

Job order cost system journal entries. The seven key journal entries, typical of a job order cost system, follow:

Journal Entry #1	*Debit*	*Credit*
Work in process inventory	1,760.24	
Raw material inventory		1,760.24
To charge material requisitions to work in process inventory.		

Journal Entry #2		
Work in process inventory	2,526.37	
Payroll clearing account		2,526.37
To charge work in process inventory with direct labor charges.		

Journal Entry #3		
Work in process inventory	1,894.77	
Manufacturing costs absorbed		1,894.77
To charge work in process inventory with overhead costs absorbed on basis of direct labor hours.		

Journal Entry #4

Cost of sales	105.23	
Manufacturing costs absorbed		105.23

To charge overhead costs not absorbed on basis of direct labor hours to cost of sales.

Journal Entry #5

Finished goods inventory	7,374.63	
Work in processs inventory		7,374.63

To charge finished goods inventory with the accumulated job costs of products manufactured on completed jobs.

Journal Entry #6

Cost of sales	7,923.81	
Finished goods inventory		7,923.81

To transfer to cost of sales the cost of goods sold during the period.

Journal Entry #7

Accounts receivable	12,649.26	
Sales		12,649.26

To record sales for the period.

The first three entries transfer the various elements of material, labor, and overhead into work in process. The details of these charges were posted to the job order cards or envelopes either as they were incurred or at some time during the month. These journal entries thus charge the control account with the total of charges already posted to the detail records during the current period. These detail records also contain charges posted in previous periods for particular job orders that had not been completed by the beginning of the current period. These latter charges represent the inventory of work in process at the beginning of the period.

The fourth entry assumes that the overhead was charged to the various job orders on the basis of the direct labor hours at a pre-determined rate, leaving an unabsorbed balance of manufacturing costs. As stated previously, this could be prorated between cost of sales and inventory, but the more general practice is to charge such variances directly to cost of sales. With this entry the credits to manufacturing costs absorbed equal the total manufacturing cost for the period.

Journal entry #5 is to charge the finished goods inventory account with completed job orders based on the detail records on completed jobs that were removed from the work-in-process account during the current period. The remaining two entries are to set up sales and cost of sales for the period.

Figure 10 shows the effect of these journal entries in such a way that the effect on the income statement and the inventory accounts can be seen more readily. In making an installation of a job cost system, it is generally desirable to prepare a schedule in this manner to determine the entries that are required and then to write the journal entries from this schedule. When all the required entries have been set forth on this schedule, the total effect of the closing entries can be seen quite clearly, and, if further entries are required, this fact will be obvious.

Journal Entry Number	Description	Income Statement			Inventory Accounts			
		Sales	*Cost of Sales*	*Mfg. Costs*	*Raw Materials*	*Work-In-Process*	*Finished Goods*	*Other Accts.*
1	To charge material requisitions to work in process inventory				(1,760.24)	1,760.24		
2	To charge work in process inventory with direct labor charges					2,526.37		(2,526.37)
3	To charge work in process inventory with overhead costs absorbed on basis of direct labor hours			(1,894.77)		1,894.77		
4	To charge overhead costs not absorbed on basis of direct labor hours to cost of sales		105.23	(105.23)				
5	To charge finished goods inventory with the accumulated job costs of products manufactured					(7,374.63)	7,374.63	
6	To transfer to cost of sales the cost of goods sold during the period		7,923.81				(7,923.81)	
7	To record sales for the period	(12,649.26)						12,649.26

Note—Amounts in parentheses denote credits.

Fig. 10. Schedule Showing Effect of Job Order Cost System Journal Entries.

A schedule prepared in this manner may also be useful at the end of each period for determining the effect of the closing entries prior to the preparation of the journal entries and their subsequent recording in the general ledger.

Process cost system journal entries. The entries for a process cost system are normally prepared from a work sheet following somewhat the form shown in Figure 11. Costs transferred from one department to another are charged to the new department and credited to the previous department. Similarly, the cost in each department reflects the work in process inventory at the beginning of the period. Some raw materials are almost always charged into the first department in the manufacturing sequence, and other raw materials may be added in later departments. Direct labor is normally charged to each department based on the work complement, and the overhead is allocated to various departments as incurred. When the completed work has been transferred to finished goods, any balances remaining represent the work in process at the end of the period.

	Work in Process	
	Dept. A	*Dept. B*
Work in process at beginning of period	$1,291.82	$ 1,968.25
Costs transferred in from other departments		6,052.84
Costs added in this department:		
Raw materials	1,731.83	
Direct labor	2,157.99	1,987.43
Overhead	1,726.39	1,391.20
Total department costs	$6,908.03	$11,399.72
Cost transferred to next department	(6,052.84)	
Costs transferred to finished goods		(9,879.05)
Work in process at end of period	$ 855.19	$ 1,520.67
QUANTITY RECONCILIATION		
Pounds in process at beginning	1,823	1,643
Pounds put in process	8,200	
Pounds transferred into department	—	8,373
Total to be accounted for	10,023	10,016
Lost in process	467	413
Available for transfer	9,556	9,603
Transferred to:		
Next department	8,373	
Finished goods		8,322
Pounds remaining in process	1,183	1,281
Unit cost	$ .7229	$ 1.1871

Fig. 11. Process Cost System Work Sheet and Quantity Reconciliation.

A quantity reconciliation, shown in Figure 11, is required in a process cost system, and, based on the assumption that inventory is carried on an average cost basis, the total departmental costs are divided by the quantities available for transfer to arrive at a unit cost. This is used to cost the quantities transferred to the next department, and the quantity remaining in the department will, in effect, be similarly priced. The example given assumes, for illustrative purposes, that all units of production (pounds) in the beginning inventory and started during the period are complete at the end of the period. Where this is not the case, the beginning and ending inventories must be evaluated in terms of equivalent complete (or incomplete) units. The equivalent unit computation used to value work in process is illustrated and explained in Chapters 7 and 10.

The following are typical of the journal entries that are required for a process cost system wherein the product flows through Departments A and B in succession:

Journal Entry #1	*Debit*	*Credit*
Work in process—Dept. A	1,731.83	
Raw materials inventory		1,731.83
To record batches of raw material put into process.		
Journal Entry #2		
Work in process—Dept. A	2,157.99	
Work in process—Dept. B	1,987.43	
Payroll clearing account		4,145.42
To charge work in process inventory with direct labor charges.		
Journal Entry #3		
Work in process—Dept. A	1,726.39	
Work in process—Dept. B	1,391.20	
Manufacturing costs absorbed		3,117.59
To charge work in process inventory with departmental overhead.		
Journal Entry #4		
Work in process—Dept. B	6,052.84	
Work in process—Dept. A		6,052.84
To record production completed in Dept. A and transferred to Dept. B		
Journal Entry #5		
Finished goods inventory	9,879.05	
Work in process—Dept. B		9,879.05
To charge work in process inventory with completed production.		
Journal Entry #6		
Cost of sales	8,966.49	
Finished goods inventory		8,966.49
To transfer to cost of sales the cost of goods sold during the period		
Journal Entry #7		
Accounts receivable	14,128.76	
Sales		14,128.76
To record sales for the period.		

These journal entries have been set up in such a way as to be comparable to the previous set prepared for a job order cost system. The first three entries are essentially the same; that is, to charge the material, labor, and overhead elements to the departments concerned. Inasmuch as the manufacturing costs are charged to either Department A or Department B, and are absorbed on the total production, there is no variance such as would normally occur in a job order cost system. There would need to be, however, an additional entry, not required in a job order cost system, to charge the production completed in the first department into the work in process for the second department. In most other respects the entries are similar.

10

Standard and Estimated Costs

CONTENTS

10

Standard and Estimated Costs

J. H. Hennessy, Jr., CPA

This chapter explains the nature of predetermined costs, both standard and estimated. It includes a discussion of how standards and estimates are prepared. The nature, analysis, and treatment of variances from predetermined costs are covered. The features of a standard job order cost system and an estimated cost system based on engineered estimates are explained in detail. A check list for the installation of a standard cost system, extremely valuable for the accountant whose client is contemplating an installation of such a system, is included in an Appendix to the chapter.

STANDARD AND ESTIMATED COSTS EXPLAINED

Standard costs. Standard costs are predetermined costs, normally developed through engineering or time study analysis, and often containing some incentive element. Standard costs are treated in the books of account as surrogates of what the actual costs should be. Variances from standards are generally treated as credits or debits to expense rather than as adjustments to the cost of products. The two major types of standards are ideal or current. Ideal standards represent goals that, although usually unattainable, can be used as a measure of current performance under very high efficiency and tight controls. Current standards, on the other hand, are intended to be realized under normal operating conditions. The current standard, determined on an engineering basis, is the type of standard described in this chapter.

Estimated costs. Estimated costs refer to predetermined costs that are usually less precisely developed than standard costs; normally reflecting historical experience. Therefore, estimated costs are not treated as the actual cost of the product, but merely are used as a means for indicating the efficiency with which production is being performed.

Advantages of a standard cost system. The advantages of using a predetermined standard cost system occur in the following areas:

1. Planning.
2. Control.
3. Pricing.
4. Data Processing.

Planning. With the aid of a predetermined standard cost system, management can develop projections of future earnings based on realistic predictions of costs. The cost of product batches to be made and sold can be forecast merely by multiplying planned quantities by their standard unit costs. The data required in setting standard costs can also be used for planning materials to be purchased, manning to be provided, and the facilities needed to meet projected demands.

Control. Standard cost systems permit the automatic preparation of control reports based on the principle of exceptions, highlighting only those facts that require management action. Unfavorable performance is immediately spotlighted and traced to the responsible factors and individuals. Early corrective action can be taken in time to prevent serious loss and before the passage of time obscures the causes of poor performance. In fact, the very process of establishing standards may bring to light costly procedures such as the unnecessary use of inefficient equipment, poor material handling practices, poor scheduling, and poor operator work habits; all of which can be corrected before the standards are established.

Pricing. As a major tool for pricing decisions, standard costs have the following advantages:

1. Improvements in operating methods are immediately reflected in variance accounts enabling management to respond quickly to take price advantages where the markets served are reasonably elastic.

2. With an accurate picture of the contribution each product makes to fixed costs, management is able to make intelligent and selective price-volume decisions.

3. Costs are not distorted by temporary changes in volume. (Under actual cost systems, products may carry greater, or lesser, amounts of fixed burden depending upon the existing activity level.)

4. Management is not misled into changing prices when higher or lower costs result merely from nonrecurring shifts in efficiency levels or unusual material procurement situations.

Data processing. Predetermined standard cost systems are useful in simplifying data processing activities related to the costing procedure:

1. Material requisitions can be accumulated by part number, the quantities footed, and costs extended with a minimum of operations.

2. Only quantities need be accounted for on inventory records and bal-

ances on hand can then be extended by their unit costs for financial reporting purposes.

3. Labor effectiveness reports can be prepared in terms of hours instead of money, eliminating time consuming and costly extensions. Further, to most shop people the comparison of standard and actual hours is considerably more meaningful than a comparison using dollar amounts.

4. Job cost summaries can be dispensed with as all jobs for a given item are costed at standard unit cost. Therefore, accumulation of individual cost elements on a job basis serves little purpose.

► CAVEAT: A significant portion of the data processing advantages of a predetermined cost system may be lost where standards or engineered estimates have been unrealistically established, or where poor performance results in large variances. It may then be necessary to distribute variances back to the products on which they originate for pricing purposes and product profitability analyses.

Limitations on the use of standard cost systems. For any comparison of actual and standard costs to be meaningful, there must be reasonable stability in methods used and the prices paid for goods and services. The major variances in costs should be the result of varying levels of performance by people repetitively carrying out the same functions. A standard cost system is seldom useful in a shop that produces highly specialized products against customer orders. Effective material price standards are extremely difficult to maintain in such situations because materials usually have to be bought in significantly different lot sizes at varying prices. The learning factor on most of the work in such shops also makes the setting of realistic labor standards a difficult, if not impossible, task. In such circumstances, a job order cost system using engineered estimates, is often the most suitable for planning, pricing and control purposes. This type of system is explained in detail later in the chapter.

► SYSTEM CHECKLIST: In the Appendix following this chapter, there is a suggested questionnaire that can be used as a guide in determining what type of cost system might be most effectively employed in any given situation. The questions in this comprehensive system survey checklist reveal what conditions should exist before an integrated standard cost system might be used, and suggest alternatives that might be considered advantageous.

ACCOUNTING FOR A STANDARD COST SYSTEM

This section contains not only an explanation of accounting for prime costs and related variances under a standard cost system, but also a brief discussion of the data processing implications and the major considerations for auditing a standard cost installation. The accounting system described is a job order cost system using standard costs. To simplify the demonstration of principles, documentation suitable for visible files has been illustrated. Decisions

BILL OF MATERIAL

FORM A

TITLE FIELD ASSEMBLY 1406-451-013

UNIT SIZE 24V DATE 5/21/__

CHARACTERISTICS SH. 1 OF 1

CUSTOMER REF. DWG 1406-451-013 BY HGN

	MAJOR ITEMS COMPONENTS	PART NAME	S/ /S	PCS. RQD.	MATERIAL SPECIFICATION
1	1406-800-003	SHELL ASSEMBLY	C	1	
2	800-0092	SHELL, FIELD	C	1	
3	104-0072	ADAPTER: field mounting	C	1	
4	275-3608	COIL, FIELD: on -3614 c/d	D	1	Buy
5	572-0311	INSULATOR, STANDOFF	B	4	Buy
6	572-0502	INSULATOR, BUSHING	B	2	Buy
7	900-0008	TERMINAL, WIRE: ring	B	1	Buy
8	797-0037	SCREW: thread cutting rd. hd.	B	1	Buy
9	698-0003	POTTING COMPOUND	B	.1667 lb	Buy
10	572-0007	INSULATOR, STANDOFF: coil	B	3	Buy
11	697-0012	PAINT, BLACK	B	A/R	Buy
12					

PART NUMBER (COMPONENT)	ORDER NUMBER	COST CTR.	PART NUMBER (SYMBOL)	OPER. NUMBER	MACHINE NUMBER	QUANTITY	PRODUCT CLASS
1406&800&003	9999	2	1406&451&013	402	501	5000	

FORM B

MATERIAL REQUISITION

PLANT NUMBER	LOCATION	QUANTITY	DATE	FILLED BY

TOTAL QUANTITY

ISC/PRYOR 52500

WARNER ELECTRIC BRAKE & CLUTCH CO. 4 2

RA.	WORK ORDER	SUPERSEDES LIST CX-13402	PRODUCTION RELEASE DATE 6/29/__	ERE 2077	APVD. PLH

DATE	ECR	LINE	CHANGE	APVD.
4/19/__	2897		REVISED & RETYPED	L
2-13-__	3179	9	PCS. REQ'D. WAS: .25	E

FORM WLB 5027-4 WARNER ELECTRIC BRAKE & CLUTCH CO. BELOIT, WISCONSIN, U. S. A.

Fig. 1. Bill of Material.

on the need for printouts and visible files will obviously depend on the nature of operations, the data processing system, and the skills and discipline of personnel.

Accounting for direct materials. Considerable convenience is provided when standard prices appear on all master documents for ordering and controlling inventory and such is assumed here. When recording purchases, price variances are calculated and only the standard values or costs are carried to the inventory accounts. Inventory records are maintained by quantities only and these quantities are extended by their standard unit costs in preparing financial reports. Standard unit quantities, derived from bills of material, appear on shop order paper and material requisitions and only such quantities are issued. In Figure 1, a bill of material and a requisition form are illustrated as Forms A and B to show how the two are used in ordering material for production. Standard issue quantities of materials contain allowances for normal scrap and other losses. Extra material needed later is issued against reprovision tickets as required and is charged to an account for material usage variance or spoiled material. The reprovision ticket under which such materials are issued is also similar to Form B, but is always clearly identified as a reprovision rather than as an original issue ticket.

When a spoiled material ticket is prepared, Form C, Figure 2, its serial number is referenced on the reprovision ticket. The spoiled material ticket then

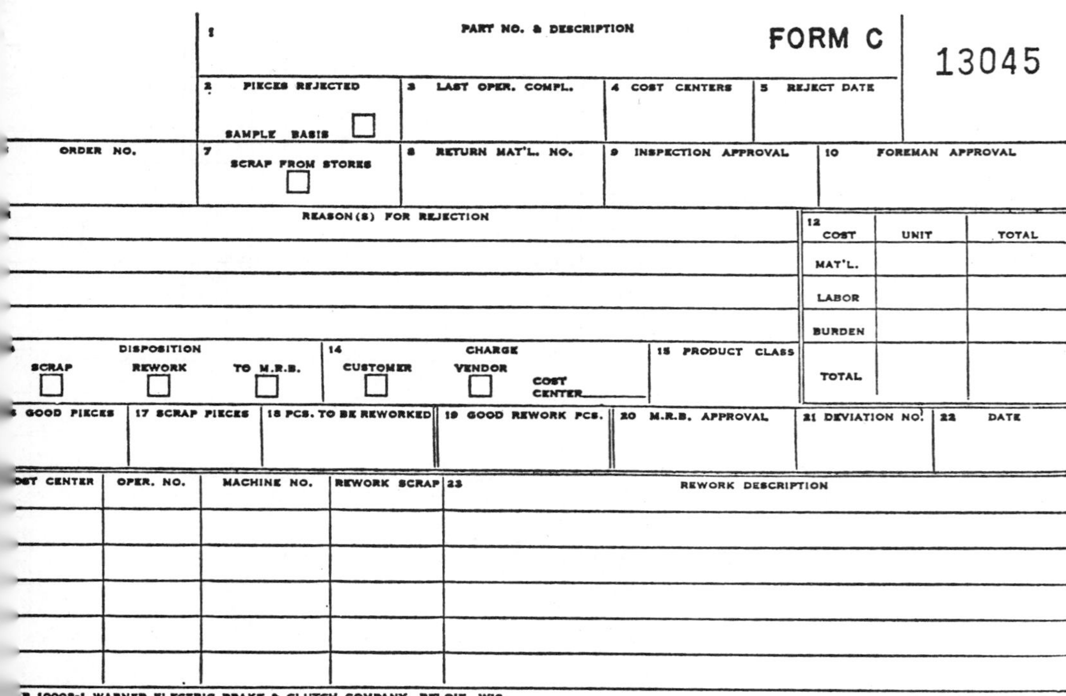

1 PART NO. & DESCRIPTION — FORM C — 13045

2 PIECES REJECTED — SAMPLE BASIS ☐ | 3 LAST OPER. COMPL. | 4 COST CENTERS | 5 REJECT DATE

ORDER NO. | 7 SCRAP FROM STORES ☐ | 8 RETURN MAT'L. NO. | 9 INSPECTION APPROVAL | 10 FOREMAN APPROVAL

REASON(S) FOR REJECTION

12 COST	UNIT	TOTAL
MAT'L.		
LABOR		
BURDEN		
TOTAL		

DISPOSITION: SCRAP ☐ REWORK ☐ TO M.R.B. ☐ | 14 CHARGE: CUSTOMER ☐ VENDOR ☐ COST CENTER____ | 15 PRODUCT CLASS

GOOD PIECES | 17 SCRAP PIECES | 18 PCS. TO BE REWORKED | 19 GOOD REWORK PCS. | 20 M.R.B. APPROVAL | 21 DEVIATION NO. | 22 DATE

COST CENTER	OPER. NO.	MACHINE NO.	REWORK SCRAP	23 REWORK DESCRIPTION

10008-1 WARNER ELECTRIC BRAKE & CLUTCH COMPANY, BELOIT, WIS.

Fig. 2. Spoiled Material Ticket.

PRODUCTION ORDER WEB 400-2 FORM D

ORDER NO.	ORDER QUANTITY	PROD. CLASS	STANDARD ORDER QTY.	START DATE	REQUIRED DATE	LEAD TIME	ASSEMBLY NUMBER	PROC. REV.	ORDER DATE
9999	5000	4	1000		6185	1	1406[illegible]451[illegible]13		618[illegible]

PAGE 1 OF 1

DESCRIPTION	ROUTER TYPE		PRIORITY
FIELD ASSEMBLY			

MASTER RATE	COST CENTER	OPER. NO.	COMPONENT REQ. QTY.	OPER. DESCRIPTION / QTY./ASSLY.	PART NUMBER	INSPECTION	OVERLAP %	LABOR CODE / UNIT/MEASURE	NO. OF MEN	TOOL NO.		MACH. NO.	STD. SET UP HRS.	PAY RATE HRS. PER 100 PCS.	PCS. PER HOUR
3360	612	402		ASSM				13007	[illegible]	7[illegible]41		9[illegible]		3[illegible]60	2976
				1	2758[illegible]8										
				2	5728[illegible]2			EA							
				3	5728[illegible]7			EA							
				1	9[illegible]8[illegible]			EA							
				1	7978[illegible]7			EA							
				1	1406[illegible]			EA							
1370	612	40[illegible]		ENC[illegible]				17099	[illegible]			7[illegible]9	[illegible]	[illegible]	7299
			8[illegible]	1	6988[illegible]8	PER 6		EA							
353	612	912													8571
122	612	511													1957

ORDER NUMBER	QUANTITY	COST CTR / OPERATION NUMBER	MACHINE NUMBER	STANDARD HOURS	PART NUMBER
9999	5000	402	9501	3360	1406451013
9999	5000	403	7389	1370	1406451013
9999	5000	912	[illegible]	350	1406451013
9999	5000	511	9502	122	1406451013

LABOR

DATE	CLOCK NUMBER	PIECES COMPLETED	ACCUMULATED TOTAL	OPERATOR'S INITIALS	DATE	CLOCK NUMBER	COMPLETED PIECES	ACCUMULATED TOTAL	OPERATOR'S INITIALS

FORM E

WARNER ELEC[illegible] BRAKE & CLUTCH

SBF-X53-53A

Fig. 3. Production Order.

stands as a special work order until final disposition is made of the material it covers. The accounting entry is made to reflect this disposition, using the spoiled material ticket as the source document. As shown in Form C, spoiled material tickets should be designed so that rework can be controlled through the shop in the same manner as regular production.

Amounts to be charged to work in process inventory are developed by footing and extending the material requisitions. An entry to take up material issues might be as follows:

Direct material in process	$150,000	
Direct material inventory		$150,000
To record standard issue of direct material to production.		

Accounting for direct labor. Labor tickets are prepared simultaneously with production orders. The most useful data to be shown on the tickets are standard hours, wage codes, operation numbers, and work center numbers. Production operations completed and their elapsed times are then recorded and extended on the tickets. Excesses over standard time are computed in hours, appropriately coded and extended at standard rates for variance recording. Differences between actual and standard rates for labor are extended by the standard hours for completed production to determine rate variance amounts. Variances are then summarized by appropriate variance classifications and analytical reports are prepared. Separate reports are prepared daily, weekly, and monthly. Their distribution within the organization varies depending upon the frequency of their issue.

Production units completed are extended by the standard unit labor costs (standard rate × allowed time) and summarized to develop charges to work in process. When there are operations for which no standards have been established, estimates are used and treated in the same manner as standards. Alternatively, actual hours can be extended by actual rates to develop the charge to work in process as in an actual cost system and memorandum records can be maintained to insure corrections are made to the finished goods inventory accounts on completion of production. Figure 3 shows a production order, Form D, and companion labor ticket, Form E. A copy of each production order and the associated labor tickets go to each work center.

A weekly direct labor distribution summary might appear as follows:

Dept.	*Standard Labor to Work in Process*	*Efficiency Variance*	*Rate Variance*	*Indirect Labor Performed by Direct Laborers*	*Set up*	*Gross Total*
1	$15,000	$ 900	$ 50	—	$3,000	$18,950
2	22,000	50	(75)	$125	1,800	23,900
3	7,000	700	100	—	500	8,300
4	12,000	1,500	125	22	900	14,547
5	8,500	100	200	—	—	8,800
Totals	$64,500	$3,250	$400	$147	$6,200	$74,497

The accounting entries to reflect the above labor distribution are as follows:

Direct Payroll

Gross wages	$74,497	
Withholding and deductions		$14,899
Net payroll accrued		59,598

Direct Payroll Distribution

Work in process	$64,500	
Efficiency variance	3,250	
Rate variance	400	
Direct on indirect	147	
Setup labor	6,200	
Gross wages		$74,497

To record distribution of the direct shop payroll, and, to record withholdings, deductions and net payroll accrual.

All direct labor performed by workers for departments other than the one to which they are regularly assigned is transferred to the department in which the work was performed. Thereafter, the total direct hours (or dollars) for each department can be used for the overhead charge to work in process.

A separate summary is prepared for all indirect wages. Included in this summary is an amount for indirect labor performed by direct laborers permitting proper allocation of direct labor and overhead to work in process.

Accounting for overhead. Actual expenses as incurred are charged to the appropriate service and production departments. Overhead applied to work in process is developed by applying to standard production hours (or standard payroll dollars) in each department the standard departmental overhead rate. This amount is credited to an applied burden account for each department. Differences between actual and applied overhead amounts are carried to volume and spending variance accounts.

Entries for finished goods and cost of sales. Total units of completed products are multipled by their respective standard unit costs to produce entries to transfer costs from work in process to finished goods inventory. Charges to cost of sales and the corresponding credits to finished goods inventory are similarly developed by extending product sales totals by their standard unit costs. In support of these unit costs, a standard product cost summary is usually maintained. Such a summary shows not only the total finished product cost but also the cost of all the assemblies that go to make up the finished product. Similar summaries are prepared for each such assembly in turn, showing all subassembly and individual component costs. Below the subassembly level, individual component cost summaries are prepared. These summaries show individual operations performed in each cost center, and set up hours, direct labor hours, labor rate, and extended costs for material, labor, and overhead. Material cost and set up cost are predicated on standard (EOQ) order quantities and run quantities respectively. A standard product cost summary is demonstrated as Form F in Figure 4.

VARIANCES FROM STANDARDS

Management by exception is achieved through comparisons of actual and standard costs. The cost accountant from a great mass of data sifts out only the significant differences between actual and standard costs which are presented to management, permitting concentration on serious problem areas.

Material variances. Material variances from standards are of two major classifications; price variances and quantity variances. In processing suppliers invoices, the quantities purchased are extended by their standard prices. Price variances are then accounted for under one of the following types of variance codes:

Vendor price difference.
Order quantity difference.
Substitute material.
Secondary supplier.
Other.

Secondary analysis is undertaken to fix responsibility and for taking corrective actions whenever the variances are significant in amount.

Material quantity variances are usually due to and can be accounted for as:

Operator error.
Faulty material.
Equipment malfunction.
Other.

Labor variances. Variances from labor standards are also of two main types. They may arise from differences in rates of pay, or differences in units produced per labor hour. Foremen assign numerical codes to the various categories of labor variances after making an investigation as to the underlying causes. For reporting purposes, all variances are grouped by departments usually under two major control codes for rate and efficiency variance. Only when these variances become excessive is an analytical report prepared for management

FORM F

STANDARD PRODUCT COST	STD. ORD. QUANTITY	ANNUAL USAGE	EFFECTIVE DATE	LOW LEVEL	PRODUCT CLASS	DESCRIPTION	PART NUMBER
	1000		03/01/[illegible]	1	4	FIELD ASSEMBLY	14068451&013

RAW MATERIAL CODE	PIECES PER UNIT OF MEAS.	UNIT OF MEAS.	CODE	POUNDS PER PIECE	POUNDS PER UNIT OF MEAS.	COST PER PIECE	COST PER UNIT OF MEAS

SEQ.	QUANTITY PER ASSEMBLY	PART NUMBER & USAGE FACTOR OR DESCRIPTION	COST CENTER	NO. OF LOADS	MACHINE NUMBER	OPER. NO.	D.L. HOURS PER 100	SET UP HOURS	LABOR RATE	LABOR	BURDEN	MATERIAL	TOTAL
5		ASSM	612	10	9501	402	3360		343	115	247		362
10	1	275&3608										891	891
15	2	572&0502										012	012
20	3	572&0007										003	003
25	1	900&0008										018	018
30	1	797&0037										009	009
35	1	14068800&003						240		174	411	464	1049
				****	SUBTOTAL		****	240		289*	658*	1397*	2344**
40		ENCA	612	10	7389	403	1370	40	343	061	131		192
45	1	698&0003 6										113	113
				****	SUBTOTAL		****	280		350*	789*	1510*	2649**
50		DEGR	612	10	1231	912	350		329	012	026		038
				****	SUBTOTAL		****	280		362*	815*	1510*	2687*
55		LOAD	612	10	9502	511	122		343	004	009		013

TOTAL SET UP	PAGE	LABOR	BURDEN	MATERIAL	TOTAL
280	1	366	824	1510	2700

14068451&013

Fig. 4. Standard Product Cost.

review. Typical codes for labor variances in a metal working shop might include the following:

Operator rate.
Nonstandard material.
Faulty material.
Operator efficiency.
Added operation.
Nonstandard operation.
Methods change.
Substitute operator.

Overhead variances. Overhead variances from standard are caused by spending or volume differences. The spending variance is the difference between actual overhead expenses and budgeted overhead expense at the actual volume experienced. The volume variance represents the difference between absorbed overhead and budgeted overhead for the actual volume experienced. Using T accounts, the basic transactions appear as follows:

A Service Cost Center

$100[1]	$ 75[2]
	25[3]
$100	$ 100

A Production Cost Center

$1,000[1]	$1,060[4]
75[2]	15[5]
$1,075	$1,075

Applied Burden

$1,060[4]	$ 900[6]
	160[7]
$1,060	$1,060

Work in Process

$ 900[6]	

Spending Variance

$25[3]	
15[5]	
$40	

Volume Variance

$ 160[7]	
$ 160	

Total Burden Expense	$1,100	($100 + $1,000)
Total Burden Applied	900	(At standard)
Total Variance	$ 200	

	Spending Variance		*Volume Variance*		*Total Variance*
Service Cost Center	$25				$ 25
Production Cost Center	$15		$160		$175
	$40	+	$160	=	$200

[1]Actual expenses charged from books of original entry.
[2]Service Center flexible budget at actual monthly activity level.
[3]Spending variance—Service Cost Center.
[4]Production Cost Center flexible budget at actual monthly activity level including the Service Center allocation.
[5]Spending variance—Production Cost Center.
[6]Applied burden at standard rate for actual production.
[7]Volume variance—Production Cost Center.

Computation of overhead variances with a flexible budget. The manufacturing expense variance computations utilizing a flexible budget are shown below in detail.

Flexible budget:				
Monthly hours at standard	2,000	2,250	2,500	2,750
Manufacturing expense flexible budget	$4,500	$4,750	$5,000	$5,175
Overhead rate per standard hour	$2.25	$2.11	$2.00[1]	$1.88

[1]Budgeted rate used for applying overhead to work in process.

Computation variances:		
Actual rate of production in standard hours: 790 units @ 3 hours		2,370 hours
Flexible overhead rate for actual production: $\$2.11 - \left(\frac{2{,}370 - 2{,}250}{2{,}500 - 2{,}250}\right) \times .11$		$2.06 per hr.
Budgeted overhead at actual production: 2,370 hours @ $2.06	$4882	
Overhead applied to work in process: 2,370 hours @ $2.00	4,740	
Volume variance (debit)		$142
Actual overhead incurred	$5,500	
Budgeted overhead at actual production	4,882	
Spending variance (debit)		618
Total variance		$760

Computer implications. It is apparent that a standard system with constant unit data lends itself particularly well to computer systemization. The basic operations involve sorting, footing, and a minimum of calculation of constant data by variable quantities. An actual cost system, on the other hand, has many more calculations and opportunities for error than a standard cost system. Constantly changing unit cost values must be accounted for and assuring the accuracy of these entries is considerably more time consuming than when using uniform standard costs.

Auditing factors. The auditing of an actual cost system is usually more difficult than the auditing of a standard cost system. In a standard cost system, the reasonableness of the standards used for the few high value usage items can normally be verified by limited test checking. Standard material quantities can be checked to blueprints and standard dollar prices traced to inventory and purchasing records. The size and frequency of variances also serve as an indication of the suitability of the standards themselves. Once the appropriateness of the standards is confirmed, the cost of goods sold can be tested by computing quantities sold by their standard unit costs. Inventory valuations can be checked simply by extending physical units on hand by their unit standard costs.

HOW TO SET STANDARDS

Engineered values are developed from study of the physical characteristics of the products to be made and the work processes to be performed. The following is a brief description of the methods used for setting material, labor, and overhead standards:

1. Material quantities are determined from engineering drawings and bills of materials. Allowances are made for that scrap or waste that can be anticipated in creating the product. To these physical quantities are applied predetermined unit costs for EOQ quantities at the current or the anticipated market price for the budget period.
2. Labor and/or machine hours are developed from analysis of methods, equipment to be used, and work to be performed. Time studied values of actual pilot runs or time values developed from standard data tables can be used. These are then converted to money amounts by applying appropriate labor rates.
3. Overhead is based upon the expected level of activity in the shop for which indirect costs are developed. Manning tables and other engineering techniques are used to develop what these indirect costs should be for the planned production level.

The mechanics of setting material, labor, and overhead standards, described briefly above, are next explored in detail.

Direct material price standards. The setting of material price standards can be rather complex. It will be discussed in terms of setting initial standards and in revising these standards when market conditions or EOQ quantities undergo change.

Setting material price standards. The establishing of direct material price standards can be thought of as a process that involves all, or some, of the following steps:

1. A forecast is made of the expected usage of each direct material item for the budget.
2. The most economical purchase lot sizes are determined.
3. These lots sizes are adjusted for such factors as limitations in storage space, transportation factors, and the reliability of the basic forecast itself.
4. Finally, a price based on the foregoing is established. This may be the existing price, or may be higher or lower to reflect reasonably predictable price movements expected to occur within the budget period.

Revising price standards. Price standards, once set, are normally maintained for an annual period. In the event of a significant change in price levels or purchase quantities to reflect major budget revisions, it may be necessary to revise the standard during a fiscal year and to revalue existing inventories. If it is possible, such revisions should be made when inventories are at a cyclical low level.

Direct material quantity standards. Material quantity standards for purchased parts are quite simple to set if prints and bills of material have been properly drawn. The standard quantity in all instances is the bill of material quantity. Any extra issues are made against reprovision requisitions.

Other aspects of material standards requiring special consideration include:

1. Raw material standards.
2. Spoiled material and usage variances.
3. By-product parts.
4. Low unit cost parts.

Raw material standards. Ideally, standard sizes and lengths of raw materials for each fabricated part should be established by industrial engineers. These sizes should seek to minimize drop-offs that cannot be reused. It is usually more practical to charge standard gross usage to work in process, and to pick up scrap recovery monthly as a reduction of direct material costs.

Spoiled material and usage variances. Opinions vary as to when charges should be made to a spoiled material account or to a material usage variance. In the opinion of the author, material usage variances should be charged only when extra materials have had to be used but no operations have been performed. For example, the use of nonstandard sized materials may result in a larger than standard material consumption which should be taken up as a variance. Material spoiled in production, through operator errors or material faults, should be charged to a Spoiled Material account at the cost through the last completed operation. It is often desirable to net out the scrap recovery in making the charge if no salvage is to be attempted. Reworked parts are taken back into inventory at regular standard cost. The related labor and overhead is charged to Rework and Salvage expense. It is possible to incur substantial losses on spoiled work. Where inspection is weak, a company can find itself paying incentive premiums for spoiled work. If spoiled work is discovered in the department where the spoilage took place, the accountant may be able to deduct it for the purposes of wage determination, if the union contract so permits. In any event, the spoilage ticket should show the last completed operation for cost purposes. All spoilage discovered past its point of origin should be charged with the full amount of labor up to its then existing completion. Units that are reworked (including disassembly and reassembly) are charged to the department making the original error.

By-product parts. These secondary parts usually result from a prime production order. The instructions on the order should call for their delivery to process inventory storage. The charge to inventory should only be for the material content, with all labor charged to the primary product.

Low unit cost parts. In many companies, there is a substantial amount of small unit value materials that are not uniformly required on different products. Therefore, these small parts cannot be equitably charged through overhead distribution. One way for handling these parts is to include them on bills of materials but issue them in bulk to the work stations where used, with a charge to a suspense account. Work in process is then charged as production is reported and the suspense account credited. Extra usage, if it occurs, will only be determined as a part of the inventory shrinkage at year end; but because of the low unit values involved, any such inventory shrink should not be significant in dollar amount.

Obviously, any standard cost system as it relates to accounting for materials, must be very carefully developed to seek a balance between:

1. Adequate control.
2. What is practical in light of existing personnel attitudes.
3. The cost of the system.

In general, controls over the few high usage value items should be comprehensive, with less stringent controls for low usage value items. In all instances, controls over spoiled material salvage and scrap should be as airtight as they can be made, consistent with the cost for doing so.

Concepts of direct labor standards. With labor contributing such a large portion of the total value added in the manufacturing process, it is only natural that pay plans have been evolved whose major objective is to provide a labor incentive for more efficient production. Although labor standards originated from such piecework incentives, later trends have been toward standard hour plans.

Piecework incentives. These provide for paying the employee a given amount per unit of finished production. This amount is often subject to downward adjustment after a worker's output exceeds a certain norm or standard, resulting in a sharing of the savings from this higher production by the worker and the company.

Standard hour plans. The use of this type of plan has increased recently due to some built-in advantages. Under this plan, labor standards are established in terms of labor time per unit of production. An employee earns extra hours by producing more than the standard. All labor savings resulting from increased production are passed on to the workman in full. The company benefits only through the reduction in unit overhead costs.

The following table illustrates how a standard hour of 100% time premium plan works:

Standard allowance	2 hours, 100 units
Actual hours worked	3 hours
Actual units produced	175 units
Hours earned	3.5 hours (1.75 × 2)
Hourly rate	$2.00 per hour
Earnings	$7.00

It can be seen from the table that the percent of efficiency in the case illustrated (earned hours over actual hours) is 116% and the incentive earnings are $1.00. Some of the advantages of this type of plan are:

1. It is easy to compute efficiency in terms of hours for both individual workers and departments.

2. Variance analysis is greatly simplified. The only variances that can be created are unfavorable variances when the employee falls below the standard.

Accordingly, this type of plan places a premium on the establishment of realistic standards. Average efficiency measurements of 115% to 130% are usually indicative of realistic standards and good productivity.

Setting labor standards. Although labor standards are generally set by industrial engineers or time study men, it is important for the accountant to know the elements included in these standards. They consist of the two basic elements of time and rate. Both factors should reflect future expectations rather than past experience. To be realistic, provisions must be made in the time allowances for personal needs and other predictable delays which will be beyond the control of operators.

Control over labor time and production reporting. Weaknesses are frequently encountered in reports on both labor hours and production output. The accountant should suggest the types of controls most likely to eliminate these weaknesses. In controlling production counts and related labor hours, major attention should be given to those items that constitute the greatest dollar value. In most cases, a relatively small number of items will absorb 80% to 90% of the total labor cost, and these are the items that require accurate piece counts and reports of elapsed hours. Possible controls include the following:

1. *For time reporting*—starting and completion times can be entered by timekeepers, dispatchers, or foremen. Elapsed time can be computed by a digital time clock and either transmitted on line to a central processor, or it can be printed, or punched, in the time card for later processing.

2. For production reporting—all counts should be verified by time keepers, inspectors, or foremen, using one of the following techniques:

   a. Weight counts for small, irregularly shaped items.
   b. Physical measurements or standard pallet loads for small, regularly shaped items that can be stacked uniformly.
   c. Individual piece counts for bulkier items.

► OBSERVATION: Where 100% count verification is too much of a job, one of the statistical sampling techniques explained in Chapter 27 may be substituted. There is a tendency for companies to resist the bother and added cost of accurate time and production reporting. However, 5% on a $1,000,000 labor bill pays for a lot of timekeepers and checkers. Considerably more than this can be lost through a combination of faulty reporting of time and production.

Overhead standards. Overhead includes all manufacturing expenses incurred to support the producing departments. These expenses are generally thought of as fixed, variable, and semi-variable, although further refinements are possible. The first step in setting standards for overhead is to prepare the overhead budget.

Developing the flexible budget. The overhead budget is flexible when budget standards are predetermined for various levels of production. In establishing the flexible budget, the following sequence of steps can be taken:

1. The production cost centers are established.

2. Service cost centers are also defined, and a method is chosen for allocating their costs to the production cost centers and to other service cost centers.

3. A chart of accounts is developed.

4. Expenses are analyzed for response to volume changes.

5. Overhead rates are established for selected increments of activity over the full range of activity anticipated to be experienced during the budget period. These rates are based on productive man hours, machine hours, or direct labor dollars for each production cost center.

These five steps are discussed individually in the following paragraphs.

Production cost centers. Before preparing the flexible budget, it is necessary to divide the plant into production cost centers, each with its specific type of work and under the direct responsibility of one person. For establishing rates, it is often best to include the largest number of production tools for which the supporting overhead expenses are uniform. For management control, several subcost centers may then be established for which these rates will apply. A flow sheet showing how products move through the plant is usually essential in establishing the cost centers to be used for cost accounting purposes. This, in fact, is a critical step if realistic overhead rates are to be established and it requires experience with plant operations in order to be properly performed.

Service cost centers. Usually these centers are defined along functional lines (e.g., repairs and maintenance, generating plant). Having made a functional analysis, the next step is to decide whether these cost centers will be treated alone or combined into larger centers. This hinges on answers to such questions as:

1. Are the services performed uniformly for other service and production centers?

2. Can the services performed for other departments be accurately measured?

3. How will costing and control over costing be affected?

► ILLUSTRATION: Repair and maintenance service costs are often significant and can vary considerably between departments. Inaccurate distribution of this expense complicates control and can distort product costs. Accordingly, this department should normally stand as an individual service center with direct allocation of its expenses through a repair order procedure. On the other hand, a cafeteria operation normally cannot distort product costs, no matter how distributed. Furthermore, control over cafeteria costs is not enhanced by any arbitrary method of distributing these costs to other departments, and accordingly, cafeteria expense is often best included as a part of the general factory overhead pool.

In keeping with the above concepts, service cost centers are studied from the point of view of services rendered to other centers. The service center that serves the greatest number of other centers should be selected for first distribution of expenses. Thereafter, each service center is distributed in order of descending number of other centers served. Techniques for finding a reasonable basis for measuring the services provided include:

1. Direct measurement, such as provided by the recording of man-hours, or by electric meters, automatic counting devices, etc.

2. Synthesized measurements, such as engineering analysis of square foot areas.

Chart of accounts. The next step in preparing the flexible budget is the development of the chart of accounts. A simple matrix can be used with

FORM G

DETAILED EXHIBIT of COST CENTERS and EXPENSES / COST CENTER ACCOUNTS	Service Centers							Production Centers			
UNIFORM EXPENSE CODE	Building	Steam Generation	Electricity Generation	General Factory	Factory Production	Repair and Betterment	Prerequisite Production	Department A	Department B section 1	Department B section 2	Department C
Direct expense	11	12	13	20	40	60	70	81	82	83	84
-01 Expense material	xx	xx	xx	xx	xx	xx	xx	xx	xx	xx	xx
-02 Supplies	xx	xx	xx	xx	xx	xx	xx	xx	xx	xx	xx
-03 Service labor	xx	xx	xx	xx	xx	xx	xx	xx	xx	xx	xx
-04 Overtime and allowances	xx	xx	xx	xx	xx	xx	xx	xx	xx	xx	xx
-05 Repairs	xx	xx	xx	xx	xx	xx	xx	xx	xx	xx	xx
-06 Fuel		xx									
-07 Inventory adjustment				xx	xx						
-31 Continuity of service	xx	xx	xx	xx	xx	xx	xx	xx	xx	xx	xx
-32 Other accruals	xx	xx	xx	xx	xx	xx	xx	xx	xx	xx	xx
-41 Supervision	xx	xx	xx	xx	xx	xx	xx	xx	xx	xx	xx
-42 Depreciation	xx	xx	xx	xx	xx	xx	xx	xx	xx	xx	xx
-43 Taxes	xx	xx	xx	xx	xx	xx	xx	xx	xx	xx	xx
-44 Insurance	xx	xx	xx	xx	xx	xx	xx	xx	xx	xx	xx
Apportioned expense											
-11 Building		xx	xx	xx	xx	xx	xx	xx	xx	xx	xx
-12 Steam generation			xx	xx	xx	xx	xx	xx	xx	xx	xx
-13 Electricity generation				xx	xx	xx	xx	xx	xx	xx	xx
-20 General factory					xx	xx	xx	xx	xx	xx	xx
-40 Factory production							xx	xx	xx	xx	xx
-60 Repair and betterment							xx	xx	xx	xx	xx
-70 Prerequisite production								xx	xx	xx	xx

Fig. 5. An Account Matrix.

expense classifications along one margin, and the service and production departments listed in order of expense redistribution across the top. To complete the matrix, departmental redistribution accounts should be listed below the expense accounts in the same order as the departments are listed across the top. By placing check marks in boxes under each department for each applicable expense, individual department charts of accounts are developed. The charts should then be reviewed carefully with shop personnel to insure against omissions. To provide flexibility, the account numbering system should permit the addition of new accounts that may be required as operations undergo expansion or change. The author highly favors the Dewey Decimal System of account numbering for this purpose. Form G, illustrated in Figure 5, represents an account matrix developed by the International Accountants Society, Inc., and illustrates well the technique described above.

Expense analysis. The utility of a flexible budget depends on accurate expense analysis—that is, in determining accurately how expenses behave in relation to shifts in volume levels. For ease in making such an analysis, overhead expenses can be classified into two major categories:

a. *Payroll.* The best analysis of payroll expense is made through the use of a manning table. To develop a manning table for establishing the flexible budget, all indirect personnel and/or man hours required at each cost center are listed by job classification. Additional personnel and/or man hours required for each successive volume level are tabulated over the full range of anticipated operations for the budget period. Although preparing a manning table may be tedious and time consuming work, it is well worth the effort as payroll often represents the greatest element of overhead expense. Once this job is completed, analysis and control of payroll and payroll burden (taxes, insurance, etc.) is greatly simplified. Form H, shown in Figure 6, illustrates a manning table that might be made up for a machining department. Figure 7 shows the same information in graphic form and adds the total labor cost for different percentages of capacity.

b. *Other expenses.* All other expenses can be budgeted in one of two ways: historical data can be statistically analyzed or an engineering analysis can be made of how expenses are influenced by volume.

Where historical analysis is employed, the most popular technique is the scatter diagram. Expense levels are plotted on one axis against volume levels on the other. Then a line is drawn through the plot points to provide an expense-volume trend line. The appropriate level of expense for the anticipated volume level can then be selected for budgeting each cost center. If a more formal method is desired, the least squares equation can be used to establish the trend line.

There are a number of hazards to recognize in using trend analyses for future planning and control. These include:

FLEXIBLE MANNING TABLE
MACHINE SHOP

Unit of Capacity: Machine Hours
100% Capacity 40.000 Machine Hours

Position	*Hourly Rate*	*Weekly Man-Hours Versus Per Cent of Capacity*										
		50%	*60%*	*70%*	*80%*	*90%*	*100%*	*110%*	*120%*	*130%*	*140%*	*150%*
Foreman	$6.50	40	40	40	40	40	40	40	40	40	40	40
Assistant foreman	5.00	40	40	40	40	40	40	40	80	80	80	80
Timekeeper	1.75	40	40	40	40	40	40	80	80	80	80	80
Setup	2.25	40	40	40	40	80	80	80	80	80	80	80
Trainee operators	1.25	40	40	40	40	40	40	80	80	80	80	120
Material handlers	1.50	40	40	40	80	80	80	80	120	120	120	120
Minor repairs	1.90	40	40	40	40	80	80	80	120	120	120	160
Cleaners	1.35	40	40	40	40	40	80	80	80	80	80	80
Expeditor	3.50	40	40	40	40	40	40	80	80	80	80	120
Dispatcher	2.25	40	40	40	40	40	40	80	80	80	80	80
		400	400	400	440	520	560	720	840	840	840	960

Fig. 6. Manning Table.

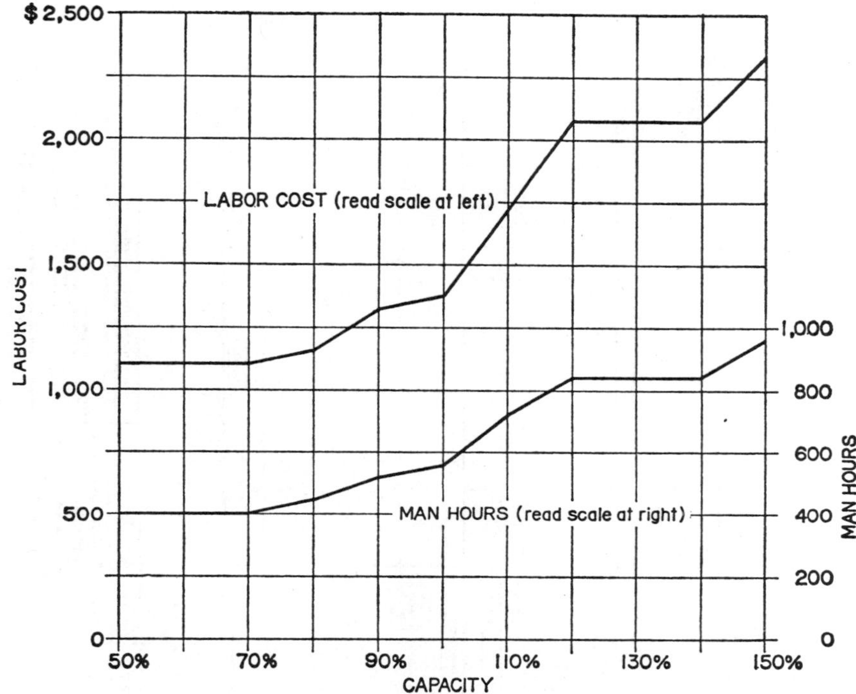

Fig. 7. Manning Table in Graphic Form.

1. Methods, policies, or organization changes which are planned may have a profound affect on past volume-expense relationships so that use of historical trend data may be highly misleading in creating significant variances if adjustments are not made for these changes.

2. If control has historically been poor, there will be little correlation between expenses and volume, and deviations may well be so large as to make any trend line only marginally useful for future planning and control purposes.

3. The independent volume variable selected may not be the predominant control variable, and if not, any correlation between volume and expense will be coincidental and of little use for future planning.

Where historical analyses cannot be used in establishing volume and expense relationships, engineering techniques must be used. Here again, if actual operations are not conducted in conformity with the engineering assumptions employed, the utility of the resulting expressions of volume to expense levels will only be marginally useful to the planner.

Using the flexible budget. Having established the standard overhead rates at the expected level of operations, they are applied by extending the hours spent in each production cost center by its individual rate.

Accounting for production and sales. The accounting for production and sales is now a relatively simple matter and can be summarized as follows:

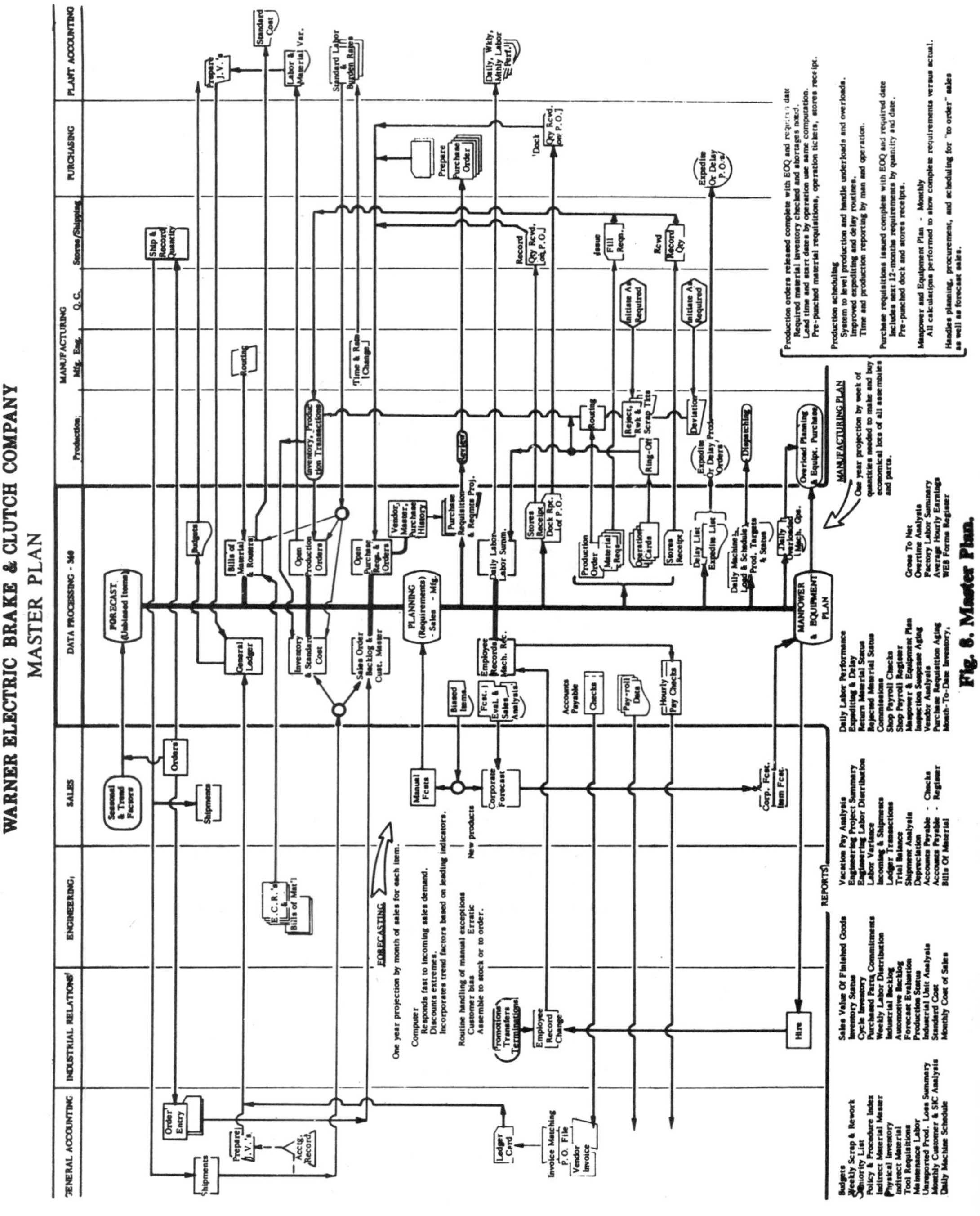

Budgets
Weekly Scrap & Rework
Seniority List
Policy & Procedure Index
Indirect Material Master
Physical Inventory
Indirect Material
Tool Requisitions
Maintenance Labor
Unreported Prod. Loss Summary
Monthly Customer & SIC Analysis
Daily Machine Schedule

Sales Value Of Finished Goods
Inventory Status
Cycle Inventory
Purchased Parts Commitments
Weekly Labor Distribution
Industrial Backlog
Automotive Backlog
Forecast Evaluation
Production Status
Industrial Unit Analysis
Standard Cost
Monthly Cost of Sales

Vacation Pay Analysis
Engineering Project Summary
Engineering Labor Distribution
Labor Variance
Incoming & Shipments
Ledger Transactions
Trial Balance
Shipment Analysis
Depreciation
Accounts Payable - Checks
Accounts Payable - Register
Bills Of Material

Daily Labor Performance
Expediting & Delay
Return Material Status
Rejected Material Status
Commissions
Shop Payroll Checks
Shop Payroll Register
Manpower & Equipment Plan
Inspection Suspense Aging
Vendor Analysis
Purchase Requisition Aging
Month-To-Date Inventory,

Gross To Net
Overtime Analysis
Factory Labor Summary
Average Hourly Earnings
WEB Forms Register

Production orders released complete with EOQ and required date
- Required material inventory checked and shortages noted.
- Lead time and start dates by operation use same computation.
- Pre-punched material requisitions, operation tickets, stores receipt.

Production scheduling
- System to level production and handle underloads and overloads.
- Improved expediting and delay routines.
- Time and production reporting by man and operation.

Purchase requisitions issued complete with EOQ and required date
- Includes next 12-months requirements by quantity and date.
- Pre-punched dock and stores receipts.

Manpower and Equipment Plan - Monthly
- All calculations performed to show complete requirements versus actual.

Handles planning, procurement, and scheduling for "to order" sales as well as forecast sales.

Fig. 8. Master Plan.

unit material costs.

1. Physical units of material going into process are extended by standard
2. Labor costs are accumulated by extending units completed in each operation by the standard unit labor cost.
3. Burden is charged by totaling the standard hours in each cost center and extending them by the selected overhead rate.
4. Finished goods and cost of sales are costed by applying the unit standard cost to the number of units completed or sold.
5. Material, labor, and overhead variances are determined and taken up in variance accounts as previously described.

Once set, standard overhead rates should be maintained for at least annual periods. However, adjustments should be made annually for:

1. Changes in price levels for indirect services.
2. Changes in factory equipment, layout, or plan of shop control.
3. Other changes that may materially affect existing rates.

How the flexible budget and standard cost system can become an integral part of the company's master plan for the budget period is shown in Figure 8.

ESTIMATED COST SYSTEMS

Estimated costs can be used in conjunction with a standard cost system or with an actual cost system, depending on:

1. The degree of standardization of basic components and assemblies.
2. The degree of refinement used in estimating the standards.

A standard cost system based on estimates is usually more desirable and useful to management. On the other hand, a combination of engineering estimates with historical costs is usually more practical where products are:

1. Highly specialized for individual customer orders.
2. Cost-estimated in arriving at selling prices.
3. Only produced against customer's orders.

A hybrid system, using such estimates together with actual costs, is discussed here in terms of:

1. Preparing cost estimates.
2. Revising cost estimates.
3. Accounting for the system.

Preparing cost estimates. The difficulties in preparing cost estimates relate to the uniqueness of the products being made. If there is no standardization, each job must be completely estimated. Usually, however, some standardization of components, subassemblies, or major assemblies exists. Estimating for products, which are repetitively produced, starts with data taken from the estimating file. For nonstandard, nonrepetitive items, estimating begins with design drawings. These drawings are used by industrial engineers to estimate:

1. The operations required.
2. Set-up hours for each operation.
3. Running hours for each operation.
4. Special tooling requirements.
5. Materials and components to be purchased.

The estimating department uses these data to prepare cost and price estimates, including mark-ups for factory overhead, selling and administrative expenses, and profits. It can be seen that estimating is more a function of engineers than of accountants, although accountants provide such data as current labor rates, material prices, and mark-up factors to be applied to the direct costs.

Form J, in Figure 9, illustrates a summary cost estimate sheet for a manufacturer of automotive equipment. It will be noted that provision is made for standard parts and subassemblies that are to be used without change. Accordingly, the bills of materials and production routings for these standard units can be used without change. For new or modified components, changes can be entered to copies of the bills of material and routings, and new masters prepared. These new masters then are filed with the cost estimate summaries.

Revising cost estimates. A standard estimating file, comprising the latest cost estimates for components and assemblies, is a valuable tool. When an order for a substantially standard component is received, the development of revisions to reflect modifications is simplified. Changes can be entered on the fact of a copy of the standard estimate file card or an adjustment card can be attached showing additions and deletions.

The standard estimate file must reflect current labor and material rates. If it is not practical to revise the entire file at one time, cards affected by changes can be tabbed. As these cards are used in making estimates, they are first updated and the tabs removed. In this manner, all cards on which there is activity are revised progressively, leaving only the balance of low usage items to be corrected as a special and separate task.

As jobs are completed, an automatic review should be made to determine:

1. Possible errors in the original estimate.

2. Any uncontrollable, nonrepetitive factors that arose in the manufacturing process.

3. The ability of the shop to meet estimates, as a measurement of the shop's general efficiency. Allowances may have to be built into the estimates, or estimates may have to be adjusted for the shop's efficiency level. The standard estimate file cards are corrected as indicated by this review.

SUMMARY COST ESTIMATE & SELLING PRICE

(PREV. EST. NO. N.A.) EST. NO. 195

ROUTING	REQUEST. BY	MGR. - PROD. PLAN	COST ESTIMATOR	MGR. - MFG. ENG.	COST ANALYST	CONTROLLER	DIVISION V.P.	DATE WRITTEN	DATE COMPLETED
→	SALES DEPT	JHK	BLJ	IRL	MNP	JHP	RLS	2/20/—	4/20/—

1 PRIORITY: RUSH ☐ 1 WEEK ☐ 2 WEEKS ☐ 3 WEEKS ☒

2 CLASS: I ☒ NEW PRODUCT; II ☐ VARIATION OR REVISION TO EXISTING PRODUCT; III ☐ COST REDUCTION - PROD. IMPROVE

3 COST & PRICE ☒ REVISE PRICE ☐ PRELIM. EVALUATION ☐

4 ☐ THIS CUSTOMER ☒ CATALOG

5 CUSTOMER N.A.
ADDRESS N.A.

6 SPECIAL PROD. NO. N.A.

7 NEW PROD. NO. 71294

8 DRAWING NUMBER(S) SEE attached list

9 PRODUCT DESCRIPTION WIDGET

10 SPECIAL COSTS (TOOLING, ETC.)

PRO-RATE ☒ QUOTE SEPARATELY ☐ TO BE REFUNDED ☐ NOT TO BE REFUNDED ☐

NEW MACHY.	TOOL DESIGN	NEW GAGING	TOTAL - SPECIAL COSTS
$ N.A.	$ 150	$ N.A.	$ 1225.00
DIE & FIXTURE $ 700	VENDOR (PURCH. PART) $ 375	OTHER $ N.A.	

11 UNIT COSTS

PART NO.	PROD. RUN	MATERIAL: ~~EST. OR~~ STD./PC	MATERIAL: COST/PC ~~w/sr #~~	S.U.: HR./PC	S.U.: COST/PC ~~w/sr #~~	DIRECT LABOR (RATE $ COMP. /HR.) NEW PARTS: HR./PC	NEW PARTS: COST/PC ~~w/sr #~~	STANDARD PARTS: HRS ~~COST~~/PC	STANDARD PARTS: COST/PC ~~w/sr #~~	TOTAL/PC DIR. LAB.	TOTAL/PC SET-UP + DIRECT LABOR
7129145	100	1	1.00	.15	.30	.75	2.15			2.15	2.45
7129143	200	2	1.50	.12	.22	1.00	2.00			2.00	2.22
7129142	200	2	1.75	.20	.60			1.50	3.00	3.00	3.60
ASSEMBLY	100	1	—	—	—	1.00	2.50			2.50	2.50

ECONOMIC FACTOR #	TYPE	%
1	CONTINGENCY	N.A.
2	PRICE	N.A.
3	SCRAP	N.A.
4		
5		

12 MFG. COSTS AND PRICING

PART NO.	PROD. RUN	ANNUAL USAGE	MATERIAL	LABOR	BURDEN 150 %	TOTAL	ADMIN. O. H. ¢ 10 %	TOTAL COST	PROFIT ¢ 20 %	NET PRICE	SPECIAL COSTS/PC	NET INCL. SPECIAL	LIST PRICE ¢ %.
7129145	100	1000	1.00	2.45	3.22	6.67	.67	7.34	1.47	8.81	.85	9.66	9.66
7129143	200	2000	1.50	2.22	3.00	6.72	.67	7.39	1.48	8.87	.19	9.06	9.06
7129142	200	2000	1.75	3.60	4.50	9.85	.99	10.84	2.17	13.01	—o—	13.01	13.01
ASSEMBLY	100	1000	—	2.50	3.75	6.25	.63	6.88	1.38	8.26	—o—	8.26	8.26

Fig. 9. Summary Cost Estimate Sheet.

It is essential to keep an historical record of the actual costs for jobs. This should be posted to show:

1. Actual cost of the job.
2. Causes of differences between actual and estimated costs.
3. Any adjustments made to the standard estimates.

Accounting for the system. In this type of estimated cost system, the forms used for estimating should be designed to provide:

1. Bills of material.
2. Process sheets for manufacturing.
3. Cost summary sheets.

Material requisitions and labor tickets are prepared by using the estimate form as a basic source document. The accounting transactions of the system are as follows:

1. Direct material and labor is charged to work in process and the related requisitions and labor tickets are filed with the cost summary sheets.

2. Monthly, or when all parts are completed, whichever occurs first, the requisitions and labor tickets are posted to the cost summary sheet for quantities used, labor hours consumed, good parts produced, and unit costs are extended.

Comparisons of actual against estimate are made visually, and significant differences are immediately investigated. Reports on such investigations are filed with the cost summary records for future reference.

As the parts are transferred to assembly, one of two practices is possible:

1. Actual costs can be posted from the parts cost summary sheets (described above) to the assembly summary sheets, eventually closing out the parts cost sheets as all parts are completed.

2. Differences between actual and estimated costs in the cost summary sheets for components can be posted to variance accounts. If this practice is adopted, the estimates for these parts appearing on the cost summary sheets are treated as standard costs. Under this method, repetitive posting of money values is avoided. More important than the clerical savings is the fact that management learns of cost overruns on each section of the job as they occur, and can seek to improve performance on the balance of the job. Furthermore, with estimates shown on shop order paper as standards, foremen know what is expected of them, and can exercise a before-the-fact control effort.

As jobs are completed, work-in-process inventory is credited and estimated cost of sales is debited with the estimated cost. The balances on the variance summary are posted to the appropriate variance accounts. The cost of sales section of the financial statements then includes:

1. Estimated cost of sales.
2. Variances from estimates.

In this system, a detailed monthly report of all jobs completed during the month is prepared showing the amount and nature of variances and their treatment (if any) in revising the standard estimate file.

► IMPORTANT: The success of the historical estimated cost system depends largely on two factors:

1. The skill with which forms are designed to minimize clerical effort.
2. The provisions made to alert management to all major differences between actual and estimated costs as production progresses.

Appendix

Check List for a Standard Cost System Installation

This check list is intended to serve in pointing up areas that require special attention in determining the applicability of a standard cost system. It also should be helpful in insuring that the system as installed will provide for the unique exception type transactions that are prevalent in most manufacturing operations.

The questions, in most instances, suggest why investigation is needed, imply what conditions should exist if the standard cost system is to function effectively, and suggest the method of approach to be followed in its installation.

Nature of the operation

1. Are proprietary products manufactured, or is the manufacturing purely of a subcontractor or job shop nature?
2. What diversity of products exists?
3. Are the manufacturing processes similar with respect to all products, or are there two or more completely distinct types of manufacture involved?
4. Are the products relatively standardized and stable with respect to design, or are they largely custom in nature with a high degree of specialized parts and assemblies that vary from order to order?
5. Are production lots manufactured, or do production orders normally call for small job lot runs?
6. Are products manufactured for stock, or are they produced against customers' orders?

From this type of review it should be possible to determine if the nature of the business is such that a completely integrated standard cost system might be installed at reasonable expense and with a reasonable chance for successful operation. It may only be practical to install a standard system for certain product lines or segments of the operations, while utilizing an actual cost system for the balance of the shop. Or it may develop that estimated standards can be used for machine loading, establishing production schedules, and estimating costs, but a completely integrated standard system tied into the general ledger cannot be made sufficiently flexible to meet the variable nature of the operations.

Identification of product

Is there a well-conceived and adequately controlled parts numbering system in operation? Specifically:

1. On what basis has the parts numbering system been developed, and what special significance, if any, is there to the arrangement of numbers or letters as they appear in a part number sequence?
2. Who is responsible for assigning parts numbers? What checks are made of the work of this person?
3. Is there a master list of outstanding part numbers?
4. What positive controls exist to insure that part numbers cannot be duplicated?
5. What controls exist to insure that the part numbers for discontinued parts are cancelled?
6. What mode of identification or numbering system is employed for experimental parts, and what controls exist to insure assignment of regular part numbers when such parts are accepted for regular production?
7. Can production work be performed on parts that are not assigned either regular or experimental part numbers? If so, how are such parts designated?
8. What means of identification, if any, are employed for indirect materials?
9. What technique is employed to identify rough castings from finished castings?
10. What numbering system is employed for assemblies and subassemblies, and do the same controls exist over these part numbers as for single piece part numbers?
11. How are modified or special parts numbered to differentiate them from the basic parts from which they were derived?
12. How are the same parts, made of different materials, designated, and what positive controls exist to prevent cross use of part numbers for such items?
13. Are part numbers used on internal requisitions, routings, and inventory records to positively identify the items involved?

The practitioner, in company with an experienced member of the client's manufacturing organization, should actually trace the part numbers and descriptions of an adequate sample of items of rough stores, process parts, and finished assemblies back to their respective bills of material, drawings, and specification sheets to insure himself that the system is functioning properly and that the chance of misidentification of product through improper assignment of parts numbers is extremely limited.

Material control

A. Purchasing

1. Is there a current and complete quotation and purchase record file—

that is, are all current parts and materials in the file, and have all discontinued parts and materials been transferred to a dead file?

2. What practices are being followed in determining economical purchase lot quantities?

3. Are production levels sufficiently stabilized so that reasonable standards can be established—based on uniform purchase lot sizes?

4. What price stability exists for the majority of parts and materials that are purchased? What special provisions, if any, must be made in establishing price standards for materials or parts with extremely volatile markets?

5. Are part numbers used on purchase requisitions and purchase orders to positively identify items to be purchased, and are the purchase orders complete as to price and terms?

6. Are engineering drawings furnished to subcontractors when outside operations are performed? How are these purchase orders priced? What allowances are made for normal scrap? What arrangements exist to charge back spoilage?

7. Is the purchasing executive furnished with a forecast of material required for production? If so:

(a) How is the period to be covered by the forecast determined?

(b) Is the forecast prepared sufficiently in advance so that purchases can be made in a timely fashion in relation to established vendor lead times?

(c) Are purchase requirements developed from exploded bills of material? If not, how are material requirements established?

(d) What provisions exist for emergency purchases in the face of material slippages on the part of regular suppliers?

8. Are all purchases made against competitive quotations? If not, what policy is observed in connection with obtaining quotations? Is there a master list of authorized suppliers for each major purchase item?

9. Does the company speculate in the procurement of raw materials? If so, what policies govern such speculation and on what economic considerations have these policies been developed?

10. What percentage of total product costs are represented by raw materials and purchased parts?

11. Are materials normally purchased for the client's account, or are they purchased for the account of customers? What safeguards exist to insure the proper accounting for customer materials?

12. Is a master material specification file in existence? Are authorized substitute materials included in the file? Are specifications referred to on requisitions and purchase orders? If a list of authorized substitute materials is not in existence, how is procurement of substitute materials controlled?

The objectives of the above investigations are to establish whether the purchasing practices being followed are sufficiently standardized to permit the development of realistic price standards for purchased materials and parts, and to determine the significance of material costs as an element of total product cost. Therefore, adequate tests of purchasing records and transactions should be made before proceeding with the establishment of material price standards.

B. *Inspection and quality control.*

1. What inspection policies are in force?

2. Are the procedures and forms in use adequate to meet the objectives of the above policies?

3. Is the raw material and purchase parts inspection function divorced organizationally from the purchasing and receiving function? Is the manufacturing inspection function divorced from the manufacturing organization?

4. Are copies of prints for castings and machine parts furnished to the inspection department with subcontract orders?

5. Are inspection standards established and in use—including statistical sampling standards?

6. Are manufactured products inspected for method as well as for quality?

7. What procedures are followed with respect to the inspection of:

(a) Reject purchase items?

(b) Reject manufactured items?

Are there positive controls in existence requiring the timely review and disposition of spoiled or rejected materials and parts?

8. What controls exist over physical counts of purchased and manufactured products? If this is not a function of inspection, what personnel are responsible for quantity verification? To whom do these personnel report?

9. What methods are employed in verifying quantities, and do these methods provide a proper compromise between accuracy and the cost of attaining the verification? (Here it would be well to run a number of test checks on quantities of purchased materials on purchase orders against receiving reports, and the quantities of production pieces against the quantities shown on time tickets. These tests should be extensive enough to include all of the various methods of quantity verification that are authorized.)

10. What procedures are followed when shortages in purchased and production parts are discovered?

11. What procedures are followed for collecting, safeguarding, disposing, and accounting for normal production scrap and spoiled materials?

C. *Material usage*

1. Are all materials issued to production against requisitions?

2. Do requisitions for materials for fabricated parts reference standard layout drawings? What controls exist with respect to ends, blank centers, and drop-offs? Is the reuse of such pieces limited to certain standard sizes and shapes? Are some pieces held for experimental, maintenance, or other indirect expense uses? How are these pieces collected, stored, and accounted for?

3. What checks are made of fabricated pieces against sheets or plates issued?

4. At what stages in the production processes are quantities of issued parts and materials verified against completed pieces and spoiled pieces?

5. Are all processed parts stored in adequately secured storage areas, and requisitioned in and out? If not, what controls exist with respect to these parts?

Methods and routings

1. Are standard operating or process sheets in existence, and being used at all production centers?
2. Are alternate methods specified for all standard operations in bottleneck areas of the shop?
3. Do routings and labor tickets reference standard operations by operation number? If not, how is this reference made?
4. How are alternative methods authorized?
5. Are operation numbers or designations entered on routings and time tickets by the scheduling department, or is this the prerogative of the foremen? What controls exist to insure the proper designation is entered?
6. Are preprinted labor tickets in use? If so, how often do methods changes require handwritten changes to these tickets?
7. Are machine feeds and speeds specified on method or process sheets? If so, who is responsible for seeing that these settings are actually employed? If not, who establishes the feeds and speeds to be used, and insures that they are followed?
8. Are dispatch centers in use? If not, how is work assigned?
9. Is production scheduling based upon some form of master planning co-ordinated with sales forecasts? If not, how are production schedules developed?
10. Have economic manufacturing lot sizes been developed? If so, what formula or basis has been employed in their development? If not, how are shop order sizes determined?
11. Are all shop orders run complete? If not, what methods are employed for controlling and accounting for partially run orders?

The obvious intent of this line of investigation is to determine whether manufacturing practices are sufficiently standardized to accommodate a standard cost system. If the methods and routing for the same parts vary from order to order, or from day to day within production centers, the procedural task of correctly accounting for the resulting variances would be extremely costly. Likewise, the data output of the cost system would have only marginal utility because of the time element involved in preparing such data. In such a situation, it is also obvious that the variances themselves would have little meaning.

Direct labor

1. Are labor standards in the form of piece rates, standard hours, or is some other unit of measure in use? If so, on what basis have these standards been developed (e.g. time study, standard data, etc.)? What incentive earnings, as a percentage of average day rates, are being earned in each work center? What incentive factors have been built into the standards, and what is the basis upon which these factors have been developed?

2. If labor incentives or standards are not in use, what basis is contemplated for the development of labor standards? Are there competent industrial engineering and time study personnel within the organization to undertake such development?

3. Are there group operations involved in any of the production processes? If so, are these operations continuous in nature, or are they susceptible to segregation or breakdown as to the functions performed by each member in the group? If this is true, would any advantage result if standards were established for each such element, as opposed to establishing group standards for the series of operations?

4. Are there any multimachine operations performed concurrently by one operator? If so, are all machines always operated together by the operator, or can one or more of these units operate without the others? If so, how is the operator's time reported in such situations? What incentives, if any, have been established for the operator, and how were they developed?

5. If labor standards or incentives are in use, how are pieces counted in determining an operator's earnings—that is, are all pieces counted, or are only good pieces counted?

6. Do operators perform their own setups, or are special crews employed to do this work? Is this class of labor classified as direct or indirect?

7. Are minor or partial setups performed by operators, with major setups assigned to special crews? If so, have standards been established for major setups as well as minor setups? If so, on what basis have these standards been established?

8. How is operating time recorded? Do operators enter their own elapsed time, or are time clocks employed? If clocks are employed, where are they located in the shop, and what allowance is made, if any, for operator's time in clocking in and out on jobs.

9. How are piece counts made:

(a) By machine counter devices?
(b) By independent checkers making physical counts?
(c) By independent weight counts?
(d) By the operator?

If counts are recorded by mechanical counters or by the operator, when and how, and by whom are verification counts made?

10. What adjustments are made to labor tickets when errors in piece counts are discovered? What is the incidence of this type of error?

11. Are down time, idle time, and waiting time being reported? If so, what percentage of productive time is represented by these classes of non-productive labor? If nonproductive time is not being reported on time tickets, how is it being segregated from actual productive time?

12. Are total hours on time tickets reconciled daily to the hours shown on clock cards? If not, what controls exist over total hours paid?

13. Are indirect workers assigned to direct labor operations or vice versa? If so, what controls exist over the reporting of the time of these employees to insure a proper segregation of direct and indirect labor costs?

14. Are workers in one department assigned to work in another department? If so, what provisions are made to transfer such labor to the using department before applying departmental burden to work in process?

There are two major objectives to be sought from this line of investigation. First, if labor standards are in use, it is necessary to determine the reasonableness of the standards that have been developed. If it is found that the standards are not realistic, then it may be necessary to give consideration to the establishment of a completely different set of standards for costing and inventory valuation purposes. Most importantly, if consistently large variances result, then the use of these standards for costing or pricing individual products could be extremely hazardous.

Secondly, if labor standards are not in use, it is important to determine whether shop operations are sufficiently standardized to permit their establishment on a realistic basis. If operating methods and machine speeds will vary widely from order to order for like parts, then it is hardly worth the effort to develop theoretical standards that will consistently be violated in actual practice.

Burden

A. Product flow

1. What is the concept of the shop layout:
   (a) Product line?
   (b) Colony?
   (c) Combination?

2. How do products flow through the shop:
   (a) All products flow through all work centers in a uniform fashion?
   (b) Products flow in an irregular pattern through different work centers, with widely varying operations performed on different products by each work center?

B. Shop organization and control

1. How are production activities organized:
   (a) In product divisions?
   (b) By major class of operation (e.g., forge, foundry, machine shop, assembly, etc.)?
   (c) Composite?

2. How are service activities organized:
   (a) For the shop as a whole?
   (b) Separately for each major division?
   (c) Composite (e.g., certain services organized under major divisions, other services organized on a shop basis, etc.)?

(d) Within the above organization structures are service activities organized functionally? If not, in what manner?

3. Within each major division, how is control exercised over the production functions:
   (a) Colonies (e.g., lathe, grinders, etc.)?
   (b) Physical areas of the shop?
   (c) Work centers (e.g., groups of diverse production units used together for specific phases of the production process)?
   (d) Product line?

4. How are the service activities controlled within each major division:
   (a) By functions?
   (b) By groups of related functions or pools?
   (c) For the division as a whole?

5. Is the organization of the shop realistic:
   (a) Presents a logical pattern for assigning costs to products?
   (b) Is appropriate for effective control?
   (c) Minimizes accounting effort consistent with effective control and realistic product costing?

C. Burden distribution

1. Have burden rates been established for each production cost center, or is a composite rate for the shop used?

2. Does the method used result in realistic distribution of burden costs to products (based on analyses of product flow and shop organization)?

3. In distributing service costs to production centers, are total service costs pooled and distributed on the basis of direct labor in each production center? If not, are the service centers distributed on a basis that realistically reflects the service performed for each activity served (both production centers and other service activities)?

4. Is maximum use made of direct charging of service expenses to using activities? How are these direct charges measured?

5. Where allocations are made, are they realistic or do they merely represent an accounting method for distributing burden to products? Can any of the allocations being made be eliminated through pooling expenses before allocation, thus reducing clerical effort without loss of accuracy in product costing or without loss of control?

6. How are overhead rates established (e.g., in terms of dollar per productive hour or as a percentage of direct labor dollars)? Is the method used the most appropriate in terms of accuracy or result and simplicity of accounting?

7. Are rates changed to reflect major changes in:
   (a) Labor rates?
   (b) Outside service costs?
   (c) Shop layout and organization?

When rates are changed, are proper adjustments made to the inventory values? What controls exist to insure changes in rates are made as required?

8. Are burden rates established to realistically reflect the anticipated level of shop activity? How are such shop activity levels forecast?

D. Flexible budgets

1. Are flexible overhead budgets in use?

2. If not, are operating levels sufficiently stable throughout the year and from year to year so that variances due to volume are not significant?

3. If flexible budgets are in use, how have they been constructed:
   (a) Payroll and related expenses, based on manning tables?
   (b) Other expenses based on engineering analysis of movements in relation to volumes?
   (c) Statistical analyses (e.g., scatter charts, least squares, etc.)?

4. How accurately have these budgets reflected actual operations in the past?

5. Where manning tables and engineering analyses have been used, what role was played by shop personnel, what role by accounting personnel? Are the work papers in support of the manning tables and the engineering analyses complete and well documented?

6. Are volume and spending variances accounted for separately in accounting reports or is this separation made on a memorandum basis for internal operating reports only? Is the basis of calculations of these variances theoretically correct?

E. Chart of accounts

1. Is there a descriptive chart of accounts in existence? Is it used? What safeguards exist to insure proper coding of charges in keeping with the chart?

2. Is the method of account numbering flexible and adequate to insure accurate cost distributions to cost centers?

3. How were the individual cost center charts of accounts constructed? Are these accounts consistent with the distribution plans? Is the distribution and account matrix maintained on a current basis? If no such matrix exists, how is the chart updated?

11

Distribution Cost Accounting and Analysis

CONTENTS

11

Distribution Cost Accounting and Analysis

This chapter explains distribution costs and distribution cost accounting, and provides step-by-step instructions for installing an effective distribution cost accounting system built around 24 key forms. These forms are illustrated and explained in detail.

DISTRIBUTION COST ACCOUNTING: WHAT IT IS AND WHY IT IS IMPORTANT

What are distribution costs? Distribution costs are the expenses involved in marketing a product after it has been manufactured. These costs include the following: securing the order from the customer, delivering the goods, accounting for them, collecting the accounts, handling the merchandise stock, and promoting sales.

These costs are both large and controllable. In many industries, distribution costs constitute a large part of the total cost of the product. Past studies have shown that the expenses involved in distributing a great many products actually exceed the cost of producing them. Management, too, generally has more control over distribution and administrative costs than over production costs, both in the amount of expenditures, and in the way they are spent.

► COMMENT: More aggressive enforcement of the Robinson-Patman Act (fair trade practices) could force companies that have put off instituting distribution cost controls to install these cost accounting systems. Distribution cost systems are essential in establishing price differentials that do not violate the Robinson-Patman Act. They provide evidence to justify the charging of different prices for a commodity because of the difference in costs of serving various segments of the trade.

What is distribution cost accounting? Distribution cost accounting is a method of accounting or cost analysis that provides for the analysis of marketing costs by product, location, customer, and the like. Although the general accounting books may be adapted to facilitate distribution cost analysis, distribution cost accounting is independent of general accounting, and actually consists of a series of cost studies.

These studies may be facilitated by setting up the ledger accounts on a *responsibility accounting* or *functional accounting* basis. The ordinary or natural general ledger accounts are converted into functional accounts; that is, separate accounts are designed in which costs are accumulated by function or purpose in each significant area of responsibility.

These general accounting figures, accumulated on a functional basis, serve as the starting point for a distribution cost analysis. They are then allocated to departments, products, territories and the like. Adjustments are made to give effect to both current and foreseeable future conditions and circumstances.

► NOTE: Because future conditions (such as sales volume, market, number of sales, personnel needed, advertising budgets, etc.) are recognized, a distribution cost study produces, as a by-product, a virtual budget of a future period.

Distribution cost accounting vs. conventional accounting. The conventional method applies distribution costs to products, territories, or classes of customers on the basis of an *overall ratio of* distribution costs to total sales. This method often results in crucial decisions being made on the basis of fallacious information. The chart in Figure 1 shows an example of the misleading results that may be obtained by the use of the conventional accounting method. Here the overall percentage of selling expenses to total sales is 5.69%, while the percentages calculated on an individual basis using distribution cost analyses vary from 3.46% to 12.56%. Obviously, the costs of distribution are different for each product and territory.

	% to Total Sales
Overall % of selling expenses to total sales	5.69
Dept. or product A1 sales	8.38
" " " A2 sales	6.90
" " " A3 sales	3.61
" " " B sales	3.46
" " " C sales	5.56
" " " D1 sales	6.19
" " " D2 sales	5.31
" " " A1 sales in territory A	10.10
" " " " " " " B	6.60
" " " " " " " A for chains	6.75
" " " " " " " A for dept. stores	7.87
" " " " " " " A for other customers	12.56
" " " " " " " B for chains	6.85
" " " " " " " B for dept. stores	4.64
" " " " " " " B for other customers	7.47

Fig. 1. Percentage of Selling Expense to Total Sales.

► NOTE: Many accountants who fully realize the clear-cut advantages of distribution cost accounting hesitate to recommend the adoption of a continuous distribution cost accounting system because they fear the difficulty of finding a practical approach to the problem. The system outlined in this chapter provides an expeditious and practical method of obtaining distribution costs for any business through the use of 24 key forms.

Purposes of distribution cost accounting. Some of the purposes and objectives of distribution cost accounting, other than compliance with Government regulations, are:

1. Revealing to management whether products are priced too high or low in view of the market and of true product costs. A price cut may add to sales volume, and increase profits.

2. Showing not only whether the company has an overall profit or loss, but determining which sales of products are profitable and which are not.

3. Facilitating pricing decisions. These decisions can be made more precisely by adding to the costs of manufacture a separate percentage to cover each function of distribution cost applicable to the said product.

4. Comparing costs in relation to levels of volume. This information may suggest the opening up of new markets for the sale of goods at lower prices than the present volume of output permits.

5. Providing management with a detailed analysis of every phase of the business. Weak spots in the operations are revealed, and management can institute the necessary corrective measures.

6. Insuring that supervisors and employees maintain high standards by putting them on notice that these studies will point up all inefficiencies, spotlighting the supervisor and department responsible for them.

7. Providing management with related figures, carefully selected and organized, on which to base decisions as to marketing policies, warehousing, delivery, and the like. Comparisons can be made between various sales districts, price groups, retail and wholesale.

HOW TO MAKE A DISTRIBUTION COST ACCOUNTING ANALYSIS

The three principal steps for making a distribution cost accounting analysis are:

1. Analyzing the primary general ledger expense accounts by function, and adjusting expense accounts to reflect current budgeted figures. This step can be eliminated if the ledger accounts are kept on the functional basis described at the beginning of the chapter.

2. Allocating expenses to functions and departments (or products).
3. Segment or secondary analysis by:
   a. Territories.
   b. Classes of customers.
   c. Order-size categories.
   d. Other desired categories.

The following distribution cost analysis of a hypothetical company that performs both manufacturing and wholesaling operations will illustrate how to proceed through the various steps and sequences of an analysis involving a great volume of data.

The illustration assumes a company of six departments. Some departments handle one commodity, product, or group of similar commodities; others handle several classes of commodities of which one or more may be manufactured on the company's premises. The products are coded: A1, A2, A3, B and C. The primary ledger accounts are *not* arranged on a functional basis.

PRELIMINARY FUNCTIONAL ANALYSIS OF GENERAL LEDGER EXPENSE ACCOUNTS

This is called a preliminary analysis because, while the accounts are grouped according to the function to which they most naturally belong, each account may contain elements of expense that are applicable to other functions. Therefore, each account will be analyzed and expenses will be redistributed in the next step of the study.

In order to make this preliminary analysis, the accountant will have to determine (1) the functional division of the business, and (2) the account classifications that should be grouped under each of these functions.

1. Functional divisions. The type of functional divisions to be set up depends upon the nature of the business. For this example we are using the following functions: factory, buying and receiving, stock handling, delivery, sales promotion, selling, administrative, rent, and payroll. Because they apply to all functions, rent and payroll are being treated as independent functions at this stage of the study to avoid assigning them, even on a provisional basis, to any one of the other functions. When the detailed analysis is made, rent and payroll expenses will be redistributed to particular functions and products.

2. Accounts classification. *Form 1,* the first of the 24 key forms, is prepared for each function (Figure 2) and in summary form (Figure 3).

The first step in filling out *Form 1* is to go through the general ledger accounts and assign to each function the accounts that seem applicable to the particular function. For each function, enter on a separate *Form 1* (Fig. 2) the general ledger balances of the expense accounts assigned to that function, adjusted to reflect current and expected conditions. Disregard cents in all the figures. After *Form 1* is prepared for each separate function, it is also prepared in summary form as shown in Figure 3.

If the general ledger accounts do not already include accruals for expenses incurred but not yet set up on the books, as well as expense items that may not be wholly chargeable to the period under review, these adjustments have to be made and posted to the worksheets. Figure 4 shows *Form 1* of the selling function after the ledger accounts have been adjusted, but before the expense accounts have been analyzed and reallocated to functions and products.

After the postings have been made, foot the columns and post the individual footings to a summary sheet. The footings of the amounts on the summary sheet have to agree with the sum of the general ledger accounts as adjusted.

► WARNING: It is essential to use the principle that *the whole is equal to the sum of its parts* to control the allocation of distribution costs. This means simply that the total of all the allocations to departments, functions, products, or classes of customers must equal the total of the general accounting figures as adjusted. This arithmetical control must be maintained every step of the way in order to insure that the resulting figures are accurate and complete.

ANALYSIS AND REALLOCATION BY FUNCTION AND PRODUCT

In the previous step, the total of each expense account was provisionally assigned to a particular function. Now a detailed analysis of the contents of each account will be made so that the portions of these accounts that are applicable to other functions can be redistributed to the functions to which they apply. While making this detailed functional analysis, we also accumulate the information that will allow the assigning of expense by product.

► NOTE: Although a product analysis is being made in this example, the same technique can be used, if necessary, to make a departmental analysis.

In the course of this analysis, costs and expenses will be charged: (1) directly to products and functions; or (2) to indirect accounts directly serving a particular product and function; or (3) to general service departments.

To make these charges it is necessary to analyze and allocate:

1. Expense bills.
2. Payroll.
3. Rent.
4. Indirect expenses.

Analyzing expense bills. To make this analysis possible, the accounting department must indicate the function, product, and service to which each bill is to be charged. This should be done at the time the invoice is first processed. These notations can be made on the invoice itself, on the voucher jacket, or on an apron pasted on the invoice. The latter is recommended because it can be torn off, filed until end of the month, and processed separately from the invoices themselves. This permits ease in handling, storing, and scheduling.

Function: SELLING

Allocation Basis No.	Account or Service	BUDGET				Primary Expense Accounts Analyzed from Aprons	Chargeable to this Function				How Charges to this Function Will Be Charged to Products									
		a/c No. or Ref.	Before Adjust-ments	J.E. Adjust-ments	As Adjust-ed		Indirect to be Allocat-ed	Charges to Products and Functions from the Aprons Analysis	Payroll Alloca-tion	Rent Alloca-tion	Direct to Dept.	Basis	Basis	Basis	Basis	Basis	Basis	Basis	Basis	Basis

Fig. 2 (Form 1) Selling Function.

Function: SUMMARY

Account or Service	a/c No. or Ref.	BUDGET			Primary Expense Accounts Analyzed from Aprons	CHARGEABLE TO THIS FUNCTION							
		Before Adjust-ments	J.E. Adjust-ments	As Adjusted		Indirect to be Allocated	Charges to Products and Functions From the Aprons Analysis	Payroll Alloca-tion	Rent Alloca-tion	To Mdse. Depts.		Non-Mdse. A/c's	

Fig. 3. (Form 1) Summary.

Function: SELLING

Allocation Basis No.	Account or Service	a/c No. or Ref.	BUDGET Before Adjust-ments	J.E. Adjust-ments	As Adjusted
19	SUNDRY SELLING EXPENSES	65	3,000	40	3,040
24	SALESMEN'S DINNER	66	900		900
24	SALESMEN'S PRIZES	67	2,000		2,000
25	BRANCH DISPLAY OFFICE	68	6,000	120	6,120
24	SALESMEN-GENERAL	69			
24	SALESMEN-INDIRECT	62			
15	PHONE-ORDER DEPT.	75		35	35
30	INVESTIGATORS (TRACERS)	76			
16	PRICE-CHECKING DEPT.	77		30	30
19	SALES ANALYSIS DEPT.	78		100	100
35	RETURNS DEPT.	79			
19	TELEPHONE A/c 65	J.E.			
	TO FIGURES 3 and 23		11,900	325	12,225

Fig. 4. (Form 1) Selling Function Completed up to Budgeted Figures as Adjusted.

The information that the accounts payable department enters on the apron is taken from the purchase order. Figure 5 shows a filled in apron.

Each month the aprons are sorted by natural account number. A tabulation of each batch is then made by product, department, function, and service. Figure 6 and 7 illustrate *Form 2* and *3,* the summaries of the apron analyses. Those amounts are then posted to *Form 1,* the function worksheet that we discussed in the prior step. Figure 8 illustrates *Form 1* after the apron analysis amounts have been posted to it. Note that many new accounts representing service departments have been added.

► NOTE: Not all expense accounts can be analyzed using the method described above. Accounts such as depreciation on equipment, postage, insurance, and telephone should be charged to products and functions on the basis of documented evidence, actual usage over a test period, and other bases appropriate under the circumstances. The techniques of finding bases of allocation are discussed further in the section *Allocation of indirect expenses.*

Analysis of payroll. The cost of salaries and wages included in distribution costs are frequently several times more than the aggregate amount of expense bills charged to such costs.

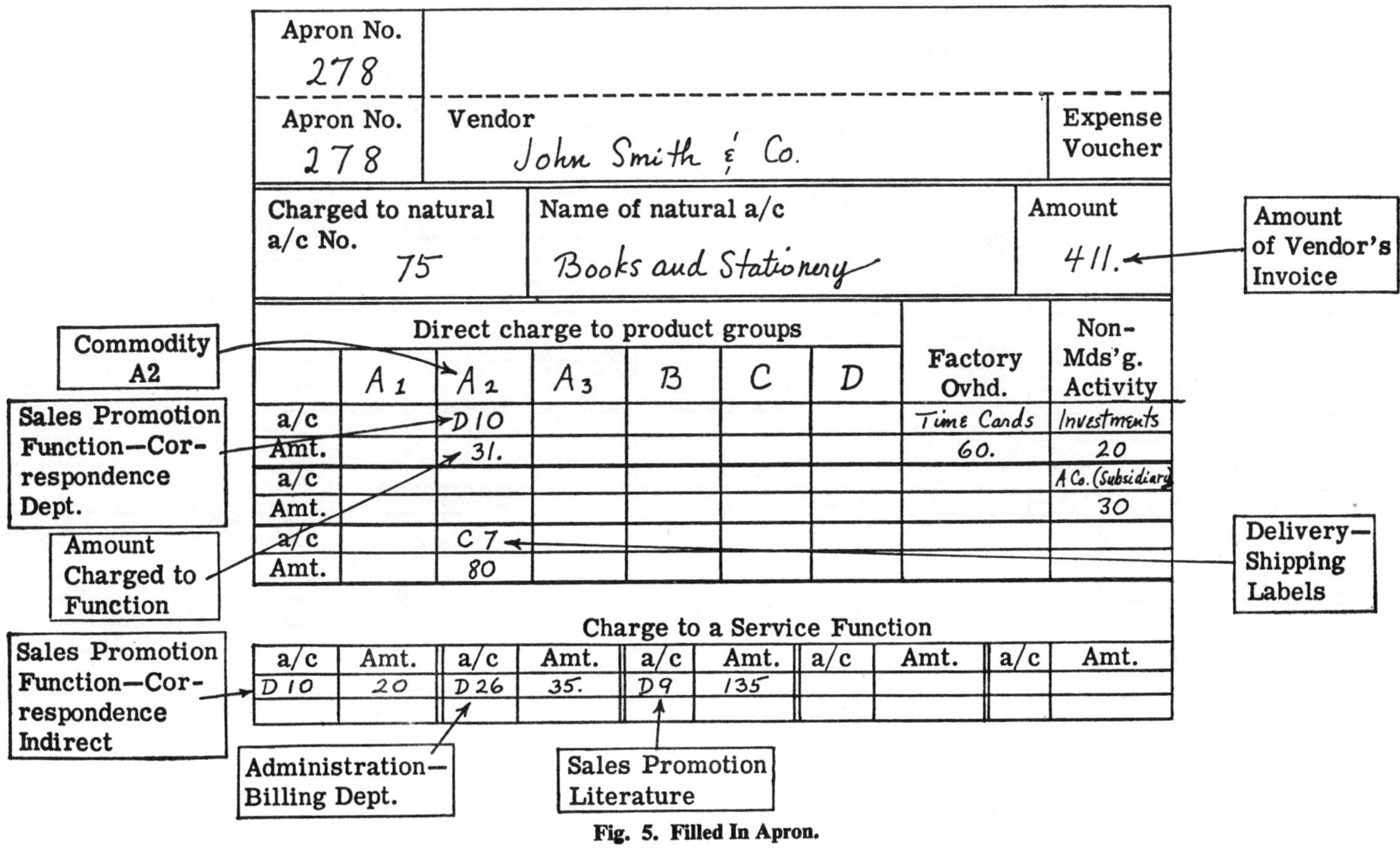

Apron No. 278		
Apron No. 278	Vendor John Smith & Co.	Expense Voucher
Charged to natural a/c No. 75	Name of natural a/c Books and Stationery	Amount 411.

Direct charge to product groups							Factory Ovhd.	Non-Mds'g. Activity
	A 1	A 2	A 3	B	C	D		
a/c		D10					Time Cards	Investments
Amt.		31.					60.	20
a/c								A Co. (Subsidiary)
Amt.								30
a/c		C 7						
Amt.		80						

Charge to a Service Function

a/c	Amt.	a/c	Amt.	a/c	Amt.	a/c	Amt.	a/c	Amt.
D10	20	D26	35.	D9	135				

Fig. 5. Filled In Apron.

APRONS SUMMARY—CHARGES DIRECTLY TO MERCHANDISE DEPTS. OR PRODUCTS

	From Nat'l. a/c No.	A1	A2	A3	B	C	D1	D2	Other	Chgd. direct to Prod.	Total all Aprons	Chgd. as Indirect
	7	4,794	58			2,879	3		644	8,378	13,119	4,741
	9	61	306							367	689	322
FACTORY		4,855	364	-	-	2,879	3		-	8,745		
	43	362	535			322				1,219	1,219	-
SALES PROM.		9,089	1,888	186	494	8,918	880	12		21,467		
	65	752				854	23	66		1,695	2,359	664
SELLING												
	81	148		1,638	616	1,136	993	223	6	4,760	14,032	9,272
	83	26			105	266	66	40		503	1,980	1,477
	89	134			7	40	22			203	334	131
ADMINISTR.		308		1,638	728	1,442	1,081	263	6	5,466		
											112	112
										67,676	98,745	31,069

Fig. 6. (Form 2) Aprons Summary—Charges Directly to Merchandise Departments or Products.

APRONS SUMMARY—CHARGES DIRECTLY TO SERVICE DEPARTMENTS

Service dept. a/c	FROM NATURAL ACCOUNT NUMBER															TOTALS
	7	7	49	51	52	53	55	65	81	83	89	MISCELLANEOUS				
7	1,206									5						1,211
59									571							375
60									98							98
61						3,582	11									3,593
																12,373
69									49							49
65								664	1,931	27						2,622
68			54						18							72
66													652			652
																3,395
105									9							9
118									339							339
122									52							52
151									194							194
																7,384
145									15					2,039		2,054
	4,741	322	543	251	7,265	3,582	18	664	9,272	1,477	131	112	652	2,039		31,069

Fig. 7. (Form 3) Aprons Summary—Charges Directly to Service Departments.

Function: SELLING

Allocation Basis No.	Account or Service	a/c No. or Ref.	BUDGET Before Adjust-ments	BUDGET J.E. adjust-ments	BUDGET As adjusted	Primary Expense Accounts Analyzed from Aprons	CHARGEABLE TO THIS Indirect to be Allocated	CHARGEABLE TO THIS Charges to Products and Functions from the Aprons Analysis	Pay all ti
19	SUNDRY SELLING EXPENSES	65	3,000	40	3,040	2,359	681	2,622	
24	SALESMEN'S DINNER	66	900		900	652	248	652	
24	SALESMEN'S PRIZES	67	2,000		2,000		2,000		
25	BRANCH DISPLAY OFFICE	68	6,000	120	6,120		6,120	72	
24	SALESMEN-GENERAL	69						49	
24	SALESMEN-INDIRECT	62							
15	PHONE-ORDER DEPT:	75		35	35		35		
30	INVESTIGATORS (TRACERS)	76							
16	PRICE-CHECKING DEPT.	77		30	30		30		
19	SALES ANALYSIS DEPT.	78		100	100		100		
35	RETURNS DEPT.	79							
19	TELEPHONE A/c 65	J.E.							
DIRECT-APRONS ALLOCATED		Form 2						1,695	
	TO FIGURES 3 and 23		11,900	325	12,225	3,011	9,214	5,090	

Fig. 8. (Form 1) Selling Function after the Apron Analysis has been Posted.

In order to make a proper analysis of payroll, the salary of every employee who affects the marketing function must be analyzed individually. The first step in this process is to request each employee, except selling personnel using *Form 8* (Figure 14), to enter on *Form 4* (Figure 9) the percentage of his time that he believes will be properly chargeable to the various departments, commodities or functions.

► HOW TO DO IT: To avoid incurring the wrath of the department head who may tend to feel that you are needlessly intruding on his domain, enlist the help of the chief executive officer in explaining your case. Have him call a conference of the department heads to explain the business reasons for making this comprehensive analysis of distribution costs and to show them how *Form 4* fits into the picture. Then you explain the mechanics of filling out the form.

The following example shows how *Form 4* is applied to payroll analysis:

Employee A's time is allocated 60% to the head of department A1; 15% to the head of department A2; 10% to factory operations specifically chargeable to department A1; and 15% to factory overhead.

Assuming a salary of $6,000 for "A," the amount columns will show the allocation of his salary in dollars as follows:

Head of Department—A1	$3,600
Head of Department—A2	900
Factory Operations Dept.—A1	600
Factory Overhead—General	900
	$6,000

EXPECTED ALLOCATION OF TIME TO BE EMPLOYED

Name of employee "A"		Code No. 215				Period 196- Amount 6,000					
a/c	Chargeable Direct to a Department or a Product	Direct to Product Group								Other	
		A1		A2							
		%	Amt.	%	Amt.	%	Amt.	%	Amt.	%	Amt.
C	Head of dept.-mds'g.	60	3,600	15	900						
C	Dept's Office										
C											
C											
	Factory operations	10	600								

CHARGEABLE TO A SERVICE FUNCTION

sub a/c	Function Group	%	Amt.	sub a/c	Function Group	%	Amt.
C	Delivery-local			D	Credit & collection		
C	Delivery-country			D	A/c's Rec. & cashier		
				D	Billing & checking		
D	Stock handling			D	Accounting dept.		
D	Packing			D	Branch office		
D	Sales promotion			D	Administrative		
D	Selling						
D	Orders- by phone				Factory overhead	15	900
D	Complaints-customers				Investments		
D	Phone-general				Other companies, etc.		
D	Correspondence dept.						

Fig. 9. (Form 4) Expected Allocation of Time to be Employed.

At first this may seem a complicated calculation with respect to the distribution of the time of each employee, but, in reality, it is so simple that the data for about 300 employees can be obtained within four or five days.

► OBSERVATION: Employees' salaries can be analyzed further according to a finer classification; that is, whether their time is spent on local, out-of-town or parcel-post shipments, or whether their time is spent in and about chain stores, department stores, and out-of-town or local customers. In such cases, these allocations should be entered by each employee when filling out *Form 4.*

Form 4 is now ready for computation. Multiply the total salary amount by the percentages indicated on the form, and enter the resulting amounts in the *amounts* columns.

The required copies of *Form 4* are arranged by employee number and then posted to summary sheets on *Forms 5, 6 and 7.* (Figures 10, 11, and 12, respectively.)

Payroll charged directly to: **Dept. Prod. A1**

Factory				Stock-factory				Stock-marketing			
Name	a/c No.	Alloc. %	Amt.	Name	a/c No.	Alloc. %	Amt.	Name	a/c No.	Alloc. %	Amt.
21	11	3.6	1,082	25	16	2.	524	25	20	2.	524
25	11	6.	1,573	40	16	24.	1,834	39	20	75.	6,186
28	14	5.	571	46	16	4.	331	40	20	2.5	172
28	8	2.5	285	50	16	3.	211	46	20	4.	331
36	14	50.	4,698	Other	16		2,637	409	20	80.	2,249
37	14	44.	3,980	Private	16		329	Other	20		15,313
40	6	5.	366				5,866	Private	20		3,573
231	13	10.5	492								28.348
200	14	16.	1,002								
192	14	18.	1,007	Delivery				Selling			
52	15	38.	1,741	28	45	2.5	236	15	62	6.	375
46	11	34.	2,977	38	46	25.	1,368	16	62	5.2	423
48	11	75.	6,975	40	30	2.6	195	17	62	5.5	430
Other	6		2,890	41	30	25.6	2,261	18	62	7.	866
"	13		687	42	30	2.5	130	21	62	24.	7,212
Private	6		7,591	220	30	55.	2,660	42	79	22.	1,122
			37,917	226	30	20.	1,025	49	62	75.	7,794
				231	44	9.	422	Other	79		477
				414	30	20.	447	Private	62		6,790
				Other	30		25,189	Salesmen	62		114,025
				Private	30		329	17	75	46.	3,873
				Other	44		1,091				143,412
Buying and Receiving							35,403				
11	1	18.	1,020								
25	1	12.	3,147	Sales promotion				Administrative			
28	5	8.	915	15	48	63.	3,939	1	117	11.	787
46	1	26.	2,315	16	48	2.5	206	1	12[illegible]	29.	2,075
226	4	10.	512	16	60	25.	2,038	3	106	40.	4,450
414	4	12.5	280	18	48	63.	7,976	4	106	10.	1,084
Other	1		3,018	19	57	38.	3,707	6	109	25.	803
"	2		962	21	48	30.	9,411	9	109	11.	953
Private	1		5,179	25	48	4.	1,049	25	30	10.	2,622
527	1		1,738	25	57	4.	1,049	31G	80	11.	8,862
529	1		2,565	28	61	2.5	290	Other	119		2,093
231	2	10.	469	46	48	7.5	661	Private	80		6,445
			22,120	566	48		1,286				30,174
				Other	54		3,489				
							35,101				

Fig. 10. (Form 5) Analysis of Time Allocations—Direct to Product.

Form 5 shows how payrolls were charged directly to Product A1 by functions. *Form 6* shows how the "Private" payroll was charged to service departments; *Form 7* shows how the entire payroll was charged directly to merchandise departments or products.

Postings are then made to *Form 1.* Figure 13 illustrates *Form 1* for the selling function at this point.

The analysis of salaries and expenses of salesmen is the next step. Not only is this generally the largest distribution cost of all, but it is usually a most important source of sales and profits. *Forms 8, 9, 10 and 11* are used to analyze and control this cost. These forms are illustrated in Figures 14, 15, 16 and 17, respectively.

NAME OR NUMBER	a/c 4	a/c 5	a/c 12	a/c 13	a/c 14	a/c 15	a/c 37	a/c 38	a/c 39	a/c 40	a/c 44	a/c 45	a/c 46	a/c 54	a/c 58
2							1,747								
7		310					103					310			310
11		828								552			276		
28	342		114	228		1,142	114	342	228	228	114			228	
40	382				153	153		153	153		153			76	
ADD'L.	-	-	-	-	-	-	721	577	577	-	-	-	-	-	-
TOTAL	724	1,138	114	228	153	1,295	2,685	1,072	958	780	267	310	276	304	310
	59	60	74	77	78	105	106	108	109	110	111	112	113	114	115
2						437			1,747						
7	619	310		309		516	206	722	516	310	310	826	309	516	309
11			276							552					
22					1,223		1,223		7,337						
1									354						
5									486						
6												195			
9												520		607	
TOTAL	619	310	276	309	1,223	953	1,429	722	10,440	862	310	1,541	309	1,123	309
	116	117	118	119	120	121	122	123	134	135	151	152			
7	516	619	310		1,238		826								
22		1,223													
2			437				5,625				1,956	5,869			
6		195	583					973			4,380	194			
9	173	2,599	433												
28				1,142		114			228	1,142		570			
40			76	76						155					
5							1,214				4,007	365			
11										276		442			
37												466			
25							2,622								
31G											9,495	2,532			
45												576			
ADD'L.											966	2,894			
TOTAL	689	4,636	1,839	1,218	1,238	114	10,287	973	228	1,573	20,804	13,908			
							TOTAL OF ABOVE						88.856		

Fig. 11. (Form 6) Analysis of Time Allocations—Indirect.

PAYROLL OF SERVICE DEPARTMENTS—INDIRECT
(NOT CHARGEABLE SPECIFICALLY TO MDSE. DEPTS. OR PRODUCTS)

	6 PRIVATE	OFFICE	OTHER	TOTAL
2 Elev. Rec'g				
4 Receiving	724			724
5 Purchasing	1,138	509		1,647
7 Fact. Exp.				
8 Labor Reports				
11 Design				
12 Nurse Fact.	114	2,769		2,883
13 Elev. Fact.	228			228
14 Mach. Shop	153		2,012	2,165
15 Personnel Fact.	1,295			1,295
21 Elev. Stock Mkt.				
32 Parcel Post				
37 Traffic	2,685	6,271		8,956
38 Shipping Local	1,072			1,072
39 Shipping Out-of-town	958			958
40 Packing Supp.	780			780
41 Sundry Del'y				
44 Elevator Shipp.	267		243	510
45 Labels	310	2,556		2,866
46 Trucks	276			276
49 Literature				
52 Other Advert.				
54 Samples	304			304
57 Advertising				
58 Sales Promotion	310	12,747		13,057
59 Mimeo.	619	6,042		6,661
60 Correspond'ce	310	8,137		8,447
61 Displays				
62 Salesmen Gen'l		5,543		5,543
65 Sales Dept.				
68 Branch				
74 Cars	276			276
75 Phone Order		19,386		19,386
76 Investi-gators		13,625		13,625
77 Price Checking	309	6,730		7,039
78 Sales Analysis	1,223			1,223
79 Returns		473		473
105 Mailing	953	4,963		5,916

	6 PRIVATE	OFFICE	OTHER	TOTAL
106 Credit	1,429	3,133		4,562
107 Initial Credit		4,173		4,173
108 Collection	722	9,944		10,666
109 Accounting	10,440	4,130		14,570
110 Stationery	862		1,986	2,848
111 Phone	310	7,926		8,236
112 Accts. Receivable	1,541	15,303		16,844
113 Filing	309	5,411		5,720
114 Cashier	1,123	8,406		9,529
115 Calculating Machine	309	15,344		15,653
116 Billing	689	24,754		25,443
117 Accts. Payable	4,636	7,825		12,461
118 Payroll	1,839	2,694		4,533
119 Mainten'ce General	1,218		2,371	3,589
120 Personnel Office	1,238			1,238
121 Nurse General	114	277		391
122 General Admin.	10,287	734	324	11,345
123 Insurance	973			973
124 Photostat		358		358
134 Elev. Gen'l	228		313	541
135 Bldg. Maint.	1,573		5,415	6,988
145 Employ. Party				
151 Investments	20,804	206		21,010
152 Other	13,908	1,149	3,070	18,127
	88,856	201,518	15,734	306,108

Fig. 12. (Form 7) Summary of Form 6.

Form 8 (Figure 14) is filled out by every salesman or executive who devotes any time to sales to customers. The salesman will indicate what his sales are expected to be for each department, or products in total, as well as for each class of customer whom he serves. He will also insert in the percentage columns the amount of time he believes he will devote to the respective products and class of customer sales. The percentages that he fills in must total to 100%. The sales manager's department will review these figures with the salesman and make adjustments thereto if necessary.

Function: SELLING

Allocation Basis No.	Account or Service	a/c No. or Ref.	BUDGET: Before Adjust-ments	BUDGET: J.E. adjust-ments	BUDGET: As adjusted	Primary Expense Accounts Analyzed from Aprons	CHARGEABLE TO THIS FUNCTION: Indirect to be Allocated	CHARGEABLE TO THIS FUNCTION: Charges to Products and Functions From the Aprons Analysis	CHARGEABLE TO THIS FUNCTION: Payroll alloca-tion	a	CHARGED TO PRODUCTS: ...s	CHARGED TO PRODUCTS: Basis	CHARGED TO PRODUCTS: Basis	CHARGED TO PRODUCTS: Basis
19	SUNDRY SELLING EXPENSES	65	3,000	40	3,040	2,359	681	2,622						
24	SALESMEN'S DINNER	66	900		900	652	248	652						
24	SALESMEN'S PRIZES	67	2,000		2,000		2,000							
25	BRANCH DISPLAY OFFICE	68	6,000	120	6,120		6,120	72						
24	SALESMEN-GENERAL	69						49						
24	SALESMEN-INDIRECT	62							5,543					
15	PHONE-ORDER DEPT.	75		35	35		35		19,386					
30	INVESTIGATORS (TRACERS)	76							13,625					
16	PRICE-CHECKING DEPT.	77		30	30		30		7,039					
19	SALES ANALYSIS DEPT.	78		100	100		100		1,223					
35	RETURNS DEPT.	79							473					
19	TELEPHONE A/c 65	J.E.												
DIRECT-APRONS ALLOCATED		Form 2						1,695						
"	-PAY ROLL ALLOCATED	Form							500,259					
	TO FIGURES 3 and 23		11,900	325	12,225	3,011	9,214	5,090	547,548					

Fig. 13. (Form 1) Selling Function After Payroll is Posted.

Thousands omitted

EXPECTED SALES AND SALESMEN'S COSTS

Salesman | Costs | Period | Form

Territory	Dept. or Prod.	Total			Chains			Dept. Stores			Out of town			Local		
		Sales	Time devoted	Salary & Expense	Sales	Time devoted	Salary & Expense									
		$	%	$	$	%	$									
A	1	66.	36.	4.1												
	2	35.	19.	2.2												
	3	-														
	4	99.	43.	4.9												
	5	-														
	6	5.	2.	0.2												
		205.	100.	11.4												

Fig. 14. (Form 8) Salesmen's Budgeted Sales and Costs.

Summary of Expected Sales and Salesmen's Costs

Terr.	Salesman	$	%	$
A	A	205.	100.	11.4

Fig. 15. (Form 9) Summary of Form 8.

SALESMAN *b*　　　TERRITORY 1　　　RECORD OF SALES, ETC.

1958 MONTH	DESCRIPTION	SALARY AND EXPENSE COST	% TO SALES ATTAINED	SALARY & EXPENSE % TO SALES	SALARY & EXPENSE % TO GROSS PROFIT	TOTALS			PRODUCT A GROSS % 20		PRODUCT B GROSS % 25		PRODUCT C GROSS % 30		TOTAL VARIANCE	
						SALES	GROSS PROFIT	GROSS PROFIT %	SALES	GROSS PROFIT	SALES	GROSS PROFIT	SALES	GROSS PROFIT	SALARY AND EXPENSE	GROSS PROFIT
	BUDGET	1,000		4.61	19.57	21,700	5,110	23.55	12,000	2,400	4,000	1,000	5,700	1,710		
JAN.	ACTUAL	1,100	92.17	5.50	23.81	20,000	4,620	23.10	12,300	2,460	3,000	750	4,700	1,410		
	VARIANCE	– 100				–1,700	–490	–.45	+300	+60	–1,000	–250	–1,000	–300	–100	–490
	BUDGET	1,100		4.78	20.37	23,000	5,400	23.48	13,000	2,600	4,000	1,000	6,000	1,800		
FEB.	ACTUAL	1,400	100.	6.09	28.00	23,000	5,000	21.73	18,000	3,600	2,000	500	3,000	900		
	VARIANCE	–300				—	–400	–1.75	+5,000	+1,000	–2,000	–500	–3,000	–900	–300	–400
CUMULATIVE VARIANCE		–400				–1,700	–890		+5,300	+1,060	–3,000	–750	–4,000	–1,200	–400	–890

+ = BETTER　　　– = WORSE

Fig. 16. (Form 10) Salesman's Record of Sales, Gross Profits, and Expenses—Budgeted and Actual.

Form 8 is computed as to costs, balanced to the total of the salesman's costs, and then posted to *Form 9* (Figure 15) Summary of Sales and Salesmen's Costs.

Form 10 (Figure 16) is a form meant to control a salesman's sales, his costs, the gross profits produced by his sales, as well as his sales mixture. The ratios of his costs to sales as well as the gross profits are good measurements of his value to the company.

Form 11 (Figure 17) is a summary of *Form 10.* It provides management with vital marketing statistics for a month or other desired period.

When salesmen recognize that management requires gross profits dollars in order to defray all distribution costs as well as earn a fair return on the company's investment, they will discipline themselves to strive for better gross profit dollars results rather than for just sales dollars. They will try to sell those products that produce the higher gross profit percentages so that the company's net profits will be satisfactory to stockholders. If salesmen are paid for their services on the basis of gross profits realized on their sales, both salesmen and company will be the happier. Incentives based on a record like *Form 10* pay off.

► Alternate Method: A company that does not wish to reveal its products' gross profit percentages to its salesmen can construct a commission rate table based on gross sales, bearing a percentage relationship to the gross margin of each product or groups of products. Thus, if a company wishes to establish a commission rate table based on 20% of the gross profit of each product group, and product groups A, B and C produce gross profits of 25%, 30% and 35%, respectively; 20% of these profit margins, or 5%, 6% and 7%, respectively, would serve as equitable incentive commission rates.

Rent Analysis. The basic purpose in analyzing rent is to ascertain the number of square feet of space now used or expected to be used in the immediate future by each merchandise department, factory, commodity or service department or any other occupant, such as a tenant or a subsidiary company. For this purpose, a columnar sheet, as illustrated in *Form 12* (Figure 18) is used.

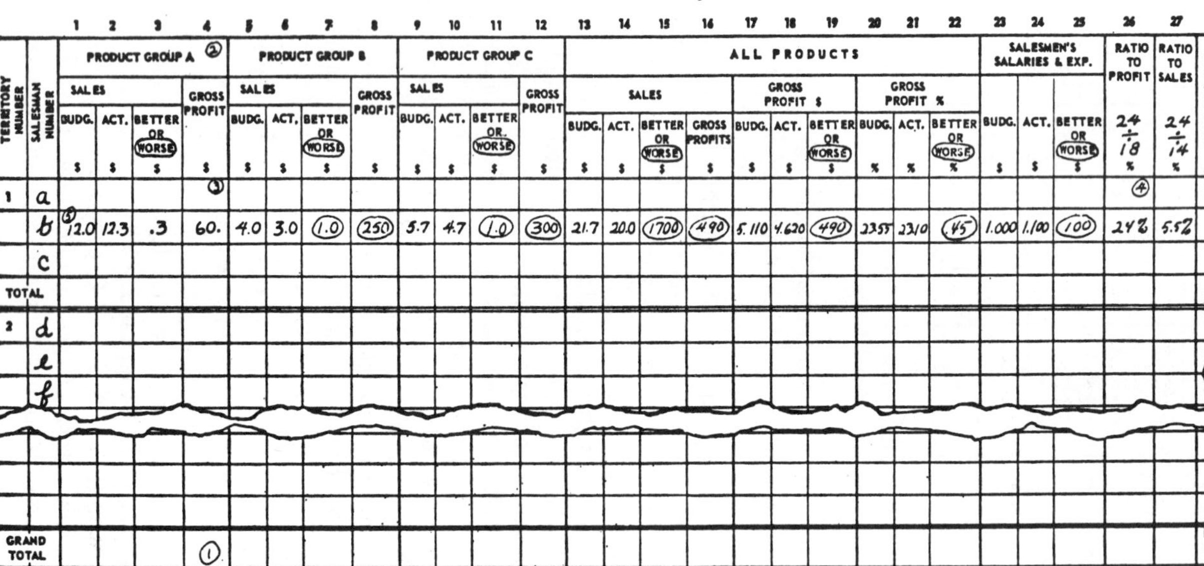

MARKETING STATISTICS FOR MONTH OF ______ 19

TERRITORY NUMBER	SALESMAN NUMBER	PRODUCT GROUP A (2)				PRODUCT GROUP B				PRODUCT GROUP C				ALL PRODUCTS										SALESMEN'S SALARIES & EXP.			RATIO TO PROFIT	RATIO TO SALES
		SALES			GROSS PROFIT	SALES			GROSS PROFIT	SALES			GROSS PROFIT	SALES				GROSS PROFIT $			GROSS PROFIT %							
		BUDG.	ACT.	BETTER OR (WORSE)		BUDG.	ACT.	BETTER OR (WORSE)		BUDG.	ACT.	BETTER OR (WORSE)		BUDG.	ACT.	BETTER OR (WORSE)	GROSS PROFITS	BUDG.	ACT.	BETTER OR (WORSE)	BUDG.	ACT.	BETTER OR (WORSE)	BUDG.	ACT.	BETTER OR (WORSE)	24 ÷ 18	24 ÷ 14
		$	$	$	$	$	$	$	$	$	$	$	$	$	$	$	$	$	$	$	%	%	%	$	$	$	%	%
		1	2	3	4	5	6	7	8	9	10	11	12	13	14	15	16	17	18	19	20	21	22	23	24	25	26	27
1	a				(3)																						(4)	
	b	(5) 12.0	12.3	.3	60.	4.0	3.0	(1.0)	(250)	5.7	4.7	(1.0)	(300)	21.7	20.0	(1700)	(490)	5.110	4.620	(490)	23.55	23.10	(.45)	1.000	1.100	(100)	24%	5.5%
	c																											
TOTAL																												
2	d																											
	e																											
	f																											
GRAND TOTAL					(1)																							

1. Gross Profit for this form means Sales less Returns, Allowances, Cash Discounts, Taxes on Sales, Costs of Material, Labor, Direct Factory Overhead, Delivery, Advertising and other costs directly applicable and chargeable to the product (but not Salesmen's Salaries and their Traveling Expenses).
2. Classification could be for Product, Product Line, Department, a group of products whose gross profits are within a range of, say, 5%, a particular class of customer, etc.
3. If it is the policy of the company for salesmen to specialize in selling to different classes of customers, as, for example, Chain Stores, Department Stores, Supermarkets, Industrials, etc., gross profits percentages will differ for each salesman.
4. Incentives in the form of cash bonuses may be given to salesmen, district managers, etc. on the basis of the figures shown in column 26, as this ratio gives effect to the better sales mixture.
5. Figures for this form come from Form 70.

Fig. 17. (Form 11) Summary of Form 10 by Territory, Salesman, and Product.

RENT—FLOOR SPACE—SQUARE FEET

Dept. Prod.	Floor 1	2	3	4	Total	$	Dept. Prod.	Floor 5	6	Total	$
Factory							Delivery				
A1	300	13,800	500		14,600	11,333		1,400		1,400	1,087
A2		1,500			1,500	1,164		250		250	194
A3								500		500	388
B								500		500	388
C	12,600	6,000	500		19,100	14,826		1,700		1,700	1,320
D1								500		500	388
D2											
Other			8,400	500	8,900	6,909					
					44,100	34,232				4,850	3,765
Stock-factory							Selling				
A1		700	5,500		6,200	4,813			250	250	194
A2		500	1,300		1,800	1,397					
A3									400	400	310
B									400	400	310
C	200		6,200		6,400	4,968			150	150	116
D1									300	300	233
D2									100	100	78
Other			2,350	800	3,150	2,445					
					17,550	13,623				1,600	1,241
Stock-marketing							Administration				
A1			1,000	5,100	6,100	4,735			500	500	388
A2				4,000	4,000	3,105					
A3			7,000	4,000	11,000	8,539			200	200	155
B				4,100	4,100	3,183			200	200	155
C	5,300	3,500	6,000		14,800	11,488			150	150	116
D1			950	7,000	7,950	6,171			50	50	39
D2				1,400	1,400	1,087					
Other											
					49,350	38,308				1,100	853

Fig. 18. (Form 12) Allocation of Floor Space—Direct to Products.

The gross space of each floor is measured first as to merchandise and service departments; then, as equitably as possible to commodities, products, or groups of products. The full square-foot area of each floor is determined.

Footage that cannot be charged to merchandise and service departments is charged to such accounts as general selling expenses, tenant *A*, subsidiary *B*, and so on. If the company occupies more than one building, a separate analysis schedule is made for each structure.

The analysis should account for the full number of gross square feet for each floor; that is to say, it should include the space taken up by aisles, columns, elevator space, stairways and so on, in all the departments on each floor.

The number of square feet for each merchandise department is entered on *Form 12*. The space occupied by service and other departments is indicated on *Form 13* (Figure 19).

After the square-foot allocation is made, and the total column as well as the square feet in the service department section add up to the total gross feet in the building, the total rent cost is distributed between the merchandise and service departments on the basis of dollar cost per square foot. The cost per square foot is derived by dividing the total square feet in the building into the total rent cost. This, of course, assumes that a square foot of space on the

RENT-FLOOR SPACE- SQUARE FEET—SERVICE DEPARTMENTS

	square feet	$					square feet	$				
2 Elev. Rec'g						106 Credit	100	78				
4 Receiving	1,000	776				107 Initial Credit	200	155				
5 Purchasing	200	155				108 Collection	50	39				
7 Fact. Exp.						109 Accounting	600	466				
8 Labor Reports						110 Stationery	250	194				
11 Design	600	466				111 Phone	150	116				
12 Nurse Fact.	300	233				112 Accts. Receivable	300	233				
13 Elev. Fact.						113 Filing	1,300	1,009				
14 Mach. Shop	2,900	2,252				114 Cashier	200	155				
15 Personnel Fact.						115 Calculating Machine	200	155				
21 Elev. Stock Mkt.						116 Billing	400	310				
32 Parcel Post						117 Accts. Payable	200	155				
37 Traffic	110	85				118 Pay Roll	150	116				
38 Shipping Local	3,380	2,624				119 Mainten'ce General						
39 Shipping Out-of-town	5,500	4,270				120 Personnel Office	300	233				
40 Packing Supp.						121 Nurse General						
41 Sundry Del'y						122 General Admin.	2,000	1,552				
44 Elevator Shipp.						123 Insurance	10	8				
45 Labels	50	39				124 Photostat						
46 Trucks						134 Elev. Gen'l						
49 Literature						135 Bldg. Maint.						
52 Other Advert.						145 Employ. Party						
54 Samples						151 Investments						
57 Advertising	200	155				152 Other						
58 Sales Promotion	200	155				94 Conveyor	100	78				
59 Mimeo.	300	233				95 Dress. Rooms	1,700	1,320				
60 Correspond'ce	200	155										
61 Displays	900	699					26,450	20,532				
62 Salesmen Gen'l							SUMMARY					
65 Sales Dept.	1,700	1,320				FACTORY	44,100	34,232				
68 Branch						DELIVERY	4,850	3,765				
74 Cars						STOCK-FACT.	17,550	13,623				
75 Phone Order	200	155				SELLING	1,600	1,241				
76 Investigators						STOCK-MKT.	49,350	38,308				
77 Price Checking	100	78				ADMINISTR.	1,100	853				
78 Sales Analysis						SERVICE DEP.	26,450	20,532				
79 Returns	200	155				TOTAL	145,000	112,554	@$.77623 per sq. ft.			
105 Mailing	200	155										

Fig. 19. (Form 13) Allocation of Floor Space—Indirect.

sixth floor is worth as much as a square foot on the first floor. If certain floor space is considered more valuable than others, the value of the space of each floor can be adjusted by a factor to give effect to this difference in value. For example, if the sixth floor is given a weight of 1, and if the first floor is worth three times that of the sixth floor, then the factor 3 is assigned to the first floor and the actual square footage occupied by each department on the floor is multiplied by 3. If the second floor is worth 2½ times that of the sixth floor, then the square footage of the departments occupying space on the second floor is multiplied by the factor 2½.

The other floors are treated similarly. By this procedure, departments are charged for space in proportion to the numbers just derived, so that the allocation of the total rental costs will then be according to their market value or location in the building.

► NOTE: If the company owns its building, such items as real estate taxes, depreciation on building, possible interest on mortgages, structural repairs and maintenance, etc., are considered in place of rent.

The rent costs are posted from *Forms 12* and *13* to *Form 1* in the columns captioned Rent Allocation. Figure 20 shows *Form 1* at this stage of completion.

Allocation of indirect expenses. After having reconciled the individual allocations to the totals of the controls, the next step involves the completion of the Allocation of Indirect Expense portion of *Form 1*. The accounts or functions that could be charged to merchandise departments or products have been entered in the columns captioned Direct Department. The other indirect accounts and functions are entered in the Basis columns. The Basis columns are numerically coded to represent the base that is going to be used to spread the indirect cost to merchandise departments or products.

► COMMENT: The selection of the proper bases for use in these allocations is probably the most important and difficult procedure in distribution cost accounting. There is no one correct way of developing bases of allocation. The bases shown in *Form 14* (Figure 21) used in the hypothetical problem were formulated through careful deliberation of a department head or group of executives.

There are 3 general methods to use in arriving at bases of allocation:

1. The statistical method.
2. The adjusted statistical method.
3. The executive-decision method.

1. *The statistical method* should be used only for activities made up of routine, continuously repetitive, comparable transactions. The number of transactions chosen should be large enough to insure a representative sample.

► EXAMPLE: The number of invoice lines on *Form 14,* line number 3 (Figure 21) is computed by actually counting the number of lines on customers' invoices for a period of 24 days, using the invoices from the first and

Function: SELLING

Allocation Basis No.	Account or Service	a/c No. or Ref.	BUDGET			Primary Expense Accounts Analyzed from Aprons	CHARGEABLE TO THIS FUNCTION			
			Before Adjust-ments	J.E. adjust-ments	As adjusted		Indirect to be Allocated	Charges to Products and Functions from the Aprons Analysis	Payroll alloca-tion	Rent alloca-tion
19	SUNDRY SELLING EXPENSES	65	3,000	40	3,040	2,359	681	2,622		1,320
24	SALESMEN'S DINNER	66	900		900	652	248	652		
24	SALESMEN'S PRIZES	67	2,000		2,000		2,000			
25	BRANCH DISPLAY OFFICE	68	6,000	120	6,120		6,120	72		
24	SALESMEN-GENERAL	69						49		
24	SALESMEN-INDIRECT	62							5,543	
15	PHONE-ORDER DEPT.	75		35	35		35		19,386	155
30	INVESTIGATORS (TRACERS)	76							13,625	
16	PRICE-CHECKING DEPT.	77		30	30		30		7,039	78
19	SALES ANALYSIS DEPT.	78		100	100		100		1,223	
35	RETURNS DEPT.	79							473	155
19	TELEPHONE A/c 65	J.E.								
DIRECT-APRONS ALLOCATED		Form 2						1,695		
"	-PAYROLL "	Form							500,259	
"	-RENT "	Form 12								1,241
	TO FIGURES 3 and 23		11,900	325	12,225	3,011	9,214	5,090	547,548	2,949
							564,801			

Fig. 20. (Form 1) Selling Function After Rent Allocation is Posted.

BASES FOR ALLOCATIONS- 19__

No.	Function	A1	A2	A3	B	C	D1	D2	OTHER
1	Number of customers orders	22.4	7.1	23.5	2.	24.5	14.2	6.3	
2	Mimeo and addressograph	25..	10.	8.	7.	34.	10.	6.	
3	Number of lines on invoices	37.06	12.98	.89	2.53	37.89	1.56	7.09	
4	Receiving	20.	10.	10.	10.	30.	15.	5.	
5	Designing	75.	20.			5.			
6	Value of merchandise inventories	16.8	6.7	20.1	8.7	32.9	6.7	8.1	
7	Country shipments-prepaid	1.2	32.			61.2	5.1	0.5	
8	Calculating machines dept.	37.06	12.98	.89	2.53	37.89	1.56	7.09	
9	Packing supplies dept.	44.	6.			44.		6.	
10	Sales- other than depts. A3 & B	28.7	10.			41.4	10.9	9.	
11	Number of local delivery stops	23.5	1.5	17.	3.	27.5	20.4	7.1	
12	Sales promotion dept.	70.	10.			20.			
13	Literature, displays, samples	70.	10.			20.			
14	Correspondence dept.	33.	13.			50.	2.	2.	
15	Phone order dept.	55.	10.			35.			
16	Price checking dept.	30.	10.	21.	1.	36.	1.	1.	
17	Credit & collection depts.	25.	6.5	12.5	12.5	26.	10.	7.5	
18	Bad debts provision	20.	2.	2.	33.	25.	8.	10.	
19	City business tax	20.4	7.1	19.4	9.2	29.6	7.8	6.5	
20	Accounting dept.	25.	12.	15.	12.	26.			10.
21	Accounts payable debt.	27.	4.	5.	14.	35.			15.
22	State franchise tax	5.	3.	79.	3	10.			
23	Machine shop	47.5	7.5			45.			
24	Salesmen's salaries	29.6	10.1	12.6	5.5	28.5	8.9	4.8	
25	Branch show room	60.	10.			30.			
26	Advertising dept.	38.	5.		1.	54.	2.		
28	Mailing dept.	32.	6.	8.	7.	33.	6.	3.	5.
29	Filing dept.	26.	9.	15.	3.	33.	9.	5.	
30	Investigator's group	38.	8.			51.	2.	1.	
31	Local telephone calls TALLY								
32	Long distance telephone calls TALLY								
33	Parcel post prepaid	18.	5.	27.	3.	41.	4.	2.	
34	Labels dept.	40.	10.			50.			
35	Returns dept.	24.	8.	20.	1.	31.	10.	6.	
36	Pay roll dept.	39.	4.	1.	0.5	40.			15.5
37	Floor areas	27.4	7.1	11.4	4.9	39.9	8.	1.3	
38	Personnel-office	37.06	12.98	.89	2.53	37.89	1.56	7.09	
39	Country-prepaid and collect	29.2	18.5		7.55	38.25	5.5	1.0	

Fig. 21. (Form 14) Allocation Bases.

third Mondays of the month. The number of invoices are in excess of 800 per day.

In the above example, the statistical method is applicable because the transactions are routine and repetitive, and the easily obtainable sample is a sufficient representation of billing department activity.

The danger is, however, that because the statistical method appears to provide a scientific, objective, and easily calculable basis for allocating indirect expenses, it tends to replace considered executive judgment and to spread to areas in which pure statistics may be invalid.

Many distribution cost accountants advocate the use of pure statistics to derive unit costs per salesman call. However, even in such a seemingly repetitive business as house-to-house bottled-milk selling, there are marked differences in the cost of making various deliveries.

► EXAMPLE: When a milkman delivers one quart to A and five quarts to B, the delivery expense per quart is different for A than for B. The difficulty is even greater when different products and services are involved. For example, a salesman gets an order from A but not from B; he helps A to dress his window but doesn't help B, C, D, and E; he has to take stock in A's store in order to make up his own order, but doesn't have to do it in the stores of his other customers, and so on.

2. *The adjusted statistical method* applies weights or factors to statistical figures in order to adjust these figures to reflect differences in operations, and to be able to compare statistically unlike figures. The factor itself may be determined by statistical study or by executives' judgment.

► EXAMPLE 1: The costs of service department Z are to be allocated to departments on the basis of gross sales of each department. However, department X's unit price per sale is higher than department Y. Therefore, although the cost of handling each unit in service department Z is equal, regardless of selling price, department X will be charged with more costs than department Y, even if department Y's unit sales are greater. This inequality is resolved by applying an activity factor based on unit number of sales to the dollar amount of sales of each department. The foregoing is illustrated as follows:

Dept.	*Sales*	*Expense Based on Sales*	*Activity Factor*	*Product*	*Expense Based on Weighted Sales*
X	$10,000	20%	4	$ 40,000	40%
Y	20,000	40%	2	40,000	40%
Z	20,000	40%	1	20,000	20%
	$50,000	100%		$100,000	100%

► EXAMPLE 2: The expenses of the buying, receiving and stock-handling functions are applied to products upon the basis of quantities of each product sold. However, the buying expenses applicable to patterned textiles are more than those applicable to solid color fabrics. This is because the floral or geometric patterns require additional attention such as designing, testing, etc. Therefore, in order to adequately reflect the numerical relationship between these two products, the quantities have to be weighted by applying a time or activity factor to the floral product. This newly-derived expression of quantity numbers is valid statistically, and is an acceptable basis for companies and allocation of buying expenses.

3. *The executive-decision method* is used in cases in which it would not be feasible to use statistical analyses. The substitution by the executive of his judgment for statistical analysis is not unscientific. If the premises upon which his judgment is based are correct and can be justified by his experience, the conclusions are valid and worthy of acceptance. In fact, in many ways, this method is superior to statistical formulas that tend to become mechanical and stereotyped.

► COMMENT: As management knows more about the internal affairs of the business than any outsider, the formulae must be the product of the managers of the business in order to insure that the study's results are valid and that management accept them. Even if adjusted or unadjusted statistics are used in developing the bases of indirect expense allocation, it is essential that their use has been assented to by management. To accomplish this, periodic meetings should be held in which proposed bases are discussed with management. Accurate and complete notes should be taken and filed away carefully. These notes together with workpapers will be used to document the choice of bases in connection with the Robinson-Patman Act.

► WARNING: The Federal Trade Commission will accept the executive-decision method only in connection with minor expenses, and then, only if you have well-documented notes of the meetings at which the decisions were made.

After the bases are determined, the Allocations of Indirect Expense column of *Form 1* can be filled in and *Form 1* can be completed as shown in Figure 22.

Indirect costs can be allocated using the bases agreed upon, and *Form 1* can be recast by product using the data from the analyses of aprons, payroll and rent. *Form 15* (Figure 23) represents the recast of *Form 1* by product. *Form 15* will be useful in performing secondary analyses, and in preparing operating reports.

SEGMENT OR SECONDARY ANALYSIS

Having analyzed costs and expenses by functions, and by products or product groups, it is now possible to use this data to further break down marketing costs into smaller segments. *Segment analysis* includes analyses of channels of distribution, order sizes, delivery methods, customer classes, sales methods, salesmen, etc. In this section, the types of segment analyses will be discussed that can satisfy the requirements of the Robinson-Patman Act by accounting for price differentials between (1) sales in one territory and another, (2) different classes of customers, and (3) different order-size categories.

Accounting for price differentials based on territories. *Form 16* (Figure 24), Costs Classified by Department and Territory, is prepared for each function using the amounts derived from *Form 15* (Figure 23).

The individual expense items charged to products are allocated to each territory. For instance, we must determine how much of the $2,513 charged to product A1 is applicable to territory A and how much to territory B. In the illustration in Figure 24, we indicated that 50% was allocable to each. Accordingly, we charged $1,256 to territory A and $1,257 to B.

Following this procedure with respect to all the other product costs, we obtain totals for each territory. For example, the total cost for the selling function of product A1 is $170,921. Since $104,961 is charged to territory A (sales volume of $1,040,000, first column) and $65,960 to territory B (sales volume of $1,000,000), the selling costs in territory A are 10.09% of sales, whereas those in territory B are 6.59%. This demonstrates the different impact that distribution costs may have on the same product depending upon where it is sold and delivered.

Accounting for price differentials based on classes of customers. Having completed the study as to the application of the "where" costs to products, we may next explore the "who" costs. *Form 17* (Figure 25) takes the selling

Function: SELLING

Allocation Basis No.	Account or Service	a/c No. or Ref.	BUDGET: Before Adjustments	BUDGET: J.E. adjustments	BUDGET: As adjusted	Primary Expense Accounts Analyzed from Aprons	CHARGEABLE TO THIS FUNCTION: Indirect to be Allocated	Charges to Products and Functions from the Aprons Analysis	Payroll allocation	Rent allocation	HOW CHANGES TO THIS FUNCTION WILL BE CHANGED TO PRODUCTS: Direct to Dept.	Basis 24	Basis 19	Basis 25	Basis 15	Basis 16	Basis 35	Basis 30	Basis 31	Basis
19	SUNDRY SELLING EXPENSES	65	3,000	40	3,040	2,359	681	2,622		1,320			4,623							
24	SALESMEN'S DINNER	66	900		900	652	248	652				900								
24	SALESMEN'S PRIZES	67	2,000		2,000		2,000					2,000								
25	BRANCH DISPLAY OFFICE	68	6,000	120	6,120		6,120	72						6,192						
24	SALESMEN-GENERAL	69						49				49								
24	SALESMEN-INDIRECT	62							5,543			5,543								
15	PHONE-ORDER DEPT.	75		35	35		35		19,386	155					19,576					
30	INVESTIGATORS (TRACERS)	76							13,625									13,625		
16	PRICE-CHECKING DEPT.	77		30	30		30		7,039	78						7,147				
19	SALES ANALYSIS DEPT.	78		100	100		100		1,223				1,323							
35	RETURNS DEPT.	79							473	155							628			
19	TELEPHONE A/c 65	J.E.											4,324						(4,324)	
DIRECT-APRONS ALLOCATED		Form 2						1,695			1,695									
"	-PAYROLL "	Form							500,259		500,259									
"	-RENT "	Form 12								1,241	1,241									
	TO FIGURES 3 and 23		11,900	325	12,225	3,011	9,214	5,090	547,548	2,949	503,195	8,492	10,270	6,192	19,576	7,147	628	13,625	(4,324)	
								564,801								564,801				

Fig. 22. (Form 1) Selling Function Completely Filled In.

SELLING FUNCTION—COSTS ALLOCATED TO PRODUCTS

SOURCE - FORM NO.	BASIS - FORM 14	ACCOUNT	NATURAL A/c NO.	CHARGE AS		DIRECT TO A PRODUCT OR GROUP							CHARGE TO A SERVICE FUNCTION GROUP						
				DISTRIBU-TABLE	DIRECT	1	2	3	4	5	6	7	24	19	25	15	16	35	30
		BUDGETED COSTS IN EXCESS OF																	
		ANALYZED APRONS:																	
1g	19	SUNDRY SELLING	65	681										681					
1g	24	SALESMENS' DINNER	66	248									248						
1g	24	SALESMENS' PRIZES	67	2,000									2,000						
1g	25	BRANCH DISPLAY OFFICE	68	6,120											6,120				
2	15	PHONE-ORDER DEPT.	75	35												35			
2	16	PRICE-CHECKING DEPT.	77	30													30		
2	19	SALES ANALYSIS DEPT.	78	100										100					
12 & 13		RENT ALLOCATION		1,708	1,241	194	-	310	310	116	233	78	-	1,320		155	78	155	
7		PAYROLL " (NOT SALES'M)		47,289	115,668	29,387	4,272	16,550	8,685	30,006	11,760	15,008	5,543	1,223		19,386	7,039	473	13,625
2 & 3		APRONS "		3,395	1,695	752	-	-	-	854	23	66	652	2,622	72				
		" "											49						
2		TELEPHONE-S. ENTRY		4,324										4,324					
4a		SALESMEN			384,591	114,025	38,671	48,448	21,331	109,686	34,331	18,059							
					503,195	144,358	42,943	65,348	30,326	140,662	46,347	33,211							
				65,930									8,492	10,270	6,192	19,576	7,147	628	13,625
		SERVICE FUNCTIONS ALLOCATED				2,513	858	1,070	467	2,420	756	408	(8,492)						
						2,095	729	1,993	944	3,040	801	668		(10,270)					
						3,715	619	-	-	1,858	-	-			(6,192)				
						10,767	1,957	-	-	6,852	-	-				(19,576)			
						2,144	715	1,501	71	2,573	71	72					(7,147)		
						151	50	126	6	194	63	38						(628)	
						5,178	1,090	-	-	6,949	272	136							(13,625)
				65,930	503,195	170,921	48,961	70,038	31,814	164,548	48,310	34,533	-	-	-	-	-	-	-

Fig. 23. (Form 15) Recast of Form 1 (Fig. 22) Allocating Indirect Expenses to Product.

function costs of each territory and shows how each cost of that function is divided among the classes of customers served in each territory. Again we have to construct suitable formulae to express numerically the extent to which each customer class equitably absorbs each cost or expense.

The results shown on *Form 17* (Figure 25) are again very revealing. Although the overall selling costs for product A in territory A were 10.09%, chain stores should be charged with 6.75% of the expense, department stores 7.87%, and other customers with 12.56%. These statistics give ample reason for price differentials between different classes of customers.

► NOTE: The other statistics shown at the bottom of *Form 17* (Figure 25) also provide valuable information for management, and are easily computed using the information provided by this and by auxiliary studies. For example, the estimated cost per shipment to each class of customer is computed by dividing the total cost for the class by the number of shipments. In this instance, the total costs (selling function) for chain stores in territory A or product A1 is $13,505, and there are 1,500 estimated shipments. The estimated cost per shipment is $9.00 ($13,505 ÷ 1,500).

Accounting for price differentials based on order-size categories. *Form 18* (Figure 26) is designed to show the average cost per shipment for product A1 by function, territory and class of customer. Before completing this form, it is necessary to obtain the following data relating to order-size categories:

1. Number of orders.
2. Cost of handling and delivery.
3. Selling and sales promotion costs.
4. Administrative costs.

1. *Number of orders.* Statistics as to the number of orders expected to be received from different classes of customers in each order-size category should be compiled. A fairly sizable test period during the current fiscal period should be used. The figures obtained from this test may then be interpolated for budgeted sales figures for each territory, customer and order-size segment, thus arriving at *Form 19* (Figure 27).

2. *Cost of handling and delivery.* Another important element in the order-size study is to determine the relative cost of handling a $10 order as against a $250 order. In the shipping or delivery area, orders may be classified on the basis of weight, bulk, distance, difficulty of handling, clerical work, and so on.

As we have already allocated our delivery costs into different territories, the distance factor has been accounted for as to all shipments. Having done so, it is impractical to differentiate, especially on local routes covering a radius of 15 miles, or less, between orders on the basis of distance covered, one mile or 15 miles. This is similar to the absence of differentiation between a passenger who travels 20 miles on the subway from Brooklyn or the Bronx, and the many passengers who ride two miles from Grand Central or Pennsylvania Station to Wall Street.

The distance or mileage factor of delivery is the costliest factor because it consumes more of the chauffeur's time, more depreciation, repairs, gas and

FROM FORM 15

SELLING Function

Budgeted Sales (000 omitted)	Dept. or Prod.	Basis 24		Basis 19		Basis 25		Basis 15		Basis 16	
		a/c	Amt.	a/c	Amt.	a/c	Amt.	a/c	Amt.	a/c	Amt.
		63	5,543	65	4,623	68	6,192	75	19,576	77	7,147
		69	49	65	4,324						
		67	2,000								
		66	900								
		%	8,492	%	8,947	%	6,192	%	19,576	%	7,147
2,040	A1	29.6	2,513	20.4	1,825	60	3,715	55	10,767	30	2,144
710	A2	10.1	858	7.1	635	10	619	10	1,957	10	715
1,940	A3	12.6	1,070	19.4	1,736					21	1,501
920	B	5.5	467	9.2	823					1	71
2,960	C	28.5	2,420	29.6	2,648	30	1,858	35	6,852	36	2,573
780	D1	8.9	756	7.9	698					1	71
650	D2	4.8	408	6.5	582					1	72
	Other										
10,000	Total		8,492		8,947		6,192		19,576		7,147
	Territory A- Local										
1,040	A1	50	1,256	50	912	80	2,972	95	10,229	50	1,072
510	A2	70	600	70	445	80	496	95	1,860	70	500
1,940	A3	100	1,070	100	1,736					100	1,501
500	B	60	280	60	494					60	43
1,960	C	70	1,694	70	1,854	90	1,672	90	6,167	70	1,801
500	D1	70	529	70	489					70	50
500	D2	80	327	80	466					80	58
6,950	Total		5,756		6,396		5,140		18,256		5,025
	Territory B- Out-of-town										
1,000	A1	50	1,257	50	913	20	743	5	538	50	1,072
200	A2	30	258	30	190	20	123	5	97	30	215
-	A3		-		-						-
420	B	40	187	40	329					40	28
1,000	C	30	726	40	794	10	186	10	685	30	772
280	D1	30	227	30	209					30	21
150	D2	20	81	20	116					20	14
3,050	Total		2,736		2,551		1,052		1,320		2,122

Dept. or Prod.	Basis 19		Basis 35		Basis 30		Basis		Basis		Basis		Basis		Basis		Basis	
	a/c	Amt.	a/c	Amt.	a/c	Amt.	a/c	Amt.	a/c	Amt.	a/c	Amt.	a/c	Amt.	a/c	Amt.	a/c	Amt.
	78	1,323	79	628	76	13,625	TOTAL INDIRECT		APRONS		SALESMEN		OTHER PAY ROLL		RENT		TOTAL	
	%	1,323	%	628	%	13,625	%	65,930	%	1,695	%	384,591	%	115,668	%	1,241	%	569,125
A1	20.4	276	24	151	38	5,178		26,563		752		114,025		29,387		194		170,921
A2	7.1	94	8	50	8	1,090		6,018				38,671		4,272				48,961
A3	19.4	257	20	126				4,690				48,488		16,550		310		70,038
B	9.2	121	1	6				1,488				21,331		8,685		310		31,814
C	29.6	392	31	194	51	6,949		23,886		854		109,686		30,006		116		164,548
D1	7.8	103	10	63	2	272		1,963		23		34,331		11,760		233		48,310
D2	6.5	80	6	38	1	136		1,322		66		18,059		15,008		78		34,533
Other																		
Total		1,323		628		13,625		65,930		1,695		384,591		115,668		1,241		569,125
Territory A- Local																		
A1	50	135	50	76	80	4,143		20,795	50	376		69,000	50	14,693	50	97		104,961
A2	70	67	70	35	80	872		4,875				36,000	70	2,990				43,865
A3	100	257	100	126				4,690				48,488	100	16,550	100	310		70,038
B	60	73	60	4				894				18,000	60	5,211	60	186		24,291
C	70	274	70	137	70	4,865		18,464	70	598		97,700	70	21,006	70	82		139,850
D1	70	73	70	44	100	272		1,457	70	16		27,000	70	8,232	70	163		36,868
D2	80	69	80	31	100	136		1,087	80	53		16,000	80	12,008	80	63		29,211
Total		948		453		10,288		52,262		1,043		312,188		80,690		901		447,084
Territory B- Out-of-town																		
A1	50	135	50	75	20	1,035		5,768	50	376		45,025	50	14,694	50	97		65,960
A2	30	27	30	15	20	218		1,143				2,671	30	1,282				5,096
A3		-		-				-				-						-
B	40	48	40	2				594				3,331	40	3,474	40	124		7,523
C	30	118	30	57	30	2,084		5,422	30	256		11,986	30	9,000	30	34		26,698
D1	30	30	30	19				506	30	7		7,331	30	3,528	30	70		11,442
D2	20	17	20	7				235	20	13		2,059	20	3,000	20	15		5,322
Total		375		175		3,337		13,668		652		72,403		34,978		340		122,041

Fig. 24. (Form 16) Costs Classified by Department and Territory.

From FORM 16

SELLING Function

Dept.
Prod. A1

Basis	a/c	Account or Service	Basis for Alloc. to Cust.	Territory A- Local							Territory B- Out-of-town						
				Total	Chains		Dept. St.		Other		Total	Chains		Dept. St.		Other	
				Amt.	%	Amt.	%	Amt.	%	Amt.	Amt.	%	Amt.	%	Amt.	%	Amt.
24	62	SALESMEN-INDIRECT	M	1,256	15	189	20	251	35	816	1,257	25	314	15	189	60	754
	69	" -GENERAL															
—	67	SALESMEN'S PRIZES															
—	66	SALESMEN'S DINNERS															
19	65	SUNDRY SELL'G EXP.	M	912	20	182	30	274	50	456	913	50	457	20	183	30	273
25	68	BRANCH DISPLAY OFFICE	T	2,972	10	297	60	1,783	30	892	743	10	74	60	446	30	223
15	75	PHONE ORDER DEPT.	M	10,229	-		-		100	10,229	538	5	27	5	27	90	484
16	79	PRICE CHECKING "	T	1,072	15	160	20	214	35	698	1,072	20	214	10	107	70	751
19	78	SALES ANALYSIS "	M	135	15	21	20	27	35	87	135	20	27	10	14	70	94
35	79	RETURN GOODS "	M	76	10	8	30	23	60	45	75	5	4	5	4	90	67
30	76	INVESTIGATORS, TRACERS	T	4,143	-		-		100	4,143	1,035	-		-		100	1,035
		APRONS	M	376	20	75	30	112	50	189	376	50	188	20	75	30	113
		SALESMEN'S SALARIES EXP.	T	69,000	15	10,350	25	17,250	60	41,400	45,025	60	27,000	15	6,750	25	11,275
		OTHER PAYROLL	T	14,693	15	2,204	25	3,674	60	8,815	14,694	40	5,878	10	1,469	50	7,347
		RENT	M	97	20	19	30	29	50	49	97	50	48	20	19	30	30
		Total costs		104,961		13,505		23,637		67,819	65,960		34,231		9,283		22,446
		Sales budget		1,040,000		200,000		300,000		540,000	1,000,000		500,000		200,000		300,000
		% of costs to sales		10.09		6.75		7.87		12.56	6.59		6.85		4.64		7.47
		Statistics:															
		Salesmen's salaries, expenses-% to sales				5.175		5.75		7.67			5.40		3.375		3.76
		Other expenses -% to sales				1.575		2.12		4.89			1.45		1.265		3.71
		Number of salesmen's calls				1,550		3,800		22,500			2,570		3,290		14,910
		Number of shipments				1,500		3,620		21,645			2,535		3,185		14,556
		Avge. total costs per shipment				$ 9.00		$ 6.53		$ 3.13			$ 13.50		$ 2.91		$ 1.54
		Avge. salesmen's salaries & exp. per ship.				$ 6.90		$ 4.80		$ 1.91			$ 10.65		$ 2.12		$ .77
		Avge. size per order				$133.33		$82.80		$24.95			$197.24		$62.80		$20.61

Fig. 25. (Form 17) Costs Allocated to Different Classes of Customers.

DISTRIBUTION COSTS PER ORDER

DEPT. A1

Territory	Cust. Class		Total	UNDER 5	5-10	10-20	20-50	50-100	100-200	200-300	OVER 300	Ref.
A	CHAINS	SALES PROMOTION & SELLING	12.70	.38	.67	1.43	3.81	7.62	15.23	24.75	42.11	21
		DELIVERY	2.04	1.08	1.20	1.35	1.63	1.90	2.17	2.72	3.26	20
		ADMINISTRATIVE	4.03	3.24	3.42	3.56	3.73	3.88	4.21	4.53	4.86	22
		TOTAL	18.77	4.70	5.29	6.34	9.17	13.40	21.61	32.00	50.23	"
	DEPT. STORES	SALES PROMOTION & SELLING	8.07	.46	.66	1.46	3.89	7.80	15.60	25.30	65.14	"
		DELIVERY	1.37	.83	.93	1.05	1.26	1.46	1.67	2.09	2.52	"
		ADMINISTRATIVE	3.03	2.55	2.70	2.81	2.94	3.07	3.33	3.57	3.83	"
		TOTAL	12.47	3.84	4.29	5.32	8.09	12.33	20.60	30.96	71.49	"
	OTHER CUST.	SALES PROMOTION & SELLING	4.174	.67	1.17	2.51	6.69	13.39	26.77	43.50	63.51	"
		DELIVERY	1.051	.82	.91	1.03	1.24	1.44	1.65	2.06	2.47	"
		ADMINISTRATIVE	1.822	1.66	1.74	1.82	1.91	1.99	2.16	2.32	2.49	"
		TOTAL	7.047	3.15	3.82	5.36	9.84	16.82	30.58	47.88	68.47	"
B	CHAINS	SALES PROMOTION & SELLING	18.41	.45	.66	1.40	3.73	7.47	14.94	24.27	37.67	"
		DELIVERY	4.36	2.00	2.22	2.53	3.03	3.53	4.04	5.05	6.06	"
		ADMINISTRATIVE	4.51	3.45	3.64	3.79	3.97	4.13	4.47	4.81	5.16	"
		TOTAL	27.28	5.90	6.52	7.72	10.73	15.13	23.45	34.13	48.89	"

Fig. 26. (Form 18) Summary of Distribution Costs per Order.

DEPT. A 1

Territory	Cust. Class		Total	UNDER 5	5-10	10-20	20-50	50-100	100-200	200-300	OVER 300
A	CHAINS	DOLLAR SALES	200,000	100	350	2,250	10,000	32,000	48,000	52,000	55,300
		NUMBER OF ORDERS	1,500	25	50	150	250	400	300	200	125
		AVGE. SALES PER ORDER	133	4	7	15	40	80	160	260	442
	DEPT. STRS.	DOLLAR SALES	300,000	240	560	7,500	60,000	64,000	80,000	20,800	66,900
		NUMBER OF ORDERS	3,620	60	80	500	1,500	800	500	80	100
		AVGE. SALES PER ORDER	83	4	7	15	40	80	160	260	669
	OTHER CUST.	DOLLAR SALES	540,000	2,000	45,500	175,500	60,000	48,000	64,000	52,000	93,000
		NUMBER OF ORDERS	21,645	500	6,500	11,700	1,500	600	400	200	245
		AVGE. SALES PER ORDER	25	4	7	15	40	80	160	260	380
B	CHAINS	DOLLAR SALES	500,000	80	350	3,000	10,000	40,000	80,000	78,000	288,570
		NUMBER OF ORDERS	2,535	20	50	200	250	500	500	300	715
		AVGE. SALES PER ORDER	197	4	7	15	40	80	160	260	403
	DEPT. STRS.	DOLLAR SALES	200,000	200	560	7,500	60,000	56,000	32,000	20,800	22,940
		NUMBER OF ORDERS	3,185	50	80	500	1,500	700	200	80	75
		AVGE. SALES PER ORDER	63	4	7	15	40	80	160	260	306
	OTHER CUST.	DOLLAR SALES	300,000	400	47,600	90,000	32,000	40,000	32,000	26,000	32,000
		NUMBER OF ORDERS	14,556	100	6,800	6,000	800	500	200	100	56
		AVGE. SALES PER ORDER	21	4	7	15	40	80	160	260	571
		TOTAL NUMBER OF ORDERS	47,041	755	13,560	19,050	5,800	3,500	2,100	960	1,316

Fig. 27. (Form 19) Customer Order Statistics.

other costs. The weight, bulk and clerical factors are not so significant from a delivery cost point of view unless they are so heavy or bulky as to require unusual amounts of space in a truck, or possibly, even a separate truck.

► OBSERVATION: A method that has found favor in this writer's experience is the assignment by the traffic manager of an activity and cost factor to each order-size category. It is practical, does not discriminate between customers within a limited territory, and is proportional as to delivery costs per shipment between one order-size category and another.

Form 20 (Figure 28) shows how the delivery expense per order is arrived at. The traffic manager starts with the "under $5" category and assigns the factor "1" to it. He now reasons:

"If 1 is the starting point with respect to an order under $5, how much more than 1 would it require in delivery costs for an order in the $5 to $10 category?" The answer is 10% more, and therefore, he assigns a 1.10 factor to the $5 to $10 category. He proceeds in this manner until he assigns cost and activity factors for each order-size category.

As delivery costs are generally dependent upon the physical characteristics of products, such as the number of trips, stops, or shipments made, these costs are allocated to order-size categories on the basis of the numerical expressions derived by multiplying the number of orders by a selected activity factor.

The remainder of *Form 20* (Figure 28) can be completed by multiplying the factors by the number of orders, allocating the resulting figures proportionately to the cost of delivery ($3,058), and then dividing the number of orders into the delivery costs of each order-size category in order to arrive at a delivery cost per order.

3. *Selling and sales promotion costs. Form 21* (Figure 29) provides for the determination of the Selling and Sales Promotion Costs per order in each order-size category.

The "under $5" category assumes an average sales per order of $4 (*Form 19,* Figure 27). There are expected to be a total $100 worth of orders in this category, or 25 orders. One hundred dollars is .05% of the $200,000 total sales to chain stores in this territory. The costs of sales promotion and selling, .05% of $19,039, is $9.52, or the costs applicable to the 25 orders. The cost of sales promotion and selling per order in this order-size category is $9.52 divided by 25, which equals $.38. The figure of $19,039 is made up of $5,534 for sales promotion costs and $3,505 for selling costs.

Since sales promotion and selling expenses are generally regarded as being most nearly variable in proportion to the sales dollars of the various products because of their close relationship with sales characteristics, it is deemed appropriate to allocate these expenses to order-size categories on the basis of the sales dollars in each such category.

4. *Administrative costs.* Administrative expenses apply to order-size categories in a physical as well as in a sales dollar characteristic manner. A basis for allocation of these expenses should therefore recognize some combination of costs having both of these characteristics that would most nearly

DELIVERY EXPENSES
BY TERRITORY, CLASS OF CUSTOMER AND ORDER CATEGORY

DEPT. A1

Territory	Cust. Class.		Total	UNDER 5	5-10	10-20	20-50	50-100	100-200	200-300	OVER 300
A	CHAINS	NUMBER OF ORDERS	1,500	25	50	150	250	400	300	200	125
		FACTOR *		1.	1.10	1.25	1.50	1.75	2.00	2.50	3.00
		RELATIVE EXPENSE IMPACT	2,837	25	55	187	375	700	600	500	375
		DELIVERY EXPENSE ALLOCATED	3,058	27	60	203	407	760	651	543	407
		" " PER ORDER	2.04	1.08	1.20	1.35	1.63	1.90	2.17	2.72	3.26
	DEPT. STRS.	NUMBER OF ORDERS	3,620	60	80	500	1,500	800	500	80	100
		FACTOR *		1.	1.10	1.25	1.50	1.75	2.00	2.50	3.00
		RELATIONSHIPS	5,923	60	88	6.25	2,250	1,400	1,000	200	300
		DELIVERY EXPENSE ALLOCATED	4,959	50	74	523	1,884	1,172	837	167	252
		" " PER ORDER	1.37	.83	.93	1.05	1.26	1.46	1.67	2.09	2.52
	OTHER CUST.	NUMBER OF ORDERS	21,645	500	6,500	11,700	1,500	600	400	200	205
		FACTOR *		1.00	1.10	1.25	1.50	1.75	2.00	2.50	3.00
		RELATIONSHIPS	27,610	500	7,150	14,625	2,250	1,050	800	500	735
		DELIVERY EXPENSE ALLOCATED	22,759	412	5,894	12,055	1,855	866	659	412	600
		" " PER ORDER	1.051	.82	.91	1.03	1.24	1.44	1.65	2.06	2.47
B	CHAINS	NUMBER OF ORDERS	2,535	20	50	200	250	500	500	300	715
		FACTOR *		1.	1.10	1.25	1.50	1.75	2.00	2.50	3.00
		RELATIONSHIPS	5,470	20	55	250	375	875	1,000	750	2,145
		DELIVERY EXPENSE ALLOCATED	11,041	40	111	505	757	1,766	2,018	1,514	4,330
		" " PER ORDER	4.36	2.00	2.22	2.53	3.03	3.53	4.04	5.05	6.06
	DEPT. STRS.	NUMBER OF ORDERS	3,185	50	80	500	1,500	700	200	80	75
		FACTOR *		1.	1.10	1.25	1.50	1.75	2.00	2.50	3.00
		RELATIONSHIPS	5,063	50	88	625	2,250	1,225	400	200	225
		DELIVERY EXPENSE ALLOCATED	6,525	64	113	806	2,900	1,579	516	257	290
		" " PER ORDER	2.05	1.28	1.41	1.61	1.93	2.26	2.58	3.21	3.87
	OTHER CUST.	NUMBER OF ORDERS	14,556	100	6,800	6,000	800	500	200	100	56
		FACTOR *		1.	1.10	1.25	1.50	1.75	2.00	2.50	3.00
		RELATIONSHIPS	17,973	100	7,480	7,500	1,200	875	400	250	168
		DELIVERY EXPENSE ALLOCATED	17,558	98	7,307	7,327	1,172	855	391	244	164
		" " PER ORDER	1.21	.98	1.07	1.22	1.47	1.71	1.96	2.44	2.93

*TO REPRESENT TRAFFIC MANAGER'S OPINION AS TO DELIVERY EXPENSE IMPACT PER ORDER.

Fig. 28. (Form 20) Delivery Expenses by Territory, Class of Customer, and Order Category.

SALES PROMOTION AND SELLING EXPENSES BY TERRITORY
CLASS OF CUSTOMER AND ORDER CATEGORY

DEPT. A1

Territory	Cust. Class.		Total	UNDER 5	5-10	10-20	20-50	50-100	100-200	200-300	OVER 300	REF.
A	CHAINS	DOLLAR SALES	200,000	100	350	2,250	10,000	32,000	48,000	52,000	55,300	
		SALES PROM. & SELL. ALLOCATION	19,039	9	34	215	952	3,046	4,569	4,950	5,264	17
		NUMBER OF ORDERS	1,500	25	50	150	250	400	300	200	125	
		SALES PROM. & SELL. PER ORDER	12.70	.38	.67	1.43	3.81	7.62	15.23	24.75	42.11	17
	DEPT. STRS.	DOLLAR SALES	300,000	240	560	7,500	60,000	64,000	80,000	20,800	66,900	"
		S.P. & SELL. ALLOCATION	29,210	27	53	730	5,842	6,230	7,790	2,024	6,514	
		NUMBER OF ORDERS	3,620	60	80	500	1,500	800	500	80	100	
		S.P. & SELL. PER ORDER	8.07	.46	.66	1.46	3.89	7.80	15.60	25.30	65.14	
	OTHER CUST.	DOLLAR SALES	540,000	2.000	45,500	175,500	60,000	48,000	64,000	52,000	93,000	"
		S.P. & SELL. ALLOCATION	90,344	335	7,612	29,362	10,038	8,031	10,707	8,700	15,559	
		NUMBER OF ORDERS	21,645	500	6,500	11,700	1,500	600	400	200	245	
		S.P. & SELL. PER ORDER	4.174	.67	1.17	2.51	6.69	13.39	26.77	43.50	63.51	
B	CHAINS	DOLLAR SALES	500,000	80	350	3,000	10,000	40,000	80,000	78,000	288,570	"
		S.P. & SELL. ALLOCATION	46,673	9	33	280	933	3,734	7,468	7,281	26,935	
		NUMBER OF ORDERS	2,535	20	50	200	250	500	500	300	715	
		S.P. & SELL. PER ORDER	18.41	.45	.66	1.40	3.73	7.47	14.94	24.27	37.67	
	DEPT. STRS.	DOLLAR SALES	200,000	200	560	7,500	60,000	56,000	32,000	20,800	22,940	"
		S.P. & SELL. ALLOCATION	16,482	16	47	618	4,945	4,615	2,637	1,714	1,890	
		NUMBER OF ORDERS	3,185	50	80	500	1,500	700	200	80	75	
		S.P. & SELL. PER ORDER	5.17	.33	.59	1.24	3.30	6.60	13.19	21.46	25.20	
	OTHER CUST.	DOLLAR SALES	300,000	400	47,600	90,000	32,000	40,000	32,000	26,000	32,000	"
		S.P. & SELL. ALLOCATION	43,609	58	6,919	13,083	4,652	5,814	4,652	3,779	4,652	
		NUMBER OF ORDERS	14,556	100	6,800	6,000	800	500	200	100	56	
		S.P. & SELL. PER ORDER	3.00	.58	1.02	2.18	5.82	11.63	23.26	37.79	83.07	

Fig. 29. (Form 21) Sales Promotion and Selling Expenses by Territory, Class of Customer, and Order Category.

numerically express the relative impact to the various products. In *Form 22* (Figure 30), an activity factor is arrived at to represent in a composite number the relative administrative expense impact per order.

Form 22 (Figure 30) shows how the administrative costs per order in each order-size category is derived.

Summary and analysis of order-size cost study. Form 18 (Figure 26) is a summarization of *Forms 20, 21* and *22* and gives the average costs per shipment for product A1 for each territory and each class of customer. The costs of the functions, delivery, sales promotion, selling, and administrative are added together. Stock marketing costs are sometimes also included to represent the total distribution costs per order for each order-size category. (See page 401.)

Form 23 (Figure 31) shows a profit and loss statement by product, territory, class of customers and order-size category. A study of this form reveals that the company has a serious "small orders" problem with respect to product A1, especially in the "other customer" class, where 87% of these customers' orders are below $220 per order. This condition is so serious and costly that immediate attention must be devoted to it.

Form 24 (Figure 32) illustrates the results of a study from which it is possible to ascertain the difference between average distribution costs allocated on an overall percentage of sales, and those based on cost analyses that give effect to cost distinctions between one group of customers and another even within the same class.

► OBSERVATION: Distribution costs based on an average of 14.05% to sales were $14 in the "under $5" category. Since the actual distribution costs, however, were $117 ($4.70 per order multiplied by 25 orders), the percentage that the actual distribution costs bear to sales is 117.5% rather than 14.05% ($117 divided by $100 sales).

By comparing the actual distribution costs percentage with the average percentage, we arrive at a difference that represents the extent of discrimination in costs in effect between different groups (order-size category) of customers within the same class (chain stores). If billings are determined on a base-price basis that does not give effect to differences in costs between order-price categories, discrimination between customers can be averted by applying plus or minus percentage rates to the invoiced amounts for each product.

► EXAMPLE: A customer whose sales for the year are from $3,000 to $4,000 and whose orders average between $100 and $200 each, should be credited with 0.54% on all his product A1 purchases. Therefore, he will pay $.9946 for each unit of the product instead of $1.00. If he buys more than one product, he may be entitled to a credit adjustment for his A1 purchases but not for his D1 purchases.

A chart similar to the one shown at the bottom of *Form 24* (Figure 32) should be prepared as a summary of adjustments to average sales price. This will be used in pricing customers' invoices.

DEPT. A1

Territory	Cust. Class.		Total	UNDER 5	5-10	10-20	20-50	50-100	100-200	200-300	OVER 300
A	CHAINS	NUMBER OF ORDERS	1,500	25	50	150	250	400	300	200	125
		FACTOR *		1.	1.05	1.10	1.15	1.20	1.30	1.40	1.50
		RELATIVE EXPENSE IMPACT	1,869	25	53	165	288	480	390	280	188
		ADMINIS. EXPENSE ALLOCATED	6,046	81	171	534	932	1,553	1,262	906	607
		" " PER ORDER	4.03	3.24	3.42	3.56	3.73	3.88	4.21	4.53	4.86
	DEPT. STRS.	NUMBER OF ORDERS	3,620	60	80	500	1,500	800	500	80	100
		FACTOR *		1.	1.05	1.10	1.15	1.20	1.30	1.40	1.50
		RELATIONSHIP	4,291	60	84	550	1,725	960	650	112	150
		ADMINIS. EXPENSE ALLOCATED	10,978	153	215	1,407	4,414	2,457	1,663	286	383
		" " PER ORDER	3.03	2.55	2.70	2.81	2.94	3.07	3.33	3.57	3.83
	OTHER CUST.	NUMBER OF ORDERS	21,645	500	6,500	11,700	1,500	600	400	200	245
		FACTOR *		1.	1.05	1.10	1.15	1.20	1.30	1.40	1.50
		RELATIONSHIP	23,808	500	6,825	12,870	1,725	720	520	280	368
		ADMINIS. EXPENSE ALLOCATED	39,446	828	11,308	21,323	2,858	1,193	862	464	610
		" " PER ORDER	1.822	1.66	1.74	1.82	1.91	1.99	2.16	2.32	2.49
B	CHAINS	NUMBER OF ORDERS	2,535	20	50	200	250	500	500	300	715
		FACTOR *		1.	1.05	1.10	1.15	1.20	1.30	1.40	1.50
		RELATIONSHIP	3,324	20	53	220	288	600	650	420	1,073
		ADMINIS. EXPENSE ALLOCATED	11,436	69	182	757	991	2,064	2,236	1,444	3,693
		" " PER ORDER	4.51	3.45	3.64	3.79	3.97	4.13	4.47	4.81	5.16
	DEPT. STRS.	NUMBER OF ORDERS	3,185	50	80	500	1,500	700	200	80	75
		FACTOR *		1.	1.05	1.10	1.15	1.20	1.30	1.40	1.50
		RELATIONSHIP	3,734	50	84	550	1,725	840	260	112	113
		ADMINIS. EXPENSE ALLOCATED	11,824	158	266	1,742	5,463	2,660	823	355	357
		" " PER ORDER	3.71	3.16	3.33	3.48	3.64	3.80	4.12	4.44	4.76
	OTHER CUST.	NUMBER OF ORDERS	14,556	100	6,800	6,000	800	500	200	100	56
		FACTOR *		1.	1.05	1.10	1.15	1.20	1.30	1.40	1.50
		RELATIONSHIP	15,844	100	7,140	6,600	920	600	2.60	140	84
		ADMINIS. EXPENSE ALLOCATED	29,674	187	13,372	12,362	1,723	1,124	487	262	157
		" " PER ORDER	2.04	1.87	1.97	2.06	2.15	2.25	2.44	2.62	2.80

*TO REPRESENT EXECUTIVE OPINION AS TO ADMINISTRATIVE EXPENSE IMPACT PER ORDER.

Fig. 30. (Form 22) Administrative Expenses by Territory, Class of Customer, and Order Category.

PROFIT OR LOSS PER SALES ORDER FOR EACH CLASS OF CUSTOMER
IN EACH TERRITORY AND FOR EACH ORDER CATEGORY

DEPT. A1

Territory	Cust. Class.			Total	UNDER 5	5-10	10-20-	20-50	50-100	100-200	200-300	OVER 300	REF.
A	CHAINS	GROSS SALES IN $	100%	200,000	100	350	2,250	10,000	32,000	48,000	52,000	55,300	19
		COST OF GOODS SOLD $	77.21	154,420	77	270	1,737	7,721	24,707	37,061	40,199	42,648	
		GROSS PROFIT BEFORE ADJUST.		45,580	23	80	513	2,279	7,293	10,939	11,801	12,652	
		CASH DISCTS. ON SALES	2%	4,000	2.	7	45	200	640	960	1,040	1,106	
		LOSSES ON ALLCES. & RET'NS.	0.4%	800	.40	1.40	9	40	128	192	208	221	
		MARK DOWNS ON OBSOLETE MDSE.	(NONE FOR CHAINS)										
		GROSS PROFIT		40,780	21	72	459	2,039	6,525	9,787	10,553	11,324	
		NUMBER OF ORDERS		1,500	25	50	150	250	400	300	200	125	19
		GROSS PROFIT PER ORDER $		27.20	.84	1.45	3.06	8.16	16.31	32.62	52.76	90.60	
		DISTRIBUTION COSTS PER ORDER $		18.77	4.70	5.29	6.34	9.17	13.40	21.61	32.00	50.23	18
		NET PROFIT OR (LOSS) PER ORDER $		8.43	(3.86)	(3.84)	(3.32)	(1.01)	2.91	11.01	20.76	40.37	
		" " AFTER DISTRIB. COSTS $		12,637	(97)	(192)	(498)	(253)	1,164	3,303	4,152	5,058	
	DEPT STRS.	GROSS SALES IN $	100%	300,000	240	560	7,500	60,000	64,000	80,000	20,800	66,900	19
		COST OF GOODS SOLD $	77.21	231,630	185	432	5,791	46,326	49,414	61,768	16,060	51,654	
		GROSS PROFIT BEFORE ADJUST.		68,370	55	128	1,709	13,674	14,586	18,232	4,740	15,246	
		CASH DISCTS. ON SALES	2%	6,000	5	11	150	1,200	1,280	1,600	416	1,338	
		LOSSES ON ALLCES. & RET'NS.	0.4%	1,200	1	2	30	240	256	320	82	269	
		MARK DOWNS ON OBSOLETE MDSE.	(NONE FOR DEPT. STORES)										
		GROSS PROFIT		61,170	49	115	1,529	12,234	13,050	16,312	4,242	13,639	
		NUMBER OF ORDERS		3,620	60	80	500	1,500	800	500	80	100	19
		GROSS PROFIT PER ORDER $		16.90	.82	1.44	3.09	8.16	16.31	32.62	53.04	136.39	
		DISTRIBUTION COSTS PER ORDER $		12.47	3.84	4.29	5.32	8.09	12.33	20.60	30.96	71.49	18
		NET PROFIT OR (LOSS) PER ORDER $		4.43	(3.02)	(2.85)	(2.23)	.07	3.98	12.02	22.08	64.90	
		" " AFTER DISTRIB. COSTS $		16,023	(181)	(228)	(1,115)	105	3,184	6,010	1,766	6,482	
	OTHER CUST.	GROSS SALES IN $	100%	540,000	2,000	45,500	175,500	60,000	48,000	64,000	52,000	93,000	19
		COST OF GOODS SOLD $	70.526%	380,841	1,411	32,089	123,773	42,316	33,852	45,137	36,674	65,589	
		GROSS PROFIT BEFORE ADJUST.		159,159	589	13,411	51,727	17,684	14,148	18,863	15,326	27,411	
		CASH DISCTS. ON SALES	1.04%	5,616	21	473	1,825	624	499	666	541	967	
		LOSSES ON ALLCES. & RET'NS.	0.4%	2,160	8	182	702	240	192	256	208	372	
		MARK DOWN ON OBSOLETE MDSE.	1.4%	7,560	28	637	2,457	840	672	896	728	1,302	
		GROSS PROFIT		143,823	532	12,119	46,743	15,980	12,785	17,045	13,849	24,770	
		NUMBER OF ORDERS		21,645	500	6,500	11,700	1,500	600	400	200	245	19
		GROSS PROFIT PER ORDER $		6.65	1.06	1.87	4.00	10.65	21.31	42.61	69.25	101.10	
		DISTRIBUTION COSTS PER ORDER $		7.04	3.15	3.82	5.36	9.84	16.82	30.58	47.88	68.47	18
		NET PROFIT PER ORDER $		(.39)	(2.09)	(1.95)	(1.36)	.81	4.49	12.03	21.37	32.63	
		" " AFTER DISTRIB. COSTS $		(8,726)	(1,045)	(12,675)	(15,912)	1,215	2,694	4,812	4,274	7,911	

Fig. 31. (Form 23) Profit or Loss per Sales Order for Each Class of Customer, Territory, and Order Category.

TERRITORY: A CUSTOMER CLASS: CHAIN STORES PRODUCT GROUP: A1

COMPARISON OF AVERAGE DISTRIBUTION COSTS BASED ON DOLLAR SALES WITH THOSE BASED ON COST ACCOUNTING PRINCIPLES. ALSO HOW AN ADJUSTMENT INDEX IS OBTAINED FOR APPLICATION TO A CUSTOMER'S INVOICE TO CORRECT "AVERAGE" SALES PRICES.

Source Form	CUSTOMER'S ORDER CATEGORY	$	Under 5.	5 to 10.	10 to 20.	20 to 50.	50 to 100.	100 to 200.	200 to 300.	Over 300.	TOTALS
		CATEGORY	-	G	F	E	D	C	B	A	
19---	TOTAL SALES IN YEAR PER CATEGORY	$	100.	350.	2 250.	10 000.	32 000	48 000	52 000	55 300	200 000.
19---	NUMBER OF ORDERS RECEIVED IN YEAR		25	50	150.	250	400	300	200	125	1 500
19---	AVERAGE AMOUNT PER ORDER	$	4.	7.	15.	40.	80.	160.	260	442.	
23---	GROSS PROFIT	$	21.	72.	459.	2 039.	6 525.	9 787	10 553.	11 324.	40 780.
	DISTRIB. COSTS AT AVGE. OF 14.05% TO SALES	$	14.	49.	316.	1 405.	4 496	6 744	7306	7 770.	28 100.
	NET PROFIT-BASED ON AVGE. COSTS	$	7.	23.	1 43.	634.	2 029	3043	3 247	3 554.	12 680.
18---	DIST. COSTS PER ORDER	$	4.70	5.29	6.34	9.17	13.40	21.61	32.00	50.23	
18---	" " ALL ORDERS	$	117.00	264.	951.	2,292	5, 360	6,483	6,400	6,279	28 147 (a)
23---	NET PROFIT OR (LOSS) - AS CORRECTED	$	(96)	(192)	(492.)	(253.)	1 165.	3 304.	4 153.	5 045.	12 637 (a)
	% DISTRIB. COSTS, BASED ON COST ANALYSIS, TO SALES	%	117.50	75.57	42.27	22.93	16.75	13.51	12.31	11.35	14.05
	DIFFCE. BETWEEN AVGE. DISTRIB. COSTS AND THOSE BASED ON COST ANALYSIS - (UNDERCHARGED) OVER-CHARGED	%	(b) (103.)	(b) (61.)	(b) (28.22)	(b) (8.88)	(b) (2.70)	(c) .54	(c) 1.74	(c) 2.70	-0-

(a) Differences are due to fractions. (b) Customers in these categories were undercharged. Corrective action should be directed to this "small orders" problem (see "Outlines" pages 186-188). If, however these small orders are occasional or infrequent and the bulk of the orders given by A, B, or C customers were orders above $100. each, no managerial action need be considered. (c) Customers in these categories were overcharged. Price adjustments should be granted to them on each one of their invoices (see below)

ADJUSTMENTS TO "AVERAGE" SALES PRICES - (SUMMARY OF FORM 24 - IN %'s)

TERRI-TORY	CUST. CLASS	PRODUCT GROUP	-	G	F	E	D	C	B	A
			ORDER CATEGORY							
A	CHAIN	A 1	(103.)	(61.)	(28.22)	(8.88)	(2.70)	.54	1.74	2.70
"	"	A 2								
"	"	A 3								
B	CHAIN	A 1								
"	"	A 2								
"	"	A 3								

CUSTOMER'S INVOICE

PRODUCT	EXTENSION	CATEGORY (c)	TOTAL
A 1	$ 1.00	.54	$ .9946
A 4	1. 00	1.74	.9826
B 5	1. 00	- 2.70	1.027

Fig. 32. (Form 24) Comparison of Average Distribution Costs to Cost Accounting Costs; Adjustment Index to Correct Average Sales Price; and Summary of Adjustments.

HEADINGS FOR OPERATING REPORTS

1. BUDGET FOR A MONTH—ALL PRODUCT GROUPS

	PROD. A		PROD. B		PROD. C		PROD. D						TOTAL ALL PRODUCTS		TRANSACTIONS OF EACH FUNCTION DURING MONTH	
	%	AMT.	%	AMT.	%	AMT.	%	AMT.					%	AMT.	PER UNIT	TOTAL TRANSACTIONS

2. ACTUAL FOR A MONTH—ALL PRODUCT GROUPS

	PROD. A		PROD. B		PROD. C		PROD. D						TOTAL ALL PRODUCTS		TRANSACTIONS OF EACH FUNCTION DURING MONTH	
	%	AMT.	%	AMT.	%	AMT.	%	AMT.					%	AMT.	PER UNIT	TOTAL TRANSACTIONS

3. ACTUAL FOR THE YEAR—PRODUCT A

	JAN.		FEB.		TOTAL 2 MONTHS		MARCH		TOTAL 3 MONTHS							
	%	AMT.	%	AMT.	%	AMT.	%	AMT.	%	AMT.						

4. VARIANCES FROM BUDGET—PRODUCT A

	JANUARY						FEBRUARY									
	BUDGET		ACTUAL		VARIANCE		BUDGET		ACTUAL		VARIANCE					
	%	AMT.	%	AMT.	%	AMT.	%	AMT.	%	AMT.	%	AMT.				

Fig. 33. Headings for Operating Reports.

FORM 15

'000 omitted — OPERATING REPORT — PRODUCT GROUP A1 — YEAR 32

Source Form	FUNCTION No.	ACCOUNT	④%	AMT.	%	AMT.	%	AMT.	%	AMT.
	A	Net Sales	100.0	1,987.						
	B	Gross Profits	25.9	514.						
	C	Direct Marketing Costs	15.6	310.						
		Contribution ③	10.3	204.						
	D	Distribution Costs (Figure 35)	7.2	143.						
		Operating Profit	3.07	61						
	C	Direct Marketing Costs								
5	C1	Payroll-Salesmen	5.7	114.0						
	C2	-Other Selling	1.5	29.4						
	C3	-Sales Promotion	1.8	35.1						
	C4	-Stock Marketing	1.4	28.3						
	C5	-Delivery	1.8	35.4						
	C6	-Administrative	1.5	30.2						
2	C7	Expenses-Delivery	.6	12.6						
	C8	-Sales Promotion	.5	9.1						
	C9	-Selling	-	.8						
	C10	-Administrative	-	.3						
12	C11	Rent-Stock Marketing	.2	4.7						
	C12	-Delivery	.1	1.1						
	C13	-Selling	-	.2						
	C14	-Administrative		.4						
	C15	Postage, Insurance, Dep'n. ②	.3	6.6						
①	C16	Telephone	.1	2.2						
	C17									
		TOTAL DIRECT MARKETING COSTS	15.6	310.4						
	E	Investment in Facilities		700.						
	F	Sales Turnover to Invstm't. ⑤ ⑧		2.8						
	G	% Net Profit to Sales		3.07						
	H	Return on Investment ⑥		8.6%						
	I	Break-Even Sales ⑦		1,393.						

NOTES: ① FORM J.E.'s; ② Insurance and depreciation on factory facilities are included in production costs; ③ Constribution to distributed expenses and return on investment; ④ Percent to sales; ⑤ A divided by E; ⑥ F multiplied by G; ⑦ D divided by 10.266%; ⑧ 2.8 times.

Fig. 34. Operating Report—Product Group A1.

OPERATING REPORTS

Operating reports can be easily prepared using the data accumulated in *Form 15* (Figure 23). These reports can take the following form:

1. Budget for a particular month for all merchandise departments or products.
2. Actual costs for a particular month for all merchandise departments or products.
3. Actual costs for a particular merchandise department or product by months and cumulatively for year to date.
4. Actual costs, budget, and variance for a particular merchandise department or product for each month and cumulatively.

The headings for these operating reports are shown in Figure 33, and the operating reports and schedules of distributed costs for a month of product A1 are illustrated in Figures 34 and 35, respectively.

► NOTE: In addition to operating reports, the costs accumulated by functions and products can also be used to provide decision-making aids such as return on investment, break-even, contribution to overhead, and other reports discussed in following chapters.

FORM 15 OPERATING REPORT—DISTRIBUTED COSTS PRODUCT GROUP A1 YEAR

Function A/C No.	Alloc. Basis No.	SERVICE OR FUNCTION GROUP	SERVICE	%	AMT.	%	AMT.	%	AMT.	%	AMT.
D1	7	Del'y.	Out. Freight & Truckers		350						
D2	33	"	Sundry Delivery		553						
D3	9	"	Packing Supplies	.1	2,767						
D4	39	"	Traffic, Shipping, Out Of Town	.2	4,453						
D5	11	"	Garage, Trucks - Local	.4	7,494						
D6	34	"	Labels & Labels Department		1,236						
			TOTAL DELIVERY	.8	16,853						
		Sales									
D7	2	Promot.	Mimeograph Department	.1	1,941						
D8	12	"	Sales Promotion Department	.5	10,387						
D9	13	"	Literature, Displays, Samples	.6	11,774						
D10	14	"	Correspondence Department	.2	3,556						
D11	19	"	Advertising	.1	2,588						
			TOTAL SALES PROMOTION	1.5	30,246						
D12	24	Selling	Salesmen's Prizes & General	.1	2,513						
D13	19	"	Sundry Selling	.1	2,095						
D14	25	"	Branch Office	.2	3,715						
D15	15	"	Orders by Phone, Dept.	.5	10,767						
D16	16	"	Price-Checking Department	.1	2,144						
D17	35	"	Returns-Salesmen's Fault		151						
D18	30	"	Complaints Department	.3	5,178						
		TOTAL SELLING (FORM 15)		1.3	26,563						
D19	19	Admin.	Sundry General Expenses	.3	6,234						
D20	28	"	Mailing Department	.1	1,970						
D21	17	"	Credit and Collection Dept.	.3	6,225						
D22	20	"	Accounting Department	.2	3,870						
D23	1	"	Accts. Rec., Cashier, Subscrip.	.7	14,115						
D24	29	"	Filing Department	.1	1,782						
D25	8	"	Calcul. Machine Department	.3	6,016						
D26	3	"	Billing Department	.6	11,097						
D27	21	"	Accounts Payable Department	.2	3,604						
D28	36	"	Payroll Dept. & Pensions	.5	10,539						
D29	37	"	Maintenance - General		985						
D30	22	"	State Franchise Tax		800						
D31	6	"	Insurance Department		166						
D32	18	"	Bad Debts Provision	.1	2,400						
		TOTAL ADMINISTRATIVE		3.5	69,803						
		TOTAL DISTRIBUTED COSTS		7.2	143,465						

Fig. 35. Operating Report for Distributed Costs—Product Group A1.

12

Cost Accounting for Service Organizations

CONTENTS

12

Cost Accounting for Service Organizations

There is neither sufficient time for the natural evolution of a new technique of accounting tailored specifically to the requirements of service organizations, nor a real need for such a technique. Our existing basic accounting principles have proven to be valid and can be readily transferred to the service industries. The accountant's next step is one of adapting and combining our present accounting techniques into modern and flexible systems for the service industries. These systems are required to meet the mounting problems of changing markets and the numerous demands on today's businesses imposed by tax laws and information-requiring statutes.

This chapter is designed to briefly describe how some of the universally accepted accounting practices such as responsibility accounting, budgeting, cost analysis and control reporting can be applied to the development of a cost accounting and management control system for nonmanufacturing businesses. Since it is not practical to cover each type of service organization in a few pages, the major emphasis in this discussion will be placed on the business and personal service group not involved in the production or handling of physical goods. In number of businesses and in total receipts, this group comprises a substantial segment of the service industries. In the interest of simplicity, in this chapter this group of business and personal service units shall be combined and referred to under the single classification of business service organizations. However, many of the concepts and techniques discussed are equally appropriate for the product handling segment of the service industries.

This chapter has been divided into three sections:

1. Cost accounting and control procedures for the service business.
2. Budgeting for the control of service businesses.
3. Illustration of cost and control techniques.

► NOTE: Cost accounting and budgeting are subjects of other chapters in this volume. They are discussed briefly in this chapter only to establish an appropriate frame of reference.

COST SYSTEMS AND CONTROL PROCEDURES FOR THE SERVICE BUSINESS

Cost accounting is highly refined and has attained its greatest development in manufacturing. However, as an orderly process of compiling detailed information about costs in relation to the operations of a business, it is as essential to service industries as it is to manufacturing enterprises. Thus, the cost systems needed by many service businesses are not fundamentally different from those required in product organizations.

The cost system must be custom designed to meet the particular requirements of the specific organization involved. Of the basic cost accounting systems used in the product producing industries—(1) specific order costs, and (2) continuous process costs—the first is generally best suited to the service industries. A characteristic prevalent in business service organizations is that each customer's order is different in its requirements and specifications from every other customer's order. Because of this, there is need for a system of compiling cost data that, to the limit of practicality, identifies and segregates each element of cost applicable to each individual order. Some of the advantages the specific order cost system offers to the business service organization are:

1. The ability to determine the profit or loss for each job.
2. The ability to improve techniques in estimating and bidding, with greater assurance that each job will yield a reasonable profit.
3. The ability to evaluate the cost control performance of the manager responsible for the service project.

Continuous process cost procedures are not appropriate for the service business that is not engaged in continuous or mass production where individual units of output lose their identity. Standard cost procedures are similarly inappropriate due to the absence of direct materials and the fact that many services are mental as opposed to physical. This makes it difficult, if not impossible, to apply industrial engineering techniques. Often, however, many of the clerical functions that support the service activities do lend themselves to methods analysis, the development of standards and finite measures of productivity. Since standards of this type and in these circumstances are usually introduced for the purposes of control in a budgeting program, they are discussed in a latter section of this chapter.

One objective of any cost system should be the accumulation and presentation of essential cost data to management for its use in controlling the operations of the business. Therefore, this discussion of cost accounting includes comments relating to control procedures.

Significant cost factors in the service business. Generally, fewer cost centers and classifications are needed in service organizations than are ordinarily required in product businesses. Also, employee costs are often the largest single element to be controlled. To illustrate, consider some of the primary factors influencing the operating costs of a business service organization and a product business. In the typical business service organization, some two-thirds of the operating costs are employee costs. Therefore, the most significant influences upon operating costs are: (1) management's ability to select personnel with the skills necessary to provide the desired quality and quantity of service, and (2) management's ability to control the utilization and productivity of the selected personnel.

These same cost influences, of course, exist in the product producing business, but are less significant because the ratio of employee costs to total costs is much lower. But of even more importance, costs in the product business that are minor or nonexistent in the business service organization are:

1. The cost of materials and production equipment.
2. The organization's skills in research and the development of new products that can be produced and marketed at a profit.
3. The organization's ability to keep abreast or ahead of its competition in technological advancement and effectiveness in manufacturing methods.
4. The organization's ability to evaluate consumer demand as a basis for effective inventory control policies and practices.

Although there are many other costs shared by both the business service and product organizations, this does not dull the fact that the management of the business service organization has a greater opportunity for absolute control of operating costs than does the management of a product business.

Assigning cost responsibility. The accountant should be warned against becoming so intrigued with the techniques of cost accounting or budgeting that he overlooks the fact that costs are controlled by people—not by highly refined systems. By organization or assignment, some *one* individual must be made responsible for *each* element of cost. Techniques to establish this accountability are popularly grouped under the term *responsibility accounting.*

One of the first steps in assigning cost responsibility is departmentalization. Many business service organizations are not adequately departmentalized. This can frequently be attributed to the fact that (1) the service they provide is not highly diversified, (2) the operational activity is directly and concurrently related to the particular service involved, and (3) many are owner-managed or operated by partners, each having very similar responsibilities. Although these circumstances may prevail, it is essential for control purposes that some form of departmentalization be established. The control of costs cannot be really effective until accountability is assigned to the individual responsible for incurring each element of cost.

The assignment of cost accountability must be done carefully. In comparison with product industries where work in process and finished goods inventories are involved, the service manager has limited flexibility as to schedule and rate of activity. The efforts of nearly all segments of the service business are directly related to the particular service being provided *currently.* Each manager, therefore, to obtain the best possible economic results from his unit, must largely depend upon other managers meeting their schedules. He should not, for this reason, be held responsible for unfavorable cost variances that are due to the failure of others over whom he has no direct control. Admittedly difficult to institute, cost responsibility is nonetheless an important element in the development of an effective cost control system.

Classifying costs aid control. It is fundamental that costs are best controlled at their source. After cost responsibility and accountability have been established, the accountant's next task is to establish classifications of costs that are responsive to control efforts. Only by this procedure can reports be prepared that will accurately demonstrate the degree of the manager's success in exercising cost and operational control.

Initially, costs should be classified broadly by the nature of the expenditure, such as salaries, supplies, communications, insurance, taxes and occupancy. Next, these major classifications should be expanded, but only to the point necessary to provide useful cost information. The list of accounts required for most service businesses will not be as complex as often needed by the product businesses.

Since specific order cost procedures are usually appropriate for service businesses, it is important to segregate direct and indirect costs. Within practical limits, all possible costs should be classified as direct. By minimizing the indirect cost allocations to each order, cost control actions can be more precise and profitability can be determined with greater accuracy.

Cost analysis and operating control reports. The development of a cost accounting system that generates a mass of financial data serves no useful purpose until the data has been transformed into effective management reports. Such reports must be adapted to the responsibilities of the manager so that he can use them for cost and operating control decisions. When this is done, the broad objectives of the cost system have been met.

► WARNING: Manufacturing management often contends, with some justification, that accounting reports do not point up the facts required to make important operating and control decisions. Since reporting techniques are less mature in service organizations, the accountant must constantly strive to understand which factors are important and require accent. He must carefully explore the specific situation and avoid accumulating and reporting marginal or useless information.

The accountant must determine *with management* what reports are needed for control purposes. To do this, appropriate consideration must be given to the factors peculiar to the situation with which he is dealing. These include:

1. Objectives.
2. Policies.
3. Organization.
4. State of development of the operations.
5. State of accounting knowledge and the management skills of the personalities involved.

6. Form, content, and frequency of reporting.
7. Special analyses and reports required for specific phases of business activity.

Pertinent information of this type will provide the accountant with the understanding required to properly integrate the cost system and reporting procedure.

Reports containing financial data become control reports when they measure the actual results of operations against some form of benchmark or standard. However, the accountant's responsibility does not end at the point where he has provided reports that include actual and standard data. The analysis and interpretation of the data included in the reports can be his most important contribution.

The management of a service business is often directly involved in the activities of business promotion and in direct work with clients. Consequently, they have little time available for the study of reports and evaluation of operating conditions. They need to be relieved of as much burdensome and repetitious detail as possible. The reports should tell them just what they want and need to know in a form that is readily comprehensible. The analysis of data in the report should immediately highlight exceptions and motivate the manager to take suitable control action.

The accountant should apply constructive thinking to the financial problems of the business, study the economic environment in which it operates, and develop the best possible means for the presentation and interpretation of economic facts. By so doing, he will establish himself as an important member of the management team. He insures this position by promptly providing highly individualized reports of what is happening and what should be happening in a manner that avoids distorted perspective and misplaced emphasis. His effectiveness is increased if he is constantly alert to the realities of the present and the probabilities of the future.

BUDGETING FOR THE CONTROL OF SERVICE BUSINESSES

A budget keyed to profit objectives and developed as a detailed operating plan is perhaps the most valuable tool management can have to assist it in directing and controlling the operations of the service business. To be effective, the budget must be the result of joint effort and collaboration by the management of the business and be adopted by that management as a definite coordinated approach to the future conduct of the business.

Forecasts. A prime function of management, and a prerequisite for effective budgeting, is intelligent planning. The accountant can provide a valuable service in the translation of plans into realistic forecasts. He does this by interpreting for management the financial objectives and policies of the business. Although the responsibility for forecasts rests with management, the accountant should check the soundness of the volume levels selected. It is advisable to forecast for a full-year period in spite of the uncertainties inherent in service businesses. When this is done, it is possible to anticipate year-end results and to replan to meet objectives as conditions change. Many businesses constantly reappraise year-end results so that surprises are avoided.

At the beginning of the year, the budget will equal the forecast in estimating expected results if it reflects the internal and external influences upon income and costs, such as:

1. Formulated policies.
2. Stated objectives.
3. Limitations of capital.
4. Limitations of the skills of management and other personnel.
5. Selling and pricing practices of competitors.
6. Economic attitudes.
7. Projections of business indices related to the service to be provided.

There is a definite need for forecast budgets in any organization. However, the accountant must be constantly alert to the limitations of this type of budget. It must be recognized, for example, that a budget cannot effectively serve in the dual capacity of a forecast and a basis for control unless each separate function of the total business operates at a rate of activity comparable to that used in developing the forecast.

Service industries are usually supported by personal expenditures and by product businesses. This, coupled with the dynamics of the economy, makes it difficult to anticipate rates of activity for each function of the business. Many businesses frequently revise and improve their forecasts throughout the year to reflect the most current and anticipated near-term conditions. Often, however, these same businesses adopt the up-dated forecasts as revised budgets without evaluating the changes against their financial policies and objectives. Thus, as continually revised, the budget is no longer a well-ordered plan that accurately tests the ability of management to accomplish predetermined goals.

Developing control budgets. In a service business subject to considerable fluctuation, it is wise to be prepared for the changes when they occur. If it is true that forecast budgets have limited value for control purposes, consideration should be given to budgeting techniques that have demonstrated value for control in product organizations. It is recognized that supplementary flexible or variable budgets overcome the shortcomings of a forecast budget for controlling manufacturing expenses (where the relation between volume and costs is most direct). In many service businesses, where the largest single cost element is the cost of employees providing the service, there is also a direct relationship between volume and cost. It is possible, then, to develop budgets that provide a basis for control by comparing actual with budgeted costs at the rate of activity or volume experienced.

Although a specific order cost system may have been established, with its requirements for a high degree of cost identification and segregation being met, it cannot be assumed that the cost classifications are entirely suitable for a budgetary control program.

► WARNING: Regardless of the type of cost system in use, it will include allocated or prorated costs. Although prorations may be sufficiently accurate for the purpose of determining profitability of a unit, prorated costs are extremely difficult to control unless the cost classifications behind them are sufficiently complete and detailed to make it possible to assign each to a cost responsibility center.

Cost classifications established for budgetary control purposes can and should be compatible with the objectives of the cost accounting system. Cost classifications should be tailored for each cost responsibility unit of the business, whether its function is a direct one of providing the specific service or an indirect one supporting the ability to provide the service. The costs accumulated for purposes of controlling the indirect functions should be prorated as necessary to meet the objectives of the cost system in use.

Selecting units of activity or volume. A distinct advantage of flexible budgets is their adaptability in providing the best possible measure of what actual expenditures should have been at the actual rate of activity. Such comparison is possible only when realistic measures of volume exist and the wholly variable costs, as well as the variable portions of other costs, have been identified.

In many service organizations, particularly those providing business and personal services, revenue is generated from the sale of time required to perform the service. This direct service unit of activity can be expressed in terms of dollars of revenue, direct service salary dollars or productive hours of the assigned staff. In most instances, productive hours would be the most stable unit of measure, because revenue and salaries are affected by fluctuations of the economy and not entirely controlled by management.

In the functions not directly involved in providing service, it is often necessary to look for other units of management. For example, if the customer is provided with a written report, the unit of measure for report preparation could be the number of pages included in the report. Other examples of units that measure the rate of activity for indirect cost centers are the number of invoices prepared by customer billing and the number of salary checks prepared by payroll.

In administrative areas, where it is difficult to identify a unit of activity that will accurately measure volume, it may be possible to use the same units selected to measure the rate of activity in other areas of the business. In some cost centers, because of management policy decisions, expenses may have little relationship with activity rates. This could be true, for example, in connection with a business promotion department where a fixed sum will be spent over a definite period of time for the purpose of stimulating the future growth of the business. Although situations of this type increase the complexity of the total budgeting program, they do not negate the value of the flexible or variable budget as an instrument of control.

► OBSERVATION: If considerable difficulty is encountered in identifying units of productivity for an indirect function, the accountant should consider the possible adaptation and application of other techniques used by product businesses.

► EXAMPLE: The control of service department costs in many manufacturing businesses has been accomplished by the use of standard costs as budgets or goals for these activities. Such standards, developed by using tested industrial engineering techniques, complement the budgeting program and provide management with improved guidance in controlling costs. Although established for control purposes, standards often also lead to cost reductions. Chapter 10 contains a complete discussion of the use of standard costs for these and other purposes.

Income factors. Control-type budgeting in manufacturing generally emphasizes the comparison of actual costs with cost goals. The importance of controlling costs cannot be denied. However, in some service businesses there are income factors that deserve equal or even greater budgetary control attention. For instance, many banks, finance, insurance and investment companies are obtaining substantial portions of their income from the effective use and turnover of customers' capital. Certainly, the budgetary control program developed for these organizations must include appropriate goals or standards for factors such as (1) the rate of return on investments, (2) capital turnover ratios, (3) maximum and minimum liquidity, and (4) minimum working funds.

In service organizations of this type, it is possible that employee cost is a relatively small percentage of gross income. Within reasonable limits, an increase in service provided with low cost clerical assistance will attract more customers' capital for investment, resulting in an increased profit. Managers in these institutions recognize the value of budgets and standards in assisting them in their efforts to control the productivity of employees and the cost of operations.

In other classes of service industries, such as transportation and communications, substantial investment in facilities and equipment is necessary. The costs connected with financing the investment, necessary replacement of facilities and equipment, and the operation and maintenance programs all require effective management control if the business is to be successful. Once again, the accountant should look to the existing control techniques that are proving successful in product organizations and modify these to meet the requirements of the service business. The accountant thus needs to be alert to the unusual nature of the prime factors in the profit-making function of the business and tailor the system to reflect these factors.

Summary. In this section, the advantages of a control-type budgetary program have been cited. Perhaps the most important of these is the strong encouragement provided management to (1) formalize and reach agreement on the policies and objectives of the business, (2) establish and assign cost and operating responsibility where it can be effective, and (3) adopt an adequate cost accounting and reporting system. When these conditions exist in an organization, the basis exists for improved measurement of performance against goals and improved managerial effectiveness through the practice of the principle of *management by exception.*

ILLUSTRATION OF COST AND CONTROL TECHNIQUES

For purposes of clarifying the concepts previously discussed, a hypothetical business service organization is depicted. This example is based on the following set of assumed facts:

1. The business is partner owned and managed; all partners devote 100% of their business efforts to the firm.
2. A single type of service is provided.
3. Clients are provided an estimate of the time and charges required to perform the service.
4. Total income is received from clients served.
5. Direct service to clients is provided by a *client staff* consisting of partners and specialists.
6. Each partner and specialist is assigned an individual hourly rate for the purpose of billing his time to clients.
7. Each partner is assigned a salary; each specialist has a salary.
8. Written reports are issued to clients at the conclusion of each assignment.

General operating objectives and conditions. In this business it is the practice to charge the client for the actual hours worked at the hourly billing rate, plus the expenses incurred by the *client staff* in the performance of the work. The expenses billed to the client are nonoperational in nature. They are incurred only because of the requirements of the work for the client, and include items such as (1) travel and subsistence, and (2) the cost of salaries and materials required in the preparation of a report.

Since the nonoperating expenses are billed to the client at cost, the billing rate of the client staff is established at a level that will cover the salaries of the staff, the cost of operations needed to support the staff, and provide a net profit that is consistent with the objectives of the firm. The billing rates are competitive with those of other organizations providing comparable services.

Each engagement is *unlike* each of the others in scope and characteristics. The average assignment requires a client staff consisting of a partner as manager and four specialists. The average length of time required to complete each assignment is two months. However, the jobs vary considerably within a range of one man for one month to teams of eight men for one year.

In order to generate a profit from the work, the partner, as manager of the project, has a responsibility to provide the required service within the maximum limit of the estimated charges to the client. As an owner of the business, he is highly motivated to accomplish this for two primary reasons. First, if the client is well satisfied with the quality and quantity of the work, he will continue to be a client each time he needs such services. Second, his actual income is finally determined by the amount of profit available for distribution to the partners at the close of each fiscal year.

What type of cost accounting should be used? Considering all factors involved in this situation, the specific order type of cost accounting system is clearly the best choice for this firm because it provides each project manager with much of the data he needs for the effective project management.

In specific order cost accounting, a project numbering system is used to segregate income and costs for each project. In this case, a simple coding system assigns the next highest number to each client as the project orders are received. Additionally, for statistical purposes, each *project* is assigned a suffix number to indicate the consecutive number of times the client has been serviced by the firm. For example, if the ABC Corporation was the fiftieth client the firm had served, the client would be identified as #50. If the firm was engaged for the tenth time by this client, the suffix code would be #—10. The complete project code in this example would be #50—10.

A project coding system similar to the one just described simplifies the accumulation of current and historical data. Where data processing equipment is used, the code is helpful in (1) accumulating individual project income and costs, (2) maintaining accounts receivable records, and (3) preparing invoices for clients. In addition, the client project code can be useful in forecasting and developing future business promotion programs where an analysis by clients is required.

Who has the cost responsibility? The project manager has been described as the person who estimates the charges for the service and is in charge of providing the service. Therefore, he is in a position to control the accuracy of estimated charges, the productivity of the client project staff, and the incidental nonoperating project costs.

The manager's project control is vital, but it, nevertheless, falls short of the mark of *complete* control. This point can be illustrated best by the basic organization of this hypothetical firm. (See Figure 1.)

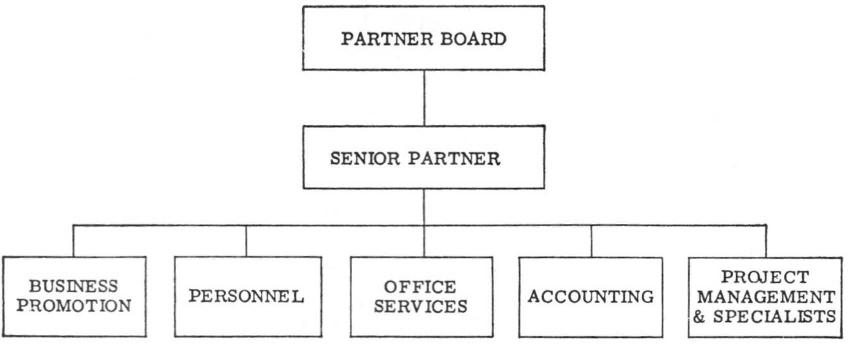

Fig. 1. Organization Chart of Hypothetical Firm.

A brief description of responsibilities follows:

1. *Partner board.* All partners are members. The group functions much as a corporate board of directors in approving policies and setting objectives.

2. *Senior partner.* Chairman of the partner board and chief administrative executive of the firm.

3. *Business promotion.* Responsibilities include the development of programs to promote the firm's services in accordance with policies, and short-term and long-range growth plans and objectives. The project managers are responsible for implementing the programs.

4. *Personnel.* Responsibilities include (a) the selection and employment of staff specialists, (b) the assignment of specialists to client projects, and (c) the administration of the salary and billing rate programs for the client staff.

5. *Office service.* Responsible for providing adequate facilities and general services necessary for operating the firm including (a) the preparation of reports, (b) travel accommodations, (c) secretarial services, (d) communications, and (e) furniture and equipment.

6. *Accounting.* Responsible for (a) general and cost accounting, (b) budgeting, (c) taxes, (d) payrolls, (e) client billing, (f) insurance, and (g) the administration of the employee benefit programs.

7. *Project management and specialists.* This is not a department in the usual sense. It is the client project staff. The project managers are responsible for selling the firm's services and managing the projects sold. The specialists are responsible for assisting the project managers in providing the firm's services.

Assuming that the organization within each of the functions has been properly developed and defined, it is now possible to establish cost responsibility at the "grass roots" level for each person having the authority to incur costs.

Classifying cost and income. The next task is an analysis of the costs and income necessary in operating the business, and the development of classifications that makes it possible to assign each cost and related income to the individual in a position to exercise control. This step is essential for cost control in spite of the fact that many of the costs will later be allocated or prorated to specific client service projects in order to determine the profit or loss of each project. Cost and income classifications will be discussed under three broad categories:

1. Direct costs.
2. Indirect costs.
3. Income.

1. *Direct costs.* In the illustration we are considering, direct costs are a combination of the salaries of the client staff and the incidental expenses necessary to provide the service required by the client. Since the firm charges its clients for time at a rate higher than actual cost but does not mark up the cost of incidental expenses, direct costs must be segregated into *at least* the two classifications of (a) incidental expenses, and (b) direct salary costs.

a. *Incidental expenses.* The level of incidental expenses required on each project is usually directly related to the nature of the service required and the location of the client. These expenses, consisting mainly of travel and subsistence for the client staff and the cost of report preparation, are not all controlled by the same individuals. The project manager controls the travel and subsistence costs. He identifies the requirements for the report. Beyond this, he relies on the manager of the report department to control these costs. Therefore, there is a need for further segregating the incidental expenses into at least two additional classifications of (1) travel and subsistence, and (2) report preparation.

b. *Direct salary costs—managers.* The level of direct salary cost for each project is determined by the amount of time the client staff actually spends on the project. This time is charged to the client project. Examination of the allocation of their total time, however, discloses a need for more than one classification. Since the project managers are involved in the management of projects and the promotion of business, and are paid for nonproductive time during vacations, holidays, and sick leave, the salaries assigned need to be segregated between:

(1) Managers' project salaries.
(2) Manager's promotion salaries.
(3) Managers' nonproductive salaries.

c. *Direct salary costs—specialists.* Because of the caliber of the specialists required and the value of their training and experience, it is not possible to employ them on a "when, as, and if needed" basis. There will be times when a specialist cannot be immediately reassigned to a new client project upon completion of each job. Nevertheless, their salaries continue during the time they are unassigned, as well as during periods of illness, vacations and holidays. The project manager has a responsibility to control the productivity of the specialists while assigned to his project. Others in the firm must be responsible for the control of the cost of the idle and other unassigned time. Consequently, there is a need for segregating the salary cost of the specialists between:

(1) Specialists' project salaries.
(2) Specialists' nonproductive salaries.

To summarize, the direct costs in this firm should be classified as follows:
(1) Travel and subsistence.
(2) Report preparation.
(3) Managers' project salaries.
(4) Specialists' project salaries.

2. *Indirect costs.* Except for the nonproductive time of project managers and specialists, the indirect cost classifications needed for this firm are comparable to those customarily used in most service departments of manufacturing businesses. Examples are administrative and clerical salaries, travel, communications, supplies, services, and occupancy.

Income. The client project ledger is charged with all of the staff time at billing rates and all incidental expenses at cost. If the total of the time and expense charges exceeds the total charges quoted to the client at the time the service was authorized, the firm must absorb the excess. The classifications of income should be (a) charges to projects, and (b) adjustments to project charges. The net of the two totals equals the amount billed to the client.

Chart of accounts. From this brief discussion of account classifications, the summary chart of accounts could be as follows:

Account No.	*Description*	
10	Income	
	11	Charges to Client Projects
	12	Adjustments to Project Charges
20	Direct Costs	
	21	Managers' Project Salaries
	22	Specialists' Project Salaries
30	Indirect Salaries	
	31	Managers' Promotion Salaries
	32	Managers' Nonproductive Salaries
	33	Specialists' Nonproductive Salaries
	34	Administrative Salaries
	35	Clerical Salaries
40*	Travel and Communications	
50*	Supplies, Services and Fees	
60*	Insurance, Taxes and Pensions	
70*	Use and Occupancy	
80*	Miscellaneous	

(*Each of these indirect cost categories should be detailed as necessary for adequate control.)

Departmental prefix or suffix codes may be used with the account classifications as needed to assign the costs to specific responsibility centers.

Budgeting. This hypothetical business, like all others, needs a forecast and a plan of action. Because of the individualistic nature of both the specific services provided to clients and the partnership form of organization, the operating plan must provide assurance that the total operation can be coordinated and that there exists a sound basis for controlling the different parts of the business. In this example, if we include the partners' income in this category, over 75% of the cost of operations are employee costs. Also, fixed costs are very low, consisting mainly of offices and office equipment. With this high degree of relationship between volume and costs, it can be seen that flexible budgets are highly desirable.

Selecting the units of volume or activity. It has been pointed out that a principal advantage of the flexible budgeting system for control purposes is the ability to determine or predetermine what the cost levels should be at any specific rate of activity. After the functions of the business are properly segregated or departmentalized and the costs are classified in a manner that makes them subject to control, the next step is to determine the units of activity or other factors that affect cost levels. With no intent of preparing an exhaustive list for this illustrative firm, some of the units and factors might be as follows:

1. *Business promotion.* The cost level in this department is not directly related to volume of business. It could be termed a managed cost. The Board of Partners approves business promotion program budgets that have been developed in accordance with the firm's policies and short-term and long-range growth objectives.

2. *Personnel.* Based on the responsibilities described earlier, more than one unit may be applied. There might be a separate budget allowance for (a) the cost of employing each specialist, (b) the cost of staffing each project, and (c) the cost of administering the salary and billing rate programs based upon a standard allowance for each member of the client staff.

3. *Accounting.* Because of equipment requirements, not all of the costs in this department are wholly variable. To avoid a lengthy discussion here, let us assume that all the equipment is needed for the normal range of business volume and are, therefore, fixed costs. The budget for variable costs may be an aggregate of many units applicable to sections of the department, such as:

a. The number of time and expense reports submitted by the client staff.
b. The number of active client accounts.
c. The number of payroll checks required.
d. The number of machine hours logged for each machine.

4. *Office services.* The principal functions aid the units of activity or other factors involved might be:

a. *Report preparation.* Several units could be used. For the typing operation, the number of masters (pages) typed; for the reproduction operation, the number of plates and copies reproduced; and for supplies, the number of plates, pages per plate and binding costs, based on the number of report copies required.
b. *Travel and reservations.* This budget might be based upon the number of travel orders placed.
c. *Secretarial services.* This budget allowance could be established as a standard ratio of secretaries to client and administrative management personnel requiring this service.
d. *Equipment and furniture.* This budget can be established on a basis that is consistent with equipment and furniture standards for the firm. The standard should be related to the number of offices and personnel required and the maintenance and replacement policies and programs.
e. *Communications.* The budget for the variable costs of communications can be related to the volume of business.

5. *Project management and specialists.* The applicable unit for the direct salary costs of this group is dollar volume of business. To facilitate control, standard ratios have been established as follows:

a. For the total group, project salaries shall equal 45% of project revenue.
b. The total time of the project managers shall be divided (a) 70% to projects, (b) 20% to business promotion, and (c) 10% to nonproductive time.

c. The total time of specialists shall be divided (a) 85% to projects, and (b) 15% to non-productive time.

The next section of this chapter includes some illustrations and discussion of the integration of the cost, budgeting and reporting procedures for the hypothetical firm used in this section.

Control reporting. Management needs information on operating results and the financial condition of the business to aid them in meeting daily requirements for objective and subjective control decisions. Accounting reports should, in large measure, fill this need. These and other types of internal reports for management are the subject of Chapter 20.

This section shall be limited to the illustration and discussion of two statements that highlight some of the concepts described in preceding sections of this chapter.

The statements selected for this hypothetical business or personal service organization are (1) Income and Expense Statement, and (2) Client Project Report.

Statement of Income and Expense. This statement is illustrated as Figure 2. It is typical in presenting actual, budget, variance and percentage ratios. There are, however, some typical features when compared to statements for product production and distribution organizations.

1. *Total charges to projects.* This amount represents the client staff productive time at billing rate plus direct project expenses. The reasons for using total charges instead of gross billings will be clarified in the paragraphs that follow.

2. *Direct project expenses.* The cost of client staff travel, subsistence and reports prepared for clients are included here. These nonoperating expenses are substantial in amount. Although the nature of the project and client location influence the amount of this expense, control is essential. Clients reimburse the firm for most of this expense. Thus, to the client it is a part of the cost of the service received. Controlling this expense is a responsibility of management and a service to their clients.

3. *Revenue charged to projects.* Reducing total charges by the amount of project expenses leaves the client staff project time priced at billing rate. The reasons for selecting this amount as the base for computing operating and expense ratios deserve comment.

First, project expenses are excluded. They are nonoperational and related to the specific projects.

Second, most of the indirect operations in this firm support the client project staff. Thus, time charged to client project ledgers is a better measure of operating volume than amounts billed to clients.

Third, the ratio of project salaries to project revenue is particularly important. There are five rates used for billing the time of the project staff. Individual salaries assigned to partners and paid to specialists are related to the billing rate most appropriate for his level of skills and performance. There is a salary range for each billing rate making it possible to reward performance,

FISCAL YEAR ENDED ____________
(000's OMITTED)

	Actual		*Budget*		*Variance over (under) budget*	
	Amount	*Per cent*	*Amount*	*Per cent*	*Amount*	*Per cent*
Total charges to projects	$4,730	112.6	$4,500	112.5	$230	5.1
Deduct direct project expense:						
Travel and subsistence	$ 480	11.4	$ 440	11.0	$ 40	9.1
Project costs	50	1.2	60	1.5	(10)	(16.7)
Total	$ 530	12.6	$ 500	12.5	$ 30	6.0
Revenue charged to projects:						
Project management	$1,200	28.6	$1,240	31.0	$(40)	(3.2)
Project specialists	3,000	71.4	2,760	69.0	240	8.7
Total	$4,200	100.0	$4,000	100.0	$200	5.0
Adjustments to project charges:						
Expense	$ 6	.1	$ 4	.1	$ 2	50.0
Revenue	50	1.2	36	.9	14	38.9
Total	$ 56	1.3	$ 40	1.0	$ 16	40.0
Operating income	$4,144	98.7	$3,960	99.0	$184	4.6
Operating expense:						
Direct:						
Salaries—manager project	$ 600	14.3	$ 560	14.0	$ 40	7.1
Salaries—specialist project	1,400	33.3	1,240	31.0	160	12.9
Total direct	$2,000	47.6	$1,800	45.0	$200	11.1
Indirect:						
Salaries—manager promotion	$ 140	3.3	$ 160	4.0	$(20)	(12.5)
Salaries—manager non-productive	80	1.9	80	2.0	—	—
Salaries—specialist non-productive	180	4.3	220	5.5	(40)	(18.2)
Salaries—administrative	350	8.3	360	9.0	(10)	(2.8)
Salaries—clerical	360	8.6	320	8.0	40	12.5
Other indirect	880	21.0	820	20.5	60	7.3
Total indirect	$1,990	47.4	$1,960	49.0	$ 30	1.5
Total operating expense	$3,990	95.0	$3,760	94.0	$230	6.1
Net operating profit	$ 154	3.7	$ 200	5.0	$(46)	(23.0)

Fig. 2. Income and Expense Statement.

although the next higher billing rate may not be justified. The midpoint of the salary range is 45% of the applicable billing rate. Thus, the ratio of project salaries to project revenue is an excellent check on the effectiveness of the administration of the salary and billing rate programs.

4. *Adjustments to project charges.* As mentioned earlier, clients are given an estimate of the project cost. Unless changed by mutual agreement during the course of the project, the estimate establishes a maximum to be billed and paid. It is, of course, not always possible to precisely predetermine the total charges to the project. Segregating these adjustments facilitates the measurement of estimating accuracy and the effectiveness of project management control.

5. *Operating income.* This is the income available for operating expenses and profit. It is the amount remaining from client billings after the cost of non-operational project expenses are deducted.

6. *Operating expenses.* These are segregated between direct and indirect for purposes of control. The classifications are self-explanatory. The *other indirect* expenses are not detailed in the exhibit, because no purpose would be served here. This item includes expenses such as:

a. Travel and communication.
b. Supplies, services and fees.
c. Insurance, taxes and pensions.
d. Use and occupancy.

7. *Net operating profit.* This is additional income to the partners in this hypothetical firm.

Client project report. This statement, illustrated in Figure 3, differs from the previous illustration of the income and expense statement in three significant ways.

First, adjustments to project charges are not permitted in the estimate. Thus, project managers are encouraged to estimate correctly and control the direct costs to avoid adjustments. When adjustments exceed 1% of the estimated project charges, the project manager must provide a written explanation to the senior partner.

Second, total operating expenses are prorated to client projects at the overall budget rate. The project managers are not held accountable for this expense. The rate will, of course, vary as overall volume changes.

Third, estimated and actual project hours are a part of this report. As indicated earlier, the personnel department is responsible for administering the salary and billing rate programs. Thus, the project manager can be held accountable only for the client staff hours on the project.

Although not illustrated, there are other reports the management of this firm needs. In view of the objective that partners shall spend 70% and specialists 85% of their time on client projects, there should be a daily report of the number of partners and specialists that are nonproductive. In addition, there should be a monthly report that indicates the percentages of productive and nonproductive time of each member of the client staff. Since the ratio of salaries to billing rates should average 45%, there should be a monthly report of the

CLIENT NAME ______________________

CLIENT NUMBER ______________________

	Project actual		*Project estimate*		*Over (under) estimate*	
	Amount	*Per cent*	*Amount*	*Per cent*	*Amount*	*Per cent*
Total charges to project	$18,200	113.0	$18,000	112.5	$ 200	1.1
Deduct direct project expense:						
Travel and subsistence	$ 1,500	9.3	$ 1,600	10.0	$(100)	(6.3)
Report costs	600	3.7	400	2.5	200	50.0
Total	$ 2,100	13.0	$ 2,000	12.5	$ 100	5.0
Revenue charged to project:						
Project management	$ 3,800	23.6	$ 4,000	25.0	$(200)	(5.0)
Project specialists	12,300	76.4	12,000	75.0	300	2.5
Total	$16,100	100.0	$16,000	100.0	$ 100	.6
Adjustments to project charges:						
Expense	$ 100	.6	$ —	—	$ 100	100.0
Revenue	100	.6	$ —	—	$ 100	100.0
Total	$ 200	1.2	$ —	—	$ 200	100.0
Project operating income	$15,900	98.8	$16,000	100.0	$(100)	.6
Deduct operating expenses:						
Managers' project salaries	$ 1,710	10.6	$ 1,800	11.2	$ (90)	(5.0)
Specialists' project salaries	5,390	33.5	5,400	33.8	(10)	(.2)
Allocated expenses *	7,890	49.0	7,840	49.0	50	.6
Total	$14,990	93.1	$15,040	94.0	$ (50)	(.3)
Project net operating profit	$ 910	5.7	$ 960	6.0	$ (50)	(6.3)
* (49% of Revenue).						
Project hours comparison:						
Manager	152	15.6	160	16.7	(8)	(5.0)
Specialists I	100	10.3	100	10.4	—	—
Specialists II	170	17.5	200	20.8	(30)	(15.0)
Specialists III	550	56.6	500	52.1	50	10.0
Total	972	100.0	960	100.0	12	1.3

Fig. 3. Client Project Report.

actual ratios by individuals at each billing rate level and for the total client staff. There are, of course, numerous other conventional accounting reports needed by the management of this firm.

Accounting reports that are timely, accurate, integrated, concise, pertinent, and individualized provide management the sense of direction needed for effective control of the business. Thus, the accountant that applies initiative in the development of reports makes a significant contribution to the success of an enterprise.

13

Using Cost Information in Management Decision Making

CONTENTS

13

Using Cost Information in Management Decision Making

Robert A. Leitch, Ph.D., CPA

This chapter will describe procedures for assembling, analyzing and using cost data for managerial decision making. Emphasis will be on cost behavior and illustrations will be given for many common managerial decisions. Moreover, the ramifications of uncertainty will be reviewed.

USES AND CLASSIFICATION OF COSTS

The collection and analysis of costs should provide management with relevant information for:

1. Income measurement.
2. Asset valuation.
3. Planning and control.
4. Decision-making activities.

Financial accounting is primarily concerned with income measurement and asset valuation. Managerial accounting on the other hand is primarily concerned with profit planning, controlling the activities of the firm and assisting management in the decision-making process by providing management with relevant information. The emphasis of this chapter will be on cost behavior and analysis concepts which relate to managerial decisions.

Management's basic objective is to predict the economic consequences for a never ending variety of decisions such as:

1. Should new equipment be purchased?
2. Should facilities be expanded?
3. Should equipment be leased or purchased?
4. Should a subassembly be manufactured or purchased?
5. What price should be charged for a product?

6. What product mix will contribute the most to profit?
7. What should be the production schedule?
8. Should a product line be dropped or added?
9. Which division is most profitable?
10. Which alternative will lead to greater profits?

The role of the controller and his staff is to provide management with relevant information pertaining to questions similar to those above. Frequently, a considerable amount of analysis is required to make marketing, production, financial and economic statistics useful to management. Moreover, the method of presentation is important for the information to be useful.

Costs can be classified as past, present and future. Those costs relevant to decision making represent expected future costs which differ for each alternative under consideration and which are measured in terms of cash flow or its equivalent.

Importance of future costs. Historical costs which represent such items as investment in inventory, plant, and equipment are irrelevant. These costs are *sunk costs* and have no direct bearing on future decisions. They are not void of information, however, for they serve as useful predictors of future cost behavior which may be relevant to a choice between alternative courses of action. Thus, any analysis using past costs should be modified to reflect future expectations such as changes in wage rates, use of new equipment and modifications in product mix.

Differential costs. The decision-making process is basically the comparison of alternatives; thus, costs and revenue which are equal for each alternative are irrelevant as past costs; they will be the same regardless of the alternative course of action chosen. As in this case of historical costs they are not void of information; however, their inclusion in management reports helps put in perspective expected future costs which differ. Allocated costs are also often irrelevant. Using this approach all costs need not be considered in evaluating alternatives. Great care should be taken, however, to include all expected costs and revenue which will differ.

► EXAMPLE: Consider a manufacturing situation where labor costs have been \$2 per unit and material costs have been \$3 per unit. The same manufacturing procedure in the future will cost \$2.25 per unit for labor and \$3.50 per unit for material. The expected cost for labor for a new process will be \$1.75 per unit; the expected material costs will be the same as that used by the old procedure. The only costs relevant to the decision as to which alternative (the current process or the new process) is better are future differential costs. In this case the difference in expected labor costs of \$2.25 and \$1.75 is the only relevant piece of information; past costs and material costs are irrelevant because they will be the same for either alternative.

► EXAMPLE: Consider a situation where a firm has \$100,000 invested in inventory and style changes or new technology renders the inventory obsolete. The firm is faced with two choices: 1) Modify the merchandise or product at a cost of \$25,000 and sell it for \$35,000 or 2) sell it for scrap for \$5,000.

Clearly, given a differential revenue of $30,000 and a differential cost of $25,000, the firm should modify the merchandise or product because the differential revenue exceeds the different cost. The historical cost of the inventory is irrelevant.

Opportunity costs. Opportunity costs are used to measure alternative uses of resources. Specifically an opportunity cost is defined as the maximum contribution to fixed costs and to profit that is foregone by using limited resources for a particular purpose. The possibility of using resources or selling them is thus relevant information in the decision-making process. Often these costs take the form of revenue foregone by not selling or renting the asset. In other words, to use the asset for manufacturing or in another case as warehouse space, you forego the rent you would have received from the asset. This is clearly a cost associated with the use of the asset for productive purposes. Opportunity costs by their very nature are generally computed and have little relationship to asset book values or other recorded cost information; they are often rough estimates. Nevertheless, they are quite relevant in the decision-making process.

► EXAMPLE: Consider a manufacturing concern which uses copper in the manufacturing process. The firm buys scrap copper, smelts it and manufactures pipe and wire. In any decision regarding the product mix of pipe or wire, the foregone revenue from selling the smelted copper is relevant information; for the market for copper may be such that the foregone revenue from not selling copper inventory may render the supposed net advantage of further processing negative. Moreover, should a firm decide to sell the inventory, the opportunity cost of lost future sales of pipe and wire to regular customers becomes relevant information, for regular customers may turn to other suppliers.

Cash flow—Time value of money. Decision makers should consider the after tax flow of resources and the accountant should make every effort to provide management with this information. Providing such information generally involves forecasting cash outlays for operating expenses, repairs, maintenance, equipment replacement and forecasting resources generated (usually in the form of cash collections) from each alternative. The effect on taxes of noncash flow expenses such as depreciation is relevant, but depreciation itself is not a cash flow and is thus irrelevant. Only the initial investment and its method of payment is relevant.

The timing of cash flow is also important to any decision. First, in today's economy and given today's tax structure, there may be financial constraints on cash flow. Second, the time value of money plays an important role in any choice of alternatives.

The effect of time on the value of money can be calculated using the compound interest formula.

$$S = PV(1 + i)^n,$$

where:

S = Future sum of money
PV = Present value of S
i = Interest rate or cost of capital
n = Number of periods

The present value of some future reserve or expenditure is thus equal to

$$PV = S/(1 + i)^n$$

Tables are provided for the present value and future value factors $1/(1 + i)^n$ and $(1 + i)^n$ respectively and with knowledge or an assumption of the interest rate i and the number of periods n and look up the discount factor. If one expects the stream of future cash flows to be equal, annuity tables are also provided. These tables will be utilized throughout this chapter. They can be found in almost any basic finance or accounting text.

► EXAMPLE: Consider a firm in the 50% tax bracket which desires to purchase some new equipment for $50,000 to be depreciated over 5 years at $10,000 annually with no salvage value. The annual operating costs will be $16,000 for the proposed system; they are currently $30,000 under the current system. The initial cost of this current system was $40,000 and its salvage value is expected to be zero. Ignoring tax consideration an investment of $50,000 will produce pre-tax earnings of $14,000. Assume that the present system's annual tax deduction (including depreciation) is $38,000. If the new equipment is bought, the annual tax deduction will be $16,000 in expenses plus $10,000 in depreciation—total $26,000. This would be $12,000 less than under the current system. Thus the after tax annual advantage would be $14,000 less .50 ($12,000) or a total of $8,000 annually. This annual advantage must then be discounted and compared with the initial investment of $50,000. If we assume that the interest rate is 8%, the present value of $8,000 is 3.993 times $8,000 = $31,944 (3.993 is the annuity factor for i = .08 and n = 5 periods). Thus the net present value of the new equipment is negative ($31,944 — $50,000 = —$19,056); thus it is not a good investment.

We can see from this example that income tax, cash flow, and time value of money are relevant to the decision.

COST BEHAVIOR AND ANALYSIS CONCEPTS

Fixed and variable costs. In the decision-making process it is often useful for management to know something about the expected behavior of various costs with respect to various levels of activity. An activity level may be defined as products manufactured, units sold, man hours used, gallons consumed, with respect to such an index of activity within an expected (relevant) range of activity. These costs are portrayed in Figure 1. As can be seen within a relevant or expected range of activity, cost behavior can be approximated by a linear function ($a + bx$) with a fixed component a, variable component b, and x indicating the level of activity. This cost function is illustrated in Figure 2 where the activity level is defined as units sold. In the case of strictly fixed and variable costs only one component is expected.

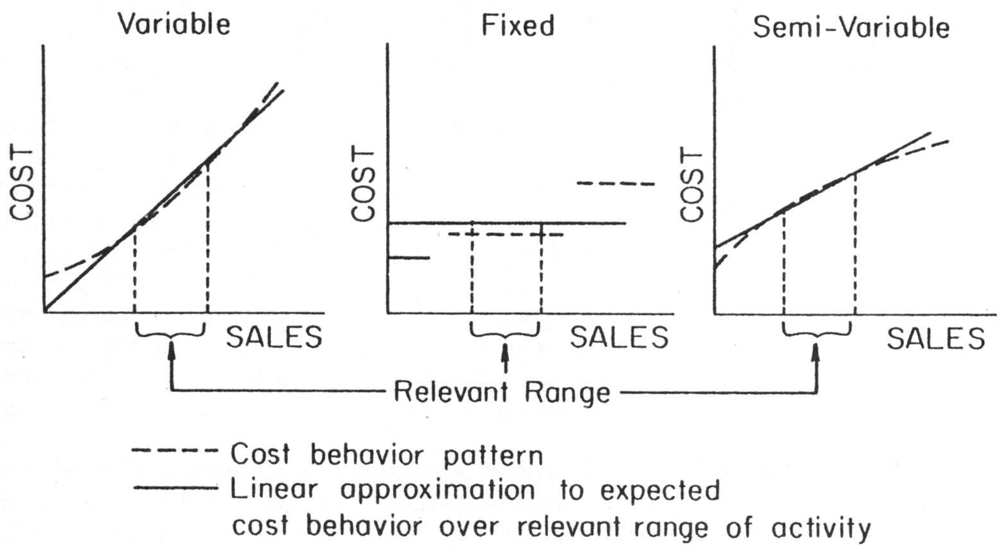

Fig. 1. Behavior of Costs.

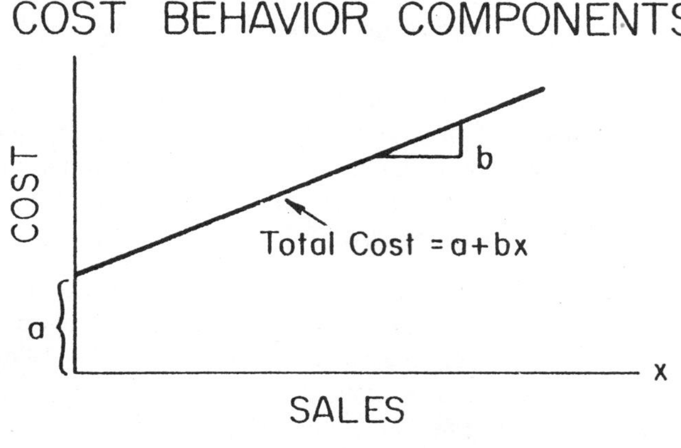

Fig. 2. Cost Behavior Componets.

Direct costing—A cost system for cost behavior analysis. The traditional financial accounting system does not provide the necessary information for management decision making. It does, however, provide an adequate framework; it can be augmented to include fixed and variable cost classifications for both product and period costs. Such an augmented system is commonly known as a direct or variable cost system. It should be noted here that direct costing is not considered generally accepted accounting practice; therefore, full costing is necessary. Essentially, a direct cost system segregates production, selling and administrative costs into fixed and variable components and provides a net contribution to fixed costs and profit. This concept is illustrated by Figure 3, and, as will be subsequently shown in this chapter, the contribution information is most useful in making many managerial decisions. Figure 3 also compares the direct costing with absorption costing income statement. The difference in net income is equal to the increase in inventory times the fixed cost per unit allocated via the absorption method. In this case the difference in net income equals 200 units × $1 per unit or $200. This is due to the fact that under absorption cost procedures some fixed costs are inventoried, whereas, under direct costing they are not. Using direct costing, all fixed costs are period costs.

Contribution analysis of division and product performance. Contribution or direct costing statements such as those shown in Figure 3 are frequently prepared by division or by product. Data in this form is useful to management in analyzing division and product performance. When this is done, fixed costs are generally further subdivided according to their degree of separability. For example, some fixed costs are *programmed;* that is, management of a certain division appropriates (budgets) a specific amount for expenses such as research, advertising, and employee training. Moreover, other fixed costs can be traced to specific divisions such as depreciation, taxes, and division staff salaries. Finally, some fixed costs can not be traced to any product or division, thus, they should not be allocated for performance evaluation. Given this type of breakdown, an income statement such as that shown in Figure 4 can be prepared to assist management in making profitability and performance decisions regarding divisions or product lines. In Figure 4 it is apparent that division B's contribution to the firm is negative, providing A and B are independent; for it may be true that A's sales depend on B's sales.

It is not easy to separate fixed and variable costs for this type of analysis. Direct material, direct labor and various discretionary or programmed fixed costs are not much of a problem. The variable portion of manufacturing overhead and selling and administrative costs poses a problem however. Mathematical techniques such as regression analysis are helpful in estimating the variable portion of these semi-variable costs. Such techniques are illustrated in most basic business statistics texts.

Cost-volume-profit analysis. Cost-Volume-Profit (CVP) Analysis or Break-even Analysis is an extremely useful technique for the analysis of cost data for management decisions regarding such diverse problems as alternative market-

Absorption Costing			*Direct Costing*		
Sales 2,000 units @ $5.00		$10,000	Sales		$10,000
Cost of goods sold			Variable manufacturing cost of goods produced @ $3.00	$6,600	
Variable manufacturing costs 2,200 units @ $3.00	$6,600		Less ending inventory 200 units @ $3.00	600	
Fixed manufacturing costs @ $1.00	2,200		Variable manufacturing cost of goods sold	6,000	
Cost of goods available for sale	8,800		Variable selling and administrative expenses	400	
Less ending inventory: 200 units @ $4.00	800	8,000	Total variable costs charged against sales		6,400
Gross margin		$ 2,000	Contribution margin		$ 3,600
Less total selling and administrative expenses		900	Less fixed costs:		
			Fixed manufacturing costs	$2,200	
Net Income		$ 1,100	Fixed selling and administrative expenses	500	2,700
			Net Income		$ 900

Fig. 3. Comparison of Absorption and Direct Costing.

ing strategies, pricing policies, alternative production processes and product mix. Most any managerial decision involving fixed costs, variable costs and price can make some use of the type of information provided by CVP analysis. Several of these will be illustrated later in this chapter.

		Division	
	Total	*A*	*B*
Net Sales	$1,000	$800	$200
Less: Variable Manufacturing Cost of Sales	500	400	100
Manufacturing Contribution Margin	500	400	100
Less: Variable Selling and Administrative Costs	100	50	50
Contribution Margin	400	350	50
Less: Fixed Costs Controllable by Division Managers	250	200	50
Contribution Controllable by Segment Managers	150	150	0
Less: Separable Fixed Costs Controllable by Others	50	25	25
Contribution by Segment	100	$125	$(25)
Less: Unallocated Costs	50		
Net income before taxes	$50		

Fig. 4. Division Performance and Profitability.

Basically, a company's breakeven point is that point where total sales are equal to total costs. Given a company's fixed costs, variable costs and selling price, the breakeven point is easy to determine using the following equation:

Selling price × Units Sold = Variable Cost × Units Sold + Fixed Cost + Profit +

or

$$SX = VX + F + P$$

where

S = Selling price per unit
X = Number of Units Sold
V = Variable Cost per unit
F = Fixed Cost per unit

► EXAMPLE: Consider a situation where a firm sells its products for $1.50/unit, its variable cost is $1.20/unit and its fixed costs are $8,000; how many units must be sold to break even? Using the formula above,

$$\begin{aligned} SX &= VX + F + P \\ 1.60X &= 1.20X + 8{,}000 + O \\ 1.60X - 1.20X &= 8{,}000 \\ .40X &= 8{,}000 \\ X &= 8{,}000/.40 = 20{,}000 \text{ Units} \end{aligned}$$

It is useful to note that *Unit Contribution* is defined as selling price per unit less the variable cost per unit. In the example above it is \$1.60 — \$1.20 or \$.40/unit. Thus it is clear that the breakeven point in units is equal to fixed costs divided by *Unit Contribution;* mathematically F/(P-V) = X = \$8,000/\$.40 = 20,000 units. The breakeven point in terms of dollars sales is equal to 20,000 units times \$1.60/unit or \$32,000. The dollar breakeven point can also be determined using the *contribution ratio*. Note that in the example the ratio of the contribution margin (unit or total as in Figure 3 may also be used) is (S — V)/S = \$.40/\$1.60 = 25%, and the breakeven point in sales dollars can be determined by dividing fixed cost by the contribution ratio; mathematically F/((S — V)/S) = \$8,000/.25 = \$32,000.

Any point above the breakeven point will yield a profit; and any point below will yield a loss as shown graphically in Figure 5. The amount of profit or loss can be determined graphically or mathematically. Likewise the volume of sales necessary to generate a particular profit may be obtained graphically as in Figure 5 or from *Profit-Volume Analysis Graph* such as the one illustrated in Figure 6. The latter is easier to use in this case for the desired profit is shown directly on the vertical axis. The expected volume above the breakeven point is known as the *margin of safety*. The volume necessary to achieve a

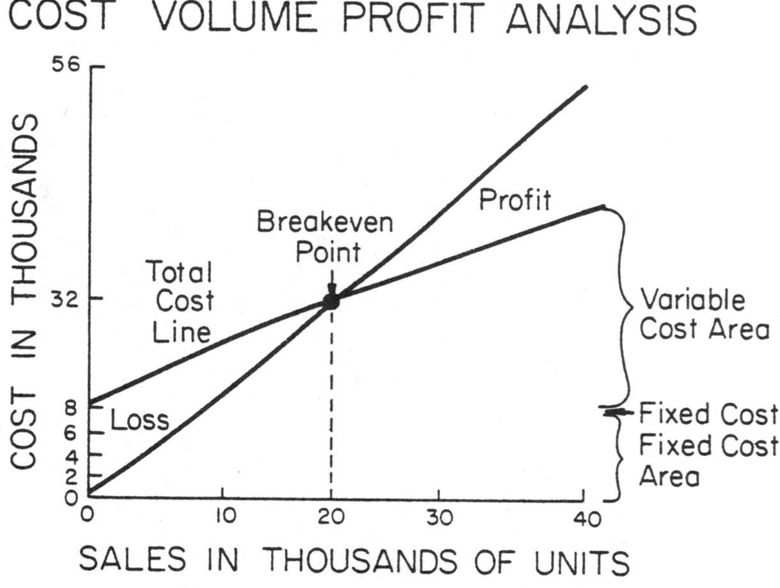

Fig. 5. Cost-Volume-Profit Analysis.

certain profit can also be determined mathematically using the breakeven equation. The volume necessary to achieve a $4,000 profit would be

$$\begin{aligned} SX &= VX + F + P \\ \$1.60X &= \$1.20X + \$8{,}000 + \$4{,}000 \\ \$\ .40X &= \$12{,}000 \\ X &= \$30{,}000 \text{ units} \end{aligned}$$

Using the unit contribution approach X is equal to $(F+P)/(S-V) = (\$8{,}000 + \$4{,}000)/\$.40 = \$12{,}000/\$.40 = 30{,}000$ units.

Several illustrations of the use of cost volume profit analysis will be presented in the application section and a brief discussion of breakdown analysis under uncertainty will be given.

Rate of return on capital. A measure of the expected return on capital expenditures is useful in making investment decisions such as: which investment yields the greatest return on capital? Will a particular investment yield a return high enough to justify the capital outlay? How long will it be before capital invested in a project is recovered?

Many methods are available to measure return on investment. Several financial accounting methods which compare net income with investment provide management with useful information for making rough estimates.

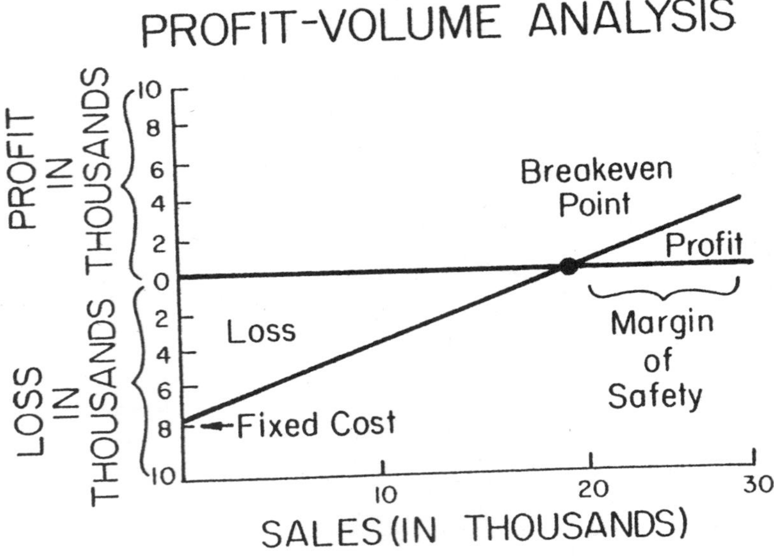

Fig. 6. Profit-Volume Analysis.

► EXAMPLE: Assume that after tax net income is estimated to be $10,000 annually and that the initial investment is $110,000 with a $10,000 salvage.

$$\text{Return on Initial Investment} = \frac{\text{Average increase in annual net income}}{\text{Initial investment}}$$

$$= \frac{10{,}000}{110{,}000} = 9.1\%$$

$$\text{Return on Average Investment} = \frac{\text{Average increase in annual net income}}{\text{Average investment}}$$

$$= \frac{10{,}000}{(110{,}000 - 10{,}000)/2}$$

$$= \frac{10{,}000}{50{,}000} = 20\%$$

The *payback* on a project in another useful measure of return. It is equal to the investment divided by the average cash flow (not net income as above) generated from operations by the investment.

► EXAMPLE: Assume that the annual average cash flow from the investment alone is equal to $22,000 per year, then the *payback* will be $110,000/ $22,000 = 5 years.

These methods are simple to use but payback does not measure profitability; all three assume uniform net income or cash flows which are often not found in practice, and neither considers the time value of money. A method which can incorporate unequal cash flows and the time value of money will necessarily give more relevant information to management even though the above methods are good for rough comparisons. Discounted cash flow techniques provide this added information.

Discounted cash flow. The rate of return computed using the discounted cash flow method is defined as the interest rate which equates expected net cash flow with the investment, (e.g., that interest rate for which the present value of a firm's net cash flow will equal the capital outlay). It is a trial and error method.

► EXAMPLE: Consider a project costing $60,000 with the annual net cash inflow shown in Figure 7 for 5 years including a salvage of 10,000 at the end of 5 years and a major overhaul of $6,000 at the end of the third year. By trial and error we see that the present value of the cash flow at 12% is greater than $60,000; therefore, the return must be in excess of 12%. We see that it is less than $60,000 for 15%; therefore, the return must be less than 15%. A linear interpolation yields an approximate value of 13.72% as shown in the figure.

The reciprocal of the payback is a first order approximation to the discounted cash flow rate computed above when the cash flows are uniform. Also, uniform cash flow annuity tables greatly simplify the calculation of the rate of return.

Net present value. When using *net present value* management calculates or estimates the rate of return (usually the cost of capital) to be used in net present value calculations. If the expected net present value is positive, this implies that the return exceeds the cost of capital or the desired interest rate.

		12%		15%	
Year	*Cash Flow*	*Factor*	*Present Value*	*Factor*	*Present Value*
0	*$60,000*	*1.000*	*$60,000*	*1.000*	*$60,000*
1	17,000	.8929	15,179.30	.8696	14,783.20
2	17,000	.7972	13,552.40	.7561	12,853.70
3	11,000	.7118	7,829.80	.6573	7,230.30
4	17,000	.6355	10,803.50	.5718	9,720.60
5	27,000	.5674	15,319.80	.4972	13,424.40
	$89,000		$62,684.80		$58,012.20

$$\text{Approximate Rate} = 12\% + \frac{2{,}684.8}{4{,}672.6}(3\%) = 12\% + 1.72\% = 13.72\%;$$

where (62,684.8 — 60,000 = 2.684.8; 62,684.8 — 58,012.2 = 4,672.6 and 15% — 12% = 3%)

Fig. 7. Computation Table for Rate of Return — Discounted Cash Flow.

UNCERTAINTY CONSIDERATIONS

It is not sufficient to present management with information about future expectations without a discussion of the degree of certainty surrounding the projected future events. While it is management's responsibility to weigh cost information and projections given an uncertain future, the controller can assist in the process by providing management with ranges, probability distributions, sensitivity analysis and weighted probabilities.

Ranges and distribution of estimates. In making the final evaluation of a course of action it is extremely useful for management to know something about the probability distribution or the range of the estimates to assess a project's risk.

► EXAMPLE: Consider two proposals, the estimated profit for one is $1,000 with an estimated standard deviation of plus or minus $500 and for the other $2,000 with a standard deviation of plus or minus $3,000. Since there is approximately a 67% chance that an event will be between plus and minus one standard deviation from the expected profit it can be said with 67% probability that the first project will have a profit between + $1,500 and + $500 and the second project will have a profit between — $1,000 and + $5,000. Thus, if management wants to avoid the probability of a loss, they should choose the first project even though its expected profit is lower than the second.

Sensitivity analysis. To further assist management in making a final decision the accountant can indicate how sensitive estimates are to various input assumptions. A good example is the traditional economic order quantity for inventory; in many cases the total cost curve is very flat and large deviations from "optimum" will not add much to the overall cost. Therefore, given some uncertainty about the input cost and product demand, management can select a satisfactory order quantity from a rather wide range of possibilities.

Probability weighting. Often several estimates are made for sales levels, costs, discounted cash flows and other relevant cost inputs. Probabilities of occurrence can be assigned to each of these, outcomes can be weighted by these probabilities, and expected outcomes can be determined.

► EXAMPLE: Consider a company that is marketing a new product which has three sales estimates: 1) optimistic 150,000 units, 2) average 100,000 units and 3) pessimistic 50,000 units with respective probalities of .3, .5 and .2. The expected sales are equal to the weighted average of the possible outcomes; specifically, expected sales equal .3(150,000) + .5(100,000) + .2(50,000) = 105,000 units. Note that the probabilities must always sum to one.

Other uncertainty considerations will be reviewed in the application section of this chapter and in the chapter on quantitative methods. Caution needs to be exercised, however, in using expected values in decisions with or without ranges and probability distributions; for, the expected value is an average which assumes that like decisions will be made several times. If this is not the case, management would be wise to place much more weight in the decision-making process on ranges, costs and probabilities of failures, and probabilities of achieving certain desired goals rather than on averages or expected values.

CAPITAL INVESTMENT DECISIONS

Management needs information on the profitability of potential capital expenditures in order to compare them with other uses of scarce capital. Estimates need to be made for the initial investment, economic life and incremental revenue and costs attributed to the potential investment. From such information the controller can provide management with information relevant to the investment decision. Mechanically accepting one alternative relative to another, based on discounted cash flow or one of the other measures of profitability, can be misleading. Other factors need to be considered such as the availability of cash, the degree of certainty surrounding the estimates and the critical nature of the project.

Basically, there are two types of projects—conflicting and competing. Conflicting proposals are mutually exclusive; management either accepts one or the other. Competing proposals *vie* for the same resources (labor, material or capital.

Evaluating competing proposals. The fundamental issue here is whether or not a project exceeds some minimum return on assets or discounted rate of return. If a project exceeds the specified minimum standard it will generally be sent to top management for consideration. At the upper management level a proposal is compared with other proposals using a system of ranking where return on assets or discounted rate of return is most always an important factor. From such a ranking projects are selected for funding. The process involves four basic steps:

1. Estimating.
2. Computing rate of return and calculating costs of capital.
3. Weighing uncertainties.
4. Ranking proposals.

Estimating. Estimates of the initial capital expenditures, net cash flows from operations and economic life need to be made by management. Generally the controller can render valuable assistance here with projections of cost behavior. Several factors are important if management is going to compare and ultimately rank these estimates. Consistency across departments is necessary. This can be aided by management setting clear objectives for the firm and basic policies for implementing these objectives. This will help insure that competing proposals have a common basis. Sometimes management must discount a department estimate if they are consistently over-optimistic. All costs and revenue should be included; those costs that are indirect must not be overlooked. For example, it is not sufficient to forecast sales of a new product without estimating the reduction in sales of current products if their markets overlap. Sufficient detail should be forwarded to management so that they can review key assumptions underlying the analysis; and when a great deal of uncertainty exists, estimates should be accompanied with relevant information about ranges, sensitivity of results to assumptions and probabilities.

Computing rate of return and cost of capital. The cost of capital is defined as the company's future, average and after tax cost of the mix of capital in the company's planned capital structure. The cost of capital is *not* the cost of debt for a particular project because the existence of debt for one project will affect the cost of equity for another project. The rate of return should exceed this average cost of capital for a proposal to be considered.

► EXAMPLE: Assume a company expects its capital structure to consist of 20% long term debt with a 3% yield after tax and 10% common equity with expected earnings on common stock of 15%; the cost of capital can be estimated using a weighted average of these. Specifically, the estimated cost of capital can be calculated as follows: $.2 \bullet 3\% + .8 \bullet 15\% = 12.6\%$. Suppose a project's expected return is 15%, since it exceeds the expected cost of capital it should be considered for implementation.

Weighting uncertainties. Uncertainties should be weighed and presented to management for consideration if assumptions about the future are uncertain and estimates are sensitive to these assumptions.

Ranking proposals. Many firms have capital budgets for various levels within the organization. For example, a plant will have a budget and the authority to approve proposals up to a predetermined budget total as long as each proposal doesn't exceed a certain limit. If they need to exceed either the project limit or the total budget, approval from higher levels is required. The job of management is to select from those proposals, which exceed a predetermined rate of return with a reasonable degree of certainty, a set of projects to be implemented providing the capital budget or other dollar value and cash flow constraints are not exceeded.

Evaluating conflicting proposals. As in the case of competing proposals several methods of evaluating return may be used to compare the alternatives. Two special problems exist, however: the measure of return using a technique such as discounted cash flow or the net present value can be misleading if the two competing projects have unequal lives or unequal investment bases.

► EXAMPLE: If discounted cash flow is used and the investment for one project is \$100,000 and the other is \$60,000 with respective return of 20% and 25%, management needs to calculate the return on the \$40,000 difference needed to equal 20% return for the larger investment. In this case it is equal to 12.5%. If this rate (12.5%) exceeds or equals the cost of capital, management should drop the smaller project (\$60,000), otherwise management should accept the larger project. This procedure should be followed starting with the smallest competing project, if there are more than two.

If net present value is used, a somewhat different approach is used.

► EXAMPLE: When projects have unequal investments a net present value index can be used to rank all competing projects on a comparable basis. The index is calculated as follows: where the net present value is \$20,000 and the required investment is \$100,000:

$$\text{Net present value index} = \frac{\text{Net present value}}{\text{Required investment}} = \frac{\$20{,}000}{\$100{,}000} = .2$$

This can be compared with a competing investment where the net present value is \$10,000 and the required investment is only \$40,000; in this latter case the net present value index is .25. Thus even though the first project has the higher net present value the second should be selected, all other factors nearly equal, because it has the greatest net present value per dollar invested or the largest index.

Unequal lives. Another problem in comparing competing investment is unequal lives. There are two ways to deal with this problem. Management must select between pieces of equipment which will perform the same manufacturing operation. Method A has a life of 10 years and B has a life of 6 years. One method of achieving equality would be to reinvest in B a sufficient number of times to equal the economic life of A; that is 1⅔ times. An estimated salvage value can be made for the fourth year of the replacement for B. The other method would be to analyze the investment over the shorter rather than the longer time span by assuming a salvage value for A at the end of 6 years. In either case the time span must be equal.

Consider Plaything Enterprises which designs and manufactures toys. Past experience indicates that the project life cycle of a toy is three years. Promotional advertising produces large sales in the early years, but there is a substantial sales decline in the final year of a toy's life.

Consumer demand for new toys placed on the market tends to fall into three classes. About 30% of the new toys sell well above expectations, 60% sell as anticipated, and 10% have poor consumer acceptance.

A new toy has been developed. The following sales projections were made by carefully evaluating consumer demand for the new toy:

Consumer Demand for new toy	*Chance of occurring*	*Estimated sales in*		
		Year 1	*Year 2*	*Year 3*
Above average	30%	$1,500,000	$2,500,000	$700,000
Average	60%	700,000	1,700,000	300,000
Below average	10%	300,000	300,000	200,000

Variable costs are estimated at 30% of the selling price. Some special machinery can be purchased at a cost of $860,000. The new machinery will be depreciated by the sum-of-the-year's-digits method with an estimated salvage value of $110,000 and will be sold at the beginning of the fourth year. Fixed expenses (including depreciation) of a cash-flow nature are estimated at $50,000 per year on the new toy. Another alternative would be for Plaything Enterprises to purchase an alternative machine for $450,000 which would need replacement at the end of two years and have no salvage at that time, but if sold after one year would have a $150,000 estimated salvage. Advertising and promotional expenses will be incurred uniformly and will total $100,000 the first year, $150,000 the second year, and $50,000 the third year. These expenses will be deducted as incurred for income tax reporting.

The management of Plaything Enterprises believes that state and federal income taxes will total 60% of income in the foreseeable future and may be assumed to be paid uniformly over the year income is earned.

The following schedules provide information relative to management's questions and decisions. Management would like to first assess probable sales of this new toy in each of the three years, taking into account the probability of above average, average, and below average sales occurring. Second, management would like to know the probable net income for the new toy in each of the three years of its life. Third, they would like the expected net cash flows from sales of the new toy for each of the years involved and for disposition of the machinery purchased for both alternatives assuming a three year time span. Assuming a minimum desired rate of return of 10%, management desires information relative to the present value of the net cash flows calculated above. The following data are relevant:

Year	*Present value of $1.00 due at the end of each year discounted at 10%*
1	.91
2	.83
3	.75

Management would like to know which investment is most profitable using the present value index.

The following schedules (Figures 8-12) should be prepared to answer the questions:

Sales if Demand is: Above average:		*Probability*	*Year 1*	*Year 2*	*Year 3*
Year 1	$1,500,000	.30	$450,000		
Year 2	2,500,000	.30		$ 750,000	
Year 3	700,000	.30			$210,000
Average:					
Year 1	$ 700,000	.60	420,000		
Year 2	1,700,000	.60		1,020,000	
Year 3	300,000	.60			180,000
Below Average:					
Year 1	$ 300,000	.10	30,000		
Year 2	300,000	.10		30,000	
Year 3	200,000	.10			20,000
Total probable sales			$900,000	$1,800,000	$410,000

Fig. 8. Schedule of Probable Sales of New Toy.

	Years		
	1	*2*	*3*
Probable Sales	$900,000	$1,800,000	$410,000
Contribution rate	.70	.70	.70
Contribution to fixed expenses and profits	630,000	1,260,000	287,000
Deduct: Advertising Depreciation	(100,000)	(150,000)	(50,000)
(SYD; C − S = $750,000)	(375,000)	(250,000)	(125,000)
Other fixed expenses	(50,000)	(50,000)	(50,000)
Taxable income	100,000	810,000	62,000
State and federal income taxes (60%)	63,000	486,000	37,200
Probable net income	$ 42,000	$324,000	$24,800

Fig. 9. Schedule Computing Probable Net Income For New Toy for First Alternative.

	Years			
	0	1	2	3
Cost of machine	$(860,000)			
Net income		$ 42,000	$324,000	$ 24,800
Depreciation (add back)		375,000	250,000	125,000
Proceeds from sale of machine				110,000
Net cash flows (after taxes)	$(860,000)	$417,000	$574,000	$259,800
Discount factor	1	.91	.83	.75
Net Present Value	$(860,000)	$379,470	$476,420	$194,850

Total Net Present Value $190.740 Present Value Index $\frac{190,740}{860,000} = .222$

Fig. 10. Net Present Value Schedule of Net Cash Flows For the First Alternative.

	1	2	3
Probable sales	$900,000	$1,800,000	$410,000
Contribution rate	.70	.70	.70
Contribution to fixed expenses and profits	630,000	1,260,000	287,000
Deduct: Advertising	(100,000)	(150,000)	(50,000)
Depreciation (SYD; = 450,000)	(300,000)	(150,000)	(300,000)
Other fixed expenses	(50,000)	(50,000)	(50,000)
Taxable Income or Loss	180,000	910,000	(113,000)
State & Federal Tax Effect (60%)	100,000	546,000	(67,800)
Probable Net Income	$ 72,000	$ 364,000	$(45,200)

Fig. 11. Schedule Computing Probable Net Income For New Toy for Second Alternative.

	Years			
	0	1	2	3
Cost of machine	$(450,000)		$(450,000)	
Net income		$ 72,000	$345,000	$(45,200)
Depreciation (add back)		300,000	150,000	300,000
Salvage			0	150,000
Net Cash Flow After Taxes	(450,000)	372,000	64,000	304,800
Discount Factor	1	.91	.83	.75
Net Present Value	$(450,000)	$338,520	$ 53,120	$228,600

Total Net Present Value $170,240 Present Value Index $\frac{170,240}{450,000} = .378$

Fig. 12. Net Present Value Schedule of Net Cash Flow For the Second Alternative.

The second alternative has the greatest expected present value per dollar of initial investment, therefore it should be selected for the manufacture of the new toy even though its total expected net present value is less than that of the first alternative.

Management needs to be sure that all reasonable alternatives are investigated. In the previous case, for example, a third alternative may be to delay the introduction of the new toy for a year in order to do some more market research given the great uncertainty surrounding the sales projections. Decisions also need to be made on different ways to finance the equipment required to manufacture and market the new product.

PURCHASE VS. LEASE DECISIONS

As in the previous case financing decisions are frequently required for new equipment. For example, management could either purchase or lease the equipment. Caution must be exercised here, however, for some leases must be capitalized with inputed interest. Several factors are relevant to the purchase vs. lease decisions. They are

1. The original cash outlay.
2. The tax reductions.
3. Other uses of the capital.
4. Leasing costs (installation, maintenance agreements and rent).

► EXAMPLE: Benson's Bakery[1] has decided to acquire a new machine either by an outright cash purchase for $30,000 or by leasing it for $7,000 per year for the life of the machine which is 5 years. It is estimated that after 5 years the machine will have a salvage value of $4,000. The machine will have an annual maintenance contract cost of $450. Benson's uses straight line depreciation for tax purposes; its estimated tax rate is 40% and cost of capital is 10%. Mr. Benson would like to know whether to purchase or lease the new machine given that the taxing authorities will permit taxation of the lease.

Since the purchase price is $30,000 and the salvage value is $4,000, the annual depreciation is $26,000/5 or $5,200; with a 40% tax rate the annual tax reduction (cash flow) related to depreciation is $2,080. Since the annual maintenance cost is $450, the after tax outflow is .6($450) = $270. Moreover, given a leasing cost of $7,000 and a maintenance cost of $450 the yearly after tax outflow for maintenance is .6 ($7,000 + $450) = $4,470. The present value analysis is completed in Figure 13.

Since the net present value cash outflow is $16,946 for leasing and $20,665 for purchasing, it is recommended that Mr. Benson lease the new machine.

---

[1]Adapted Problem—AICPA and Matz and Usry.

PRODUCT AND MARKETING DECISIONS

In many situations prices are determined by the market, but in making decisions about price, product mix, promotional expenses, manufacturing methods and distribution channels it is useful for management to be as fully informed as possible about the effect of their decision on the profit picture of the firm. In the final analysis all costs must be considered over the long run for a firm to be profitable, but in the process of making decisions it is important for management to consider cost behavior patterns. Thus, direct costs rather than full costs should be used; otherwise management may base conclusions on misleading information.

Contribution approach to pricing. One of the major decisions facing management is whether or not to accept new business. Many factors need to be considered in such a situation: (1) Does the firm have sufficient capacity? (2) How will it affect other customers? (3) Can management justify price differences under the Robinson-Patman Act? (4) How much will the new business contribute to the profitability of the firm? An analysis of a product or customer's contribution is quite useful to this type of decision; if the contribution is positive, management should generally accept the business.

Alternative	*Years*	*Cash (Outflow) or Inflow*	*P.V. Factor*	*Net Present Value*
Purchase	0	$3,000 initial investment	1.0	$(30,000)
	1-5	$2,080 depreciation tax reduction	3.791	7,885
	1-5	$270 after tax maintenance	3.791	(1,024)
	5	$4,000 salvage	.621	2,481
		Total		$(20,665)
Lease		$4,470	3.791	(16,946)

Fig. 13. Benson's Bakery
Purchase or Lease Cash Flow Analysis.

► EXAMPLE: Jefferson Mills[2] had the following operating characteristics in 19XX:

Basic production data at standard cost	
Direct materials	$1.50
Direct labor	1.70
Variable overhead	.30
Fixed overhead ($150,000—Expected volume 100,000 units)	1.50
Total factory cost at standard	$5.00

Sales price, $6.00 per unit—selling and administrative expenses are assumed fixed at $75,000 yearly, except for sales commisions which are 5% of dollar sales.

[2]Illustration Adaption—C. J. Horngren.

In 19XX, a Jefferson Mills salesman had asked the president for permission to sell 1,000 units to a particular customer for $4.50 per unit. The president refused, stating that the price was below factory cost. Based solely on the information given, what is the effect of the president's decision on 19XX net income?

The refusal of the order diminished net income by the amount of the lost contribution margin, the contribution foregone because the sales price of $4.50 exceeds the relevant unit cost of $3.73 as shown in Figure 14.

Sales, 1,000 units × $4.50		$4,500
Variable manufacturing costs, 1,000 × $3.50	$3,500	
Variable selling expense, 5% of $4.50 or $.23 per unit. 1,000 units × $.23	230	
Total variable costs		3,730
Contribution margin		$ 770

Fig. 14. Jefferson Mills Contribution Cost Analysis.

By not accepting the order, short-run profits will be $770 lower. Therefore, the $770 foregone represents the amount Jefferson Mills is willing to invest now to preserve an orderly long-run price structure. The fact that the $4.50 selling price is less than the $5.00 total factory cost is not relevant to this decision.

Cost-volume-profit analysis. In the process of determining the effect of various marketing plans, it is useful to the decision maker to know the effect on profit marketing plans and the necessary sales levels required to attain certain profit levels. An analysis of the interrelationships of costs, volume and profit will illustrate this effect. This type of analysis is called Cost-Volume-Profit Analysis.

► EXAMPLE: Pocket Camera[3] was disappointed with the profit experienced on the sale of 100,000 cameras even though this represented a record number of sales with a net profit of $600,000. Competition from other firms was causing management to worry about its market position. Management was also concerned about the possibility that variable costs would increase in the next year. Total fixed costs amounted to $1,700,000; and they, too, were expected to increase. At the moment an average price of $48 was received for the product. A break-down of fixed and variable costs per unit is shown in Figure 15 and the income statement is shown in Figure 16.

An 8% decrease in prices and an 8% increase in fixed costs has been considered. An analysis of past conditions indicates that variable costs have been increasing at a rate of 8% each year. The management is interested in some information regarding the percentage increase in volume necessary under each of the possible outcomes to maintain the same $600,000 profit. Specifically

[3]Illustration Adaptation—Matz and Usry.

Variable Costs	*Per Unit*	*Fixed Costs*	*Total*
Direct materials	$12	Fixed factory overhead	$ 600,000
Direct labor	7	Selling and advertising	400,000
Variable factory overhead	6	Administrative and general	700,000
Total variable costs	$25	Total fixed costs	$1,700,000

Fig. 15. Pocket Camera Cost Statistics.

Sales		$4,800,000
Cost of goods sold:		
Direct materials	$1,200,000	
Direct labor	700,000	
Factory overhead	1,200,000	3,100,000
Gross profit on sales		$1,700,000
Selling and advertising expenses	$ 400,000	
Administrative and general expenses	700,000	1,100,000
Net Income		$ 600,000

Fig. 16. Pocket Camera Income Statement.

management is interested in the breakeven point, the contribution margin and the net income if: (a) prices are reduced 8%, (b) variable costs increase 8%, and (c) fixed costs increase 8%. What increases in volume are necessary to offset each of the changes in a, b, and c, and which change is most influential on the net income? This information is tabulated in Figure 17.

	No Change	*8% Price Reduction*	*8% Var Cost Increase*	*8% Fixed Cost Increase*
Sales	$4800	$4416	$4800	$4800
Variable Costs	2500	2500	2700	2500
Contribution Margin	2300	1916	2100	2300
Fixed Costs	1700	1700	1700	1836
Net Income	500	216	400	464
Breakeven Point* =	$3548	$3003	$3886	$3525

Fig. 17. Pocket Camera Contribution, Net Income and Breakeven Analysis. (1000's)

Product mix and contribution to profit. Management is often faced with decisions regarding product mix. It is thus important for management to have some information on the effect of various mixes on the operating profit of the firm. Cost-Volume-Profit Analysis and Contribution Analysis can be useful techniques for providing information relevant to decisions such as which product lines should be continued, increased or decreased.

*Breakeven Point = Fixed Cost/(1 — Variable Costs/Sales)

► EXAMPLE: The officers of Maxwell Printing Company[4] reviewed the profitability of the company's four products and the potential effect of varying the product mix. Excerpts from the 19XX income statement are shown in Figure 18.

The officers of Maxwell Printing would like to know the effect on net income of four different product mix and pricing alternatives none of which will result in any major change in fixed costs. The unit contribution margin can be used effectively for providing the officers with useful information in each of these cases.

	Totql	*X*	*Y*	*Z*
Sales	$44,500	$10,725	$21,775	$12,000
Cost of Goods Sold	25,600	4,600	8,000	13,000
Gross Profit	18,900	6,125	13,775	(1,000)
Operating Expenses	9,100	2,300	2,800	4,000
Net Income Before Taxes	$ 9,800	$ 3,825	$10,975	$ (5,000)
Units Sold		1,100	1,300	1,500
Sales Price Per Unit		$ 9.75	$ 16.75	$ 8.00
Variable Cost of Goods Sold Per Unit		2.00	2.50	7.80
Variable Operating Expenses Per Unit		2.00	1.30	.80
Contribution Margin Per Unit		$ 5.75	$12.95	$ (.60)

Fig. 18. Maxwell Printing Company
Excerpts from 19XX Income Statement.

Case 1: If product Z is discontinued, the effect on net income would be to eliminate the $.60 negative unit contribution for 1500 units. Thus net income would increase by .60(1500) = $900.

Case 2: If by discontinuing Z in Case 1, Maxwell also causes a customer loss of 166 units of Y, the additional effect on net income would be a loss of $12.95 contribution of Y for 166 units or $12.95(166) = $2,150 decrease in net income. Add this to the $900 increase in Case 1 and the net change in net income would be $1,250.

Case 3: If product Z's sale price is increased to $9.20 with a decrease in the number of units sold to 1400 with no effect on other products, the contribution margin would change from $.60 to a position of $.60 per unit. Thus the contribution margin changes from a negative $900 (see Case 1) to a positive contribution margin of .60(1400) = $840; the net change is $900 + $840 or a $1,740 increase in profit.

[4]Adapted Problem—AICPA.

Case 4: If a second shift is added so that 640 more units of product X can be produced, higher wages will result in variable costs of goods sold increasing from $2.00 to $3.00 per unit for the second shift. If this happens net income will be increased by the contribution margin of the additional units (9.75 − 5.00) times the additional number of units (640) or 4.75(640) = $3,040.

► EXAMPLE: *P/V Chart and Sales Mix:* The Carter Company manufactures two products A and B with respective contribution margins of $3.50/unit and $1/unit. The current product mix is 2 units of A for every 3 units of B. Management would like to know how many units of A and B are needed to break even if the mix stays the same and if they changed the product mix to 2 units of A for every 8 units of B if fixed costs are $3,000 the average contribution per unit for the current 2 to 3 mix is 2($3.50) + 3($1.00) which yields $10 per 5 units on $2 per unit; for the new 2 to 8 product mix it is 2($3.50) + 8($1.00) which yields $15 per 10 units on $1.5 per unit. The respective breakeven points are calculated by dividing fixed costs by the average contribution margin per unit; for the 2 to 3 mix and the 2 to 8 mix the respective breakeven points are: $3,000/$2 = 1,500 units and $3,000/$1.5 = 2,000 units. The respective product mixes will thus be for the 2 to 3 mix 900 of A and 600 of B (for every 5 units, 3 are A) and the 2 to 8 mix 400 of A and 1,600 of B (for every 10 units 2 are A). The Profit Volume graph in Figure 19 clearly shows the effect of this shift on Net Income or Profit of $2,000 to $750 at a volume of 2,500 units.

ALLOCATION OF SCARCE RESOURCES

Often management must decide between two alternatives requiring the use of scarce resources. Monetary resource limits were discussed earlier in this chapter where management had limited investment capital. Constraints on labor, materials and plant capacity may also limit options. The controller, therefore, must present management with information on the ramifications of various alternative courses of action. Ideally management would like to optimize the overall contribution to profit; operations research techniques such as linear programming are useful for this type of analysis. These will be discussed later in this book. A simple analysis of a product's contribution per limiting factor will often suffice, however, where there is only one limiting factor and other constraints are not complex. The basic idea is to select that product mix which will result in the greatest contribution to profit and fixed costs per unit of limiting factor.

► EXAMPLE: In the last several years, Madison Pump has manufactured all of its required components; however, in 19XX only 28,000 hours of otherwise idle machine time can be devoted to the production of components. Thus some parts must be purchased from outside suppliers. In producing parts, factory overhead is applied at $1 per standard machine hour. Fixed capacity costs, which will not be affected by any make or buy decision, represent 64% of the

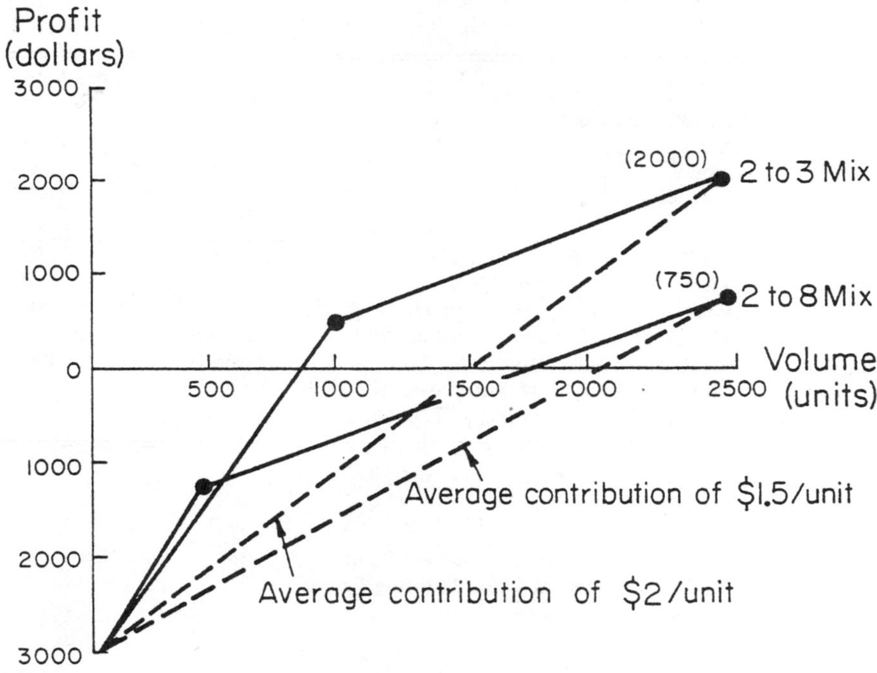

Fig. 19.

applied factory overhead. How can Madison Pump schedule the available machine time to maximize its potential cost savings, if the standard costs and other relevant information for the two major component parts are as shown in Figure 20?

Contribution per limiting factor information will prove useful in this decision; the limiting factor is machine hours. From the analysis in Figure 21 it can easily be seen that the greatest per hour savings is for manufacturing part B; therefore, Madison Pump should manufacture 13,000 units of B and 666 units of A and purchase the remaining 6,534 units of A.

	A	B
Direct Materials Per Unit	$ .50	$ 7.76
Direct Labor Per Unit	.95	5.00
Factory Overhead Per Unit	4.75	3.00
Total Standard Cost Per Unit	$ 6.20	$ 15.76
Units Needed Per Year	7,200	13,000
Machine Hours Required Per Unit	3	2
Unit Cost If Purchased	$ 4.75	$ 15.60

Fig. 20. Madison Pump Component Cost Information.

(a) Unit Cost if Purchased	$ 4.75	$ 15.60
(b) Relevant Production Costs		
Direct Material	.50	7.76
Direct Labor	.95	5.00
Factory Overhead (36% Variable)	1.71	1.08
Total	$ 3.16	$ 13.84
(c) Potential Cost Savings Per Unit (a-b)	1.59	1.76
(d) Machine Hours Required Per Unit	3	2
(e) Potential Cost Savings Per Machine Hour (c/d)	.53	.88[1]
(f) Machine Hours of each Part Manufactured	2,000[3]	26,000[2]
(g) Number of Parts Manufactured (f/d)	666	13,000
(h) Machine Hours of each Part Purchased (i * d)	19,602	—
(i) Number of each Part Purchased (7200-666)	6,534	—

[1]Largest savings per machine hour.
[2]Make as much of B as possible.
[3](28,000 hours — 26,000 hours) = 2,000 hours.

Fig. 21. Madison Pump Analysis Using Limiting Factor.

MAKE OR BUY DECISION

Management is frequently presented with a decision on making a product or buying a product. This is clearly a case where these are mutually exclusive alternatives and should be analyzed in a fashion similar to that illustrated in the conflicting investment or the purchase vs. leasing section of this chapter. There are, however, many other factors to be considered. A brief listing which is not at all inclusive follows:

1. Does the firm want to be in a different type of business?
2. Does the firm have the necessary expertise, equipment and capacity to make the product?
3. How reliable is the supply of parts which are to be purchased?
4. What are the entry barriers such as equipment, technology, economics of scale, skilled labor and raw materials?

These and similar factors must be given very careful attention by management; it is often not enough to base a decision such as this on a comparison of net present values of alternatives.

SELL OR PROCESS FURTHER— DIFFERENTIAL SALES AND REVENUE ANALYSIS

As indicated earlier in this chapter strict attention should be given to those costs and revenues which will be different in the future. Historical costs and future costs which are incurred up to the decision point of whether to sell or process further are irrelevant. Often these include allocated joint costs.

► Example: Bogart Fertilizer Company produces three products — X, Y and Z from a joint chemical process. Each may be sold at the point of split-off or processed further and additional processing requires no special facilities. Production costs of further processing are variable and traceable to the fertilizer products involved. In 19XX, these products were processed beyond split-off and joint production costs for the year were $52,000 and they were allocated to the products in proportion to the relative physical volume of output. Data for 19XX are shown in Figure 22. Should Bogart Fertilizer process any products beyond the split-off point? A brief analysis, also shown in Figure 22, which compares added sales value and added costs indicates that Bogart Fertilizer should subject only Product X to additional processing in order to maximize profits because the added sales value of $17,300 exceeds the added costs of $8,200. However, for both Products Y and Z, the added costs exceed or only cover the added sales value.

		Sales Value			
Product	*Units Produced*	*If Processed Further —*	*At Split-off =*	*Added Value*	*Added Cost*
X	8,000	39,400	22,100	17,300	$8,200
Y	4,600	41,500	38,300	3,200	7,400
Z	3,000	34,000	25,000	9,000	9,000

Fig. 22. Bogart Fertilizer 19XX Product Data, Added Sales Value and Cost Comparison.

14

Budgetary Control Systems

CONTENTS

14

Budgetary Control Systems

This chapter embodies a general approach to modern budgeting. As part of this approach, past and present trends in accounting are reviewed as they relate to budgeting.

In addition to such material as the various types of budgets and the installation of budget systems, the problems of selling management on the use and advantages of budgets are discussed.

To avoid the idea that a typical budget system is sufficient for all purposes, some deficiencies in long-term budgeting are pointed out, as well as techniques to overcome these deficiencies. Budgeting sometimes degenerates to *after-the-fact* comparisons of budgeted and actual expenditures. For this reason, a discussion of *pre-control procedures* for *before-the-fact* control of costs is included.

The chapter should be read in conjunction with Chapter 15, *How to Budget Business Operations*. While the general theory and approach to budgeting is covered in this chapter, the detailed aspects of working with budgets are covered in Chapter 15.

MAKING THE MOST OF MODERN BUDGETING

Accounting—past and present. Accounting has long been considered as historical in character (i.e., principally concerned with recording the past). Its chief functions have been those of correctly recording business transactions and periodically producing financial statements. These financial statements permit comparison with those for other accounting periods. Their contribution as aids to management, however, is very limited. They are of but minor importance in the control and improvement of the operating results of a business enterprise.

In recent years management accounting has come to be emphasized. Management accounting is modernized accounting that is designed to assist management in its planning, control, and administrative functions. Historical accounting is gradually being revamped into a form and technique of accounting that is dedicated to a new function—that of planning and evaluating the operating results of a business in comparison with preplanned objectives. Three of the principal ingredients of management accounting are the following:

1. It aims at efficiency of operations.
2. It fixes responsibility for achievement.
3. It requires a budgetary control system.

In this evolution of accounting, the public accountant finds himself frequently called upon to develop and coordinate a budgetary system. With his background of extensive knowledge of his client's accounts, the public accountant can be of invaluable assistance to management in this area. The installation of a budget system provides a natural bridge from the traditional role of the accountant to providing expanded management services in the advisory field. The established client relationship, the accountant's familiarity with his client's business, and his professional training and experience, all qualify him to plan and implement a new budgetary system.

The accountant, of course, must keep up with the times by learning modernized budget techniques. In the budgetary systems of 20 years ago, particular emphasis was placed on control by dollar amounts or by percentages. Modern techniques in budgeting developed within the past several years utilize unit control instead of dollars or percentages. Unit control is the effective use of a stipulated number of units of labor in terms of hours or work days, and the control of materials through the number of units to be used or sold. As an example of unit control, consider a restaurant endeavoring to budget the cost of food sold. Under methods previously used, management might strive to attain a 40% food cost in relation to sales. The percentage actually experienced becomes known only after the costs have already been incurred. Under a system of unit cost control, the cost of each meal is predetermined by establishing a standard portion size for each of the component parts of the meal, priced at current market costs. Standard meal recipes are developed, and the sales price is set to provide the desired cost of sales. Modern planning and forecasting also involves setting similar standards of labor performance to improve and to control the results of client's operations, as will be discussed later under payroll pre-control.

What budgeting accomplishes. Before going any further, it may be well to discuss what an effective budget system can accomplish. Primarily, the budget provides a well-organized plan based on facts. It provides definite objectives with regard to future operations. At the same time, executive policies for the future are formulated and clarified. The budget is a convenient yardstick for measuring the efficiency of overall operations as well as analyzing detailed segments of operations.

The budget fixes the responsibility for achieving each estimated result on some individual or department. Employees are encouraged to attain the objectives set by the budget. There is no better method of coordinating financial, sales, and operating results than through budgetary control.

Effective budgetary control strengthens the system of internal control. Frequent comparisons of projected and actual figures serve to check the correct recording of transactions and events in the accounts. Errors are often disclosed as a result of a department head or a foreman questioning the charges against his operation.

A well defined flexible budget cushions the effect of adverse developments. If unexpected events cause decreased sales, expenses can be reduced promptly when operating results are evaluated in comparison with preplanned results. The budget provides for coordinated efforts by all sections of a business. It serves as a communications tool that enables each section to know what its role is in achieving the overall objectives.

One of the most important advantages of budgeting is the aid it affords in planning working capital needs and cash availability. Financial planning, whether on a long or a short-term basis, is largely founded on anticipated operating results. A budget system sounds a prompt alarm whenever previously formulated plans are not being carried out and require modification.

Selling the budget. Despite the efficacy of a budget system, it frequently must be sold to management. It is the duty of public accountants to impress upon their clients the value and necessity of financial planning. The best way to do this is to identify budgeting with the profit-making objectives of management. Public accountants should encourage the adoption of a budget system as a useful and necessary tool in attaining profit goals.

The size of the business has little bearing upon the necessity for planning and budgeting. Budgeting is effective in both small and large operations. Although the small businessman often considers budgeting unsuited to his requirements, budgeting procedures are fundamentally the same in a small or a large business. They are, in fact, much simpler in their application by a small organization.

Numerous misconceptions about budgeting exist and these must be corrected. Here are some frequently voiced objections to budgeting that are based on such misconceptions:

1. "It is too costly and involved."
2. "We don't have a large enough staff to administer it."
3. "The budget will restrict our operations and hamper our growth."
4. "It will involve a lot of useless paper work."
5. "We don't need a budget—we know how we are doing without one."

These incorrect notions can be refuted by pointing out the following:

1. Experience has shown that the increased profits resulting from a well-administered budget are frequently far in excess of its cost.

2. Even inexperienced employees can be trained in budget work. Once installed, its operation is quite simple.

3. A budget can and should be flexible. This is even more true in the case of a small business.

4. The paper work can be minimized and procedures instituted to produce the desired budget data routinely and effectively.

5. Planning and control can make even the most active management, with all details of the business in its grasp, more successful.

The principal types of budgets. Each revenue and expense activity of a business can be budgeted. In addition, there are all kinds of special purpose budgets. A listing of the various kinds of budgets, however, would serve no purpose. Instead, the principal types of budgets will be explained. One or another of these types of budgets can be used for any budgeting purpose.

1. Long-term budgets.
2. Short-term budgets.
3. Fixed budgets.
4. Variable budgets.

Long-term budgets. Long-range budgets are usually the basis for planning over a period of years. A long-term budget may be used for any one of the following purposes:

1. To determine long-range plans for capital expenditures.
2. To plan profit potentials.
3. To forecast cash position in relation to anticipated cash needs by specific dates.
4. To implement market development for a new product.
5. To guide in determining research projects that may be initiated.
6. To schedule expansion and growth.

As long-range planning is necessarily a top management function, long-term budgets require the active participation of top level executives.

Short-term budgets. These budgets for shorter periods are most often used for estimates of income and expenses. They generally involve the coordinated planning of all aspects of operations for a forthcoming period. Various phases of short-term budgeting may be placed under the direct responsibility of second level management personnel, such as department heads or foremen.

Fixed budgets. In this type of budget, estimated levels of income and expense are established in advance and these levels are not raised regardless of the actual levels experienced. Fixed budgets require accurate forecasting and analysis of each budget item. This type of budget is best suited for manufacturing companies producing items that can be inventoried.

Variable budgets. The variable budget, or flexible budget as it is sometimes called, is actually a group of budgets, each based on a different operating level of volume or prices. It is set up by estimating sales volume at various levels, and estimating manufacturing costs, distribution costs, other expenses, and other income at the differing amounts considered applicable to each anticipated level of sales. Variable budgets are most effective as a means of controlling costs in a business whose rate of activity fluctuates daily or weekly.

Installing a budget system. While no two budget installations are alike, there are standard steps that are part of the routine of installing and making operative any budget system. Some of these steps will be discussed and a checklist for a budget installation will follow. The checklist will necessarily be general in order to apply to a variety of situations.

Define the objectives. The principal aim of budgeting is increased profits. This goal must be communicated to every individual who participates in budgeting. In order to obtain their full cooperation, this philosophy must be communicated to all employees. Attainable concrete goals must be set both for the overall business and for its component elements. It is preferable to set goals for both long- and short-term objectives.

In addition to the profit objective, the budget is designed to provide an overall plan of coordinated action. It also is designed to provide a basis for comparing actual performance with anticipated results. It aims at holding operations to a previously charted course, and measures the extent of any departure from the original plan.

The budget serves to coordinate the activity of all the groups within the organization, keeping each in proportion with relation to the basic budget objectives.

Analyze the situation. Historical facts relating to prior operations must be studied and interpreted in the light of new conditions before the budget is prepared. It is also essential to prepare an organization chart and to clearly define areas of responsibility.

Estimates of the company's future should be tempered in the light of general economic conditions. Data regarding general economic factors may be obtained from such business periodicals as *The Wall Street Journal, Business Week, Nation's Business, Federal Reserve Bulletins,* and various economic indicators published by the U.S. Government Printing Office. Trends in the particular industry must also be considered. These trends are reflected in surveys and projections made by trade associations. They include cycles within the industry and demand and price fluctuations for particular products.

Estimate sales and income. In estimating sales for the coming year, you should proceed as follows:

1. Start with a study of sales or income for prior years. Sales data should be as detailed as possible by periods of the year, source of sale, territory, etc.
2. Analyze and evaluate all non-recurring business obtained last year.
3. Add this year's scheduled and estimated non-recurring business.
4. Consider and evaluate the current trend of business to the extent that it differs from that of prior years.
5. You can now estimate the sales or income for the ensuing year.

While the procedure is somewhat oversimplified here, the approach is basic. Such other factors as the effect of advertising campaigns, or other special promotional plans of management, while difficult to estimate, must also be taken into account.

In estimating volume, three distinct levels must be considered:

1. The general economy as a whole.
2. The trend in the particular industry.
3. The outlook for the particular company, in relation to its past history and its future prospects.

Estimate costs and expenses. In this fourth step of a budget installation, it is best to start with an estimate of fixed costs and expenses. The estimate should be based on a review and projection of overhead expenses, with due consideration being given to just how essential each item actually is.

Variable expenses usually consist of material and labor costs in the main. Certain variable costs and expenses, of course, will bear a fairly constant relationship to sales. Expenses of this type are estimated in relation to the sales forecast previously prepared. Specific material requirements, particularly, are projected based upon the amounts necessary to meet the forecasted sales volume. Allowances for waste of materials must be carefully estimated and variances from anticipated losses must be adequately accounted for.

Standards of material usage can be established based upon the unit, group lot, or bulk amount, whichever is applicable to the type of product made. Actual usage must then be compared with the planned potential usage.

The control of labor costs, frequently the most important single element of costs, will be discussed later.

► WHAT TO DO: The actual installation of a budget system is always preceded by a planning period in which consideration must be given to things that, at first glance, seem not to be involved in the installation of a budget system. The checklist that follows is very useful in this planning stage as well as in the actual installation of the system.

CHECKLIST FOR A BUDGET INSTALLATION

1. Prepare organizational chart.
2. Assign responsibility for preparation of preliminary budget.
3. Determine management reports to be prepared.
4. Decide what sales estimates are to be made and by whom.
5. Analyze types of products or services to be sold.
6. Substantiate sales estimates by relating them to past experience or changed current conditions.
7. Review adequacy of facilities to produce estimated sales.
8. Estimate expected profits in relation to sales.
9. Determine adequacy of expected profits as representing a sufficient return on invested capital.
10. Complete the budget preparation by refining estimates of sales, costs, and expenses, utilizing one or more of the following techniques, as applicable:

a. Increasing sales by increasing prices, adding or changing products, expanding markets, or increasing volume by lowering prices.
b. Developing standard costs for all products.
c. Applying unit control procedures to direct labor and direct material costs.
d. Determining minimum fixed overhead.
e. Determining variable costs in relation to sales increases or decreases.
f. Determining break-even point.
g. Analysis of desired inventory turnover ratios and minimum stock requirements.

11. Finalize individual budgets for each phase of operations.
12. Implement the use of the various management reports.
13. Prepare summary reports comparing budget with actual operating results.
14. Analyze reasons for variances between objectives previously set and actual operating results.
15. Take indicated action to correct either future objectives or operating conditions, as determined by the foregoing analysis.

BUDGETING ADDITIVES

Although the advantages to be gained from budgeting have been fully discussed, it must also be said that these benefits are not always completely realized. Additional procedures are often necessary to achieve the maximum benefits from budgeting. Why this is especially true of budgeting on a short-term basis and some additional procedures that will help in attaining the full potentials of budgeting will be discussed next.

Some deficiencies of long-term budgeting. Unfortunately, only too often businesses are not using the budget tool to maximum advantage on a short-term basis. Too often management seems content to deal with budgets only on an annual or monthly basis. This is the traditional approach and consists of projecting income and expenses for the coming year or month.

No doubt, the traditional budgeting approach is essential as a guide to management in determining policies of pricing, advertising, and standards of service. It does serve as an aid to management with regard to financial programming by determining the cash availabilities. However, it is often overlooked that a monthly budget by itself is insufficient to provide management with the day-to-day plans and controls it needs for its expenditures. In other words, as a tool in assisting management to maximum profits, the monthly budget has two serious drawbacks:

1. It operates too late to be entirely efficient as a profit control tool. The application of a monthly budget system involves: (a) budgeting, (b) accounting for the actual dollars spent, and (c) comparing dollars spent with

budgeted amounts to determine any variances. If the reason for any variance is that forecasted volume did not materialize, it probably will be 15 days after the end of the month before sufficient information is obtained to take remedial action. Obviously, it is then too late—some damage has already been done.

2. Even the fact that actual costs may have equalled budgeted costs doesn't mean that maximum monthly profits were realized. It may well be that past inefficient operations were continued into the period under consideration. Budget estimates themselves often reflect nothing more than past operating and management inefficiencies that have been restated at current cost levels.

If maximum profits are to be obtained, some additional element must be introduced into budgeting that will operate more quickly than the usual budget report.

Pre-control procedures. Modern budgeting stresses the pre-control system designed for the very purpose of assisting in the achieving of maximum profit potentials. Pre-control, as the word implies, means the adoption of procedures that prevent unwarranted costs by controlling these costs where they should be controlled—at their origin. In this way, costs are not first incurred and later compared with a budgeted amount, but are incurred only if necessary. Instead of operating blindly for a month or longer, pre-control procedures provide management with day-to-day controls.

Day-to-day planning and controls are particularly necessary where the volume of business changes frequently and may even fluctuate greatly within an average month. This often requires daily or weekly changes in the labor force in order to attain maximum profits. Where a business does not produce a product that can be inventoried, stored, and used at a later date, each man-hour of labor not utilized productively represents a direct loss. This is particularly true in the service industries.

It should be emphasized that pre-control systems, particularly for controlling payroll and material costs, are not substitutes for the traditional monthly budget. They are valuable adjuncts—each within its own sphere contributing to efficient and profitable operations. It is, therefore, proper to consider pre-control techniques in this chapter, especially those pre-control techniques that are helpful in short-term budgeting.

Payroll pre-control. There is no doubt that labor is one of the most difficult items of expense to control. Such being the case, the area of labor costs has been selected to illustrate the workings of pre-control techniques.

Payroll pre-control is predicated on the theory of maintaining a predetermined standard of work productivity. This means that a specific number of personnel is related to a specific work load or volume. Payroll pre-control forecasts work loads on a day-to-day basis, not on a historical basis. It projects staff requirements to meet the daily work loads of each department. The performance of departments is evaluated by comparing actual personnel used with the established standards.

► EXAMPLE: Under the payroll pre-control method, the rooms department staff of a hotel would predetermine a standard number of rooms to be serviced per maid per day. Then, based on day-to-day forecasts of expected occupancy, only the number of maids needed to service the occupied rooms would be called to work.

There are six elements that are prerequisites in any system of payroll pre-controls. These are listed and explained in the following paragraphs:

1. *Establish job number control.* The first element of payroll pre-control is the individual job. Job number control of each job is installed as a fundamental part of any payroll pre-control system.

2. *Set work performance standards for each job classification.* This second major element of payroll pre-control requires a study to determine standards of work performance in every job classification. These measures of performance are used to predetermine staff requirements in forecasting work loads. Such standards are also used in measuring performance by calculating standard staff requirements in comparison with actual staff used as recorded by each department head.

3. *Determine work load forecast.* Payroll pre-control's third element is the forecast of the expected work loads a week in advance, with necessary corrections being made on a day-to-day basis. These forecasts are expressed in terms of the number of units of sales or anticipated sales volume. The sales information so forecast is the foundation for staff planning in all departments.

4. *Prepare daily payroll reports for each department.* This requires the establishment of accurate daily payroll reports for each department. These payroll reports do not record dollars of payroll costs. They merely reflect the number of full-time employees in each job classification.

5. *Controlling the hiring of extras and overtime.* The fifth principle of the system is the establishment of a formal controlling device for the hiring and use of extra employees and of overtime. In order to provide effective control, the procedure for hiring extra employees and the authorization of overtime must be subject to management's review and possible veto. Therefore, this element of formal requisitioning becomes an integral part of the system. Specific authorization by management is necessary before additional labor costs are incurred. Incidentally, this requisition also serves as an authorization to the payroll department to make payment for the services so approved.

6. *Report on actual performance as compared with forecasts.* The sixth element of the system of payroll pre-control requires measurement of performance by means of a formal report at the end of each week. This report projects the number of employees over or under the standards that have been previously set for each department and for the entire business.

There are, of course, many refinements that are necessary in an effectively functioning system of payroll pre-control. This presentation covers only the basic techniques or fundamentals that are inherent in the day-to-day budgetary control of the principal elements of cost in business operations.

Maintaining the budget system. The budget will be effective only as long as it has the complete approval and support of the organization's top executives. They must understand thoroughly what it will accomplish and must insist that it be adhered to throughout the company. Budgeting philosophies formulated at the top level must be sold down the line throughout the company. In this sense, the success of a budget system depends more on human relationships than on accounting techniques.

The budget system needs periodic follow-up and review from time to time by both management and the public accountant. Procedures and forms must be up-dated to meet changing conditions. The budget prepared last year can become obsolete if the company adds a new product or makes changes in its departmental setup. Business is fluid and budgeting and planning must be reviewed continuously for needed adjustments to meet new conditions.

It is the benefits that are derived from a properly functioning budget that serve to insure its continuance. The company that plans ahead moves ahead. The very adoption of a budget, with the consequent necessity to plan, is sometimes spoken of as the major advantage gained from budgeting.

The changing role of the accountant requires that you play an important part in aiding management to forecast, plan, control, and improve operating results. In performing this management service, you yourself will benefit greatly through continuing growth, and through the greater satisfaction you will derive from your work. Such services to management offer variety, challenge and opportunity, and, if well handled, a means of real and lasting satisfaction to you, the professional accountant. It is these areas that present your greatest challenge and the fullest opportunity for the exercise of your creative talents.

15

How to Budget Business Operations

CONTENTS

15

How to Budget Business Operations

Bertrand J. Belda, CPA

A budgetary system is easier to understand when the budgets and reporting forms are illustrated, instead of merely explained through textual material. For this reason, budgets and underlying source data for various sections of a typical company are interspersed throughout the chapter. These presentations, together with examples of budget reports, are included in order to give the reader a clear perception of how this useful management tool can be developed and applied.

This chapter aims to present the important subject of budgeting in a manner that is most useful to accountants serving both large and small enterprises. Hence, a full budgetary control system for a "medium" sized manufacturing business is illustrated on the theory that the more modest requirements of smaller organizations may be met by subtracting some details, and the needs of larger ones can be satisfied by expanding the material. In any discussion of budgeting, executives, such as the Controller and the Budget Coordinator are key individuals who should be intimately involved.

The independent accountant can often provide helpful counsel to his clients in budgeting matters. Also, by reviewing budget performance data, the auditor may observe variations that merit special attention.

This chapter also covers and explains the special techniques applicable to budgeting for project-type expenditures, such as plant and equipment acquisitions and research.

THE ESSENTIALS OF BUDGETING

Before entering into the actual mechanics of bugeting, it is important to review the factors that contribute to the success of a budget system. It is important, also, to discuss some of the approaches that are often helpful in organizing a budget program. These essentials of budgeting are covered under the following headings:

1. Elements of budgeting.
2. Elements of a budget program.

Elements of budgeting. The classic roles of management are to plan, organize, execute, and report. Forecasts and budgets are both planning and control mechanisms which can provide organized systems for developing sound business programs. By measuring results against these plans, management is able to assess the progress (or lack of it) in meeting objectives, and direct attention to problems and/or opportunities so identified. Thus, forecasts and budgets are major tools for "profit planning."

A forecast is a dollarized representation of both revenues and expenses of an enterprise over a fairly long period ahead. Forecasting methods are discussed subsequently in this chapter. Budgets, on the other hand, are more attuned to planning and controlling costs and expenses on a current, shorter-term basis. In essence, forecasts may be likened to *strategic* planning, while budgets are *tactical* programs to reflect pre-determined policies of what should be attained under prevailing circumstances that may differ from those contemplated when the forecast was developed. Thus, a sound budget system should be flexible enough to measure performance under varying conditions of operations.

Control of operating costs and expenses is the primary aim of business budgeting. This control may be achieved by incorporating four distinct elements into the internal accounting and reporting system. These are listed and discussed as follows:

1. Cost and expenses are classified into clearly defined functional groupings in a manner that will provide meaningful and consistent analyses.
2. Departments and operating centers are identified in terms of the managers responsible for their respective operations.
3. Quantitative goals or objectives are established for each specific cost and expense classification and according to departmental responsibilities.
4. Timely compilation and reporting of costs and expenses incurred in comparison with established goals is vital.

Classification of costs and expenses. The system of classifying costs and expenses for budgetary control purposes should indicate the sources of the principal components of these charges. Expense accounts such as repairs and maintenance or supplies, that include charges from payroll, vouchers, journals, etc., all combined, may not be adequate for budgetary planning and control. Thus, the account classifications should be developed in a manner that will clearly show management those separate costs that stem from labor effort, physical quantities of materials or supplies consumed, journal entries, etc.

Identification of departments and operating centers. The next essential element of a successful budget program is the separation of costs and expenses according to the scope of responsibility of individual managers. It is axiomatic to effective control that each manager be keenly aware of and understand just what costs are incurred in operations under his jurisdiction. The accounting arrangement should conform to the organizational chain of command in the enterprise so that budgets for a group of subordinate supervisors can be combined into a total for all units under the direction of the senior executive. Cost centers utilized for product cost accumulations may not always conform to these managerial authority and responsibility divisions. In such instances, it is important that the chart of accounts be revised to provide information that clearly reflects the span of control for each level of management.

Establishing goals or objectives. Budgeting involves the definition of an operating plan that sets forth specific cost and expense "allowances" for a particular period, under defined conditions. These allowances are expressed in monetary terms for a given period of time, for a unit of activity, and/or a combination of these factors. The cost elements, determined, first, in "physical" dimensions (gallons, pounds, labor hours, etc.), are then translated into dollar amounts for various levels of activity. This process is accomplished through the joint efforts of departmental managers and accounting staff so that the responsible supervisors are familiar with the nature of the expenses generated under their respective jurisdictions, both in total and for segments thereof. This kind of "participative" management contemplates that the budget allowances reflect reasonable goals that each manager believes to be attainable and is willing to have used as a measure of performance. When expenses incurred are measured against budget allowances, so determined, managers and their executive superiors alike are given a current yardstick to gauge the progress achieved in reaching the pre-planned objectives.

Timely management information. Performance reports, prepared and issued at frequent intervals (monthly, at least), showing actual expenses compared to budget allowances, and made available promptly after the close of each interval, are essential to effective cost control. In addition to reporting complete, itemized information on a regular schedule, it is often important to compile and report certain key data on a more current basis. For example, man hours worked, kilowatt hours of power consumed, materials requisitioned, etc., when tabulated at the close of each shift or each day, and compared with the quantities of such items contemplated in the budget for them, can be valuable indicators of prospects for successful performance for the period, and signal the need for management attention to any areas that merit it.

Elements of a budget program. While the budgeting of business operations involves the knowledge and application of specialized techniques of planning, measuring, and reporting, the most important feature is the method of organizing the program. In establishing a budget program, the budget technician is only the catalyst; the line executives and managers have the key role in successful budgeting. Accordingly, it is essential that all members of the management team understand the plan's principal features, respect them, and support its use and application.

The final authority for setting budget allowances must rest with the chief executive officer of the enterprise. Similarly, all departmental and divisional budgets must have the full cognizance and approval of the respective managers of those units. Much of the detail, rationale, and computations of specific allowances can be developed by the budget co-ordinator, but the program is not likely to achieve good results unless the line managers agree to the measurement bases and accept them as equitable performance evaluators.

Usually, administration of a budget program is a function of the Controller's Office. The tasks involved in organizing the system, compiling budget allowances, and reporting results are traditionally accounting functions and should be the "natural" location for this responsibility. Among others, there are two reasons for placing the budget function under the Controller that merit mention. These are the following:

1. The Controller has the basic function of translating business activities into monetary amounts and of measuring and reporting them on an objective basis. Budget data are an integral part of this process.
2. Compiling, classifying, and summarizing underlying source information often involves the handling of extensive quantities of paper work and processing which are routine functions in the accounting and bookkeeping operations of the Controller's Office.

The individual appointed to handle the day-to-day responsibility for administration of a budget program can be identified by one of a variety of suitable titles. These designations include: Budget Director, Budget Administrator, Manager of Budgets, Budget Co-ordinator, and other. Regardless of the specific title given this position, it is highly important that the authorities of this individual be limited to interpretation of operating requirements of each organizational unit, translating them into useful measures, and compiling reports on budget performance. He should *not* have authority to establish the budget allowances or to enforce conformity to them. These are clearly the responsibilities of line management; the budget is a tool for operating officials and not an accountant's straight-jacket to be imposed upon other executives of the enterprise.

Although operating budgets can be developed for all areas of a business, it may be prudent to commence the program by establishing budget allowances for a limited number of key areas, initially. After these have been successfully instituted, the program can be extended to other areas.

In manufacturing companies where a standard cost system is in use, the standards for prime manufacturing costs (component materials and direct productive labor) usually can be used to represent the budget allowances for these cost elements. These costs tend to increase or decrease in direct proportion to the unit volumes of production attained, and may be budgeted accordingly. These are customarily referred to as "variable," since they rise or decline in proportion to varying production volumes. In certain industries (merchandising, insurance, banking, etc.) where standard costs are not employed, the task of developing budget allowances for variable costs is likely to involve more extensive analyses to ascertain what measures are suitable.

As indicated previously, an operating budget program should provide performance measures that "flex" to conform to the conditions at hand. While variable costs may be budgeted on the basis of allowances related to the volume of activity, other charges are not likely to respond to the ebb and flow of activity. Frequently, the most difficult problem encountered in budgeting is the identification of the behavior patterns of certain expense categories. Also, while all expenses of a business are aimed at producing profitable revenues, either presently or in the future, many charges incurred do not readily relate to products or services currently being marketed. Administrative expenses and the costs of facilities acquired in periods past are typical items of this nature. These types of charges may not be expanded or contracted as production of goods or services increases or decreases. Costs fitting this description are referred to as "fixed" costs and tend to remain relatively constant from period to period, within a reasonable range of activity. These are usually budgeted by allowances established per period of time, rather than per unit of activity volume.

Another category of cost behavior, and this applies to a substantial number of items in most businesses, is "semi-variable" or "semi-fixed." These items may be expected to vary somewhat with changing activity levels, but not in *direct* proportion to production or sales outputs. Many indirect and overhead expenses are characterized by these behavior tendencies and are sometimes referred to as "mixed" costs. After suitable study, mixed costs can be budgeted so as to provide a fixed amount, per period of time, plus a variable amount per unit of activity; the combination of both elements providing the total budget for the item, as calculated from the pre-set conditions.

In some businesses, certain expenses, such as maintenance, may be deferred during periods of high activity and scheduled for incurrence when operating volume falls to low levels. Expense behavior for such items tends to increase or decrease in inverse relationship to volume and may be referred to as "inverse variables."

Finally, certain business activities are programmed with a view to very long periods ahead on a basis that does not fit any of the patterns discussed above. These are usually "project-type" programs involving product development or construction and acquisition of additional or replacement facilities. Budgetary control of these costs is usually developed through special appropriation methods that are tailored to the objectives of the program.

THE SALES FORECAST — THE FOUNDATION FOR BUDGETING

The preparation of an operating budget usually begins with a forecast of sales or other revenues that may be reasonably expected over a representative period ahead. This estimate of prospective sales volume is necessary in order to develop plans to acquire and/or produce the goods and services necessary to support these revenues, together with the underlying costs and expenses that are required to meet the projected demand. Thus, inventory levels of raw materials, work-in-process and finished goods, personnel staffing, marketing programs, and all other activities should be keyed to expected customer demand. Moreover, the range of prospective sales volumes is a fundamental consideration in management decisions relating to the acquisition and/or construction of physical facilities necessary to produce and market the merchandise expected to be sold.

The sales forecast should include a reasonably detailed estimate of future sales for each major product line or type of service revenue, and should reflect any seasonal or other month-to-month variations in terms of physical units, as well as dollar amounts.

As sales forecasts are predictions of probable future events, they cannot be prepared with any assurance of complete accuracy. Nevertheless, past experiences, carefully evaluated and related to probable causative factors, can provide a basis for rational projections of probable demand.

Industry-wide forecasts. Companies which can be identified as being a part of a specific industry will find it advantageous to begin their own sales forecast by making an appraisal of the prospects for the entire industry. When this has been developed, the share of that market which may be expected by the individual enterprise within that broad category may be calculated.

As an example, consider the approach that might be used by a manufacturer of an item of clothing for high school students. It would appear that the demand for this merchandise is likely to depend upon such factors as the general economic climate, style preferences, etc., of the sub-adult group, the number of individuals in that group, pricing policies, and similar considerations. Using just some of these factors, for example, a simple approach to a forecast of the industry-wide sales for the clothing item under consideration might begin with a study of past experience over a representative period of time. For this purpose, assume that trade association data are available and they show the following patterns:

NATIONAL VOLUME OF PRODUCTS
(In Thousands)

Year	*Unit shipments*	*Dollar Shipments*
0	25,845	$15,507
1	24,428	14,657
2	25,541	15,325
3	25,944	15,566
4	27,608	16,565
5	24,943	14,966
6	28,575	18,574
7	29,565	19,217
8	29,969	19,480
9	29,798	19,369
10	32,308	22,616

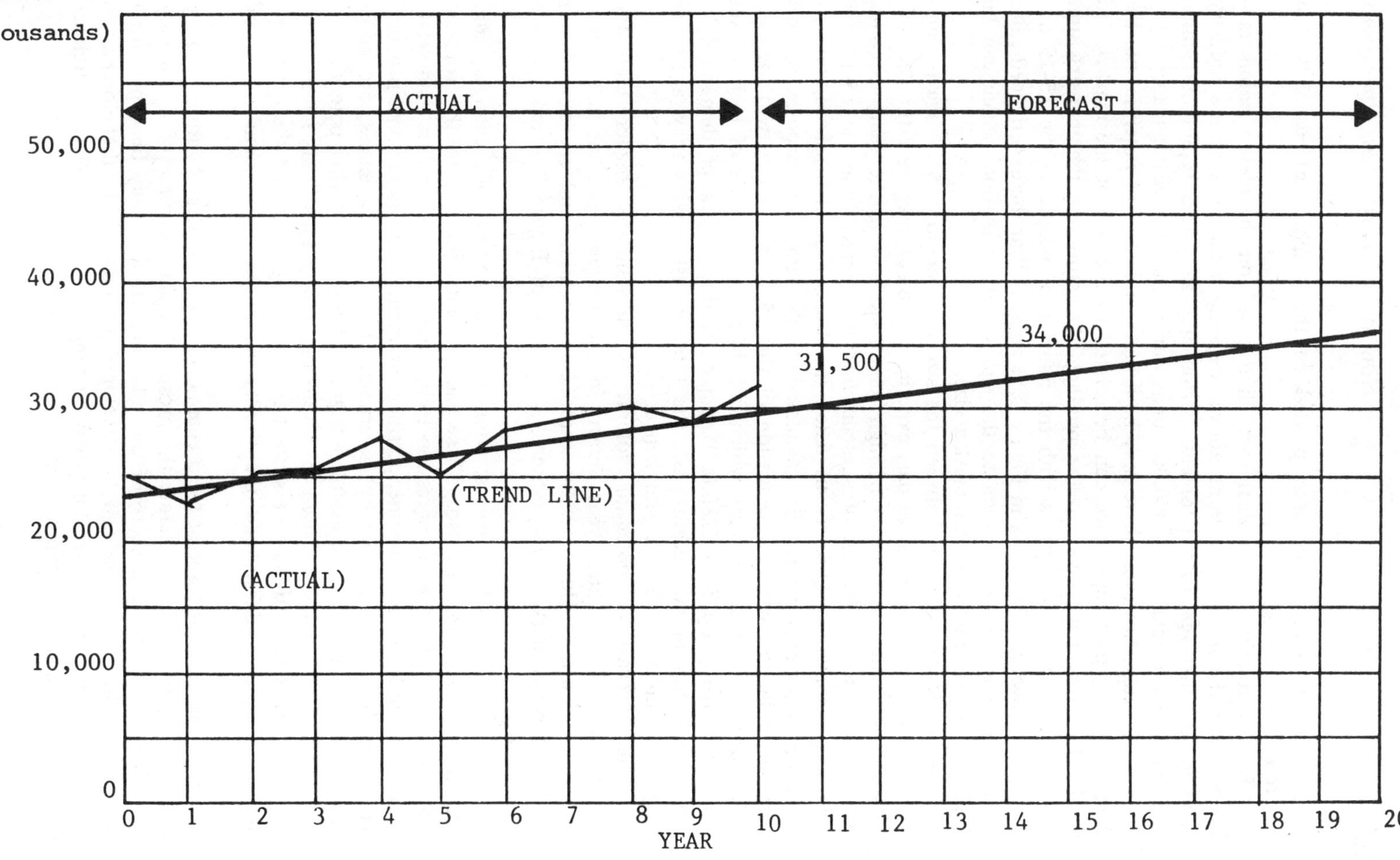

Fig. 1. Industry Shipment of Product by Years.

The above information has been plotted on the graph chart, as shown in Figure 1.

By constructing a statistical trend line based on the eleven points tabulated from the industry patterns above, we may ascertain that the industry sales for the first year of the forecast period may aggregate 31,500,000 units, and may reach a total of 34,000,000 units during the fifth year ahead.

In this case, however, there may be a better indicator of potential market demand, if the past experience can be related to the *size* of the market and the level of patronage given to the product. By comparing the industry unit sales for the past eleven years with the number of people in the 15-19 age group, as shown on the graph in Figure 2, it appears that the experienced sales patterns have a close correlation to the age 15-19 population, which can be deemed as representative of the market size.

Using the relationships between the size of demand (15-19 age population) and industry unit sales of past experience, we can prepare estimated unit volumes for future populations of high school students in the years to come. Based upon the distribution of ages in children younger than the 15-19 age bracket (as shown by U.S. census data) the number of high school students in future years may be readily calculated. Such data, for purposes of this example, indicates that the population of the 15-19 age group will increase 28% during the next five years which will bring the number of high school population group up to 17,280,000 people. If the pattern of demand continues as it has in the recent past, the total industry sales may aggregate 41,400,000 units in the fifth year hence.

This forecast of potential volume is substantially higher than the 34,000,000 units for that year shown in the simple trend-line calculation shown in Figure 1. However, by introducing an additional causative factor (size of specific market), the estimate developed in Figure 2 seems to have superior logic.

Other variables, such as prices, competitive pressures, style changes, etc., may merit consideration, also. These can be introduced into the forecast through the use of multiple regression techniques. Macro economic data relating to disposable personal income, pertinent segments of gross national product, retail sales, etc., as predicted by governmental economic agencies, are additional elements that may be useful indicators of industry market potential.

Whatever methods are used in developing a forecast of this nature, it is paramount that the rationale be such that the management find the basis sensible and understandable, and the results acceptable as a sound basis for planning purposes.

Preparing a sales forecast for a company. The estimates of future industry demand may be used to generate the prospective sales volume of a company within that industry. The share of the total market that may be experienced by an individual enterprise can be developed by quantifying that company's traditional portion as adjusted for possible changes in pricing policies, merchandising strategies, and competitive strengths and weaknesses.

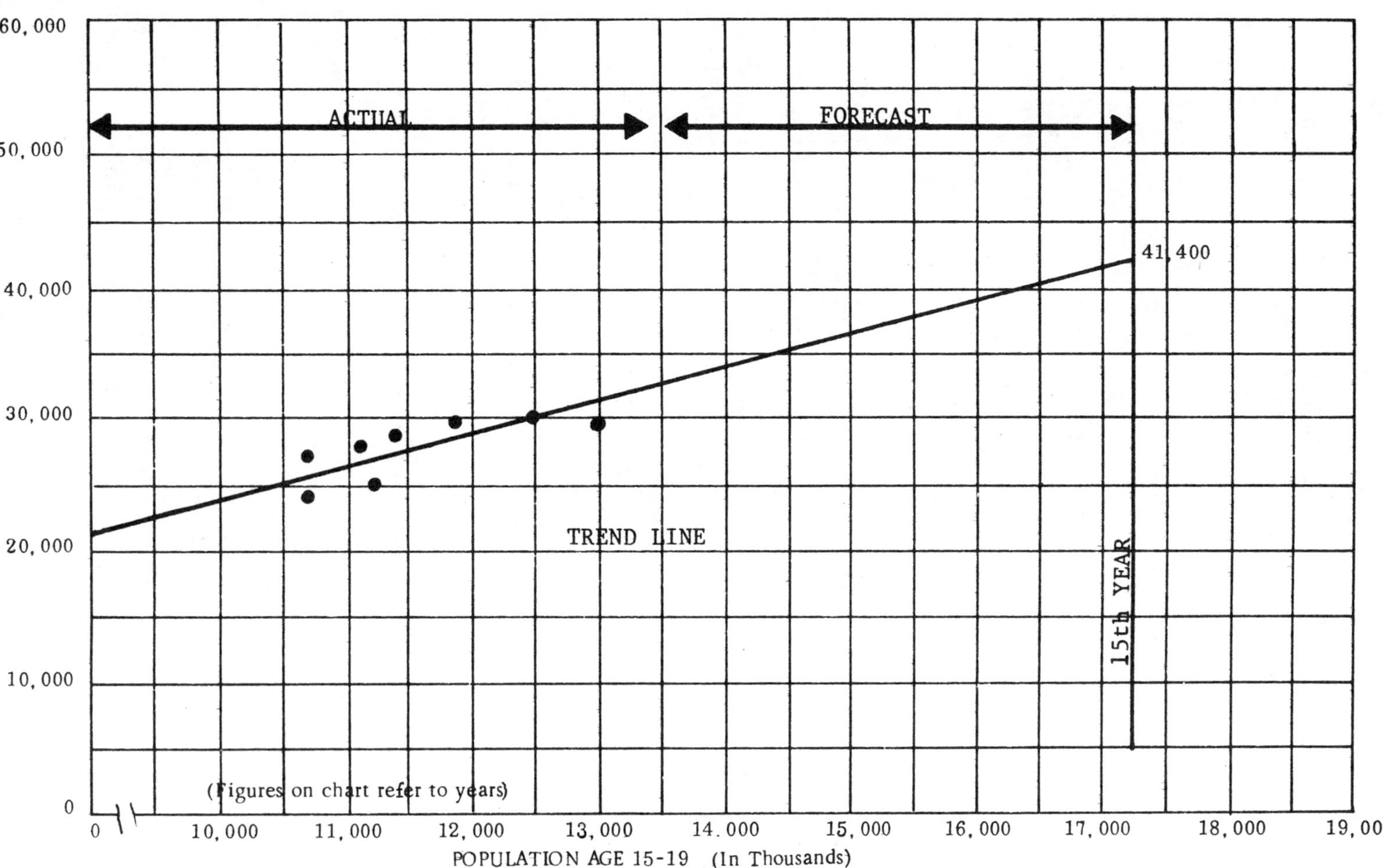

Fig. 2. Industry Shipments of a Product as Related to Population Age 15-19.

Without detailing all of these considerations, a company might develop its own sales forecast, using industry data referred to previously, along the following lines:

Year	Industry Shipments (Thousands of Units)	Company Shipments (Thousands of Units)	Company Share of the Market	Company Dollar Sales (Thousands of Dollars)
Actual:				
5	24,943	2,544	10.2%	$2,125
6	28,575	3,143	11.0%	2,768
7	29,565	3,311	11.2%	2,940
8	29,969	3,386	11.3%	2,922
9	29,798	3,397	11.4%	2,938
10	32,308	3,780	11.7%	3,528
Forecast:				
11	33,300	3,930	11.8%	3,660
12	35,000	4,130	11.8%	3,920
13	37,300	4,440	11.9%	4,220
14	40,000	4,760	11.9%	4,665
15	41,400	4,970	12.0%	4,970

The particulars supporting the gradual increase in market share during the forecast years are not reviewed here. However, it is important that supporting rationale for such pattern adjustments as the expected gradual increase in market share and prices be carefully documented, including any costs that may be incurred in achieving the estimated sales increases. The annual sales data, for the first year of the forecast period at least, should be converted into shorter periods for short-term comparisons of results and expectations. To the extent that actual sales exceed or fail to meet the forecasts, it may be desirable to revise future revenue expectations and take prompt tactical actions to meet the circumstances.

BUDGETING COSTS AND EXPENSES

Direct (variable) costs. After completing a reasonable sales forecast, the prime costs of producing the goods or services expected must be determined. Customary cost accounting methods for ascertaining the unit direct materials and direct labor are usually adequate to calculate the estimated cost of these elements. An integrated standard cost system can be quite effective as a basis for these calculations. Where the variety of products is extensive, or where unit costs are not readily available, it may be practical to utilize percentages of revenue dollars to establish the budget allowances for the prime costs. However, if sales dollars are used, care should be taken to recognize the impact of potential price inflation which may not affect costs in the same proportion as that applicable to selling prices.

Budgeting labor costs. Employee compensation costs, including salaries and wages of all personnel, can be budgeted effectively by first identifying the number of people, specific skills, and rates of pay for the staff required in each department or other unit of the business. The customary approach to this analysis is the preparation of a "manning table" that lists the personnel complement of each organizational unit. In preparing this table, it is essential to specify the operating volume that is expected to prevail. This may be done by first determining the quantities of expected unit production, and then translating these into a suitable common denominator for each unit. Assuming that a standard cost system is employed, production units frequently use measures such as "standard labor hours produced"[1] as indicative of the quantity of production volume attained. In some departments, the quantity of materials processed may be an alternative volume measure.

In order to illustrate methods for developing and using an operating budget system, a manufacturing enterprise has been selected. It is assumed that the company's products are fashioned from metal components and other materials which are assembled into a variety of finished units.

Compiling a manning table. Figure 3 illustrates a manning table as it might appear for a typical factory department. It contains an analysis of all the personnel in a machine shop, classified as to types of skills employed in both direct and indirect labor categories, and these are identified in column (1). Compensation rates are shown in column (2). It is assumed that production schedules are planned on a week-to-week basis, therefore, the data are compiled for weekly periods. Columns (3), (4) and (5) are used to display the staffing in the department as it is presently set. This can be of assistance in developing realistic budget allowances. The present operating level (1760 Standard Direct Labor Hours produced[1]) is slightly below the "normal" volume of production.

In columns (6), (7), and (8), respectively, are set forth the staff requirements, time worked and payroll costs for a "normal" production volume. The normal operating volume represents the output necessary to support the sales forecast over the weeks ahead. The normal weekly labor hours are determined by the Machine Shop Foreman and the Budget Co-ordinator, working in concert and, using Standard Direct Labor Hours as the measure of departmental activity, the staffing requirements have been established at 1846 SDLH per week.

After the personnel requirements for the normal operating level have been established, staffing needs and hours and costs for selected other production volumes, below and above the normal activity, are determined. In Figure 3, these have been detailed to show the pre-planned manpower requirements at six other volume levels which have been developed for points at 10% inter-

---

[1]Standard Direct Labor Hours (SDLH), as used here, represents the direct labor hours planned or budgeted for the performance of each production operation. The total SDLH produced is determined by multiplying the quantity of production by the SDLH requirement for each operation.

MANNING TABLES--MACHINE SHOP
WEEKLY STAFFING REQUIREMENTS

(1)	(2)	(3)	(4)	(5)	(6)	(7)	(8)	(9)	(10)	(11)	(12)
		PRESENT STAFF			"NORMAL" STAFF			STAFFING AND BUDGET AT AT 110%			
JOB CLASSIFICATION	Standard Hourly Wage Rate	Number Of Employees	Weekly Hours	Standard Cost	Number Of Employees	Weekly Hours	Standard Cost	Number Of Employees	Weekly Hours	Standard Cost	Number Of Employees
DIRECT LABOR:											
Drill press	$ 9	11	440	$ 3,960	11	440	$ 3,960	12	480	$ 4,320	13
Milling machine	11	8	320	3,520	8	330*	3,630	9	360	3,960	9
Lathe	10	10	400	4,000	11	450*	4,500	12	490*	4,900	13
Boring mill	11	6	240	2,640	6	266*	2,926	7	280	3,080	8
Gear cutter	10	5	200	2,000	5	200	2,000	5	221*	2,210	6
Grinding machine	9	4	160	1,440	4	160	1,440	5	200	1,800	5
TOTALS--DIRECT LABOR		44	1,760	$17,560	45	1,846	$ 18,456	50	2,031	$ 20,270	54
INDIRECT LABOR:											
Supervision	$ (A)	4	160	$ 2,860	4	160	$ 2,860	4	160	$ 2,860	4
Clerical	(A)	4	160	1,210	4	160	1,210	4	160	1,210	4
Inspectors	12	2	85*	1,020	2	90*	1,080	2	100*	1,200	3
Stock handlers	7	4	160	1,120	4	170*	1,190	5	200	1,400	5
Machine set-up	14	3	120	1,680	3	120	1,680	3	130*	1,820	3
Clean-up	6	3	125*	750	3	130*	780	3	140*	840	4
Dept. maintenance	11	2	80	880	2	80	880	2	80	880	2
Other	(B)	1	40	470	1	40	470	1	40	470	1
TOTALS--INDIRECT LABOR		23	930	$ 9,990	23	950	$ 10,150	24	1,010	$ 10,680	26
OTHER LABOR OVERHEAD:											
Overtime premium*				40			250			150	
Shift differential				-0-			-0-			-0-	
TOTALS--LABOR OVERHEAD				$10,030			$ 10,400			$ 10,830	
MONTHLY BUDGET ALLOWANCES (WEEKLY TOTALS CONVERTED TO MONTHLY TOTALS @ 4-1/3 WEEKS (ROUNDED)):											
Standard direct labor hours							8,000 Hrs.			8,800 Hrs.	
DIRECT LABOR BUDGET (STAND. COST)							$ 80,000			$ 87,800	
INDIRECT LABOR OVERHEAD BUDGET							45,000			47,000	
TOTAL MONTHLY LABOR COST BUDGET		67			68		$125,000	74		$134,800	80

Fig. 3. Manning Table of a Factory Department.

(13)	(14)	(15)	(16)	(17)	(18)	(19)	(20)	(21)	(22)	(23)	(24)	(25)	(26)
ACTIVITY LEVELS IN EXCESS OF NORMAL					STAFFING AND BUDGET AT ACTIVITY LEVELS BELOW NORMAL								
AT 120%			AT 130%			AT 90%			AT 80%			AT 70%	
Weekly Hours	Standard Cost	Number Of Employees	Weekly Hours	Standard Cost	Number Of Employees	Weekly Hours	Standard Cost	Number Of Employees	Weekly Hours	Standard Cost	Number Of Employees	Weekly Hours	Standard Cost
530*	$ 4,770	14	570*	$ 5,130	10	380	$ 3,420	9	360	$ 3,240	7	260	$ 2,340
385*	4,235	10	400	4,400	7	280	3,080	7	280	3,080	7	280	3,080
520	5,200	14	560	5,600	10	400	4,000	9	360	3,600	8	320	3,200
320	3,520	9	370*	4,070	6	240	2,640	5	200	2,200	4	160	1,760
240	2,400	6	260*	2,600	5	200	2,000	4	160	1,600	4	160	1,600
220*	1,980	6	240	2,160	4	160	1,440	3	120	1,080	3	120	1,080
2,215	$ 22,105	59	2,400	$ 23,960	42	1,660	$ 16,580	37	1,480	$ 14,800	33	1,300	$ 13,060
160	$ 2,860	5	200	$ 3,500	4	160	$ 2,860	4	160	$ 2,860	4	160	$ 2,860
160	1,210	4	160	1,210	4	160	1,210	4	160	1,210	4	160	1,210
120	1,440	3	120	1,440	2	80	960	2	80	960	2	80	960
200	1,400	5	200	1,400	3	160	1,120	2	80	560	2	80	560
140*	1,960	3	150	2,100	3	120	1,680	3	120	1,680	3	120	1,680
160	960	4	160	960	3	120	720	3	120	720	2	80	480
90*	990	2	90*	990	2	80	8[illegible]	2	80	880	2	80	880
40	470	1	40	470	1	40	470	1	40	470	0	-0-	-0-
1,070	$ 11,290	27	1,120	$ 12,070	22	920	$ 9,900	21	840	$ 9,340	19	760	$ 8,630
	270			200			-0-			-0-			-0-
	-0-			330			-0-			-0-			-0-
	$ 11,560			$ 12,600			$ 9,900			$ 9,340			$ 8,630
	9,600 Hrs.			10,400 Hrs.			7,200 Hrs.			6,400 Hrs.			5,600 Hrs.
	$ 95,800			$103,800			$ 71,800			$ 64,100			$ 56,600
	50,100			54,600			42,900			40,500			37,400
	$145,900	86		$158,400	64		$114,700	58		$104,600	52		$ 94,000

PREPARED BY: T. E. Anderson (Budget Co-ordinator)
APPROVED BY: J. W. Hemphill (Dept. Foreman)
AUTHORIZED BY: J. M. McKeon (Plant Superintendent)

Fig. 3. Manning Table of a Factory Department. (Continued.)

vals, above and below normal. Columns (9) through (17) reflect weekly staffing details when production volumes exceed the normal level, and columns (18) through (26) provide similar data for staff needs when production output is below normal.

When these detailed plans have been completed to the satisfaction of the Department Foreman and the Budget Co-ordinator, they are presented to the Plant Superintendent whose final authorization is required to establish the budget allowances for each department under his jurisdiction. Weekly data is then converted to monthly information as shown in the lower portion of Figure 3. This has been done so that the budget allowances conform to the system of compiling performance reports on a monthly basis.

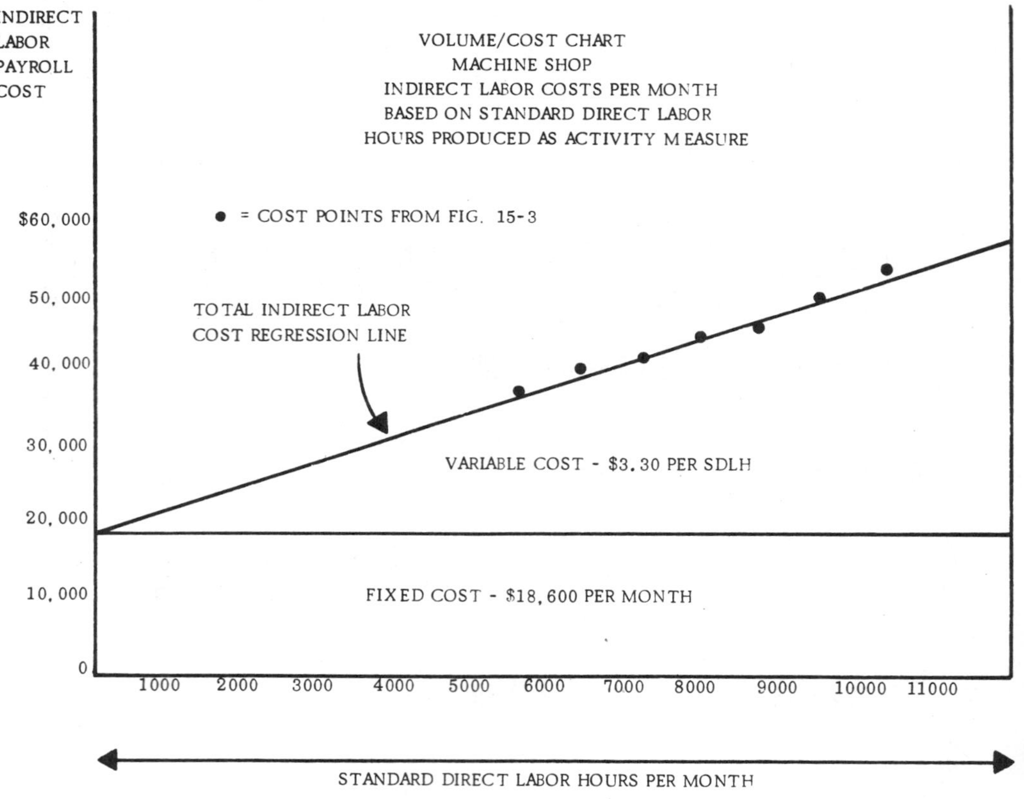

Fig. 4. Volume/Cost Chart.

Plotting the volume/cost chart. Figure 4 displays the cost behavior variations as developed for payroll charges for seven varying production levels in the manning table, as measured by Standard Direct Labor Hours Produced.

By applying the "least squares" method, a regression line can be inserted on the graph which indicates that the "fixed" cost element for indirect labor is $18,600 per month and the "variable" cost rate is $3.30 per SDLH produced. Using these data for flexible budgeting, the Machine Shop Foreman can be aware that his budget plan allows for these costs. Thus, if production schedules for a coming month contemplate that the department will generate, say 9000 SDLH, his manpower budget will total $90,000 for direct labor costs, and $48,300 for indirect labor ($18,600 fixed cost, plus $29,700 variable cost, the latter developed by multiplying 9000 SDLH by $3.30). With this information at hand, the Foreman can arrange his staff complement and work hours in a manner that will conform to the budget plan that he, himself, has had a major part in preparing.

Budgeting non-labor costs. Budgets for departmental charges for costs other than personnel compensation should be developed with much the same kind of analytical study as that used for the labor portion. Figure 5 displays a summary of nonpayroll departmental costs as they might be determined for the same seven volume levels used in Figure 3 for the same Machine Shop. As these charges are usually accumulated in the accounting records on a monthly basis, the analysis has utilized a monthly period (without weekly detail). For each expense category, as shown in column (1), this example shows some past experience results in column (2). Column (3) sets forth the budget bases for each expense item. These bases, it is assumed, were developed from more detailed studies of the individual items. For example, the budget for electricity costs would be based upon the kilowatt hours required for plant illumination and operation of continuous equipment to determine the fixed amount of power consumption, while the variable power costs would be based on the kilowatts consumed per hour of machine operations in production. These units of electrical power, extended at utility rates in effect, produce the $400 monthly fixed expense, and the $0.70 rate per SDLH variable expense for budgeted electricity costs.

It will be noted that Figure 5 distinguishes between two categories of departmental expenses. The first group are departmental items that are incurred as a result of actions taken within the department and, presumably, under the direct supervision of its Foreman. The other category (Allocated Departmental Expense) is comprised of overhead items which are distributed to the Machine Shop for product costing purposes, but relate to non-current management decisions (depreciation) and general Company policies, rather than direct departmental actions.

Column (4) of Figure 5 sets forth the result of calculations of budget allowances for "normal" operating activity (8000 SDLH per month). Columns (5) through (7) show the budget for three points above normal volume, and columns (8), (9), and (10) display budgeted expenses for three levels below the normal operating rate. It will be observed that Standard Direct Labor Hours are used as the measure of production. The nonlabor departmental

MACHINE SHOP

NON-LABOR DEPARTMENTAL BUDGET ALLOWANCES

(1)	(2) Monthly Average Last Quarter	(3) Budget Bases
ACTIVITY MEASURE - STANDARD DIRECT LABOR HOURS PRODUCED	7,600	
Departmental Charges (Controllable):		
Labor fringe benefits--		
Payroll taxes	$ 9,700	8% of payroll
Vacation and holiday pay	7,700	6% of payroll
Pensions	4,800	4% of payroll
Group life and health insurance and miscellaneous	2,700	$40 per employee
Total Labor fringe benefits	$ 24,900	
Perishable tools, fixtures, etc.	6,700	$500 plus $0.80 per S.D.L.H.
Electricity	5,850	$400 plus $0.70 per S.D.L.H.
Other Utilities	3,460	$300 plus $0.40 per S.D.L.H.
Lubricants	2,520	$200 plus $0.30 per S.D.L.H.
Manufacturing supplies	2,370	$1,000 plus $0.20 per S.D.L.H.
Staff charges for direct services:		
Factory maintenance	4,800	$1,100 plus $0.50 per S.D.L.H.
Industrial engineering	1,750	$480 plus $0.20 per S.D.L.H.
Miscellaneous	2,150	$400 plus $0.20 per S.D.L.H.
Scrap and spoiled work (excess over std.)	5,300	$0.50 per S.D.L.H.
TOTAL CONTROLLABLE CHARGES	$ 59,800	
ALLOCATED DEPARTMENTAL EXPENSES:		
Depreciation-Machinery and Equipment	$ 5,700	$5,700 per month
Insurance	1,960	$1,200 plus $0.10 per S.D.L.H.
Local taxes	1,700	$1,700 per month
Space charges	3,000	$3,000 per month
General Factory-Overhead	2,600	$2,600 per month
TOTAL ALLOCATED EXPENSES	$ 14,960	
TOTAL NON-PAYROLL CHARGES	$ 74,760	
ADD INDIRECT LABOR (FIG. 15-3)	43,340	
TOTAL DEPARTMENT OVERHEAD	$ 118,100	

STANDARD DEPARTMENTAL OVERHEAD RATE ($120,000 ÷ 8,000 SDLH)

(4)	(5)	(6)	(7)	(8)	(9)	(10)
	Budget At Activity In Excess Of Normal			Budget At Activity Less Than Normal		
"Normal"	At 110%	At 120%	At 130%	At 90%	At 80%	At 70%
8,000	8,800	9,600	10,400	7,200	6,400	5,600
$ 10,000	$ 10,780	$ 11,670	$ 12,670	$ 9,180	$ 8,370	$ 7,520
7,500	8,090	8,750	9,500	6,880	6,280	5,640
5,000	5,400	5,840	6,340	4,590	4,180	3,760
2,720	2,960	3,200	3,440	2,560	2,320	2,080
$ 25,220	$ 27,230	$ 29,460	$ 31,950	$ 23,210	$ 21,150	$ 19,000
6,900	7,500	8,180	8,820	6,260	5,620	4,980
6,000	6,560	7,120	7,680	5,440	4,880	4,320
3,500	3,820	4,140	4,460	3,180	2,860	2,540
2,600	2,840	3,080	3,320	2,360	2,120	1,880
2,600	2,760	2,920	3,080	2,440	2,280	2,120
5,100	5,500	5,900	6,300	4,700	4,300	3,900
2,080	2,240	2,400	2,560	1,920	1,760	1,600
2,000	2,160	2,320	2,480	1,840	1,680	1,520
4,000	4,400	4,800	5,200	3,600	3,200	2,800
$ 60,000	$ 65,010	$ 70,320	$ 75,850	$ 54,950	$ 49,850	$ 44,660
$ 5,700	$ 5,700	$ 5,700	$ 5,700	$ 5,700	$ 5,700	$ 5,700
2,000	2,080	2,160	2,240	1,920	1,840	1,760
1,700	1,700	1,700	1,700	1,700	1,700	1,700
3,000	3,000	3,000	3,000	3,000	3,000	3,000
2,600	2,600	2,600	2,600	2,600	2,600	2,600
$ 15,000	$ 15,080	$ 15,160	$ 15,240	$ 14,920	$ 14,840	$ 14,760
$ 75,000	$ 80,090	$ 85,480	$ 91,090	$ 69,870	$ 64,690	$ 59,420
45,000	47,000	50,100	54,600	42,900	40,500	37,400
$ 120,000	$ 127,090	$ 135,580	$ 145,690	$ 112,770	$ 105,190	$ 96,820
$ 15						

PREPARED BY - T. E. Anderson (Budget Co-ordinator)
APPROVED BY - J. W. Hemphill (Department Foreman)
AUTHORIZED BY - J. M. McKeon (Pl[illegible] Superintendent)

expenses, as budgeted for seven levels of production volume, are plotted on a volume/cost chart in the same manner as shown for the labor costs. The non-labor expense behavior is depicted in Figure 6. This analysis indicates that the nonlabor components of the Machine Shop expenses have a "mixed" behavioral pattern that is comprised of $23,860 in fixed costs per month, plus $6.40 per Standard Direct Labor Hour, in various costs.

Summarizing the departmental flexible operating budget. The budget plan for the Machine Shop labor and other expenses, as derived from Figures 3 and 5, may be summarized as follows:

	VARIABLE (Per SDLH)	*FIXED (Per Month)*
Direct Labor	$10.00	$ —0—
Indirect Labor	3.30	18,600
Non-labor direct Expenses	6.30	9,660
Non-labor Allocated Expenses	10	14,200
TOTALS	$19.70	$42,460

With these factors as the total departmental budget basis, the budget allowances can be readily calculated for any reasonable level of activity in the Machine Shop, ranging from a low of 70% of normal to 130% of normal. Of equal significance, the expected behavior of expenses can be utilized for other important management studies, also. For example, if the standard costs in this department, for labor and overhead (conversion costs) are set on the basis of "normal" activity, product cost analysis for use in determining contribution margins on items produced in this department can be readily ascertained. The standard conversion cost, in this case, would be determined as follows:

	Standard Cost Rate
Direct Labor	$10.00
Variable Overhead	9.70
TOTAL VARIABLE MACHINE SHOP COSTS	$19.70
Fixed Overhead = $42,460/8,000 SDLH	5.30
TOTAL STANDARD CONVERSION COST RATE	$25.00

Assuming that inventories are carried at standard cost, developed on an "absorption cost" basis, each Standard Direct Labor Hour produced in the Machine Shop would be added to inventory value at the $25.00 Standard Rate, with product costs also determined on that basis. However, if studies are undertaken to ascertain the probable impact of changing operating volumes, such as a new sales order for products requiring, say 1,000 SDLH of Machine Shop production, management can be aware that the "out-of-pocket" standard

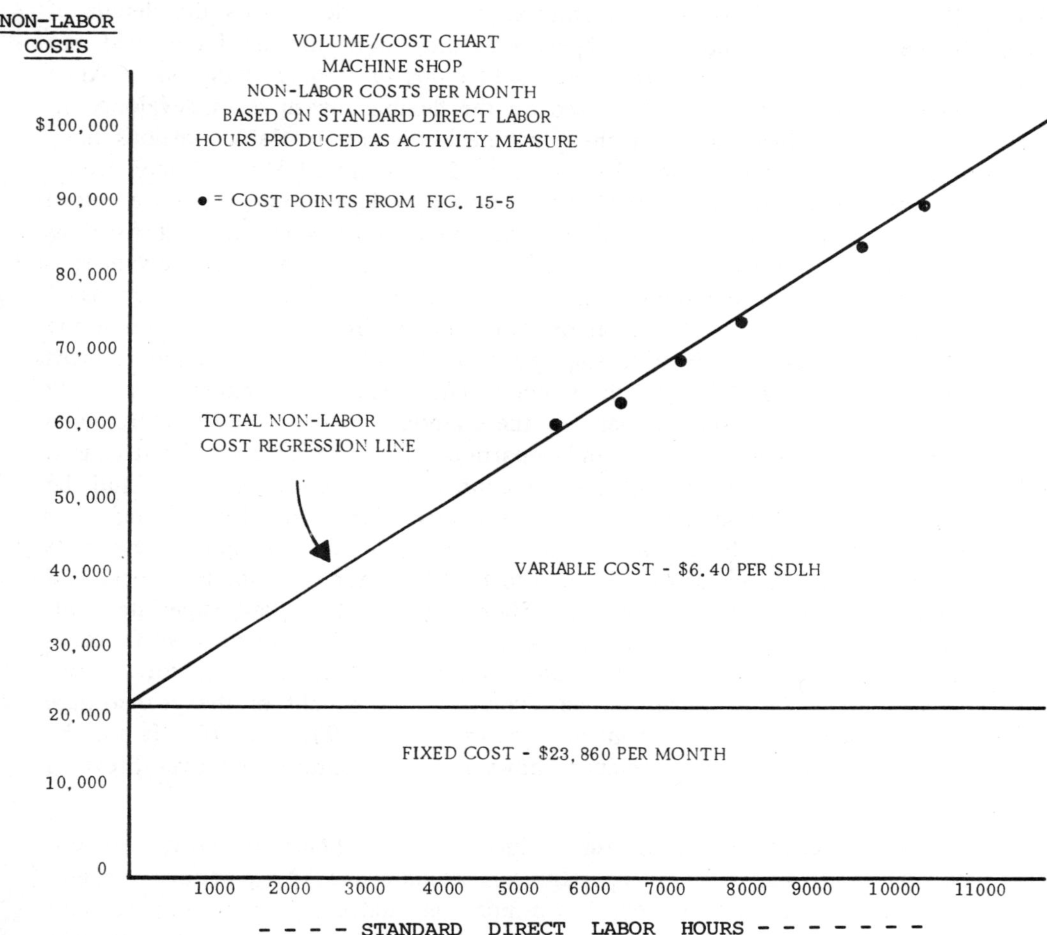

Fig. 6. Volume/Cost Chart for Nonlabor Expenses in Machine Shop.

conversion costs will be $19,700.When this total, plus direct material costs, are compared to prospective selling prices, the probable change in gross profit can be readily ascertained.

Periodic budget performance reports. The regression line analyses for indirect labor and nonlabor department expenses shown in Figures 4 and 6 provide behavior patterns for two broad groupings of departmental expenses. However, it is usually desirable to determine the fixed and variable elements for each expense category. If this is done (in the same manner as that shown for groups) budget reports can pinpoint budget variations in a way that management can give attention to the specific areas that merit it. Figure 7 illustrates a monthly budget performance report which shows the details of budget allowances and actual expenses as they might appear if the fixed and variable components are pre-determined in this fashion. The month of April budget allowances have been based on the flexible measures as developed in the previous illustrations for the Machine Shop. The variable portions have been extended at the respective rate for 8200 Standard Direct Labor Hours generated in the month (2-½% above normal volume), and these are shown in column (3). Monthly fixed expense amounts budgeted are set forth in column (4). The sum of the variable allowances and the fixed allowances is used to determine the total budget for the month, and these data are listed in column (5). Thus, the total operating budget for April, based upon the plans developed in advance, aggregates $204,000, under the circumstances experienced during the month. Column (6) displays the expenses actually incurred, and the variations between these amounts and the budgeted amounts are shown in column (7). Overall departmental performance for April (based on budget and actual amounts for the controllable charges) is 97.4% and the expense overrun aggregates $5,350 for controllable items. By glancing over the variances in column (7), it can be noted that the principal excess costs were incurred in the categories of direct labor, scrap and spoiled work, and industrial engineering. The Machine Shop Foreman, the Plant Superintendent, and other concerned management people can use this information to focus attention on these problem areas and concentrate their efforts to solve them. The monthly performance can be examined in the light of the year-to-date performance data which are given in columns (8), (9), and (10). It may be noted that the April performance shows a slight improvement over previous months.

The accounting system for budgeting. As emphasized throughout this chapter, budgeting business operations is accomplished by planning expenses for each unit of a company, based upon estimated operating requirements which are, primarily, made by the managers of the individual departments. Through the assistance of the Budget Co-ordinator, the planned actions are organized to reflect monetary measures that automatically adjust to the levels of activity actually prevailing. However, the measures and performances need to be incorporated into the company's accounting and data processing systems in order to regularize the program in a consistent manner. In this way, the program can be administered so that timely, useful, and complete information is compiled and reported.

In a manufacturing enterprise, such as one having a Machine Shop Department like that used in the budget illustrations, it is desirable to integrate the budget data, as well as the incurred expenses into the company's chart of accounts. This can be done if the budget allowances are regarded as being equivalent to standard costs, and are recorded in a manner that will accumulate variances by department and expense category, and to reflect volume variances within the general ledger accounts.

MACHINE SHOP--BUDGET REPORT

APRIL, 19

Foreman: J. W. Hemphill

April Volume: 8200 Standard Direct Labor Hours (SDLH)

(1)	(2)	(3)	(4)	(5)	(6)	(7)	(8)	(9)	(10)
	Month Of April						Year-To-Date (4 months)		
	Budget Allowance								
	Variable								
Category	Per SDLH	Amount	Fixed Amount	Total Budget For Month	Actual Expenses For Month	Budget Variance: Better Or (Worse)	Budget Allowance	Actual Expense	Budget Variance: Better Or (Worse)
CONTROLLABLE ITEMS:									
Direct Labor	$10.00	$ 82,000	$ -0-	$ 82,000	$ 84,600	$ (2,600)a	$318,600	$331,000	$(12,400)b
Indirect Labor	$ 3.30	$ 27,060	$ 18,600	$ 45,660	$ 46,100	$ (440)	$179,540	$180,500	$ (960)
Non-payroll items:									
Labor fringe benefits	$ 2.50	$ 20,500	$ 5,280	$ 25,780	$ 26,750	$ (970)	$100,770	$103,500	$ (2,730)
Perishable tools	.80	6,560	500	7,060	6,800	260	27,490	27,380	110
Electricity	.70	5,740	400	6,140	6,200	(60)	23,900	24,000	(100)
Other utilities	.40	3,280	300	3,580	3,400	180	13,940	13,700	240
Lubricants	.30	2,460	200	2,660	2,560	100	10,360	10,220	140
Supplies	.20	1,640	1,000	2,640	2,400	240	10,370	9,900	470
Scrap and spoiled work	.50	4,100	-0-	4,100	6,200	(2,100)	15,390	24,800	(9,410)
Direct staff charges:									
Maintenance	.50	4,100	1,100	5,200	4,650	550	20,330	19,000	1,330
Indust. engineering	.20	1,640	480	2,120	3,170	(1,050)	8,290	7,800	490
Miscellaneous	.20	1,640	400	2,040	1,500	540	7,970	8,100	(130)
TOTAL NON-PAYROLL	$ 6.30	$ 51,660	$ 9,660	$ 61,320	$ 63,630	$ (2,310)	$238,810	$248,400	$ (9,590)
TOTAL CONTROLLABLE	$19.60	$160,720	$ 28,260	$188,980	$194,330	$ (5,350)	$736,950	$759,900	$(22,950)
ALLOCATED EXPENSES	.10	820	14,200	15,020	15,200	(180)	59,990	60,040	(50)
DEPARTMENT TOTALS	$19.70	$161,540	$ 42,460	$204,000	$209,530	$ (5,530)	$796,940	$819,940	$(23,000)
BUDGET PERFORMANCE									
(Based on Controllable Department Charges):						97.4%			97.2%

Notes on direct labor variance:

	Efficiency	Rate	Total
a. Month	$ (2,000)	$ (600)	$ (2,600)
b. Year-to-date	(11,000)	(1,400)	(12,400)

Fig. 7. Monthly Budget Report for Machine Shop.

A simple but effective approach to using this procedure can be illustrated by summarizing the general ledger accounting entries that would record the Machine Shop operations for April, as set forth in Figure 7, as follows:

Direct labor control	$ 84,600	
Accrued payroll		$ 84,600
To record machine shop direct labor cost incurred		
Work in process inventory	82,000	
Direct labor absorbed—at budget		82,000
To record standard cost and budgeted cost of direct labor applicable to production (8200 SDLH @ $10.00 = $82,000)		
Factory overhead control	124,930	
Various accounts		124,930
To record machine shop overhead costs incurred.		
Work in process inventory	123,000	
Factory overhead absorbed—at budget		122,00
Volume variance		1,000
To record machine shop overhead to inventory at standard cost of production (8200 SDLH @ $15.00 = $123,000) and to record favorable variance due to production in excess of normal (8200 SDLH—8,000 SDLH = 200 SDLH @ $5.30 fixed overhead = $1,000 rounded)		

Summing up the foregoing entries, the ledger amount totals conform to those shown on the Machine Shop budget performance report for April (Figure 7) as shown below:

	Absorbed at Budget	*Actual*	*Variance*
Direct labor	$ 82,000	$ 84,600	$(2,600)
Factory overhead	122,000	124,930	(2,930)
TOTALS	$204,000	$209,530	$(5,530)

Company-wide budget reports. The explanations and illustrations given for a Machine Shop are intended to demonstrate how an operating budget can be developed and used in but *one* of *many* departments of a company. These same principles and techniques should be applied to all other units of the organization, also. In this way, all operating plans and performance against those plans can be monitored by individual unit managers, their supervisors, and top executives of the enterprise.

AMERICAN MFG. CO.
COMPANY-WIDE BUDGET REPORT

APRIL, 19XX

	Performance for the Month			Year To Date Performance		
	Budget	Actual	Actual Better Or (Worse) Than Budget	Budget	Actual	Actual Better Or (Worse) Than Budget
MANUFACTURING OPERATIONS						
Productive Departments:						
Machine shop	$204,000	$209,530	$ (5,530)	$ 796,940	$ 819,940	$(23,000)
Press	173,200	174,000	(800)	663,200	665,300	(2,100)
Forge shop	48,500	49,200	(700)	183,560	184,200	(640)
Paint and plating	51,300	51,000	300	198,300	199,330	(1,030)
Assembly	146,500	148,000	(1,500)	571,700	572,400	(700)
Packaging	38,600	41,400	(2,800)	148,600	156,830	(8,230)
TOTAL PRODUCTIVE	$662,100	$673,130	$(11,030)	$2,562,300	$2,598,000	$(35,700)
Service and other overhead:						
Maintenance	$ 17,300	$ 19,200	$ (1,900)	$ 67,800	$ 69,200	$ (1,400)
Industrial engineering	7,500	8,300	(800)	30,000	29,100	900
General factory	8,400	8,500	(100)	32,800	33,000	(200)
Space costs	10,200	10,100	100	40,800	41,000	(200)
Local taxes	4,800	4,800	-0-	19,200	19,200	-0-
Insurance	5,100	5,000	100	20,400	20,000	400
Depreciation--machinery and equipment	14,200	14,400	(200)	56,800	56,000	800
	$ 67,500	$ 70,300	$ (2,800)	$ 267,800	$ 267,500	$ 300
Less amounts applied to other units	67,500	67,500	-0-	267,800	267,800	-0-
NET SERVICE AND OTHER	$ -0-	$ 2,800	$ (2,800)	$ -0-	$ (300)	$ 300
Totals--Manufacturing	$662,100	$675,930	$(13,830)	$2,562,300	$2,597,700	$(35,400)
MATERIALS PURCHASE PRICE VARIANCE	$ -0-	$ 3,870	$ (3,870)	$ -0-	$ 6,300	$ (6,300)
MARKETING OPERATIONS:						
Home office sales	$ 8,300	$ 8,400	$ (100)	$ 32,900	$ 34,600	$ (1,700)
Branch offices--sales	17,200	16,700	500	67,000	63,800	3,200
Market research	5,100	5,200	(100)	20,400	20,600	(200)
Warehouse and distribution	23,400	21,900	1,500	93,000	91,700	1,300
Advertising and promotion	14,500	16,200	(1,700)	58,000	55,300	2,700
	$ 68,500	$ 68,400	$ 100	$ 271,300	$ 266,000	$ 5,300
ADMINISTRATIVE OPERATIONS:						
Accounting	$ 13,200	$ 13,800	$ (600)	$ 52,000	$ 53,800	$ (1,800)
Treasury	3,800	3,700	100	15,200	15,000	200
Purchasing	7,100	7,200	(100)	28,200	28,500	(300)
Personnel	4,900	5,100	(200)	19,600	20,000	(400)
General executive	18,300	18,000	300	73,200	72,600	600
	$ 47,300	$ 47,800	$ (500)	$ 188,200	$ 189,900	$ (1,700)
TOTAL--ALL OPERATIONS	$777,900	$796,000	$(18,100)	$3,021,800	$3,059,900	$(38,100)

Fig. 8. Summary of Company-Wide Budget Performance.

An illustration of a company-wide summary budget report, which includes the Machine Shop as one of the units, for the month of April is displayed in Figure 8. A review of the data in this exhibit will disclose that Machine Shop operations in April, and for the year-to-date, have resulted in the largest dollar amount of unfavorable variances. However, on a percentage basis, the Packaging Department has generated a higher proportionate amount of costs in excess of budget during both periods shown. These comparisons can provide meaningful signals to management of the most important problem areas needing attention.

Monthly operating reports. The flexible budgetary control program presented in this chapter is based upon the integration of budget allowances with standard costs of direct materials, direct labor, and factory overhead. The system assumes that the costing of inventory accumulations and dispositions is based on standards established for normal volume levels of production.

Hence, the variance between budgeted manufacturing costs that include both fixed and variable elements, and standard costs, represents a gain or loss attributable to production volumes which exceed, or are less than, normal levels. This is called, appropriately, a "volume" variance, and is reflected in the internal periodic summary of operating results.

A monthly operating report, prepared in the manner as shown in Figure 9, summarizes. Undoubtedly, an internal monthly report of this nature would usually include a breakdown of sales (and standard cost of sales) according to product lines or other meaningful elements. However, since the emphasis here is on budgeting of costs and expenses, these details have been omitted from the exhibit. It should be noted that Figure 9 displays the budgeted amounts for each major operating charge against earnings for the month, and the year-to-date, and the variances from budget, in order to highlight the significant areas where the incurred expenses differed from the budget plan.

Although comparisons of current operating results with past periods are often useful, the method of reporting shown in Figure 9 utilizes *forecast* data in order to focus on progress (or lack of it) in attaining the company's profit targets.

This example may be helpful in clarifying the essential difference between operating budgets and forecasts. Among other things, the illustration shows that the forecast *anticipated* that certain budget variances would occur, and these are provided for in the forecast data. Thus, in essence:

1. The forecast is an estimate of all revenues and operating charges that are expected in future periods, while,
2. The budget is a control device that measures the effectiveness of management's efforts to keep costs and expenses in line with plans that flex with changing volumes of operations.

Both forecasts and budgets are valuable management tools, and both are essential to sound planning and control.

AMERICAN MFG. CO.
MONTHLY OPERATING REPORT

APRIL, 19XX

	Month			Year To Date		
	Forecast	Actual	Actual Better Or (Worse) Than Forecast	Forecast	Actual	Actual Better Or (Worse) Than Forecast
NET SALES	$1,214,000	$1,140,000	$ (74,000)	$4,780,000	$4,500,000	$ (280,000)
COST OF PRODUCTS SOLD:						
Budgeted (Standard) Cost:						
Raw materials	$ 412,000	$ 385,000	$ 27,000	$1,625,000	$1,530,000	$ 95,000
Direct labor	248,000	234,000	14,000	974,000	918,000	56,000
Manufacturing overhead	372,000	351,000	21,000	1,461,000	1,377,000	84,000
TOTAL STANDARD COST	$1,032,000	$ 970,000	$ 62,000	$4,060,000	$3,825,000	$ 235,000
Standard gross profit	$ 182,000	$ 170,000	$ (12,000)	$ 720,000	$ 675,000	$ (45,000)
Variances from standard cost:						
Materials price	$ -0-	$ (3,870)	$ (3,870)	$ -0-	$ (5,400)	$ (5,400)
Direct labor	(2,500)	(4,030)	(1,530)	(9,700)	(17,200)	(7,500)
Factory expense - Budget	(6,900)	(13,100)	(6,200)	(27,100)	(48,300)	(21,200)
Factory expense - Volume	(600)	3,300	3,900	(2,200)	(500)	1,700
NET VARIANCES	$ (10,000)	$ (17,700)	$ (7,700)	$ (39,000)	$ (71,400)	$ (32,400)
ACTUAL GROSS PROFIT	$ 172,000	$ 152,300	$ (19,700)	$ 681,000	$ 603,600	$ (77,400)
OTHER OPERATING EXPENSES:						
Budgeted amounts:						
Marketing	$ 69,300	$ 68,500	$ 800	$ 275,000	$ 271,400	$ 3,600
Administration	47,300	47,300	-0-	189,000	189,000	-0-
TOTAL BUDGET	$ 116,600	$ 115,800	$ 800	$ 464,000	$ 460,400	$ 3,600
Budget variations:						
Marketing	-0-	100	100	-0-	800	800
Administration	-0-	(500)	(500)	-0-	(1,600)	(1,600)
ACTUAL OTHER OPERATING EXPENSES	$ 116,600	$ 116,200	$ 400	$ 464,000	$ 461,200	$ 2,800
OPERATING PROFIT	$ 55,400	$ 36,100	$ (19,300)	$ 217,000	$ 142,400	$ (74,600)
FINANCIAL AND OTHER ITEMS						
Interest expense	$ (11,000)	(10,000)	1,000	$ (43,000)	$ (38,000)	$ 5,000
Miscellaneous	1,600	1,900	300	6,000	5,600	(400)
PRE-TAX INCOME	$ 46,000	$ 28,000	$ (18,000)	$ 180,000	$ 110,000	$ (70,000)
INCOME TAXES	23,000	14,000	9,000	90,000	55,000	35,000
NET INCOME	$ 23,000	$ 14,000	$ (9,000)	$ 90,000	$ 55,000	$ (35,000)

Fig. 9. Company Monthly Operating Report Showing Comparison with Forecast.

The examples used in this chapter relate, primarily, to an industrial enterprise. However, the principles involved and the techniques suggested can also be used in developing and using flexible budgets in other types of companies. The important point to keep in mind when organizing and establishing a budget system for operating expense control is that the budget measures should be pre-determined in terms of amounts per period of time or per unit of activity, or a combination of both of these elements, depending upon the expected behavior patterns of the costs and expenses involved.

Revising budget allowances. Change is common in business operations. New methods, automation, and revised procedures are introduced frequently as enterprises constantly seek to improve productivity and gain greater efficiency. These events, coupled with ever-changing price levels in wages, supplies, and services, can obsolesce budget measures unless the system can quickly adjust to current conditions.

Revisions of budget allowances can and should be arranged for as a fundamental part of a practical flexible budgetary control system. These revisions should, preferably, be developed and instituted much in the same way that the existing allowances were established. This contemplates that revisions may be initiated by any one of the three key individuals who prepared, approved, or authorized the existing budget allowances. Thus, in the Machine Shop Department example given in the previous sections of this chapter, the Department Manager, the Budget Co-ordinator, or the Plant Superintendent may propose a change in the budget allowance. Regardless of which of these concerned parties suggests a change, each of the other two should subscribe to it before it is incorporated into the budget measures.

An organized way to handle budget revisions is to provide a suitable form to be completed by the person instigating the proposed change. This would include a clear statement of the old and new budget allowance, the reasons for the revision, and supporting calculations. When formally signed by the required individuals, the new allowances would be used as of the date indicated in the form.

In cases where the budget allowances and standard cost data are integrated as companion elements of a co-ordinated system, a budget change would, preferably, be incorporated into revised standard costs. These revisions could have an impact on costing into, and out of inventories, and the chief accounting officer should be alert to the possible need to reflect them in determining interim inventory valuations.

Up-to-date allowances result in better, more equitable measures of operating performance.

BUDGETING IN A SERVICE INDUSTRY

While it is feasible to develop an effective budget program for any type or size of business enterprise, the system must, of course, be tailored to fit the needs of the particular business to which it is applied. In a service industry, for example, the principles already described for a manufacturing concern are substantially the same as those which can be used in organizations in the service, rather than the physical product field. The main difference is likely to lie in developing appropriate volume measures for variable expenses, and in how they might be used.

Budgeting for a banking institution. For purposes of illustration, a bank has been selected as an example of a service institution. Figure 10 shows how a flexible budget system might be applied and reported in a department of a banking enterprise. In this example, it is assumed that the budget allowances have been established with the approval of the department head by techniques similar to those used in a manufacturing department, previously explained. In this presentation, however, a larger portion of the expenses in a bookkeeping department are of a "fixed" nature which are not expected to change as a result of increases or decreases in activity. Those expenses that are variable and those that are "mixed" (elements of fixed and variable) are expected to have behavior tendencies of two distinct kinds: (1) Variables which are expected to increase *only* after activity volume exceeds normal levels and (2) Variables which are expected to increase or decrease in proportion to the measure of total activity. Thus, the payroll costs are based on a "normal" staffing requirement for the volumes of transactions expected in the ordinary course of operations. It is only after the activity exceeds those levels that the budget allowances are increased. For other types of expenses, such as stationery and supplies, the variable portion of the budget allowance is increased or decreased in proportion to the total department activity.

For budgeting purposes, the measure of operating volume selected for the bookkeeping department has been the number of transactions processed. Other departments are likely to have other measures. For example, business loans may have a volume measure based on a combination of the number of new loans made as weighted by type and amount.

It should be emphasized that, in each case, work objectives are analyzed, methods required to perform the tasks are determined, and the manpower, equipment charges, and other requirements are scheduled in accordance with predetermined specific plans. These factors, together with appropriate activity measures, provide the bases for planning and controlling operating expenses for clerical and similar types of routine business functions.

The other bank departments, segregated according to each branch or other managerial responsibilities, are summarized in a fashion similar to that shown in Figure 8 for an industrial company. In this way, a bank's top executives are provided periodic summaries of the performance of each major segment of the institution, and can focus attention to those areas that indicate opportunities or problems.

It may not be feasible to develop variable budget elements for some departments in relation to operating activity. In such cases, it is likely that the bulk of expenses will be budgeted on a fixed basis. However, it is often desirable to link budget plans with some suitable measure, even if it shall be based on "what can be afforded." For example, advertising and promotion may be budgeted, in part, on the basis of profits. By using pre-planned flexible budget allowances, expenses can be programmed in a way that automatically contracts them when necessary, thus avoiding sudden, unexpected edicts to cut costs indiscriminately in crisis periods.

PROJECT-TYPE BUDGETS

Nonroutine projects undertaken by businesses are often unrelated to current operating activity and, accordingly, do not have "variable" cost behavior characteristics comparable to those suggested for planning and controlling day-to-day business affairs. Typical projects of a nonroutine nature are product development programs and additions or replacements of physical facilities. Although capital expenditures do not, ordinarily, have an immediate impact on company earnings, the amounts involved and future consequences can be significant. Development projects may also require substantial expenditures and may have a profound effect on future operating success.

Both capital outlays and research projects should be planned and controlled with the same degree of attention as that given to current operating costs. Indeed, it is axiomatic that, unless *all* cost and expense elements are controlled, it may be difficult to control *any* of them; the time to do this is when the expenditure commitment is made, and during the course of the program, itself.

Capital expenditure budgeting. Many companies find it useful to plan and program expenditures for new facilities for a relatively long period ahead, say five or ten years in advance. Some phases of the long-term plan can be geared to known replacement or expansion needs (the sales forecast, as described earlier in this chapter, may be an important consideration); other capital expenditures may be planned on the basis of anticipated funds available, and after consideration of operating needs and debt and dividend policies.

Regardless of the extent of forward planning that may be appropriate in a given situation, it is important that all major capital expenditures contemplated in the near future be carefully budgeted. This involves the establishment of internal policies and practices relating to recommendations for facility acquisitions, approval procedures, appraising prospective results, and, finally, techniques to be used in determining the amount of the budget. Facilities budgets should be formalized into individual defined projects and, after approval, given an identifying appropriation designation.

A project-order cost accounting system should be established (with project numbers assigned) that is suitable to accumulate all costs applicable to each project. Cost estimates, prepared in advance of authorization, should be detailed as to principal elements, and appropriate evaluation of benefits expected should be calculated. The itemization of expected costs for each project should be organized into sub-projects that facilitate comparison of budgeted amounts against actual costs as each phase is completed. Thus, a capital project for

DEPT.--Main Office Commercial Accounts
MGR.--V. Panichi
ACTIVITY UNITS FOR MONTH: 167(A)

	(1)	(2)	(3)	(4)	(5)	(6)	(7)	(8)	(9)
	Budget For The Month								
	Variable								
	Per Unit(A)	Amount	Fixed	Total Budget	Actual Expense	Actual Better Or (Worse) Than Budget	Budget	Actual	Actual Better Or (Worse) Than Budget
CONTROLLABLE ITEMS:									
Employee regular pay	$300(B)	$ 5,100	$ 40,000	$ 45,100	$ 45,600	$ (500)	$219,400	$218,100	$ 1,300
Overtime	30(B)	510	-0-	510	1,210	(700)	1,400	2,340	(940)
Part-time pay	80(B)	1,360	5,000	6,360	5,900	460	26,900	23,200	3,700
Interdept. trans. pay	25(B)	425	-0-	425	890	(465)	1,500	2,800	(1,300)
Payroll fringes	80(B)	1,360	9,000	10,360	10,600	(240)	50,100	49,200	900
Supper money	10(B)	170	-0-	170	420	(250)	600	960	(360)
Telephone	10(C)	1,670	2,000	3,670	3,500	170	14,800	13,900	900
Postage and express	5(C)	835	3,000	3,835	3,920	(85)	15,900	16,200	(300)
Stationery and supplies	15(C)	2,505	1,000	3,505	3,400	105	14,500	14,100	400
Equipment rentals	40(C)	6,680	18,000	24,680	23,500	1,180	114,600	113,500	1,100
Equipment maintenance	10(C)	1,670	4,000	5,670	5,500	170	24,500	26,100	(1,600)
Miscellaneous	5(C)	835	1,000	1,835	1,900	(65)	5,800	6,000	(200)
TOTAL--CONTROLLABLE		$ 23,120	$ 83,000	$106,120	$106,340	$ (220)	$490,000	$486,400	$ 3,600
ALLOCATED EXPENSES:									
Examinations		$ -0-	$ 500	$ 500	$ 500	$ -0-	$ 2,500	$ 2,500	$ -0-
Depreciation		-0-	8,000	8,000	8,000	-0-	40,000	40,000	-0-
Insurance		-0-	500	500	520	(20)	2,500	2,580	(80)
Space charges		-0-	5,000	5,000	5,150	(150)	25,000	25,520	(520)
TOTAL--ALLOCATED		$ -0-	$ 14,000	$ 14,000	$ 14,170	$ (170)	$ 70,000	$ 70,600	$ (600)
TOTAL--ALL EXPENSES		$ 23,120	$ 97,000	$120,120	$120,510	$ (390)	$560,000	$557,000	$ 3,000
PERFORMANCE RATING						99.7%			100.5%

(A)--Activity unit = each 10,000 entries (checks and deposits).

(B)--Variable factor = applies to activity units in excess of 150 only.
("Normal" volume = 150 units.)

(C)--Variable factor = applies to all activity units.

Fig. 10. Operating Report and Budget for a Bank.

AMERICAN MFG. CO.
STATUS REPORT--CAPITAL EXPENDITURES BUDGET

JUNE 30, 19X0

	Total Budgeted	Expended To Date	Remaining Budget
SUMMARY--ALL PROJECTS			
Measurable return:			
Major items	$3,640,000	$1,132,400	$2,507,600
Minor items	187,000	61,200	125,800
TOTAL MEASURABLE	$3,827,000	$1,193,600	$2,633,400
Non-measurable return:			
Major items	$ 430,000	$ 112,300	$ 317,700
Minor items	28,000	10,100	17,900
TOTAL NON-MEASURABLE	$ 458,000	$ 122,400	$ 335,600
GRAND TOTAL	$4,285,000	$1,316,000	$2,969,000

PROJECT DETAILS:

Project No.	Description	Pay-Out (Years)	Total Budgeted	Expended To Date	Remaining Budget
350	Mach. Shop--Minor	2.2	$ 30,000	$ 18,000	$ 12,000
351	Press--Minor	2.4	20,000	7,000	13,000
352	Paint and plate--Minor	2.0	10,000	8,000	2,000
353	Assembly--Minor	1.8	25,000	11,000	14,000
392	Plating system	3.2	187,500	-0-	187,500
398	New foundry building	8.4	923,000	315,000	608,000
401	5-ton press	4.2	74,500	-0-	74,500
403	Land acquisition Plant #1	-	122,000	-0-	122,000
410	Refurnish President's off.	-	27,000	23,000	4,000
412	New waste disposal syst.	-	165,000	-0-	165,000
	GRAND TOTAL		$4,285,000	$1,316,000	$2,969,000

Fig. 11. Status Report—Capital Expenditures Budget.

construction of a factory building might, for example, have detailed budgets for distinct phases, such as: (1) site clearance, (2) excavations, (3) foundation, (4) utility lines, and many other elements essential to final completion of the project.

In many businesses, it is desirable to distinguish between major projects and those of a minor nature; usually, the amounts involved are the criteria for separating them. Major projects may be subject to approval by the chief executive officer, the board of directors, or its finance committee. On the other hand, approvals of minor projects may require only the approval of a department head or divisional supervisor, within broad generalized allotments over a period of time. This procedure avoids the need for top management to attend to matters of lesser consequence.

In considering a capital expenditures program, it is desirable to separate those projects which are expected to contribute directly to company profits from those which are made for other reasons. Capital expenditures aimed at increasing revenues or reducing operating expenses are regarded as having a measurable return. Other projects undertaken for reasons of safety, employee comfort, governmental regulatory demands, or enhanced company prestige, etc., may not have any measurable return.

Estimated Budget Variance Over-(Under)	Total Remaining Cost	Year Of Expenditure 19X0	19X1	19X2	19X3	19X4
$ 83,200	$2,590,800	$1,315,400	$ 518,300	$ 312,100	$ 280,000	$ 165,000
-0-	125,800	75,800	30,000	20,000	-0-	-0-
$ 83,200	$2,716,600	$1,391,200	$ 548,300	$ 332,100	$ 280,000	$ 165,000
$ (11,500)	$ 306,200	$ 163,000	$ 103,200	$ 40,000	$ -0-	$ -0-
-0-	17,900	17,900	-0-	-0-	-0-	-0-
$ (11,500)	$ 324,100	$ 180,900	$ 103,200	$ 40,000	$ -0-	$ -0-
$ 71,700	$3,040,700	$1,572,100	$ 651,500	$ 372,100	$ 280,000	$ 165,000
$ -0-	$ 12,000	$ 12,000	$ -0-	$ -0-	$ -0-	$ -0-
-0-	13,000	13,000	-0-	-0-	-0-	-0-
-0-	2,000	2,000	-0-	-0-	-0-	-0-
-0-	14,000	14,000	-0-	-0-	-0-	-0-
-0-	187,500	-0-	187,500	-0-	-0-	-0-
61,000	669,000	474,000	195,000	-0-	-0-	-0-
-0-	74,500	74,500	-0-	-0-	-0-	-0-
-0-	122,000	-0-	-0-	122,000	-0-	-0-
4,000	8,000	8,000	-0-	-0-	-0-	-0-
-0-	165,000	-0-	165,000	-0-	-0-	-0-
$ 71,700	$3,040,700	$1,572,100	$ 651,500	$ 372,100	$ 280,000	$ 165,000

Fig. 11. Status Report—Capital Expenditures Budget (Continued).

Measurable return projects are evaluated by considering the estimated contribution to profits in relation to their costs. This is sometimes referred to as the "pay-out" and may be expressed in terms of the probable time required for the benefits to equal the amount of the investment. In a true sense, expenditures for facilities represent an "investment" and the expected return may be calculated in a manner suitable to appraise the desirability of the venture. Some companies use the time values of the resources to be committed to each project, and calculate "present values" of cash flows to be generated as a decision tool.

Typical capital expenditures budgets. After the basic policies and procedures for capital expenditure budgeting have been established, the system for accumulating and classifying the budget items and reporting the status of the program should be devised. Notwithstanding the degree of sophistication used in making a decision to proceed on a capital expenditure project, it is sometimes found that the actual costs of an undertaking exceed the budget by a substantial amount. Control of expenditures, by monitoring incurred costs against the plan on a timely basis through sound budget procedures, is aimed at providing management with information necessary to prompt remedial action, where indicated.

AMERICAN MFG. CO.
MONTHLY PROGRESS REPORT--MAJOR PROJECTS

JUNE, 19X0

Project Number	Authorized Budget	Previous Expenditures	Expended This Month	Expended To Date	Estimated Cost To Complete	Estimated Total Cost	Indicated Variance (Over)-Under
Measurable Return							
392	$ 187,500	$ -0-	$ -0-	$ -0-	$ 187,500	$ 187,500	$ -0-
398	923,000	264,000	51,000	315,000	669,000	984,000	61,000
401	74,500	-0-	-0-	-0-	74,500	74,500	-0-
403	122,000	-0-	-0-	-0-	122,000	122,000	-0-
416	137,000	16,600	114,000	130,600	13,200	143,800	6,800
418	120,000	38,300	24,700	63,000	52,000	115,000	(5,000)
419	260,000	112,000	62,000	174,000	86,000	260,000	-0-
Non-measurable Return							
410	$ 27,000	$ 12,000	$ 11,000	$ 23,000	$ 8,000	$ 31,000	$ 4,000
412	165,000	-0-	-0-	-0-	165,000	165,000	-0-
428	75,000	30,000	26,000	56,000	18,000	74,000	(1,000)
TOTAL--MAJOR PROJECTS	$4,070,000	$ 848,500	$ 396,200	$1,244,700	$2,897,000	$4,141,700	$ 71,700

Fig. 12. Monthly Progress Report—Major Projects.

Periodic reporting of key data for capital budget purposes may cover programs from two vantage points: (1) the long-term view of planned projects, and (2) the perspective of current projects in progress. In Figure 11, an example of a summary of planned expenditures over a five-year period is presented. This displays the commitments that have been authorized in a manner that indicates the year in which the expenditures are scheduled to be made. This summary is useful for cash flow projections, as well as for expenditure control purposes. It will be noted that the data are classified into major and minor projects and, also, according to measurable and non-measurable return categories. Below the summary information, specifics for each project are given, and the "pay-out" estimates are shown. The long-term analysis, such as illustrated in Figure 11, may not be necessary each month. However, in critical, constantly changing situations, it would seem desirable to prepare it on a quarterly basis, at least.

The long-term projections, as shown in Figure 11 are not likely to provide adequate budgetary control over capital expenditures. As projects often require several months, even years to complete, it is important to keep abreast of the progress and probable outcome at frequent interim intervals. An assessment of current status and prospective results, promptly determined and reported, can provide the information to management so it can take such steps as may be needed to curb cost overruns, or even revise or cancel the commitment before it is too late. Figure 12 is intended to provide an example of a typical monthly status report that displays the kind of information useful for control purposes. This report shows the activity of major projects during the period covered, the circumstances at the close of the period, and an estimated cost to complete each project. Assuming that each project has been budgeted in detail for each phase, any differences between the actual and budgeted cost for each such phase can be taken into account in preparing the estimated cost to complete. Also, other changes resulting from revisions in plans, unexpected problems or cost cuts applicable to phases not yet finished, can be incorporated into the estimate of additional expenditures in prospect. In this way, a revised total project cost can be ascertained, and the expected amount of overrun or savings brought to management's attention for such action as may be appropriate.

Development projects budgeting. The principles and techniques described for capital expenditure budgeting are also generally applicable to development projects. The fundamental task is to plan and evaluate each project in advance, and to determine the amount to be appropriated. However, whatever difficulties are encountered in preparing cost estimates for facility additions, the problems of developing comparable projections for a development project are likely to be much more complex.

Development projects should be identified and classified, and a cost accumulation system should be established in the same manner as that suggested for capital items. However, in budgeting a project, such as development of a new product, the sub-phase specifications can be more critical. The "pay-out" calculations for developing a new product usually include estimates of the size of the market demand and duration, probable product selling prices and costs, among other considerations. These data can be used as helpful parameters for budgeting a development project and serve to establish practical limits of what a company can *afford* to spend to create the product.

Thus, a notion to develop a new machine-tool product, for example, might be based on an indicated market demand that would support annual sales of 100 units, priced at $100,000 each, for a ten year period. Assuming that the costs of the investment in facilities and risk dictate that the target unit cost should not exceed $70,000, including applicable development costs, some perspective of reasonable development expenditures may be determined. If, in this case, experiences with other machine-tool products indicate that the production cost for the item will range in the area of $68,000 per unit, it appears that $2,000 per unit is a reasonable estimate of the development costs that can be absorbed. Although "present value" concepts applied in this situation would modify the computation, the expected sales of 100 units each year over a ten year period would produce a total development budget of $2,000,000 that can be afforded for the project (100 x 10 x $2,000).

With this maximum in mind, the development budget might be prepared by allocating a portion of that total into three major phases: (1) Concept definition, (2) Manufacture and test of an experimental prototype, and (3) Redesign into a production model and testing. Each of these phases should, in turn, be sub-classified into manageable tasks, each having a defined cost and point of completion. Continuing with this example, assume that the concept definition phase (probably subdivided into tasks such as mechanical, electrical, etc.) is allocated 10% of the total development budget, or $200,000. As the project work proceeds, incurred costs, compared with budget estimates for each task, are reported on a monthly basis. It isn't unusual for the initial phase to be the most troublesome, and assume that, after expending 90% of the concept phase budget, a company may find that no satisfactory definition has been achieved. In evaluating this information about the project, the management may consider increasing the appropriation if there is sufficient promise of success or, if not, may cancel it. The key point to be emphasized through the use of this example is that the phasing process provides interim information as to the project feasibility *before* exhausting the entire development budget, when it may be too late to learn that it is not an economical venture.

SUMMARY

Budgeting business operations, as explained and illustrated in this chapter, is based upon the fundamental concept of "Plan your work, and work your plan." As a practical management accounting tool, plans are translated into money values, and organized in a fashion that will consistently compare actual results with the budgeted amounts in a manner that will highlight differences that may merit management action. Moreover, by incorporating automatic budget adjustments as are pre-determined to meet changing levels of activity, department managers and top executives, alike, have agreed upon courses of action that should be taken when business conditions require expansion or contraction of operating volume. In this way, a company may be able to avoid much of the confusion, uncertainty, and costly errors that often stem from "panic-button" decisions made without prudent forethought. Thus, a sound budget program supplies both the definition of the plans and feasible alternatives as well as the signals for action necessary in implementing and/or modifying them.

16

Accounting and Data Analysis for Financial Decision Making

CONTENTS

16

Accounting and Data Analysis for Financial Decision Making

P-H Editorial Staff

J. K. Pescow, CPA, Editor

This chapter will discuss methods by which the accountant can plot how much cash will be needed to carry out the plans and programs of a business. The available sources of short- and long-term funds will be enumerated and discussed. Finally, the problem of protecting the funds already raised will be considered.[1]

PLANNING THE FINANCIAL REQUIREMENTS

The accountant must be able to translate the plans and programs of a business into what they will cost. He must also be able to interpret the cost in terms of where the money should come from. This will provide a basis for a judgment as to the best course to be followed in implementing the overall program or any particular part of it.

► COMMENT: A company with insufficient working capital cannot operate efficiently, with the result that it will not continue in business for any appreciable length of time. But we should not forget that a company with too much capital

---

[1]Portions of this chapter were adapted, with permission, from "Satisfying Your Company's Need for Capital and Employing It Effectively," *N.A.A. Bulletin* (National Association of Accountants), by P. M. Chiuminatto.

has failed to make full use of its expansion opportunities—in effect, it is also operating inefficiently.

How to determine the cash requirements. There are three basic methods of determining the cash requirements for a business. They are:

1. The cash receipt and disbursement method.
2. The balance sheet projection method.
3. The graphic method.

1. *Cash receipt and disbursement method.* The simplicity of this method makes is particularly suitable for a small business. All the known major sources of income and expenditures are listed and are assigned amounts based on actual management decisions or on past experience. A balancing figure sufficient to take care of all unlisted items is estimated from past experience. Figure 1 is an illustration of the cash receipt and disbursement method of determining cash requirements. The term "safety factor" on the illustration refers to the balancing figure mentioned above.

► NOTE: If inventories and accounts receivable have a tendency to vary in a wide range, it will be necessary to include an estimate according to their behavior pattern.

► WHAT TO DO: In order to make this kind of forecasting more accurate and of more value to management, you should compare each month's estimated figures with the actual experience for that month. This will indicate any errors so that the necessary corrections can be made. A new forecast should be prepared each month based on the corrected amounts for the previous months' forecasts. Quarterly estimates would be broken down into months at the beginning of the quarter. Semiannual forecasts would first be broken down into quarters, then into months.

2. *Balance sheet projection method.* Although a small business can also use this method, it is more commonly employed by large and medium-size concerns. It provides more detailed accuracy than the cash receipt and disbursement method. If the accountant can predetermine what the company's balance sheet and profit and loss statement will look like at the end of a stated period, he will actually be forecasting the amount of capital that the company needs. The first step in preparing these *pro-forma* statements is to lay down the "ground rules" that are to apply. These ground rules are based on management decisions, past experience, and comparison with competition. Each rule should be backed up with detailed facts and plans. Figures 2 and 3 show, respectively, pro-forma profit and loss statement and a pro-forma balance sheet, and list the ground rules that were applied in the preparation of each statement.

	(Thousands of Dollars)					
	Jan.	*Feb.*	*Mar.*	*Apr. to June*	*July to Dec.*	*Total Year*
RECEIPTS						
Opening balance	100	103	106	99	106	100
Estimated profits	10	10	10	45	75	150
Depreciation	3	3	3	9	18	36
Sale of securities				15		15
Sale of common stock					50	50
Total	113	116	119	168	249	351
DISBURSEMENTS						
Bonds retired				10		10
Bond interest				2		2
Machinery & equipment					50	50
Dividends			10	10	20	40
Income taxes	5	5	5	25	40	80
Safety factor	5	5	5	15	30	60
Total	10	10	20	62	140	242
CLOSING CASH BALANCE	103	106	99	106	109	109

Fig. 1. Cash Receipts and Disbursements Method of Financial Forecasting.

► COMMENT: If the cash position is such that constant supervision is necessary, a monthly format may have to be adopted. The format can also be on either a quarterly or a semiannual basis, in addition to the annual basis that was used for the illustration. No matter which format is followed, there should be a periodic comparison between actual experience and the predetermined ground rules.

How to apply the cash receipt and disbursement method or the balance sheet projection method. Either the cash receipt and disbursement method or the balance sheet projection method will tell the accountant whether or not there will be sufficient money to do the things management has planned. And, if the schedules are properly set up, either method will also tell in what months or quarters or years such funds will be required.

But it is not enough to merely know that a business needs a certain amount of capital at certain times. The accountant must determine what part of the needed funds is required for short-term use and what part is required for long-term use. This division will indicate where the money should come from.

Short-term funds—that is, funds for quick-turnover or variable assets such as minimum cash balance, accounts recevable, and inventories—should be raised from sources that can be increased or liquidated as business conditions change. This insures that there will be no excess capital or permanent cost to the business beyond the time the funds can be profitably used.

Long-term funds are those required for slow-turnover or fixed assets such as land, buildings, and machinery and equipment. They should be raised from sources that do not expect payment for some time in the future, or, at the very

(Thousands of Dollars)

	Current Year	*Next Year*	*Second Year*
Gross sales of present products	600	720	864
Gross sales of new products	—	600	600
Total sales	600	1,320	1,464
Cost of goods sold	300	600	672
Gross profit	300	720	792
Selling expense	90	198	220
Admin. expense	60	132	147
Research & development	18	40	44
Adv. & sales promotion	30	66	74
Other income & expense	15	15	15
Total expenses	213	451	500
Net profit before taxes	87	269	292
Federal income taxes	44	135	146
Net profit after taxes	43	134	146

1. Normal products will show a sales increase of 20% a year.
2. New products now in development will bring in an additional volume of \$50,000.00 a month.
3. New products will gross 60% while present products will gross 50%.
4. Selling expenses will be 15% of gross sales.
5. Administrative expenses will be 10% of gross sales.
6. Research and development expenses will be 3% of gross sales.
7. Advertising and sales promotion expenses will be 5% of gross sales.
8. Other income and expenses will total \$15,000.00 annually.

Fig. 2. Pro-Forma Profit and Loss Statement and the Applicable "Ground Rules" for the XYZ Manufacturing Co.

(Thousands of Dollars)

	Current Year	*Next Year*	*Second Year*
Assets			
CURRENT ASSETS			
Cash	100	109	119
Accounts receivable	70	55	61
Inventories	300	100	112
Total current assets	470	264	292
FIXED ASSETS			
Land	15	15	15
Buildings	40	190	190
Equipment	750	1,500	1,500
Total fixed assets	805	1,705	1,705
Less depreciation	300	430	555
Net fixed assets	505	1,275	1,150

1. Cash on hand should not be less than 50% of the current liabilities.
2. Accounts receivable will not be larger than one-half month's sales.
3. Inventories will turn-over six times a year.
4. It is no longer necessary to advance money to supliers of raw materials.
5. The company now owns enough land for future expansion.

Fig. 3. Pro-Forma Balance Sheet and the Applicable

OTHER ASSETS			
Advances to suppliers	30	—	—
TOTAL ASSETS	1,005	1,539	1,442

Liabilities

CURRENT LIABILITIES			
Accounts payable	100	67	73
Accrued taxes other than income	13	27	28
Accrued income taxes	44	135	146
Total current liabilities	157	229	247
CAPITAL & SURPLUS			
Common stock	600	600	600
Surplus	248	282	328
Total capital and surplus	848	882	928
Shortage in financial requirements	—	428	267
TOTAL LIABILITIES	1,005	1,539	1,442

6. A $50,000 expansion in present buildings will provide sufficient space for the expected sales volume.
7. A new warehouse costing $100,000 will be needed because of the way the new products will be sold.
8. An additional investment of $750,000 in machinery and equipment is required to take care of the expected sales volume.
9. The company will take advantage of the double-declining depreciation deduction allowed under the tax law.
10. Accounts payable should be approximately 60% of the average monthly sales.
11. There will be no increase in the rate for real estate and personal property taxes.
12. Income taxes will continue to be 50% of taxable income.
13. A dividend of $100,000 will be paid annually.
14. Return on investment will be one turn-over of assets a year with a minimum profit of 10%.
15. Expenditures for capital additions should return a minimum of the average cost of money in the business, and should have a payout period of not more than three years.

"Ground Rules" for the XYZ Manufacturing Co.

most, expect annual or periodic payments that the business can meet without difficulty.

► EXAMPLE: Suppose that a company made a 10-year financial forecast by either of the methods discussed and had arrived at the following "shortages" in cash position:

Year of Forecast	*Cash Shortage*
1	$200,000
2	$428,000
3	$267,000
4	$350,000
5	$450,000
6	$600,000
7	$800,000
8	$500,000
9	$700,000
10	$400,000

The largest deficit will be $800,000. At the end of the 10-year period there will still be a shortage of $400,000. Therefore, the company has to borrow: (1) a minimum of $400,000 on a long-term basis for a period of at least ten years, and (2) an additional $400,000 through a five-year revolving credit loan. The revolving credit loan would take care of temporary cash shortages.

3. *Graphic method.* This method is used principally for making long-range forecasts of a general nature. The accountant plots the total assets in use in the business against the sales volume. Then, by drawing a trend line that intersects most of the plotted points on the graph, he arrives at the fixed capital requirements of the business. Another line is drawn straight across the graph to indicate the separation of fixed and variable capital requirements. Therefore, the area within the trend line and the dividing line represents the amount of variable capital required at any of the given sales levels. When this variable factor is translated into a percentage of sales, it is simple to compute the amount of capital required for any estimated increase in sales.

► EXAMPLE: Figure 4 is an example of the graphic method. It tells the accountant that the business needs 28.4 cents of capital for each additional sales dollar. With this information, the following computation can be made:

(Thousands of Dollars)

Estimated Increase in Sales	*Additional Capital at 28.4%*	*Possible Plant Additions*[1]	*Total*
500	142	——	142
800	227	——	227
1000	284	600	884
1200	341	600	941
1500	426	1000	1426

[1]This would be management's best estimate of the additional facilities needed to reach a sales volume of over $800,000.

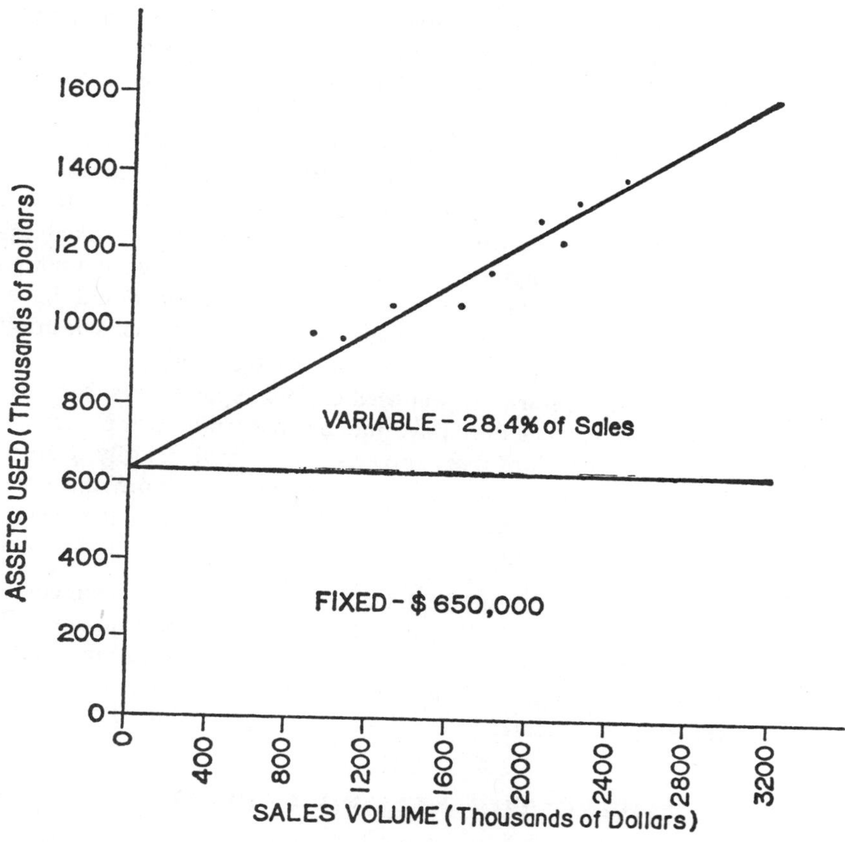

Fig. 4. Graphic Method of Financial Forecasting.

► SUGGESTION: Since individual assets act differently at varying sales levels, it is better to chart each asset separately. Otherwise, the particular activity of any asset will be hidden in the overall average, with the result that there will be no way of knowing how much capital is needed for a certain asset. In drawing these individual graphs, a semi-variable asset should be broken down into two or more accounts so that each account will be variable or fixed in its own right.

How to apply the graphic method. Liabilities can be charted in the same way that assets are. This will indicate how much working capital is automatically generated by means of accounts payable and accrued items as the sales of the business go up. By deducting this figure from the total capital required, the accountant can determine the actual amount that will be needed to accomplish a stated increase in sales. For example, let us refer again to Figure 4, which shows that 28.4 cents of capital is required for each additional dollar of sales. Assume that the liabilities have also been charted, and the accountant has come up with a figure of 14.4% variable. This means that the business will automatically generate 14.4 cents of capital for each additional sales dollar. Therefore, the business will be "short" 14.0 cents of capital for each additional sales dollar.

We will further assume that the company realizes 14.0% on its sales after taxes. The accountant can then conclude that the only additional permanent capital needed to finance an increased sales volume will relate to the expansion of facilities—in other words, required additions to such fixed assets as land, and machinery and equipment. However, if the business were a marginal one with a profit of only 5.0% after taxes, the accountant would have to recognize that 9 cents of capital must be raised for every additional sales dollar, in addition to the funds needed for the expansion of facilities.

How to determine the return on proposed capital expenditures. Most companies have more projects than they have money to spend, so the accountant must advise management which of these projects should have priority. Naturally, the available money should be spent on projects that will return the greatest amount to the company. *The discounted cash flow method* is the generally accepted procedure for calculating the return on capital expenditures.

► OBSERVATION: To have any real value, the return on investment must be considered in conjunction with the pay-out period. It is not a matter of how soon the investment is returned, but how much it continues to make after it has been returned. For example, it is better to get 18% on your money for 25 years than to get 30% for 5 years.

RAISING THE NEEDED CAPITAL

After the financial needs have been determined and a general appraisal of the company's status with regard to raising the capital has been made, the accountant must be able to point out the specific areas from which funds are available. We will consider:

1. Internal sources of funds.
2. Equity financing.
3. Borrowing from outside sources.
4. Special and unconventional methods of fund raising.

INTERNAL SOURCES OF FUNDS

A company can, of course, obtain additional working capital through an increase in actual profits. This is naturally the preferred and cheapest method of financing. However, it will seldom provide a complete answer to the problem of raising the capital needed to carry out the plans and programs of a business, because an actual increase in profits is generally dependent on those very plans and programs. Some progress might be made in the area of cost reduction, or through the implementation of better pricing policies.

There are other methods by which a company can raise funds internally. It can:

1. Pay out less money in taxes by means of
   a. The depreciation deduction.
   b. Inventory control and pricing.
2. Decrease the amount of capital presently invested in
   a. Inventories.
   b. Accounts receivable.
   c. Fixed assets.
3. Retain earnings by issuing stock instead of cash dividends.
4. Control the outflow of cash.

The depreciation deduction. The more depreciation a business can take, the more dollars it can save in taxes, with the result that additional capital will be currently available.

Of course, a number of factors enter into the decision as to which depreciation method is better for a particular company. Of interest here is the fact that the declining-balance methods do provide a higher deduction over the initial years of life of the asset.

► EXAMPLE: A small business buys a large machine costing $50,000 and having a useful life of 30 years. Depreciation for the first 5 years under the various permissible methods would be as follows (salvage value has not been taken into consideration for the purposes of this example):

Year	*Straight-line method*	*Double declining-balance method*	*Sum-of-years'-digits method*
1	$1,665	$ 3,330	$ 3,226
2	1,665	3,108	3,118
3	1,665	2,901	3,010
4	1,665	2,708	2,902
5	1,665	2,528	2,795
Total	$8,325	$14,575	$15,051
Cash savings over straight-line method (based on 52% tax rate)		$ 3,250	$ 3,497

► OBSERVATION: Unless the business takes the higher depreciation only as a deduction on its tax return and does not reflect it on the books, the accountant will have to weigh the immediate tax savings and cash build-up against the effect that lower reported earnings will have on the company's ability to raise funds from outside sources.

Inventory control and pricing. Any reduction of inventory will result in a reduction of taxes and an increase in cash. Inventories can be written down to the lowest possible level through elimination of all obsolete and slow-moving items. The fact that cash might be received in the process of eliminating these items—through mark-downs, for example—is also worth noting.

In instances where a constant inventory is being priced at an ever increasing market price, taxes can be reduced and the cash position improved by means of a switch to one of the LIFO methods of inventory valuation. Naturally, a change of this nature should involve a careful study of a great many factors, such as the course of future price movements, variations in tax rates, possible changes in the amount and type of inventories, and the effect upon reported income.

► EXAMPLE: If a business in 1970 had a particular inventory that was priced at $20 a unit for 10,000 units, and this price has now risen to $40 a unit, the book inventory for the same number of units has increased by $200,000. This increase could have been reflected in the cost of goods sold if LIFO had been used. Assuming that the tax rate has been 50%, the business has paid out $100,000 that it could have retained.

Decreasing the amount of capital invested in inventories. By maintaining and enforcing proper inventory turn-over ratios, a company can do the greatest amount of business on the least amount of capital. This leaves capital that might otherwise be tied up in inventory free for other purposes. Figure 5 illustrates an Inventory Control Worksheet from which minimum and maximum inventories can be established. In the example used in this exhibit, it is determined that the maximum sulphur inventory to be carried at any time, unless conditions change, is 96,000 pounds. The minimum inventory should equal the days of safety factors, which in this case number 7, for a minimum inventory of 56,000 pounds. If we assume that sulphur costs $40 a ton, the maximum amount of cash that should be tied up in inventory is $1,920 and the minimum cash requirement for inventory is $1,120. Deliveries should be scheduled so that they arrive on the day the inventory reaches its minimum amount.

Consideration should also be given to the question of buying certain items instead of making them. If it costs less to purchase some inventory components than to make them, the advantage is obvious. But even if this is not the case, the purchase of components can increase the immediate working capital by reducing the amount of cash that must be invested in inventory.

Decreasing the amount of capital invested in accounts receivable. The accountant should make sure that the company is using its cash flow to the best advantage. Cutting down the float time of customers' checks in transit will allow the company to operate with less actual cash. The faster the customer's money gets to the bank, the sooner the company can use it.

Many companies receive all their funds at one spot and then disburse them to various banks in different cities in relation to the needs of the plants in those cities. If the company does a nation-wide business, it might be as long as four or five days from the time some customers mail their checks until they arrive at the local bank and are available to the company. If this time can be cut in half, funds would be available two to three days earlier, which would enable the company to pay pressing bills and do a greater amount of business with less cash.

Date *January 15, 19—*

1. ITEM: *Sulphur* MILL: *Jones Mfg. Co.*

2. LBS. PER SHIPMENT: *40 000*

3. RATE OF USAGE: (Pounds per day of operation)

From scheduled operation	8000
Estimated	8500
From past usage figures	7500

---

4. TRANSPORTATION TIME: (Average number of days)	14	Use smallest figure
5. NUMBER OF DAYS SUPPLY A SHIPMENT REPRESENTS:	5	

6. SAFETY FACTORS:
(Add extra days for each pertinent item)

A. Shipping delays	2
B. Allowance for nonstandard items	—
C. Allowance for receiving defective materials and/or lost shipments*	—
D. Importance of items to production, inventory cushion	2
E. Allowance for increased rate of usage	2
F. Allowance for supplier failures	1

*Allow number of days a shipment represents in terms of daily usage. Not to exceed figure, paragraph 2.

(Adjust total days if:)

G. Material is in speculative class (minus or plus)	—
H. Material is in high risk inventory (minus)	—
I. Storage limitations (minus)	—
TOTAL DAYS (4 or 5 + 6)	12

7. RESULTS

12 multiplied by *8000* equals *96 000*
TOTAL DAYS, DAILY USAGE, INVENTORY LEVEL

Fig. 5. Inventory Control Worksheet.

The most common method of reducing cash float is the *"lock-box" plan.* Under this system, checks from customers within a certain sales area are mailed to a nearby bank that deposits them to the credit of the company, then notifies the company's home office of the amount deposited. The excess balances can be invested or they can be distributed where they might be needed. Thus, funds are available two to three days sooner than normally.

If the credit of the company is good, it is possible to operate on the *guaranteed overdraft system,* under which a bank will honor checks even though the company maintains no balance at that particular bank. The amount of the guarantee is limited and the company pays a fee for the service. By using this system, the company is able to pay out money as needed, so that large amounts do not have to be tied up.

► EXAMPLE: A company has three plants, each of which normally needs $90,000 a week to operate. The company supplies its plants with the necessary funds, totaling $270,000, at the beginning of each week. If a guaranteed overdraft system were used, the following type of situation could occur during an average week:

	Actual cash requirements	*Cash available for other use*
Monday opening	$ ——	$270,000
Monday closing	40,000	230,000
Tuesday	70,000	160,000
Wednesday	50,000	110,000
Thursday	65,000	45,000
Friday	45,000	——

Tighter credit and collection policies will also enable a company to do more business while needing less cash. For example, say that a company has $1,500,000 worth of outstanding accounts receivable representing 15 days' sales. If the average collection period can be reduced to 14 days, the company can increase its available cash by $100,000.

► OBSERVATION: Where contracts are of long duration from the start to the completion of the manufacturing process, it is quite in order to ask for interim payments as the work progresses. This procedure was prevalent during the war in connection with Government contracts, and there is no reason why it cannot be extended to civilian work as well.

Decreasing the amount of capital invested in fixed assets. More funds can be made immediately available if certain fixed assets are leased rather than purchased outright. More and more kinds of industrial and other equipment are becoming available on lease arrangements. Leasing has particular advantages for companies engaged in activities where there is a danger of being caught with a heavy investment in obsolete equipment, or where equipment is needed only for a specific purpose or a limited period of time, or where expert servicing of the equipment is required.

► NOTE: Sale and leaseback of property is a popular device for raising capital.

Retaining earnings by issuing stock instead of cash dividends. By issuing a stock dividend in lieu of a cash dividend, a company can retain and possibly reinvest its earnings while still giving the stockholders a return on their money. A dividend record is maintained, but there is no outflow of cash. Of course, this increases the amount of stock on which future dividends will have to be paid, and it may also decrease the market value of the stock.

Controlling the outflow of cash. The outflow of cash can also be controlled so that more working capital will be available. Care should be exercised to make sure that all or most of the obligations of the business do not come due in a relatively short space of time. A periodic payment system in which invoices are paid once a week or four times a month will not only save time, but it will also make a dollar go further.

EQUITY FINANCING

If long-term funds are needed, it is possible to obtain them by expanding the ownership of the business. Partnerships can do this by adding new partners; single proprietors must change their form of organization. Corporations, of course, can sell capital stock. Mergers, joint ventures, and the use of venture capital firms are other methods by which funds may be brought into the business through equity or equity-type financing. This type of financing does not burden the company with a fixed charge, and there is ordinarily no obligation to repay or return the sums invested in the business. In addition, no special restrictions are placed on the use of the funds.

One point that should be stressed is the importance of cultivating and maintaining good stockholder relations. Quarterly reports on earnings and future prospects of the business are a must if the company wants to retain the goodwill of its stockholders and thereby encourage them to increase their investment.

► OBSERVATION: The sale of convertible bonds can also be considered a method of equity financing, at least to the degree that the bonds are actually converted into stock. The point can further be made that the sale of bonds that are convertible into stock is a means of selling the stock for more than the present market value. For example, assume that the stock of a company is selling for $80 a share. If the company sold 100,000 shares at that price and the marketing costs were $200,000, the net proceeds would be $7,800,000. In the same kind of market the company could sell $8,000,000 of convertible bonds, making them convertible into stock on the basis of $100 a share. Again, say that the marketing costs are $200,000, leaving net proceeds of $7,800,000.

Now, the net proceeds are the same, but when the bonds are converted into stock at $100 a share, only 80,000 shares will be issued. The company has, in effect, sold stock for $100 a share, or $20 more than the market price at the time of the original sale. The interest paid on the bonds has been tax deductible, and there will be dividend requirements on 20,000 less shares.

There is, of course, a chance that earnings will be poor and consequently the bondholders will not want to make the conversion. Still, the company might be able to retire the bonds at par, and the advantage of the interest deduction will have been gained.

BORROWING FROM OUTSIDE SOURCES

When negotiating a loan, it pays to have all the required information carefully worked up in advance so that it can be placed before the lender. Proper sales forecasts, budgets for production and expenses, and pro-forma statements are not enough. The individual responsible for negotiating the loan must be prepared to discuss such things as (1) the basis for valuation of assets, (2) the kind and degree of inventory control, (3) credit policies, (4) the effectiveness of cost control, (5) the provisions for internal financial control, (6) the ability and reliability of present and potential management personnel, (7) the use to be made of the borrowed funds, and (8) how the funds are to be repaid. A conservative, realistic, and positive approach will usually bring the best results.

A good accountant will not wait until the company must actually borrow funds. He will prepare for this eventuality long before the need occurs by maintaining good relations with the banker, the broker, the insurance company, or anyone else who controls a possible source of funds. He will see that these parties, especially the banker, receive the latest financial information at regular intervals. He will also discuss financial problems with them, and he will make sure that each of them receives a fair share of the client's business. A close and personal working arrangement between the accountant and potential lenders is one of the most important prerequisites for a good financial program.

Outside sources for long-term funds. Long-term funds can be raised from the following outside sources:

1. Long-term bonds.
2. Bank loans.
3. Insurance companies.
4. Sale and leaseback of property.
5. Government agencies.

Long-term bonds. There probably is no end to the kinds and combinations of long-term bonds that can be used to finance a business. However, when you analyze them, they fall into three principal classes:

1. Income bonds.
2. Debenture bonds.
3. Mortgage bonds.

Income bonds. These bonds have no security behind them. They constitute a promise to pay the principal at some future date, with a provision that interest will be paid only to the extent that it is earned. Therefore, there can be no default or foreclosure until maturity. Such bonds are ordinarily used in reorganizations. They are issued to previous bondholders or other preferred security holders in return for their old securities, and in payment of back interest and dividends. Since the interest charges on income bonds are flexible in relation to income, the reorganized company is not forced to take upon itself the fixed charges of the old company.

Debenture bonds. There is no security behind a debenture bond either, but fixed interest payments must be made. Of course, this interest is tax deductible, and some companies will sell debentures rather than issue stock because of this. Another factor to be considered is that debentures can reach a market that stocks cannot—trusts, banks, insurance companies, etc., are often prohibited by law from purchasing stock, but they can purchase a debenture.

Mortgage bonds. Mortgage bonds are a lien against all or part of presently owned fixed assets and, in certain cases, a future lien on fixed assets subsequently acquired. Any default in interest or sinking fund payments results in foreclosure and the operation of the business by a bondholders' committee. The trust indenture generally contains provisions that restrict management.

► NOTE: Mortgage and debenture bonds are sometimes convertible into other securities within a certain period of time at a stipulated price.

Bank loans. There is only one loaning agency, so it is possible to talk over any problems and work out a solution. This type of financing maintains the stockholders' interest in the business. In addition, any increased profits resulting from the loan accrue to the stockholders.

► OBSERVATION: Of course, bank loans can also be a source of short-term funds.

Insurance companies. There is hardly any difference between borrowing from an insurance company and borrowing from a bank. Both usually require the same restrictions in the areas of working capital, salaries, dividends to be paid, sale or merger, etc. The interest rates do not vary greatly. Insurance companies usually exact a penalty for early retirement of the loan while banks do not. On the other hand, money can be borrowed from an insurance company for much longer terms than a bank permits. Long-term for bank loans generally means five to seven years, as opposed to the 15 or 20-year terms of loans from insurance companies.

Sale and leaseback of property. A business can sell some of its fixed assets and then lease them back from the purchaser. This will result in an immediate lump sum increase in capital, represented by the proceeds from the sale less the tax on any profit realized. The tax can frequently be computed at capital gains rates. There is a substitution of the rental deduction for the otherwise available depreciation deduction. This method of financing would be particularly advantageous when a company has fully depreciated certain property on its books for tax purposes.

► EXAMPLE: Assume that a company has a building that was purchased 30 years ago at a cost of $40,000. The building has been fully depreciated, but it has been well maintained so, with inflation, the present market price is $80,000. The company needs $60,000 additional working capital; however, no one will loan over 50% of the value of the property, or $40,000.

If the company sells the building for $80,000 it will realize a profit of $80,000, since the property is fully depreciated. After a capital gains tax of 28%, the net proceeds of $57,600 is available for use in the business. At the present time, the company is getting no deduction for depreciation, but under the new arrangement it will be able to deduct the rent paid to the purchaser.

Of course, the company should be sure that it can earn more on the $57,600 in additional working capital than it will pay out in rent after taxes. If the purchaser demanded 10% as a rental fee, which would be about 5% after taxes, the rate of return on the $57,600 should be considerably in excess of 5% or there would be no reason to sell the property. Also, it should be pointed out that the sale and leaseback can seldom be arranged for buildings that are attached to one another for an integrated manufacturing process. The lessee usually wants a building that can be used for general purposes in the event something goes wrong and the property has to be repossessed.

► WARNING: When a company enters into either a straight leasing arrangement or a sale and leaseback, it should do so by an arm's-length transaction. Otherwise the agreement will be construed as a purchase by the Bureau of Internal Revenue and all benefits will be lost. If the lease contains a buy-back provision at a nominal price, and the rental just about equals the net sound value of the asset at the termination of the lease, the company will be in trouble. To be safe, there should be no buy-back provision.

Government agencies. A number of Federal agencies lend money or insure or guarantee loans to businesses for special purposes. If the concern qualifies, the Small Business Administration is often a lender of last resort. States and municipalities increasingly are also providing funding for businesses.

► SUGGESTION: Contact your Congressman or Senator whose staffs can usually tell you which agencies can offer the appropriate financial help. Frequently, they will establish the contact with the agency for you. In some cases, it might be easier to make a direct contact with the local office of the agency, or with the agency itself.

Borrowing from outside sources for short-term purposes. If the need is for short-term funds, the following outside sources are available:

1. Trade creditors.
2. Bank loans.
3. Trade acceptances.
4. Commercial finance companies.
5. Factoring.
6. Commercial paper.
7. Field warehousing.

Trade creditors. It may mean the loss of discounts, but arrangements can be made with regular business creditors to obtain an additional 30 or 60 or 90 days on their invoices. Also, merchandise can be obtained on a consignment basis, where payment is made each month for the merchandise sold.

Bank loans. If the credit of the business is good, it will be possible to negotiate a bank loan for a period long enough to tide it over for any short-term capital needed. However, collateral is sometimes necessary. Such collateral would take the form of the assignment of inventories or accounts receivable, cash value of life insurance, or any other asset the business owns that the bank will accept as security. A bank loan is usually the cheapest and easiest way to raise short-term funds from an outside source.

Trade acceptances. Instead of going to a bank and giving them a note, a business can give its vendors a note or trade acceptance. The vendors accept these notes and discount them at their own bank. This method of raising funds can be used if the notes are paid at maturity. If the notes are renewed too often, or are not paid at maturity, this avenue of fund raising is immediately closed. In using trade acceptances the business is frequently able to take a cash discount for prompt payment, thus offsetting a substantial part of the interest cost.

Commercial finance companies. Financing arrangements with a commercial finance company are usually on a secured basis, involving the assignment of accounts receivable or the pledge of inventories, or both. Periodic liquidation is not normally required, with the result that loans outstanding can be fairly continuous over long periods of time against revolving security. On the other hand, interest rates are much higher than for the ordinary revolving bank loan.

Factoring. Certain commercial finance companies engage in the specialized business of purchasing accounts receivable with or without recourse to the seller. Previously, it was thought that a disadvantage of this method of raising funds was that customers would learn about the financial condition of the business. However, now many factors employ non-notification plans, eliminating this drawback. Then too, the wide usage of factoring in many industries has relieved this method of financing of its former stigma. Although interest rates are higher than for other forms of financing, many firms make use of this method, particularly during their busy seasons.

Commercial paper. A well-established business may elect to finance some part of its seasonal or temporary requirements by selling short-term unsecured notes in the open market through a commercial paper broker. This is almost the same as going directly to a bank, but the interest rate is lower.

► SUGGESTION: Before advising a company to embark on this method of financing for the first time, be sure to discuss it with the company's banker. Set a policy on how much of the short-term needs the banker will provide and how much will be commercially financed. The banker is always available to help, while the commercial paper market is strictly a market place for those who can qualify. Today you are in, tomorrow you are out. It is not so with the banker—he will stick with you much longer. There is a happy medium where the banker can be satisfied, and the company's overall interest can be substantially reduced.

Field warehousing. When sales are seasonal, field-warehouse financing is a good way of both raising capital and providing for sustained production throughout the year. Under this form of financing, inventory is used as loan collateral, but the goods still remain on the borrower's premises and for practical purposes are subject to his direction. Since a bonded field-warehousing concern takes legal custody of the inventory, banks and other lenders who otherwise would not handle this type of loan will now do so. Although rates are high, greater sales potential is created due to inventory build-up, and lower costs usually result because of sustained production.

SPECIAL AND UNCONVENTIONAL METHODS OF FUND-RAISING

In smaller firms, it is sometimes impossible to raise the funds needed by the methods already discussed. There are other methods that can be recommended on the principle that when the ship is sinking everything should be done to keep it afloat. Some of these methods are:

1. Have the officers, directors, or partners pledge collateral on a personal basis.
2. Rely on endorsements and guarantees by the officers, directors, or partners.
3. Subordinate debts due to the officers, directors, or partners.
4. Borrow against the cash value of life insurance policies.
5. Borrow from employees.
6. Obtain second and third mortgages.
7. Sell part of the business.

PROTECTING THE FUNDS ALREADY RAISED

It is important to know how much capital is needed. It is also important to know where and how to get this additional capital. But all this is worthless if the accountant is unable to show management how to protect the funds once they have been raised. The following areas should be carefully watched and analyzed:

1. Profits.
2. The dividend policy.
3. The ratio of equity to borrowed capital.
4. The cost of money used in the business.
5. The insurance program.
6. Reserves.
7. Taxes.
8. Investment of excess funds.

Profits. The accountant must make sure that the company is operating at a profit that is in line with the amount of funds invested in the business. This can be done by keeping track of the return on total investment. One of the most effective ways of obtaining a proper return is to insure that selling prices are adequate but not excessive. If the company has only one product line, or the accountant does not feel that it is necessary to price for individual products, an overall method of price determination can be used. This method consists of (1) taking all the assets that relate to sales volume and dividing them individually by the budgeted sales volume, (2) taking all the assets that relate to the manufacturing process and dividing them individually by the budgeted production cost, (3) factoring the results of (1) and (2) by the percentage of desired return, and (4) dividing one plus the ratio to cost by one minus the ratio to sales (after adding to the ratio to sales a figure representing selling and general expenses), in order to obtain the percentage of mark-up over cost that is needed to attain the desired return.

► EXAMPLE: Assume that the budgeted sales volume of a company is $1,000,000 and the budgeted production cost is $600,000. The following computation can be made:

		Ratio to Sales	*Ratio to Mfg. Cost*
$ 50,000	Cash	.0500	
40,000	Accounts receivable	.0400	
49,300	Raw material inventory		.0833
49,300	Finished inventory		.0833
591,700	Plant and equipment		1.0000
$780,300	Total assets ratios	.0900	1.1666
	19% (desired profit)	.0171	.2216
	Add selling and other expenses budget to sales	.2600	
Total		.2771	.2216

$$\frac{1 + .2216}{1 - .2771} = 1.69$$

If the cost of any product is multiplied by 1.69, we will arrive at a selling price that will return the required amount on the investment.

However, often it is not feasible to price all of the products at the same rate, because the amount of material, labor, and other expenses that go into them are not constant. In such cases, the products can be separated into like lines according to their cost make-up. Budgeted figures and the amount of total assets employed in producing the product permit the accountant to compute the ratio of sales to material cost and the ratio of labor and expense to material cost. By applying the turnover period for material to this information, a determination can be made as to how the particular product should be priced.

► EXAMPLE: Assume that the following computation has been made for "Product Line A":

	Product Line A
Budgeted sales	$20,400
Material cost	$ 8,000
Labor and expense	6,000
Total cost	$14,000
Total assets employed to produce this product	$32,000

Return on investment		
Gross profit / Capital used	$ 6,400 / $32,000 =	20%
Ratio of sales to material cost		255%
Ratio of labor and expense to material cost		75%

Now, if the elapsed time from when the raw material for this product line is received until payment is received for the finished product is six months, then in order to earn an annual return of 20%, the company will have to make 10% each time the material is used. Therefore, the required ratio of material profit is 110% of costs. By deducting the ratio of material profit from the ratio of sales to material cost, and dividing the result by the ratio of labor and expense to material cost, we come up with the required ratio of profit on labor and expense—in this instance, 193⅓%. Therefore, the proper pricing for "Product-Line A" is 110% of material cost plus 193⅓% of labor and expense. Proving this on the above computation, we have:

$8,000 × 110%	$ 8,800
$6,000 × 193 1/3%	11,600
Total sales price	$20,400

The dividend policy. The accountant should be certain that dividends are not being paid out of the capital of the business. Just because dividends paid are not in excess of the earnings is no reason to conclude that the capital is not being impaired. For example, let us assume that the following situation exists:

Fixed assets	$10,000,000
Depreciation at a rate of 5%	$ 500,000
Replacement cost	$20,000,000
Earnings after taxes	$ 1,400,000

If the company has a divided policy of paying out 50% of its earnings and retaining the balance, it should, at first glance, pay out $700,000 in dividends and retain $700,000 in the business. But if it does this, it will be paying dividends out of its capital. The accountant should make the following computation:

Assuming a 50% tax rate, the earnings of the company before taxes were	$2,800,000
Add back depreciation deducted	500,000
Deduct depreciation based on replacement value	(1,000,000)
Adjusted earnings for dividends	$2,300,000
Less actual taxes due	1,400,000
Earnings after taxes for dividend purposes	$ 900,000
Dividends to be paid on 50% payout	$ 450,000

The additional $250,000 that might have been paid out is really a distribution of the capital. Over a period of years the cumulative effect of such dividend errors could be disastrous.

The ratio of equity to borrowed capital. Sometimes the financial plans of a company are limited by factors beyond its control, such as the size of the company, its access to money markets, and the amount of security that must be pledged. These factors could cause the ratio of owners' capital to creditors' capital to get out of balance. But in the long run, if a business is to be successful it must adhere to the ratios of its competitors, or at least the top three or four in the industry. When these competitors operate on the basis of, for example, 60% equity capital and 40% borrowed capital, the company should attempt to keep its financial house in the same order.

The cost of money used in the business. The accountant has to know the cost of money used in the business, so that he can determine whether additional borrowings will increase the overall costs. In any business, the cost of money is a combination of the cost of borrowed money and the cost of equity capital. The more borrowed capital, the lower the cost of money. However, the financial structure will be less secure, because in times of recession or depression the fixed interest and sinking fund payments can be the straw that breaks the camel's back. Fortunately there is a happy medium that a business should strive to attain. What the proper ratio is depends upon the individual company.

Many companies consider the cost of money borrowed from institutional lenders to be the going interest rate at which the money was borrowed. This is not the true cost. Not only the interest, but also the cost of underwriting, the bond discount, if any, the premium on redemption, and most of all the average life of the loan are factors in determining the cost of money.

► EXAMPLE: A $5,000,000, 30-year bond issue bears an interest rate of 4%. The cost of underwriting was $150,000, and the redemption price is 104. The cost of the $5,000,000 (before taxes) will be:

5.40% if the bonds are redemed in five years.
4.70% if the bonds are redeemed in 10 years.
4.35% if the bonds are redeemed in 20 years.

The cost of equity financing would be the average earnings per share divided by the present market value of the stock, with a factor added for the cost of underwriting. If the average earnings per share are $5 and the market value is $55, the cost would be 9.1% plus marketing costs. This ratio of average earnings to market price must be maintained so that the market value will not drop, with the result that new stockholders would be hurt and would probably be lost as a future source of funds.

When the accountant knows the cost of borrowing and the cost of equity financing, he can determine how much any particular financing method will cost. Then he can compare this information with the cost of the money presently invested and advise management of the proper course to be followed.

► EXAMPLE: A company has present capitalization of $1,000,000 in common stock, $500,000 in 6% preferred stock, and $1,000,000 in bonds that have a total cost of 5%. The accountant has ascertained that any bond financing will now have a total cost of 4.5%. Assuming a 50% tax rate, the bonds will have a cost after taxes of 2.25%. The cost of common stock financing will be 9.1% plus the cost of underwriting. Therefore, a financing consisting of half bonds and half common stock would cost at least 5.67%. The cost of the money presently invested can be computed as follows:

		Cost of money	
Security	*Amount*	*Before taxes*	*After taxes*
Common stock	$1,000,000	9.1%	9.1%
6% preferred stock	500,000	6.0%	6.0%
Bonds	1,000,000	5.0%	2.5%
Total	$2,500,000	6.8%	5.8%

To preserve the present cost of money in the business (5.8%), the company would have to issue half bonds and half common stock, which would cost 5.67% plus marketing costs for the common stock.

The insurance program. A proper insurance program is a must for any business. Clearly the actual assets should be insured. But it is also important to insure the person or persons responsible for the fullest utilization of those assets —in other words, the brain power and know-how of the company. Key-man insurance will protect the company from loss of profits until a good replacement is found, and it will often pay for the cost of training replacements. In a more human vein, it will also take care of the obligation that the company may feel it owes the widow of a man who has given long and faithful years of service to the company.

The actual assets of the company should be covered by the following types of insurance:

1. Fire and extended coverage at replacement value.
2. Use and occupancy.
3. Boiler and machinery.
4. Business interruption.
5. Fidelity.
6. Liability.

Besides these general coverages, there may be specific and special coverages that apply to a particular industry. Doing business with a reputable insurance agent will enable the company to get expert advice and a sound program.

Reserves. Reserves should be set up to take care of all known contingencies. Although many of these contingency reserves should not be included in reports issued outside of the company, they will let management know the financial position of the company if any of the contingencies do occur.

Under this particular heading come reserves for:

1. Future inventory losses.
2. Possible law suits.
3. Income taxes.
4. Depreciation on a replacement basis.

The reserves for inventory losses and law suits could be book reserves only, unless the amount is so large or the liability so certain that cash reserves are necessary to avoid financial embarrassment. Income tax reserves should always be covered by tax certificates or some other form of investment rather than a book entry only. Book reserves are not much help when the tax payments come due.

If possible, it is a good idea to follow a cash policy in connection with depreciation. The amount of annual depreciation can be put into an investment fund. Against this fund can be charged all capital expenditures. When there are not sufficient funds in the account to take care of any intended programs, management knows that some financing must be arranged. The problem is recognized early, and there is time to adjust the program to keep it in line with the funds available.

Taxes. A business cannot conserve its working capital unless it has a good tax department or a good outside source of tax advice. Taxes now take more than half of all that most businesses make. The time to save taxes is not after a transaction has been effected, but before the deal is made, by making sure that it will be handled in the proper manner.

► WARNING: The tax consequences of any action should not be the sole guide. Sometimes it is better to pay more taxes immediately in the interests of a long-range business benefit.

Investment of excess funds. If a business is in the enviable position of having too much capital available, even for a short time, the problem of investing it is much the same as getting it. First of all, it is necessary to divide the excess funds into short-term and long-term, i.e., funds that will be needed within the next six months and funds that will not be needed for at least six months.

For short-term funds, the best investments are:

1. Commercial paper.
2. Tax certificates.
3. Short-term government securities.
4. Short-term municipal securities.
5. Paying off bank loans.
6. Time deposits.

The best investment for long-term funds are government and municipal bonds.

Investments in any of these areas should be controlled so that the funds will come due when the company needs them. Purchasing with the proper maturities in mind will eliminate the possibility that investments may have to be sold before they achieve the desired profit, or even at a loss.

► OBSERVATION: Some corporations are becoming bankers in their own right. They lend money to a bank, obtain government securities from the bank as 100% collateral, then collect the interest on the government obligations as long as the loan is outstanding. In most cases this arrangement gives a business a higher interest return than the bank could legally pay on a time deposit. Also, it does not subject the business to some of the inconvenient requirements for time deposit accounts.

► NOTE: Smaller companies are now turning to the use of money market mutual funds to invest short-term funds. These no-load funds usually allow withdrawal of funds by check which enables firms the flexibility of investing and withdrawing funds with little or no advanced planning and no commissions.

17

Accounting Data and Analysis for Organizational Decision Making

---

CONTENTS

17

Accounting Data and Analysis for Organizational Decision Making

Robert A. Wofsey, CPA

The proper kind of organizational planning will enable a business to organize its command and communications functions rationally. Such a structure can be created for either a centralized or decentralized organization. In either case, however, there must be controls that management can use to direct the organization. It is our aim to show how such an organization can be developed and controlled most effectively.

This chapter also contains sections describing how to make an organizational study, starting with the organization of the study group, continuing with procedures to use in making the study, and ending with presenting the results of the study in the form of a study report.

THE RELATIONSHIP OF ACCOUNTING DATA TO ORGANIZATIONAL PLANNING

A company's organizational plan provides the practical framework within which management can assign the tasks of planning and directing operations. An integral part of the plan should be a system of management controls to insure that responsibilities that have been delegated are being carried out as intended. Although minimum planning and control requirements can sometimes be met without a formal program of organizational planning, most well-run companies have found that a systematic approach offers the following advantages:

1. A formal program helps management achieve a better understanding of the problems involved.

2. It reduces the likelihood of costly duplication of effort.

3. It helps to prevent the overlooking or neglecting of any essential management functions.

Basic principles of accounting controls. Accounting data is the essential tool in planning, directing, and controlling operations. In preparing and presenting accounting information for management purposes two principles have come to be recognized as basic; without them accounting cannot be of maximum benefit to the organization. These principles are known as:

Responsibility accounting. This means aligning accounting data in such a way that the accounts and reporting system parallel the organizational plan. Thus, operational areas can be identified with operating responsibilities.

Management by exception. This principle requires the highlighting of exceptional conditions or variations between actual results and budgeted plans. Thus, busy executives are enabled to devote their time to solving problems rather than identifying them.

Before it is possible to apply either of these principles, a certain amount of organizational planning is required.

THE BASICS OF ORGANIZATIONAL PLANNING

Organization is dynamic in most companies, rarely remaining unchanged for any period of time. There are always organizational problems to deal with and, usually, more than one workable solution. Hard and fast laws that can be applied to constantly evolving and changing organizations do not exist. Rather, there is a framework of general rules that are useful as guides, and also as a checklist of practical considerations in organizational planning. These general rules that are basic to organizational planning will be discussed under the headings of:

1. Fundamental considerations of organizational structure.
2. General rules for delegation of authority.
3. Defining executive responsibilities.

Fundamental considerations of organizational structure. Naturally, the first objective in organizational planning is to tailor the organization structure to the particular needs of the company. Doing this effectively requires that:

1. Responsibilities for directing activities be subdivided to the point where one person can effectively administer each subdivision.

2. The number of people supervised be varied according to the nature of the supervision required.

3. Provision be made for the orderly development and promotion of junior executives.

In subdividing responsibilities, the operations of certain areas may involve administrative decisions based on simple considerations that can be grasped quickly. These areas may be combined, with each manager directly supervising a relatively large number of subordinates.

In highly technical areas, such as research and design engineering, executives must spend more time becoming familiar with the facts on which decisions must be based. Likewise, in a growing company where conditions are changing so that past experience may not apply to future operations, executives must evaluate the future implications of present decisions more thoroughly. Under these circumstances more organizational subdivisions will be required to provide more men for the executive team. As a result, the number of people reporting to a single executive, sometimes referred to as the span of supervision, will vary depending upon how much time an executive must spend with each subordinate. In practice, the span of supervision usually ranges from six to ten subordinates. Where subordinates are well trained and experienced in their jobs, spans will be larger. Where problems are varied or exceptional talents are required, spans of even less than six may be best.

The plan of organization may also be affected by the need for developing junior executives. The development of capable younger men is required to attract and retain the kind of younger men who can efficiently manage current operations and is essential for the future vitality of the organization. The organizational structure can provide for this in two ways:

1. Executive positions in each major corporate function should be arrayed in steps of increasing responsibilities so that junior executives have a logical promotion ladder.

2. Staff positions should be established in which junior executives can gain broad experience in the various management functions required for top level positions.

► WARNING: If the organization structure forces the company to fill its top level positions from the outside, the incentive for junior executives to remain and develop themselves is destroyed.

General rules for delegation of authority. Many of the decisions involved in planning the organization structure are based on the location of the power of decision. Good rules to follow in delegating the authority to make decisions are:

1. The power of decision should rest as close to the point of action as is reasonable.

2. Authority to act should be the responsibility of an individual rather than a group.

Decisions affecting several groups must be made at the organizational level that is responsible for the activities of these groups. However, unnecessarily bucking decisions up the line of command delays action and increases the difficulty of accurately determining the facts of the case. To avoid this, and to provide a guide for their subordinates, executives at the decision-making levels should clearly spell out, wherever possible, their operating policies and practices.

Making use of committees. Committees are often set up to deal with problems in areas where several equally important organizational responsibilities are involved. Two rules should be followed if such committees are to function effectively.

1. They should be used to coordinate individual actions rather than to make decisions.
2. The functions of each member of the committee should be defined beforehand so that each individual's role in making committee decisions is clearly understood.

Committees have been used effectively for such projects as improving management communications, studying proposed projects, and selling new ideas and programs.

Defining executive responsibilities. The most detailed phase of organizational planning is the definition of executive responsibilities. It is at this point that the responsibilities of specific individuals are related to their positions in the organization structure and to the authority delegated to them. A complete definition of an individual's responsibilities should include the following:

1. The broad objectives of his position.
2. The bases on which his performance will be evaluated.
3. The specific areas of operations in which the individual has primary executive responsibility.
4. Those areas of operations in which the individual should consult with or advise other individuals.

Note how these criteria are met in the duties and responsibilities of a treasurer-controller shown in the following job description.

TREASURER-CONTROLLER: DUTIES AND RESPONSIBILITIES

Reports To: President.

Basic Functions:

To direct the planning and evaluating of the financial aspects of Company operations, to direct the Company's budget activities, and to be responsible for the actual supervision of Financial Department operations, including the implementation of new programs, systems and procedures, and to safeguard the assets of the Company.

Specific Responsibilities:

1. To develop and administer a system of short-range and long-range budgets.
2. To advise the Executive Committee on matters pertaining to budgeting and to attend all of its budget meetings.
3. To work with all levels of supervision in developing an understanding of budgets, to coordinate planning and to increase use of control reports.
4. To review and appraise departmental budgets in light of basic Company objectives.

5. To supervise the preparation of budget summary reports and to report to the Executive Committee on the effects of the proposed plan of operations.

6. To develop and install practical procedures for collecting and recording general accounting, cost accounting and statistical information required for control purposes; to accumulate significant information by functions and by departments.

7. To see that accurate and meaningful financial statements and operating reports are prepared and distributed on a timely basis.

8. To assist in the interpretation of operating results, the determination of factors underlying results, and the formulation of recommendations for action to be taken to improve operating results.

9. To be responsible for the preparation and filing of tax returns and all matters relating to taxes.

10. To initiate and control the continuous audit of all accounts, records, and procedures of the Company.

11. To assist in developing plans and recommendations for all aspects of the Company's financial structure.

12. To direct the management of cash funds.

13. To develop the Company's credit policy and to assist in the determination of terms of sales.

14. To provide for the safekeeping of funds and securities.

Reporting to the Treasurer-Controller Are:
Budget Accountant
Internal Auditor
Credit Manager
Assistant Controller—Funds and Billing
Chief Accountant
Assistant Controller—Foreign Accounting
Tax Manager

Responsibilities of all executives. In addition to responsibilities which relate to a particular position, the definition of responsibilities should include general responsibilities that are common to all executives. Some of these are:

1. Planning the activities of their organization.
2. Directing long-range and day-to-day operations.
3. Keeping up with outside developments in their field.
4. Managing and developing the personnel assigned to them.

► WARNING: The organization plan should not be so rigid as to hamper operations. Executives should be free to contact directly the individual with the necessary authority to act on specific matters. However, it is the subordinate's responsibility to keep his superior advised of such contacts, and to secure approval for action where necessary.

The basics of organizational planning consist of the general rules that you have just read. How are these rules applied in practice? Several kinds of organizational structures have evolved to apply these general rules in the varying circumstances under which different businesses function. The various forms that organization structures take will be discussed in the following section.

VARIOUS ORGANIZATIONAL FORMS

Basically, organizational forms fall into the broad categories of centralized and decentralized structures. In a centralized organization, there is a single top management group that administers all phases of operations. In a decentralized organization, the top management function is divided among several groups. One group is a central staff that coordinates overall planning and in some cases performs certain staff functions for the organization as a whole. The other groups are teams of operating executives responsible for directing the activities of two or more relatively independent divisions of the company.

► WARNING: The company's activities may be physically situated in one place or in scattered locations. Do not infer from this that the company's organization is correspondingly centralized or decentralized.

The following discussion of the two categories of organizational forms will be in terms of:

1. Choosing between a centralized and decentralized organization.
2. Planning a centralized organization.
3. Planning a decentralized organization.

Choosing between a centralized and decentralized organization. As is so often the case, the relative advantages of one form correspond to the disadvantages of the other. An understanding of this relationship can be obtained from the following chart that shows the form of organization that best meets various management requirements.

TABLE OF MOST SUITABLE ORGANIZATION FOR VARIOUS MANAGEMENT REQUIREMENTS

Management Requirement	*Form of Organization Usually Best*
1. Unified control of management decisions.	centralized
2. Versatility in managing diverse operations.	decentralized
3. Flexibility in adjusting top level policies and objectives to widely varying conditions.	decentralized
4. Speed in dealing with day-to-day operating problems.	decentralized
5. Consolidation of workload to make use of costly equipment or facilities.	centralized
6. Most effective use of limited management or technical talent.	centralized
7. Greatest opportunity for executive development.	decentralized

(Note: In many cases a partially decentralized organization can provide an effective answer to conflicting organizational requirements.)

A centralized form of organization is generally the simplest. For small organizations, or for large organizations carrying on a relatively limited variety of operations, a centralized organization involves less administrative expense. As operations become more widespread, diversified, or complex, the central management group finds it increasingly difficult to keep abreast of all company activities. When this occurs, portions of the top-level managerial responsibilities must be delegated to units closer to the scene of operations. These shifts to decentralized operations generally increase the number of executive positions and lead to some duplication of functions among divisions. Offsetting this, the decentralized organization offers more direct incentives to divisional managers, by means of:

1. Broader responsibility for divisional performance.
2. Competition among divisions.
3. Greater prestige within the organization and in the community.

Similarly, the greater number of management positions at the divisional level provides a correspondingly greater opportunity to cultivate broad gauge, top-level managers.

► SUGGESTION: In most companies the transition from a centralized to a decentralized organization is a difficult one. Sometimes, this is best accomplished in two stages. The first stage makes use of features of both forms of organization in that combination best suited to the company's current needs and abilities.

Planning a centralized organization. Centralized organizations should be subdivided primarily according to basic functions. The grouping of similar or closely related functions usually makes it easier to coordinate operations and to fill executive positions with men who are experienced in all of the functions assigned to them.

The basic functions most commonly required are marketing, product design, production, finance, and administration. In different industries, other basic functions may exist that are equivalent to these only in the broadest sense. For example, product design may be an engineering activity in a manufacturing company, an underwriting activity in an insurance company, and a merchandising activity in a retail chain.

Subdivisions of functions. In a small company the basic functions may provide all of the subdivisions required for assigning management responsibilities to individuals. In larger companies further subdivisions will be required at least in some areas. These further subdivisions may be based upon such factors as:

1. Detailed functions or activities.
2. Products or services.
3. Geography or location of facilities.
4. Customer groups.
5. Channels of distribution.

As in other phases of organizational planning there is no firm rule about subdividing basic functions. Frequently, combinations of factors provide the best answer in a particular situation. As an example, the sales organization might be subdivided geographically into branch territories. And yet, within branches, salesmen may be assigned by types of customer.

In order to illustrate the subdivision of functions, a centralized manufacturing company and a partly decentralized chain store operation will be described in turn.

A centralized manufacturing company. A typical centralized organization for a manufacturing company is shown in Figure 1. This chart outlines the top levels of the organization structure.

1. Top management is represented by the five largest blocks consisting of the president and his four vice presidents, each of whom is responsible for one basic function.

2. Middle management is represented by the smaller blocks and consists of the various executives responsible for more detailed functions within the areas of the vice presidents' basic functions.

3. Operating management is represented by the activities listed under management positions. Each activity might be headed by a junior executive.

In the company we have illustrated, the entire organization is built around a single manufacturing operation. The responsibilities for managing this operation are divided entirely by function so that no two executives are performing similar jobs. This eliminates duplication of management effort and makes for a high degree of executive specialization.

Collaboration is required on matters involving several functions, but with activities confined to a single operation this is usually not a major problem.

A partially decentralized chain store operation. A partially decentralized organization is illustrated by the organization chart for a restaurant chain shown in Figure 2. In this organization there is a distinct difference between the operating organization and the central staff.

The operating organization must manage numerous physically separated stores and is, therefore, decentralized with subdivisions based on locations. At both the district supervisor and store manager levels, responsibilities for all of the operating functions have been subdivided so that operating management can be closer to the activities supervised.

The central staff performs certain service or control functions for the company as a whole. Consequently, it is organized on a functional basis to make the best use of highly skilled executives in directing specialized functions.

The type of organization shown in Figure 2 is an example of the combination of centralized and decentralized forms of organization, retaining the major advantages of each form. The particular requirements for managing the various activities determine which organizational form is used.

Administrative and functional responsibility. Frequently, a staff executive's responsibilities require that he report to more than one top-level executive on certain matters. In such cases he should have administrative responsibility to one executive and functional responsibility to the others. These types of responsibilities are defined as follows:

Administrative responsibility is the responsibility for performing work promptly and effectively.

Functional responsibility is the responsibility for performing work in accordance with company policy and/or in a technically sound manner.

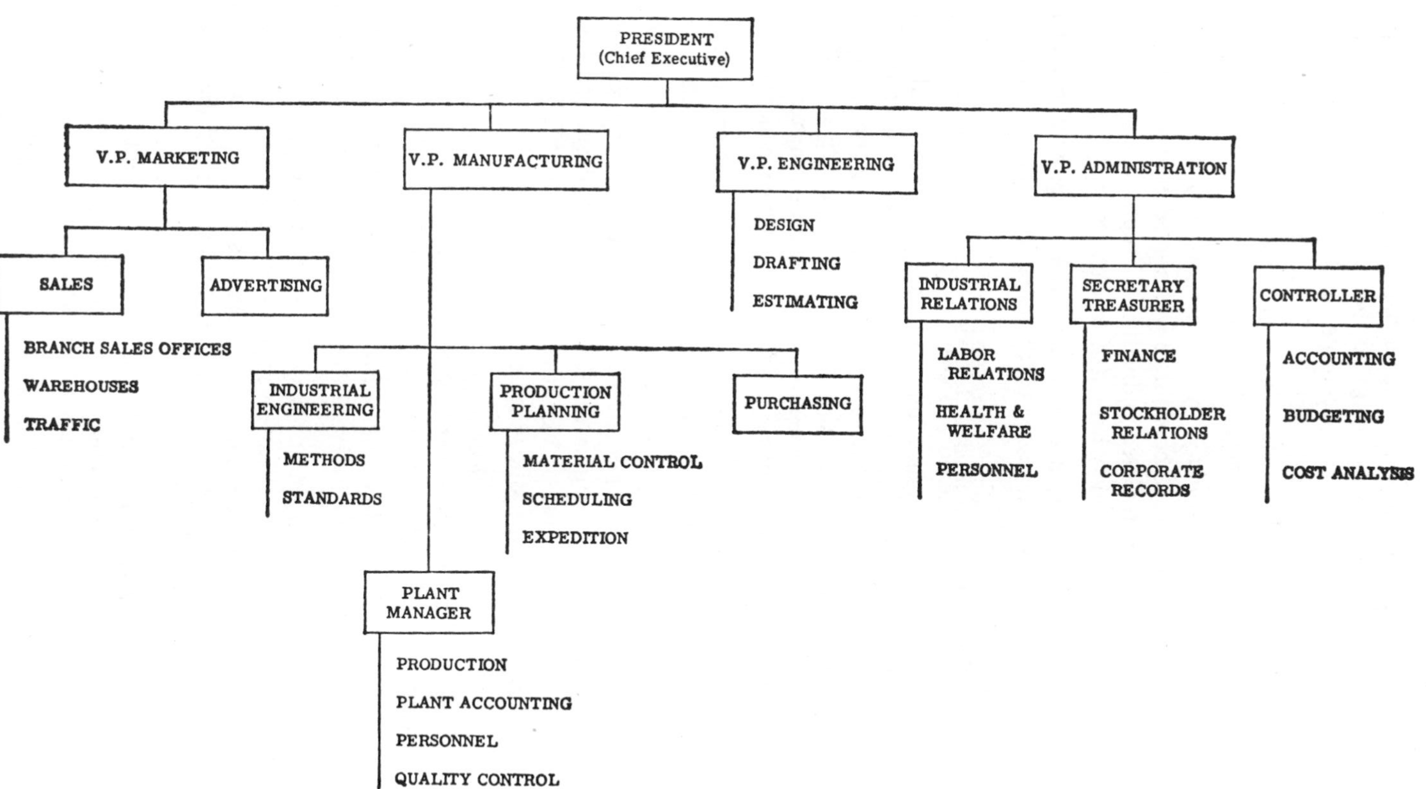

Fig. 1. A Centralized Manufacturing Organization.

A common example of this dual responsibility is in the job of plant controller. The plant controller is responsible to the plant manager for providing required management control data in accurate, usable form at reasonable expense. At the same time, he is responsible to the company controller for using basic accounting methods and records that are in keeping with sound accounting practice and meet corporate policy requirements.

Use of functional responsibility. As an organization decentralizes, functional responsibility can be used to coordinate widespread activities and to make more effective use of highly talented individuals. Emphasis on functional responsibility is most often desirable where staff executives in the operating units:

1. Perform technical services that require specialized knowledge and ability.
2. Administer specialized functions that require close coordination throughout the company.
3. Serve as liaison between a central service unit and a decentralized operating unit.

Functional responsibility may be required in managing decentralized accounting activities for all three of these reasons. It may also be useful in engineering, marketing, personnel, purchasing and similarly specialized staff services.

Planning a decentralized organization. In a fully decentralized organization the primary division of responsibility is based on the two concepts of:

1. Segregating the company into relatively autonomous operating units, and
2. Delegating profit responsibility to managers of these units.

The application of these concepts results in a top-level organization that is basically different from the functionally divided centralized organization. This is illustrated by the organization plan for the fully decentralized and diversified company that is shown in Figure 3. Various aspects of a decentralized organization will be discussed under the following headings:

1. Main subdivisions of a decentralized organization.
2. Bases for establishing business or service units.
3. Delegating profit responsibility.

Main subdivisions of a decentralized organization. Management responsibilities in a decentralized company are divided among three groups. These are:

1. *The central staff* consisting of the chief executive and those senior officers of the company who assist him. This group sets overall corporate objectives in various fields, directs general corporate programs such as public relations, research and new product developments, and furnishes specialized technical assistance to business unit managers.

2. *Business and service unit managers* consisting of unit heads who are responsible for directing all functions of their relatively independent units so that the units achieve desired management objectives.

3. *Financial planning and control group* consisting of the accounting and related financial sections that are responsible for coordinating the financial plan-

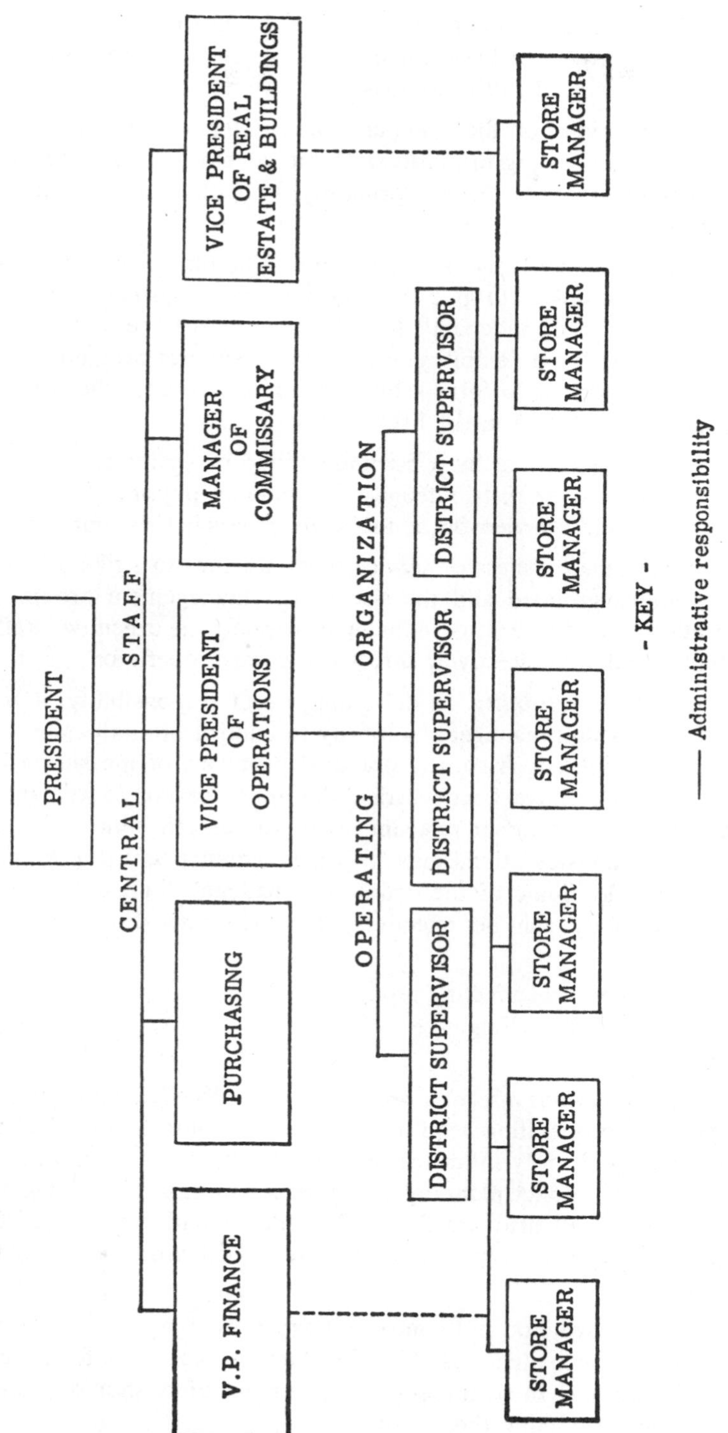

Fig. 2. A Partially Decentralized Restaurant Chain.

ning of all units. This group is also responsible for the financial reporting and analysis activities that provide a basis for evaluating the performance of each business or service unit as well as the company as a whole.

All operating functions of the company are performed by business or service units. Those units dealing primarily with the general outside market are considered business units. Units dealing primarily with other units within the company are service units.

Bases for establishing business or service units. The objective in establishing a business or service unit is to give the unit manager a business entity that he can manage effectively and independently. In this way, a large company can achieve much of the speed and flexibility of action of a smaller company. When activities are grouped together to form a business or service unit, the bases for groupings are likely to be found in the list below:

1. Products or services used by a common group of customers.
2. Products produced or distributed using the same physical facilities.
3. Company activities carried on at the same physical locations.

► NOTE: In forming business or service units, attempt to strike a balance between the operations grouped and the size of the management group. The volume of operations should be large enough to support an executive staff of the size and ability needed to effectively direct and control operations.

Delegating profit responsibility. In delegating profit responsibility, it is essential that the business unit manager's authority to control profits be commensurate with his responsibilities. Also, the practical problems of measuring how well profit responsibilities have been carried out must be considered in any sound organizational plan. Another relevant factor to keep in mind is the possibility that divisional considerations may, at times, conflict with the needs of the company as a whole. Some of the conditions that may limit the extent to which profit responsibility can be effectively delegated are discussed below under the headings:

1. Control over functions affecting profits.
2. Inter-unit buying and selling.
3. Nonprofit operations.

1. *Control over functions affecting profits.* In order to effectively carry out profit responsibilities, an operating head must effectively control all of the operating functions that significantly influence his profits. These functions generally include marketing, and product planning and production activities that govern income and costs. Included also are financial planning and control activities that enable the manager to measure the profit effects of his different activities and decisions.

Some business managers do not control all expenses charged to their business units, particularly such items as the allocation of central staff expenses, corporate income taxes, etc. In such cases, profit responsibility should be measured by profits before deducting these costs.

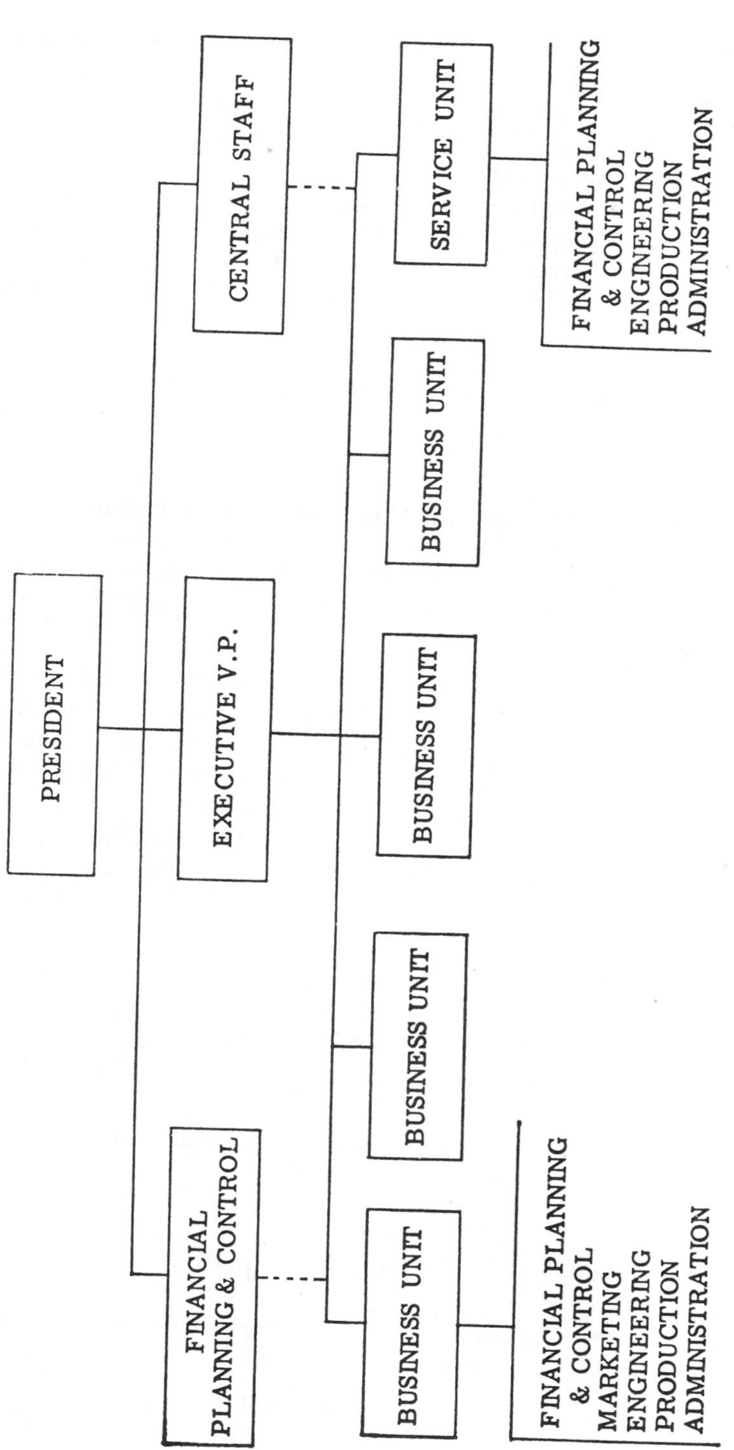

- KEY -
——— Administrative responsibility
- - - - Functional responsibility

Fig. 3. Fully Decentralized Diversified Organization.

2. *Inter-unit buying and selling.* In general, transactions between business or service units should be priced at the general market price for similar items or services. However, there are situations in which this sort of objective measure of profits cannot readily be developed. Perhaps overall company policies dictate that business units must purchase certain products or services from other company units in order to make economical use of facilities, develop and retain valuable skills, or achieve long-range marketing objectives. In turn, the supplying unit is obligated to provide these items as requested. Also, there are often no general market prices established upon which to base prices for such inter-unit transactions. Or, where market prices are available, the supplying unit may not be able to meet them profitably although the fixed expenses absorbed by such production would increase overall company profits. In such cases, the most practical approach is to price these inter-unit transfers on the basis of the best available predetermined cost estimates or rates.

► WARNING: An alternative approach used in pricing inter-unit transactions is to negotiate the prices after costs are known. In practice this usually results in delays and time-consuming conferences. Such a procedure defeats the basic objective of segregating profit responsibilities into manageable segments.

3. *Nonprofit operations.* In operating units established to develop new products or services, management may recognize that profits cannot be achieved in the immediate future. In the case of certain service units, such as the purchasing department in the partially decentralized organization shown in Figure 2, operations are grouped because of specialized or technical requirements for which profit is not a good measure. In such cases, profit responsibility cannot be delegated to the service unit manager. Instead, he must be responsible for accomplishing operating objectives as measured by budgets or cost estimates prepared and approved in advance.

► WARNING: A major pitfall in the delegation of profit responsibility is the danger of achieving divisional profits by sacrificing long-term profits for the organization as a whole. To avoid this, top management must establish far-sighted profit objectives for business unit heads that recognize in reasonable ways the needs for current expenditures to insure future profits. Some of the management control tools that are used to do this are enumerated in the next section.

AREAS OF ORGANIZATIONAL CONTROLS

The previous discussion of organizational decision-making has implied the need for management controls in three areas. These are:

1. *Organizational controls* establishing responsibilities and bases for evaluating performance,

2. *Financial controls* providing for review and advance approval of operating plans for carrying out these responsibilities, and

3. *Accounting policy controls* comparing actual performance with approved operating plans.

It is important to become familiar with the main management tools used in each of these three areas.

Organizational controls. The objectives of organizational controls are:

1. To clearly define the delegations of authority and responsibilities.

2. To establish reporting and working relationships among the various positions in the organizational hierarchy.

3. To assure that all necessary functions and activities are provided.

4. To provide for the development, advancement, and replacement of management personnel.

The basic vehicle for accomplishing these objectives is the company organization manual. The working tools here are the organization charts contained in the manual. Where necessary, the manual should also contain detailed position descriptions clarifying the general responsibilities depicted in the charts. Other types of organizational controls include the following:

1. *A management development program* matching the management positions that must be filled currently and in the foreseeable future with potential candidates for the positions. The program should indicate when the positions should be filled and, where necessary, should outline requirements for supplementing candidates' present qualifications by additional training or special assignments.

2. *A job evaluation program* to provide an objective basis for equating positions of similar responsibility in different areas of the organization.

3. *A management compensation program* to assure that executive compensation is equitable and sufficient to attract and retain able individuals.

Financial controls. The primary organizational objective of financial controls should be to provide top management with means by which they can assure themselves that the responsibilities and authority they have delegated are being effectively implemented. A budget program can provide the framework for accomplishing this providing it recognizes the following essentials:

1. Top management should establish the overall objectives that budgets are planned to attain.

2. The budgets that each manager prepares for his operation should be supported by specific plans for accomplishing the budgeted goals.

3. Budgets should be reviewed and approved (with modification and resubmission if necessary) before the budgeted operations take place.

4. Budgets should be revised currently to reflect major changes in operating conditions not originally anticipated.

In using various techniques for evaluating budgets and operating performance, management must take certain organizational considerations into account. An example of this was discussed in connection with selecting objective bases for determining costs and prices as a factor in measuring profit responsibility.

Organizational problems also arise in setting profit objectives for operating units. For example, the return-on-investment that a business unit manager can achieve may be limited by the cost of facilities furnished to him, or by organizational restrictions on the products he may make or markets he may serve. Thus the evaluation of the return on an investment should not be based solely on an overall standard applied equally to all units. Rather, it should be based on that unit's particular potential and place in the overall organization. Other organizational questions arise in determining bases for allocating central staff or service unit expenses to other units. Where there is no practical basis for allocating such expenses in a way reasonably related to the delegation of authority, financial controls should make clear the effects of such allocations on the reported budgets and performance of each level of the organization.

Accounting policy controls. Accounting policy controls are used to align the treatment of accounting data with organizational responsibilities and management planning. The four main tools and their uses are described in the following section.

1. *Accounting policies and procedures manual.* The accounting policies and procedures manual embodies management decisions as to accounting objectives. It usually describes the treatment and procedures for handling various transactions. In some cases a manual is assembled over a period of time by indexing instructions and memoranda that were prepared as problems arose. In whatever form a manual is developed, the following should be provided for:

   a. Consistency in the accounting methods for handling similar transactions.
   b. Recognition of the accounting needs of the company as a whole.
   c. Coordination and exchange of information on common problems of different organization units.

2. *Top level system of reporting.* The top-level system for reporting the plans and performance of the primary divisions of the organization should be designed to provide for the uniform presentation of key data for all divisions. Where profit responsibility is delegated, key data for divisions should include:

   a. Balance sheets.
   b. Profit and loss statements.
   c. Other control data:

      (1) Receivables.
      (2) Sales and backlogs.
      (3) Inventories.
      (4) Departmental expenses.
      (5) Cash forecasts.
      (6) Return on investment and turnover of funds.

Where profit responsibility is not delegated, some balance sheet, profit statement and return-on-investment items may not be applicable. In practice, the problems encountered in developing uniform reports often lead to the first clear recognition of major needs for planning or clarifying organizational relationships.

3. *Uniform chart of accounts.* The uniform chart of accounts should be closely related to accounting policy and top-level reporting system. It should specify and define the control accounts required for top level reporting. In a decentralized organization, however, the uniform accounts should be kept broad enough so that each division can develop the subsidiary accounts that best suit its particular needs. For effective management reporting, it is also important to code control accounts in a way that will speed the preparation of consolidated statements and facilitate the use of data processing equipment.

4. *Accounting staff control units.* Accounting staff units such as the internal audit, or systems and procedures groups, frequently provide a valuable means for aligning accounting data with organizational requirements. They can review operations to assure adherence to established policies and procedures. They can also be of valuable assistance in developing specific methods for aligning accounting data with organization planning.

MAKING AN ORGANIZATIONAL STUDY

A major practical problem in organization planning is that organizational decisions are complex and require careful study. As a result, there is a strong tendency to get used to and live with organization problems rather than to solve them. One way to overcome this tendency is by establishing an organization study group with the specific responsibility of recommending an organization plan for the operation as a whole. This section outlines how such a group can be established and how it should do its job. Specific steps and techniques that might be used in making such a study are presented under the following headings:

1. Staffing an organizational study.
2. Gathering the facts.
3. Developing recommendations.

Staffing an organizational study. The organizational study group can vary in size depending upon the size of the organization studied, and the manpower available. Within this group, responsibilities fall into three main levels for which different positions may be established. *The director* heads the study and is responsible for its recommendations. *Organization analysts* conduct the necessary fieldwork and formulate recommendations. *Assistant analysts* perform specific research tasks and assist in preparing material for presentation. Further details on the responsibilities and qualifications for each of these positions are outlined below:

Typical Outlines of Responsibilities and Qualifications for Members of Organization Study Group

DIRECTOR

Responsibilities:

1. To formulate the specific program for the study.
2. To arrange and maintain effective working relationships between the study team and the organization studied.
3. To direct studies and coordinate the development of recommendations.

Qualifications:

1. Seasoned management man with sound knowledge of the basic principles of organization and administration.
2. Accurate knowledge of company objectives and practical grasp of its operating problems.
3. Respect of the operating heads of the organization.
4. Ability to view management problems objectively.
5. First-hand acquaintance with key operating heads is desirable but should not take priority over other qualifications.

ORGANIZATION ANALYSTS

Responsibilities:

1. To determine the specific facts required to evaluate organizational requirements.
2. To conduct interviews with key operating heads.
3. To formulate specific organizational recommendations.

Qualifications:

1. Practical understanding of basic principles of organization and administration.
2. Skill in survey techniques of interviewing, preparing questionnaires, etc.
3. Ability to express thoughts clearly in writing and verbally.
4. It is desirable that organization analysts have a level of competence close to that of the operating heads with whom they deal.

ASSISTANTS

Responsibilities:

1. To assist in the gathering and analysis of detailed facts.

Qualifications:

1. Thoroughness and accuracy in the determination and summarization of detailed facts and operating statistics.
2. Skill in graphic presentation for preparation of visual aids, organization charts, statistical data, etc.
3. Wide knowledge of company operating procedures and practices is desirable to aid in locating and evaluating records reflecting desired data.

One man may act in one or more of these capacities depending upon the amount of work and the availability of suitable people. Preferably, analysts and assistants should devote full time to the study. As with any long-range project, organization study work tends to bog down if it is combined with responsibilities for current operations.

Using outside consultants. Individuals to fill all or some of the positions in the study group may be recruited from within the organization. However, in many cases it is desirable to call upon outside consultants for assistance, particularly during the initial phases of the study. Some of the reasons for doing this are:

1. There is a need for the objectivity an outsider can bring to the study.
2. A consultant's special skills in survey techniques enables him to develop and evaluate facts relatively quickly and present recommendations more effectively.
3. Qualified individuals within the company cannot be made available full-time for the study because of their important operating responsibilities. If consultants are used, it is esssential that they work closely with at least one senior member of management.

Gathering the facts. Facts concerning the present organization will provide the foundation for planning since the present organization must be the point of departure in planning any organization changes. Wherever possible, the reasoning process should be supported by the facts and statistics on which it is based. Needless to say, judgments as to those areas requiring changes or clarification, and the suggested way to accomplish these changes, should also be based on facts.

Fact-gathering techniques. It is best to use a straight-forward approach in gathering facts relating to an organization. Otherwise, it is difficult to get all of the required information. Also, the accuracy of facts uncovered indirectly may later be challenged. Various methods and approaches that are useful for fact-gathering in an organization study are discussed under the following headings:

1. Questionnaires.
2. Personnel interviews.
3. Checking existing records.
4. Questions to ask.

Although the items discussed under each heading have certain major limitations if used alone, if used jointly they usually provide all of the necessary information.

1. *Questionnaires.* Questionnaires provide an effective means of quickly gathering together a large amount of relatively simple information. They are most valuable in the initial stages of a study when they can be used to get a general picture of the size and form of the present organization. A sample of a questionnaire used for this purpose is shown in Figure 4.

Questionnaires should be distributed through the organization's customary channels of command, accompanied by a brief explanation of their purpose. Filled-in questionnaires should be reviewed by interested superiors. Copies should be retained by persons completing them.

ORGANIZATIONAL STRUCTURE
QUESTIONNAIRE

1. NAME		2. DEPARTMENT	
3. TITLE		4. SUPERVISING OFFICER	
5. CHECK COMPANIES OF WHICH YOU ARE AN OFFICER OR COMPANIES WHICH YOUR DEPARTMENT REPRESENTS ☐ ALL CO'S. ☐ ABC CO. ☐ XYZ COMPANIES ☐ ________		6. NUMBER OF PERSONNEL SUPERVISORY ________ CLERICAL ________ TECHNICAL & PROFESSIONAL ________ TOTAL	

7. FURNISH THE INFORMATION REQUESTED FOR THE PRESENT RESPONSIBILITIES OF YOUR POSITION		
A) RESPONSIBILITIES: FUNCTIONS, TRANSACTIONS ACTIVITIES OR SERVICES PERFORMED	B) TERRITORY: COUNTRYWIDE EXCEPT PACIFIC, ETC.	OPERATIONS: XYZ, GROUP, ABC
1.		
2.		
3.		
4.		
5.		
6.		
7.		
8.		
9.		
10.		
11.		
12.		
13.		
14.		
15.		
16.		

8. LIST OTHER UNITS WITH WHICH YOUR ORGANIZATION IS IN MOST FREQUENT CONTACT, INDICATING SUBJECT OF CONTACT	
UNIT	SUBJECT OF CONTACTS
1.	
2.	
3.	
4.	
5.	

Fig. 4. Front of a Sample Questionnaire.

In evaluating responses to questionnaires it is essential to recognize that even the most simple questions are liable to be interpreted in different ways by different people. Differences in terminology, confusion with similar questions from other sources, and unforeseen ambiguities are all common sources of misunderstandings. Provisions should be made to answer questions raised by people as they are completing questionnaires. In addition, any facts on which major decisions are based should be checked carefully by means of other fact-gathering techniques.

ORGANIZATIONAL STRUCTURE
QUESTIONNAIRE – SIDE 2

NAME		DEPARTMENT	
9. WHAT MANAGEMENT CONTROL REPORTS DO YOU EITHER CREATE OR REVIEW? INCLUDE ONLY THOSE SUMMARY REPORTS WHICH ENABLE MANAGEMENT TO EXERCISE OVER-ALL CONTROL			
A) DESCRIPTION: TITLE, SOURCE AND FREQUENCY CHECK (✓) THOSE WHICH YOU CREATE.	(✓)	B) CONTENTS: INFORMATION SHOWN, REPORTING CLASSIFICATIONS, ETC.	C) PURPOSE FOR WHICH YOU USE REPORT
1.			
2.			
3.			
4.			
5.			
6.			
7.			
8.			
9.			
10.			
11.			
12.			
13.			
14.			
15.			

10. LIST COMPANY OR TRADE GROUP OPERATING COMMITTEES ON WHICH YOU SERVE INDICATING PURPOSE, SCOPE OF ACTIVITIES, AUTHORITY

11. COMMENTS, SUGGESTIONS OR PROBLEMS RELATING TO THE ORGANIZATION OF YOUR UNIT.

Fig. 4 (Continued). Back of a Sample Questionnaire.

2. *Personnel interviews.* Interviews are the major source of information in an organization study. They should be used to gather details concerning present duties and responsibilities; to determine management objectives, major problems, and present methods of controlling operations; and to explore suggestions for changes or new approaches to organization.

First interviews should be with top executives to learn their organizational objectives and plans, and to determine which problems they believe will require the greatest study. Top executives can also help the analyst to select the people whom he should interview and to advise him of the subjects on which these people are best informed. However, the analyst should reserve the right to speak to whomever he wishes, and he should be sure to cover all areas of the organization.

Where the organization presently appears sound and without problems, this can be verified by brief interviews with executives whose positions give them contact with all parts of the operation.

a. *Conducting the interview.* It is generally desirable to have a senior member of the organization studied introduce the analyst and assure the executive to be interviewed that he should answer questions freely. In addition, the analyst should spend a few minutes describing his role in the organization study, and outlining briefly the general program that is being followed. If it is appropriate, he should also give subjective assurances that comments will be kept confidential.

   It is usually necessary to take notes in order to be sure that facts are retained accurately. If this is done in an open manner it will not disturb most people. However, avoid the appearance of writing down every word as this will slow down the interview.

b. *Starting and closing the interview.* The first few questions in an interview should be questions that the interviewee can answer easily. For example, ask about the history of the department or about his or her own working experience. It is also a good practice to cover all routine factual questions early in the interview to avoid the need for interrupting free discussion later on.

   When it appears that all of the major subjects have been covered, the analyst should signal the end of the meeting, closing his notebook or thanking the executive for cooperating. At this point, the executive will frequently volunteer many thoughts which he or she hesitated to express during the "official" conversations. Often, this post-closing discussion will prove to be the most valuable part of the interview.

3. *Checking existing records.* Accounting and related statistical records, where they can be used, are the best sources of information. These records are usually the most integrated and accurate source of detailed data in an organization. Their use reduces the complications that arise from piecing together fragments of data from unrelated sources and makes it easier to relate results to established financial statements.

Accounting classifications such as cost center and departmental codes are frequently helpful in outlining the framework of the present organization structure.

Payroll records are another valuable source of information. Payroll registers provide an accurate list of the names and the number of employees in the organization at any given time. Departmental classifications and payroll distribution data can give further indications of the activities in which these employees are engaged and the cost of some operations. Finally, the methods or formulae used for allocating expenses may in some cases be indicative of organizational responsibilities or of areas where relationships require classification.

It is important not to overlook any other records that may be used to verify statistical judgments or estimates offered by management to support their views. While such estimates are very valuable, they may be incorrect because they give undue weight to exceptional items or items that, by their nature, are more likely to receive attention. Records that are often of value for this purpose include:

a. Special management studies or transaction counts.
b. Personnel records.
c. Company census reports.
d. Production schedules.

In addition, counting the items in records such as mailing lists, data files or journals and accounts may provide statistical data not otherwise available. Other sources of information include management manuals, telephone directories listing personnel by department and title, and various company sales catalogs and brochures.

4. *Questions to ask.* There is no simple checklist of questions to ask in making an organization study. The specific questions that are worth exploring will vary in each organization. Therefore, it is generally best to use a flexible approach, probing first for problem areas. Some general questions for this purpose are shown below. This list is intended to be suggestive of opening questions rather than all-inclusive. Under each question some of the items that might be considered are listed.

Basic Checklist of Questions for an Organizational Study

1. What are the corporate objectives and philosophy?
   a. Technical pre-eminence in specialized field?
   b. Diversification?
   c. Mass-produced, economy product?
   d. High measure of quality or individualized service?
2. What makes for success?
   a. Product quality?
   b. Marketing pre-eminence?
   c. Production know-how?
   d. Finance and administration?
3. How is the organization now divided?
   a. Functionally?
   b. Geographically?
   c. Types of customers?
   d. Types of product?
   e. Skills or processes?

4. What are the basic measures of performance?
   a. Profit?
   b. Budgetary controls?
   c. Attainment of physical goals?
   d. Growth of operations?
   e. Personal charm?

5. What specific activities are performed in each organization?
   a. Bookkeeping?
   b. Manufacturing operations?
   c. Order processing?
   d. Other?

6. What are the natures of major communications between organizational units?
   a. At what operating level do contacts arise?
   b. Which units communicate most often?
   c. What are the purposes of the contacts?
      (1) Exchange facts.
      (2) Coordinate operations or request service.
      (3) Secure approval or counsel.
   d. What are the specific subjects of communications?

7. What are the skills, backgrounds and capabilities of present managers?
   a. Formal education?
   b. Special training?
   c. Positions held?
   d. Years with the company?
   e. Current earnings?

Developing recommendations. The first step in developing organizational recommendations is to outline an "ideal" plan based exclusively on considerations of the functions and activities to be performed. This involves choosing between a centralized or decentralized organization, determining whether the primary divisions of the organizations should be functional, geographic, etc., and establishing the basic operating divisions desired.

Next, the "ideal" plan must be modified by taking practical problems into account. For example, it may be necessary to group together several smaller divisions or functions in order to achieve a large enough volume of activity to support necessary administrative or technical services or to make the most economic use of the available facilities. For some functions, such as sales, product service, or plant accounting, the physical problems of properly serving customers or other units of the organization will require that activities be decentralized even though this may undesirably complicate the organization plan.

After considering those practical limitations that must be recognized, the modified plan that results represents the company's ultimate organizational objectives. As such it should be the practical plan best suited to the long term needs of the company.

Staffing considerations. Before the ultimate organization plan can be put into effect, staffing problems must also be evaluated. Are individuals presently available within the company for the executive positions called for by the plan? Are they competent enough to justify the desired responsibilities to be delegated to them? Do they possess the required combinations of skills?

Where the answers to these questions are negative, it may be necessary to fill some positions from outside the company. This too is subject to the availability of competent individuals. Also, it is important to consider the effects of such action on valuable present employees.

Use of interim plans. Frequently, the best approach to achieving ultimate organizational objectives is to develop one or more interim plans, each of which brings the present organization progressively closer to the ultimate plan. These interim plans must be workable at the time they are put into effect, but they are judged less desirable than the plan representing ultimate objectives. To serve as effective stepping stones, these plans should be related by a clear program for developing the management capabilities required to progress to the ultimate objectives.

PRESENTING THE PLAN

Work from the top down. Approval of organizational changes must be secured first at the top levels of the organization for several reasons. First, some of the proposed changes may affect present bases for delegating top level responsibilities. Secondly, approval of organizational objectives frequently involves clarifying or redefining company policies. In both cases, top level participation is required to resolve conflicts in responsibilities at lower levels in such a way as to best serve the interests of the company as a whole.

► PRACTICAL NOTE: For the reasons mentioned, organization studies are often made a level at a time in this order:

Top level—those positions reporting directly to the chief executive.

Middle management—the positions and groups reporting to top level executives.

Operating levels—the supervisory positions in production and clerical groups that report to middle management.

It is not always necessary to study all areas in detail. If the study leaves responsibilities at the top or middle management levels substantially unchanged, and operations appear satisfactory, management may decide to forgo further assistance in organizational planning.

Selling the plan to lower levels. There are obvious problems in disclosing specific organizational recommendations to lower level managers before securing top level approval. However, it is essential to review with the managers involved, the facts and reasoning on which the recommendations are based. This is a valuable way to verify the practicality of the conclusions, and to determine questions that will be raised regarding the proposed plan.

Such reviews with lower level managers can also lay the foundations for selling the plan. To do this effectively, the reasoning behind the recommendations must be clearly brought out, and the people involved must have a genuine opportunity to point out factors that may have been overlooked.

What to include when presenting the plan. The executive who receives organizational recommendations has probably not had the opportunity to think about these problems intensively. It is important, therefore, to brief him on the essential stages of thinking that led up to the proposed plan. Undoubtedly, he will want to satisfy himself about the effectiveness and thoroughness of the study before accepting its results. After he has gone through the recommendations, he will want to know what specific concrete action is next required.

Sections of an organization report. A typical form of report that contains recommendations for revisions in the organizational structure, and that provides for the needs of executives reviewing the report, includes four sections. A listing of the content of each section follows:

1. *The approach and scope* of the study should be outlined and should include the following:
   a. A brief description of the specific sources of the facts used and the extent of the survey.
   b. An outline of the considerations judged most important in developing the proposed plan.
   c. A clear definition of the objectives of the plan.
2. *The present situation* should be reviewed to:
   a. Show charts of the present organization and define departmental or other designations used in the discussion.
   b. Describe how the present organization is intended to work.
   c. Outline the specific operating problems or organizational deficiencies, citing facts indicating the extent or nature of them.
   d. Summarize the conclusions regarding present problems.
3. *The proposed organizational plan* should be described fully as follows:
   a. State the basic form of organization recommended, indicating whether it is centralized or decentralized, and whether its primary division is functional, geographic, etc.
   b. Define the main elements of the plan, outlining positions at each organizational level and describing the duties and responsibilities of major functions.
   c. Show the details of the plan using charts outlining the organization structure and key functions of each unit. Where necessary for clarity, include descriptions of key positions and illustrate types of controls and operating reports.
   d. Outline how the plan could deal with the present problems that were previously described.
4. *The program* required to establish the recommended plan should be outlined. Specifically, the program should:

a. List those policy decisions required to implement the proposed organization plan.
b. Indicate a sequence of changes that would bring about an orderly transition from the present organization to the proposed plan.
c. Outline plans for changes in staffing, indicating the extent of training, recruiting, or relocation and reassignment of personnel that will be necessary.
d. Provide measures to insure that necessary management controls are established and maintained during the period of transition.
e. Define specific projects that must be next undertaken to implement the recommendation.

The report itself. Reports on organization normally will be difficult to prepare. Consideration must be given to all the technical and physical aspects of operations, the problems of management planning and control, as well as the less concrete, but nonetheless important aspects concerning people, their liabilities, and their ambitions. The same reasons that make these reports difficult to prepare may make them difficult to understand. Therefore, the report should be in the form that offers the clearest and simplest way of presentation. Visual aids, including organization charts, statistics, and lists of key points, are essential in order to represent the large number of facts involved. In many cases, a verbal presentation which provides an opportunity for questions and answers will be most effective.

Presenting the report. The final report should be previewed by the top executive who is primarily responsible for making the necessary decisions. Then, if he wishes, he can make special provisions for disclosing the plan and his decisions to various of his managers. If this is done, it should be kept in mind that the general management group will be anxious to learn the results of the study as soon as possible. To avoid uncertainty and to prevent the spread of rumors, it is often desirable to arrange a group presentation at which all managers may hear the report together.

If possible, such a presentation should be introduced by the top executive. In his introduction he should state his reasons for authorizing the study, he should indicate that he believes the recommendations are worthy of serious consideration, and he should recognize the effects of the plan on the positions of certain individuals. The consideration he will give to any personal problems that may arise should also be indicated.

► FINAL NOTE: This chapter has discussed organization planning in terms of a formal study of specific duration. It is important to recognize, however, that organization planning is a continuous function in any vital company. The planning process may include a study to develop a comprehensive plan, as has been described. But, organization is a changing thing—and there is no *one* answer. A complete solution of all organizational problems is never achieved. Organization study is worthwhile, therefore, if it succeeds in pointing the way to changes in the right direction.

18

How to Design and Install Accounting Systems

CONTENTS

18

How to Design and Install Accounting Systems

George E. Hunt, Jr., CPA

HOW TO GET THE SYSTEMS ENGAGEMENT MOVING

The know-how and the ability to design and install accounting systems is a field where the accountant has no. peers. Others may do as good a job at preparing income tax returns, but the accountant is the only professional with wide experience in working with *various* businesses and observing first hand their accounting systems. This field *is* exclusively yours, but you must constantly strive to improve your techniques and abilities in this field.

This chapter is a step-by-step checklist that you can use to design and install accounting systems. It will enumerate certain "pitfalls" that you may encounter along the way. Sometimes you can avoid them if you know others have fallen into them before. Sometimes you must experience them yourself. Try to adapt your own experiences to the guidelines shown.

A systems design and installation engagement begins with a call from a client (or prospective client) and this initial contact is most important. Like the architect who must *first* determine *what the owner wants,* the first step for you here is to arrange a conference.

What does the owner want from the accounting system. Sometimes the owner has definite wants and sometimes he asks you to answer his first question—"What do I want?" To get the conversation on solid ground, you might begin with his most usual want—profit. Would he like to know his profit monthly, quarterly, or yearly? Is he interested in this one figure only, or does he want a detailed statement showing how the profit was obtained? How often, if ever, would he like the other information such as:

1. Summary of Cash on Hand
2. Summary of Accounts Receivable
3. Summary of Accounts Payable
4. Inventory Totals
5. Salaries Expense
6. Advertising Expense, etc.

Make this first conference as rewarding as possible for the client as well as yourself. Take along to this first meeting a sample monthly reporting form similar to that illustrated in Figure 1.

The advantage of using a sample report such as this one is that it often provides a good base on which to begin your discussion. The owner can better visualize what information he would like to have from his accounting system.

► EXAMPLE: A paint store owner calls you in to discuss his accounting system. He tells you that he never knows until the end of the year whether he has made any money or not. He wants more information.

You show him your sample monthly reporting form. He tells you that he likes the idea, but that he is not interested in all of the information that this sample includes. Start with the first item, sales, and see if he is interested in that information. If he isn't, cross it off. Continue down the list in this manner.

You now ask him if there is other information that he would like to have. He says that he is interested in his utility expenses also. Add that to your list. Check to see that the monthly report is what he wants. Maybe he prefers some other interval.

At this first meeting, find out what information his records already supply. You do not want to spend time working out methods to give him what he already has. Concentrate on what he needs and doesn't have. Possibly he needs reports for interested parties such as stockholders and banks. Be sure to note all types of reports that he needs.

Explain the basic requirements of a good accounting system. Use this first conference to point out what a good system contains. Caution your client against the possible consequences of an inadequate system—embezzlement, tax troubles, unreliable reports.

You want to keep the system simple. You want it to supply the information for the required government reports. You want it to have built-in controls to help prevent embezzlement.

Since you will be connected with the system you design and install for a long time, you will benefit yourself as well as the owner by discussing the basic requirements of a *good system*. You must do your "homework" well. You need to have well fixed in your mind the three basic requirements: simplicity, satisfaction of legal requirements, and safeguards.

A good system is as simple as possible. You prefer a doctor who uses English rather than Latin when he talks with you. The client will prefer a simple accounting system that he can understand. A simple system will also require less time to maintain and will require fewer personnel.

In your conversations with the client, keep your word usage on his level. If he has had no previous accounting language exposure, do not just refer to a "journal." Say, "We will need a journal to record the checks written." Remember that the best professional is the one who not only knows, but who can also communicate.

A. B. C. CLOTHING COMPANY
Comparative Statements
For the Eight Months Ending September 30,

	This Year	*Last Year*
Sales	$	$
Cost of Sales	______	______
Gross Earnings	______	______
Freight Expense		
Salesmen's Salaries		
Advertising Expense		
Insurance Expense		
Depreciation Expense		
Rent Expense		
Other Expenses	______	______
Total Expenses	______	______
Net Earnings	$______	$______
Cash in Banks	$	$
Accounts Receivable		
Inventory		
Notes Payable		
Accounts Payable		

Fig. 1. Monthly Reporting Form.

Accountants have been accused of setting up complicated systems so that their services will always be needed. Systems do become complicated at times. This is more often the fault of management requesting too much data than of ulterior motives of the accountant. This is why you must explain at the very beginning the advantages of a simple system. Make your position clear.

► EXAMPLE: You are called in for a systems discussion by a department store owner. He has 20 departments and 10 clerks. You can describe to him the usual departmental code procedure for making sales tickets. This will give him a breakdown of sales by departments. You can then outline the department recording procedures for inventories and cost of sales. These are basic facts that you feel he must have to know department gross profit percentage and inventories.

He asks about further departmental breakdowns for rent, salaries, utilities, etc. Explain that this additional information will complicate the system and require additional personnel. Let him know also that some of these breakdowns will be "educated guesses." This is particularly true of such expenses as rent, utilities, etc. Tell him that you would prefer to start with a simple system and then expand it later if he thought it worth the additional accounting costs.

The system must meet governmental requirements. Every business today has a not-so-silent partner, the government. Explain to the owner that his system must provide certain information for governmental reports. Although it is not necessary to enumerate all of these reports to him, it would be well to have a list of them with you in case he would like to discuss them. This list might include:

1. Annual Federal Income Tax Return
2. Monthly Sales Tax Returns
3. Monthly, Quarterly and Annual Payroll Tax Returns
4. Yearly Personal Property Tax Return
5. Capital Stock Tax Return
6. Pension and Profit Sharing Plan Forms
7. Bureau of Census Forms
8. Economic Stabilization Forms

► NOTE: Governmental reporting requirements change from time to time and you must be ready to adjust your system to such changes. This is part of keeping the system in good health.

A good accounting system will provide the necessary information for any reports required with as little additional work as possible. Should the owner refuse to supply the government or others with such required information, it is best to refuse the engagement—your professional reputation is at stake. However, most businessmen have accepted the government and other agencies as part of life.

► EXAMPLE: You have been called in by a candy vending machine operator to discuss a system. You and he are both aware that monthly sales tax returns must be sent to the state. He indicates to you that he would prefer just to "estimate" the figures for the sales tax returns. He says that he doesn't want to hire extra people just to satisfy the government. Explain to him that his estimate practice could:

1. Lead to fraud charges by the agent.
2. Have him pay more taxes than necessary.
3. Have lengthy government investigations that would disrupt his business operation.

Show him the various methods that he could use to segregate his non-taxable sales. Show him how it can be worked into his system so that the data for the reports can be taken directly therefrom without any additional personnel.

Design the system so that the government auditors will have a clear trail to follow. Make it easy to find where the reported information came from. These clear trails will save the client's time as well as yours should a tax audit come up.

Do not look upon government agents as "enemies." They have a difficult job to perform and most of us would not care to trade places with them. You will find that if you try to help the agents work, they can help you and your client by making their audits short and painless. Give them the best kind of accounting system you can devise. You will be of real service to the owner by cooperating with the government agents and by satisfying them. In the long run, this may be the most valuable task you will perform for your client.

► EXAMPLE: You are called by two brothers in the contracting business. They inform you that they have spent the past several months at the Internal Revenue Service answering questions when they should have been working. They ask you to: "Set up an accounting system that will keep us out of trouble."

You review the revenue agent's report of the difficulties and correct the shortcomings of the books. You find it best to set up a completely new system. You inform the brothers that it is very possible that the books, however set up, will be reviewed again.

You volunteer to meet with the revenue agent yourself if they are contacted again. A good job by you will save them many hours in the future—hours that they can best use doing their building. This saving of their time will be the most appreciated service that you can render to them. This is really public accounting—serving the public.

A good system safeguards the business through internal controls. The third basic requirement of a good accounting system is adequate internal controls. This should really appeal to your client. Does he know that many losses through embezzlement can be traced to poor internal controls? When explaining to him the need for internal controls be sure to point out that you can have good internal controls and still have a simple system.

Embezzlement is a word understood by all because of wide newspaper coverage. You need not explain what this word means—just how a good system can help prevent it. Even in the smallest operation it is possible to build in some controls.

► EXAMPLE: Take the case of a small office with only a receptionist and a bookkeeper. The system could provide for the receptionist to open the mail and to list all of the cash receipts by name and amount. The bookkeeper would then count the money and make out the deposit ticket independently. He would also control and mail out the accounts receivable statements.

The receptionist's list and the deposit ticket duplicate give the owner his control. This system would require collusion for embezzlement.

Internal control is too large a subject to cover completely in this initial conversation with the client—just let him know that you consider it important. Let him know that you are not suspicious of anyone, but that it is just sound business practice to build as many controls into the accounting system as possible. Most people are basically honest, but why tempt a good employee to turn bad?

What to do when you meet a new problem. In systems work, you will often meet new situations. Each business is different from others in some respect, and you must tailor make each system. However, you cannot expect yourself to be an expert in every area. You will have to seek help when you just do not know.

Use all the help you can get. Don't feel "dumb" if you have to ask for help. The accountant does it every day—especially in systems work. The following list includes the sources of information available to you:

1. Your own workpapers of similar businesses.
2. Systems textbooks.
3. Other accountants.
4. Accounting societies.

If you still need an answer, go outside the profession to:

1. Business machine salesmen.
2. Attorneys, bankers, and the like.

There is one more source that is available to you. It could well be the best source, and what is more, it's free. This is the trade association. Most businesses belong to one. You can contact them through your client. For example, here's how the laundry association came to the rescue.

► THE PROBLEM: A laundry client's business had grown to the point where the girls in his office just couldn't get the posting work done. Each bundle of laundry had a three-part ticket which was copied on a daily sheet. The copy process was taking too much time.

► THE SOLUTION: We asked the association what they did in other laundries. They described an adding machine tape procedure that could be used in place of the copy process, and gave us names of laundries that were using this system successfully. After checking with the other laundries, we made the change. It works. My client is now up-to-date.

You have taken the preliminary steps for a systems engagement. You have met with the owner to determine what information he wants from the system. You have explained to him the basic requirements that a good system should have—simplicity, satisfaction of governmental requirements, and safeguards. And you have researched his type of business.

► NOTE: As with any engagement, you must agree on a fee arrangement before starting work. Give him as close an idea as possible how much this is going to cost. State your hourly rates for doing systems work. Now you are ready to design the system and then install it.

HOW TO DESIGN A SYSTEM

Designing a system for a new business is different from designing one for an established business. In this section we will discuss each of these separately. As an architect finds it easier to plan a new house than to remodel an old one, so you will usually find it easier to design a system for a new business.

How to design a system for a new business. In your discussions with the client, you found out the type of business he was forming and other particulars such as the number of employees. Rarely is such information complete. You must start somewhat in the dark and be ready to roll with the punches.

No owner can forecast exactly how much a business may or may not grow. Therefore, your system must allow for expansion. This can be accomplished by having a flexible chart of accounts. Setting up a chart of accounts is the first step in designing a system for a new business.

Working up the chart of accounts. Although a chart of accounts is the basic structure of any accounting system, the individual accounts will, of course, vary from business to business. In the usual chart, the accounts are numbered and grouped somewhat as follows:

#100 accounts—Assets
#200 accounts—Liabilities
#300 accounts—Capital
#400 accounts—Income
#500 accounts—Expenses

Generally the individual accounts are arranged in the order of financial statement presentation, but this is not a hard and fast rule. You may prefer another arrangement in some circumstances.

Leave room for expansion. The beginning of the chart will probably resemble the following:

#100 Petty Cash
#102 Cash in First National Bank
#110 Accounts Receivable—Trade

Note that #101 and #103—109 have been left blank. This is to allow for any more accounts that may be needed. There is no harm if some of the account numbers are never used. It is better to leave blanks than to end up with accounts numbered #100A, #100B, and the like.

Tailor the chart for each client. Keep in mind any special accounts that the owner has told you he is especially interested in. List them. Show them to him. Let him know that you are designing a system especially for him.

► EXAMPLE: Suppose your client has requested detailed information on advertising expense. You might set up accounts for:

Advertising—Newspapers
Advertising—Radio
Advertising—TV
Advertising—Display Material
Advertising—Signs
Advertising—Postage
Advertising—Printing
Advertising—Booklets
Advertising—Flowers
Advertising—Cut Service

The chart of accounts is basically the story of the business. The terminology you use is that which will appear in the accounting records and reports. Keep it accurate, simple, and descriptive.

Since this is a new business, you will change the chart of accounts from time to time as the operations of the business change. You will probably fill in some of the blank spaces and change some of the account titles. This is part of keeping the design current.

When you have completed the chart of accounts, you should ask the client to go over it with you. Explain what the various accounts are for and how this arrangement suits his particular needs.

Selecting and setting up the books. Since the system for the new business is not really designed until it is ready for use, you must prepare it for operation. You can buy the ledger and journals from the office supplier recommended by the client and have the supplies charged to him or, if he has no preference, use your own supplier.

You have had experience working with various types of ledgers and journals and will probably have definite preferences. Get what you like best. You may personally prefer a three-column ledger sheet. If so, buy this type. There is no one best type of record book. Buy what you feel will work best.

If the bookkeeper has already been hired, ask him about his preference. He is the one who is going to work with the records so he might as well have what he's most comfortable with.

► EXAMPLE: During your design work, you find that the bookkeeper has had many years of experience with general ledgers using four columns. You have always preferred a three-column ledger since there is only one balance column instead of two. You feel that it is easier to take a trial balance with only the one column.

Tell him that you prefer the three-column ledger and why. He may not know that there is more than one kind. If he still prefers to keep the four-column type, let him. *He* is the one that must use it, not you. He will respect you for seeing *his* side. He can be a valuable ally to you later in your systems installation.

Most bookkeepers develop an intense pride in the neatness and accuracy of their work. Give them a neat set of books to begin with. Type headings where possible, or at least, print in ink. Don't scribble. This is your opportunity to set a good example. Make the most of it.

The various types of accounting records available cannot be discussed here at length. You must decide on the types of records and numbers of columns that you will need. You can then have the supply people show you the various types available.

There are several grades of paper and binders available, but the cheapest is usually the most expensive in the long run. Supply costs are only a small part of the systems cost. Buy supplies that will last. These are to be permanent records.

If you are designing a machine bookkeeping system, you can use the service of the machine salesmen and technicians. Explain to them what you want and they will help design the records. This service is included in the cost of the machine. But remember that this is *your* system. You are the one that the owner is counting on. Do not turn all the work over to the machine salesmen—they have a product to sell. You are designing a system for the business. Salesmen tend to build a system around the machine.

Putting the system into action. You have prepared the chart of accounts and headed up the books. You have the product ready. Now you must explain how it is to be used. Do not make the mistake of doing this verbally. It is easier this way, but it can also be disastrous. Write out the instructions for your system. Make sure your instructions are simple and complete.

Keep your instructions simple. We have all had experience in buying kits with instructions "so simple that a child can assemble." Sometimes we end up by calling an electrician to help us with the radio kit or we find that Christmas day is here before the bicycle or train is together. Look over your instructions several times. Would you understand them if someone else had prepared them for you to follow?

► EXAMPLE: When writing instructions for the accounts receivable bookkeeper, don't just say, "Post all transactions each day and prove." Enumerate the duties as follows:

1. Post each day's charge sales tickets as debit on the accounts receivable card.
   A. You *do not* post *cash sales* to the accounts receivable cards.
   B. If you find a charge sales ticket and no accounts receivable card, get permission from your superior to make a new card. Be sure it has the proper address.
2. Post each day's cash received on charge accounts as a *credit* to the accounts receivable card.
3. Post any charge sales return slips as a *credit* to the accounts receivable card. Use the symbol RET on these postings.
4. Run a total of the accounts receivable balances after completing each day's posting.
5. This total must agree with the total at the beginning of the day, plus the day's charge sales total, minus the day's sales returns total, minus the day's cash received on account total.
6. If you are unable to prove out in step number 5, see your superior before starting the next day's posting.

I cannot emphasize too strongly how important such instructions are. I have seen some bookkeepers keep typed instructions for a number of years. You should do your best to outline all bookkeeping procedures in detail.

Format varies, but usually instructions are broken down into duties:

Daily
Monthly
Quarterly
Annually

Try to imagine yourself in the bookkeeper's job and list the instructions in the most logical sequence. You may even make the first few entries yourself so that the bookkeeper has a pattern to follow. This also assures you that your system is workable.

Be precise in your wording. Use language that can be understood. Your instructions may well determine if your system will succeed or fail. Get your system off to a good start.

► EXAMPLE: Avoid such vague language as, "After filling a page" or "at the end of the month, crossfoot all totals." Your instructions should state:

1. Total all columns:
   A. When each page is completed, and
   B. After all items for a month are posted—even though a page hasn't been completed.
2. The totals of columns #1 through #4 must equal the totals of columns #5 through #10.
3. If they do, your journal is in balance.

Your system planning for the new business is now complete. You are now ready to install your system. First, however, let us explore the design procedures for an established business. Let us see how this is different from the new business design work. Installation procedures will be discussed later.

How to design a system for an established business. An established business may be one that has been in business a number of years or just a short time. Either way, an accounting system is in operation. The owner may know that the present system is deficient or he may just want you to check it over to be sure that it is in good shape.

Again, the first conference with the owner is important. You must determine his exact reasons for calling you if you are to render him the best service. Make sure the owner realizes that a particular ailment may be caused by many different things. To make an accurate diagnosis you may need to make a complete examination. Again you are like a doctor, seeing where the system is sick.

► EXAMPLE: You are called in by a magazine publisher who wants you to check out his accounting department. He tells you that too many customers are complaining about their subscriptions. The customers think that they have paid for more issues than the accounting department does. You are asked to investigate.

When you look into the system of recording magazine subscriptions, you notice that code letters are used. This practice has been in use for many years. You inquire if the actual date of the subscription expiration couldn't be used instead of the code letters. The accounting department says it is fine with them if the label machine can be so adapted.

You now report your findings back to the owner and request permission to clear this matter with the label machine people and the sales department. This is granted. Your survey also leads you to other departments such as circulation.

This apparently simple reform actually affected the whole organization. However, be sure to check with the owner before entering other departments. It is wise to proceed through channels.

Studying the system in use. A certain amount of attitude adjustment is in order before you enter the client's bookkeeping department. Remember that you are an outsider looking in. If the procedures presently used are good, admit it. If you come across something that looks bad, go slow. Don't jump to conclusions. Keep an open mind until you have completed your study.

► EXAMPLE: You have been called in to review the accounting system of an automobile dealership. You notice several blank checks that have been signed by the owner. You find out from the bookkeeper that this is often done when the owner is out of town.

You know that this procedure is dangerous, but avoid discussing it any further with the bookkeeper. Make a note of this practice for your future recommendations. If the bookkeeper asks you if this is a bad procedure, tell him, "It is usually not a good practice but I'll have to complete my study before coming to any conclusion."

There are several reasons for not going into this signed check matter with the bookkeeper now:

1. You owe it to the owner to discuss such matters with him first. He hired you. He is responsible for the business. He will have to make the final decision on the matter.
2. You should not point out embezzlement possibilities to the bookkeeper. Hold your fire until your recommendations are ready and approved.
3. You may find that this practice is a calculated risk that the owner feels he must take. Don't turn the employees against him.

Meet the employees and find out what they do. Ask the owner for the names and duties of the bookkeeping staff. A diagram of desk placement is also useful for orienting yourself. Be formal with the employees; address them as Mrs., Mr., Miss or Ms. Ask that you be introduced to each member of the staff. Make sure your client understands that it is important that his employees know who you are and why you are there.

In a systems review of an established business, you are entering a going concern with its own rules and regulations. Make an effort to fit in. The employees will not appreciate being kept overtime. Neither will the owner. Try to obtain the employees' cooperation. They are usually proud of their work and willing to talk about it. Let them know that you are a "fact finder." Do not spend a lot of time discussing baseball scores or office scuttlebutt. Be professional. Be courteous. Learn their names. Use them.

You may come across employees who are curious about you and accountants in general. Answer their questions in a friendly way. These are excellent opportunities for promoting yourself and your profession.

► EXAMPLE: You have been introduced to Mr. Jones, the accounts payable bookkeeper. You start out by asking him to show you how he records the payables. Where does he get his information? From whom? Does he have an assistant? What notations does he make on the invoices to indicate that he has seen them? What does he do with them when he is finished? Is it his responsibility to authorize payments or to make the disbursements? Mr. Jones asks you a few questions about yourself and your profession. Would you advise his son to be an accountant? Do you enjoy your work? Answer his questions. Be pleased that he cares. You will obtain better cooperation from him.

Use an internal control questionnaire to organize your study. Now that you know the employees and what they do, you are ready to move into their offices and find out how they do their work. You need a plan to insure that your investigation is thorough. One of the best tools that you can use in your investigation is an internal control questionnaire.

Use an internal control questionnaire similar to those you use in your audit work. This will be invaluable in framing the questions you will ask the employees. If employees are curious about your questionnaire, explain that they are normally used in making a systems survey. If it's a normal procedure, they are apt to be a bit more relaxed with you. Do everything you can to put the employees at ease. It is only natural for them to become a bit edgy when someone is looking over their shoulder.

As you fill out the form, make frequent notations. Don't just check "yes" or "no." Note the names of the employees giving you the information. Be on the alert for any ideas or complaints the employees may have about their jobs. Their thoughts might contribute to solving the problem.

► EXAMPLE 1: Your questionnaire includes a question, "Are incoming merchandise shipments checked at the receiving door?" Instead of just checking "yes" if that's the case, note the name of the man responsible. If you can, observe him performing this task. Does he appear to be conscientious? Does he initial the receiving ticket? Does he record the items received in a book of some sort? Talk to him. Does he have any suggestions? What does he do with the tickets and merchandise after checking them in? Use the margins of your questionnaire to note such information.

► EXAMPLE 2: You are filling out a questionnaire on your local United Fund accounting system. You find massive records of contributions. You notice that each volunteer worker lists the names of contributors and amounts contributed on an envelope. These are audited before the deposit is made, and then a master list of all contributions is prepared.

The bookkeeper asks you if you think it is necessary to include contributions under $5 in the master list. You examine the list and find the contributions under $5 comprise about 50% of the total list.

You discuss the matter with the fund director and find that these lists are maintained in case the Internal Revenue Service wants to check any particular contribution. You ask if the volunteer worker's envelope listing wouldn't satisfy the revenue agent. He agrees that it would be sufficient. However, the records have always been kept this way and the director tells you that he couldn't make the change without the approval of the board of directors.

You agree to recommend this change to the board, thereby implementing the suggestion of the bookkeeper as well as contributing to the efficiency of the bookkeeping system.

How to conduct survey interviews. You have familiarized yourself with the existing operation, and have an organized way of conducting your investigation. Now you are ready to interview the personnel. Generally, you should start with the supervisory personnel and filter down to the operating personnel. To obtain the most information from your interviews, here are a few guidelines to follow:

1. *Be thorough.* Impress the interviewee that this is not a perfunctory operation which you must go through to fill either time or paper. Let him know that the details are important.
2. *Be tactful, but exhibit skepticism.* Impress him that you "trust everyone, but that you like to cut the cards." Rather than take flat exception to what he might say, just note his answer and try with other questions to expand on any point which you think he has not covered thoroughly or honestly.
3. *Be patient.* While it may seem, at times, that he is just griping to you, the interviewee may reveal a point or two that does bear on the subject under investigation. However, do not turn these sessions into general discussions. Do not let them wander into a discussion of politics, sports, religion, and so on.
4. *Be a listener.* Since you are gathering information, you must spend most of your time on the receiving end of the interview. Control the urge to dispute with the interviewee his ideas about company policy, other employees, or working conditions. If you answer in any way or try to justify an opposing point of view, he may feel that you are not interested in his information and he may become uncooperative.
5. *Be efficient.* Prepare yourself before the interview. Knowing something about the person you will be talking to will help you both during the interview and in the analysis of information later on. This might be done while you are obtaining his superior's permission for the interview, or by reviewing the personnel file.

   Prepare an outline of the questions you will ask each individual based on your internal control questionnaire. Make every effort to get all the information you need in "one shot."
6. *Be prompt.* When you make an appointment for an interview, let the other person set the time and place whenever possible. Keep in mind that you are intruding upon his time—time which he may feel could be better spent performing his regular job. Always make sure that he has

been informed of the need for the interview by his superior so that you do not catch him unaware.

Start the interview on time and terminate it at a pre-arranged time or sooner. Do not feel that you have to give everyone "fifteen minutes," but if you do set a time limit for a particular interview, stick to it. Try not to hold people past their regular lunch or quitting time.

Obtain copies of the forms used in the bookkeeping department. As you interview employees, they will show you what forms and reports they work with. You will need copies of each of these forms when you evaluate the system. Getting a copy of each form now will save time for you and the employee. You will not need to bother him a second time.

Since many forms are pre-numbered, have the employee mark the one given to you "void—auditor use." Insisting on the voiding procedure will impress on the employee the importance that you place on accountability. He may be uneasy about removing a form from the series. If he wishes to obtain the O.K. of his supervisor, encourage him to do so.

How to account for pre-numbered forms you take. You need a sample purchase order blank from the pre-numbered series. Give the clerk a sheet of paper the size of the order blank on which you indicate that purchase order #4681 was given to you on such and such a date.

As you accumulate the forms, indicate on the form itself what information it contains, who records it, and where it goes next. Examine completed forms, and obtain the reasons for initials, code letters, and rubber stamp impressions used. These may be considerations in redesigning the form. Note them on your sample form—be sure not to overlook them.

Diagram the paperwork flow. Once you have collected the information, you must arrange it in such a way as to get a picture of the bookkeeping operation. Flow charts are most useful for this purpose. They illustrate the path of work through the office.

Flow charting techniques in systems work serve in much the same way as drafting techniques in engineering. They are a universal shorthand useful in depicting the often complex interrelationships of various procedures.

Flow charts are much more informative than written descriptions. A well-drawn flow chart also has great impact because it can show more clearly the simultaneous paths taken by, say, each part of a set of multiple forms. Even more important, however, is the fact that flow charting forces you to trace the steps in a procedure flow to a satisfactory conclusion. By comparing the flow chart of the existing system with your revised system, you can make sure that you have not omitted any necessary steps.

The symbols used in flow charting vary widely. Several manufacturers of data processing equipment have developed their own system of symbols, as have a number of forms manufacturers. Unfortunately, no single system has achieved universal recognition.

A satisfactory set of symbols is designed so that the *do* functions (presumably of a productive nature) are separated from the *check* or *store* functions (which may not be productive). A simplified set of symbols would include:

The move symbol	▽
The check symbol	□
The story symbol	△
The do symbol	○

Appropriate mnemonic symbols can be used to describe the nature of each function in abbreviated form. For example, arithmetic symbols (as A for add, M for multiply) may be used in conjunction with functional symbols to describe what is being done. Symbols can also be used to indicate something about the form itself.

In certain situations, you will find it useful to depart from the usual procedure, and show flow chart symbols and descriptive text on the same page. If you are not an old hand at flow charting, this is probably the best method for you to use. This technique is illustrated in Figure 2.

The flow chart is an excellent tool for analyzing existing procedures. It provides a means for questioning the need for, and method of performance of, each listed step in an existing procedure. Steps described by symbols of a non-productive nature such as copying, sorting, filing, or checking would come under detailed scrutiny to see if they can be eliminated, combined, reduced in scope through sampling, and the like.

Evaluating the system in use. At this point you are like a doctor who has completed a physical examination. You have the facts — now for the diagnosis. The system is sick in places, and you must prescribe. Remember that the patient will probably not follow all of your advice, but you are duty-bound to point out your findings.

Evaluation of an accounting system is knowing what the system now does for management in contrast to how it could do the job better.

The best approach is to compare the existing system with the criteria embodied in general principles of system design. This approach is greatly superior to one of comparing the existing system with several other similar systems. The approach of making comparisons with other systems is definitely limited by your knowledge and past experience. Using proven principles is less limited and tends to produce more creative systems design.

Proven principles used in new, imaginative ways produce systems that fit specific situations better than a "canned" system superimposed on a new situa-

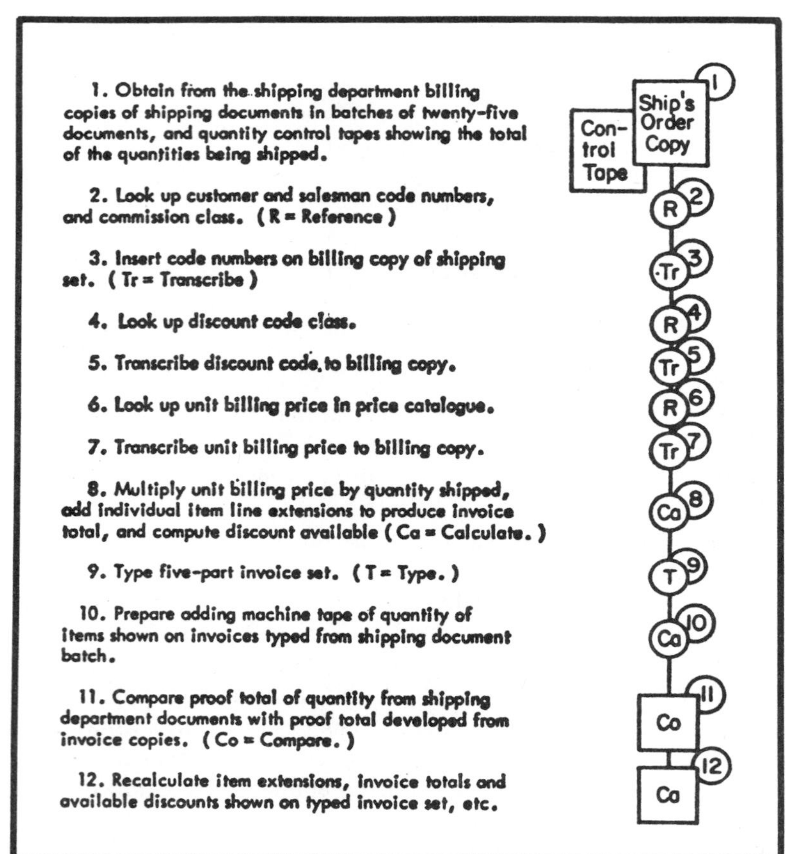

1. Obtain from the shipping department billing copies of shipping documents in batches of twenty-five documents, and quantity control tapes showing the total of the quantities being shipped.
2. Look up customer and salesman code numbers, and commission class. (R = Reference)
3. Insert code numbers on billing copy of shipping set. (Tr = Transcribe)
4. Look up discount code class.
5. Transcribe discount code to billing copy.
6. Look up unit billing price in price catalogue.
7. Transcribe unit billing price to billing copy.
8. Multiply unit billing price by quantity shipped, add individual item line extensions to produce invoice total, and compute discount available (Ca = Calculate.)
9. Type five-part invoice set. (T = Type.)
10. Prepare adding machine tape of quantity of items shown on invoices typed from shipping document batch.
11. Compare proof total of quantity from shipping department documents with proof total developed from invoice copies. (Co = Compare.)
12. Recalculate item extensions, invoice totals and available discounts shown on typed invoice set, etc.
Ship's Order Copy
Con-trol Tape
R
Tr
R
Tr
R
Tr
Ca
T
Ca
Co
Ca

Fig. 2. Flow Chart for Billing Procedure.

tion. This doesn't mean that the approach of making comparisons with other systems has no value. But it has the most value after the present system has been measured against the criteria of good systems design.

The following checklist is based on accepted principles of system design. This checklist will indicate inefficiencies in the existing system. These inefficiencies, in turn, can be used as a second checklist, to insure that an alternative system does not have the same failings.

Checklist of principles of systems design.

1. Is the existing system designed with a view to excessive precision? Unnecessary emphasis on accuracy of certain types of data usually generates costs that are out of line with the benefits produced.

2. Is the work load so arranged and scheduled that a substantially equal amount of effort is called for at all times? Experience indicates that an insuffi-

cient volume of work is itself a cause of low productivity. Solutions to this peaking problem may be found in cycle processing as used, for example, in a retail credit billing plan.

3. Is there too much breaking down of job functions, resulting in time-consuming rereading of data that must be understood before it can be processed? The ultimate in assembly line techniques—splintering the job into many small segments, each performed by a different person—is inefficient for many types of clerical work. Time-consuming assimilation of the meaning of data shown on documents, though not apparent, must be done by each employee involved in the procedural flow.

4. If the same basic information is reproduced several times to serve the requirements of a given procedural flow, is such data captured initially in such a way that it can later be reproduced without requiring manual recopying?

5. Is paperwork processing scheduled so as to allow optimum timeliness in processing and reporting? Although internal delay in processing paperwork has a price tag, needlessly fast or frequent processing also costs money.

► Example: Excessive time taken to prepare sales invoices slows down cash flow and may even affect collections. Delays in paperwork processing for the purchasing department may cause unnecessarily long procurement lead time. This can result in excessive inventory safety cushions and larger carrying costs.

Work scheduling, therefore, should aim at having paperwork stop at as few desks as possible, at enlarging individuals' job knowledge, and at pumping work through the department at a rapid rate. Where batch accumulation is necessary, batches should not be allowed to be of excessive size, and should be scheduled in layers. This allows processing at the next work station to begin without waiting for the first batch to be completed.

6. If identical information must be shown on several types of documents, is it being recorded simultaneously?

7. Are procedural cycles too short? Frequently, paperwork is done at too frequent intervals. For example, checks to vendors may be prepared for each purchase invoice, instead of accumulating several invoices and paying them in groups.

8. Is constant information used repetitively, rather than being reintroduced each time it is needed? Many systems require the communication of constant specification-type data—part numbers, operation descriptions, etc.—each time a transaction cycle is begun. This type of information should be provided, as a by-product of its initial creation, and should be mechanically reproduced for each subsequent use.

9. Is there an indication that procedural duplication exists? In certain cases, duplication of effort is not readily apparent because the results being obtained are dissimilar in form (though not content), and are used in different ways. Nevertheless, elimination together with combination of data can produce a single set of documents or procedures that can serve all needs, at lower cost.

10. Can definite justification be established for all functions that are not

"doing" functions, but have to do with checking, review, rearrangement, storage, transport, etc.? Numerous techniques exist to eliminate *nonproductive* functions. For example, checking and review functions may be entirely eliminated as a calculated risk. Document storage and transport functions may be eliminated, based on accepting the risks of isolated losses of information, difficulty of location, and the like. Techniques using statistical approaches can also greatly reduce the extent of nonproductive functions.

Presenting your recommendations. You have spent many hours in conducting the survey and drafting an improved plan. Now you have to sell it. The following are rules to guide you in presenting your recommendations. They are tricks of the trade for giving your critique in as acceptable a way as possible.

1. The owner's time is valuable—don't abuse it.
2. Be professional—this is not the time for after-dinner jokes.
3. Begin with something good—that the cooperation was good—if it was—and/or that many parts of the present system are good—if they are.
4. Present your recommendations in order of importance. Start with the most important one.
5. Have your recommendations typed. Give the client a copy and discuss them with him in order listed. Explain "why" you make each recommendation.

► EXAMPLE: You have made a recommendation that the owner pay his employees by check rather than cash. Explain to him that you recommend this, ". . . because checks provide evidence of payment and will reduce chances of embezzlement." Only the recommendation need be typed.

You can give your reasons orally.

6. Do not rattle off your recommendations with machine gun rapidity. Give the owner time to absorb your recommendation and to ask questions.
7. Present your recommendations as improvements, and avoid belaboring your criticisms of the present operation to the point that someone is offended. If possible, try to give the impression that those concerned agree to the improvement.

► EXAMPLE: You are making recommendations to a church pastor in the presence of his bookkeeper. Your recommendations include an improved method for preparing recapitulations of each member's annual contribution. Remind the pastor of the system now being used. He may have forgotten or never known. Phrase your remarks to the effect that you have discussed another method with the bookkeeper and that you both agree it would be an improvement. Describe the new method. Tell him why it is better.

In this manner you have included the bookkeeper as a co-proponent of the new plan. He feels that you have both worked together, rather than being told by you what is wrong with the old system. His cooperation is necessary. Promote it. The next move is up to your client. He may:

1. Ask you for additional information.
2. Tell you to go ahead.
3. Ask for time to think it over.

Here again you must be ready to roll with the punches. Don't try to force the client to come to a decision. If he wants time, this is his prerogative. Let him know, however, when you will be available to make the installation. Don't assume for instance that he knows you will be tied up from January through April with income taxes.

HOW TO INSTALL THE SYSTEM

The plans have been drawn and approved and you are now ready to build. You have been architect and salesman in the system planning stage and now you are also the contractor. Your chief foreman is the head bookkeeper. Work closely with him. Be open to suggestions from him. You must have his help.

In the design phase we were able to follow rather logical steps:

1. Determining what the owner wanted.
2. Explaining to the owner the requirements of a good system.
3. Combining the above wants and requirements.

The installation phase cannot be listed in any such logical order. It is similar to playing bridge. You have thirteen cards. You know that all must be played, but you must be prepared to adjust to the situation. Sometimes it is better to play a diamond before a spade. Sometimes it isn't. About the only logical step in design installation is to do it. Install your system. Which part you install first will vary with the situation.

Installing an accounting system for a new business. When installing a system for a new business, you become an integral part of the "business birth" process. You will begin the records. You may also be asked to give your opinion of other facets of the business—Do you think we should expand into other lines? Do you think we should advertise more? You must help to the best of your ability. You are being asked because of your experience with similar situations in other businesses. Be truthful. If you don't know, say so.

► EXAMPLE: You are installing a system of accounts for a new shopping center. The owner calls you into his office. He asks your opinion as to the rental he should charge for a vacant location. You find out from him that each store in the center has separate and different types of leasing arrangements.

You can indicate to him that his decision is like a horsetrade—get the most you can. If he wants cost figures to help him with his decision, provide them. This work is not systems work, but you must be ready to help your client in any way that you can. He may have no other person whom he trusts as much as you. Merit his trust. Help him if you can.

You have your chart of accounts and the necessary records for your system. You are now ready to install the system—to enter the business transactions. Plan to be at the client's office at least a part of each day during the first week. You may prefer to make the first entries yourself. At least you should work closely with the bookkeeper when he makes the first entries.

The first few days can be rough. You will find many difficulties the first days of operation. Consider them as challenges, not obstacles. Observe each operation—pricing of inventory, employees' time records, preparation of sales tickets, etc. You are probably the only one there who is fully aware of the end results your system requires. See that your system is properly installed—as you designed it.

New business installations should be broken down to those with experienced and inexperienced personnel. Your installation job will be easier with experienced personnel, but close supervision is needed in any case to make sure that *your* system is being followed—not theirs. Part of your task will be to train the personnel properly. You may even be asked to interview new applicants.

► EXAMPLE: You have worked with the creation of a new bowling alley corporation. The building is finally built, your accounting system is ready, and opening day is here. The bartender is experienced, the bowling manager is experienced, but your bookkeeper is the owner's sister—experienced with books—but not with bowling alley books.

After the first day's operation, you find that the bookkeeper is confused about handling money from the bar, tickets from the bar, money from the alleys, lane usage sheets, charge slips, merchandise sales tickets, and the like.

You must again roll with the punches. Be prepared to improvise on the spot and to train the personnel. This is part of properly installing your system.

You may be a jack-of-all-trades these first few days. Some tasks that you may have to take care of at first include:

1. Securing the bank signature cards.
2. Buying adding machine tapes and other supplies. You may be supplying your own adding machine for a while.
3. Checking in new merchandise.
4. Arranging desks and files in the office.
5. Giving instructions on setting up file folders and the filing system.

These duties may not seem very professional, but they can be the most important part of your whole system design and installation—making it work.

Check for compliance with governmental reporting requirements. The installation of an accounting system in a new business is not only books, columns, and figures. It also includes a myriad of other matters. Among these are the various governmental rules that must be complied with. Never assume that your client is aware of these technicalities. Make sure by using a checklist. Naturally, your checklist will vary with the state and municipality.

Ask the following questions:

1. Has he filed for his employer's social security identification number?
2. Has he obtained the social security number of each employee?
3. Does he need to apply for a state sales tax number?
4. Has he checked into state unemployment tax reporting?
5. Does he understand the correct method for withholding income taxes from employees' pay?

6. Has he obtained any licenses or tax stamps that he needs?
7. Has he checked into the current government stabilization rules regarding the posting of prices?
8. Is he familiar with federal and state employment regulations regarding minimum rates of pay and allowable hours of work?
9. Is he up-to-date on current economic stabilization rules regarding prices, wages, dividends, and interest?

Naturally, for any "no" answers, see what you can do to give him a hand.

Installing an accounting system for an established business. When you enter an established business to install a system, the wheels are already turning. The extra tasks that may have been required of you in the new business are already being taken care of. You can concentrate on "professional" work.

Installing an accounting system in an established business is somewhat different than it is in new business. In the established business there is already a system in use. You have designed "improvements." Your installation is two-fold. Like the contractor, you must rip out the bad planks before nailing in the new. This can be a very challenging assignment.

► EXAMPLE: You are ready to install your new accounting system in a hospital that has been operating for a number of years. Through your previous study of its accounting operations, you learned that billing of accounts receivable is slow and that the statements are hard to understand. Your recommendations for improvements have been approved by the board of directors of the hospital, and they have urged you to continue to use the present bookkeeping machines where possible.

Your first step should be to call in the machine salesmen who installed the present bookkeeping machines in the hospital. Explain to them your problem. Ask them if their machines can be adapted to give you the results you seek. You will find machine salesmen can be of great help to you. They want your confidence so that you will recommend them for work in the future.

When you have decided the machine changes needed and have obtained the cost figures from the machine salesmen, you should report back to the board for authorization to proceed. You must abide by the board's decision, but be sure to explain the limitations on your installation if you are restricted by them. It is better to keep all parties informed so that misunderstandings will not develop.

From your use of the internal control questionnaire you have noted the bad spots of the present system. You have used your professional judgment and experience to plan corrections of the bad spots. You have sold the owner and the head accountant on the fact that the changes should be made. You may also have to convince the employees who will do the work. Do not rely on the boss to pressure the employees into making the changes, if you can avoid it. He has other matters needing attention. You have been hired to install the system changes. Do it with as little upheaval as possible.

► HOW TO DO IT: Mr. Plante, who is in charge of the perpetual inventory cards for a factory, is unhappy about your improvements. He has had his own little island for a long time and hates changes. Take time to explain to Plante the reasons behind your changes. Indicate that you are making changes in other departments so that he won't feel alone. Although there is no one *best* approach, do whatever you can to win him over.

But whatever develops, *never* give up. You have spent long hours developing your system. Your client wants it installed. Do not let Plante block your way. If all other things fail, and only then, go to the head accountant and owner and ask them to "have a word" with Plante.

Work closely with the head accountant. While installing the system, the head accountant should be your chief ally. His cooperation with you and concern for good installation are imperative. Cultivate his assistance. Let him know that you are a friend—not an enemy. If you can, have him make your recommended changes. It will probably be done more efficiently since he knows better than you the capabilities and natures of the accounting personnel. The employees are used to taking instructions from him. Just like a good committee chairman, you will do your job best when you can get others to do the work for you. Your responsibility is to see that it gets done and according to your plan.

► EXAMPLE: You have been engaged by a meat market owner to look over his accounting system. The head accountant has worked with the company for 30 years. He has been at his job longer than you have been alive. Don't let this fact deter you. You don't care if your doctor is young—as long as you have confidence in his ability. You must sell the head accountant on *your* ability.

Let him know that you have no thought of changing anything until you have examined everything thoroughly. Tell him that you are not there to make changes. Your purpose for being there is to look over the system and recommend improvements, if you discover any. You would like the accountant to show you what he does and to suggest to you any improvements that *he* would like to have made.

► EXAMPLE: Some years ago I was doing systems work for a machine tool manufacturing company. The chief accountant was an elderly man whom we shall call Mr. Towry. He was wary of me. He seemed to resent me. From hints he dropped, I discovered why. It wasn't me. It was public accountants in general.

Towry had seen and heard of other men, in similar positions to his, being replaced by independent public accountants who had been doing systems or audit work. He felt that any public accountant in his office might replace him. After I dropped several hints, we got along fine. I told him that public accounting gets into your blood. I said, "I guess I could never be happy doing the *same* thing in the *same* office every day." He soon realized he had nothing to fear from me. He didn't. We got along fine.

Be open to suggestions for changes and improvements. The best planned accounting system may not work quite as well in practice as it did on paper.

Welcome any suggestion from the employees, the owner, and your ally, the head accountant. Be willing to change your mind if you are wrong. Be ready to give an inch to save a mile.

Although your planning was thorough, you may now discover a procedure that you hadn't observed earlier. Don't let it upset you. Take it in stride. Use this new knowledge to improve your system. This is a fine opportunity to show your professional competence—that you will use every scrap of information to help your client.

► EXAMPLE: You have devised a system for a lumber yard that classifies sales as either charge or cash. This classification of sales was approved by both the owner and head accountant. However, when you are installing the system, you find many wholesale sales that have a different mark-up percentage than regular sales. This is something that you had overlooked in your planning.

Discuss the matter with the head accountant and owner and suggest adding another sales and cost of sales account for wholesale sales. Explain that their profit percentage information will be clearer with these additional accounts and that the system can be altered without difficulty. Being willing to revise in this manner is a continuation of your professional service to your client.

Keeping your system in good repair. Let's assume that you have completed your installation. But are you finished? Are you ever finished? The answer, of course, is "no." You cannot walk away never to return. Any system must be looked over once in a while to see that it continues to operate as well as when it was installed. A car that never has a change of oil will soon need a new motor. An accounting system that is not reviewed at intervals may have to be scrapped. Impress this on the owner before you leave your installation work.

Every business operation changes with time. Your system must change with it. If you don't look at the patient every so often, he will soon drift back to the sorry state that you were asked to correct. A system installation is never an accomplished fact—it is always a continuing challenge.

► EXAMPLE 1: You are called in by a clothing retailer who thinks that his office personnel spend too much time sorting and posting sales tickets. He thinks that they may need a machine to replace this hand work. You have investigated the situation and have found a machine to do the job. You have the machine salesman demonstrate the machine to the personnel. They seem to understand how to use it and you assume that you have done your job.

Several months later you make a visit. You find the machine in the corner with a cover on it You find the personnel doing the same hand work that they did before. You are criticized by the owner. You should be. You should have made sure that the machine would do the work or gotten rid of it. You did an installation but did not follow through.

► EXAMPLE 2: In installing a payroll system for a doctor's office, you make a detailed instruction list for the bookkeeper. You explain the use of the individual earnings records and the ceilings on unemployment and social security taxes.

He says he understands. He says that he can prepare the quarterly payroll tax returns without further help from you.

At the end of the year, when helping him with the annual payroll tax returns, you find that he had forgotten the ceiling figures. Who is to blame is not important—you are now forced to do much extra work to make the corrections. I think that you are to blame. You should have made a few visits during the year to discover if he was forgetting or not.

► EXAMPLE 3: You install a retail perpetual inventory system for a dress shop in place of the old cost method The items are simple to count now, but you forget that the employees have never worked with the retail method. This is new to them.

You have two choices. Either you must work closely with them and make it work, or throw it out. It is better to have a poor system than none at all. It is your responsibility to see that they have the best they can handle.

Follow-up procedures after the system installation. Not long ago, I received a phone call from the same laundry owner client, whose business had grown with the population growth and who was concerned that his office girls were getting behind in their posting work.

I revised his system several years ago when a cash shortage was discovered. I installed several new internal controls. Now I will have to look the system over again. Maybe I installed too many controls. The owner and I will probably have to reach a compromise. We will have to weigh several factors: personnel, paperwork, and controls.

Systems work is never an accomplished fact. A perfect design and installation today may not be satisfactory tomorrow. If we can't keep our clients satisfied, other accountants will. We should explore the several means by which we can review from time to time the effectiveness of our system.

1. **Review the system throughout the year.** Many of your clients rely on you for year-round services. They expect you to keep them posted on any changes in taxes or other matters that affect them. Use these everyday inquiries to see how their system is working. Ask the owner if his system is supplying him with the information he wants. Would he like you to drop by every month to discuss the systems operation with his head accountant?

Some owners may hesitate to call you. Drop by and see them. Let them know that you have a continuing interest in their accounting system. You do. Your professional reputation is at stake. You would rather have him tell you its bad features than have them discussed with his associates. Cultivate the owner's confidence in you. It is the best asset you can have.

2. **Review the system during your annual audit.** More and more companies are realizing the advantages of annual audits. More banks and governmental agencies are requiring annual audited reports. Use your annual visit to the company to check the system's operations. You are going to cover most

phases of the accounting operation in your audit anyway, so why not kill two birds with one stone?

Many public accountants fill out a new internal control questionnaire during each annual audit. Others merely review the questionnaire that had been filled out previously. Whichever method you prefer, note any changes in the accounting system. Keep a memo sheet of matters which you believe should be brought to the owner's attention.

3. **Make recommendations for system changes.** When you discover that your accounting system is not functioning properly, write a letter to the owner. You have not done professional work if you discover a fault and do nothing about it. You must communicate your findings. Do it in writing. Verbal communications can lead to misunderstandings.

Your letter should state clearly the change that you think necessary. Even if you have suggested the same change before, do so again. Sometimes a repeated suggestion will be acted upon. At least you have brought it to the owner's attention. If he does not want to act on your suggestion for one reason or another, you can not help that. You have done your part.

HOW TO DESIGN AND INSTALL AN ACCOUNTING SYSTEM FOR A REGULATED INDUSTRY

We have discussed the design and installation of accounting systems for nonregulated businesses. Our primary objectives were to design a system that was simple and yet produced all the necessary information for the owner and governmental agencies. We have based our system on accepted accounting principles. Such principles have been developed over the years by accountants.

Regulated industries are those controlled by Interstate Commissions and the various state commissions. The design and installation procedures discussed already are applicable, but we must add one more step in our thinking. We must tailor our system to the commission requirements. We must keep in mind the accepted accounting principles as well as the commission requirements, and we must be able to satisfy both.

Obtain a copy of the uniform system of accounts for the regulated business. You should obtain a copy of the commission's uniform system of accounts before having your first conference with the owner. You can obtain copies of the Interstate Commission booklets from the U.S. Government Printing Office. State booklets can be obtained from the state commission offices or the state printing office.

These booklets will describe the uniform system of accounts required by the various commissions. They will also describe in detail each account and what the commission wants included therein. A thorough reading of this pamphlet before your first conference with the owner will help you become familiar with this particular business. It will make you better able to use correct terminology in your conference.

► EXAMPLE: You have been called by the owner of a trucking firm to design an accounting system for him. Whether or not you have had previous experience with trucking firms, you should obtain a Uniform System of Accounts for Motor Carriers of Property. You should become familiar with the account classifications shown in the booklet, and the terminology used in the trucking industry. Then, you will be more able to discuss with the owner his system needs.

Set up a conference with the owner of the regulated business. The first conference with the owner of the regulated business will follow the same pattern as that for a nonregulated business. Find out from him how often and what types of reports he desires. Explain to him what a good system should have. Outline the desirability of as simple a system as possible that will satisfy both the government and the owner. Explain the basic factors of internal controls.

You must also be able to discuss the requirements of the Commerce Commissions. There are several ways that you can bring this matter into the discussion. One of the best methods is to have a copy of the annual report to the Commerce Commission that will be required. This report is rather lengthy for larger companies. You will find that there are several different types of reports required depending on the size of the company. Be familiar with these. Be able to tell the owner at this first meeting which report his company will probably be required to file. You can obtain blank copies of these reports from the Commission Offices.

The owner may now be in a dilemma. He can not see how he could possibly have a simple system and still provide the mass of detail necessary for the Commerce Commissions. He is not sure how much business his company will do and which reporting form will be required. He wonders if perhaps you could set up a system without following the commission's chart of accounts. These questions are easier to answer than they may appear. Let's answer one at a time.

"How can I have a simple system and still furnish all of this detail to the commission?" Explain that a simple system in his case will be one that can satisfy everyone at once. Tell him that it will be better for him if you design the system along the lines outlined by the commission. Explain that if he wants additional information as time goes on, it should not be too difficult to supply. If the commission's classifications are followed to the letter, as they should be, the owner's chief accountant can usually provide any additional data needed. Tell the owner the advantages of setting up a system exactly as required by the Commerce Commission.

1. The commission manual will then provide his chief accountant with detailed information as to the types of transactions that should be entered in each account. This should reduce the times that he need call in his public accountant. It will reduce his accounting costs. The only necessity for calling you would be to help him interpret sections of the commission's booklet.
2. It will make it easier to file correct reports with the Commerce Com-

mission. His accounts will already be as prescribed by the commission.

3. He *must* comply in order to continue operating his business under the certificates issued by the commissions. If the reports sent to the commission are not accurate and filled in completely, questions will be asked. Time will be required to dig out additional information for the commission. It will be to the owner's benefit to keep these questions to a minimum.

"How can I tell how good business will be?" The owner will be uncertain as to the future size of his business. How can he be sure which report to send to the commission at the end of the year? He probably can't know for sure. You should suggest that it is not necessary to know this now. The proper report can be determined at the end of the year.

The decision necessary now is whether to design the system so that any size commission reports can be obtained therefrom in the future. This is desirable. Ask the owner to allow you to design the system so this can be done. It will then be adaptable for any reports needed.

► EXAMPLE: The XYZ Trucking Co. is starting in business. You are having your first conference with the owner and his chief accountant. You open the Commerce Commission booklet to the chart of accounts. You recommend that the accounts be set up and numbered according to the largest classification. You explain that there are many accounts that will not be needed now but which could be used later if necessary.

You explain that any size report to the commission can be made up from this system. The system will not have to be changed later. Explain that if you set up the smaller system it is possible that it would all have to be thrown out and replaced later. The simple system here is to use the largest classification! Explain that you will use only the parts necessary.

"Why do I have to do it that way?" His last question concerned setting up a system that did not follow the commission's chart of accounts. Explain to the owner that you can do this, but that this would mean two sets of books. He must have one set that follows the commission requirements. This will usually settle the matter.

Some businesses do maintain separate records for internal reporting purposes. This is usually done for correct reporting of such items as depreciation expenses. The fast methods for depreciation may be used for income tax purposes and straight-line methods for the internal reports.

Some companies do use a separate set of records for the commission reports. You probabaly should not recommend this, however, until you can be sure that one set cannot do the job. Start as simple as possible. Even this may not prove as simple as you would like.

How to design an accounting system for a regulated business. You have had your conference with the owner of the regulated business. You have learned his desires for the system. You have explained to him what you think he should have. You have shown him the report forms that he will have to file with the Commerce Commissions. He has hired you to design his system.

Your first step is *to study the special accounting problems inherent in this type of business*. You can refer to your own files if you are now doing work on similar businesses. You can use systems textbooks that list various types of businesses. You can combine this information with your study of the commission booklet on procedures.

Your second step is *prepare a chart of accounts*. Your primary source for this work will be the commission booklet's chart of accounts. You will not need all of the accounts listed. Start with only the bare necessities. This will make it easier to explain your system to the head accountant. You can show him how additional accounts can be added from the commission's chart of accounts when needed.

Your third step will be *to purchase the accounting books for your system*. They need be no different from the books for a nonregulated business.

Your last step will be *to type instructions for the head accountant*. You should follow the procedures already outlined for a non-regulated business with one addition thereto. Your instructions relating to account classifications must constantly refer to the Commerce Commission's uniform system of accounts booklet. You should give the head accountant a copy of this booklet along with your typed instructions. They are an integral part of the regulated business's accounting system. They should be available and used by the company accountant at all times.

How to install an accounting system for a regulated business. You have completed your system design and are now ready to make the installation. Previous mention has been made of sources of help to you in your design and installation work. These have included:

Company Attorneys
Business Machine Salesmen
Insurance Agents
Internal Revenue Agents
Bankers

In a regulated business you will have one more man who can help. He is the Commerce Commission field accountant. He has many companies to work with and may not always be available when you want him. But if you have questions, write or call him. If you want him to visit you to help with the system, request this. He can help. He has had wide experience in his particular field. Use his help. It is free.

► EXAMPLE: The ABC Trucking Co. has had an accounting system that they have used a number of years. They are a small firm doing local moving work. The accounting system was not set up by you, but you have reviewed it a number of times during the years. You have never been satisfied with the system because it is on the cash basis. No records were maintained of account receivables or account payables. It has been impossible to prepare a proper financial statement.

The ABC Co. has now grown larger and is requesting certification by the Commerce Commission. You are asked to design and install a system that will be acceptable to the Commission. The head accountant is balking at your installation of a system that will show receivables and payables. You need help.

You call Mr. Smith, the Commission field auditor. You go over your new system with him and request that he help you show the head accountant how to keep the accounts receivable and accounts payable properly. Smith has done this many times before. He speaks the language of the trucking industry. He knows how to answer objections of the bookkeeper. Use his help. Go to ABC Co. with him. You can learn also. You can also be sure that his suggestions fit in with *your* plans.

Smith will be doing himself a favor as well as you. If he can help establish a system that will require fewer visits and letters by him in the future, it will be time well spent for him. Work with him. Introduce him to the ABC Co. as the friend of the company that he is.

Your installation work of a regulated business has the same requirements as a nonregulated business. In brief, they are to:

—work closely with the bookkeeper at the beginning.
—be open to suggestions from the owner and the head accountant for changes and improvements.
—impress on the owner and the head accountant to call you on any question.

Accountants are ideally trained for the highly technical work of design and installation of accounting systems. From observation of the various businesses with which you work, you are aware of the good and the bad. You have seen the pride that employees take in their work with a good system. You have seen the lack of pride where the employee does not know exactly what he is supposed to do and nobody seems to care.

You have seen how often a successful business has a good system and a sick business a poor system. There is no question about the importance of a good system. You must be able to convince your clients of this importance. The increasing awareness of the public to embezzlements and government regulations helps you to some extent. You must also constantly improve your methods of design and installation.

Each business is different from others in some respect. You must tailor-make each system. Each owner has the human characteristic of wanting something a little different from his accounting department than other owners. Each accounting department is made up of human beings. They are different from the ones you worked with on your last assignment.

You must determine what the business wants. You must assess what they have. You must recommend what they need. You are the doctor. Prescribe.

You may find at least part of the system now in use as good as, if not better than, any you have previously encountered. Do not change it unless you can better it. Be ready with compliments as well as criticism. When you do criticize, do so in a professional manner. Let all concerned realize that you are there to help—not to hurt. You want the business to succeed, and you are using your special talents to help them achieve this.

Keep up with improvements in accounting machines—a new one might be able to help your system. Attend at least one machine convention each year. Encourage the chief accountants of your clients to attend also. You must be aware of the new developments in order to properly advise your clients. Let them know that you are keeping current. Ask to review their system periodically. This will demonstrate your interest in the continued success of the system that you have designed and installed.

You are an expert in the field of design and installation of accounting systems. Take advantage of this fact. Continually seek self-improvement. You are valuable to your client. Believe it yourself. Demonstrate it to your client.

19

Forms Control, Design and Management

CONTENTS

19

Forms Control, Design and Management

Francis C. Dykeman, CPA, and
William N. McNairn, CPA

Well over 50,000,000 different forms are currently estimated to be in use in government and business organizations in the United States. Billions of hours of employees' efforts are required to fill in, process, correct, and file the several million copies of these forms that are handled each week. In addition, thousands of hours of high-cost processing time on computers, automated data input equipment, realtime processing systems, and time-sharing terminals are required. Each one of the more than 50,000,000 forms is a link in a chain of procedures for accomplishing work. As such, each affects the efficiency with which the procedures can be carried out. Thus viewed, the overall volume of work activity associated with forms is awesome. Clearly, the direct costs of procuring these forms and the indirect costs of using them represent a staggering sum in the total costs of running government and business organizations throughout the country.

With the vast number of forms in use—and with constantly increasing wages for forms users—costs arising from inadequate forms quickly reach prohibitive levels of waste in any organization tolerating this type of inefficiency. And with overall operating costs continuing their upward climb, more and more businessmen and administrators are becoming aware of the need for solutions to forms problems and are turning to their professional counselors for assistance in evaluating and instituting programs of forms management.

As an aid to the professional accountant who wishes to counsel his clients on forms matters, this chapter provides comprehensive answers to such frequently asked questions as: What is forms management? When does an organization need a forms management program? How do I set up a forms management program? What continuing actions are needed to maintain a forms management program? The wide spectrum of detailed forms management information that is described in answering these questions should provide the professional accountant wishing to counsel in this field with a valuable background for undertaking the work.

WHAT IS FORMS MANAGEMENT?

Forms management is the function of *providing, improving,* and *controlling* the forms that an organization needs to perform its activities *with maximum efficiency.*

Eight subfunctions, or skill areas, are involved in carrying out the forms management function. These, with brief descriptions of their purposes, are listed below:

Subfunction	*Purpose in relation to forms management*
1. Work Analysis	To get all the facts describing the work flow in which the forms are used.
2. Work Simplification	To simplify, reduce the costs, and improve the effectiveness of work performed in connection with forms.
3. Forms Standardization	To specify the materials, styles, and formats to be used for forms.
4. Forms Identification	To systematize the numbering, titling, and cataloging of forms.
5. Forms Analysis	To examine and evaluate forms in order to identify opportunities for eliminating weaknesses and making improvements.
6. Forms Design	To develop and specify the physical details of forms.
7. Forms Inventory Control	To order and maintain stocks of forms so that they will be available for use when needed.
8. Records Management	To control the filing, retention, and destruction of forms.

In practice, in carrying out the forms management function, there is considerable blending and overlapping of these eight subfunctions. Work analysis, work simplification, forms analysis, and forms design, for example, are closely related subfunctions, between which there is close interaction when specific work assignments are being carried out. Being aware of the more important details which make up each of the individual subfunctions is useful for acquiring the understanding which is the primary key to their blending and successful use in forms management. For this reason, each of the subfunctions is reviewed at length in a separate section below.

WORK ANALYSIS

Work analysis is the process of subdividing work into its component tasks and seeking to learn, for each task and for the overall group of tasks, all pertinent facts that will be helpful in improving the efficiency of the work.

For analytical purposes, work is frequently considered to have three subdivisions. The smallest subdivision is a "task" which is defined as a group of work steps used to perform a single identifiable segment of work. The next larger subdivision is a "procedure" which is a group of tasks directed to accomplishing a specific purpose. The largest work subdivision is a "function," which is a group of interrelated procedures linked to accomplish a basic objective of the organization. The term "system" is sometimes used as a synonym for "function."

Examples

TASK

Checking the clerical accuracy of sales invoices.
Filing sales orders.
Reviewing personnel applications.

PROCEDURE

Preparing accounts payable checks.
Preparing sales invoices.
Making shipments to customers.
Maintaining an inventory of productive materials.

FUNCTION

Production of manufactured products.
Distribution of products to warehouses and customers.
Providing qualified personnel for organizational activities.

Work analysis may be directed to a task, a procedure, or a function, depending on the extent of the results being sought.

In seeking facts about work being analyzed, the six basic questions—What, Who, Where, When, How, and Why— should be used unsparingly. The answers obtained will come from two sources:

First—from the persons involved in carrying out the work or in using its results.

Second—from the documents which describe the forms and procedures in use, including instruction manuals, flow charts, study reports, and training materials.

Some of the questions that can be asked to elicit work analysis information are:

1. How does it begin? What is done next? How does it end?
2. What is its purpose and why? Is it necessary? Is it worth the cost?
3. Who performs each step and why? Organizationally and occupationally, are these the appropriate persons? Does each step serve a purpose and produce a desired result?
4. Where is each step performed and why? Can it be combined with similar work? Can it be performed elsewhere to advantage?
5. When is each step performed and why? Why are the steps in that particular order? Can peak loads be levelled off by better scheduling or staffing?
6. How is the work done and why that way? Are the most efficient methods and equipment being used for the job?

Before carrying out interviews of persons having knowledge of the work, background documents should be read and notes made of pertinent questions to be asked. Simple notes should be kept of facts and opinions obtained during interviews. The notes should include the names and titles of the persons interviewed, and the dates and times of the interviews. In collecting information, it is important to make a conscious distinction between "opinion" and "fact." It is desirable to obtain copies of typical forms and specific examples of problems or operating constraints. These forms are usually highly useful for reference during subsequent work simplification and forms design phases. When problems are described during interviews, some measure of their frequency and extent should be obtained. There is often a tendency for interviewees to mention exceptional events as problems when, in fact, their occurrence may be so infrequent as to make special consideration unnecessary. On the other hand, no problems should be dismissed without consideration since seemingly isolated conditions can sometimes be clues to important exceptions that must be provided for if procedures are to function satisfactorily.

Use graphic forms. Tables, flow charts, graphs, decision tables, and other ways of *graphically* portraying information should be used wherever handy for concisely recording information obtained during work analysis. Affixing a sample form with typical entries to a large sheet of paper and entering background facts on the large sheet with arrows to the spaces on the form to which they relate is one fact-gathering technique that is often useful. Much of the information obtained during interviews may later appear cryptic and perhaps even undecipherable because of the need to write fast when information is being given in a hurry. For this reason, interview notes should be reviewed, clarified, and put in order soon after each interview, while memory of the discussion is still fresh.

WORK SIMPLIFICATION

Work simplification is the process of reducing work to its most efficient essentials. It is applied to a specific work situation by examining the facts obtained during work analysis and challenging the need for each work step and task.

In general, the basic questions that must be answered in seeking to simplify work are:

Can any work be *eliminated?*
Can any work be *combined* with other necessary work?
Can the *time sequence* of work steps be changed?
Can the *physical sequence* of work steps be changed?
Can the *work methods* be improved?

Work simplification offers an interesting challenge to find simpler and easier ways to perform forms work. A step-by-step questioning of each task, looking for opportunities to *eliminate, combine, change sequence,* and *improve methods* will generally disclose opportunities for simplification. In applying general simplification techniques to the forms management area, the following types of questions should be asked and answered:

1. Should the form or any part or copy of it be eliminated? Is the form worth the costs, including procuring and storing the form?
2. Is there another source of the same information available?
3. Should the form or any part of it be combined with another form or forms?
4. Should the sequences of information on the form be changed?
5. Should the sequence of the procedural flow of the form or its copies be changed?
6. Should the readability of the form be improved?
7. Should additional information or copies be added to the form?
8. What alternatives are there for handling the work if the form were not available?
9. Should the work methods used in preparing, processing or filing the form be improved, including the use of more or less equipment?

To avoid wasteful pursuit of minor improvements, one should, of course, maintain a practical outlook during work simplification activities. It is important, therefore, to periodically assess the value of additional simplifications against the cost of pursuing and implementing them. When a point of diminishing returns is reached, simplification efforts should move on to other tasks or areas. Also, it is desirable to shun any tendency to view each step or task in isolation. The overall perspective of a form and its use in a set of procedures should be kept in mind. For example, adding information to a particular form in any early step may permit the elimination of several steps later in the overall work flow at a saving that more than offsets the cost of adding the information.

FORMS STANDARDIZATION

Left to the individual preferences that exist in any organization (and subject to the random influence of forms salesmen), the forms purchased by an organization over a period of time usually develop an interesting, although costly, variety. Special sizes, special papers, special colors, and special bindings quickly appear. To control unnecessary variety in forms, forms standards are required.

These standards are specifications for the physical aspects of forms, and cover such factors as the following:

Sizes
Weight, grades, and colors of paper
Print styles and ink colors
Layouts and margins
Procurement quantities
Bindings
Identifications

The purpose of establishing forms standards is to obtain a practical balance between the usefulness of forms and the cost of forms. The higher costs of small quantity orders, special handling and storage, individual filing arrangements, and additional design efforts are some of the penalties paid for unnecessary variety. With standards set for the physical factors, these costs can be minimized, and consistently better forms will result for use in the organization. Because the standards represent a set of physical guidelines established after careful consideration, their observance by forms designers forces attention to basic factors that might otherwise be overlooked, and results in forms that are more economically procurable and more efficiently usable.

An example of forms standards as used in one medium-sized manufacturing organization are shown below:

Forms Standards

Form Sizes

Select form sizes that will fit standard storage and filing equipment, standard office machines, and standard-size envelopes.

Forms should be designed to be cut from standard paper stock without waste. File cards should be of standard sizes.

Paper Weights and Grades

Forms to be kept on file for seven years or longer—use 25% rag content, bond paper, of 20# weight.

Forms to be kept on file for less than seven years—use sulphite paper of 20# weight.

Paper Colors

Colored papers should be used only for special emphasis when their use is economically justified by more efficient sorting, handling, or filing. Whenever possible, use bold symbols, headings, or other devices to make colored paper unnecessary.

Ink Colors

Black ink should be used for all forms, unless use of colored inks can be economically justified by increased efficiency in form use.

Identification

Headings should be centered at the top of the form where they can be easily seen for filing and retrieval.

Form numbers should be placed in the lower left corner of forms.

Margins

Binding margin—1 inch

Typewritten fill-in margins—top line 1-¼ inches; bottom line ¾ inch.

Printing margin—⅜ inch on all sides of form for possible gripper use by printer.

Form Arrangements

Arrange information for sequential entry, minimizing the number of tabular stops that will be required if the typewriter is used.

Place serial numbers in the upper right hand corner of forms.
Group related information.
Use check boxes whenever feasible.
Provide spaces for entry of information that fit the typewriters or other machines that will be used to enter information.

Punching

3 holes—space 4-¼ inches from center to center, and ⅜ inch from edge of form.
2 holes—space 2-¾ inches from center to center, and ⅜ inch from edge of form.

Two-Sided Forms

Two-sided forms should be avoided unless economically justified by reduced handling, filing, or other operations.
When used, two-sided forms should be arranged for ease of reference, in use and in filing. Two-sided forms that are to be bound, for example, should have the top of one of the forms opposite the bottom of the other so that they can be viewed easily when being turned in the binder.

FORMS IDENTIFICATION

There are a number of forms classification systems in use. All of these systems can work satisfactorily as long as they are understood by everyone responsible for classifying the forms.

Systems family. Probably the classification system that is most often used, particularly in small companies, is the systems family grouping. Under this system, the forms are separated according to the systems of which they are a part.

Almost any small company's forms could be fitted into the following systems families:

Personnel and payroll
Purchasing
Manufacturing
Sales
Accounting
Communications

It is easy to see that this classification would not be satisfactory for a large company having 5,000 or 6,000 forms. The group of forms comprising each system family would be too large to be workable since forms performing the same function within a systems family would not be easily available for analysis. However, if the forms in each systems family were further subdivided according to what they do, we would have workable groupings.

Business factors. There is another type of classification system used by many large companies and government agencies. Under this system, the forms are first identified by business factors, and secondly by function. The advantage of using business factors instead of systems families is that all forms can be identified with a principal business factor, whereas there is often confusion about where a specific form belongs.

FORMS RELATING TO PRODUCT OR SERVICE

Includes forms relating to all aspects of the company's products or services which are offered for sale to customers.

Adjustments	Financing	Prospects
Advertising	Franchises	Quality
Agreements	Handling	Quotations
Analysis	History	Reliability
Assembly	Identification	Reporting
Bidding	Import	Requirements
Breakdown	Inspection	Return
Cancellation	Installation	Routing
Charges	Instruction	Salvage
Claims	Inventory	Sales
Commissions	Labeling	Sampling
Complaints	Layout	Scheduling
Compliance	Location	Servicing
Control	Loss	Shipment
Credit	Marketing	Simplification
Damage	Measurement	Specifications
Defects	Methods	Standards
Delivery	Operation	Statistics
Design	Orders	Storage
Display	Packing	Taxes
Distribution	Packaging	Testing
Estimating	Patent	Transfer
Evaluating	Planning	Value
Experimenting	Prices	Warranty
Export	Production	Withdrawal
Failure	Promotion	

Fig. 1. Forms Relating to Product or Service.

The business factors selected for classifying purposes should be broad in scope and few in number. A small number of factors is not a problem because each group of business factors will be further subdivided, as will be explained subsequently.

The forms used in any business may be considered from the standpoint of whether they deal with physical factors or abstract factors. For example, the following is a set of business factors that might be selected for the purpose of classifying all forms:

Physical Factors	*Abstract Factors*
Product or service	Performance
Employees	Communications
Materials	
Property and equipment	
Money	

The business factors selected, though few in number, should be sufficient to form the basis for an entire system of forms classification. The types of forms included in the foregoing classifications may be defined in the following manner:

Product or service. The type of forms classified in this category relates to all products or services that are offered for sale to customers. This includes forms for designing, manufacturing, storing, shipping, selling, granting credit, etc.

Employees. There would be forms connected with all aspects of employing people in the business; for example, hiring, training, evaluating, promoting, providing benefits, terminating, etc.

FORMS RELATING TO EMPLOYEES

Includes forms relating to all aspects of employing people in the business.

Absence
Accidents
Addresses
Agreements
Applications
Attendance
Awards
Benefit Plans
Bonding
Changes
Claims
Complaints
Conduct
Contracts
Death
Deductions
Demotion
Disability
Discharge
Discipline
Elections
Enrollment
Examination
Exit Interviews
Fingerprints
Grievances
Handbooks
Hiring
History
Identification
Interviewing
Insurance
Inventions
Job Analysis
Job Description
Job Evaluation
Layoff
Leave
Manuals
Medical Treatment
Memberships
Merit Rating
On-The-Job Training
Overtime
Parking
Pay Increases
Performance Rating
Probation
Profit Sharing
Promotion
Records
Recruiting
References
Reporting
Requisitioning
Retirement
Safety Rules
Salary Admin.
Scholarship
Seniority
Sickness
Social Security
Statistics
Suggestions
Testing
Training
Transfers
Travel
Tuition
Turnover
Unemploy Compen.
Union Agreements
Vacations
Wage Admin.
Wage Surveys
Withholding Taxes

Fig. 2. Forms Relating to Employees.

Materials. Forms classified under this factor have to do with raw materials, purchased parts, merchandise acquired for resale, supplies, services, scrap, etc. They would relate to all aspects of procuring, receiving, handling, storing, requisitioning, issuing, recording, analyzing, reporting, etc.

Property and equipment. In this area we would find forms relating to the procurement, construction, installation, ownership, protection and disposal of tangible property such as plants, land, buildings, machinery, equipment, and transportation and communication facilities. It also includes forms relating to the procurement, ownership, protection and disposal of intangible property such as patents, copyrights, leases, licenses, franchises, trademarks, trade names, brand names, and secret processes.

Money. This takes in forms relating to all aspects of raising, receiving, handling, banking, disbursing, recording, analyzing, and reporting on money.

Performance. Here would be forms concerned with the functions of organizing, planning, budgeting, coordinating, controlling, reporting, analyzing, and interpreting the results of all operations. This also includes forms concerned with the chief executive's task of reporting on performance to such external groups as stockholders, customers, the public, unions, trade associations, and Federal, state, and local government agencies.

Communications. Within this area are the forms relating to general purpose communications, both internal and external, such as letterheads, envelopes, telephone message slips, long distance charge slips, interoffice memorandum forms, mailing labels, mailing lists, etc.

Examples of the types of forms that would be included in the categories of physical business factors are shown in Figures 1 through 3—Forms Relating to Business Factors.

Functions of company forms. The next step in classifying the forms in the systems family and business factors groupings is to further subdivide them according to the functions they perform. For this purpose, 16 verbs are used to express the purposes for which the forms are used. These verbs are:

To acknowledge
To agree
To apply
To authorize
To certify
To classify
To follow up
To identify
To instruct
To notify
To order
To record
To report
To request
To route
To schedule

It is, of course, possible to expand the list of verbs, should this be necessary to more clearly express the actions taken. It may also be feasible to eliminate some of them. In either event, the meaning of each action verb should be defined to guide those who will determine the functional classifications of the forms. Specific examples of functional uses are also helpful in this respect. The following chart contains definitions of the 16 action verbs and examples of the functions each performs.

FORMS RELATING TO MATERIALS

Includes forms relating to all aspects of receiving, handling, storing, requisitioning, issuing, recording, analyzing and reporting on raw materials, purchased parts, merchandise for resale, supplies, services, scrap, etc.

Agreements	Issuance	Records
Analysis	Labeling	Release
Bidding	Loan	Requesting
Compliance	Location	Reporting
Delivery	Movement	Requirements
Disposal	Packing	Return
Forwarding	Packaging	Shipment
Identification	Purchase	Stock Control
Inspection	Quotations	Traffic
Inventory	Receipt	Transfer

FORMS RELATING TO PROPERTY AND EQUIPMENT

Includes forms relating to the procurement, construction, installation, ownership, protection, and disposal of tangible property such as plants, land, buildings, machinery, equipment, transportation and communication facilities, etc.

Accidents	Installation	Receipt
Applications	Instruction	Records
Agreements	Insurance	Registrations
Bidding	Inventions	Release
Compliance	Inventory	Rental
Contracts	Leases	Repair
Delivery	Loan	Reporting
Disposal	Location	Requirements
Document security	Maintenance	Return
Engineering Notebooks	Movement	Safety
Grants	Operation	Servicing
Ideas	Plant Security	Shipment
Identification	Purchase	Specifications
Inspection	Quotations	Transfer

FORMS RELATING TO MONEY

Includes forms relating to all aspects of raising, receiving, handling, banking, disbursing, recording, analyzing and reporting on money.

Accounts	Credits	Payrolls
Accounts Payable	Customers' Accounts	Petty Cash
Accounts Receivable	Debits	Premiums
Advances	Debts	Prepayments
Allowances	Deposits	Quotations
Amortization	Depreciation	Receipt
Analysis	Disbursements	Records
Appropriations	Discounts	Refunds
Assessments	Distributions	Reporting
Auditing	Dividends	Requesting
Awards	Donations	Revenue
Bidding	Drafts	Royalties
Bonds	Earnings	Savings
Cash	Expenditures	Scrap
Certificates	Expenses	Stamps
Certification	Financial Acctg.	Statements
Charges	Government Acctg.	Statistics
Charts	Income	Stocks
Checks	Interest	Stop Payment
Collection	Investments	Taxes
Commissions	Journals	Transporting
Contracts	Ledgers	Verifying
Contributions	Loans	Withdrawal
Cost Accounting	Notes	
Coupons	Payments	

Fig. 3. Forms Relating to Physical Business Factors.

THE FUNCTIONS OF FORMS

Functions	Definitions	Examples
To acknowledge	To report receipt of To admit or make known	To acknowledge receipt of materials, payments, wages To acknowledge acceptance of orders
To agree	To accept To come to terms To promise	To agree to specifications To agree on a settlement of a claim To agree to make payment
To apply	To ask for To use	To apply for a permit, employment, insurance To apply a credit balance against a future purchase
To authorize	To empower or permit To approve	To authorize a leave of absence, a special price to customer To authorize return of product, purchase of equipment
To certify	To attest authoritatively To testify (in writing)	To certify to the actual cost of a contract, product, etc. To certify to the end use of materials
To classify	To group or segregate in classes that have a systematic relation; also to codify or catalog and to arrange in order	To classify forms by function To classify charges on accounts payable invoices To classify expense accounts, products, inventories
To follow up	To pursue—by taking supplementary action To remind oneself of an original or subsequent action to be taken	To follow up on a late shipment by review of purchase order To follow up on completion of employment papers by check list To follow up on operations completed (manufacturing orders)
To identify	To establish the identiy of	To identify employees (I.D. cards) To identify products (labels, tags, etc.) To identify shipments of materials (receiving report)

Functions	Definitions	Examples
To instruct	To impart knowledge or to explain To inform or command (action to be taken)	To instruct employees by furnishing written procedures To instruct employees to obey safety rules To instruct a common carrier where to deliver products (bill of lading)
To notify	To give notice of To give notice to To tell, transmit or convey information To announce, publish or proclaim To furnish information of interest or concern	To notify a supervisor of a new employee (hiring notice) To notify an employee that his employment is terminated To notify a customer that his order will be shipped in one week To notify the public in advertising of a new product To notify a person of a telephone call received for him
To order	To give an order to To give an order for To direct with authority	To order the plant manager to repair the roof To order forms from the storeroom To order the bank to issue savings bonds to employees
To record	To commit to writing, printing, etc. To enter To register To reproduce information	To record form titles and numbers on control cards To record entries in the accounts receivable ledger To record visitors' names in book To record or make a record of sales—as with tabulating equipment
To report	To give an account or accounting of	This function is generally limited to forms reporting comparative, analytical or interpretative performance data
To request	To ask for some thing or action To requisition	To request credit ratings of specified customers To request preparation of a vacation schedule To request or requisition purchase of equipment

FUNCTIONS	DEFINITIONS	EXAMPLES
To route	To send, forward, or transport To arrange an itinerary To specify or direct the order and course of action in a procedure	To route customers' orders to the credit department To route shipments of products to customers (traffic) To route production orders for manufacture of products
To schedule	To designate, list or outline times, dates and places	To schedule production To schedule salesmen's calls To schedule delivery of merchandise

It should be kept in mind that all classification systems are to some degree arbitrary, and difficulties will be encountered from time to time in fitting a particular form into the correct category. These difficulties arise from two principal sources:

1. A common tendency to confuse *names* with *purposes*.

The name that a form is called is not necessarily indicative of its purpose. For example, a purchase order copy used as a receiving report serves the function of a receiving report (to acknowledge receipt) and should not be confused with the purchase order (to authorize purchase).

2. Multipurpose forms that serve several functions.

For example, the dinner check prepared by a maitre d'hotel at the time he takes a customer's order might be used to perform all of the following functions:

To notify the chef to prepare a specific meal.

To order the waiter to deliver the meal.

To record the items delivered (for food control).

To notify the customer to pay the charges.

To record the sale, the receipt of cash, and the sales tax.

The form has several important functions. None can be ignored. All should be shown for the form when it is classified, with cross-referencing between categories.

Each form should be assigned a code number for quick and positive identification. This number will be useful for ordering, inventorying, and referring to the form.

One widely used form numbering system assigns a two-digit code to each system family or a single-digit code to each business factor (depending on which identification system is used). Then, suffix numbers are assigned sequentially, as needed, to forms in each category. For example, a bill of materials form might be assigned a form number as follows:

Business factor code		*Sequential number suffix*
1	—	273

Minor changes in forms specifications do not require that a new form code number be assigned to each modification of the form. However, the date of the last change in form specifications should always follow the form number to identify the specific version of the form. Hence, a form number should always consist of the following:

Business factor code		*Sequential suffix number*		*Date of last change*
1	—	273	—	6/25/x3

The date should be changed only when a design change occurs. It should not be changed with each ordering of the form if the form remains the same in design.

One copy of each form should be filed in numerical order by form number for reference.

FORMS ANALYSIS

Forms analysis and work simplification are closely related activties. Forms analysis deals with the physical characteristics of forms; work simplification deals with the procedures associated with using the forms. Because of the close, complementary relationship of the two, much of the discussion and many of the questions asked in performing work simplification are similar to those used in performing forms analysis.

Forms analysis is the process of critically reviewing the physical characteristics of forms in order to discover improvements. The fact-finding questions of What? Who? Where? When? How? and Why? are the mental tools needed for forms analysis work. Some typical questions that can be useful in discovering forms improvements are:

Can the form, or any part or copy of it, be eliminated? Is it worth the costs it will create, including procurement and storage costs? Is the same information available elsewhere? Is all the information necessary?

Can the form, or any part of it, be combined with another form or forms?

Who needs the information? Is it needed for after-the-fact analysis or for current action? Are all those who need the information getting it? Do all those who get the information use it?

Who prepares the form? Is it laid out in a format that is efficient for entry of information?

Where is the information for entry obtained? Could any of the copying of information from the source be simplified or eliminated?

Who receives the form? Is it laid out in a format that is efficient for extracting the information needed? Is it laid out in a format that is efficient for mailing to users?

When is the form first prepared? When is it transmitted and processed? When is it filed or disposed of? Is it needed as frequently as in the past?

How is the form prepared? Is it suited to the spacing and type size of any machines used for its preparation or processing? Should it be prepared by less expensive methods?

How is the form ultimately filed? How frequently is it referred to after filing? Is key information easy to find and read?

Forms analysis questions are aimed at discovering opportunities for improving the efficiency with which the forms can be used. All aids and short-cuts that can be devised should be considered in evaluating the existing forms. The results of the forms analysis work are a direct input to forms design activities.

FORMS DESIGN

Forms design is the process of determining within the forms standards established for an organization the exact specifications for a form's physical characteristics. Forms design is the final step in a sequence of steps that have been taken to develop the form. It is, therefore, heavily dependent on the quality of the outputs of the preceding steps for success. With good information from work analysis, work simplification and forms analysis, good forms design becomes possible.

Based on the information obtained from the fact-finding steps, the following should be available to the forms designer when he begins his work:

1. The purpose of the form and its related procedures.
2. The data to be entered on the form (and on the back of the form, if necessary), and the sequence in which this data will become available for entry.
3. The need for special type faces to emphasize instructions or key information.
4. The method (handwritten, typewritten, addressographing, etc.) by which data will be entered on the form.
5. The number of copies needed, and any special identification, description, or block-out needed on any copies.
6. The carbon paper or other copy-producing requirements.
7. The numbering, punching, and perforating requirements.
8. The filing requirements during processing and for reference.

With this information, the forms designer can tentatively lay out the form. For this operation, he generally uses a special forms layout graph paper with lines which conform to pica or elite typewriter spacing (1/6″ horizontally).

The design of simple forms to be produced in small quantities is not a difficult technical process, and common sense is an adequate guide. However, the design of large-volume forms to be prepared by hand or by machines can require technical knowledge of paper and printing to achieve an efficient design. One method of obtaining competent assistance with technical matters is to contact forms-printing companies. If they are invited to submit bids for the finished forms, they will usually welcome the opportunity to render technical help in design.

Considerations in form design. Important factors to be considered by the forms designer are described and discussed below:

1. *Form size.* The overall size of the form is determined by these factors:
   a. The quantity of information to be entered.
   b. The method of preparation (manual vs. machine).
   c. Requirements imposed by margin policy, office machines, files, binders, window envelopes, etc.
   d. The necessity of arranging the spaces so that data may be entered or used in logical sequence.
   e. The company's policy with respect to standard sizes for forms (8½ × 11, 8½ × 5½, 4¼ × 5½, etc.).

2. *Form image.* The image is the size of the printed and ruled part of the form in which the data will be entered. The factors governing image size are the same as those governing form size.

3. *Margins.* Margins are the open spaces at the top, sides, and bottom of the form, outside of the form image. The size of these spaces depends upon:

   a. Whether the form is to be bound at the sides, top, or bottom.
   b. Requirements imposed by office equipment (e.g., duplicating machines).
   c. Company policy preference.
   d. Printing requirements. A minimum margin of ⅜ of an inch on the sides, top, and bottom usually avoids any printing press difficulties.

4. *Form title.* The title should be short, yet descriptive of the purpose and function of the form. For example, the title "Operating Report" is not specific enough, since there are many types of operating reports. The titles "Production Report" and "Material Usage Report" are more specific and hence more useful.

The title should be at the top of the form. Usually, the best position is in the left corner of the form.

5. *Space requirements.* The space allotted for the entry of a single item of data depends upon:
   a. The inclusion of the printed caption in the space.
   b. The method of entry (manual or machine).
   c. The quantity of data to be entered (number of alphabetic or numeric characters). To conserve space, printed captions should be included in the space allotted for the entry.

Like this

Name (First,	Middle,	Last)

Not this

Name

(First, Middle, Last)

The space allotted for each letter or number depends primarily on the manner of entry. If accounting machines are used, for example, the equipment's printing specifications will govern the space requirements. If entries are made manually or by typewriter, the following table may be used as a guide.

	Manual Entries	*Typewriter Entries*
Horizontal	1/8 inch per character.	10-12 characters per inch.
Vertical	1/3 inch if the caption is included in the space, or ¼ inch if the caption is outside the space.	1/3 inch if the caption is included in the space, or 1/6 inch if the caption is outside the space.

PURCHASE REQUISITION FOR STATIONERY

TITLE		FORM NO.
ORIGINAL SUPPLIER	LEAD TIME	ORDER QUANTITY

ACCOUNTS TO BE CHARGED

%	NO.	%	NO.	%	NO.	%	NO.

REQUISITION		ORDERED				NEXT PURCHASE DATE
DATE	QUANTITY	DATE	P.O. NO.	QUANTITY	SUPPLIER	

Fig. 4. Purchase Requisition for Stationery.

Where the form is to be filled in by typewriter, the horizontal entry spacing should be coordinated with the tabulating stop system on the typewriter.

6. *Vertical side headings.* Space can be conserved by using vertical side captions when both primary and secondary headings are required. Figure 4 illustrates both the usual design and the space-saving design.

7. *Check boxes.* Check boxes are useful when a limited number of predetermined answers can be preprinted on the form. A large number of check boxes may require excessive eye travel to pick out the preprinted answer. In such cases, a satisfactory grouping can usually be devised to assist eye travel.

8. *Company form numbers.* All forms should be assigned numbers to facilitate requisitioning, purchasing, and storing. The best position for the form number is in the lower left corner. In this position, the number is visible without removing the forms from the storeroom shelves. When completed forms are filed vertically by form number (not used extensively), the numbers may be placed at the top of the form, under the title.

9. *Serial numbers.* The position of serial numbers is important. The usual position is in the upper right corner where the numbers are first seen when the form is in a file drawer. When the forms are filed in a post binder, however, it is sometimes advantageous to have the serial number in the lower right corner. Many business forms companies furnish serial numbering in one position at no additional cost; the charge for furnishing the number in a second location is usually nominal.

10. *Paper.* The weight and quality of paper used is a cost factor that should not be ignored. The choice of weight and quality depends primarily on how the forms are processed and filed. Other factors that might influence the selection of paper include: the number of copies to be prepared, the method of preparation (pencil, pen, typewriter, etc.), filing space requirements (thickness), the possible necessity of preventing data on the reverse side of a form from showing through, the appearance requirements, and the retention period of the form.

It is advantageous for each copy of a multi-part form to be a different color. This facilitates routing and aids in detecting misfilings. Pastel shades are preferable to dark colors because they are easier to read.

11. *Type faces and line weights.* The selection of type faces and line weights are technical matters. They are best left to the business forms company representative. It is usually sufficient to indicate the various distinctions desired on the draft or layout copy of the new form.

FORMS INVENTORY CONTROL

A system for centralized control of stocks of forms is an essential element of effective forms management. Inventory investment can be kept at a minimum when the stocks of forms are under the control of the forms manager. The centralization of control gives greatest assurance that forms will be available when they are needed and, at the same time, prevents the accumulation of excessive stocks in employees' desks and filing cabinets.

A system should be established for requisitioning from the central storeroom. Some companies have a rule that all requisitions cover a month's usage. Others are more realistic and require that only small-volume forms be ordered monthly, while larger-volume forms may be requisitioned either weekly or biweekly. In all cases, the forms required should be identified by form title, and by company form number, if one has been assigned

Some companies require that stationery requisitions be priced and extended. These companies use the requisitions to obtain the accounting distribution of stationery costs. Most companies, however, distribute the costs of forms to appropriate accounts at the time that purchase invoices are recorded or paid. The distribution is usually made by using predetermined allocation factors. These are calculated based on a sample of usage for a representative period.

The stationery storeroom should have adequate space and be equipped with either wooden shelving or adjustable steel shelving. Forms should be stored in form number sequence to facilitate receiving, issuing, and inventory control.

Physical inventories should be taken once or twice each year. Companies using the charge-out method previously mentioned should, of course, adjust the stationery inventory balance in the general ledger account to the physical inventory amount. In all cases, the physical counts should be reviewed in relation to the purchases recorded on the permanent requisitions, which are described below, to determine if there are obsolete or overstocked items. If there are surpluses, notations should be made on the requisitions so that additional stocks will not be ordered.

When stocks are to be replenished, the forms manager sends unit purchase requisitions, copies of the forms to be ordered, and the forms control cards to the purchasing department. A permanent requisition form should be used, similar to that illustrated in Figure 4.

The purchasing department enters the date, purchase order number, quantity ordered and the name of the supplier on the permanent requisition before returning it to the forms manager. Upon return from purchasing, the forms manager establishes the date when the next purchase is to be made, using as a basis the quality currently ordered, the purchase lead time, and the current stock on hand. He then enters a date approximately one week prior to the next procurement date on the requisition and files it by such date. Each day, he should select the requisitions from the date file and visually inspect the stocks of the items to determine if a purchase should be made. If so, he will enter the date and quantity on the requisition and send it to the purchasing department. If the stock on hand is such that immediate action is not required, the forms manager should redetermine the next procurement date, change the date on the requisition, and refile it accordingly.

It is usually desirable to give special inventory control attention to high-volume usage forms and long lead time forms. These are the two types of forms that most often give rise to availability problems. A special file for these forms removes them from the volumes of less difficult forms and minimizes the chance that their timely procurement may be overlooked (Figure 4).

RECORDS MANAGEMENT

The legendary small businessman who kept all his papers filed in a cigar box has disappeared from the modern scene, a victim of the growth in governmental controls and taxes as well as the availability of low-cost, fast-copy equipment. These developments have formed all organizations to deal with the problems of paper flow in some practical way or to be engulfed in paper confusion. Records management is the outgrowth of the need for controlling organizational records. It covers all records used in an organization—forms as well as correspondence, legal documents, tax returns, and all other papers. Forms management is, therefore, vitally concerned with records management as it relates to forms. This section will discuss the objectives of records management and the basic factors important to accomplishing these objectives, with particular emphasis on their relationship to forms.

Records management programs have the following principal objectives:

1. To minimize the filing equipment and space required to store active records.
2. To improve filing methods, including classifying and indexing systems which permit prompt retrieval of material relating to a particular subject.
3. To identify vital records and provide for their protection against fire, flood, sabotage, or other disasters.
4. To provide economical storage of inactive files which is adequately indexed to permit requests for the material to be handled expeditiously.
5. To establish retention periods which satisfy legal and operating requirements.
6. To provide procedures for destroying records which are no longer needed.

Basic factors important to accomplishing the above objectives are discussed below, under the captions: filing facilities, filing methods, vital records protection, inactive records storage, establishing retention periods, and destruction of inactive records.

Filing facilities. Centralized filing is generally desirable in organizations having significant volume of material to be filed. Under a fully centralized plan all files are maintained at one central location. Under a partially centralized plan, headquarters' records and records of major legal or operating importance are maintained at one or more centralized locations, while other records are maintained at decentralized filing locations under standard practices specified by the records manager. It is common in the growth phase of smaller organizations that they reach a point where loosely defined, decentralized filing arrangements no longer can keep pace with the needs for controlling and making information available. Some form of centralized filing then usually becomes mandatory.

There is a variety of filing equipment available for meeting the needs of each organization. Shelf files, drawer files, transfer files, visible index files, and motorized files are some of the types that can be used. For most smaller and medium sized organizations, the salesmen from equipment suppliers can be good sources of information on what is available. Also, there is usually excellent information in a number of office management trade magazines regarding filing devices.

Basic considerations in selecting filing equipment are:

Space utilization. What is the capacity of the equipment—how many records will it hold? How much space for opening drawers is required? How well will the units fill the available vertical and horizontal space?

Accessibility. Can a record be filed or found easily? Is it easy to remove or insert a record without disturbing other records in the file?

Security. Will the equipment adequately safeguard the records from access by unauthorized personnel? Can the units be locked and are the locks sufficiently strong to prevent theft?

Protection. Will the equipment provide enough protection against dirt, moisture, smog, or other environmental hazards? Will the records be adequately safeguarded against wrinkling, tearing, and abrasion during filing and retrieval? Will the equipment provide protection of the records in the event of a major disaster such as a fire, flood, explosion, or wind storm?

Cost. What is the initial investment cost of the equipment? What is the annual maintenance cost of the equipment?

Spacing your equipment. The way in which equipment is arranged in the filing area is also important. The space available for filing should be accurately measured and a scale diagram prepared for use in evaluating alternative layouts. Doors and windows should be shown on the diagram, with the direction of door opening indicated. Templates of the filing equipment to be used should be prepared and used for experimental layouts. The following list of allowances for spacing equipment has been used in several organizations:

ACTIVE FILES

File cabinets. Allow at least 3 feet and preferably 5 feet between the drawer fronts of facing file cabinets. Allow enough space in front of file drawers to permit full access to the contents of the drawer. If the aisle into which the drawer opens is a busy aisle, allow an extra 18 inches.

Shelf files. Allow at least 28 inches between facing shelf files.

INACTIVE FILES

File cabinets. Allow 3 feet between the drawer fronts of facing file cabinets.

Shelf files. Allow 24 inches between facing shelf files.

Work flow in the filing area should be considered in arranging the equipment so that necessary equipment is readily available. Since it is usually necessary to plan for future increases in filing work loads, it is desirable to assign adequate space to the filing operations rather than to cram them into minimum space and have them quickly reach an overload condition.

FILE METHODS

There are three basic elements in any filing system:

1. Units of material to be filed.
2. A classification system for filing and indexing the materials.
3. Filing facilities to contain the materials.

The units of material to be filed may be a particular type of document such has been discussed in the preceding section.

The units of material to be filed may be a particular type of document such as a sales invoice, a production order, or a receiving report. They may also be a group of documents that are related by a common element, such as a case file covering legal matters in litigation. Whatever the unit of material to be filed and retrieved, whether a paper, a book, a catalog, a file folder, or some other record or object, it should represent the unit of information usually of greatest interest to the users of the file. The unit of material for filing purposes will, therefore, vary with different types of files. Single sales invoices may be the filing units in a sales history file, for example, while case folders may be the filing units in an attorney's litigation file.

A classification system must be established to give coherence and usefulness to the units of material on file. The classification system may be alphabetic, numeric, or chronological, but it should arrange the filed materials into a pattern which is useful for filing and retrieving them. A file of customer invoices might be arranged alphabetically according to the customers' names, or if customer account numbers have been assigned to customers the file might be arranged numerically by customer account numbers. The classification system for a particular file should be suited to the individual needs of that file. If most of the needs for reference are alphabetic, the file should be arranged alphabetically. If most of the needs for reference are by account number, the file should be arranged numerically. A cross-reference file of names and account numbers should be maintained for use when only the name and not the number is known by the person seeking information. Classification systems are usually established by subjects, geographic areas, time periods, or some type of individual entities. Subclassifications are often made within major classifications. Sales may be classified by geographic areas, with subclassifications by products within each geographic area.

Use of color coding within files will facilitate the filing and retrieval of records. In an employee's personnel file, for example, different colored tabs or folders may be used to identify subsections of the file containing applications, tests, job history, counseling notes, awards, or other matters.

A manual of standardized filing practices which specifies the files to be maintained, the steps to be followed in maintaining them, the equipment and supplies to be used, and any special instructions required, should be prepared in all but the smallest organizations. The manual will not only be useful for training new filing personnel but should help to maintain consistency in the organization's filing practices.

Vital records protection. Vital records are those essential to the continuation of the organization's activities. There are few records that cannot to some degree be reconstructed if they are destroyed. The reconstruction may be costly but it can usually be done, to at least a substantial degree, from copies of source documents or other sources of basic information. However, during a period of attempted reconstruction of destroyed records, normal operations may be seriously interrupted and delayed, and the costs of the reconstruction may be prohibitively expensive or beyond the financial resources of the organization affected. Consequently, it is desirable to identify the records which would have a seriously crippling effect on the organization's activities, and to take steps to protect them against major hazards such as fire, explosion, flood, sabotage, and similar disastrous events. Some of the records often classified as "vital" are listen below—although the specific records so classified will vary with each organization.

Legal documents—Deeds, titles, contracts, licenses, patents, copyrights, leases, etc.
Administrative records—Bylaws, minutes of directors meetings, stock records, bond records, tax returns, capital investment records, etc.
Operating records—Specifications, drawings, bills of material, patterns, inventories, etc.

Three principal approaches are used to safeguard vital records:

1. The vital records are identified and are segregated for special protected storage in a location remote from the principal place of business.
2. Vital records are stored in safes or insulated files, and the storage areas are protected with fire extinguishers, sprinkler systems, and smoking restrictions.
3. Vital records are identified and segregated for storage at a public vital records center.

Inactive records storage. It is generally recognized that provision be made for the storage of inactive records, and that this storage space should cost as little as possible. Many companies do not recognize, however, that time and money can be saved by insisting on some degree of formality in the filing and control of inactive records. Too often, inactive storage turns out to be a dark, dusty, poorly ventilated room with unidentified paper cartons and wooden boxes strewn indiscriminately on the floor or piled on top of each other. Too often, a clerk who is asked to retrieve a three year old invoice, labor ticket, or purchase order, is gone from the office for hours. He returns dirty and sweaty only to say, "I couldn't find it."

The inactive storage area should be clean, ventilated, and well lighted. It should be equipped with wooden or steel shelving and supplied with cardboard transfer cases of a uniform size. Each section of shelving should be numbered consecutively.

The employee responsible for inactive storage should maintain a control card for each type of record filed in inactive storage. The control card should identify the record by title and form number (if any), it should show the approved retention period, and it should provide spaces for entry of the following data:

Date of transfer to inactive storage.
Transferring office or department.
Inclusive dates of records transferred.
Storage location code (section and shelf).
Scheduled destruction date.
Date destroyed.

Establishing retention periods. For this phase of records management, an inventory of the contents of the files in all parts of the organization should be made. The purpose of the inventory is to determine those forms and records for which retention periods should be established. A secondary purpose is to ascertain if there are forms and records filed in individual departments that might better be stored in a central fileroom.

The principal factors to be considered in establishing retention periods for forms and records are as follows:

1. The identification of records which are important and must be retained indefinitely. Such records include:

   Corporate charter and bylaws
   Stockholder records
   Board and committee minutes
   Accounting records
   Insurance policies
   Powers of attorney
   Contracts
   Important legal documents

2. The requirements of executives, department heads, and others for retaining forms and records that will be needed and useful in years to come.
3. The requirements of Federal, state, and local laws and regulations for retaining records.
4. The requirements for microfilming large-volume forms and records that otherwise would be retained and occupy valuable filing space for many years.

The first step in establishing a retention period for all forms and records is, of course, the preparation of retention schedules. Naturally, such retention schedules should be reviewed by legal counsel to insure compliance with legal requirements. The treasurer and other company officials should also review the retention schedules to make sure that all company needs will be met. After making any necessary revisions, the tentative schedules should be adopted as official company policy. As such they should be, in common with other policies, subject to revision whenever conditions change.

The cardboard transfer cases containing the inactive files should be labeled on the outside so that it will not be necessary to open them to ascertain their contents. The cases should then be placed in the next unused shelf location, and the location codes entered on the cases and the control cards.

Destruction of inactive records. Although retention periods have been carefully established after approval by all concerned, it is nevertheless prudent to consult those who originate forms and records before the files are destroyed. This is usually accomplished by circulating a list of the records to be destroyed, with the request that interested parties sign the list to indicate that they approve of the destruction. Such lists may be prepared monthly, quarterly, or annually, as warranted by the volumes of materials to be destroyed. They should contain the following basic data:

1. Titles and form numbers.
2. Inclusive dates of the records.
3. Departments or offices that transferred the records to inactive storage.
4. Scheduled destruction dates.

A common method of destroying records is by cremation. Some organizations bale their records, in their original form or after shredding, for sale as scrap paper. The practice of shredding records is growing, as there is a ready market for such scrap in some localities. Many organizations cremate records of a confidential nature and sell the rest. The control cards should indicate the date, location, and method of destruction.

WHEN DOES AN ORGANIZATION NEED A FORMS MANAGEMENT PROGRAM?

The determination of the need for managing forms is largely dependent upon the size of the business. The owner-operator of a very small enterprise where few forms are required often keeps informed of business operations by his own observations, without needing elaborate paperwork reporting systems. Furthermore, the financial aspects of a very small enterprise may require only the simplest of bookkeeping systems. Here, where no major forms problem exists, the informal approach is clearly indicated. On the other hand, when the business is no longer a one-man operation and cannot be controlled by the "seat of the pants" method, a formal program is necessary to ensure effective communication and economical clerical operations.

Few, if any, new businesses come into existence with a complete plan for forms management. In the majority of cases, the initial accounting system and the first forms and procedures needed for communication purposes are designed and installed by the owner of the enterprise, the public accountant, and sometimes the bookkeeper. As the tempo of operations increases and new communications problems arise, these people change the system in order to meet the added requirements. As new people are added to the organization, those engaged in operating functions (manufacturing, engineering, sales, purchasing, etc.) either install their own paperwork system or, at least, participate in establishing forms and procedures to meet their needs.

The preceding situation is typical of the informal approach to forms management. This informal approach is almost a necessity for the new business that begins on a modest scale. The approach is satisfactory as long as the business remains small, communications are uncomplicated, relatively few forms are used, and the clerical force is small.

It is not always easy to recognize when a business reaches the point where formal controls should be installed, although there are a number of recognizable factors that serve to indicate the need for a formal program. Unfortunately, the factors that indicate the need for a change might not be recognized in the case of a very small company. This may be due to a lack of centralized responsibility for systems, procedures, forms, etc., or perhaps to a lack of experience in such matters. In these situations, management frequently turns to the public accountant for advice and help.

Whether or not management has specifically requested the public accountant's assistance or advice, he should be alert to note any deficiencies in clerical and operating procedures. The public accountant can watch for areas where improvement is needed while making his audit of financial transactions. Ordinarily, this does not entail any extension of normal auditing procedures since the public accountant is already familiar with his client's operations, the availability and timeliness of information, the condition of the files, and the need for labor-saving devices. Much of this information comes to him as a by-product of the examination for forms, documents, and reports, and through inquiry into operating and accounting methods—both procedures being integral parts of the usual audit.

The factors listed below are indicative of a need for formal control. These factors are symptoms that there is need for a review of the paperwork procedures, the forms, and the retention and destruction programs. If all factors were present at the same time, the situation would indeed be chaotic. Isolated deficiencies in one or two areas might be indicative of nothing, and, in any case, are easily corrected. Certainly, if there are a number of deficiencies, a survey should be made to determine the extent of the corrective action that should be taken. The factors that indicate a need for formal controls are:

1. Dissatisfaction of all or some levels of management with the nature, timeliness, or reliability of operating reports they receive.
2. Repetitive requests for types of financial and operating information not produced by or readily available from the present system.
3. Weaknesses in the internal control over important financial transactions.
4. Numerous clerical errors in documents of original entry and in other records.

5. Chronic backlogs of incomplete clerical tasks.
6. Absence of written clerical procedures and constant changes in the procedures.
7. Excessive clerical turnover.
8. Requests for additional clerical help.
9. Voluminous manual posting jobs that could be performed more economically on bookkeeping machines or with punched card equipment.
10. Employees using "homemade" forms and keeping records of certain types of data for their personal use, usually for "alibi" purposes.
11. Using numerous small, single-purpose forms for communicating data abstracted from other forms.
12. Using two or more forms containing similar basic data when one form could serve all purposes; for example, using separate forms for shipping orders, packing lists, and sales invoices.
13. Preparing and distributing more copies of a form than are needed for effective communication and control.
14. Preparing too few copies of a form so that recipients are required to retype the data or otherwise duplicate the form to obtain the number of copies needed for their sphere of activity.
15. Using unit sets rather than continuous forms for large-volume, repetitive typing jobs such as invoicing.
16. Using pads of multicopy forms where carbons must be inserted manually when precarboned unit set forms would result in sufficiently lower clerical preparation costs to more than offset the additional form costs.
17. Using expensive printing processes and high grade paper when less costly printing and paper would be satisfactory.
18. Loosely controlled stationery stockroom.
19. All clerical employees keeping large stocks of blank forms in their desks and filing cabinets.
20. Requests for more filing space and equipment.
21. Inadequate provision for storing inactive files.
22. Inability to locate inactive files needed for reference due to poor housekeeping.
23. Inactive files constantly increasing—the storage area "bursting at the seams."

HOW TO SET UP A FORMS MANAGEMENT PROGRAM

This section will describe the steps to be taken in setting up and implementing a formal program of forms management. The steps are discussed in the same order that they should be undertaken, as listed below:

1. Introducing the program.
2. Defining the forms to be furnished.
3. Information to be furnished with forms.
4. Filing the forms.
5. Establishing forms control records.
6. Analyzing the forms in use.

Introducing the program. The decision to inaugurate a formal forms management program must be made by management. In a small company, there will be no difficulty in explaining the program and obtaining the cooperation of all employees engaged in paperwork activities. If the company has a complex organizational structure consisting of several divisions, plants, offices, etc., the intention to begin the program should be communicated in writing.

This first communication is most important. It should come from the top administrative officer, and identify the employee who will be responsible for implementing the program. It will define what is meant by forms and request each employee to submit two copies of all forms that he originates as well as certain basic information regarding the forms. The communication sets deadlines for completing the more important phases of the program and informs the employees of the objectives of the program, which are:

1. To identify all forms in use.
2. To eliminate unnecessary forms.
3. To improve clerical efficiency by redesigning forms.
4. To centralize responsibility for forms design and procurement.
5. To reduce inventories of unused forms.

Defining the forms to be furnished. It is important that employees have a clear understanding of the forms to be furnished. A forms management program should cover forms of every type and description used in the business. A definition, such as the following, is not sufficient:

> A form is any tangible evidence, usually paper with prescribed spaces for entering data that is used to communicate information between people in a uniform manner.

It is usually necessary to supplement this definition with more explicit information, such as the following:

1. All forms purchased from outside printers, including but not limited to the following types of items:

Checks	Letterheads
Coupon books	Labels
Envelopes	Payrolls
Identification cards	Purchase orders
Invoices	Receiving reports
Requisitions	Tickets
Tags	Time cards

2. All stock forms purchased from stationery stores, including but not limited to the following:

File folders	Pads of lined paper
Index cards	Petty cash slips
Inventory sheets	Stock cards
Ledger sheets	Telephone call slips

3. All forms printed on company-owned duplicating equipment.
4. Regularly used worksheets and file cards on which column headings and space identification data are entered manually or by typewriter.

Information to be furnished with forms. The information needed regarding the forms submitted by employees in the various departments, divisions, offices, etc., is not voluminous or difficult to obtain. At the time the forms are collected, only the following is usually requested:

1. **The purpose or use of the form.**
2. The department where the form originates.
3. The number of copies in each form set and their distribution.
4. A copy of the instructions or a reference to the company manual or directive (if such exists) that prescribes the use of the form.
5. The number of form sets normally used each year.
6. The retention period for each copy of the form, if already established.

More information may be obtained later, when the forms are analyzed, regarding the clerical procedures for originating and processing them.

The method of furnishing the information regarding forms varies. Companies that have many divisions and use several thousand forms may develop a standard *form data sheet.* All sections of the company would use the form data sheet to list the required information for each of their forms. The data sheet would be attached to the forms when they are submitted to the employee responsible for implementing the forms management program. In other cases, the required information may be entered directly on the form. This latter method has both advantages and disadvantages. The advantages include a reduction in the volume of paper to be handled and filed. Also, subsequent analysis of the forms is easier since the forms can be examined and the data reviewed at the same time. Disadvantages, on the other hand, are: the data may not be presented uniformly, some data may be omitted since there are no specified blank spaces to be completed, and some forms may be too small to enter all the information needed.

Filing the forms. In the usual situation, forms from all departments arrive at the same time. The employee responsible for installing the control system, whom we shall call the forms manager, is immediately faced with a filing problem. It is usually possible to make a reliable advance estimate of the number of forms in use. Using this estimate as a basis, the forms manager should prepare himself by obtaining the file cabinets and file folders that will be needed for the job.

In determining the quantities of file cabinets required, a good rule of thumb is to figure one four-drawer letter-size filing cabinet for each 1,500 forms. Slightly more file folders will be required than the number of forms to be filed. File folders of the least expensive type, without printing on the tabs, are adequate. All folders should be letter-size and have right hand tabs. A file folder should be prepared for each form submitted.

Before the forms manager can file the forms, he must decide on a forms identification system, as discussed in the "Forms Identification" section of this chapter. He should use whatever system has been decided on for identifying and filing the forms. If he is using, for example, the systems family or business factors classification system, the forms manager then reviews the forms to determine (1) the systems family or business factor to which each form relates, and (2) the primary function performed by each form. It is practical to use alphabetical codes to identify systems family or business factors classifications and numerical codes to identify the functional classifications. As the forms are classified, the codes should be entered on the file folders.

A separate file drawer (or section of a drawer if the number of forms is small) should be labeled and set aside for each systems family or business factor. The form files (which are still in form number sequence) should now be segregated and filed by systems family or business factor. The files in each systems family or business factor group should then be sorted into functional classification code number sequence. When this is completed, the forms manager should prepare a set of functional classification index guides for each systems family or business factor file. The regular file folders with the right hand tabs can be used for the index guides by entering the action verbs of the functional classifications on the reverse side of the tabs. When the guides are placed in the file drawers, the functional classifications will be visible on the tabs along the left side of the file drawer and the form titles will be visible along the right side of the drawer.

When the process of classifying and filing the forms has been completed, the form files will be arranged in the following order.

1. By systems family or business factor
2. By function
3. By form number and title

The files within each functional group should be rearranged alphabetically by form title. If the form titles are reasonably descriptive of the actual functions performed, forms of like character should now be together. When the number of forms of like character is large, it is sometimes desirable to use an additional set of index guides to identify the kinds or types of forms.

Figure 5 illustrates the arrangement of a file drawer with functional and form-type index guides.

Establishing forms control records. After completing the files, related groupings of forms will be available for review and analysis. This phase of the program, however, should be deferred temporarily. There will be requests for

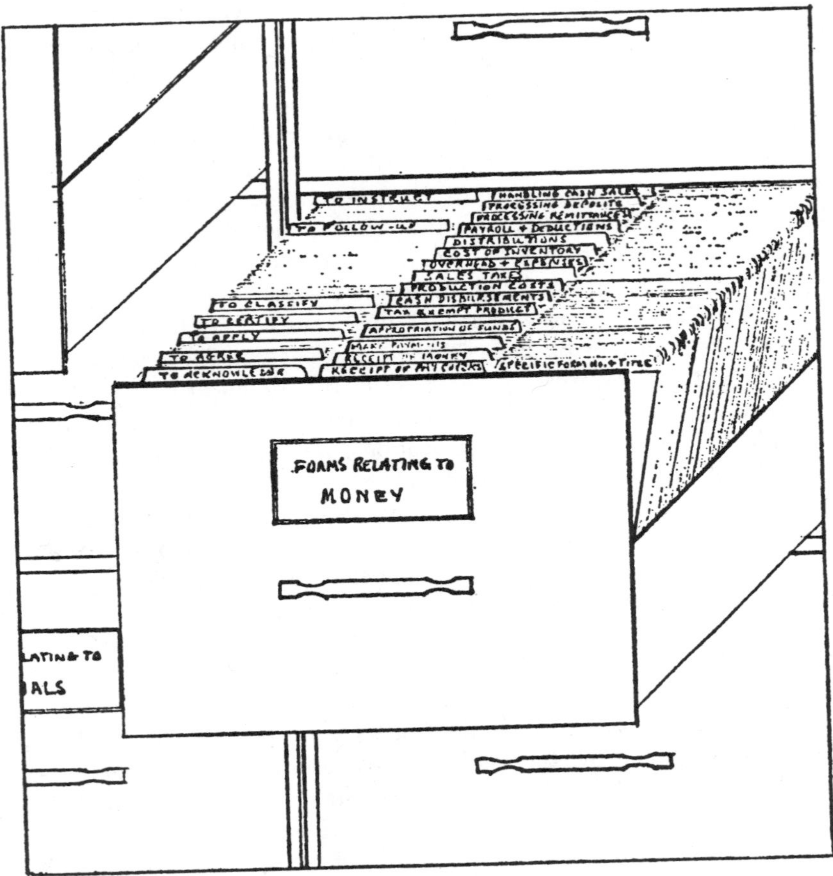

Fig. 5. File Drawer with Functional and Form-Type Index Guides.

new forms and stock replenishments before the analysis work could be completed. It is most important, therefore, that appropriate control records be established as early as possible.

A forms control record should contain the following basic data for each form:

1. Form title
2. Systems family or business factor and function codes
3. Company form number
4. Name of each organization using the form
5. Estimated annual usage by each organization
6. Name of original printer
7. Price-break quantities and prices originally quoted
8. Lead time requested by printer
9. Economical order quantity established on the basis of price-break, lead time and total annual usage

10. Physical characteristics:
    a. Make-up (unit set, continuous, fan-fold, pad, single sheet)
    b. Number of parts or copies in each set and the following with respect to each part:

        Size
        Paper weight and color
        Color of ink
        Special printing on copies (yes or no)
        One-time carbon (short, cut-out, uniform)
        "Carbonless" paper
        Punching required (yes or no)
        Numbering required (yes or no)

The above should be considered as minimum requirements. Some companies may wish to include the date the form was originated, the dates of revisions, the names of employees requesting revisions, actual annual usages, unit cost prices, the accounts to be charged at time of purchase, etc.

The form of the control records or data sheets is a matter of personal preference. The data may be entered on specially printed 5 × 8 cards, Kardex records, ledger sheets, 8½ × 11 paper forms, or any other appropriate forms.

Analyzing the forms in use. It is now practicable to return to the important task of analyzing the forms in use. The first step in analyzing the forms gathered during the implementation of the forms management program is to determine the number of forms in each classification. This is a simple job and takes little time. Nevertheless, it is an important one because it reveals the classifications having many forms. This information is the starting point for finding forms that can be eliminated immediately because they are duplications or are not needed for other reasons.

A survey of forms of one large company disclosed approximately 5,000 forms in use in the company's principal divisions and subsidiaries. An analysis of forms by business factor and function uncovered areas where abnormally large numbers of forms were used for the same purposes. Figure 6, Distribution of Forms in Company X, gives the approximate quantities of forms by business factor and by function as found by the survey.

It was decided that the forms in the business factors categories of employees and communications should be analyzed first. These factors were selected because it was felt that they offered the greatest opportunity for obtaining uniformity in both forms and clerical procedures.

The analysis uncovered serious breaches of good forms management. Some of the more glaring violations were:

Employees:

22 forms to apply for employment
21 forms to apply for hospital and medical insurance
19 forms to apply for leave of absence
36 forms to notify attendance time
33 forms to notify termination of employment

Communications:

13 varieties of *while you were out* telephone message slips
28 varieties of inter-office memorandum pads
34 varieties of inter-office memorandum letterheads
80 varieties of letterheads
180 varieties of envelopes
17 varieties of general purpose mailing labels

It is not difficult to recognize duplications in these forms. It is also not difficult to determine the actions that should be taken to correct the situation. The cost savings from eliminating the obvious duplications are important, and can even be substantial, as they were in the case of Company X. More important savings, however, can usually be obtained by a thorough and sophisticated ánalysis of all of the forms in use, whether or not they are complete or partial duplications of others. A complete analysis covers not only the physical features of forms and their primary purposes, but also includes an analysis of the procedures for preparing and processing them.

WHAT CONTINUING ACTIONS ARE NEEDED TO MAINTAIN A FORMS MANAGEMENT PROGRAM?

Changes occur over time in all systems. Work procedures and their associated forms as part of an organization's operating system are no exception. They are subject both to the obvious changes that occur dramatically within an organization, such as new product lines or new plant locations, and to the subtle changes that occur gradually, such as declining numbers of production personnel as automation increases in the plant.

In maintaining a forms management program, there are, therefore, needs to deal with new forms to meet new requirements resulting from changes in the organization's operations. There are also needs to deal with old forms and to modify or discontinue those that no longer efficiently serve the organization's needs.

Effective forms management requires that the centralized control system provide procedures that govern the creation of new forms. This does not mean that systems specialists, accountants, department managers, and others should not determine and sketch the forms they need and the clerical procedures for preparing and processing them. It does mean that when new forms are required, requests for them should be submitted to the forms manager. The requests should be accompanied by drafts of the forms and related clerical procedures, and should provide the following information:

Proposed form title
Purpose or use of the form
Estimated annual usage

Purpose or Function Performed	FORMS RELATING TO						
	Product or Service	Employees	Materials	Property and Equipment	Money	Performance	Communication
TO ACKNOWLEDGE	50	5	2	5	15		
TO AGREE	15	5		5	15		
TO APPLY	5	80	5	10	5		
TO AUTHORIZE	10	40	15	5			
TO CERTIFY	25	35	15			5	
TO CLASSIFY	150	10			200		
TO FOLLOW-UP	200	70	10	10	40		10
TO IDENTIFY	200	20	2		5	2	10
TO INSTRUCT	40	10	1	1	10		
TO NOTIFY	1020	330	115	30	340	3	15
TO ORDER	70		60	25	130		
TO RECORD	210	65	10	40	325		
TO REPORT	30	2		5	55	190	
TO REQUEST	20	30	45	4	70		
TO ROUTE	105	8			10		380
TO SCHEDULE	75						
TOTAL	2225	710	280	140	1220	200	415

Fig. 6. Distribution of Forms in Company X.

Physical characteristics (same as those entered on the forms control records)
Date the new procedure is to be installed
Proposed retention periods for the various copies of the form
Form or forms that will be made obsolete by the new form

Upon receiving such requests, the forms manager should review the forms control records and the forms file to determine if a similar form is already in use. If so, he should remove a copy of the form from the file, and meet with the creator of the new form. At this meeting, the forms manager can determine if the existing form will serve the purpose outlined in the request, or if the proposed new form can be redesigned to serve both purposes.

If the forms manager determines that there is not a similar form presently in use, he should:

1. Review the proposed form for adequacy of design considering all of the basic forms management subfunctions described in the first part of this chapter.
2. Assign a form number to the new form.
3. Classify the form as to systems family or business factor, and function.
4. Prepare a forms control record.
5. Prepare a purchase requisition for stationery.
6. Send the purchase requisition and the draft copy of the new form to the purchasing department.

When the new forms are received from the printer, they should be placed in the forms storeroom. Two copies should be filed in the forms file by classification, and whoever requested the form should be notified that a supply is available for use.

Conditions affecting forms needs can often change without notification of the forms manager. A periodic review (say, annually) of the higher volume-higher costs forms in use should, therefore, be made to make certain that the forms are still efficiently meeting the needs of users.

CONCLUSIONS

One of the most important functions the manager of an organization has is communicating. Communicating with customers, with suppliers, and with employees is the linking process that enables an organization to accomplish useful results. By making it easier to communicate, by reducing errors in communication, and by cutting costs of communication, forms management makes a sizable contribution to the communication process, and, hence, to the overall performance and profitability of any working organization.

The professional accountant who has availed himself of the forms management information in this chapter is in an improved position to assist his clients with obtaining the many benefits of better forms management. During his visits to clients' offices he can observe their systems with increased awareness of opportunities for communication and cost improvements.

20

How to Set Up Internal Reports for Managerial Purposes

CONTENTS

20

How to Set Up Internal Reports for Managerial Purposes

James A. Cashin, CPA

Internal reports are playing an ever increasing role in the planning, direction, and control of company operations. As the amount of money to be realized or lost on each decision increases, the necessity of making the right decision becomes more crucial. And for management to make the right decision, it is essential that the right information reach the right individual at the right time.

Therefore, modern managerial control requires that significant facts affecting company operations be provided to management promptly, accurately, and efficiently. The public accountant, with his training, experience, and independent outlook, is eminently suited to devise an effective system of reports through which his client can achieve this objective. With this in mind, we will consider the procedures and problems pertinent to the implementation of such a system.

First, we will outline the basic requirements for effective reporting. Next, we will discuss and illustrate the various kinds of reports. Finally, we will suggest techniques that can be used to design an effective reporting system. This final section will be supplemented by an Appendix consisting of a check-list of reporting techniques.

BASIC REPORTING REQUIREMENTS

In planning the design of an effective internal report system, it is important to consider each of the following factors:

1. Profit responsibility.
2. Content of the reports.
3. Management preference of report form.
4. Timing of the reports.
5. Distribution of reports.

Determining profit responsibility. The first step in setting up reports for managerial purposes is to determine the lines of responsibility in the particular organization. A reporting system, to be effective as a control device, must follow profit responsibility on the basis of departments, plants, divisions, and other responsibility units. If performance has not been up to expectation and action needs to be taken, there should be little doubt as to where the responsibility lies.

Organization charts should be obtained or prepared both for the company itself and for each of its responsibility units. Then a reporting system should be developed that will provide the pertinent information to each person who has a particular area of responsibility.

What should go in the reports? Naturally, the content of the reports will depend on the needs of the company. In planning to meet these needs the following principles should be recognized:

1. *Purpose of the reports.* The selection from a mass of data of the significant information that will best serve management's needs is one of the most important considerations in reporting. To do this properly, the accountant must determine exactly what each report is to accomplish. If the information is to be meaningful, it must be directed toward achieving action that will align operations with company objectives.
2. *Adequacy of information.* Under normal circumstances, it should not be necessary for the recipient of a report to request additional information. If special circumstances cause him to request further details, supplementary reports or the work papers should be readily available.
3. *Pertinency of information.* Adequacy does not mean "to the nth degree." Only those facts that are pertinent should be included, and such facts should be stated concisely and clearly, with all unnecessary detail and extraneous information excluded.

► IMPORTANT: Construct the report in accordance with what the recipient considers pertinent rather than with what you might think is more relevant. After all, he is the one who has to read and act upon the information.

4. *Arrangement of information.* The material included in a report should be so arranged that it will be a direct aid in motivating the recipient. Thus, significant data, trends, and developments should be prominently shown in order to make easily discernible any deviation from what was expected. Comparisons, ratios, and relationships are valuable in this respect, so they should be set out separately, and areas where improvements can be made should be clearly indicated.

Management preference of report form. All the effort and expense of preparing the best possible report will be of little avail unless management makes use of the report. In other words, there must be communication. To accomplish this, the general presentation has to have management's approval.

Management frequently does not know the exact type of data or form of report that will suit its needs. But they often have very definite ideas concerning the kind of report they do not want. For example, a visual presentation might be indicated where there is a comparison or trend over a number of periods. However, management's preconceived dislike for a chart or graphic presentation would suggest that some other method has to be developed.

► WHAT TO DO: Difficulties of this nature are generally the result of a lack of understanding of the advantages of a particular presentation. Discussion with a sample report as the focal point often overcomes opposition that originally existed.

Timing of the report. If information is not provided at proper and consistent intervals, much of its effectiveness is lost. Generally, reports should be timed so as to produce the quickest action. For example, reports showing the units produced and the units of material and labor used would be sent to the responsible department head daily. Upper levels of management might receive the same information on a weekly basis.

The trend in recent years is to get reports out as quickly as possible after the information is available. It has been found that striving to obtain an unnecessary degree of mathematical exactness can destroy the value of a report by causing a time-lag that makes action difficult. A realistic approach to compilation and computation is essential if reports are to have immediate as opposed to historical application.

Distribution of reports. One of the first problems encountered in the operation of a report system is the preparation of a distribution list for each type of report. It is important that all persons who are charged with responsibility for any of the operations reported on should receive a copy of the report. Those who have no primary responsibility should not, under ordinary conditions, receive the basic or detail report.

There is often a tendency for too many people to receive too many reports. Executives may receive so many reports that adequate time cannot be devoted to those that should receive attention. Obviously, this practice is confusing and expensive. Following is a summary of the various levels of reporting, with comments on the type of reports that should be provided at each level:

1. *Board of directors.* The regular reports required by the board of directors are generally in a more summarized form than those required by the top company officers. The nature of these reports and the degree of summarization will depend, to a large extent, on the knowledge the directors have of company operations. In most cases, company officers make up a large part of the board membership. Since they have close contact with operations and probably have already received much up-to-date information, it is not necessary to duplicate the reports made to management. Some companies have found that the same set of statements can be used for the board of directors and for top management. Certain statements can be removed from the set before it is submitted to the board. In fact, in some cases the reports are so numbered that the supporting

or direct responsibility statements bear a subnumber. Thus, the primary series of numbers can be retained for the board of directors' reports. Where special reports may be required, or where the board meets quarterly and quarterly reports are required, a separate set of statements is, of course, prepared.

2. *Officers.* The reports submitted to top management are generally in a more summarized form than those submitted to lower levels of management. More interpretative information and comments are ordinarily required.

Executives in the top management group include the president, the vice-presidents, the secretary, the treasurer, and the controller. When the chairman of the board is the chief executive officer of the company, he receives the same report as other top company officers. The information for the vice-presidents would be concerned primarily with their particular area of responsibility. For example, one vice-president may be responsible for sales, another for manufacturing, and so on. The information each receives would be determined on that basis. The treasurer requires information relating to financial matters, such as current cash status and future cash requirements. Data as to credits and collections, budgets, and capital commitments, all of which have a direct bearing on cash availability, would also be of special interest to the treasurer. The controller ordinarily has the responsibility for accumulating the necessary accounting data and for preparing the reports.

3. *Staff and operating managers.* The reports for staff and operating managers should contain data relating to their respective areas of responsibility. Where, for example, the staff man has functional responsibility for a particular activity such as industrial relations, he would be interested in receiving information concerning the number of employees, labor costs at various plants, the increased costs where new contracts may be in negotiation, safety records at the plants, and similar employees matters.

The manager of a plant would be primarily interested in matters pertaining to the plant. Depending on the organizational setup, he may be in charge of sales as well as manufacturing at the particular plant. In any case, he will have the various department heads in the plant reporting to him. Hence he will want reports relating to all these departments in order to determine how the department heads are carrying out their responsibilities.

4. *First-line supervisors.* The kind of information the first-line supervisor receives depends on the nature of his work and his assigned area of responsibility. Whether he is in a sales, an operating, or a financial area, he will usually be responsible for the supervision and leadership of the employees in his unit, and for the general efficiency of his activity. Even though he may not be responsible for the general personnel policies, he is directly responsible for employee performance and morale. If the output of a department is below expectation, the supervisor must answer to management. Since he works closely with the day-to-day problems of output, he is at the point where corrective

action can be taken quickly. Consequently, the reports should be prepared on a daily or weekly basis. Generally, output is compared with a standard, and any significant variance from standard should be promptly investigated.

► SUGGESTION: Many of the physical problems connected with the distribution of reports can be solved by preparing the reports in such a way that sections can be detached and sent separately.

KINDS OF REPORTS AND THEIR APPLICATION

Since management reports must be designed to suit the particular organization, there is a wide variety of reports as among various companies. However, certain basic reports are common to most companies. Representative reports in this latter category will be described and illustrated as follows:

1. Financial reports.
   a. Balance sheet.
   b. Supplementary statements.
2. Operating reports.
   a. Profit and loss statement.
   b. Sales department reports.
   c. Production department reports.
3. Special reports.
   a. Short-term reports.
   b. Long-term reports.

FINANCIAL REPORTS

The financial report reflects the financial position of the company at a given date. Therefore, it is a summary of the records as of a certain date and does not account for changes that occur in the period between two financial reports. Such changes are shown in the profit and loss statement.

Balance sheet. With the greater emphasis on operations in recent years, the attention given to the balance sheet has declined. However, it is still the basic financial report. In contrast to the various kinds of operating reports, the balance sheet is seldom prepared more frequently than monthly.

More detail is shown when the balance sheet is prepared for management purposes than when it is intended for outside use. For example, comparative data (previous month, beginning of year, etc.) and supporting data (working capital, current ratio, etc.) are frequently included on a balance sheet for internal distribution. For this internal distribution, the balance sheet is usually prepared in report form—that is, in a vertical arrangement. For reports to outsiders, the account form that was common in former years still predominates. In the account form, assets are shown on the left and liabilities and owners' equity on the right. Figure 1 illustrates a balance sheet prepared in the report form.

BALANCE SHEET
APRIL 30, 19__

	April 19__	March 19__	December 19__	Inc. or (Dec.) Month	Inc. or (Dec.) To Date
ASSETS					
Current Assets					
Cash	245,351	230,217	215,332	15,134	30,019
Notes and accounts receivable (net)	617,833	604,600	541,136	13,233	76,697
Marketable securities	151,875	149,785	135,415	2,090	16,460
Inventories	941,675	925,415	815,714	16,260	125,961
	1,956,734	1,910,017	1,707,597	46,717	249,137
Other Assets					
Non-current receivables	77,785	67,576	66,945	10,209	10,840
Deposits	10,500	10,500	10,500	—	—
Cash surrender value—life insurance	54,884	52,784	50,484	2,100	4,400
	143,169	130,860	127,929	12,309	15,240
Property, Plant and Equipment					
Land and buildings	110,000	110,000	110,000	—	—
Machinery and equipment	375,875	353,410	322,150	22,465	53,725
Construction in progress	55,932	45,975	34,835	9,957	21,097
	541,807	509,385	466,985	32,422	74,822
Less accumulated depreciation	198,861	194,317	182,515	4,544	16,346
	342,946	315,068	284,470	27,878	58,476
Prepaid Expenses and Deferred Charges	59,525	49,432	48,755	10,093	10,770
	2,502,374	2,405,377	2,168,751	96,997	333,623
LIABILITIES					
Current Liabilities					
Notes and accounts payable	315,471	306,835	285,918	8,636	29,553
Accrued federal taxes on earnings	175,617	157,867	151,409	17,750	24,208
Accrued other taxes, wages, ins., etc.	167,641	161,814	155,895	5,827	11,746
	658,729	626,516	593,222	32,213	65,507
STOCKHOLDERS' EQUITY					
Capital Stock					
Preferred stock	200,000	200,000	200,000	—	—
Common stock	800,000	800,000	800,000	—	—
Total	1,000,000	1,000,000	1,000,000	—	—
Capital Surplus	250,000	250,000	250,000	—	—
Retained Earnings	593,645	528,861	325,529	64,784	268,116
Total stockholders' equity	1,843,645	1,778,861	1,575,529	64,784	268,116
	2,502,374	2,405,377	2,168,751	96,997	333,623

Fig. 1. Balance Sheet (Report Form).

Supplementary statements. A number of other types of financial statements supplement or support related items on the balance sheet. Examples of these statements are:

1. Cash report.
2. Accounts receivable report.
3. Inventory analysis.
4. Capital expenditure progress report.
5. Change-in-cash-position reports.

Before discussing these individual reports, it should be pointed out that they are used in many different combinations and arrangements as needed by the particular company. For example, some firms now prepare only one daily report that includes both financial and operating data. Generally, all the data are on one sheet of paper for quick preparation and easy handling. Figure 2 is an example of this *combined form*.

DAILY MANAGEMENT REPORT
APRIL 19__

	Today	*Month to Date*	*Year to Date*
SALES			
Shipments—units	215	4,283	18,415
Billings—dollars	28,616	595,000	2,350,000
PRODUCTION—UNITS			
Production	190	4,157	19,105
Bookings	220	4,398	19,875
Backlog	30	241	770

	Debit	*Credit*	*Closing Balance*
CASH AND RECEIVABLES—$			
Cash	35,675	31,708	276,304
Accounts receivable	37,615	48,694	624,817

	Today	*Last Week*	*Last Month*
EMPLOYEES—NO.	3,150	3,147	3,045

Fig. 2. Daily Management Report (Combined Form).

However, *individual forms* are used by many companies. This is often more satisfactory, especially when there is relatively wide distribution of the report and many of the recipients are responsible for only one item.

1. *Cash report.* A daily cash report is prepared in practically every company. It is primarily a report for the treasurer or his assistant, but others in top management might request a copy. This report is especially important in companies that operate with a minimum of working capital. Under such conditions, a very close control of cash disbursements is necessary. And most companies do try to keep working capital at a minimum, having found that they are able to carry on greatly expanded operations with little or no increase in working capital. To maintain working capital at a minimum, it is necessary to develop effective cash budgeting and cash forecasting routines. When such procedures are operating and tight cash control is maintained, a weekly cash report rather than a daily cash report may be sufficient. Figure 3 illustrates a form frequently used for the daily cash report.

DAILY CASH REPORT
(Stated in Dollars) **DATE April 10, 19__**

Bank	*Opening Balance*	*Deposits* (*Day's Activity*)	*Disbursements* (*Day's Activity*)	*Closing Balance*
Bank A	91,705	25,718	6,707	110,716
Bank B	36,807	5,746	11,666	30,887
Bank C	49,876	12,817	17,577	45,116
Bank D	17,671	3,875	6,549	14,997
	196,059	48,156	42,499	201,716
Lock box #1	11,500	4,000	15,500	—
Lock box #2	25,350	19,965	7,065	38,250
Lock box #3	21,750	3,708	3,708	21,750
	58,600	27,673	26,273	60,000
Total	254,659	75,829	68,772	261,716

Cash Summary

Receipts and Disbursements	*Today*	*Month To Date*
Receipts		
Cash sales	11,647	105,716
Accounts receivable	18,978	168,519
Other	5,867	48,705
Total	36,492	322,940
Disbursements		
Trade creditors	13,467	126,812
Payrolls	14,815	151,387
Other	3,785	28,908
Total	32,067	307,107
Net increase	4,425	15,833

Cash Position	*Today*	*1st of Month*
Cash	261,716	245,351
Receivables	478,671	517,615
Market securities	157,811	151,875
Total	898,198	914,841
Current liabilities	718,158	769,411
Net	180,040	145,430

Fig. 3. Daily Cash Report.

2. *Accounts receivable report.* The accounts receivable information may be included in either of two general kinds of reports: (1) the *daily control report,* and (2) the *monthly analytical report.*

The daily control report summarizes the information in the same general manner as was illustrated for cash—that is, the opening balance, the billing, cash received, and the closing balance are shown daily. In addition to the daily and month-to-date amounts, forecasted data is often provided.

The monthly analytical report is generally a supplementary statement that supports the balance sheet. The accounts receivable are analyzed according to due dates. This information is prepared in practically all companies, but often no formal report is prepared. Figure 4 illustrates this type of report.

ACCOUNTS RECEIVABLE
MONTHLY ANALYTICAL REPORT

(Stated in dollars) March 31, 19__

Division	Total	Current	Days Past Due 30	60	90
A	265,817	215,685	29,897	14,813	5,422
B	147,895	127,877	11,676	3,786	4,556
C	87,615	69,384	10,784	6,477	970
D	16,288	9,685	5,647	847	109
Total	517,615	422,631	58,004	25,923	11,057
%	100	82	11	5	2

Fig. 4. Monthly Analytical Report.

3. *Inventory analysis.* Ordinarily, the inventory figure on the balance sheet will be supported by an analysis of the principal items making up the total. A comparison of the component balances with those at the end of the previous month and at the beginning of the year is desirable to show the total amount of change and the area accountable for the principal changes. Also, these balances should be related to appropriate significant data such as the rate of turnover, the trend of inventory, and unfilled orders.

4. *Capital expenditure progress report.* With the present high cost of capital equipment, a control of capital expenditures is more necessary than ever before. Such control is effectively exercised through a capital budget and a close follow-up of jobs by means of a capital expenditure progress report. This report shows the status of all open appropriations and indicates whether funds are being expended according to management's plan. Figure 5 shows the type of progress report that many companies use.

5. *Change-in-cash-position reports.* There are various reports that reflect the change in cash position from one period to another. One form that is in general use is the *source and application of funds statement.* This report shows the source of funds, such as net profit (adjusted for depreciation and other non-cash charges), sales of assets, and new capital received. Against this total is offset the amount of funds applied to the purchase of fixed assets, the retirement of debt, and similar expenditures. The difference between the total funds provided and the total funds applied is the increase or decrease in working capital. This report is usually prepared monthly or quarterly.

CAPITAL EXPENDITURE REPORT

(Stated in dollars)		MONTH OF APRIL 19__							Plant A	
				Expended		Unexpended			Physically Completed	
Job No.	Date Auth.	Description	Authorized	Month	To Date	Committed	Non-Committed	Overrun	%	Date
101	2/__	Field coils	20,000	3,855	16,560	6,310	—	2,870	70	—
108	4/__	Air compressor	18,435	2,415	18,435	—	—	—	100	4/__
121	6/__	Reed distiller	8,683	1,516	5,315	1,500	2,868	1,000	90	—
136	7/__	Safety guard	5,608	—	—	3,705	1,903	—	0	—
148	9/__	Brass roll	8,421	878	4,679	2,177	1,565	—	50	—
			61,147	8,664	44,989	13,692	6,336	3,870		

Fig. 5. Capital Expenditure Report.

OPERATING REPORTS

The operating report shows the result of operations and the sources and causes of profits and losses. Since there is ordinarly a greater difference between companies in the operating area than in the financial area, there is far more variation in operating reports than in financial reports.

Profit and loss statement. The principal operating statement is the profit and loss statement, which summarizes operations for the period. With the greater use of machines, earlier cut-offs, and the use of standards, there is a significant trend towards getting the profit and loss statement to management more quickly.

In those companies that have developed reliable cost standards, a weekly profit and loss statement is now prepared. Since the profit and loss statement is of such interest to management, the financial officer will frequently review the pencil draft or discuss the figures with top management before typing is begun.

The condensed profit and loss statement includes the operations for the entire company. Generally, the current results are compared with the budget for the current month and year to date. When budgets are not used, such comparisons are made with the month and year to date for the previous year. The condensed report, illustrated in Figure 6, discloses how well the various functions such as sales, production, and purchasing have been carried out, and how well selling expenses and general administrative expenses have been controlled. Individual analyses of these activities and their variations from standard or budget performance are prepared.

Further supplementary reports to support the condensed profit and loss statement are required as the company increases in size and more products are added. Following are the usual types of supplementary profit and loss reports. These are classified according to:

1. Product.
2. Division.
3. Type of sales distribution.

1. *Product profit and loss statement.* In order to localize responsibility, it is necessary to provide more detail than is available in the condensed profit and loss statement. Where more than one product is produced, the contribution of each product toward the established company goal must be reflected.

Generally, the product profit and loss statement is presented in much the same form as the condensed profit and loss statement. The totals of the product statements should tie into the condensed totals.

2. *Division profit and loss statement.* The same principle of pinpointing responsibility for favorable or unfavorable results holds true with respect to division profit and loss. When the division management has responsibility for one or more products or activities and these activities are arranged into a separate group, it is necessary to report how well that responsibility has been discharged. Because the trend in recent years has been toward decentralization, divisional reporting has become more and more important.

This report is also presented in much the same form as the condensed report, with comparisions to budgets and divisional quotas.

3. *Type-of-sales-distribution profit and loss statement.* When more than one type of sales distribution is employed or may be considered, a profit and loss statement according to type of distribution is desirable. A comparison of results obtained through the use of company salesmen and results obtained through the use of distributors, retailers, or other channels of distribution is of special value to sales management.

Sales department reports. Adequate control of the sales function requires that a great deal more sales information be available than is obtainable from the condensed and supplementary profit and loss statements. This information is provided to the sales manager or his assistant through various forms of reports. The principal reports according to type of data are:

1. Sales analysis.
2. Bookings, billings, and backlog report.
3. Bookings, billings, and backlog analysis.
4. Salesmen's performance report.
5. Selling expense analysis.

1. *Sales analysis.* The principal control report, after the profit and loss statement, is the analysis of sales. This type of report is prepared in many different forms according to the needs of the company. Generally, however, sales data are broken down according to (1) product, (2) territory, (3) salesman, (4) branch, (5) store, and (6) customer.

Very often, the report will be arranged to combine several different factors—for example, sales by product, by type of customer, and by territory. In order to evaluate the extent of price fluctuations, physical units are shown along with dollar amounts. Actual sales are compared with established quotas and past performance.

2. *Bookings, billings, and backlog report.* In practically all companies it is desirable to prepare a daily report reflecting sales operations. Shipping or

PROFIT AND LOSS STATEMENT
MONTH OF APRIL 19__

	Month				Year to Date			
	Amount		% of Sales		Amount		% of Sales	
	Actual	*Budget*	*Act.*	*Bud.*	*Actual*	*Budget*	*Act.*	*Bud.*
Sales	$	$			$	$		
Gross	595,000	625,000			2,453,271	2,500,000		
Less: Returns, etc.	25,000	25,000			103,271	100,000		
Net sales	570,000	600,000	100.00	100.00	2,350,000	2,400,000	100.00	100.00
Cost of Sales								
Material	189,297	192,000	33.21	32.00	763,400	756,240	32.48	31.51
Labor	121,695	120,000	21.35	20.00	489,063	498,000	20.81	20.75
Overhead	91,599	90,000	16.07	15.00	383,718	386,880	16.33	16.12
Total	402,591	402,000	70.63	67.00	1,636,181	1,641,120	69.62	68.38
Standard gross profit	167,409	198,000	29.37	33.00	713,819	758,880	30.38	31.62
Variances—material —usage	15,000		2.64		65,000		2.77	
" —price	10,000		1.76		(38,000)		(1.61)	
" —labor —efficiency	5,000		.88		21,000		.89	
" —rate	2,000		.35		9,000		.38	
" —overhead—volume	(15,000)		(2.64)		(30,000)		(1.28)	
" —price	3,000		.52		8,000		.34	
Total	20,000	—	3.51	—	35,000	—	1.49	—
Gross profit	147,409	198,000	25.86	33.00	678,819	758,880	28.89	31.62

Fig. 6. Condensed Profit and Loss Statement.

PROFIT AND LOSS STATEMENT [Continued]
MONTH OF APRIL 19__

	Amount		% of Sales		Year to Date			
					Amount		% of Sales	
	Actual	Budget	Act.	Bud.	Actual	Budget	Act.	Bud.
	$	$			$	$		
Operating Expenses								
Administration	6,250	6,000	1.10	1.00	26,500	25,000	1.13	1.04
Selling	12,475	12,000	2.19	2.00	53,708	50,000	2.29	2.08
Advertising	20,150	19,000	3.54	3.17	79,814	75,000	3.40	3.12
Research and development	8,750	9,000	1.53	1.50	32,373	35,000	1.37	1.47
Total	47,625	46,000	8.36	7.67	192,395	185,000	8.19	7.71
Operating Profit	99,784	152,000	17.50	25.33	486,424	573,880	20.70	23.91
Income Credits	30,000	15,000	5.27	2.50	78,411	70,000	3.34	2.91
	129,784	167,000	22.77	27.83	564,835	643,880	24.04	26.83
Income Charges	5,000	10,000	.88	1.66	48,719	50,000	2.08	2.09
Profit Before Fed. Inc. Taxes	124,784	157,000	21.89	26.17	516,116	593,880	21.96	24.74
Provision for Fed. Inc. Tax	60,000	75,000	10.53	12.50	248,000	300,000	10.55	12.50
Net Profit	64,784	82,000	11.37	13.67	268,116	293,880	11.41	12.24
Units Sold—M	4,283	4,444			18,415	17,777		
Average Price	13.31	13.50			13.35	13.50		

Fig. 6. Condensed Profit and Loss Statement. (Continued.)

billing data are usually accompanied by booking and backlog information. This is generally arranged to show, by product, the bookings and billing data for *today, this month to date,* and *last month to date.* The backlog data are usually shown for *today* and for *same day last month.*

3. *Bookings, billings, and backlog analysis.* Booking and backlog data are particularly important for control purposes and for scheduling future operations. For example, an analysis of billing and backlog data can reveal that special energies must be directed to one area to achieve a balance of products. The analysis might also indicate a future bottleneck in one part of the factory and idle capacity in another part.

4. *Salesmen's performance report.* In order for the sales manager to effectively supervise the salesmen responsible to him, it is necessary that he have data concerning individual sales efforts. This is usually done by means of a weekly or monthly salesmen's performance report that shows budgeted and actual direct expenses incurred by each salesman. Further control data is provided when the standard gross profit is shown on the form; in this way, the individual salesman's contribution towards profits is shown more directly. Thus, efforts are measured not on volume alone, but on *profitable* volume. Figure 7 illustrates the type of report used in many companies.

5. *Selling expense analysis.* Another control report that is of value to the sales manager is an analysis of direct sales expense by product and by type of customer. The direct charges are obtained by product and the indirect or general expenses are then applied in order to arrive at the total product selling expense.

Sales expense can also be analyzed by the type of expense. Thus, for the given period, the actual expense is compared to budgeted expense and actual expense for preceding periods. Generally, this type of report is prepared monthly as a part of the operating reports.

Production department reports. There is a wide variety of production data that may be presented in many different types of reports. Generally, these data are reported on two bases: (1) totals by departments; and (2) totals by type of expense for all departments. When standards are used, it is common to include an analysis of variations from these standards.

Since there is a broad range of responsibility from the division manager to the section manager, production reports are needed for each level of responsibility. Therefore, the reports usually fall into the following general classes:

1. Cost summaries by:
   a. Division.
   b. Factory.
   c. Department.
2. Analyses by cost element:
   a. Material.
   b. Labor.
   c. Overhead.

SALESMAN'S PERFORMANCE REPORT

DIVISION A | Month of April 19__

	Sales				*Gross Profit*				*Expenses*			
	Amount		*% of Sales*		*Amount*		*% of Sales*		*Amount*		*% of Sales*	
Salesman	$ *Actual*	$ *Budget*	*Act.*	*Bud.*	$ *Actual*	$ *Budget*	*Act.*	*Bud.*	$ *Actual*	$ *Budget*	*Act.*	*Bud.*
Baird	73,435	95,000	12.9	15.8	18,415	32,000	25.1	33.7	3,838	2,500	5.2	2.6
Hamburg	55,250	55,000	9.7	9.2	19,565	22,000	35.4	40.0	978	1,000	1.8	1.8
Harter	45,525	100,000	8.0	16.7	19,475	24,000	42.8	24.0	3,281	2,200	7.2	2.4
Johnson	87,475	75,000	15.3	12.5	30,315	30,000	34.7	40.0	478	900	.6	1.2
Knowles	85,375	85,000	15.0	14.2	22,465	23,000	26.3	27.0	1,283	1,500	1.5	1.7
Reed	95,425	75,000	16.7	12.5	20,875	27,000	21.9	36.0	775	1,800	.8	2.4
Smith	68,950	65,000	12.1	10.8	17,721	19,000	25.7	29.2	978	1,200	1.4	1.8
Straus	58,565	50,000	10.3	8.3	18,578	21,000	31.7	42.0	864	900	1.5	1.8
Total	570,000	600,000	100.0	100.0	167,409	198,000	29.4	33.0	12,475	12,000	2.2	2.0

Fig. 7. Salesman's Performance Report.

1a. *Cost summary by division.* Where a number of plants are grouped into a division, a cost summary is prepared to show the production costs for those factories responsible to the division manager. Comparisons are ordinarily made of individual plant costs for the purpose of localizing areas in which corrective action should be taken.

1b. *Cost summary by factory.* The factory manager has the responsibility for all production departments in the factory; therefore, the factory report is a summary of all factory costs. Generally, the production costs are shown by the various departments through which the products pass. Actual costs are compared with standards, and significant variances are analyzed. Figure 8 is a type of summary often used in the factory.

FACTORY COST SUMMARY BY EXPENSE CLASSIFICATION

Month of April 19__

	Month			*Year to Date*		
(Stated in dollars)	*Actual*	*Standard*	*Gain or (Loss)*	*Actual*	*Standard*	*Gain or (Loss)*
CONTROLLABLE						
Material						
Raw material into production	168,637	165,000	(3,637)	700,431	640,000	(60,431)
Usage variance	15,160	—	(15,160)	36,015	—	(36,015)
Total material	183,797	165,000	(18,797)	736,446	640,000	(96,446)
Labor—Direct						
Performance	109,195	108,000	(1,195)	425,815	432,000	6,185
Efficiency variance	5,000	—	(5,000)	18,000	—	(18,000)
Rate variance	2,000	—	(2,000)	6,000	—	(6,000)
Overtime premium	10,500	10,000	(500)	31,500	40,000	8,500)
Total direct labor	126,695	118,000	(8,695)	481,315	472,000	(9,315)
Overhead						
Salaries and wages	44,448	45,000	552	196,715	180,000	(16,715)
Maintenance	15,615	15,000	(615)	85,244	60,000	(25,244)
Supplies	12,465	12,000	(465)	70,415	48,000	(22,415)
Social security taxes	1,631	1,600	(31)	5,861	6,400	539
Provision for vacation	2,200	2,400	200	8,433	9,600	1,167
	76,359	76,000	(359)	366,668	304,000	(62,668)
Volume variance	(15,000)	—	15,000	(50,000)	—	50,000
Price variance	3,000	—	(3,000)	10,000	—	(10,000)
Total overhead	64,359	76,000	11,641	326,668	304,000	(22,668)
TOTAL CONTROLLABLE	374,851	359,000	(15,851)	1,544,429	1,416,000	(128,429)
NONCONTROLLABLE						
Material price variance	15,500	—	(15,500)	65,000	—	(65,000)
Fixed charges	28,500	28,000	(500)	115,000	112,000	(3,000)
Total noncontrollable	44,000	28,000	(16,000)	180,000	112,000	(68,000)
GRAND TOTAL	418,851	387,000	(31,851)	1,724,429	1,528,000	(196,429)

Fig. 8. Factory Cost Summary.

1c. *Cost summary by department.* Each department head receives regular reports according to his responsibility. These reports compare the actual cost charged to his department with standards or with the budget. Generally, expenses the foreman can control are separated from those that are fixed. This separation of variable expenses provides an excellent picture of the effect of volume on profits. Various graphic presentations can be developed, such as a chart of the breakeven point and the curve of variable costs.

2a. *Analyses by cost element—material.* Material usage—that is, the amount actually used as compared to what should have been used according to standard specifications—is a significant control factor. The number of units of good production and the number of units of scrap are also important. Other significant data are the total units received, the average cost per unit, and the quantity and value of the closing inventory. Where standards are used, appropriate data such as material consumption and price variances should be reported.

2b. *Analyses by cost element—labor.* The number of direct and indirect employees, the direct and indirect total wages paid, and the amount of overtime premium paid, along with total direct and indirect hours, are important for measuring efficiency. Information as to lost time due to absenteeism and lateness should also be reported. The variance accounts, such as number of production hours lost because of below-standard operation and the dollar variance due to higher rates than standard, have significance for control purposes. Figure 9 illustrates one type of *direct labor summary*.

DIRECT LABOR SUMMARY

PERIOD: April 19__

Department	*Units Reported*	*Total Hours*			*Variance Due to*			
		Actual	*Standard*	*Variance*	*Low Product.*	*Machine Break.*	*Lack of Material*	*Employee Training*
		$	$	$	$	$	$	$
A	5,561	4,500	4,000	500		300	200	
B	4,675	9,180	10,000	(820)	(920)	100		
C	16,451	12,804	13,000	(196)	(196)			
D	17,813	11,617	9,747	1,870	1,270	200	300	100
		38,101	36,747	1,354	154	600	500	100

Fig. 9. Direct Labor Summary.

2c. *Analysis by cost element—overhead.* As the investment in machinery and equipment increases, there is a corresponding increase in depreciation, maintenance, power, and similar expenses. And as competition becomes keener, it is necessary to have closer control of both quantity and quality. This has brought about an increase of staff departments for such functions as production control, material control, and quality control.

Overhead may be grouped into two general classes—*fixed* and *variable*. Variable or semi-variable costs, generally, vary directly with volume, while fixed costs do not. Therefore, variable costs can be applied to operating period with reasonable accuracy, while fixed costs must be assigned by more arbitrary methods. The responsibility for variable costs rests largely with production heads; fixed costs are usually the responsibility of general management.

► DIRECT COSTING: Greater emphasis is being placed on the segregation of fixed and variable expenses because of the increased use of direct costing. Under the direct costing concept, variable manufacturing costs are applied to the product and fixed costs are applied to income during the period when incurred.

SPECIAL REPORTS

Often, special reports are needed to supplement or follow-up the regular reports. In other instances, a special report may result from an assignment to provide information on a matter upon which a decision must be reached.

Short-term reports. A short-term report is designed to provide answers to specific questions. Examples of the types of short-term reports that are frequently prepared are:

1. Cost studies.
2. Inventory studies.
3. Return on capital report.

1. *Cost studies.* This is the most common area for special reports. Extensive studies of material, labor, or overhead are frequently necessary. Product studies, comparison of cost elements, and similar analyses are also required. These reports are prepared in order to reveal to management why an expected result did not materialize.

► EXAMPLE: Management may want to know why actual costs are exceeding estimated costs. To do this, it might be necessary to make a further study of cost variances to ascertain the particular order or product with which the variance is identifiable.

2. *Inventory studies.* Since questions arise that require an entirely different emphasis from month to month, there are many aspects of inventory control that cannot be effectively presented in a regular report. For example, if the regular reports show that there has been a slow inventory turnover for the period, it might be necessary to pinpoint the class of inventory and even the specific items that caused the slow turnover. Sometimes quantitative data will be sufficient, but frequently it must be supplemented by dollar amounts. In another instance, management may want to know the carrying cost of inventory, requiring information as to storage cost, inventory cost, financing cost,

and the like. Then again, the effect of a change in inventory valuation—from FIFO to LIFO, for example—might have to be analyzed.

3. *Return on capital report.* The return on the investment of capital is a valuable gauge or measure with which to evaluate the performance of division or unit managers. If the return in a particular division or unit is too low, then it may be more profitable to employ those funds in some other manner. However, various factors have to be considered in order to maintain reasonable standards among the different units. For example, if the productive capacities are comparable, the gross fixed asset might be the most equitable base. In other cases, the net book value may be more equitable. Also, the degree of control allowed the manager should be taken into account, because each division or unit manager should be charged only with the capital investment and expenses over which he has direct control. A good way to reduce the need for arbitrary allocation is to set up the accounts to show capital invested and expenses by unit, so that charges may be made direct to the unit. Thus, if the unit is responsible for inventory but purchasing is controlled from headquarters, the unit manager will not be held accountable for any excess inventory included in capital that is the direct responsibility of headquarters.

► EXAMPLE: Management sometimes controls divisional production from divisional headquarters by allocating orders to individual plants according to the overall benefit that will accrue to the company. Therefore, materials are purchased to meet production requirements that are based on a decision by higher management.

Figure 10 is a type of return on capital report that is often used.

RETURN ON CAPITAL REPORT

April 19__

Capital Factors	*Plant Number* #1	#2	#3
		(Stated in Dollars)	
1. Capital invested	1,000	1,500	2,000
2. Sales	2,000	1,000	500
3. Net earnings	200	120	100
Earnings			
% on capital	20.0	8.0	5.0
% on sales	10.0	12.0	20.0
Turnover			
Sales/capital	2.0	.67	.25

Fig. 10. Return on Capital Report.

Long-term reports. This group includes reports covering a three-year, five-year, ten-year, or even a longer period. Obviously, long-term trends and patterns are particularly important. Information of this nature can often be best presented in a chart.

Examples of long-term reports are:

1. Three-year cash projection.
2. Five-year capital budget.
3. Long-term product trend.

1. *Three-year cash projection.* A long-term cash projection is now accepted as an important tool in fully utilizing available funds. Unless close review is made of the cash requirements, it is likely that a less than adequate return will be obtained. And with the present day trend toward a minimum amount of cash working funds, it is vital that the cash needs be anticipated well in advance. This is especially true in cases where financing is required to carry normally high seasonal inventories. The three-year cash projection is also required when a more permanent method of financing is under consideration.

2. *Five-year capital budget.* The long-term capital budget is an important factor in the long-range planning of every company, especially industrial companies that must make heavy expenditures for property, plant, and equipment. Future requirements must be known in order to provide adequate long-term financial planning.

This budget should be closely coordinated with the annual capital budget. Certain capital items can be transferred to the current annual budget as funds become available.

3. *Long-term product trend.* The long-term activity of a product or group of products is generally best shown by some form of visual presentation that eliminates the need for a great amount of detail. The units may be stated as percentages, sales dollars, quantities sold, produced, registered, etc. For example, a chart for a product may show for a ten-year period the percentage of the total market that the product receives each year. The trend may also be expressed in sales dollars, tons produced, units registered, or other pertinent units.

TECHNIQUES FOR DESIGNING AN EFFECTIVE REPORTING SYSTEM

The first section discussed in a general way the fundamental aspects of reporting, or what might be more aptly described as the objectives and problems that must be kept in mind when planning the installation of a reporting system. It will be the purpose of this section to provide methods of attaining these objectives and overcoming the problems. The Appendix to this chapter consists of a check-list that summarizes all the major techniques as covered in the text and adds a number of other useful procedures, thus furnishing complete coverage.

We will consider:

1. Action reports.
2. Visual presentation.

Action reports. As management's need to exercise control over an operation increases, the need for convenient, effective tools, such as action reports, increases proportionately. Action reports may be defined as *those reports that motivate management to take prompt corrective action.* Therefore, such reports differ substantially from purely historical reports in purpose, content, and timing. Following are some of the major methods of developing a system of action reports:

1. *Use significant figures.* The figures that are most significant to the recipient of the report should be emphasized. These significant figures may be volume, rate, or dollar information indicating performance. Very often these reports will supplement or confirm what the supervisor already feels or suspects. Therefore, the facts can be presented briefly and with a minimum of descriptive data.

Included in the category of significant figures are performance indicators, cost indexes, personnel statistics, inventory analyses, and similar data. Certain elements of cost may have more significance, depending on the nature of the business. For example, if labor is a high percentage of cost, various kinds of significant figures relating to direct and indirect labor performance should be provided.

2. *Relate the figures to standards of performance.* In order that management can know when performance is below normal, it is necessary to have a yardstick by which to measure the performance. With such a yardstick, it is not necessary to spend time investigating performance that is normal or expected —such efforts can be directed to off-standard performance. Thus, the *principle of exception* is used and the greatest effort is applied to the exceptions.

It is common practice to show such data as standard allowance, standard hours, and efficiency ratings as part of the report. With the great advances made in electronic equipment in recent years, many of the detailed computations can now be carried out by machine. In fact, in some cases, control reports that may not have been feasible formerly can now be prepared on the computer.

3. *Report to lowest appropriate level of supervision.* Because of the growth of decentralization and the shifting of responsibility to a lower level, it is esssential that information be provided from the first line of supervision to the top management level. If certain action can be taken by the foreman, he must be provided with the necessary information to take such action. If the foreman has the responsibility for taking the necessary action, the plant manager should not be called upon to do it.

Thus, the foreman may take action where the production is not up to standard, where employees are absent, or where scrap is excessive. To carry out his responsibility, he must be provided with information as to where in particular the production is deficient, by section, unit, and individual. It is important that such information be provided promptly.

4. *Use available methods of speeding-up the reporting cycle*. As we have previously indicated, reports tend to decrease in effectiveness in direct proportion to the time taken in preparation. Important information and a good system of reports may be rendered useless because of an inefficient method of report preparation.

Various means have been developed in recent years to meet the need for a speed-up in action reports. In some cases, electronic data processing has helped to get reports out faster. An early cut-off date and the use of standard or direct costs are other devices that can reduce the preparation time. It may even be necessary to review and overhaul the entire accounting system so that the underlying information will be provided promptly in the form required for the report.

But one of the most prevalent and effective methods in use today is the *flash report,* which is made available a day or two after closing. The flash report, of course, lacks the detail of a final statement, but it gives management a quick picture of the result of operations for the period. Action can then be taken much sooner and, consequently, much more effectively.

► How to Do It: Sales data are based on actual sales, while the cost of sales is estimated to the degree necessary. The figures are rounded, making the report more valuable on an overall, quick-action basis. Comparisons are made with the budget or with actual results for prior periods. Although balance sheet accounts could be shown on a flash basis, it is seldom practical or necessary to do so as many of the key figures (cash, accounts receivable, etc.) are available in subsidiary records.

Further reports showing in more detail the results of operations by department, plant, or division should follow the flash report within a few days. Even in a large company, it is possible to get a very effective picture no later than five working days after closing.

5. *Gear the accounting system for reporting*. In order that action reports can be prepared accurately and promptly, the accounting system must be geared to such preparation. It is important to remember that the primary purpose of the accounting system is to facilitate the flow of the necessary data from the records into the various management reports. Therefore, records are a means to an end, not the end in itself. The records must be organized and operated so that the required information can be assembled and reported in the quickest possible time. For example, if labor efficiency is falling, it is essential that management know about it promptly. The system, then, should be designed for the benefit of management, not the accounting department.

► Observation: The report that the accounting system issues is its product, just as a product results from the operations of other departments. So the judgment of management as to the quality of the accounting system depends on the kind of report the system produces. This is especially true for action reports since so many nonaccounting people will be involved. There have been many good accounting systems that were greatly underrated because of the poor quality of the action reports issued. On the other hand, even a mediocre system that nevertheless produces well-planned action reports can make the various levels of management conscious of effective control tools. Often, a supervisor will find such an action report indispensable in controlling his operation.

Visual presentation. Charts and graphs are a very effective means of presenting data to management in a simple, clear, and convenient form. Often, more meaning can be conveyed to the reader by means of a chart than by any other form of report. Physical perspective that cannot be shown by figures alone can be accomplished by a visual presentation. Various changes, movements, and relationships can effectively be shown by charts, especially where large amounts of data are involved. A wide swing of a line or the concurrent movement of two lines on a chart is often far more meaningful than the same data shown by figures only.

Every accountant should keep these points in mind when he is considering the presentation of data to management. However, it should be pointed out that some executives may not be familiar with charts and some of the effectiveness of the visual presentation may be lost. Again, charts may sometimes be very complicated, especially where three or more variables are shown on the chart. As far as possible, a simple presentation should be used at the beginning until the particular executives understand the advantages of visual presentation.

The principal advantages of a visual presentation may be summarized as follows:

1. *Saves executive time.* The time of the executive is saved since the essential points in large amounts of statistical data can be readily seen.
2. *Easier to remember.* Relationships shown visually are generally easier to remember.
3. *Creates interest.* Well-designed charts generally create interest and have more appeal to the reader than other forms.
4. *More comprehensive.* A more comprehensive and understandable presentation of two or more relationships can be shown by the use of charts than by the tabular or textual form.
5. *Stimulates analysis.* Charts and graphs help to stimulate analysis and to bring out hidden facts and relationships.

A wide variety of charts is now being used to meet a wide range of needs. There are also a great many ways of classifying charts—for example: those that relate to time and those that relate to other factors; also, those that use an arithmetic scale and those that use a ratio scale. These and other bases of classification are fully described in various standard texts on the subject.

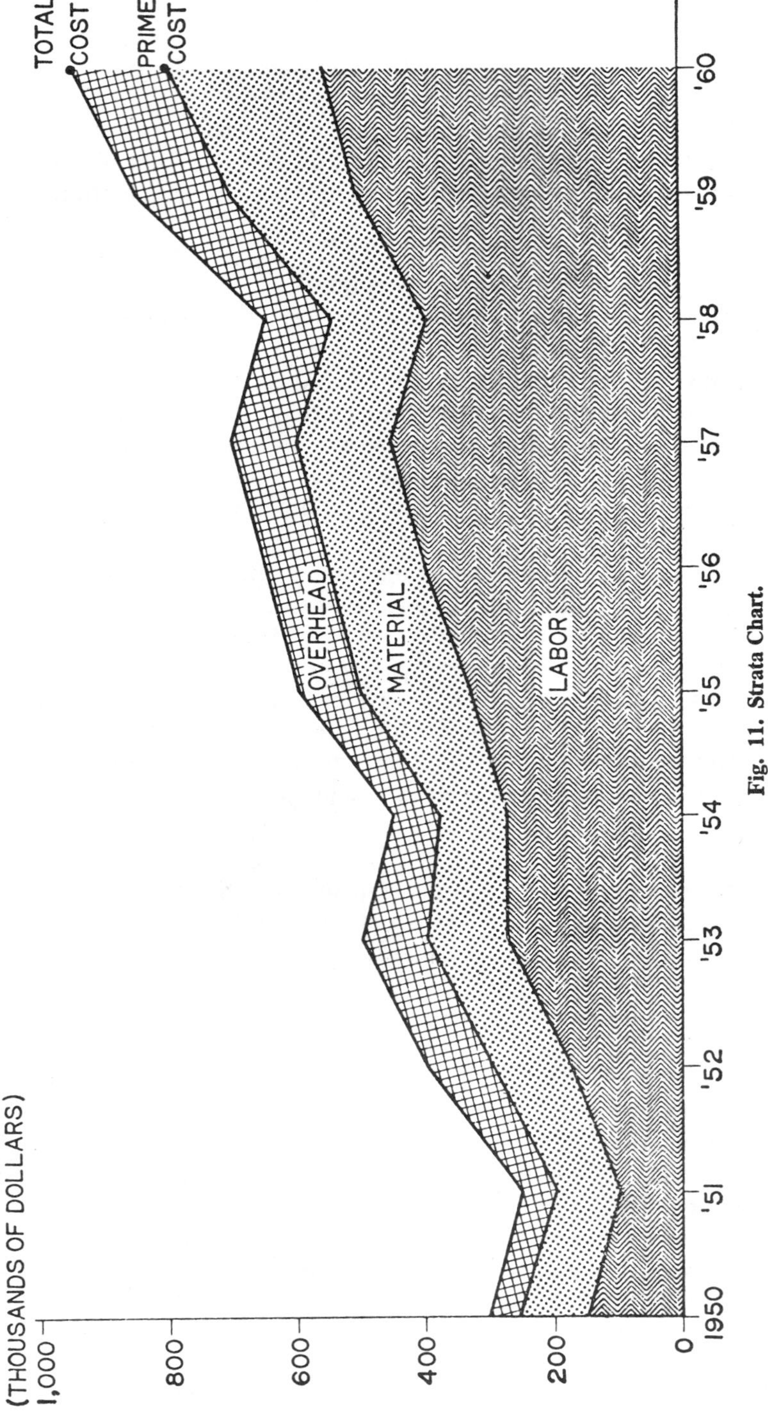

Fig. 11. Strata Chart.

For our purposes it is more useful to discuss the principal types of charts that have proven to be most effective in presenting information to management. Following are the types of charts most commonly used for this purpose:

1. *Line chart.* The most widely used chart for presenting data to management is the line chart. This chart may be prepared as a *simple line chart,* or as a *strata chart* (see Figure 11) of two or more horizontal lines to show several factors. The line chart is most frequently used to show changes and variations occurring with time. For example, sales may be shown by means of a line drawn across regular intervals of a time series represented by weeks, months, years, etc. Line charts are satisfactory for most presentation of figures except where the figures are of such different values that significant comparisons are difficult. In such cases the figures can be converted to index numbers or percentages that permit a direct comparison of two distinct series of figures. While this commonly-used chart, ruled on the arithmetic scale, meets most needs, it is not as suitable for some purposes, such as percentage comparison, as the semilogarithmic scale chart.

2. *Semilogarithmic chart.* This is a form of ratio chart in which the hozizontal ruling is equally spaced or arithmetic, but the vertical ruling is spaced according to the logarithms of numbers, similar to slide rule spacing. This chart is especially suitable where two or more widely varying series of numbers are to be plotted.

The logarithmic ruling shows the *relative* change or *rate* of change rather than the change in absolute values shown by the arithmetic scale. For example, on the logarithmic scale the distance between 100 and 200 is the same as the distance between 1,000 and 2,000 since the ratio is the same.

The semilogarithmic chart is particularly effective when two related series of data such as production and scrap are plotted. The built-in ratio feature can readily show that scrap moves up and down faster than production. In other words, the *percentage* of scrap increases faster than the rate of *increase* of production. Figure 12 is an example of a semilogarithmic chart.

3. *Bar chart.* The bar chart is essentially a line chart except that the lines are vertical rather than horizontal. This form is convenient for comparison of absolute quantities. It also has the advantage of easy preparation. Generally, the bars represent total amounts. However, it is becoming more common to show two or more separate components within each bar.

4. *Pie chart.* The pie or circle chart shows relationship to a total that is pictured as a whole pie or circle. The pie is divided into sectors, each of which represents a slice or component of the total. Frequently the pie chart is used to show the percentage distribution of the total without showing the total amount. For example, the distribution of the sales dollar is shown as so many cents each for salaries and wages, materials and supplies, taxes, dividends, and retained earnings.

5. *Scatter chart.* The scatter chart is frequently used to show the relationship between two variables. The time factor is not important here as it is in

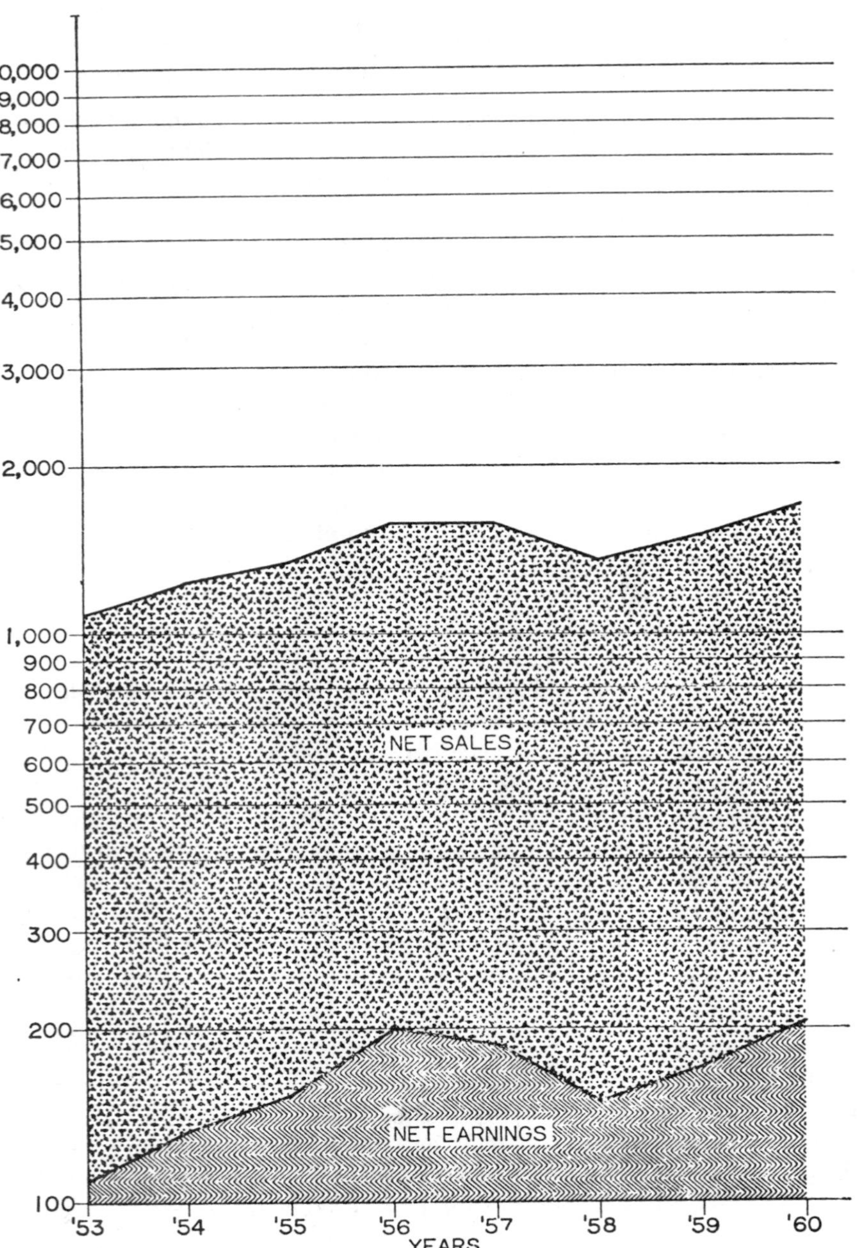

Fig. 12. Semilogarithmic Chart.

most of the other types of charts we have discussed. Thus, the relationship between monthly direct labor hours and dollars of clerical expense may be charted. One of the principal purposes of the scatter chart is to show whether there is, or is not, a definite correlation between two variable factors. This type of chart is especially useful in presenting cost information to management.

6. *Special purpose charts.* In addition to the basic charts, there are a wide range of special purpose charts that are especially suited to a particular purpose. Examples are the *break even chart, the profit control chart,* the *Gantt chart,* the *profit graph,* and the *fixed and variable cost chart.*

Checklist for Better Reports

A. *Suit report to recipient.*
   1. Find out what management wants and what they can digest. Is management oriented towards figures and accounting?
   2. The language and terms used should be familiar to the recipient. For example, operating terms such as "machine hours" are more significant than financial terms to production personnel.
   3. Relate amount of detail to responsibility. More detail for the lower levels of management; summarized data for the upper levels.
   4. Data should cover a period to meet the needs of the recipient.

B. *Make reports timely.*
   1. Determine whether reports should be made daily, weekly, or monthly.
   2. Control reports, such as for spoilage, should generally be daily.
   3. Long-term analyses and trends are usually monthly, quarterly, or annually.
   4. Combine two reports where possible.

C. *Make system flexible.*
   1. Revise reports as conditions change.
   2. Emphasis must be changed as needed.
   3. Change in management may require change.
   4. Special reports may be included when necessary.
   5. Set expiration dates for special reports.

D. *Include only essential data.*
   1. Keep in mind the purpose of the report.
   2. Emphasize important elements.
   3. Be sure that sufficient facts are provided.
   4. Eliminate unnecessary detail.
   5. Group less important items into significant totals.
   6. Regular reports should minimize need for special reports.

E. *Standardize presentation, forms, etc.*

1. Style of presentation should be consistent.
2. Provide standard binder, properly titled.
3. Size of form should fit conveniently into binder.
4. Color can be used to differentiate reports.
5. Forms and paper should be uniform.
6. Use tabs for easy reference.
7. Use uniform page sequence.
8. Use uniform column headings.

F. *Issue reports earlier.*

1. Make flash reports when practical.
2. Issue more important reports first.
3. Organize accounting system to expedite reports.
4. Set definite time schedule for underlying data.
5. Make earlier cut-offs.
6. Use direct costing and standards.
7. Prepare certain data during slow periods.
8. Issue rough drafts and pencil copies for top management.
9. Use mechanical methods of duplication.
10. Use preprinted headings, titles, and comparative data.
11. Release as prepared rather than waiting for full set.

G. *Pinpoint responsibility.*

1. Determine responsibility area of each recipient.
2. Report should relate facts to responsibility.
3. Individual responsibility should be apparent.
4. Charge controllable costs to responsibility area.
5. Uncontrollable costs should be separately shown.

H. *Keep reports accurate.*

1. Reports must present facts.
2. The facts must be accurate.
3. Specify source of data.
4. Reports to all levels should tie in.
5. Avoid extreme accuracy in details.

I. *Simplify and clarify.*

1. State facts concisely.
2. Arrange data in logical sequence.
3. Report should stand by itself.
4. Avoid technical language.
5. Explain and interpret significant data.
6. Omit complicated statements.
7. Use short titles.
8. Use guide lines, capitals, and indentations.

9. Eliminate cents, dollar signs, and commas.
10. Round off excessive decimal places.
11. Avoid prorates where possible.

J. *Show comparisons, ratios, and trends.*
1. Compare current and cumulative data to last year.
2. Compare actuals with standards and budgets.
3. Utilize principle of exception.
4. Classify increases or decreases as favorable or unfavorable.
5. Show unfavorable amounts in red. Explain large variances.
6. Develop ratios and percentage data; relate expenses to sales.
7. Relate investment to operations.
8. Compare data with industry trend.
9. Compare data with general economic trend.

K. *Use visual aids.*
1. Visual presentation conserves time of executives.
2. Relationships and trends may be shown more clearly than by statistical presentation.
3. Consider advantages of each type of chart: (a) Line (b) Semi-logarithmic (c) Scatter (d) Bar (e) Pie.
4. Visual aids may be used to supplement reports.
5. Use trend indicators—daily, weekly, to date, etc.

L. *Consider cost.*
1. Reports should be regular part of accounting process.
2. Carefully consider cost of special art work, etc.
3. Examine amount of time required in gathering data for various reports—make sure cost is justified.
4. Avoid duplication of effort where report covers same data but prepared from different sources.
5. Investigate alternative methods of presentation, reproduction, etc., to reduce costs.

M. *Control distribution.*
1. Distribution should include person responsible for the activity.
2. Don't overload any one person with reports. Tendency will then be to ignore them all.
3. Fix responsibility for control of distribution.
4. Additions to distribution list should be properly approved.
5. Keep distribution list up to date.

21

Quantitative Methods in Accounting

CONTENTS

21

Quantitative Methods in Accounting

Frank J. Fabozzi, Ph.D.

The prevailing attitude by some accountants is that the application of mathematical techniques to accounting is too abstract to deal with "real world" accounting problems. Some accountants have even referred to management science as "management science fiction."

However, although fears may have been warranted, such fears can be removed once accountants realize two important facts. First, the basic nature of the quantitative approach is systemic rather than mathematical. The essence of quantitative models is to reflect managerial problems, and not to be mathematical. Second, one of the key individuals in a management science staff is the accountant. It is this individual who can convey the problem to the management scientist. Once the management scientist believes that an appropriate model has been formulated, it is the accountant who must verify that all factors were properly considered and if modifications of the model are necessary. Accountants need not know the necessary mathematics for determining the optimum solution to such models just as the management scientist need not be an expert in accounting. What the accountant must know is what quantitative tools are available, how they can be applied, the limitations of each, and when to seek the aid of a management scientist.

The purpose of this survey is to highlight some of the mathematical techniques which have been applied to accounting problems. No attempt is made to provide mathematical rigor or cover all management science techniques. The mathematics, and resulting theorems, is deeper and more abstruse than the material covered in this survey, and it will not be possible to elaborate on the full implications of each technique.

THE METHODOLOGY OF MANAGEMENT SCIENCE

For all business problems management must determine some course of action to be taken. There are several courses of action or alternative decisions that are available to the decision maker. The decision maker will generally try to choose that decision which would best realize the goal or objective set by management. Hence, it would be valuable to examine the possible consequences of each alternative decision in advance.

The consequences or outcomes of a decision depends not only on controllable factors available to the decision maker but also the environment or states of nature which cannot be controlled by the decision maker. For example, if the decision maker is trying to determine which capital investment projects should be undertaken, the consequence of the decision will depend on future economic conditions since such conditions will determine the future cash flows for each project and therefore the rate of return earned on the project. Of course, the decision maker has no control over future economic conditions.

Forecasting and good judgment can aid the decision maker in reducing the uncertainty about the environment or states of nature. Nevertheless, there still exists alternative decisions that must be analyzed for each possible environment that could exist. For example, if the decision maker in the previous example believes that the four possible states of nature or environments are recession, no economic growth, moderate economic growth and economic boom then each capital investment project must be analyzed for each environment.

Using the outcome matrix. This procedure can be conceptualized by using an outcome matrix or outcome table. Figure 1 provides an illustration of this table. The top row of this table shows the different environments or states of nature that the decision maker believes could exist. In the table it is assumed that there are m possible environments or states of nature. In the first column the alternative decisions or courses of action are presented. There are n such alternatives assumed. Each cell in the table represents the outcome or consequence of a decision for the environment at the top of the column.

The outcomes could be measured as profits, costs or opportunity losses. If the outcomes were measured as dollar profits the table would be referred to as a pay-off

Alternative Decisions (X_i)	Alternative Environments or States of Nature (Y_j)		
	Y_1	$Y_2 \ldots$	$Y_j \ldots Y_m$
X_1	E_{11}	$E_{12} \ldots$	$E_{ij} \ldots E_{1m}$
X_2	E_{21}	$E_{22} \ldots$	$E_{2j} \ldots E_{2m}$
.	.	.	. .
.	.	.	. .
.	.	.	. .
X_i	E_{i1}	$E_{i2} \ldots$	$E_{ij} \ldots E_{im}$
.	.	.	. .
.	.	.	. .
.	.	.	. .
X_n	E_{n1}	$E_{n2} \ldots$	$E_{nj} \ldots E_{nm}$

E_{ij} = expected outcome for decision i given environment j.

Fig. 1. Outcome Matrix.

table or pay-off matrix. The yardstick of performance employed to measure the outcome is called the *decision criteria.*

The primary contribution of management science is providing the decision maker with the outcome matrix. A function can be developed to show the relationship between the decision and environments, and the decision criteria. This formulation is referred to as a model. When expressed in mathematical terms it is called a mathematical model. If we let X_i be the decision made, Y_j the environment and E_{ij} the outcome we can write $E_{ij} = f(X_i/Y_j)$ which means the outcome E_{ij} is a function of (depends on) the decision made given the environment. (The "/" is used to denote the word "given.")

▶ EXAMPLE: Deciding how many cakes to order. Suppose that the manager of a retail store must decide on how many cakes to order at the beginning of the week for resale. Assume that for each cake sold a profit of \$.30 is realized, but for each cake not sold by the end of the week the price must be reduced by \$.40 so that the store realizes a loss of \$.10 on each such cake. (Assume that all cakes will eventually be sold.)

The manager of the store has estimated from sales over the past year that the demand per week for these cakes is never less than 100 cakes but never more than 500 cakes. Rather than considering the whole range of values between 100 and 500, let us restrict the environments to increments of 100 units. Also assume that the alternative decisions are to order in the same quantities.

Figure 2 presents the outcome matrix. In this problem the decision criteria has been selected to be profits measured in dollars. Hence Figure 2 is called a pay-off table or pay-off matrix.

A mathematical model that expresses the relationship between the states of nature or environments (Y_j, $j=1, \ldots, 5$) which represents the possible demands and the decision variable (X_i, $i=1, \ldots 5$) which represents the number of cakes ordered is:

$$E_{ij} = \$.3\, Y_j - \$.1\,(X_i - Y_j) \quad \text{if } Y_j < X_i$$
$$E_{ij} = \$.3\, X_i \quad \text{if } Y_j \geq X_i$$

OUTCOME MATRIX FOR CAKE ORDERING PROBLEM:
PAYOFF MATRIX

Alternative Decisions (X_i) [Number of cakes ordered]	Alternative environments (Y_j) [Number of cakes demanded]				
	(Y_1) 100	(Y_2) 200	(Y_3) 300	(Y_4) 400	(Y_5) 500
(X_1) 100	\$30	\$30	\$30	\$30	\$30
(X_2) 200	20	60	60	60	60
(X_3) 300	10	50	90	90	90
(X_4) 400	0	40	80	120	120
(X_5) 500	−10	30	70	110	150

Fig. 2. Outcome Matrix for Cake Ordering Problem.

For example, if 300 cakes are ordered (X_3) and demand turns out to be 200 cakes (Y_2) then the outcome is:

$$E_{32} = \$.3\,(200) - \$.1\,(300 - 200)$$
$$= \$50$$

If 300 cakes are ordered (X_3) but 400 cakes are demanded (Y_4) then the outcome is:

$$E_{34} = \$.3\,(300) = \$90$$

Note that in the last example the store lost the opportunity to earn $120 if 400 cakes had been ordered. Thus there was an opportunity loss of $30. Rather than use the decision criteria as profits, the decision criteria could have been the opportunity loss and the outcome matrix would have included such losses.

Four steps in setting up the outcome matrix. The management scientist goes through several steps in helping the decision maker in setting up the outcome matrix. Let us briefly discuss these steps.

First, the management scientist must understand the problem faced by the decision maker. In turn the management scientist must help orient the decision maker as to the restrictions imposed by the methodology.

Second, a decision criteria must be selected. This is not always as simple as it seems. Sometimes it may be difficult to quantify the decision criteria. Not-for-profit entities typically face this problem. Further, multiple objectives might be set and some of these objectives might even be conflicting objectives.

Third, the different states of nature or environments which can be expected to influence the outcome of a decision must be enumerated and then these factors must be described by a set of parameters. Forecasting techniques are useful in this phase. Depending on the environment we can distinguish three types of models. When the environment is known with certainty, that is, there is only one environment, then we have a *deterministic model*. In *stochastic* or *probabilistic models* alternative environments exist and the decision maker is assumed to be capable of assigning probabilities for the occurrence of each environment. If more than one environment exists but probabilities of occurrence cannot be assigned to the environment we have a *distribution free model*. Probability theory will be discussed in a later section.

Development of the decision alternatives or the courses of action the decision maker should consider is the *fourth* step. Once the four steps above are complete, the management scientist can construct the model or functional relationship between the decision criteria, the alternative environments and the alternative decisions. The cells in the outcome matrix can then be determined by solving the model for the decision variable. Some models can be simple to solve such as the model illustrated above. Yet, some models may involve complex computational techniques best handled by a computer.

SOME BASIC MATHEMATICS

The role of calculus. Most undergraduate accounting majors and graduate students in business take a course in basic calculus. What is the use of calculus in business decision-making? Because calculus deals with changes in variables, and more specifically, with the rate of change of variables, it can be used to help solve business problems in which the optimization of some function is sought. Moreover, incremental or marginal concepts are derived from certain "operations" on functions.

Calculus in inventory models. An explanation of the techniques of calculus will not be given here. Instead, an illustration of how calculus can be used to find the optimal value for a function will be presented.

Later we shall discuss inventory models. The basic objective of the inventory model is to minimize total inventory cost which in a simple deterministic model is made up of two costs. First, the total cost of carrying inventory such as the cost of capital, insurance and storage. Second, the total cost of ordering. Each of the two costs can be reduced separately if we are prepared to increase the other. For example, total ordering costs can be reduced by carrying a larger inventory and hence reducing the number of times it is necessary to reorder. On the other hand, total carrying costs can be reduced by ordering more frequently hence increasing total ordering costs. The objective is to find a balance between these two costs which minimizes the total inventory costs.

For a simple (deterministic) inventory problem, the expression for total inventory costs, which will be explained in more detail when inventory models are discussed, is:

$$C = \frac{SQ}{2} + \frac{AP}{Q}$$

where C = total inventory costs;
Q = number of units of the product ordered at each ordering;
P = ordering costs each time an order is placed;
S = carrying costs per unit, and;
A = number of units demanded over the time period.

The first expression on the right hand side of the equality represents the total carrying cost while the second expression represents the total ordering costs. Since the values for S, P and A are assumed to be known by the accountant, it can be seen that total inventory cost depends upon only one variable, Q, the number of units to order. The values S, P and A are referred to as parameters in this model, that is, they are fixed. The standard notation for the above expression is:

$$C = f(Q)$$

which is read as "total inventory cost is a function of the number of units ordered."

To find the value for Q which minimizes the above function, we would take the first "derivative" of the function, set it equal to zero, and then solve for the value(s) which satisfies the resulting equation. The mechanics of obtaining the derivative or equivalency, the process of differentiation is explained in calculus textbooks. For our purposes, it need only be understood that the first derivative of a function is the rate of change of the value of the function with respect to a change in the value of the variable. In the above function, the first derivative represents the rate of change for total inventory cost with respect to a change in the number of units ordered for a particular level of Q. When we refer to the rate of change of total inventory costs we are talking about incremental or marginal cost for a given change in the number of units ordered at each level of Q.

If the first derivative of the inventory model is taken, set equal to zero and solved, we have the familiar expression for the economic order quantity (EOQ):

$$\text{EOQ} = Q^* = \sqrt{\frac{2\,A\,P}{S}}$$

How do we know that the optimal value for Q, Q*, is the value which minimizes the function rather than maximizes it? A theorem from calculus assures us that if the second derivative of the function is a positive value at the point Q* then we have a minimum.

To illustrate how the "marginal" concept is developed from calculus suppose that the accountant estimates the relationship between cost and production as follows:

$$C = .50\,X + 40$$

where C represents total production cost and X the number of units produced. A technique for estimating such relationships will be discussed later.

In the above relationship, 40 represents the fixed cost. When 100 units of X are produced, the total cost is:

$$\begin{aligned} C &= .50\,(100) + 40 \\ &= 90 \end{aligned}$$

The average cost of producing a unit is then:

$$\text{average cost} = \frac{.50\,X + 40}{X}$$

Hence, if 100 units are produced the average cost is:

$$\begin{aligned} &= \frac{\$90}{100} \\ &= \$.90 \end{aligned}$$

The average cost represents the total cost distributed equally over all units produced. The marginal cost, on the other hand, is the additional cost of producing an additional unit. The marginal cost relationship for the cost function is found by taking the first derivative of the cost function which is:

$$\text{marginal cost} = .5$$

As can be seen, as production increases the marginal cost per unit remains constant. This implies that the variable cost per unit is unchanged with the level of output. In this case the marginal cost is $.50 per unit.

Calculus can be used to find the optimal value for a function if there are constraints or restrictions in the model as long as these constraints are represented by equalities, e.g., $X + Y = 50$. When inequality constraints or restrictions are imposed, e.g., $X + Y \leq 50$, then mathematical programming must be used. Mathematical programming will be discussed later on.

Probability theory–objective vs. subjective approach. In stochastic or probabilistic models probabilities of alternative environments must be estimated. Probabilities can be determined through objective or subjective analysis. The objectivist's approach to probability basically maintains that probabilities relate to long-run frequencies of occurrence. That is, the objective or *a priori* probability of an outcome or event can be defined as the relative frequency with which an event would occur given a large number of observations. The objectivist would assign a probability of 1/6 to the outcome or event that a value of "1" would appear if a fair die is rolled and a probability of 4/52 to the outcome or event that an ace of any suit would be drawn from a fair deck of 52 cards.

It is difficult in most business decisions to apply the objectivist approach. For example, suppose that a company is considering the expansion into a new product line such as when Union Carbide was considering whether to develop the laser for commercial application. Little data was available for determining development costs and specific applications. Hence, how could cash flow and rates of return probabilities be estimated for capital budgeting purposes? It is in such situations that the subjectivist approach to probability theory can be employed.

The subjective approach basically asserts that probabilities measure the decision maker's degree of belief in the likelihood of a given outcome. Hence this approach is very broad and flexible allowing probability assignments to outcomes for which no objective data may exist or for which there may be a combination of objective data and subjective belief.

Preliminary concepts in probability theory. Let us discuss some preliminary concepts in probability theory. The following holds regardless of whether the objective or subjective approach is taken.

Simple and compound events. Suppose an experiment is performed which involves tossing a fair die. There are then six possible outcomes: 1, 2, 3, 4, 5 or 6. Each of these outcomes is referred to as a simple event. The characteristic of a simple event is that it cannot be decomposed into other events. On the other hand, a compound event refers to an event which can be decomposed into simple events. For example, an outcome which defines an even number occurring when a fair die is tossed is a compound event since it can be decomposed into three simple events of getting a 2, 4 or 6.

Mutually exclusive events. If two events or outcomes have nothing in common they are referred to as mutually exclusive events. That is, if an experiment can result in only one of the two events occurring, then the events are mutually exclusive. For example, if in the experiment of tossing a die the probability of a 1 and a 2 occurring is zero. Both cannot appear simultaneously. Hence the events defining an outcome of 1 and an outcome of 2 are mutually exclusive.

Three basic postulates. Let us now consider the three basic postulates of probability theory.

(i) Given an experiment with n possible simple events or outcomes denoted by $E_1, E_2, \ldots, E_n$, a nonnegative number is assigned to each outcome and referred to as the probability of the outcome. This is denoted mathematically by:

$$P(E_i) \geq 0$$

(ii) The sum of the probabilities of all possible simple events is one, that is,

$$P(E_1) + P(E_2) + \ldots + P(E_n) = 1$$

and,

(iii) for two mutually exclusive events E_i and E_j the probability of either occurring is the sum of the two probabilities. That is,

$$P(E_i \text{ or } E_j) = P(E_i) + P(E_j)$$

Conditional probabilities. Conditional probabilities are probabilities obtained after the initial conditions have changed. For example, the probability of obtaining an ace if a card is selected from a fair deck of 52 cards is 4/52. However, suppose that you draw a card from the deck and it is not an ace. If you then select another card without replacing the original card in the deck, what is the probability of now obtaining an ace? The probability is now 4/51. This probability is a conditional probability since it is conditional on the withdrawal and nonreplacement of a card that is not an ace. In probability notation we denote the probability of some event E_i conditional on the occurrence of some other event E_j by $P(E_i/E_j)$.

Joint probabilities. Joint probabilities refer to the probability where more than one event occurs simultaneously. For example, suppose an experiment is performed which involves selecting a card from a deck and we define one event as selecting an ace and a second event as selecting a card which is a heart. Then the joint event of the two events defined above is selecting the ace of hearts. The probability of this joint event is 1/52. In probability notation the joint probability of two events E_i and E_j is denoted by $P(E_i \& E_j)$.

Statistically independent events. Two events are statistically independent if the occurrence of one does not effect the probability of the other. That is, suppose a fair coin is tossed twice. Define the first event as a head appearing on the first toss and the second event as a head appearing on the second toss. If a head does in fact appear on the first toss how does this affect the probability of obtaining a head on the second toss? It does not since we will still assign a probability of 1/2 to a head occurring on the second toss. Hence, the two events are statistically independent. When two events E_i and E_k are statistically independent then we can write:

$$P(E_i / E_k) = P(E_i) \quad \text{or} \quad P(E_k / E_i) = P(E_k)$$

Alternatively we can state that two events are statistically independent if the following holds:

$$P(E_i \& E_k) = P(E_i)\,P(E_k)$$

That is, if two events are statistically independent we can obtain the joint probability by multiplying the probabilities of the two events.

Rules for calculating conditional and joint probabilities in cases where statistical independence does not hold will not be given here. The interested reader can refer to an elementary statistics textbook to expand his or her knowledge of probability theory.

Bayesian decision theory. Suppose that we are going to make a decision utilizing a set of initial probabilities that were obtained through either the objective or subjective approach. But suppose that before we make our decision we somehow obtain additional information or data that is relevant to the problem at hand. That is, this information or data would affect the initial probabilities that we are using. How can this data be utilized to revise our initial probabilities?

An English Presbyterian minister and mathematician, Reverend Thomas Bayes (1702-1761), considered this problem. His theorem, known as Bayes' Theorem, provides a formula for revising initial probabilities. A considerable body of literature known as Bayesian decision theory has developed in the post-World War II years to help solve problems involving decision making where risk exists.

Statistical measures of a probability distribution. In the previous section the elements of probability theory were discussed. In this section statistical measures of a probability distribution that will be useful in quantifying risk will be discussed.

A probability distribution or probability function is defined as a function in which the possible values that a random variable can take on are assigned probabilities. For example, suppose that two coins are tossed simultaneously. The following outcomes are possible: (head, head), (head, tail), (tail, head) and (tail, tail) where the notation in parentheses represents the side of the coin that appears on the first and second coin respectively. If we let X be the random variable which represents the number of heads that appears when the coins are tossed, then X can take on the value of 0, 1 or 2. The probability distribution or function for this experiment is shown as follows:

PROBABILITY DISTRIBUTION FOR THE NUMBER OF HEADS
APPEARING IN THE TOSS OF TWO COINS

Number of Heads (X)	*Probability*
0	.25
1	.50
2	.25

▶ EXAMPLE: Decision to expand facilities. To understand statistical measures of a probability distribution consider the case of a transportation company which is considering a capital investment. The company is considering whether to expand its present facilities in Atlanta. The probability distribution for the rate of return on the capital investment under alternative economic environments that might exist in the future is presented as follows:

PROBABILITY DISTRIBUTION FOR THE RATE OF RETURN
ON A CAPITAL INVESTMENT PROJECT

Economic environment	*Probability*	*Forecasted rate of return*
Boom	.1	.20
Slow growth	.4	.10
Zero growth	.4	.05
Recession	.1	−.10
	1.0	

The first measure that we will consider is the expected value of a probability distribution. The expected value is simply the weighted average of the distribution. The weights in this case are the probabilities associated with the random variable X. The expected value of a random variable is denoted by E(X) and is computed by the following expression:

$$E(X) = P_1 X_1 + P_2 X_2 + \ldots + P_N X_N$$

where P_i is the probability associated with the random variable X_i.

For the example above the random variable is the rate of return. Applying the expression for E(X) to the probability distribution illustrated above, we have:

$$\begin{aligned} E(X) &= .2\,(.1) + .1\,(.4) + .05\,(.4) + (-.1)\,(.1) \\ &= .07 \end{aligned}$$

The expected return for the project is therefore 7 percent.

Dispersion and risk. A decision maker is not only interested in the expected value of a probability distribution but also the dispersion of the random variable around the expected value. A measure of dispersion of a probability distribution is the variance of the distribution. The variance denoted by var (X) is computed by the following expression:

$$\begin{aligned} \text{var}\,(X) = {} & [X_1 - E(X)]^2\,P(X_1) + [X_2 - E(X)]^2\,P(X_2) \\ & + \ldots + [X_N - E(X)]^2\,P(X_N) \end{aligned}$$

The variance of the random variable X for the probability distribution in the above example is:

$$\begin{aligned} \text{var}\,(X) = {} & [.2-.07]^2\,(.1) + [.1-.07]^2\,(.4) + [.05-.07]^2\,(.4) \\ & + [(-.1) - .07]^2\,(.1) \\ = {} & .0051 \end{aligned}$$

The problem with using the variance as a measure of dispersion is that it is in terms of squared units of the random variable. Consequently the square root of the variance called the standard deviation is used as a measure of dispersion and is also employed as a measure of risk. The greater the standard deviation the greater the risk. The standard deviation for the illustration above is .071 or 7.1 percent.

Assuming that the probability distribution is normally distributed, the expected return and the standard deviation can be used to measure the relative risk of alternative capital investment projects. For all investments with the same expected return, the capital investment project with the smallest standard deviation is the one which has the least relative risk. For example, suppose that the transportation company is considering another capital investment project which is an alternative plan for the expansion of the Atlanta terminal facilities. It is estimated that the expected return on this project is 7 percent but the standard deviation is 5 percent. Then the risk involved in the second project is less than the risk involved with the first since both have the same expected return but the second project is less dispersed around the expected return. Similarly, if we have two investment projects with the same standard deviation then the one with the larger expected return is the project with the lower relative risk.

In real world situations alternative investment projects have both different expected returns and standard deviations. To measure relative risk in such cases the decision maker can use a statistical measure called the coefficient of variation which is measured by:

$$\text{coefficient of variation} = \frac{\text{standard deviation}}{\text{expected value}}$$

Relative risk is thus measured by the standard deviation relative to the expected return and can be considered a risk-reward ratio. The larger the coefficient of variation the greater the dispersion relative to the expected return and hence the greater the risk.

Figure 3 illustrates three cases comparing two hypothetical probability distributions representing two capital investment projects.

Choosing between alternative decisions. Let us now illustrate how the expected value of a decision can be employed to assist the decision maker in selecting between alternative decisions. In the payoff matrix represented by Figure 2 we have the dollar profit for alternative environments (number of cakes demanded) for each possible decision (number of cakes ordered). Let us suppose that the manager of the store has determined from cake sales during the previous 52 weeks that the probability distribution for the random variable which in this case is the number of cakes demanded (Y_j) is as shown below. Then the expected value (pay-off) of each decision can be computed as follows:

PROBABILITY DISTRIBUTION FOR THE WEEKLY DEMAND FOR CAKES

Alternative environment	*Probability*
(Y_1) 100 cakes demanded	.4
(Y_2) 200 cakes demanded	.2
(Y_3) 300 cakes demanded	.2
(Y_4) 400 cakes demanded	.1
(Y_5) 500 cakes demanded	.1

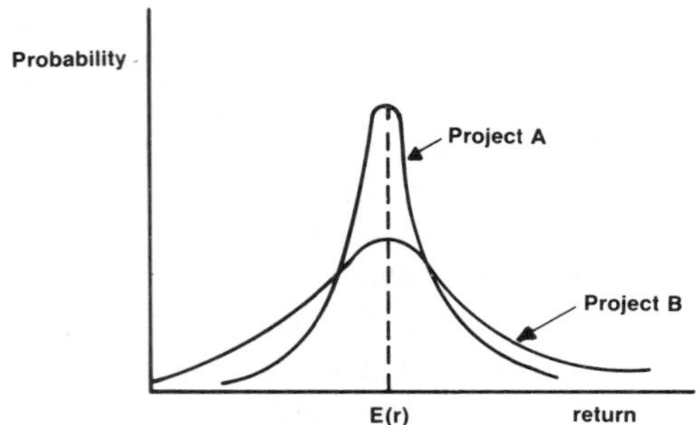

COMMENT: The expected return for Project A and B are equal. The standard deviation for Project A is less than Project B. There is less risk for Project A. Hence, Project A is preferred.

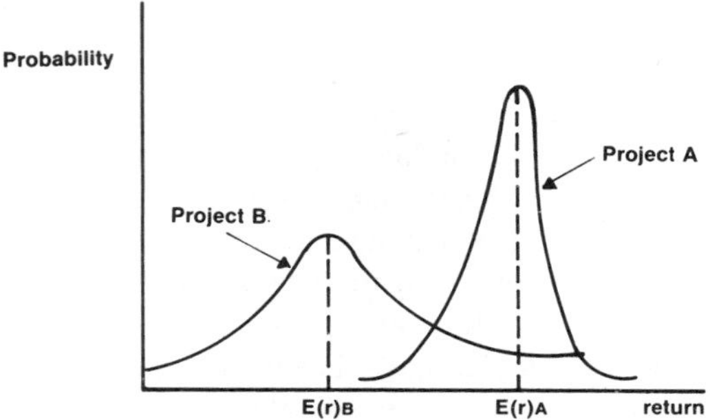

COMMENT: The expected return for Project A is greater than that for Project B. The standard deviation for Project B is greater than for Project A. Hence, Project A is preferred to Project B.

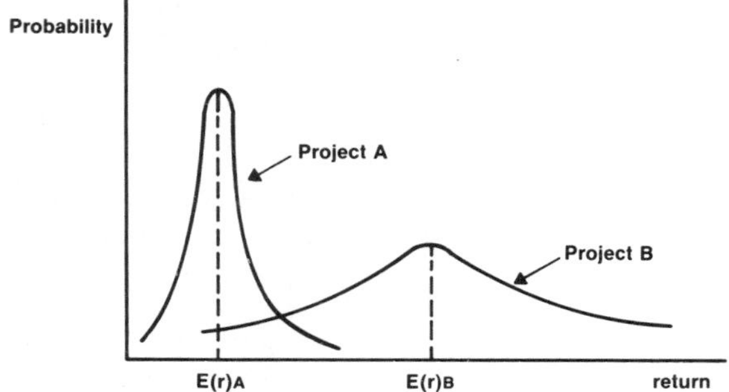

COMMENT: The expected return for Project B is greater than for Project A. The risk for Project A is less than the risk for Project B since A's standard deviation is less. The coefficient of variation can be used to look at the risk-reward ratio in order to select the more attractive project.

Fig. 3. Comparisons of Two Capital Investment Projects.

Expected value of X_1 (order 100 cakes):

$$E(X_1) = \$30(.4) + \$30(.2) + \$30(.2) + \$30(.1) + \$30(.1) = \$30$$

Expected value of X_2 (order 200 cakes):

$$E(X_2) = \$20(.4) + \$60(.2) + \$60(.2) + \$60(.1) + \$60(.1) = \$44$$

Expected value of X_3 (order 300 cakes):

$$E(X_3) = \$10(.4) + \$50(.2) + \$90(.2) + \$90(.1) + \$90(.1) = \$50$$

Expected value of X_4 (order 400 cakes):

$$E(X_4) = \$0(.4) + \$40(.2) + \$80(.2) + \$120(.1) + \$120(.1) = \$48$$

Expected value of X_5 (order 500 cakes):

$$E(X_5) = -\$10(.4) + \$30(.2) + \$70(.2) + \$110(.1) + \$150(.1) = \$42$$

The decision maker could then select the decision which represents the largest expected value or pay-off. In this case it would be to order 300 cakes.

Estimating relationships. Many times it is necessary to estimate relationships between variables in order to forecast certain variables. For example, management is interested in forecasting sales, costs, and cash flows in order to facilitate planning and budgeting. One of the most widely used techniques to estimate relationships for forecasting is regression analysis or the method of least squares.

▶ EXAMPLE: Sales forecast for electric can openers. To illustrate the technique, let us consider the case in which we have only two variables. Suppose that the Household Appliance Corporation is trying to forecast sales for a particular product line for the forthcoming year. The product line it is interested in is electric can openers. Management believes that the level of sales of its electric can openers is dependent upon the amount of advertising done by the company in that year on that product line, and is interested in formulating an equation which can be used to forecast sales given the amount of advertising for that product. In this case, the level of sales is called the dependent variable and advertising is the independent or explanatory variable. The linear relationship management is interested in can be expressed as

(1) $Y = b_1 + b_2 X + u$

where Y = annual sales of electric can openers (in thousands of units);
X = dollar annual advertising expenditures on electric can openers (0000 omitted);

b_1, b_2 are parameters to be estimated and;

u = stochastic or random error term.

It is because of this last variable that the regression model is called a stochastic or probabilistic model. The justification for introducing a random error term is that there are many variables in addition to advertising that will affect the sales of the firm's electric can openers which have not been included in equation 1. For example, the amount of advertising by a competitive company, the firm's sales force, the number of marriages each year, the income level of families, etc.

Annual data from 19X1-19X8 for both X and Y from which the relationship will be estimated is given in Figure 4. Each point is then plotted on Figure 5. When actual data are plotted in this fashion, the resulting diagram is called a *scatter diagram*.

Equation 1 can be rewritten to allow for the observation as:

$$(2)\quad Y_t = b_1 + b_2 X_t + u_t$$

where the subscript t denotes the t-th observation. The objective is to estimate equation 2.

One possible way of obtaining an approximation to equation 2 is by simply drawing a line through the points which the investigator feels best represent the relationship. Selecting two points on this line will determine the estimated relationship. This technique is called the *free-hand method*. The obvious pitfall of this technique is that there is no established criteria for drawing the estimated line and hence different investigators could obtain different estimates of equation 2 with the same data.

Regression analysis. An alternative method which can be used to find an approximation to equation 2 is the *method of least squares* or *regression analysis.* This method requires that we estimate a linear equation such that the sum of the squares of

ANNUAL SALES OF ELECTRIC CAN OPENERS AND ADVERTISING EXPENDITURES ON PRODUCT: HOUSEHOLD APPLIANCE CORPORATION, 19x1 – 19x8

Year	t	Dollar Advertising Expenditures (0000 omitted) (X)	Annual Sales (in thousands of units) (Y)
19x1	1	4	138
19x2	2	8	141
19x3	3	29	146
19x4	4	19	154
19x5	5	36	158
19x6	6	31	152
19x7	7	34	153
19x8	8	39	158

Fig. 4. Annual Sales of Electric Can Openers and Advertising Expenditures.

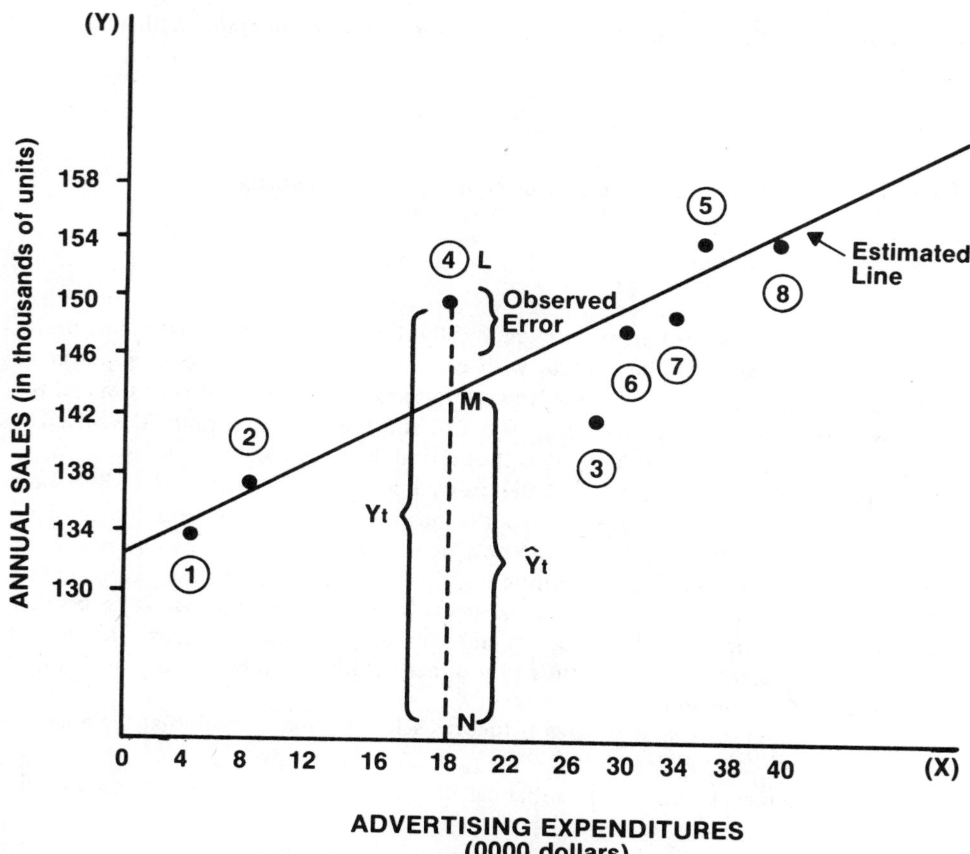

Fig. 5. Scatter Diagram for Annual Sales of Electric Can Openers and Advertising Expenditures on Product: Household Appliance Corporation.

the difference between the observed value and the value obtained from the model is a minimum. That is, we want to estimate a linear equation

$$(3)\quad \hat{Y}_t = \hat{b}_1 + \hat{b}_2 X_t + e_t$$

where $\hat{b}_1$ and $\hat{b}_2$ are estimates of the true b_1 and b_2 of equation 2;

$\hat{Y}_t$ = an estimate of Y_t from equation 3 and;

e_t = the observed error term.

The aim of the method of least squares then is to find a value of b_1 and b_2 such that the sum of the squares of the observed error term is a minimum. Mathematically, we want to minimize

$$\sum_{t=1}^{8} e_t^2$$

which from equation 3 can be seen to be equivalent to minimizing

$$\sum_{t=1}^{8} (Y_t - \hat{Y}_t)^2$$

To see the observed error term graphically, Figure 2 has an estimated line drawn in. Take any observed point, say L, with coordinates (X=19, Y=154). Suppose we drop a perpendicular from L to the X axis intersecting the estimated line at M and the X axis at N. Then the observed value Y is LN, and the estimated value Y is MN. The observed error term which is $Y_t - \hat{Y}_t$ is the vertical distance LM.

From Figure 5 we can see that all observed points below the estimated line show where the estimated line overestimated the observed Y and vice versa for observed points above the estimated line. It can now be seen why we square the observed error term. Since observed error terms can be both positive and negative, by just summing the observed error we could have large negative errors canceling out large positive errors. By squaring the observed errors and summing, this cannot occur. The sum of the squared observed errors will thus vary directly with the deviation of the observed points from the estimated line.

The principle of least squares is then to select $\hat{b}_1$ and $\hat{b}_2$ such that the quantity $\sum_{t=1}^{8} e_t^2$ is minimized. From differential calculus the two equations for computing the value of $\hat{b}_1$ and $\hat{b}_2$ that minimizes that quantity can be derived. These two equations are

$$(4)\quad \hat{b}_2 = \frac{\sum_{t=1}^{T} X_t Y_t - \frac{1}{T} \sum_{t=1}^{T} X_t \sum_{t=1}^{T} Y_t}{\sum_{t=1}^{T} X_t^2 - \frac{1}{T}\left(\sum_{t=1}^{T} X_t\right)^2}$$

and

$$(5)\quad \hat{b}_1 = \overline{Y} - \hat{b}_2 \overline{X}$$

where T = total number of observations;

$$\overline{X} = \frac{\sum_{t=1}^{T} X_t}{T} = \text{mean of X and;}$$

$$\overline{Y} = \frac{\sum_{t=1}^{T} Y_t}{T} = \text{mean of Y.}$$

Using the data from Figure 4, the necessary sums are computed on Figure 6. As can be seen from Figure 6,

$$T = 8 \quad \sum_{t=1}^{8} X_t = 200 \qquad \sum_{t=1}^{8} Y_t = 1{,}200$$

$$\sum_{t=1}^{8} X_t Y_t = 30{,}604 \quad \sum_{t=1}^{8} X_t^2 = 6{,}216$$

$$\overline{X} = \frac{200}{8} = 25$$

$$\overline{Y} = \frac{1{,}200}{8} = 150$$

Substituting into equation 4, we have

$$\hat{b}_2 = \frac{30{,}604 - \frac{1}{8}(200)(1{,}200)}{6{,}216 - \frac{1}{8}(200)^2}$$

$$= .4967105.$$

To find $\hat{b}_1$ we substitute the above data into equation 5. Thus we obtain

$$\hat{b}_1 = 150 - .4967105(25)$$
$$= 137.58224$$

The equation which can then be used to predict annual sales of the firm's electric can openers given planned annual advertising expenditures on that product line is

$$\hat{Y}_t = 137.58224 + .4967105\, X_t$$

WORKSHEET FOR ESTIMATION OF PARAMETERS OF THE RELATIONSHIP BETWEEN HOUSEHOLD APPLIANCE CORPORATION'S ANNUAL SALE OF ELECTRIC CAN OPENERS AND ANNUAL ADVERTISING EXPENDITURES FOR PRODUCT.

t	X_t	Y_t	X_t^2	Y_t^2	$X_t Y_t$
1	4	138	16	19044	552
2	8	141	64	19881	1128
3	29	146	841	21316	4234
4	19	154	361	23716	2926
5	36	158	1296	24964	5688
6	31	152	961	23104	4712
7	34	153	1156	23409	5202
8	39	158	1521	24964	6162
SUM	200	1200	6216	180398	30604
MEAN	25	150	—	—	—

Fig. 6. Worksheet for Estimating Parameters.

Suppose that next year the planned advertising expenditure for the product line is \$450,000, then what would be the estimated relationship project for total annual sales? Since planned advertising expenditures are \$450,000, X_t is thus 45. Substituting $X_t = 45$ into the estimated relationship, we obtain:

$$\hat{Y}_t = 137.58224 + .4967105(45)$$
$$= 159.93421$$

Hence projected annual sales for the firm's electric can openers would be 159,934 units.

Remember that by using any set of data for two variables we could obtain a value for $\hat{b}_1$ and $\hat{b}_2$. However, we are interested in how "good" the relationship is. Statistical tests determine in some sense how "good" a linear relationship exists between two variables. A measure of the "goodness of fit" of the relationship is the *coefficient of determination*.

To illustrate the meaning and measurement of the coefficient of determination, consider Figure 7. The independent or explanatory variable, X, is being used to try to

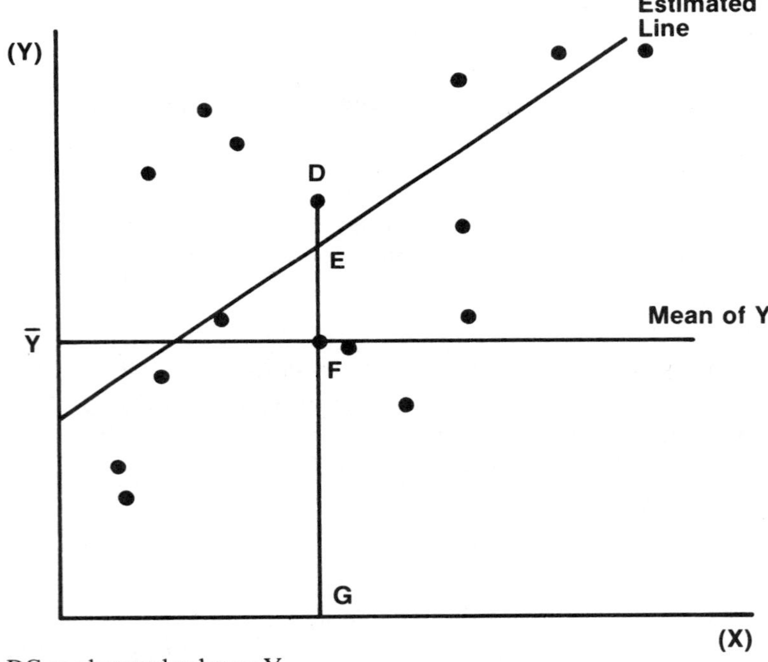

DG = observed value = Y_t
EG = estimate of Y_t given by the regression line = $\hat{Y}_t$
FG = mean of Y = $\overline{Y}$
DF = deviation of the observed Y_t from its mean = $Y_t - \overline{Y}$
EF = amount of deviation of Y_t from its mean explained by X = $\hat{Y}_t - \overline{Y}$
DE = amount of the deviation of Y_t from its mean that is still unexplained = $Y_t - \hat{Y}_t$

Fig. 7. The Value of the Regression in Explaining the Variation in Y.

explain movements in the dependent variable, Y. But what movements is it trying to explain? What we are interested in explaining by using the variable X is why the variable Y would deviate from its mean. It can be shown that if no independent variable were used to try to explain movements in Y, the least squares method would give the mean of Y as the value by which to estimate Y. Thus what we are interested in is the ability of X to explain the deviations of Y from its mean.

As can be seen from Figure 7, the observed value of Y at point D measured by the distance DG, deviates from the mean of Y measured by FG by the distance DF. It is the deviation of Y from its mean, that is DF, that the variable X is trying to explain.

The difference X is trying to explain, DF, is made up of two components. The first component is EF which is the difference between the value estimated by the regression line and the mean value of Y. This distance is the amount of the deviation from the mean of Y explained by X or equivalently explained by the regression line. The second component is DE which is the deviation of Y from its mean which is still unexplained.

This can be expressed mathematically as

$$DF = EF + DE$$

where

$DF = Y_t - \overline{Y}$ = deviation of the observed Y_t from its mean;
$EF = \hat{Y}_t - \overline{Y}$ = amount of the deviation of Y_t from its mean explained by X;

and

$DE = Y_t - \hat{Y}_t$ = amount of the deviation of Y_t from its mean still unexplained.

Thus we have

$$Y_t - \overline{Y} = (\hat{Y}_t - \overline{Y}) + (Y_t - \hat{Y}_t)$$

which is in fact an identity. Squaring both sides, and summing over all T observations it can be shown that

$$(6) \quad \sum_{t=1}^{T} (Y_t - \overline{Y})^2 = \sum_{t=1}^{T} (\hat{Y}_t - \overline{Y})^2 + \sum_{t=1}^{T} (Y_t - \hat{Y}_t)^2$$

The term on the left hand side of equation 6 is the total deviation of the observed Y_t's from the mean of Y squared. This sum will be referred to as the *total sum of squares* and denoted by TSS. The first term on the right hand side is the total deviation of the observed Y_t's explained by X squared. This sum will be referred to as the *explained sum of squares* and denoted by ESS. The second term on the right hand side is the total deviation of the observed Y_t's still unexplained squared. This sum will be referred to as the *residual sum of squares* and denoted as RSS. Thus, equation 6 can be expressed as:

$$TSS = ESS + RSS$$

To compute the total and explained sum of squares, the following equations can be used:

$$(7)\quad TSS = \sum_{t=1}^{T} (Y_t - \overline{Y})^2 = \sum_{t=1}^{T} Y_t{}^2 - \frac{1}{T}\left(\sum_{t=1}^{T} Y_t\right)^2$$

$$(8)\quad ESS = \sum_{t=1}^{T} (\hat{Y}_t - \overline{Y})^2 = \hat{b}_2\left(\sum_{t=1}^{T} X_t Y_t - \frac{1}{T}\sum_{t=1}^{T} X_t \sum_{t=1}^{T} Y_t\right)$$

The residual sum of squares is then found by subtracting from the total sum of squares the explained sum of squares.

The coefficient of determination is then defined as the percentage of the total sum of squares explained by X. Thus, denoting the coefficient of determination by R^2 we have

$$(9)\quad R^2 = \frac{ESS}{TSS}$$

R^2 can take on any value between 0 and 1. The coefficient of determination can be interpreted from three viewpoints. First, it shows the percentage of the total sum of squares explained by using the explanatory variable X. If all the observed points lie along a straight line then the residual sum of squares is zero and thus the total sum of squares would equal the explained sum of squares. Hence, R^2 would be equal to one. A second interpretation of R^2 is that it indicates the closeness of fit between the regression line and the observed points. The closer the observed points to the regression line, the closer R^2 will be to 1. On the other hand, the greater the scatter of observed points from the regression line, the closer R^2 will be to zero. A third interpretation of R^2 similar to the closeness of fit interpretation is the degree to which the observed points resemble a straight line. In this case R^2 is a measure of the degree of linearity. The closer R^2 is to 1, the more the observed points resemble a straight line, whereas a value of R^2 close to 0 will be the opposite from resembling a straight line.

Two warnings are in order for interpreting R^2. First, suppose that all the observed values of Y were equal to the same number, say K. Then the mean of Y would be equal to K as is shown in Figure 8. Thus the Y values would fall along the horizontal line $Y = K$. Since all observed points fall along a straight line, it would seem that we have a perfect fit and R^2 equals 1. On the other hand, there is no variation in Y to be explained by X. Hence it may seem that R^2 equals 0. The problem here is that the observed Y's do not have a distribution and hence we cannot apply the regression model in this case. Thus, the observed Y values must be scattered in order to apply the regression technique.

The second warning is against interpreting an R^2 value of close to 0 as meaning no relationship between X and Y. The third interpretation of R^2 tells us that an R^2 value close to 0 means that the observed points do not resemble a straight line. This does not mean that there is no relationship between X and Y, but instead means there appears to be no *linear* relationship between X and Y. For example, consider Figures 9 and 10. In both cases, a regression line could produce an R^2 value close to 0. Clearly, in both cases one cannot say there is no relationship between X and Y. In

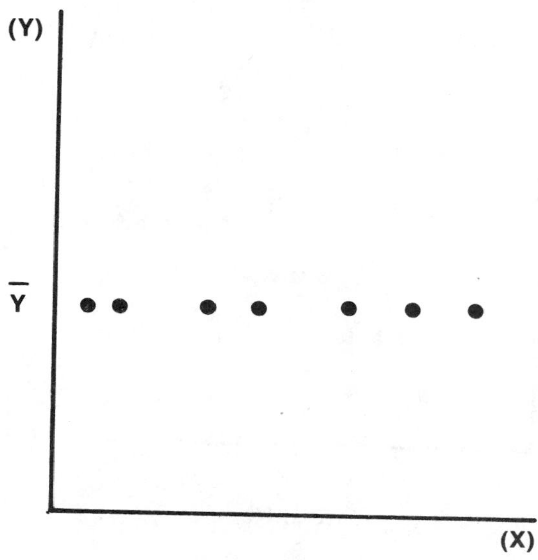

Fig. 8.

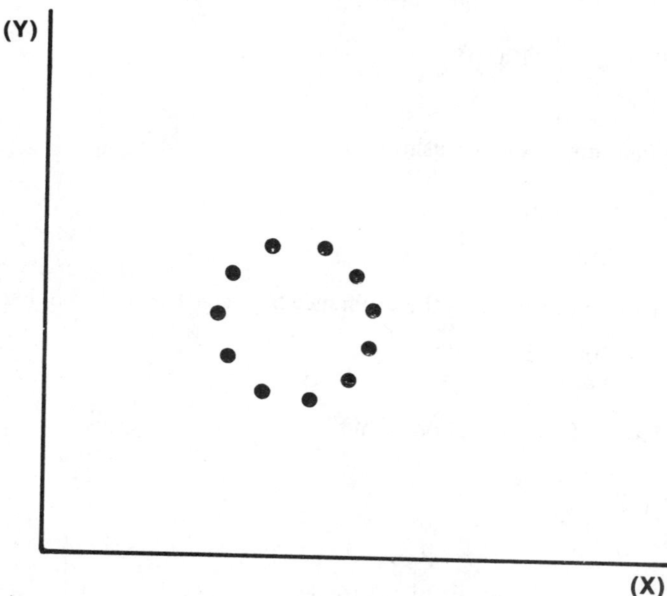

Fig. 9.

Figure 9 we have the equation of a circle, whereas in Figure 10 we have a step function. Thus it is important to keep in mind this linearity interpretation of R^2.

To illustrate the computations required to obtain the coefficient of determination, consider the data in Figure 6.

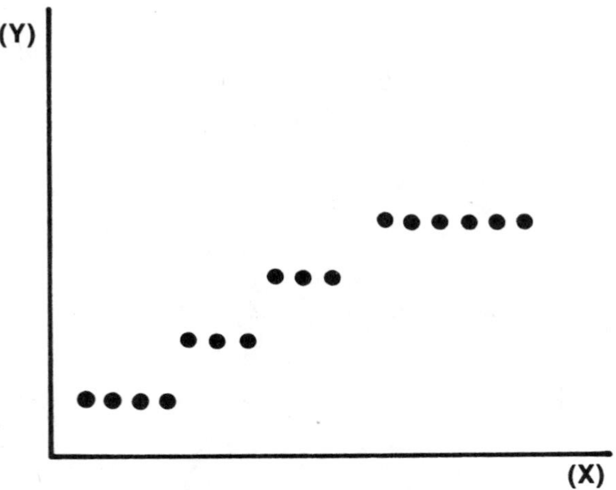

Fig. 10.

The total sum of squares using equation 7 is

$$\text{TSS} = 180,398 - \frac{1}{8}(1200)^2$$
$$= 398$$

The explained sum of squares using equation 8 is

$$\text{ESS} = (.4967105)\ [30604 - \frac{1}{8}(200)(1200)]$$
$$= 300.01314$$

The residual sum of squares is the difference between TSS and ESS, hence

$$\text{RSS} = 398 - 300.01314$$
$$= 97.98686$$

The coefficient of determination is thus

$$R^2 = \frac{300.03314}{398}$$
$$= .758$$

This means that almost 76 percent of the total variation in the annual sales of electric can openers is explained by annual advertising expenditures.

The regression model can be used when there is more than one explanatory or independent variable. The computations for obtaining the parameters of the model are difficult to compute once we have more than two explanatory variables. However, most computer companies and time-sharing services provide regression programs.

MATRIX ALGEBRA

The aim of this section is to present the essentials of matrix algebra. As will be seen, matrices provide a decision maker with a convenient way to express a linear system of equations. The rules, or *algebra*, for manipulating matrices is therefore known as *matrix algebra*.

Matrix defined. A *matrix* is defined as a rectangular ordered array of elements. As an example, consider the matrix A:

$$A = \begin{bmatrix} a_{11} & a_{12} & \cdots & a_{1n} \\ a_{21} & a_{22} & \cdots & a_{2n} \\ a_{m1} & a_{m2} & \cdots & a_{mn} \end{bmatrix}$$

A typical element of the matrix A can be written as a_{ij} where the first subscript represents the i-th row and the second subscript the j-th column of the matrix.

Order of the matrix. The number of rows and columns of the matrix tells us the *order* or *size* of the matrix. The matrix A shown above is of order (m×n), that is, there are m rows and n columns.

As an example, let

$$A = \begin{bmatrix} 1 & 3 \\ 6 & -8 \end{bmatrix} \qquad B = \begin{bmatrix} 5 & 9 & 3 & 2 \\ 1 & -7 & 0 & 6 \end{bmatrix} \qquad C = \begin{bmatrix} 4 & 2 & 6 \end{bmatrix}$$

Then A is of order (2 × 2), B is of order (2 × 4) and C is of order (1 × 3).

Given the matrices of A, B and C what are the following elements: a_{21}, b_{23}, and c_{12}?

For matrix A, a_{21} represents the element in the second row and first column which is the number 6.

For matrix B, b_{23} represents the element in the second row and third column which is the number 0.

For matrix C, c_{12} represents the element in the first row and second column which is the number 2.

We shall now go on to discuss and define special cases of the general (m×n) matrix.

When the number of rows are equal to the number of columns, that is when m=n, the matrix is said to be *square*.

We define a *vector* as a matrix with only one row or one column. If m=1, we have a row vector; while if n = 1, we have a column vector.

A special case of all the above matrices occurs when both m and n equals 1. These are the usual numbers we use. We define the (1×1) matrix as a *scalar*.

If we let

$$D = \begin{bmatrix} 6 & -7 & 9 \\ 4 & 5 & 0 \\ 3 & 2 & -9 \end{bmatrix} \qquad E = \begin{bmatrix} 2 & 3 & -6 & 5 \end{bmatrix} \qquad F = \begin{bmatrix} -1 \\ 6 \end{bmatrix} \qquad G = \begin{bmatrix} 4 \end{bmatrix}$$

then, D is a square matrix of order 3, that is (3X3); E is a row vector; F is a column vector and; G is a (1X1) matrix called a scalar.

In a square matrix, if all the a_{ii} elements are equal to one the matrix is called an identity matrix. The matrix I_3 below is an example of an identity matrix of order 3.

$$I_3 = \begin{bmatrix} 1 & 0 & 0 \\ 0 & 1 & 0 \\ 0 & 0 & 1 \end{bmatrix}$$

Transposing a matrix. When we interchange the rows and columns of a matrix, we are performing the operation of transposing a matrix. We denote the transpose of a matrix, say A, by A′. The transpose of the matrices A, B and C given above is:

$$A' = \begin{bmatrix} 1 & 6 \\ & \\ 3 & -8 \end{bmatrix} \qquad B' = \begin{bmatrix} 5 & 1 \\ 9 & -7 \\ 3 & 0 \\ 2 & 6 \end{bmatrix} \qquad C' = \begin{bmatrix} 4 \\ 2 \\ 6 \end{bmatrix}$$

Matrix addition and multiplication. Having defined a matrix, we now turn to fundamental operations with matrices. The basic operations are matrix addition and multiplication.

The addition of two matrices *of the same order* is a matrix whose elements are the sum of the corresponding elements of the matrices which are to be added. In short hand notation, given the (mXn) matrices $A = a_{ij}$ and $B = b_{ij}$ then

$$A + B = a_{ij} + b_{ij}$$

For example, if

$$A = \begin{bmatrix} 5 & 3 & 6 \\ 7 & 9 & 4 \end{bmatrix} \qquad \text{and} \qquad B = \begin{bmatrix} 1 & 12 & 8 \\ 16 & 3 & 1 \end{bmatrix}$$

then

$$A + B = \begin{bmatrix} 5+1 & 3+12 & 6+8 \\ 7+16 & 9+3 & 4+1 \end{bmatrix} = \begin{bmatrix} 6 & 15 & 14 \\ 23 & 12 & 5 \end{bmatrix}$$

Note again that the two matrices must be of the same order. That is, if one matrix is (mXn) while another matrix is (mXr) where $n \neq r$ then we cannot perform the operation of addition with these matrices. When the two matrices are of the same order, they are said to be comformable with respect to addition.

As an introduction to matrix multiplication, let us first define the multiplication of a row vector by a column vector. We define this operation for a (1Xn) row vector ***a*** given by

$$a = [a_1 \quad a_2 \quad a_3 \quad \ldots \quad a_n]$$

and an (n×1) column vector b given by

$$b = \begin{bmatrix} b_1 \\ b_2 \\ \cdot \\ \cdot \\ \cdot \\ b_n \end{bmatrix}$$

as

$$ab = a_1\, b_1 + a_2\, b_2 + \ldots + a_n\, b_n$$

That is, the multiplication of a row vector by a column vector in which the row vector has the same number of columns as the column vector has rows, is just a scalar (number). This scalar is found by multiplying the kth element of the row vector by the kth element of the column vector and then summing over all products. For example, the multiplication of the following row and column vector:

$$\begin{bmatrix} 7 & 4 & 9 & 3 \end{bmatrix} \qquad \begin{bmatrix} 8 \\ 1 \\ -2 \\ 5 \end{bmatrix}$$

is

$$\begin{aligned} &= (7)(8) + (4)(1) + (9)(-2) + (3)(5) \\ &= 56 + 4 - 18 + 15 \\ &= 57 \end{aligned}$$

Note again that the row vector must have the same number of columns as the column vector has rows.

Let us now define matrix multiplication, that is, the multiplication of one matrix by another matrix. To illustrate how matrix multiplication is done consider the matrices A and B. Since in matrix algebra multiplication is *not* commutative, we cannot simply say "multiply matrix A and B." It is necessary in the multiplication of matrices to consider the order in which the matrices are being multiplied. That is, we could have A times B (AB) or B times A (BA). AB will not necessarily be equal to BA and in fact even if we can multiply A times B we may find that B times A does not exist. Therefore, instead of saying "multiply A and B," we say "premultiply (or postmultiply) A by B." For example, for AB we can say either A is being postmultiplied by B *or* B is being premultiplied by A. Similarly, for BA we can say either B is being postmultiplied by A *or* A is being premultiplied by B.

Now let us see how matrix multiplication is defined and what requirements must be met before we can multiply two matrices. Let the matrix A be of order (m×r) and the matrix B be of order (r×n) and we want to find AB, that is,

$$\begin{bmatrix} a_{11} & a_{12} \cdots & a_{1r} \\ a_{21} & a_{22} & a_{2r} \\ \cdot & \cdot & \cdot \\ \cdot & \cdot & \cdot \\ \cdot & \cdot & \cdot \\ a_{m1} & a_{m2} \cdots & a_{mr} \end{bmatrix} \text{ times } \begin{bmatrix} b_{11} & b_{12} \cdots & b_{1n} \\ b_{21} & b_{22} & b_{2n} \\ \cdot & \cdot & \cdot \\ \cdot & \cdot & \cdot \\ \cdot & \cdot & \cdot \\ b_{r1} & b_{r2} \cdots & b_{rn} \end{bmatrix}$$

To perform matrix multiplication, we think of each row in matrix A as a row vector and each column in matrix B as a column vector and then perform the operation of multiplying a row vector and a column vector to get the elements of the matrix A B using the following rule: when you multiply the i-th row by the j-th column this scalar will be the ij-th element of the matrix we desire.

Since we are initially performing the operation of multiplying a row vector by a column vector we must remember that we can only define this operation when the number of columns in the row vector is the same as the number of rows in the column vector. This requirement in turn gives us the condition which must be met for matrix multiplication. The condition is that the number of columns in the first matrix must be the same as the number of rows in the second matrix. When this condition holds, the matrices are said to be conformable with respect to multiplication.

We can also tell from the order of the two matrices what the order of the resulting matrix will be. The resulting matrix will have the same number of rows as the first matrix and the same number of columns as the second matrix.

Let us now illustrate matrix multiplication and confirm the statements made above with some examples.

If we define A and B as:

$$A = \begin{bmatrix} 4 & 1 \\ 5 & 2 \\ 6 & 10 \end{bmatrix} \text{ and } B = \begin{bmatrix} 12 & 3 & 7 \\ 9 & 0 & 15 \end{bmatrix}$$

then what is AB?

The first question to ask is: Are the two matrices conformable with respect to A postmultiplied by B? Since A is of order (3×2) and B is of order (2×3), the two matrices are conformable since the number of columns in A is the same as the number of rows in B. That is, the number of columns in A is two and the number of rows in B is two and hence the two matrices are conformable with respect to the multiplication AB.

The second question to ask is: What is the order of the resulting matrix AB? We know that the resulting matrix AB will have the same number of rows as the first matrix A, and the same number of columns as the second matrix B. In this example, A has three rows and B has three columns therefore the matrix AB is of order (3×3).

The third question to ask is: How do we find the elements of the matrix AB? To find the element of the first row and first column of the matrix AB we simply multiply the first row of A by the first column of B which gives:

$$\begin{bmatrix} 4 & 1 \end{bmatrix} \begin{bmatrix} 12 \\ 9 \end{bmatrix} = 4\,(12) + 1\,(9)$$

$$= 48 + 9$$
$$= 57$$

To find the element of the first row and second column of the matrix AB we multiply the first row of A by the second column of B which gives:

$$\begin{bmatrix} 4 & 1 \end{bmatrix} \begin{bmatrix} 3 \\ 0 \end{bmatrix} = 4\,(3) + 1\,(0)$$

$$= 12 + 0$$
$$= 12$$

Similarly, we can follow this procedure to find each element of AB so that AB is then

$$AB = \begin{bmatrix} 57 & 12 & 43 \\ 78 & 15 & 65 \\ 162 & 18 & 192 \end{bmatrix}$$

The multiplicative inverse of some matrix, say A, in matrix operations is that matrix Y such that

$$AY = YA = I$$

The matrix Y is called the *multiplicative inverse* and is denoted by A^{-1}. We define the multiplicative inverse *only for square matrices*. The multiplicative inverse of a square matrix may not always exist. What we are interested in is knowing when the inverse can be found and how to compute it.

Let us now see how we can use matrix notation to formulate different mathematical expressions and operations.

In high school algebra, we encountered a system of simultaneous linear equations. That is, the system of simultaneous linear equations consisted of two linear equations and two unknowns or three linear equations and three unknowns. For example, the following is a system of simultaneous linear equations with two equations and two unknowns:

$$5X_1 + 5X_2 = 8$$
$$X_1 + 2X_2 = 7$$

The system is linear because each of the unknowns X_1 and X_2 is only raised to the first power.

Using the matrix operations defined in this chapter we can rewrite the system of two linear simultaneous equations by letting:

$$X = \begin{bmatrix} X_1 \\ X_2 \end{bmatrix}, \quad A = \begin{bmatrix} 5 & 5 \\ 1 & 2 \end{bmatrix} \text{ and, } b = \begin{bmatrix} 8 \\ 7 \end{bmatrix}$$

Then, we can write

$$AX = b$$

Decision makers constantly work with a system of linear equations. By rewriting such systems in matrix notation it will be easier to manipulate such systems mathematically.

To see the power of matrix algebra, let us see how we can use it to solve a system of simultaneous linear equations with n equations and n unknowns. Again, the system can be written:

$$AX = b$$

We are interested in solving for the value of each X_i given the matrix A and the column vector b. Since A is a square matrix, this can be done by premultiplying AX and b by the inverse of A, A^{-1}, that is,

$$A^{-1}(AX) = A^{-1}b$$
$$(A^{-1}A)X = A^{-1}b$$
$$X = A^{-1}b \qquad \text{since } (A^{-1}A)X = IX = X$$

The matrix $A^{-1}b$ will then give the solution for the value of each x_i. The solution obviously depends upon whether the inverse of A exists.

For example, for the system of linear equations

$$5x_1 + 5x_2 = 8$$
$$x_1 + 2x_2 = 7$$

We can solve for x_1 and x_2 algebraically. The reader can verify that the solution is $x_1 = -3.8$ and $x_2 = 5.4$.

Now using matrix notation we can write

$$AX = b$$

where

$$X = \begin{bmatrix} x_1 \\ x_2 \end{bmatrix}, \quad A = \begin{bmatrix} 5 & 5 \\ 1 & 2 \end{bmatrix} \text{ and, } \quad b = \begin{bmatrix} 8 \\ 7 \end{bmatrix}$$

To solve for X we have shown

$$X = A^{-1}b$$

The inverse of

$$\begin{bmatrix} 5 & 5 \\ 1 & 2 \end{bmatrix} \text{ is } \begin{bmatrix} .4 & -1 \\ -.2 & 1 \end{bmatrix}$$

thus

$$X = \begin{bmatrix} x_1 \\ x_2 \end{bmatrix} = \begin{bmatrix} .4 & -1 \\ -.2 & 1 \end{bmatrix} \begin{bmatrix} 8 \\ 7 \end{bmatrix}$$

$$\begin{bmatrix} x_1 \\ x_2 \end{bmatrix} = \begin{bmatrix} .4(8) + (-1)(7) \\ -.2(8) + 1(7) \end{bmatrix}$$

$$\begin{bmatrix} x_1 \\ x_2 \end{bmatrix} = \begin{bmatrix} -3.8 \\ 5.4 \end{bmatrix}$$

thus $x_1 = -3.8$ and $x_2 = 5.4$ as would be found by using ordinary algebra. For a large system of equations, it is difficult to solve for the x_i values algebraically. However, if we cast the system of linear equations in matrix notation and solve for the inverse of the A matrix then $A^{-1}b$ will give us the value of each x_i.

Using matrix algebra in cost allocation. To illustrate how matrix algebra can be applied to solve business problems, consider the problem of cost allocation faced by an accountant. To illustrate the problem, consider a commercial bank with the following four departments which provide revenue for the bank: mortgage loans, commercial loans, consumer loans and credit, and trust department.

Each of these departments have certain direct costs such as salaries for personnel in that department, telephone expenses, etc. In addition, there are certain indirect costs as a result of charges from departments which provide only services to the bank and no revenue themselves. Departments which provide revenue will be referred to as revenue departments while those departments which provide only services to revenue departments will be referred to as service departments.

Let the service departments of the commercial bank be: Electronic Data Processing (EDP), accounting, and advertising. The problem of cost allocation is then the task of allocating the total costs of the service departments to the revenue departments. Complications arise because each service department may provide services to each other. For example, the EDP department provides bookkeeping tasks for the accounting department and possibly computerized mail labeling for advertising. Using matrix algebra the interrelationship between indirect costs can be handled.

Direct monthly costs for the three service departments and four revenue departments are given in Figure 11. The total cost is the sum of the direct cost and indirect cost. Since the indirect cost is not known, the total cost for each department is not known. To solve the cost allocation problem, the total cost for each service department must be found and then distributed to each revenue department.

As an estimate of indirect costs, management must make some estimate of the percentage of total cost of each service department that should be allocated to other departments. For example, the EDP department can easily provide such estimates for its own department by classifying each department by a code number and when computer time is used the system can keep a record of the amount of time used by a particular department.

Figure 11 includes the commercial bank's accountants estimate of indirect cost by service department as a percentage of total cost. Each column shows the allocation of total cost of the service department appearing at the top of that column to the department appearing in the row. For example, reading down column 3 of Figure 11 labeled EDP, shows that 10 percent of EDP total costs should be allocated to the advertising department, 40 percent should be allocated to the accounting department, none to the EDP department itself, etc.

Based on this data, we can now start model building. The aim, remember, is to find the total cost of each revenue department. Total cost is the sum of direct and indirect costs. Direct costs are known whereas indirect costs for each department are not. Once we find the total cost for each service department, the indirect costs can be allocated to the revenue departments.

Let X_i denote the total cost of each service department. The total cost is the sum of both direct and indirect costs. For the three service departments the total cost can be expressed as follows:

$$\text{(S.1)} \qquad \begin{aligned} X_1 &= .00X_1 + .18X_2 + .10X_3 + 1500 \\ X_2 &= .00X_1 + .00X_2 + .40X_3 + 4700 \\ X_3 &= .00X_1 + .15X_2 + .00X_3 + 4000 \end{aligned}$$

Letting X, C, and D denote the following matrices:

$$X = \begin{bmatrix} X_1 \\ X_2 \\ X_3 \end{bmatrix} \quad C = \begin{bmatrix} .00 & .18 & .10 \\ .00 & .00 & .40 \\ .00 & .15 & .00 \end{bmatrix} \quad D = \begin{bmatrix} 1500 \\ 4700 \\ 4000 \end{bmatrix}$$

System 1 can be expressed as

$$\text{(S.2)} \qquad X = CX + D$$

Solving for X we find:

$$\text{(S.3)} \qquad X = (I-C)^{-1}D$$

where I is an identity matrix of order 3.

Given the above data, I–C is

$$(I-C) = \begin{bmatrix} 1.00 & -.18 & -.10 \\ .00 & 1.00 & -.40 \\ .00 & -.15 & 1.00 \end{bmatrix}$$

DIRECT AND INDIRECT MONTHLY COSTS FOR EACH DEPARTMENT OF A COMMERCIAL BANK

	Allocation of Indirect Cost of Each Service to Each Department as a Percentage of Total Cost			Direct Monthly Cost ($)
Department	(1) *Advertising*	(2) *Accounting*	(3) *EDP*	
(1) Advertising	.00	.18	.10	1500
(2) Accounting	.00	.00	.40	4700
(3) EDP	.00	.15	.00	4000
(4) Mortgage Loans	.20	.22	.16	3500
(5) Commercial Loans	.40	.15	.12	4200
(6) Consumer Loans and Credit	.35	.18	.18	3000
(7) Trust	.05	.12	.04	5300

Fig. 11. Monthly Costs for Commercial Bank Departments.

The inverse of (I–C) is

$$(I-C)^{-1} \begin{bmatrix} 1.000 & .207 & .183 \\ .000 & 1.064 & .426 \\ .000 & .160 & 1.064 \end{bmatrix}$$

From system 3, the total cost vector of the service departments can be found by

$$X = (I-C)^{-1}D$$

$$= \begin{bmatrix} X_1 \\ X_2 \\ X_3 \end{bmatrix} = \begin{bmatrix} 1.000 & .207 & .183 \\ .000 & 1.064 & .426 \\ .000 & .160 & 1.064 \end{bmatrix} \begin{bmatrix} 1500 \\ 4700 \\ 4000 \end{bmatrix}$$

$$\begin{bmatrix} X_1 \\ X_2 \\ X_3 \end{bmatrix} = \begin{bmatrix} 3204.9 \\ 6704.8 \\ 5008.0 \end{bmatrix}$$

Once the total cost vector for each service department is known, the indirect cost for each revenue department can be found by allocating the total cost of each service department to the revenue departments as given in Figure 11. The total cost for each revenue department is then found by adding the indirect cost to the direct cost.

Let Y_1 denote the total cost of each revenue department. Again, the total cost is the sum of both direct and indirect costs. For the four revenue departments total cost is

$$\begin{aligned} Y_1 &= .20X_1 + .22X_2 + .16X_3 + 3500 \\ Y_2 &= .40X_1 + .15X_2 + .12X_3 + 4200 \\ Y_3 &= .35X_1 + .18X_2 + .18X_3 + 3000 \\ Y_4 &= .05X_1 + .12X_2 + .04X_3 + 5300 \end{aligned}$$

Using matrix notation, and letting

$$Y = \begin{bmatrix} Y_1 \\ Y_2 \\ Y_3 \\ Y_4 \end{bmatrix} \qquad B = \begin{bmatrix} .20 & .22 & .16 \\ .40 & .15 & .12 \\ .35 & .18 & .18 \\ .05 & .12 & .04 \end{bmatrix}$$

$$E = \begin{bmatrix} 3500 \\ 4200 \\ 3000 \\ 5300 \end{bmatrix} \qquad X = \begin{bmatrix} X_1 \\ X_2 \\ X_3 \end{bmatrix}$$

we can write the above system as

$$\text{(S.4)} \qquad Y = BX + E$$

Substituting for the X vector the values found above, the total cost to the revenue departments can then be found. From system 4 we have

$$Y = \begin{bmatrix} Y_1 \\ Y_2 \\ Y_3 \\ Y_4 \end{bmatrix} = \begin{bmatrix} .20 & .22 & .16 \\ .40 & .15 & .12 \\ .35 & .18 & .18 \\ .05 & .12 & .04 \end{bmatrix} \begin{bmatrix} 3204.9 \\ 6704.8 \\ 5008.0 \end{bmatrix} + \begin{bmatrix} 3500 \\ 4200 \\ 3000 \\ 5300 \end{bmatrix}$$

Carrying out the above operations we obtain

$$\begin{bmatrix} Y_1 \\ Y_2 \\ Y_3 \\ Y_4 \end{bmatrix} = \begin{bmatrix} \text{total cost of mortgage loans dept.} \\ \text{total cost of commercial loans dept.} \\ \text{total cost of consumer loans \& credit dept.} \\ \text{total cost of trust dept.} \end{bmatrix} = \begin{bmatrix} 6417.3 \\ 7088.6 \\ 6230.0 \\ 6465.1 \end{bmatrix}$$

Notice that the sum of the total cost for all revenue departments is $26,201 and the total direct cost of all departments from Table is $26,200. The discrepancy of $1.00 is due to rounding errors.

Suppose that in the next month the following direct costs are assigned to each department:

Department	*Direct Cost in Following Month ($)*
(1) Advertising	2000
(2) Accounting	5000
(3) EDP	4200
(4) Mortgage Loans	3800
(5) Commercial Loans	4000
(6) Consumer Loans & Credit	3200
(7) Trust	5000

The allocation of indirect cost of each service department to each department is assumed to be the same as in the previous month. Then using system 3, (I–C) inverse remains the same, while D becomes

$$D = \begin{bmatrix} D_1 \\ D_2 \\ D_3 \end{bmatrix} = \begin{bmatrix} 2000 \\ 5000 \\ 4200 \end{bmatrix}$$

hence,

$$X = (I-C)^{-1}D$$

$$= \begin{bmatrix} X_1 \\ X_2 \\ X_3 \end{bmatrix} = \begin{bmatrix} 1.000 & .207 & .183 \\ .000 & 1.064 & .426 \\ .000 & .160 & 1.064 \end{bmatrix} \begin{bmatrix} 2000 \\ 5000 \\ 4200 \end{bmatrix}$$

$$\begin{bmatrix} X_1 \\ X_2 \\ X_3 \end{bmatrix} = \begin{bmatrix} 3803.6 \\ 7109.2 \\ 5268.4 \end{bmatrix}$$

The total cost of each revenue department is then found by using system 4. The matrix B is unchanged in system 4 while the vector X is now the new total cost vector of each service department found above and the matrix E is

$$E = \begin{bmatrix} 3800 \\ 4000 \\ 3200 \\ 5000 \end{bmatrix}$$

From system 4 we have

$$Y = \begin{bmatrix} Y_1 \\ Y_2 \\ Y_3 \\ Y_4 \end{bmatrix} = \begin{bmatrix} .20 & .22 & .16 \\ .40 & .15 & .12 \\ .35 & .18 & .18 \\ .05 & .12 & .04 \end{bmatrix} \begin{bmatrix} 3803.6 \\ 7109.2 \\ 5268.4 \end{bmatrix} + \begin{bmatrix} 3800 \\ 4000 \\ 3200 \\ 5000 \end{bmatrix}$$

$$\begin{bmatrix} Y_1 \\ Y_2 \\ Y_3 \\ Y_4 \end{bmatrix} = \begin{bmatrix} 6967.7 \\ 7220.0 \\ 6759.2 \\ 6254.0 \end{bmatrix}$$

The sum of the total cost for all revenue departments is $27,200.9 which only differs from the total direct costs which is $27,200 by $.9 due to rounding.

Using matrix algebra to prepare pro forma financial statements. As another illustration of how matrix algebra can be applied to business problems consider how a conventional accounting system can be translated into a system of simultaneous equations which can assist management in examining how the balance sheet will change as a result of some assumed level of operation, that is, preparing a pro forma balance sheet. From this balance sheet the financial manager can foresee future financial needs of the firm and thus take appropriate steps to assure that these needs are met. For example, as sales increase, the firm will require additional cash, inventory, and fixed assets to produce that level of sales. Also, the firm will have to support a higher level of accounts receivable. All this will result in an increase in total assets. But by the well known accounting principle, "total assets equals total liabilities plus net worth," this requires that total liabilities and net worth must increase to support the higher dollar level of assets.

The Richardson Manufacturing Corporation, a hypothetical firm, will be used to illustrate how a conventional accounting system can be translated into a mathematical system and how the model can be used for financial planning. For simplicity we shall assume that only eight accounts are set up by the firm's accountants: (1) cash, (2) accounts receivable, (3) inventory, (4) net fixed assets, (5) liabilities and net worth, (6) cost of goods sold, (7) other expenditures, and (8) sales. We shall also assume that depreciation is 1 percent of the net fixed assets existing at the end of the accounting period, the firm's accounting period is the calendar year, and the firm is in the 50 percent tax bracket. The balance sheet for our hypothetical firm for the year that just ended is given below:

RICHARDSON MANUFACTURING CORP.

Balance Sheet

December 31, 19XX
(in millions)

Assets		Liabilities & Net Worth	
Cash	$ 300	Liabilities & Net Worth	$1700
Accounts Receivable	400		
Inventory	200		
Net Fixed Assets	800		
Total	$1700		$1700

What the accountant is interested in is how sales will affect the other accounts and, as a result, the balance sheet.

Last year's bookkeeping transactions which resulted in debits and credits between accounts and the balance sheet given above is summarized on Figure 12. The following notation will be used:

X_i = total debits to account i during the accounting period;

X_{ij} = debits to account i which are credited to account j during the accounting period;

and Y_i = debits to account i which are credited to the sales account.

To understand the notation used above, let us interpret some of the elements in Figure 12. The X_{12} element with a value of 300 means that of the $580 million debited to the cash account, $300 million was credited to accounts receivable. This obviously resulted from transactions in which receivables were paid off in cash. The element X_{56} with a value of 100 means that of the $150 million debited to the cost of goods sold account, $100 million was credited to the liabilities and net worth account. That is, $100 million of the cost of goods sold was purchased by increasing liabilities or net worth or both. What specific liability might have been used is unknown because of the broad classification of this account. It could have been accounts payable or short-term bank loan, etc. Y_2 from Figure 12 is 200 which means that there was a debit of $200 million to the receivable account that was credited to the sales account due to sales on credit.

SUMMARY OF BOOKKEEPING ENTRIES FOR
RICHARDSON MANUFACTURING
DURING PREVIOUS YEAR
(in millions of dollars)

Debit to:	Credit to: (1) Cash	(2) Rec.	(3) Inv.	(4) Fixed Assets	(5) Liab. & NW	(6) CGS	(7) O.E.	Y Sales	Total Debits
(1) Cash	0	300	60	0	120	0	0	100	580
(2) Acct's Rec.	0	0	0	0	150	0	0	200	350
(3) Inventory	50	0	0	0	70	0	0	0	120
(4) Fixed Assets, Net	200	0	0	0	100	0	0	0	300
(5) Liab. & NW	40	0	0	0	80	0	0	0	120
(6) Cost of goods sold	50	0	0	0	100	0	0	0	150
(7) Other Exp.	50	0	0	0	40	0	0	0	90
Total Credits	390	300	60	0	660	0	0	300	1710

Fig. 12. Summary of Entries for Previous Year.

The total debits for each account can then be expressed as

$$
\begin{aligned}
X_1 &= X_{11} + X_{12} + \ldots + X_{17} + Y_1 \\
X_2 &= X_{21} + X_{22} + \ldots + X_{27} + Y_2 \\
&\vdots \\
X_7 &= X_{71} + X_{72} + \ldots + X_{77} + Y_7
\end{aligned}
\qquad \text{(S.5)}
$$

The assumption that shall be made here is that the credit to account j as a result of a debit to account i is a fixed percentage of the total debits to account j. That is,

$$X_{ij} = a_{ij} X_j$$

Substituting $a_{ij}\,X_j$ for X_{ij} in system 5 we have

$$\text{(S.6)}\qquad \begin{aligned} X_1 &= a_{11}\,X_1 + a_{12}\,X_2 + \ldots\ldots + a_{17}\,X_7 + Y_1 \\ X_2 &= a_{21}\,X_1 + a_{22}\,X_2 + \ldots\ldots + a_{27}\,X_7 + Y_2 \\ &\;\;\vdots \\ X_7 &= a_{71}\,X_1 + a_{72}\,X_2 + \ldots\ldots + a_{77}\,X_7 + Y_7 \end{aligned}$$

In matrix notation, system 6 can be expressed as

$$\text{(S.7)}\qquad X = AX + Y$$

where

$$X = \begin{bmatrix} X_1 \\ X_2 \\ \vdots \\ X_7 \end{bmatrix},\; A = \begin{bmatrix} a_{11}\ a_{12} \cdots a_{17} \\ a_{21}\ a_{22} \cdots a_{27} \\ \vdots \\ a_{71}\ a_{72} \cdots a_{77} \end{bmatrix} \text{and, } Y = \begin{bmatrix} Y_1 \\ Y_2 \\ \vdots \\ Y_7 \end{bmatrix}$$

What is of interest to the financial accountant is given that the A matrix is fixed, how will the sales vector, Y, affect the total debits of each account and in turn how will it affect debits and credits between accounts. To answer this question, it is first necessary to solve system 7 for the vector X of total debits. Solving we obtain

$$\text{(S.8)}\qquad X = (I-A)^{-1}Y$$

Once we solve for the total debits vector X, we can then find the debits and credits between each account. From the total debits and credits between accounts both a proforma income and balance sheet statement can be computed.

FOR THE RICHARDSON MANUFACTURING CORPORATION
DEBITS OF ACCOUNT I CREDITED TO ACCOUNT J
AS A PERCENTAGE OF THE TOTAL DEBITS OF ACCOUNT J

	Credit to:						
	(1)	(2)	(3)	(4)	(5)	(6)	(7)
Debit to:	Cash	Rec.	Inv.*	Fixed Assets	Liab. & NW	CGS	O.E.
(1) Cash	.000	.857	.500	.000	1.000	.000	.000
(2) Acct's Rec.	.000	.000	.000	.000	1.250	.000	.000
(3) Inventory	.086	.000	.000	.000	.583	.000	.000
(4) Fixed Assets, Net	.345	.000	.000	.000	.833	.000	.000
(5) Liab. & NW	.069	.000	.000	.000	.667	.000	.000
(6) Cost of goods sold	.086	.000	.000	.000	.833	.000	.000
(7) Other Exp.	.086	.000	.000	.000	.333	.000	.000

Fig. 13. Debits and Credits as a Percentage of Total Debits to Account J.

Continuing with the Richardson Manufacturing Corporation, the elements of account i credited to account j as a percentage of the total debits of account j are shown in Figure 13. The matrix, A, is then

$$A = \begin{bmatrix} .000 & .857 & .500 & .000 & 1.000 & .000 & .000 \\ .000 & .000 & .000 & .000 & 1.250 & .000 & .000 \\ .086 & .000 & .000 & .000 & .583 & .000 & .000 \\ .345 & .000 & .000 & .000 & .833 & .000 & .000 \\ .069 & .000 & .000 & .000 & .667 & .000 & .000 \\ .086 & .000 & .000 & .000 & .833 & .000 & .000 \\ .086 & .000 & .000 & .000 & .333 & .000 & .000 \end{bmatrix}$$

therefore,

$$(I-A) = \begin{bmatrix} 1.000 & -.857 & -.500 & .000 & -1.000 & .000 & .000 \\ .000 & 1.000 & .000 & .000 & -1.250 & .000 & .000 \\ -.086 & .000 & 1.000 & .000 & -\ .583 & .000 & .000 \\ -.345 & .000 & .000 & 1.000 & -\ .833 & .000 & .000 \\ -.069 & .000 & .000 & .000 & .333 & .000 & .000 \\ -.086 & .000 & .000 & .000 & -\ .833 & 1.000 & .000 \\ -.086 & .000 & .000 & .000 & -\ .333 & .000 & 1.000 \end{bmatrix}$$

The inverse of (I–A) can be shown to be

$$(I-A)^{-1} = \begin{bmatrix} 2.139 & 1.833 & 1.070 & .000 & 15.180 & .000 & .000 \\ .554 & 1.475 & .277 & .000 & 7.685 & .000 & .000 \\ .442 & .379 & 1.221 & .000 & 4.890 & .000 & .000 \\ 1.107 & .949 & .554 & 1.000 & 10.359 & .000 & .000 \\ .443 & .380 & .222 & .000 & 6.148 & .000 & .000 \\ .553 & .474 & .277 & .000 & 6.427 & 1.000 & .000 \\ .332 & .284 & .116 & .000 & 3.353 & .000 & 1.000 \end{bmatrix}$$

Suppose that management forecasts that in the current year cash sales will be \$150 million and sales on account will be \$290 million. To predict what the balance sheet and income statement will look like for the current year, the effect of sales on each account must be projected.

Using system 8, the vector Y is now

$$Y = \begin{bmatrix} 150 \\ 290 \\ 0 \\ 0 \\ 0 \\ 0 \\ 0 \end{bmatrix}$$

and (I–A) inverse is given above. To determine the total debits to each account system 8 tells us to premultiply the vector Y by the inverse of (I—A). Hence, we have

$$X = (I-A)^{-1} \begin{bmatrix} 150 \\ 290 \\ 0 \\ 0 \\ 0 \\ 0 \\ 0 \end{bmatrix} \qquad X = \begin{bmatrix} X_1 \\ X_2 \\ X_3 \\ X_4 \\ X_5 \\ X_6 \\ X_7 \end{bmatrix} = \begin{bmatrix} 852.42 \\ 510.85 \\ 176.21 \\ 441.26 \\ 176.65 \\ 220.41 \\ 132.01 \end{bmatrix}$$

Remembering that

$$X_{ij} = a_{ij} X_j$$

the debits and credits between each account can be determined. For example X_{35} which is a debit to the inventory account and a credit to the liabilities and net worth account is 102.99 found by multiplying a_{35} which is .583 by X_5 which is 176.65. Using this procedure debits and credits to each account can be found. These forecasted transactions are shown on Figure 14. The discrepancy between the total debits appearing in Figure 14 and those in the total debits computed above is due to rounding errors when computing the inverse of (I—A).

From Figure 14 the balance sheet and income statement for the current year can be forecasted. To forecast the balance sheet we must see what happens to each asset and the liabilities and net worth account. Figure 15 shows the total debits and credits to each account appearing on the balance sheet. Column 3 shows whether a debit or credit exists between these transactions. Column 4 gives the opening balance for each account. These balances are simply the amount shown on the balance sheet of a year ago. The closing balance is shown on Column 5. Such balances are found by adding Columns 4 and 5. Credits are shown in brackets.

From the balances shown in Column 5, a pro forma balance sheet can be completed. This balance sheet is shown below:

RICHARDSON MANUFACTURING CORP.

Pro forma Balance Sheet
(in millions)

Assets		Liabilities & Net Worth	
Cash	$ 579.73	Liabilities & Net Worth	$2494.75
Accounts Receivable	473.01	Financing Required	74.96
Inventory	288.19		
Net Fixed Assets	1228.78		
Total	$2569.71	Total	$2569.71

As can be seen from the pro forma balance sheet, the financial manager of the firm must secure funds to the extent of $74.96 million in order to support cash sales of $150 million and sales on account of $290 million.

PROJECTED DEBITS AND CREDITS BETWEEN ACCOUNTS FOR THE RICHARDSON MANUFACTURING CORPORATION FOR THE CURRENT YEAR
(in millions of dollars)

Debit to:	Credit to: (1) Cash	(2) Rec.	(3) Inv.	(4) Fixed Assets	(5) Liab. & NW	(6) CGS	(7) O.E.	(8) Sales	Total Debits
(1) Cash	0	437.80	88.11	0	176.65	0	0	150	852.56
(2) Acct's Rec.	0	0	0	0	220.81	0	0	290	510.81
(3) Inventory	73.31	0	0	0	102.99	0	0	0	176.30
(4) Fixed Assets, Net	294.08	0	0	0	147.15	0	0	0	441.23
(5) Liab. & NW	58.82	0	0	0	117.83	0	0	0	176.65
(6) Cost of goods sold	73.31	0	0	0	147.15	0	0	0	220.46
(7) Other Exp.	73.31	0	0	0	58.82	0	0	0	132.13
Total Credits	572.83	437.80	88.11	0	971.40	0	0	440	2510.14

Fig. 14. Projected Debits and Credits

A pro forma income statement of the firm is given below:

RICHARDSON MANUFACTURING CORP.

Pro forma Income Statement

Sales	$440.00
Cost of goods sold	(220.46)
Gross margin	219.54
Depreciation	(12.41)
Other expenses	(132.13)
Earnings before taxes	75.00
Taxes (50%)	(37.50)
Earnings after taxes	$ 37.50

The treasurer can similarly forecast the balance sheet and income statement for any level of sales.

WORKSHEET FOR PRO FORMA BALANCE SHEET OF
RICHARDSON MANUFACTURING CORPORATION
(in millions of dollars)

Account	(1) Total Debits	(2) Total Credits	(3) Balance	(4) Opening Balance	(5) Closing Balance
(1) Cash	852.56	(572.83)	279.73	300	579.73
(2) Acct's Rec.	510.81	(437.80)	73.01	400	473.01
(3) Inventory	176.30	(88.11)	88.19	200	288.19
(4) Net Fixed Assets	441.23	(0)	441.23	800	1228.78*
(5) Liab. & Net Worth	176.65	(971.40)	(794.75)	(1700)	(2494.75)

*Total net fixed assets would be $1241.19. However, it was assumed that depreciation is 1 percent of total net fixed assets at year end. Thus, this account would be credited by the amount of depreciation, $12.41, and this amount debited to a depreciation account.

Fig. 15. Worksheet for Pro forma Balance Sheet.

MANAGEMENT SCIENCE TECHNIQUES

In this section those management science techniques which have found commercial acceptance will be discussed. The techniques that will be discussed are mathematical programming, network models, inventory models and simulation.

Mathematical programming models. Mathematical programming models are used to solve problems which involve the allocation of resources in such a way so as to optimize a quantifiable goal. The nature of allocation problems is that a large number of acceptable solutions which satisfy the constraints or restrictions imposed upon the decision maker may exist but there may be an optimal or best solution which optimizes the value of the specified goal. Mathematical programming has been applied to determine the optimal product mix, allocate overhead costs and determine transfer prices. Moreover, mathematical programming can be used in connection with break-even analysis, incremental cost analysis, financial planning and budgeting.

The mathematical programming models discussed below are (1) linear programming, (2) integer programming, (3) nonlinear programming, (4) goal programming, and (5) dynamic programming.

1. Linear Programming. The first step in all mathematical programming models is to define the variables about which a decision must be made. These variables are referred to as *decision variables*. The second step is to mathematically specify the objective the decision maker seeks to optimize. The mathematical expression is termed the *objective function*. In linear programming the objective function is linear. The third step is to establish the constraints under which the objective function is to be optimized. Again, in linear programming each constraint must be expressed as a linear relationship. The final step is to solve for the optimal solution. The decision maker and the management scientist participate in the first three steps. The management scientist must then develop a computational procedure to solve for the optimal solution. Fortunately, a computational procedure to solve a linear programming problem is available. The algorithm is called the *simplex method*.

▶EXAMPLE: Production scheduling of Linear Programming. The following hypothetical example will illustrate a linear programming problem.

A major automobile manufacturer also produces two types of trucks which we shall denote as Type I and Type II. All of the trucks are produced in one plant in the eastern part of the United States. Each month the production manager of the plant must determine how many units of each truck to produce. The Type I truck generates a profit of $220 per unit, while on the Type II truck a profit of $420 is realized. The production of both trucks must go through the following phases: (i) engine construction; (ii) chassis assembly and; (iii) inspection. Production requirements for production of a Type I truck are 3 man-hours of engine construction, 8 man-hours of chassis assembly, and 2 man-hours of inspection. The production of a Type II truck requires 9 man-hours for engine construction, 5 man-hours for chassis assembly, and 3 man-hours for inspection. The production manager has available each month 8,100 man-hours for engine construction, 12,000 man-hours for chassis assembly, and 3,600 man-hours for inspection. The sales department informs the production manager that demand is sufficient to handle any number of Type I trucks produced; however, he is also told that only 800 Type II trucks can be sold. Assuming that the production manager is interested in maximizing profits, how many Type I and Type II trucks will he schedule to produce, given the conditions specified above?

Let us express the above problem in mathematical terms. The relevant data is summarized in Figure 16. The two decision variables are the number of units of Type I and Type II to produce. The objective of the production manager is to maximize profits. Since a profit of $220 per unit is earned on each Type I truck, the total profit for all Type I trucks produced is $220 multiplied by the number of Type I trucks produced. Since a profit of $420 is earned on each Type II truck produced, the total profit for all Type II trucks produced is $420 multiplied by the number of

Type II trucks produced. The total profit of the plant for the month is then:

Total profit = \$220 (number of Type I trucks produced)
+ \$420 (number of Type II trucks produced)

If we let X_1 represent the number of Type I trucks produced and X_2 represent the number of Type II trucks produced then the previous expression can be written as:

$$\text{Total profit} = \$220\, X_1 + \$420\, X_2$$

It is this expression that the production manager seeks to maximize. Hence, it is the objective function for the problem. Notice that the objective function is linear (i.e., the exponent of each decision variable is equal to 1).

	Type I Truck	*Type II Truck*	*Capacity man-hours per month*
engine construction	3 man-hours	9 man-hours	8,100
chassis assembly	8 man-hours	5 man-hours	12,000
inspection	2 man-hours	3 man-hours	3,600
maximum		800 units	
profit per unit	\$220	\$420	

Fig. 16. Summary Data: Linear Programming Example.

The production manager however faces limitations imposed by the production and sales department. For example, only 8,100 man-hours for engine construction are available in the month. Since each Type I truck requires 3 man-hours of engine construction, the total number of man-hours required for producing Type I trucks in the engine construction department is equal to 3 multiplied by the number of Type I trucks produced. Similarly, 9 man-hours of engine construction are required to produce each Type II truck, and hence the total number of man-hours for producing Type II trucks in the engine construction department is equal to 9 multiplied by the number of such trucks produced. The total number of man-hours utilized in the engine construction department can therefore be expressed as:

$$\text{Total man-hours for engine construction} = 3\, X_1 + 9\, X_2$$

The limitation imposed on the production manager is that the above total man-hours must be less than or equal to 8,100, that is,

$$3\, X_1 + 9\, X_2 \leq 8{,}100 \text{ man-hours (engine construction constraint)}$$

We have just expressed the engine construction man-hour constraint mathematically. Notice that the engine construction constraint is linear.

In the same way we can express the constraints imposed with respect to the number of man-hours in the chassis assembly and inspection department as:

$$8\, X_1 + 5\, X_2 \leq 12{,}000 \text{ man-hours (chassis assembly constraint)}$$
$$2\, X_1 + 3\, X_2 \leq 3{,}600 \text{ man-hours (inspection constraint)}$$

In addition to the resource constraints, there is also a sales constraint which specifies that the production of Type II trucks be limited to 800 units. This can be expressed as:

$X_2 \leq 800$ units (sales constraint)

Finally, two constraints are necessary for the problem to make sense. These two constraints require that the number of Type I or Type II trucks be greater than or equal to zero, that is, a negative value for X_1 or X_2 is not permitted. Obviously, a negative value for either of the decision variables is meaningless. The two contraints are then:

$X_1 \geq 0$ units (nonnegativity constraint)
$X_2 \geq 0$ units (nonnegativity constraint)

The linear programming problem facing the production manager can then be expressed mathematically by:

Maximize: Total profits $= \$220\ X_1 + \$420\ X_2$

Subject to the following constraints:

$3\ X_1 + 9\ X_2 \leq$ 8,100 man-hours (engine construction constraint)
$8\ X_1 + 5\ X_2 \leq$ 12,000 man-hours (chassis assembly constraint)
$2\ X_1 + 3\ X_2 \leq$ 3,600 man-hours (inspection constraint)
$X_2 \leq$ 800 units (sales constraint)
$X_1 \geq$ 0 units (nonnegativity constraint)
$X_2 \geq$ 0 units (nonnegativity constraint)

The computational procedure employed to solve a linear programming problem is the Simplex method. Although the Simplex method will not be described here, the principle behind the method will be explained by means of a graph. It should be pointed out that the graphical method is also used to solve simple linear programming problems. However, in problems with more than two decision variables the graphical method generally cannot be used.

The shaded areas in Figures 17 (a)-(d) indicate the areas which satisfy the designated constraints. Each figure is limited to the quadrant of the $X_1\ X_2$ plane where both X_1 and X_2 are nonnegative since the nonnegativity constraints require that we limit our search for the optimal solution to this quadrant. Since all constraints must be met simultaneously, the optimal solution must lie in the shaded area that is common to all constraints. This area is shown on Figure 18. All points along the boundary and within the region ABCDEF satisfy all the constraints simultaneously. The region ABCDEF is therefore called the feasible region. Each of the corner points (A,B,C,D,E,F) on the region can be found by solving for the point at which two of the constraints intersect.

To find the optimal solution, we can apply the basic theorem of linear programming which states that: If a linear programming problem has an optimal solution, this solution must occur at a corner point of the feasible region. Because of this theorem we can limit our search for the optimal solution to the corner points.

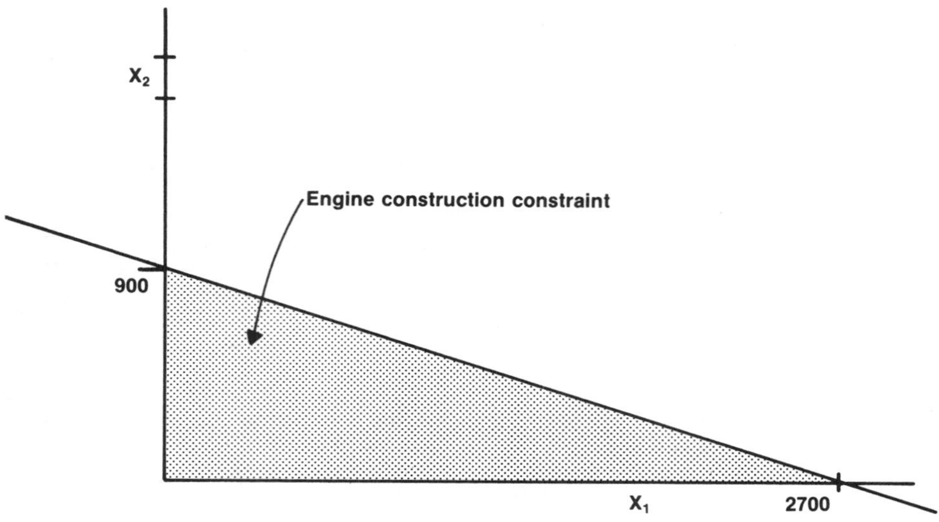

Fig. 17a.

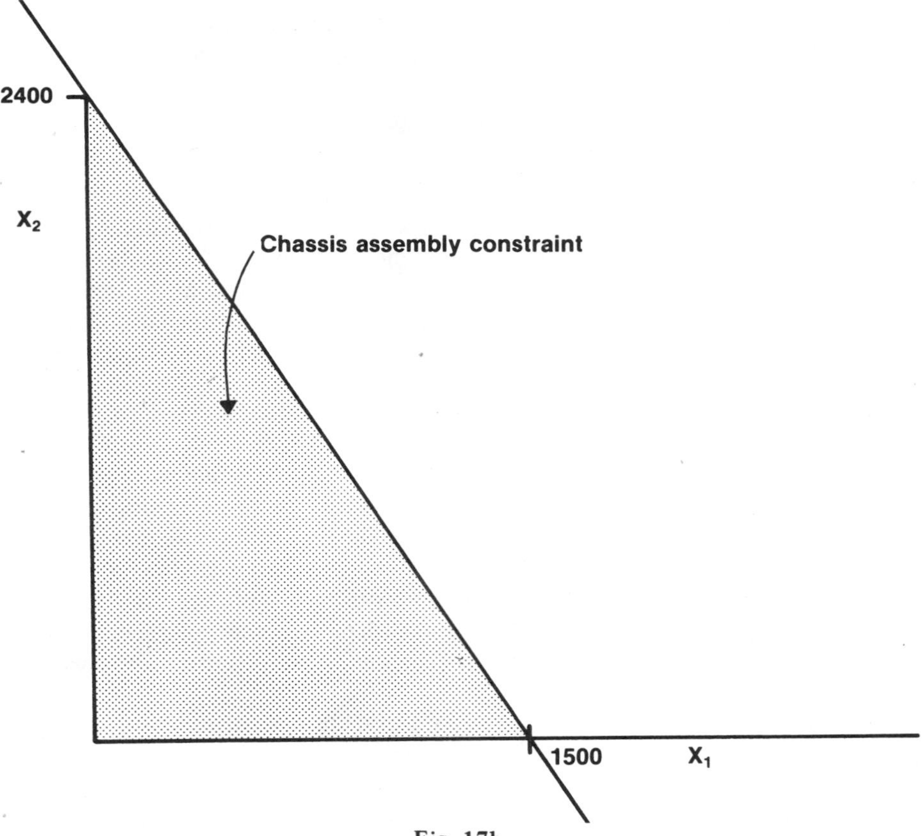

Fig. 17b.
Constraints for the Linear Programming Problem.

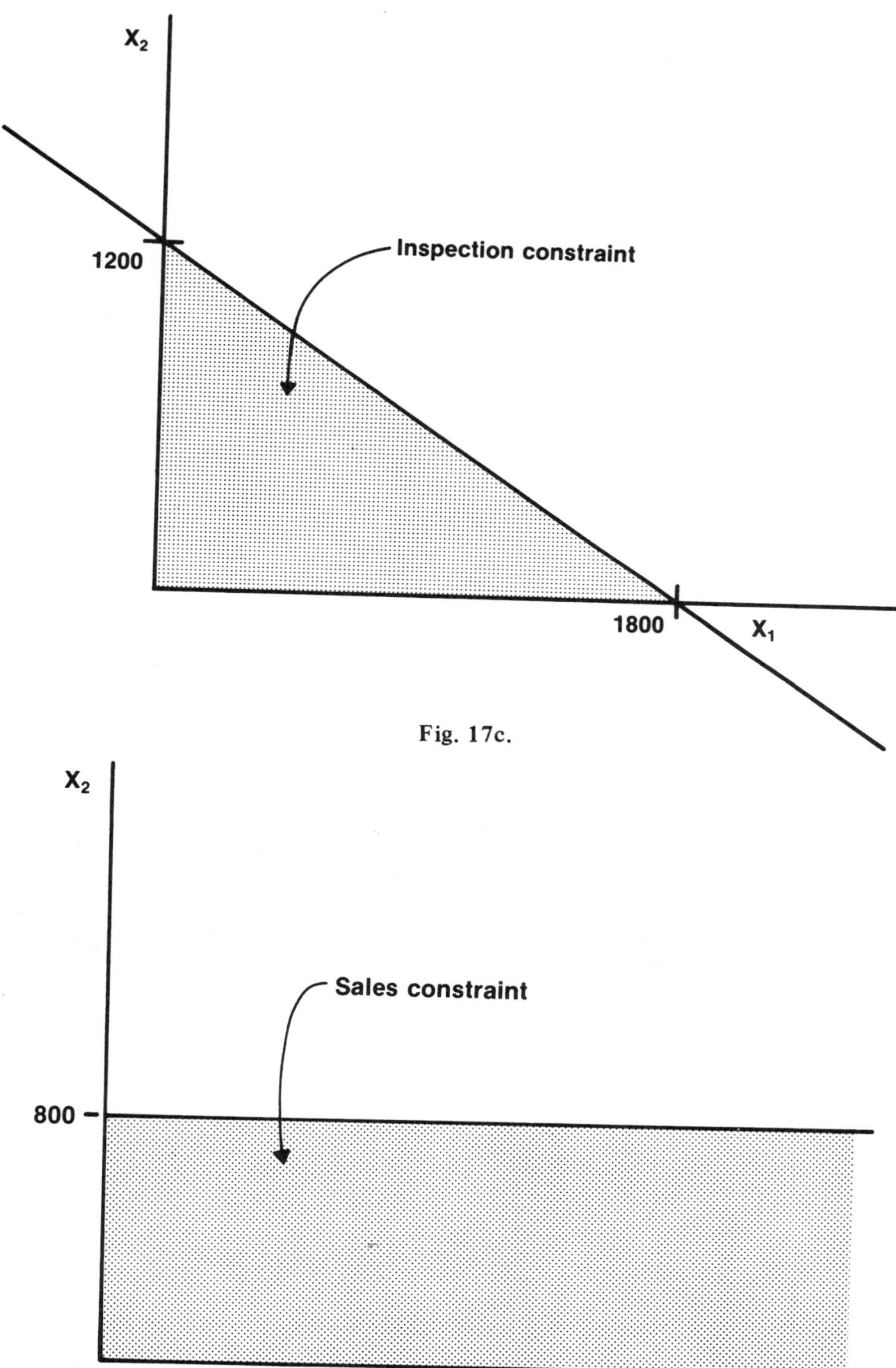

Fig. 17c.

Fig. 17d.

Constraints for the Linear Programming Problem (Continued).

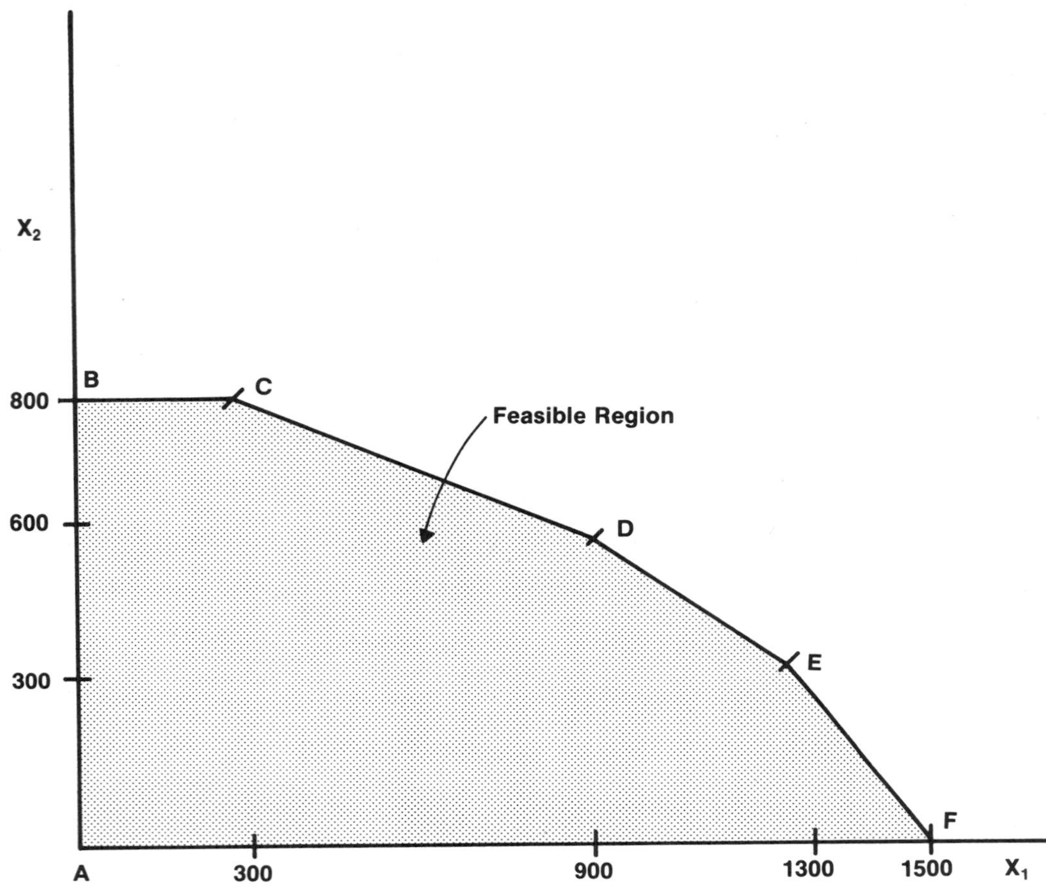

Fig. 18. Feasible Region for the Linear Programming Problem.

Figure 19 indicates the profit level for each of the corner points of the feasible region. As can be seen, the maximum profit is at corner point D requiring the production of 900 units of Type I trucks and 600 units of Type II trucks and yielding a profit of $450,000.

Corner point	Value of X_1	X_2	Profit ($)
A	0	0	$ 0
B	0	800	336,000
C	300	800	408,600
D	900	600	450,000*
E	1,285.7	342.9	426,872
F	1,500	0	330,000

*Optimal value

Fig. 19. Profit Level at Each Corner Point.

The Simplex method, first developed by G.B. Danzig in 1947 and later further refined by him and others, is an iterative procedure which searches corner points in such a way that the value of the objective function is improved at each iteration until the objective function can no longer be improved, that is, the optimal solution is reached. Numerous "canned" computer programs using a form of the Simplex method are available from computer manufacturers as part of their software services. A partial, and by no means exhaustive, list of such programs is given below:

- IBM 1410 Basic Linear Programming System
- IBM 1620-1311 Linear Programming System
- Honeywell 800/1800 Advanced Linear Programming System
- General Electric 225 Linear Programming
- Control Data Corporation 3600 Ophelie Linear Programming

Each program has advantages and disadvantages which the accountant should investigate before selecting a program.

For every linear programming problem in which a maximization of the objective function is sought there exists a symmetrical linear programming problem in which a minimization of the objective function is sought. It is convention to call one the "primal" problem and the other the "dual" problem.

The concept of "duality" is important in mathematical programming for two reasons. First, the solution to the dual generally contains valuable economic information. Second, it is sometimes easier to solve the dual than the primal, or original, problem.

The dual of the original problem illustrated above is:

Minimize: $K = 8{,}100\ W_1 + 12{,}000\ W_2 + 3{,}600\ W_3 + 800\ W_4$

Subject to the following constraints:

$$3\ W_1 + 8\ W_2 + 2\ W_3 + 0\ W_4 \geq 220$$
$$9\ W_1 + 5\ W_2 + 3\ W_3 + W_4 \geq 420$$
$$W_1 \geq 0, W_2 \geq 0, W_3 \geq 0, W_4 \geq 0.$$

It can be seen from the above how the dual is generated from the primal. First, the objective function is changed from maximization to minimization. The number of decision variables in the dual is equal to the number of constraints (excluding the two nonnegativity constraints) in the primal and the coefficients in the objective function in the dual are equal to the right hand side values for the respective primal constraints. There are two constraints in the dual which corresponds to the two decision variables in the primal and the right hand side values of the dual constraints are equal to the respective coefficients in the objective function of the primal. The two constraints in the dual are "greater than or equal to" type whereas in the primal they are the "less than or equal to" type.

The optimal solution of the dual can be found by using the Simplex method directly on the dual linear programming problem. Alternatively, the dual solution is generally provided as a byproduct of the Simplex method applied to the primal linear programming problem. For the dual problem above, the optimal value of the dual variables are:

$W_1 = 20, W_2 = 0, W_3 = 80$ and $W_4 = 0$.

The optimal value of the objective function for the dual is 450,000. Note that this is the same value that the optimal solution to the primal yields. The question is then how do we interpret the value of the dual variables.

In the primal problem the objective was to maximize profits by selecting the number of units of each type truck to produce given the resource and sales constraints. The dual problem is a mathematical abstraction and its interpretation is not straightforward. Hence, it is only possible to give an intuitive interpretation at this point. One way of looking at the dual problem is to ask how much of the profit is contributed by each of the firm's resources? We would like to assign artificial per unit prices to each of the resources in such a way so as to totally distribute profits. That is, from an accounting point of view there will be no accounting profit since we will be assigning values to each resource so as to leave zero profits. This is why the dual variables are referred to as "shadow prices" or "accounting prices."

Given this interpretation, a man-hour of engine construction and a man-hour of inspection time are assigned a shadow price of \$20 and \$80 respectively. Why do the other dual variables – W_2 and W_4 – have a zero shadow price? To understand why let us examine the value of the primal constraints when the optimal solution is obtained. By substituting $X_1 = 900$ and $X_2 = 600$ into the primal constraints it can be seen that all of the engine construction and inspection man-hours are used. However, only 10,200 chassis assembly man-hours and less than 800 units of Type II trucks are sold. Since the two constraints are not fully utilized the two dual variables are assigned zero shadow prices.

Another useful way to interpret the dual variables is that they indicate the incremental change in the objective function if an additional unit of a specific resource or constraint is permitted. For example, suppose that the production manager obtains 10 additional man-hours for engine construction, what would happen to the value of the objective function? The objective function would increase by the dual value assigned to a man-hour of engine construction times the increase in the number of man-hours. Hence, the objective function would increase by \$200 (10 man-hours times \$20). For this reason, the dual variables are sometimes referred to as the "opportunity costs." Notice that if the number of man-hours for chassis assembly is increased, the value of the objective function would not change.

2. *Integer Programming*. In the linear programming model it was assumed that the decision variables are divisible. That is, a solution of say 555.4 Type I trucks is a possible solution. It is difficult to perceive of many products in business being divisible. It is sometimes thought that simply rounding off the optimal solution so that all the values are integers will eliminate the problem. However, to see why rounding off will not necessarily result in the optimal solution consider the following linear programming problem:

Maximize: Total profits $= 40\ X_1 + 200\ X_2$

Subject to the following constraints:

$$4\,X_1 + 40\,X_2 \leq 80 \quad \text{(labor constraint)}$$
$$4\,X_1 \leq 8 \quad \text{(sales constraint)}$$
$$X_1 \geq 0 \text{ and } X_2 \geq 0$$

where X_1 and X_2 are two products.
The optimal solution is to produce two units of X_1 and 1.8 units of X_2. The optimal profit is then $440. If X_2 is not divisible then it is not possible to produce .8 units of the product. We cannot roundoff X_2 to two since it is not possible to produce two units of both X_1 and X_2 since it violates the first constraint. We can round X_2 down to one unit so that the solution would be two units of X_1 and one unit of X_2 yielding a total profit of $280. However, there is a better solution than the rounded linear programming solution. If two units of X_2 are produced and no units of X_1 are produced then the value for the objective function is $400. Notice that this solution is not as good as the linear programming solution but it is better than the solution found by rounding off the values for the decision variables in the linear programming problem.

To handle problems in which all decision variables must take on integer values, the technique of integer linear programming is used. To further illustrate the applicability of integer linear programming consider the following capital budgeting problem:

$$\text{Maximize: Total net present value} = 230\,P_1 + 160\,P_2 + 234\,P_3 + 204\,P_4 + 130\,P_5$$

Subject to the following constraints:

$$21\,P_1 + 18\,P_2 + 24\,P_3 + 21\,P_4 + 15\,P_5 \leq 90$$
$$27\,P_1 + 21\,P_2 + 30\,P_3 + 24\,P_4 + 24\,P_5 \leq 104$$
$$33\,P_1 + 24\,P_2 + 36\,P_3 + 27\,P_4 + 21\,P_5 \leq 112$$
$$0 \leq P_i \leq 1 \qquad (i = 1,2,3,4,5)$$

and each P_i is an integer that can be either 1 or 0.

The objective function is to maximize the total net present value generated from the five capital investment projects (P_i). The constraints represent the estimated costs for each project in each of the next three years. The right hand value for each constraint represents the total funds available to support projects in each year. Linear programming cannot be applied since P_i can only take on a value of zero or one. That is, it is not possible to take on a fraction of a project. A value of one means the project should be accepted whereas a value of zero means that the project should not be undertaken.

Suppose that two projects, P_4 and P_5, are mutually exclusive which means that the acceptance of one project will result in the rejection of the other. Then this requirement can be imposed by adding the following constraint:

$$P_4 + P_5 \leq 1$$

Hence, it is only possible for one of the two projects to be accepted since the value of P_4 and P_5 are restricted to be either zero or one.

In a capital budgeting problem one project may be contingent on the acceptance of another project. This can easily be included into an integer programming model.

Suppose that project two is contingent on the acceptance of the third project, then the following constraint will ensure that the solution will consider this requirement:

$$P_2 - P_3 \leq 0$$

In certain problems it is possible that some of the decision variables must take on integer values while other decision variables can take on any nonnegative value. Such problems are called mixed integer programming problems. Real life problems may also require that decision variables be limited to discrete values (e.g., .1, .2, .3, . . . or 1/5, 1/10, 3/5, . . .). One example of such a problem is when the decision variable may be the number of quarts of a liquid product to produce. Such programming problems are called discrete programming problems. A discrete programming problem can be transformed into an integer programming problem by simple scaling of the decision variables.

Computational techniques are not as simple for integer programming problems compared to algorithms employed to solve linear programming problems. Several researchers have experimented with and/or developed computer programs to handle integer programming problems. Some programs can handle up to one hundred decision variables and fifty constraints. When compared to some computer programs to solve linear programming problems which can handle several thousand decision variables and constraints, the integer programming computer programs are quite modest. Moreover, the computer time required to solve even a small integer programming problem may be prohibitive.

3. Nonlinear Programming. The restriction made in employing the linear programming model is that both the objective function and the constraints be linear. For example, in a linear programming problem the unit profit margin does not vary with the level of output or the price per unit does not vary with volume. However, in many real life problems, nonlinear relationships exist. It is often found that as volume increases the price per unit of the product decreases. Or, in the production process the average cost per unit varies with the level of output as a result of economies or diseconomies of scale. When nonlinear relationships are encountered in either the objective function, the constraints, or both, we have moved into the realm of nonlinear programming.

The mathematics involved in comprehending nonlinear programming is more complex than in linear programming. Remember that in linear programming the optimal solution was found by examining the corner points of the feasible region. In nonlinear programming the solution cannot be found as easily. The optimal solution can lie anywhere along the boundary of the feasible region or even within the feasible region. Hence, an efficient algorithm for solving general nonlinear programming problems is yet to be developed.

▶ EXAMPLE: Solving a product mix problem by nonlinear programming. To illustrate a nonlinear programming problem let us consider the product-mix problem of the truck manufacturer. Suppose that it is determined that the price per truck is dependent on the number of each truck produced. An investigation of the market indicates the following demand function for each type of truck:

$$\text{price of Type I truck} = 7{,}000 - 2\,X_1$$

and

$$\text{price for Type II truck} = 8{,}500 - 4\,X_2$$

Assume further that the cost of producing each truck is \$5,400 and \$6,000 respectively for Type I and Type II trucks respectively and that the cost does not vary with the level of output.

The total profit from the production of each type truck is then:

$$\begin{aligned}\text{total profit from Type I trucks} &= (\text{price per unit})\,(\text{quantity}) - (\text{cost per unit})\,(\text{quantity})\\ &= (7{,}000 - 2\,X_1)\,(X_1) - (5{,}400)\,(X_1)\\ &= 1{,}600\,X_1 - 2\,X_1^2\end{aligned}$$

and

$$\begin{aligned}\text{total profit from Type II trucks} &= (8{,}500 - 4\,X_2)\,(X_2) - (6{,}000)\,(X_2)\\ &= 2{,}500\,X_2 - 4\,X_2^2\end{aligned}$$

The total profit is then:

$$1{,}600\,X_1 - 2\,X_1^2 + 2{,}500\,X_2 - 4\,X_2^2$$

The above expression for total profit is therefore the objective function. The constraints are the same as before. We therefore have a nonlinear programming problem in which the objective function is nonlinear while the constraints are linear.

We could modify the above problem by assuming that the average cost per unit varies with the level of output rather than remaining constant. For example, suppose the production department estimates that the average cost per unit for the two type trucks is:

$$\text{average cost per unit for Type I trucks} = 2{,}000 + 3\,X_1 + 60{,}000/X_1$$

and

$$\text{average cost per unit for Type II trucks} = 4{,}500 + X_2 + 63{,}000/X_2$$

The total profit expression is then:

$$5{,}000\,X_1 - 5\,X_1^2 + 4{,}000\,X_2 - 5\,X_2^2 - 123{,}000$$

The above expression would then be the objective function resulting in a nonlinear programming problem.

4. Goal Programming. One of the problems with the mathematical programming models discussed above is that they do not permit multiple objectives to be considered by the decision maker. For example, the mathematical programming models above will find the optimal solution when a single objective is specified. However, if there are multiple objectives some of which may be conflicting, say maximization of profits and the desire to minimize employee layoffs, then the mathematical programming models discussed above cannot handle the situation.

In goal programming instead of having constraints we have goals. That is, each constraint is transformed into a goal. Each goal is then given a priority level which is specified in ordinal terms. Within a given priority level, there may be several goals.

5. Dynamic Programming. The mathematical programming techniques thus far discussed deal with solving problems involving a single point in time or a single stage. Dynamic programming is a technique for solving certain types of sequential problems where the parameters of the model vary from period to period or from stage to stage.

Such multistage (or multiperiod) problems appear frequently in business problems. For example, the optimal policy for investing capital expenditures this year depends on how the cash flows generated from current capital expenditure can be employed in future years. As another example, consider a company's maintenance policy. The policy followed for the firm's machinery in the present year depends upon what management intends to do with machinery in future years.

Although the technique of dynamic programming is much more powerful than the previous mathematical programming techniques discussed, computational techniques are much more involved and time-consuming even for small-size problems. Unlike the other mathematical programming techniques discussed, no standard form for dynamic programming exists.

Network Models. What do PERT, CPM, PRISM, IMPACT, SCANS, PEP, PLANNET, PAR, ICON, RAMPS, LESS, SPERT, TOPS, TOES, MPACS and GERT have in common? One guess might be that they are acronyms for federal government agencies. The correct answer is that they are acronyms for network techniques that have proven useful in solving problems for planning and controlling long-term, nonrepetitive projects such as the construction of a plant, the development of a new product line or the establishment of a new production system.

A network itself represents a diagram of the interrelationships of a complex time series of activities or jobs. The object of each technique is to help determine potential bottlenecks and continually monitor the progress of the project. The difference in many of the techniques listed above arises as a result of the emphasis of the specific job under consideration. The two most common techniques are the Critical Path Method (CPM) and the Program Evaluation and Review Technique (PERT). The former technique is a deterministic model while the latter is a probabilistic model.

CPM and PERT were developed about the same time. CPM originated in the private sector by E.I. duPont de Nemours and Company and Remington Rand in planning the construction of a plant. PERT was developed in 1958 by the U.S. Navy Special Projects Office and the consulting firm of Booz, Allen and Hamilton in connection with the U.S. Navy's *Polaris* project. Some estimates suggest that PERT saved up to two years in the completion of the *Polaris* project. Since then PERT has become an important managerial tool in private industry. In accounting PERT has been used in revising standard cost data, scheduling the closing of books, scheduling the time elements for preparing departmental budgets, preparing the annual profit plan, and analyzing cash flows.

Algorithms for solving network models can be found in standard textbooks in management science. Hence, such computational techniques will not be discussed below. Canned computer programs are also available.

1. Critical Path Method (CPM). The essential characteristics of projects to be analyzed by the critical path method are: (i) a well defined set of jobs (or activities) which when all completed mark the end of the project; (ii) within a given sequence a job can be started and stopped independently of other jobs, and; (iii) jobs must be completed in a specified technological sequence.

▶ EXAMPLE: For illustration purposes, eight jobs necessary to complete a project will be assumed. Each job is denoted by a letter ($a, b, \ldots, h$). A specification of the sequence in which the jobs must be completed is given in the following table along with the time (in days) that it takes to complete the job.

DATA FOR NETWORK MODEL PROBLEM

JOB NAME	IMMEDIATE PREDECESSORS	TIME (DAYS)
A	–	3
B	A	3
C	B	4
D	B	3
E	D	6
F	C	3
G	E,F	7
H	G	3

The above provides a network diagram which represents the sequential technological relationship specified in the foregoing table. In the circles (or nodes) the job and the number of days necessary to complete the job are given. From Figure 20 it can be seen, for example, that jobs *e* and *f* must be completed before job *g* can be started.

Notice that there are two paths which lead to the completion of the project: *a-b-d-e-g-h* and *a-b-c-f-g-h*. The former path takes 23 days to complete while the latter path takes 25 days to complete. What is the shortest time that the project can be completed? Obviously the project cannot be completed in less than 25 days under the conditions specified above. Hence, the critical path that management must concentrate on is *a-b-c-f-g-h* since any delay in a job on this path will delay the project from being completed in 25 days.

This information will prevent management from following a crash program on all jobs if it wants to reduce project time, and instead, concentrate on shortening the time of jobs on the critical path. Management also can determine where jobs can slide for a while if that is advantageous in that it will not reduce the completion time. For ex-

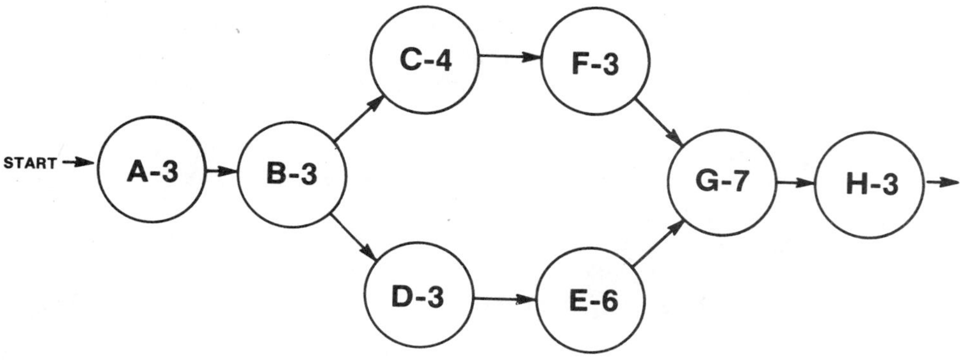

Fig. 20. Illustration of a Network.

ample, job *d* could be delayed by two days without changing the time that the project can be completed. Such time is referred to as *slack* time.

If data was supplied for the cost of each job it would be possible to compute the cost of carrying out the project. It is then possible to compute the trade-off between cost and the amount of time by which the project completion can be decreased.

2. Program Evaluation and Review Technique (PERT). CPM assumes that the completion time for each job is known with certainty. This is why CPM is a deterministic model. More realistically, management may have several estimates for the time of a job with different degrees of confidence. PERT frequently involves three estimates for each job: most optimistic, most pessimistic, and most likely.

Given the three estimates by management, the estimate for a given job is then usually obtained by

$$\frac{\text{most pessimistic} + 4 \text{ times most likely} + \text{most optimistic}}{6}$$

For example, for job *d* management might believe that the most pessimistic time is 7 days while the most optimistic time is 2 days. If the most likely case is 3 days, then the time for job *d* is:

$$\frac{7 + 4 \text{ times } 3 + 2}{6} = 3.5 \text{ days}$$

This would be the number of days used in the network model.

Inventory Models. The major objective of inventory management is to determine the optimal amount of investment in the firm's inventory. Carrying an excess amount of inventory will result in a lower rate of return on total assets of the firm and consequently a lower rate of profitability as measured by the rate of return on stockholders' equity or rate of return on total assets. On the other hand, carrying insufficient inventory can result in lost sales or the closing of the firm's plant with the result that the profitability rate will decline. The objective of this section is to discuss the basic principles of inventory control models and to present several models. The derivation of each model will not be presented here.

All inventory models basically deal with the problems associated with storing something to meet future demand. This need not be restricted to the storing of raw materials or finished inventory. It applies equally to cash and plant capacity. In the discussion below the case in which a firm must determine how much to order from a supplier will be given.

The three costs associated with inventory are order costs, carrying costs and shortage costs. Order costs include transportation costs, clerical costs for ordering and handling costs when the goods are delivered. The cost of capital, risk of obsolescence, insurance costs and storage space are examples of carrying costs. Shortage (or stock-out) costs represent the contribution margins on lost sales due to inventory shortages and the loss of goodwill resulting from the inability to supply customers or supply them with a considerable delay.

The objective is to minimize total inventory costs. There is a trade-off between

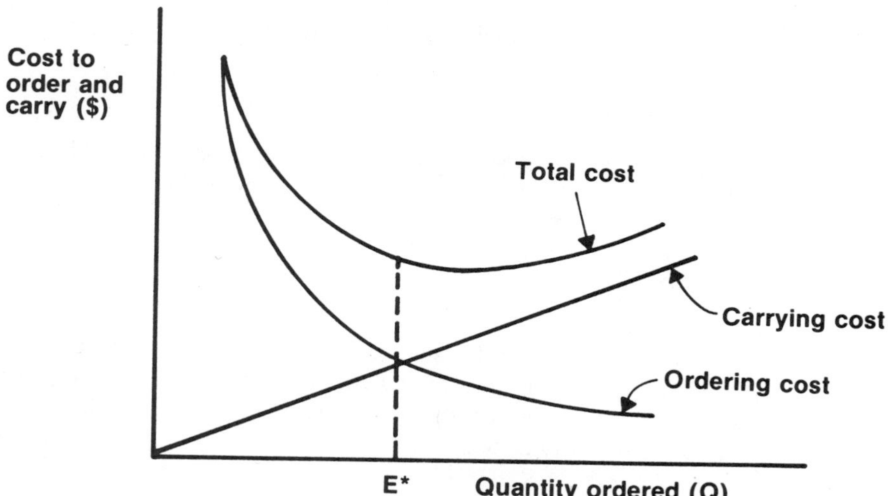

Fig. 21. Graphic Illustration of the Economic Order Quantity.

the components of total cost. For example, the more inventory carried the lower will be the total ordering costs since the firm can order less times. On the other hand, in this instance the total carrying costs will increase. The trade-off between these two costs is illustrated on Figure 21. The inventory models below will assist the decision maker in finding a balance between these costs.

There are deterministic and probabilistic inventory models. In a deterministic model the demand for the firm's inventory is known with certainty. When the demand is not known with certainty but can be estimated by a probability distribution, we have a probabilistic model. Also when the lead time to have an order filled by a supplier fluctuates we have a probabilistic model.

1. Deterministic Models. There are several deterministic inventory models. Let us consider the simplest model.

▶ EXAMPLE: Assume that a wholesale firm has contracted to supply a customer with a certain number of units of some item for the next year at a uniform rate over the year. Assume that no shortages are permitted and that inventory orders are filled without delay. Let

C = total inventory cost
Q = number of units of the product ordered by the firm at each ordering
P = ordering costs each time an order is placed
S = carrying costs per unit
A = number of units contracted for (demanded) over the year.

It can be shown that total carrying costs $= \frac{SQ}{2}$ and

total ordering costs $= \frac{AP}{Q}$

Therefore, total inventory costs are equal to the sum of the two costs. That is,

$$C = \frac{S\,Q}{2} + \frac{A\,P}{Q}$$

The optimal quantity to order, Q* (economic order quantity), can be found by using differential calculus. The economic order quantity can be found to be equal to

$$(1)\ \ Q^* = \sqrt{\frac{2\ AP}{S}}$$

Point E represents Q* on Figure 21.

To illustrate the use of equation (1) suppose that the wholesale firm contracted to supply 4,000 units during the entire year at a uniform rate. Ordering costs are estimated to be \$100 per order and the carrying costs per unit are estimated to be \$20 per unit. The economic order quantity is found from equation (1) to be

$$Q^* = \sqrt{\frac{2(4{,}000)\,(100)}{20}} = 200 \text{ units}$$

The firm would therefore order 200 units each time it places an order and it would order twenty (4,000/200) times during the year. If we assume 360 business days, this means that the firm will order every eighteen days (360/20).

In the above model it was assumed that the wholesale firm would replenish its stock immediately. That is, no lead time between the placing of the order and its delivery was assumed. The model above for determining the economic order quantity is not affected if there is a lead time and the lead time is known with certainty. For example, if the firm in the above illustration faced a lead time of eight days it would still order 200 units each time it ordered but it would place its order twelve days after delivery of the previous order.

Consider what would happen to the economic order quantity if the assumption that shortages are not permitted is relaxed. (Note that the assumption that shortages are not permitted is tantamount to stating that shortage or stockout costs are infinite). If we let L be equal to the shortage costs per unit per time period then the economic order quantity can be shown to be

$$(2)\ \ Q^* = \sqrt{\frac{2AP\,(S + L)}{SL}}$$

Other deterministic models can be developed. For example, if the demand is not assumed to be uniform over the time period but instead is rapid at the beginning of the inventory cycle and slows down, an appropriate model can be developed. This model will be modified depending upon whether we permit shortages.

2. Probabilistic Model. In deterministic models the rate of demand for the firm's product and the lead time is known with certainty. If either is not known, we have a probabilistic model. Let us consider the case where the demand is not known with certainty.

▶ EXAMPLE: Consider the problem of a general manager of a retail store chain who must decide on how many cakes to order per week. Suppose that each cake sells for \$1.30 and costs \$1.00. If any cakes are not sold by the end of the week these cakes are sold for \$.90. The loss of \$.10 per cake not sold during the week is referred to as the "overstock" cost. The general manager believes that demand per week can be between 0 and 1,000 cakes.

Suppose that the general manager believes that the number of cakes (Q) demanded per week follows a probability distribution given by

$$P(Q) = 0.000002\ Q \quad \text{for} \quad 0 \leq Q \leq 1{,}000.$$

The aim then is to maximize the expected profit.

Using calculus and probability theory, the optimal number of cakes to order can be found by using the following equation:

$$\textbf{(3)}\quad Q^* = 1{,}000{,}000\sqrt{\frac{\text{Profit per unit}}{\text{Profit per unit} + \text{overstock cost per unit}}}$$

To see how to use equation (3) let us substitute the information in our illustration. Since profit per cake is \$.30 if sold within the week and the overstock cost per cake is \$.10, then

$$Q^* = 1{,}000{,}000\sqrt{\frac{.3}{.4}}$$

$$= 866 \text{ cakes}$$

Equation (3) can be applied for any profit per unit and overstock cost per unit as long as the probability distribution is $P(Q) = 0.000002\ Q$. If the probability distribution changes a general formula similar to equation (3) can be developed.

In many inventory problems management faces the possibility of being out of inventory stock. The costs of being out of stock are referred to as "shortage" costs or "stockout" costs. In such instances management will probably follow a policy of maintaining a safety or buffer stock. Given a probability distribution for the usage per time period, carrying cost per unit and stockout cost per unit, the expected total cost for alternative levels of safety stock management is considering can be determined. Management can then select the optimal level of safety stock, i.e., the level which results in the lowest expected total cost. Rather than trying to estimate stockout or shortage costs management may set a maximum probability that it will accept for running out of stock.

If the lead time to replenish stock is not known with certainty, further refinements in the model must be made. Given a probability distribution for lead time, this information can be utilized to determine the optimal level of safety stock.

Simulation. In most business problems the number of noncontrollable variables may be large. Each noncontrollable variable may take on a range of values. Hence, to evaluate solutions in each possible case to obtain the optimal solution may become impractical. For example, suppose a decision maker is considering a capital investment.

The yield on the capital investment will depend on the noncontrollable variables management faces. Suppose that management believes that the nine most important noncontrollable variables are: market size for the product, market price for the product, market growth rate, eventual market share, total investment required over time, useful life of the project, scrap value of the project, operating costs and fixed costs. Suppose that each of these noncontrollable variables can take on seven possible values. Then to evaluate this project, that is compute its yield, for all possible combinations of the noncontrollable variables, 4,782,969(9^7) cases must be considered. Furthermore, each possible outcome for a noncontrollable variable may not have an equal probability of occurrence.

At the other extreme, the decision maker can take the "best estimate" for each noncontrollable variable and compute the yield for these values of the noncontrollable variable. The decision maker might consider this to be the "best estimate" for the yield on the project. To understand the shortcomings of the "best estimate" approach suppose that for each noncontrollable variable the probability of the "best estimate" is 75%. Assuming that the probabilities for the noncontrollable variables are independently distributed (which in this problem they would not be) then the probability of occurrence for the "best estimate" yield would be 7.5% ($.75^9$). The decision maker would not want to place a great deal of confidence in this "best estimate" yield.

Between the "best estimate" approach and the complete enumeration approach we have the simulation approach. Simulation is more of a procedure than a model. The solutions obtained will not give us optimal solutions to problems such as linear programming, but rather provides us with information about the problems we are analyzing. Simulation is analogous to the wind tunnel used by aeronautical engineers to design ideas in the laboratory.

When probability distributions are assigned to the noncontrollable variables the procedure is referred to as Monte Carlo simulation. To understand how Monte Carlo simulation works suppose that we consider one of the noncontrollable variables in our previous example, say the dollar investment required. The following table shows the seven possible values for the dollar investment required along with management's subjective probability distribution for this noncontrollable variable.

PROBABILITY DISTRIBUTION FOR THE INVESTMENT REQUIRED AND TWO DIGIT NUMBERS ASSIGNED

Investment required	Probability	Two digit numbers
$100,000	.05	0–4
125,000	.15	5–19
180,000	.20	20–39
200,000	.25	40–64
245,000	.18	65–82
275,000	.10	83–92
300,000	.07	93–99
	1.00	

In the third column of the table we see two digit numbers assigned to each possible value for the noncontrollable variable. The numbers are assigned in a certain way. There are 100 numbers which range from 0 to 99. Each possible outcome is assigned enough numbers so that the ratio of the number of numbers assigned to 100 will equal the probability of the outcome. For example, for the outcome of $100,000 five numbers are assigned (0 to 4) because the ratio of five to 100 is 5%. This 5% represents the probability of obtaining an outcome of $100,000, that is, the investment required will be $100,000. For $245,000, eighteen numbers are assigned (65-82) since the probability of a required investment of $245,000 is 18%. The reason for assigning these numbers will be explained shortly. It is important that you understand that you can assign three digit numbers to each possible outcome but the ratio of the number of numbers assigned to the total number of numbers (1000) must be equal to the probability of occurrence for the particular outcome. Each noncontrollable variable will be assigned numbers in the same manner.

The reason for assigning numbers will now be explained. We can now perform an experiment using a random number table. This table is simply a table of digits generated by a random process. Using a random number table we select a random number with the appropriate number of digits for each noncontrollable variable. Hence, the process of selecting random numbers will tell us which values for the noncontrollable variables to use in the experiment. We next substitute these values into the model (or formula) for computing the yield on a capital investment.

Once the yield is computed, we repeat the experiment by selecting random numbers for each noncontrollable variable again. This experiment is repeated a number of times. The frequency or number of times each yield is observed can be recorded and a frequency or probability distribution for the yield can be obtained.

For most problems it would be very time consuming to perform the experiment enough times to get a meaningful distribution. Fortunately, computer programs are available for simulating models. Simulation is also used to examine the sensitivity of other management science techniques to changes in the parameters of the model. It is a powerful tool that has gained wide acceptance.

Conclusion. Accountants offer a wide range of management advisory services to their clients. The tools discussed in this chapter are part of the arsenal that accountants can use as an aid for management decision-making.

22

Integrated Data Processing—Machines and Mechanical Devices

CONTENTS

22

Integrated Data Processing—Machines and Mechanical Devices

Marvin Bachman, CPA

Integrated data processing (IDP) essentially consists of recording and processing information *without* rerecording of repetitive data. Recording and processing can be achieved through many media and procedures, examples of which are the following:

1. Carbon or pressure sensitive paper.
2. Punched-paper tape or tags.
3. Typewriter keyboards.
4. Punched cards.
5. Optical character recognition (OCR).
6. Key-to-tape, key-to-disk.
7. Computer and minicomputer processing.

CONSIDERATIONS IN APPLYING INTEGRATED DATA PROCESSING

Use of IDP can be applied to any business, no matter how large or small. The nature of the business and its record keeping requirements, as well as its size, can determine the type of integrated data processing to use.

For example, the record keeping of an Investment Company (or Mutual Fund) and the associated detailed computations was converted from a manual pen-and-ink journal and ledger system to a system utilizing a minicomputer which automatically recorded all activity on sales journals, cash receipts journals, and shareholder and dealer ledger cards with magnetic tape strips. Also, this minicomputer printed out confirmations for mailing to dealers and shareholders, describing the details of the transaction.

The computations and the record keeping were so detailed that, not only was this minicomputer needed to maintain the bookkeeping of the shareholder and dealer transactions, but also to perform day-to-day detailed computations of investment share values which then provided a per share value of the investment company.

This minicomputer was, in effect, a general purpose tool for all accounting records of a relatively small business. It performed the functions of an electromechanical accounting machine and, with the flexibility of stored programming, performed even more than what could be done on an accounting machine with external program bars or wiring.

In effect, this minicomputer could, through one keyboard entry, perform many processes and functions; and its current price was comparable to electromechanical accounting machines.

It is reasonable to state that there has been an ever-increasing trend toward the use of keyboard entry minicomputers in the use of integrated data processing. Their improving price performance with the corresponding labor saving has made them not only general purpose resources for small business, but also special or specific purpose machines for medium and large businesses with larger volume and/or more detailed record keeping to do.

While there has been an ever-increasing trend toward the use of desk size minicomputers and keyboard entries, there is still equipment which is used in functions designed to reduce keystriking—still the slowest and most error vulnerable form of data recording. Such equipment as character scanning (OCR and MICR), transaction reorders, and prerecorded data can reduce the amount of individual keystroking.

For example, if in the case of the Investment Company, the confirmation was printed through the minicomputer (under stored program control) in a specific manner so that certain information on the confirmation could be optically read automatically when cash was received for the sale, a copy of the confirmation document could be automatically read through the "scanner" and the keystroking reduced.

Needless to say, in addition to the above, the proper design and use of forms, both single and multicopy, can be an important factor in effective IDP, whether these forms are processed by people or equipment.

CONDUCTING A FEASIBILITY STUDY

While there are many component facets of a feasibility study, the following are three major component phases that will be discussed:

1. Survey of company needs.
2. Justification of resources—includes both personnel and equipment.
3. Comparative evaluation of competitive equipment and software.

The following are some of the important elements of the above three phases:

1. Determining the extent of the survey.
2. Surveying present data processing activities and costs.
3. Estimating future costs of the present system.
4. Determining the benefits expected from a new system.

5. Evaluating the expected benefits.
6. Determining the requirement of a new system.
7. Estimating the costs of the proposed system.
8. Making an economic evaluation.

While the scope and depth of the above may vary, it is important to identify the facts, problems, assumptions supporting conclusions, and ultimate decisions.

Survey of company needs. The benefits to be expected by management are primarily the factors that will contribute to increased profits for the organization. These factors include the following:

1. Reductions in data processing costs.
2. Improved management controls and better information. This may contribute to such reductions as inventory carrying costs, etc.
3. Improved customer relations. The president of one small consumer goods manufacturer stated that if he could get the information he was requesting timely and accurately, he could be more specific about delivery commitments to customers and it would increase sales 20%.
4. Improved personnel relations. If the existing system makes unreasonable demands on personnel (e.g., substantial periods of overtime) and results in a high employee turnover, improvements can increase individual productivity and reduce turnover.
5. Improved competitive position. Better information through improved systems enabled one bank to concentrate its trusteeship marketing efforts toward more profitable clients.
6. Reduction in working capital requirements. Improved cash flow through faster billing and collection.

Evaluation of the above benefits. In the past, expected benefits have been classified as tangible or intangible.

Tangible benefits are more susceptible to analysis for determining anticipated savings. Intangible benefits are those that are expected to improve the profit picture, but cannot be measured in terms of dollars.

It is this writer's contention that there are no purely tangible benfits and there are no purely intangible benefits, but merely degrees of accuracy to which the benefits can be evaluated.

Each and every one of the above described factors can be quantified. The reliability of the estimates can vary but, nevertheless, inventory carrying costs, the impact of a 20% improvement in sales, reductions in personnel turnover, and the benefits of better marketing and improved cash flow can all be estimated.

It is important to make these estimates. For example, in the case of the consumer goods manufacturer whose president estimated sales increases of 20% with the installation of a general purpose minicomputer, he was willing to accept a $50,000 annual increase in systems costs to achieve a net increase of $250,000 in profits through increased sales.

Justification of resources. Determining the requirements of a new system. Probably the most important consideration for any system is its adaptability by the people who will use it. Other important considerations, more technical in nature, include the practicality of a particular equipment resource to the system in question. Some factors are:

1. Possible need for processing alphabetical and/or numerical information.
2. Volumes of data records and files.
3. Specified time limits for processing.
4. Complexity of processing such as computations, reporting, sorting, and merging.
5. Inquiry requirements—level of service to customers and users.
6. Equipment users.
7. Compatibility with other equipment.

► OBSERVATION: Frequently, organizations present requirements for immediate inquiry response which may or may not be necessary. Such response requires expensive use of random and direct access equipment. In many cases, there would be little or no sacrifice of customer service if inquiries were more economically batch processed and the responses received within 24 hours.

Estimating the continuing annual costs of the proposed systems. Before the implementation of any proposed system is undertaken, its ongoing costs should be estimated. Included in the elements of cost are:

1. Timing of various equipment processing.
2. Equipment rental or purchase.
3. Personnel required not only to operate equipment, but also auxiliary personnel such as production control.

These estimates should be made conservatively, under the assumption of the most realistically projected circumstances.

Estimating implementation costs. Once the continuing costs and benefits of a proposed system have been estimated and evaluated, and it appears likely that the comparative costs to the present proposed system indicate a potential for a significant continuing improvement in operating profits, it is necessary to consider the one-time preparation and conversion costs. If the one-time costs are significant enough so that it requires many years for the savings to overcome them, then the proposed system may either not be feasible, or it may be desirable to break the proposed system into subsystems and try to achieve the greatest benefits in the earlier phases.

Evaluation of competitive equipment and software. There are several major factors that can contribute to a comprehensive evaluation of competitive hardware and software. Some desirable procedures that should be followed for reasonable measurements include:

1. Outline systems specifications and invite manufacturers to submit proposals.
2. Evaluate manufacturer's proposals.

3. Evaluate personnel handling of equipment.
4. Pilot test equipment and software under realistically simulated conditions of operation. Use these tests to assist in estimating the timing of jobs in the system to be run.
5. Relate equipment and software to solutions of management's problems, both short- and long-term.
6. Evaluate costs of implementing the particular hardware-software configuration for the system under consideration.
7. Request and evaluate proposals from several hardware-software suppliers. While these proposals may tend to emphasize the advantages of the respective products and services of each manufacturer, they can provide useful information upon which to base a decision.

The proposal request: when manufacturers (or suppliers) are invited to submit proposals, a typical request should include the following:

1. A brief description of each application.
2. A general and, if necessary, semi-detailed flow chart for each relevant application showing input documents, output documents, files and data bases.
3. Data sheets for each input-output, file and data base showing volumes, frequency of processing (periodicity), data descriptions (including size and composition of data fields) overall format, etc.
4. Brief description of the required processing steps.
5. A statement as to the form and content of the proposal and representations to be made to the manufacturers.

The above considerations and procedures should be guidelines for constructive and meaningful decision making and assurance that the best possible selections for the organizations are made.

To insure management's objectivity and comprehensiveness of examination, it has become customary to establish a management committee consisting of representatives of marketing production and financial management to participate in the investigations and evaluations.

THE TOOLS OF INTEGRATED DATA PROCESSING—MANUAL SYSTEMS

Manual systems, as used in this chapter, cover processing other than that defined as automatic processing and include the following:

1. Handwritten systems.
2. Augmented handwritten systems.
3. Reproducing equipment.
4. Typewritten systems.
5. Augmented typewritten systems.
6. Imprinting systems.
7. Accounting machine systems.

Each of these manual systems will be discussed separately. The various tools and devices that are available for use in each manual system will be described and, in some instances, illustrated below.

Handwritten Systems. Although handwritten systems are generally associated with small businesses, both medium-sized and large businesses may find occasion to use them too. For example, a confidential payroll may be used on an accounting board by a company having large scale EDP equipment. Integrated handwritten systems generally involve the simultaneous production of two or more forms used for different purposes, or the production of one form that can be used for two or more purposes, or a combination of the two. The tools or devices available for use in handwritten systems include the following:

1. Accounting boards.
2. Preshingled forms.
3. Multicopy forms.
4. Edge-notched cards.
5. Distribution slips.
6. Pegboard slips.

Accounting boards. There are a number of different types of accounting (or posting) boards on the market. Some are very simple devices to hold forms in alignment. Others are quite complicated and have the ability to realign forms so that, for example, three lines written on a pay check will generate one line on a check register.

Through accounting boards, one is able to record data on several documents or forms for the effort of one entry. For example, in writing on a pay check, one can simultaneously make an entry in a transaction register, and post to a ledger sheet. Accounting boards are used for accounts receivable, accounts payable and inventories as well as payrolls. (See Figure 1.)

► TYPICAL APPLICATION: The board is prepared by shingling payroll checks over a payroll register as shown in Figure 1. As each check and pay statement stub are written, the employee's earnings record is aligned under the statement stub. The earnings record is a carbon copy of the earnings, deductions, and net pay that are recorded on the statement. A carbon copy is also transmitted to a payroll register.

Preshingled forms. Some further advantages of accounting boards can be obtained from the use of forms that are preshingled over a register sheet.

► TYPICAL APPLICATION: In a check writing application, the vendor's name and the amount of the check are written on the top edge of the check and entered via carbon paper onto the check register. The check is then detached (exposing the next check which is positioned to provide entry to the check register one line below the preceding check).

Multicopy forms. Many integrated data processing systems make use of carbon paper, or NCR paper to produce additional copies. The number of

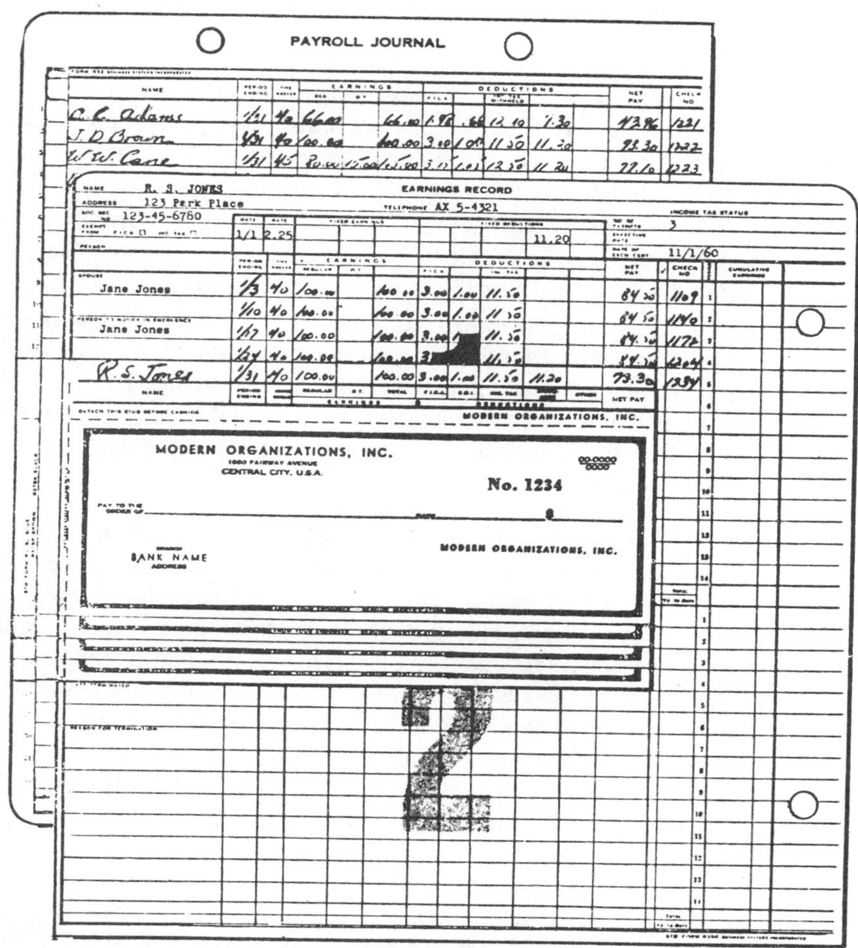
PAYROLL JOURNAL

C. C. Adams 1/31 40 66.00 66.00 1.98 .66 12.10 7.30 43.96 1221
J. D. Brown 1/31 40 100.00 100.00 3.00 1.00 11.50 11.20 73.30 1222
W. W. Case 1/31 45 80.00 15.00 95.00 3.15 1.05 12.50 11.20 77.10 1223

EARNINGS RECORD

NAME R. S. JONES
ADDRESS 123 Park Place
TELEPHONE AX 5-4321
SOC. SEC. NO. 123-45-6780
1/1 2.25 11.20
3
11/1/60
SPOUSE Jane Jones
PERSON TO NOTIFY IN EMERGENCY Jane Jones

1/3	40	100.00	100.00	3.00	1.00	11.50	84.50	1109
1/10	40	100.00	100.00	3.00	1.00	11.50	84.50	1140
1/17	40	100.00	100.00	3.00		11.50	84.50	1172
1/24	40	100.00	100.00	3.		11.50	84.50	1204
1/31	40	100.00	100.00	3.00	1.00	11.50	11.20 73.30	1234

R. S. Jones

MODERN ORGANIZATIONS, INC.

MODERN ORGANIZATIONS, INC.
CENTRAL CITY, U.S.A.
No. 1234
BANK NAME
MODERN ORGANIZATIONS, INC.

2

Fig. 1. Accounting Board Payroll Application.

additional copies is limited to the number that can be legibly produced. The purpose of the copies may determine whether this use of handwritten multicopy forms is desirable. For example, some company managements object to handwritten documents being sent to customers. However, as in the recording of orders by salesmen or order clerks, it is possible to obtain order, shipping, and invoice documents in one operation. The detailed data on each of the documents is the same. Each document has a preprinted heading that is different.

► Typical Application: Orders received by telephone are recorded on a three part "snap-out" form. The two carbon copies are sent to the shipping department, one to serve as a shipping report and the other as a packing slip. After the shipment has been made, the original copy and the shipping report are priced, extended and totaled. The original is then mailed to the customer as an invoice and the shipping report becomes the medium for posting accounts receivable.

Edge-notched cards. One aspect of most business transactions is that they occur in unrelated sequence and several transactions (such as inventory items shipped) may be recorded on one document. Consequently, these transactions must be sorted to enable analysis for management control and other purposes.

The use of edge-notched (or keysort) cards provides a manual system with some of the manipulative abilities of a punched-card system. They are particularly useful where several distributions are to be made.

Edge-notched cards are perforated along each margin with each group of perforations representing a distribution code. Four perforations are required to represent *one* decimal digit. The coding is accomplished by cutting through the card margin to the perforation (notching) so that notched cards will drop off the sorting needle. Repetitive information (date, department number, part, etc.) can be grooved into several cards simultaneously.

► TYPICAL APPLICATION: In a factory job cost application, machine operations are provided with a deck of cards that are prenotched with their respective clock numbers and department numbers. For each job worked on, the machine operator writes on a card the job number, operation code, starting and stopping time each day, and quantity produced. At the end of the production shift, cards are sent to the cost department where elapsed time is computed and the job number and operation code are notched as shown in Figure 2. The cards are then sorted in job number sequence, totaled and posted to cost records. Each week the cards are sorted into departmental sequence for preparation of employee pay and departmental labor distribution reports.

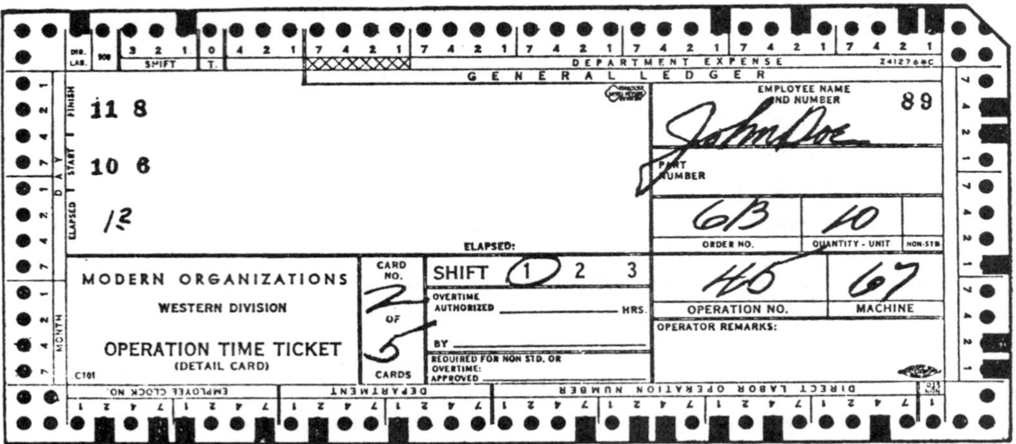

Fig. 2. Job Ticket Using Edge-Notched Cards.

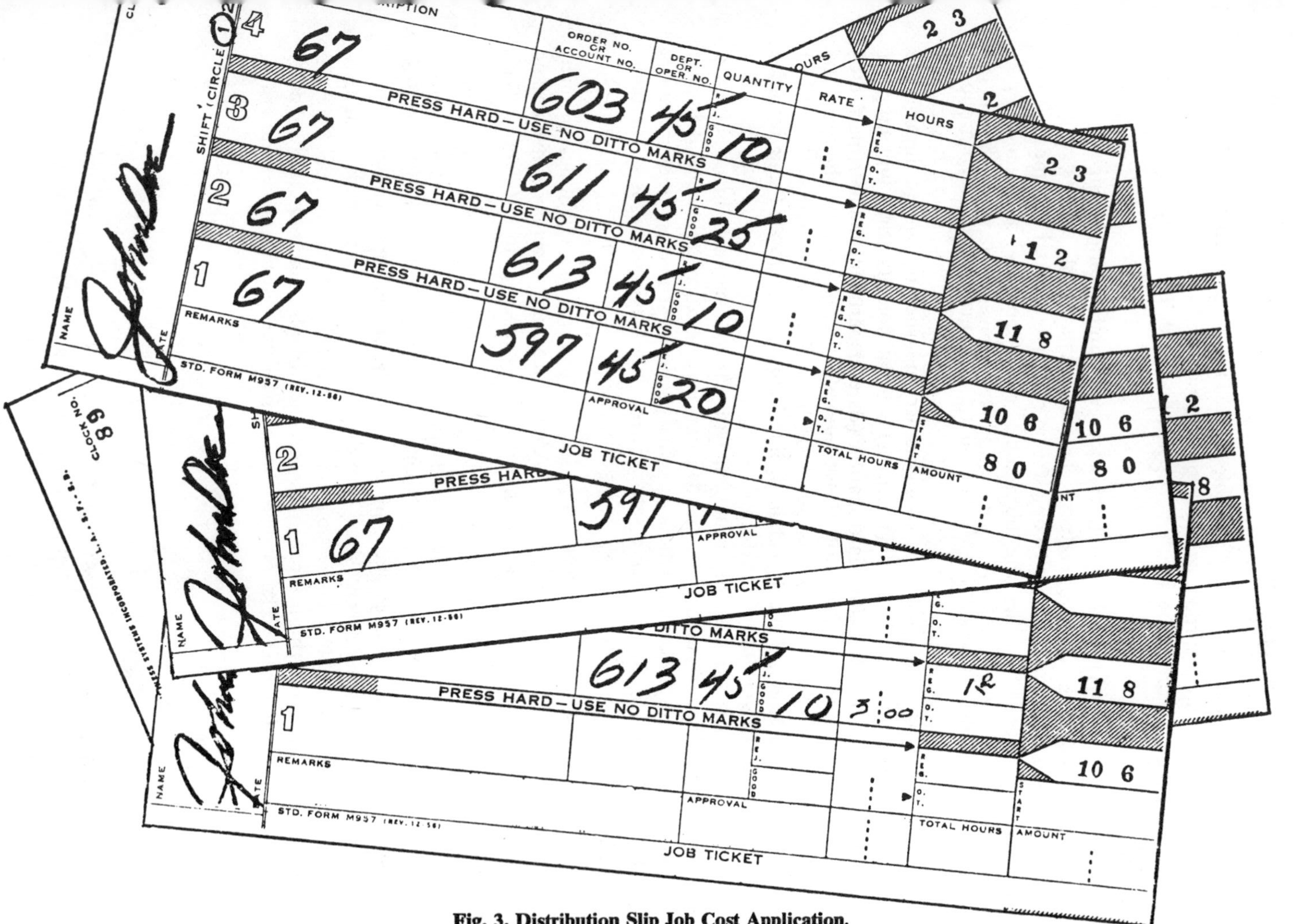

Fig. 3. Distribution Slip Job Cost Application.

Distribution slips. Another method of obtaining unit documents for sorting purposes is the use of multicopy forms designed to reproduce on each copy the reference data and one line of variable data. This is achieved through the use of spot carbon, strip carbon, or block out of undesired data. Thus, the first line of the original appears on the first copy, the second line on the second copy, etc.

► TYPICAL APPLICATION: In this job cost application (see Figure 3) slips are prepared by machine operators. The date, department, and clock number are entered and appear on all copies. For each job worked on, the machine operator writes on one line the job number, operation code, and quantity produced. The cost department computes and enters elapsed time for each job. The original copy serves as an attendance card and the carbon copies are sorted by job number, totaled, and posted to the cost records.

Pegboard Strips. When distribution classifications are constant and relatively few in number, pegboard strips provide a convenient method for making distribution analysis. Distribution classifications are preprinted on the form and quantities or amounts are entered in the right or left margin (or both). When the strips are shingled on a pegboard, line items can be totaled and recorded without rearrangement of the forms.

Pegboard strips may be combined with other documents in a multicopy form to provide, for example, a handwritten invoice for merchandise delivered as well as a strip for sales analysis or other purposes. The most frequent use of pegboard strips is for recording sales orders, but they can be used for other applications.

► TYPICAL APPLICATION: A salesman records the quantities of merchandise ordered on a pegboard strip. After processing to produce invoice and shipping documents, strips are shingled on a pegboard to produce a sales analysis.

Augmented handwritten systems. Imprinting and reproducing devices are frequently used to augment handwritten systems. Fixed data that is required periodically, such as names and addresses, can be stored in an embossed plate and used to imprint forms, thus eliminating the need for handwriting this information. Additional copies of handwritten documents can be obtained without any more writing through use of photographic photoelectric, or other reproduction processes. The devices that can be used to augment handwriting include:

1. Imprinters.
2. Microfilm.
3. Reproducing equipment.

Imprinters. There are two general approaches to the use of imprinters in connection with a handwritten system. Documents may be imprinted using semi-automatic equipment and then distributed to the individuals who will prepare the documents. This may be practical for a delivery route application, but is not practical in a retail store. The second approach involves imprinting at the time the transaction is recorded.

There are many successful applications of imprinters, the most familiar being credit cards. Other successful applications include their use in hospitals for imprinting the patient's name and other reference data on documents and charge slips. One important advantage of imprinters is that the customer number and other reference data are always reproduced accurately.

► TYPICAL APPLICATIONS: In a delivery route application, the route salesman takes with him a tray containing an embossed plate for each customer on his route. Where a delivery is made, quantities are entered on a sales form and are priced, extended, and totaled. The customer's name, number, and other reference data is recorded by use of an imprinter mounted in the truck. The original copy of the form is given to the customer as an invoice and the duplicate is used in accounting for the load and for posting to accounts receivable.

Microfilm. When it is necessary to submit sorted documents in support of a billing it is frequently less expensive to microfilm the documents than to make additional document copies. This procedure is commonly used by retail stores, gasoline companies, and others who return copies of charge slips with a monthly statement. The microfilm record becomes the reference copy.

► TYPICAL APPLICATION: In a retail cycle-billing application, handwritten sales slips are dropped into the customer's file, after being totaled, by cycle, to obtain controls. At the end of the cycle, sales slips are posted to the customer's statement and ledger, microfilmed, and mailed to the customer with his statement.

Reproducing Equipment. There are five general types of reproducing equipment that are effective in data processing applications. Since this equipment can be used in either handwritten or typewritten systems, the discussion that follows covers both:

1. Spirit duplicators are widely used because the original and supply costs are relatively low and a number of copies can be produced in a short period of time. The duplicating master is prepared by writing or typing on a master that is backed by a sheet containing an aniline dye. Reproduction is from the mirror image on the back of the master.
2. Photocopy machines are popularly thought of as machines that produce a copy from an original document. In its true sense, photocopying involves the use of special cameras that enable documents to be enlarged or reduced. However, most photocopy equipment requires the preparation of a sensitized paper negative (which is in direct contact with the original) and the transfer of the image from the negative to the finished copy. Although not a photographic process, thermal copiers, which operate on the principle that dark colors absorb heat more rapidly than light colors, serve the same function and are referred to

as photocopy equipment. The photocopy process is relatively slow and is seldom used where large volumes are involved.

3. Offset duplicators are widely used when the quality of the reproduction is important. Many public accounting firms use this type of equipment for reproducing reports. Offset masters are prepared by writing on the master with a special pencil having a high oil-content "lead" or by typewriting using special ribbons. In printing, the master is first moistened (the oily image repelling the moisture) and then inked (the moistened surfaces repelling the ink. The image is then printed on a rubber blanket (mirror image) which, in turn, transfers the image to the finished copy.
4. The diazo process is similar to photocopy except that different chemical processes are involved and a negative is not required. Copies can be made directly from masters prepared on a translucent paper.
5. The xerography process involves fairly expensive equipment and is used primarily where it is necessary to reproduce documents originating outside the company. Its most frequent use is for the preparation of offset duplicating masters. The processing involves "photographing" the copy using a positively charged metal plate instead of a sensitized negative. After exposure, the image remains positively charged and thus attracts negatively charged powder sprinkled on it. This powder is then transferred to the finished copy and is fused to form a permanent print.

Application for Accountants. In public accounting firms that use offset duplicators, staff accountants prepare tax returns using masters on which the tax forms are preprinted. The handwritten masters are then run to produce copies for filing.

Typewritten Systems. With aid of properly designed forms, the typewriter can be one of the most versatile machines used in manual integrated data processing systems. Although typewritten systems are generally limited to the production of multicopy forms, there are several approaches to integration using a typewritten system. Two common approaches that can be combined in an integrated system are:

1. Using form copies as ledger sheets.
2. Using copies to eliminate entries into ledgers.

Form copies as ledger sheets. The use of document copies as ledger sheets has been an accepted procedure for many years. Usually copies of invoices, time sheets, or inventory activity are placed in a tub file. There is special filing equipment designed specifically for this type of application.

There must be careful physical and accounting control of these documents because of the ever-existent danger of loss. But this type of ledgerless bookkeeping can save a substantial amount of clerical effort in the proper environment.

► TYPICAL APPLICATION: A company that sells merchandise from warehouse stock prepares a multicopy form consisting of an invoice, accounts receivable copy, shipping report, packing slip, and delivery copies. When merchandise is shipped, the invoice and accounts receivable copies are completed, totaled, and entered as an addition to the accounts receivable control. Accounts receivable copies are then filed by the customer.

Upon receipt of remittances from customers, the related accounts receivable copies are pulled from the file and totaled. If a partial payment is received, a remittance slip is filed and the accounts receivable copies are *not* removed. The total of pulled accounts receivable copies and remittance slips, after comparison with the deposit, is entered as a deduction from the accounts receivable control.

At the end of the accounting period, a trial balance listing all open invoices for each customer is prepared and balanced with the control. Open item statements are prepared if they are required.

Eliminating entries into registers. The elimination of the check register through the practice of filing copies of checks in chronological sequence has been widely accepted for many years. Using this basic procedure, only the daily total of disbursements is recorded. Remittance advices are also used as voucher registers to a lesser extent.

► TYPICAL APPLICATION: A company that normally pays invoices on the tenth of the month enters invoice data in the remittance advice section of a four-part voucher check (see Figure 4). At the end of the month, the remittance advice and check are completed and the first two copies consisting of the check and check register are stripped off and held for release. The third copy is filed chronologically with a recap of the expense distribution and serves as the voucher register. The fourth copy is filed alphabetically with the related vendor's invoices.

When checks are released, check numbers are assigned and posted to the related voucher register copies. The second copy, filed by check number, serves as the check register. At any time, the voucher register copies that do not show a check number represent the detail of accounts payable.

Augmented typewritten systems. Handwritten systems, as has been described, may be augmented by the use of imprinting, microfilming, and reproducing equipment. Similarly, typewritten systems may be augmented by the use of the same kinds of equipment. Reproducing equipment is used most frequently to augment typewritten systems.

Reproducing equipment. Reproducing equipment is frequently used where more copies of a form are required than can be produced with a typewritten multicopy form. With such a system, the form may be printed on the master. This is particularly applicable with spirit duplicating and offset printing equipment.

In other systems, repetitive information may be combined with variable information. For example, a production order may be prepared by adding quantities, completion dates, etc., to a standard schedule of operations. The superimposition of variable data on a transparent master, using the diazo process,

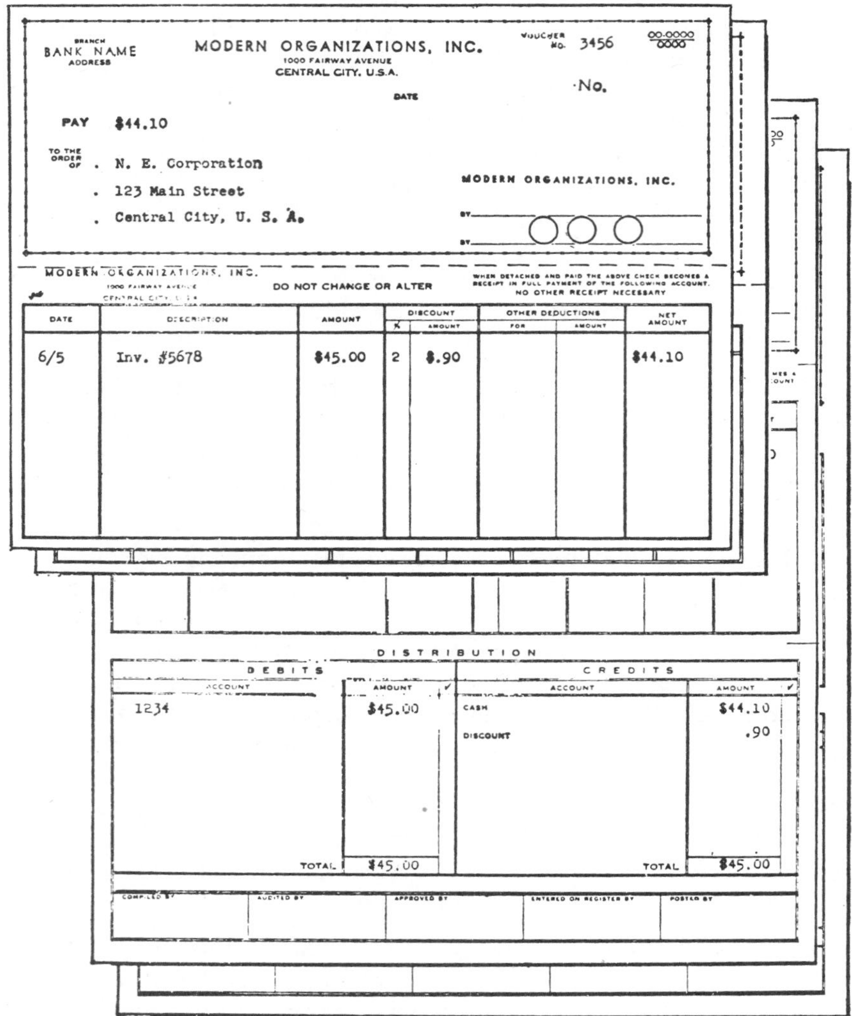

BRANCH BANK NAME ADDRESS

MODERN ORGANIZATIONS, INC.
1000 FAIRWAY AVENUE
CENTRAL CITY, U.S.A.

VOUCHER NO. 3456

00-0000 0000

No.

DATE

PAY $44.10

TO THE ORDER OF
N. E. Corporation
123 Main Street
Central City, U. S. A.

MODERN ORGANIZATIONS, INC.

BY

BY

MODERN ORGANIZATIONS, INC.

DO NOT CHANGE OR ALTER

WHEN DETACHED AND PAID THE ABOVE CHECK BECOMES A RECEIPT IN FULL PAYMENT OF THE FOLLOWING ACCOUNT. NO OTHER RECEIPT NECESSARY

DATE	DESCRIPTION	AMOUNT	DISCOUNT %	DISCOUNT AMOUNT	OTHER DEDUCTIONS FOR	OTHER DEDUCTIONS AMOUNT	NET AMOUNT
6/5	Inv. #5678	$45.00	2	$.90			$44.10

DISTRIBUTION

DEBITS ACCOUNT	AMOUNT	CREDITS ACCOUNT	AMOUNT
1234	$45.00	CASH	$44.10
		DISCOUNT	.90
TOTAL	$45.00	TOTAL	$45.00

COMPILED BY	AUDITED BY	APPROVED BY	ENTERED ON REGISTER BY	POSTED BY

Fig. 4. Registerless Bookkeeping Application.

permits adding the varying data without destroying the fixed data. This may also be accomplished using variable masters with spirit duplicating equipment.

When additional information is required on some copies of a document, the use of variable masters or the addition of the information to the original master may be feasible. Spirit duplicating or diazo process equipment is usually effective in systems of this type.

► Typical Application: In a purchase order application, the master is sent to the receiving department after the necessary purchase order copies have been prepared. Upon receipt of the merchandise, the receiving clerk records on the master the quantities received and then receiving report copies are prepared.

Imprinting systems: Although imprinting systems are generally used in conjunction with other systems, it may be feasible to create a system based on imprinting equipment alone where there is a need for the periodic reproduction of fixed data. Some imprinting plates are designed to permit the use of signals to designate data such as the billing month. However, such equipment is not essential.

► TYPICAL APPLICATION: A membership organization bills its members for an annual fee that varies with the class of membership. Embossed plates are prepared and filed by the billing month. These plates show the member's name and address, billing month, and the amount of the fee.

Controls are established and maintained by the billing month. After bills for the month have been run, the plates are segregated and serve as the accounts receivable file. When remittances are received, the plates are pulled and used to imprint a cash receipts register. Thereupon, they are refiled by billing month. At any time, a run of the plates remaining in the accounts receivable file provides a trail balance of the open accounts.

Accounting Machine Systems. Accounting machines are defined in this section as equipment that, under program control, can process data entered in:

1. A keyboard.
2. A typewriter terminal.
3. A video terminal.

This processing can be accomplished in the following ways:

1. *Interchangeable program bars* control the movement of a carriage, the addition (or subtraction) of data to accumulator or register totals, the printing of register totals, and the clearance of registers to zero. Data may be added to or deducted from two or more registers, or may be added to some registers and deducted from others.

2. *Electronic balance-pickup machines.* One of the basic operating principles of accounting machines is the pickup of ledger balances prior to posting, and the repeat of this pickup to obtain proof of posting accuracy. This requirement is eliminated in electronic balance-pickup machines.

Ledger cards used in this type of equipment are printed with stripes of magnetizable material on the back. During the operation of the accounting machine, the accountant number and account balance are recorded as magnetized spots that can be read and printed automatically the next time the ledger card is used.

3. *Calculating accounting machines.* In applications that involve computations, a calculating accounting machine may be efficient. Some machines combine small externally programmed electronic computers with accounting machines or typewriters. Others use electromechanical calculators.

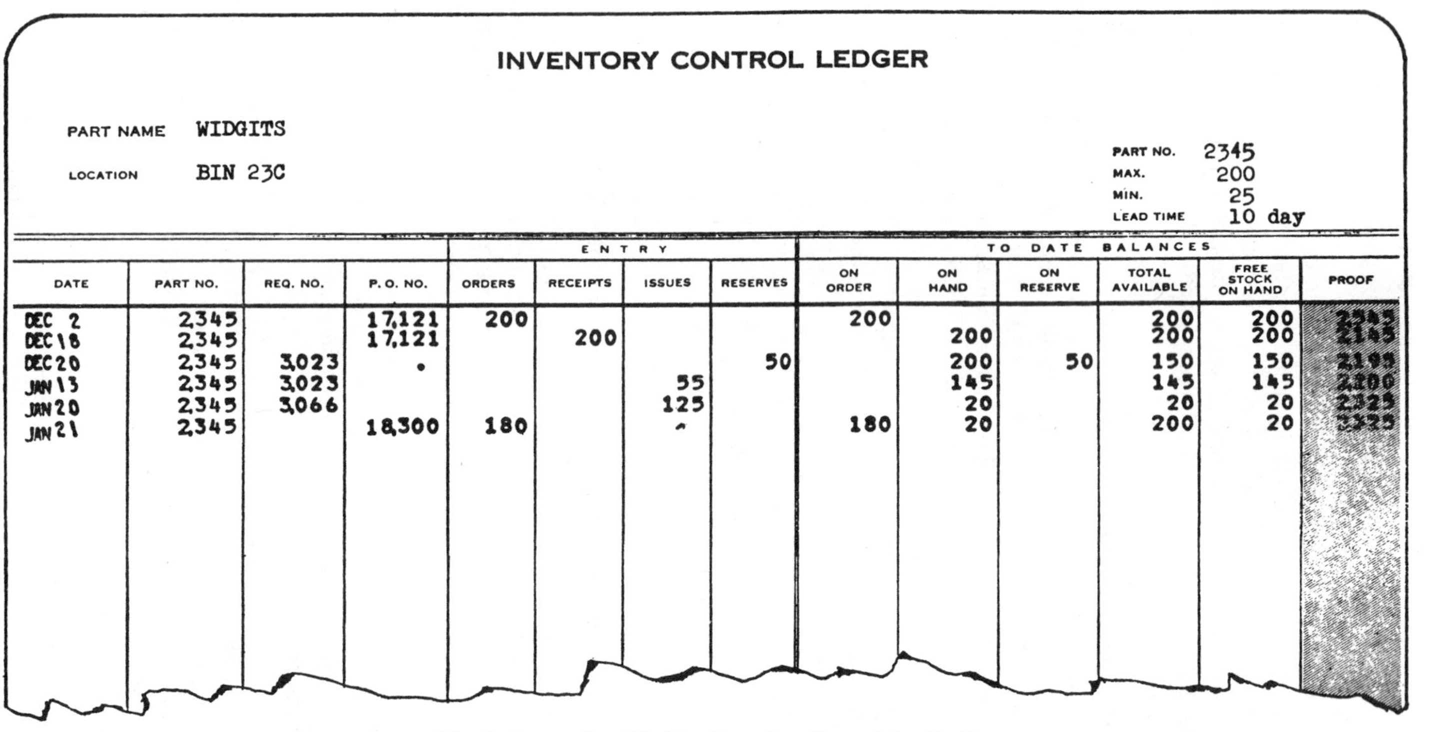

INVENTORY CONTROL LEDGER

PART NAME WIDGITS
LOCATION BIN 23C

PART NO. 2345
MAX. 200
MIN. 25
LEAD TIME 10 day

				ENTRY				TO DATE BALANCES					
DATE	PART NO.	REQ. NO.	P. O. NO.	ORDERS	RECEIPTS	ISSUES	RESERVES	ON ORDER	ON HAND	ON RESERVE	TOTAL AVAILABLE	FREE STOCK ON HAND	PROOF
DEC 2	2,345		17,121	200				200			200	200	2345
DEC 18	2,345		17,121		200				200		200	200	2145
DEC 20	2,345	3,023	•				50		200	50	150	150	2195
JAN 13	2,345	3,023				55			145		145	145	2200
JAN 20	2,345	3,066				125			20		20	20	2325
JAN 21	2,345		18,300	180				180	20		200	20	2325

Fig. 5. Accounting Machine Inventory Record Application.

In addition to calculating ability, some machines of this type have 100 or more registers or storage units and have the ability to make decisions.

4. *Stored program minicomputers.* This form of accounting machine is replacing the above three. As price performance improves through improved electronic hardware and software, and improved reliability, durability, and flexibility, this machine can perform all the functions required, utilizing carriage printers, magnetic strip ledger cards, typewriters, video terminals, and magnetic tapes and disks.

Applications utilizing these minicomputers were described at the beginning of this chapter (see Figure 5). The use of mini and microcomputers in an accounting practice is treated in Chapter 37.

THE TOOLS OF AUTOMATED SYSTEMS FOR INTEGRATED DATA PROCESSING (OTHER THAN EDP)

Automated data processing, as defined in this chapter, involves machines that can communicate with one another. There are several means of communication among machines and, frequently, two or more communications media are used in one system.

The principle types of media for communicating and typical codes used are discussed in the following paragraphs:

Standard punched cards. One of the most common media for communication among machines is the punched card. It is, of course, the medium used for communication by punched-card machines. In addition, it can be read by other types of equipment.

Figure 6 shows an 80-column card. In this medium, numerical digits are represented by positions on the card. Alphabetical characters are represented by a numeric punch (1 through 9) and a zone punch (0, 11, 12 with zones 11 and 12 above 0 zone). There are also 90-column cards and 96-column cards (not illustrated). The 90-column card uses one or two punches to represent numerical characters and two or three punches to represent alphabetical characters. The 96-column card uses 1 to 8 hole punch combinations for each numerical and alphabetical character.

Punched-paper tape. This type of medium has declined in importance. It is used on teletypes, flexowriters and for occasional low-volume data recording.

Except for five-channel tape, the most common character representation is the binary-coded decimal. In this coding the bottom hole (binary digit or bit) has a value of one. The next bit has a value of two; the third, four; and the fourth, eight. The decimal three, for example, is represented by holes in the first and second channels. In alphabetical representation, there are punches in one or both of the fifth and sixth channels together with a numerical character punching.

Most punched-paper tape codes (other than the five channel code) provide for a check or parity bit that may be on either an odd or even basis.

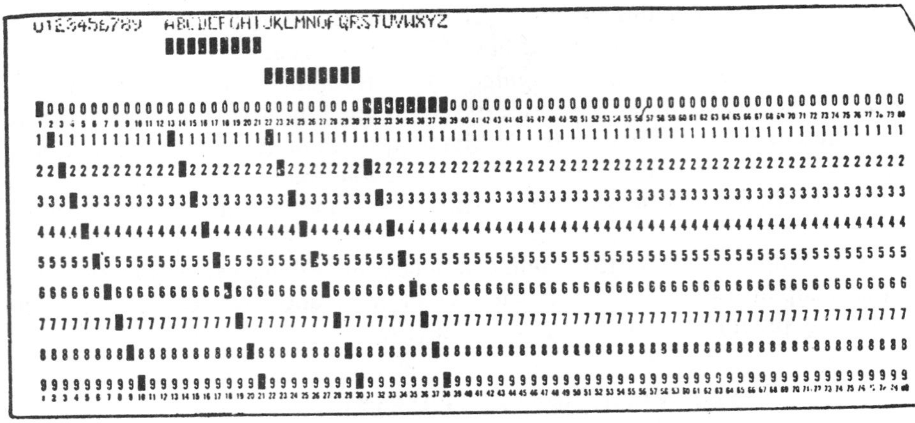

Fig. 6. 80-Column Punched Card.

If, for example, parity is odd, a hole is punched in the seventh channel whenever the number of bits in channel one through six is even. Machines that use such tape check each character to determine that there are an odd number of bits, and stop themselves if there is a parity error.

In the eight channel tape shown in Figure 7, the eighth channel is used for machine operating codes.

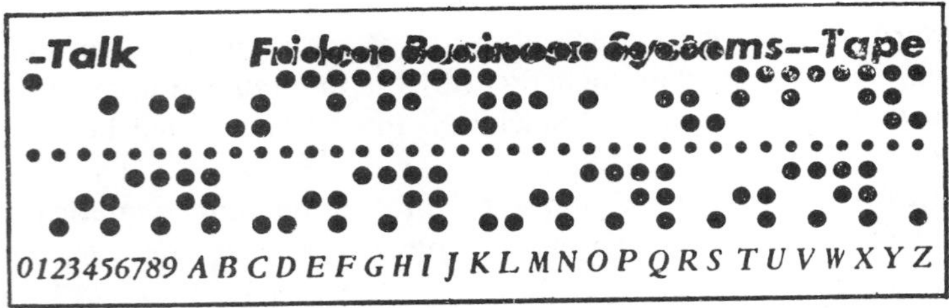

Fig. 7. Eight-Channel Punched Paper Tape.

Five channel tape is used primarily for teletype transmission. It does not have a parity check, and a bit dropped in transmission may result in receiving a valid but incorrect character.

Edge-punched cards, used by some equipment, are a variation of punched-paper tape and can be produced and read by the same punches and readers used for punched-paper tapes. They are usually used to store repetitive information (such as customer name and address) required as input to the system.

Machine-recognizable printed characters. These media have been used increasingly in many environments, such as banking, publishing, and retailing.

There are two basic types of character recognition equipment: optical (OCR) and magnetic ink (MICR). The optical equipment scans the character and recognizes the presence or absence of ink in predetermined grid positions, and thereby establishes the character. The specific type must be "known" to the equipment. A typical typeface is shown in Figure 8.

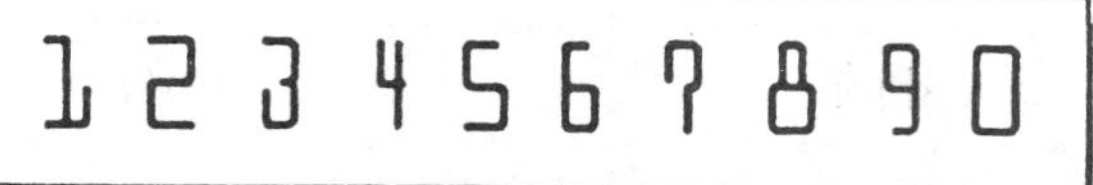

Fig. 8. Optically Recognizable Characters.

Reading magnetic ink characters involves the recognition of differences in intensities of magnetism. For this reason portions of some characters are exaggerated to provide greater intensity and permit differentiation. The typeface adopted by the American Bankers Association is shown in Figure 9.

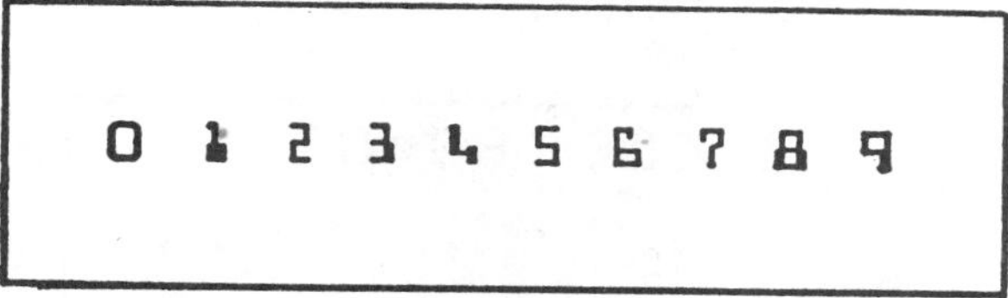

Fig. 9. Magnetic Ink Characters.

Imprinting requirements are extremely rigid for both OCR and MICR. However, the requirements for MICR are even stricter than for OCR, and for this reason, banks and similar organizations that can enforce rigid imprinting requirements are the primary users of MICR.

Machine-recognizable printed codes. The printed code (mark reading) is another means of optical character recognition (OCR). Various codes have been devised for this purpose. An example of a typical code that makes use of bars is shown in Figure 10.

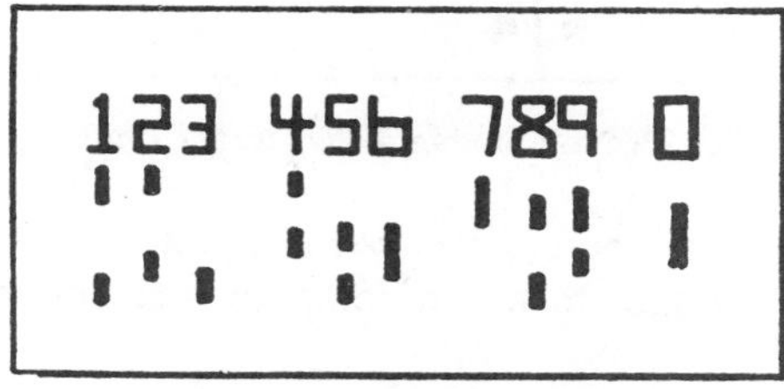

Fig. 10. Optically Recognizable Printed Code.

Machine-recognizable perforated characters. As described above (punched paper tape), these characters represent a machine sensible medium. They are recognized by specifically positioned hole punches (or specifically positioned combinations of hole punches) and are used in a variety of industries. The retail industry, with a "Kimball" ticket is an example of the use of a perforated tag for recording specific sales.

Figures 11 to 13 illustrate specific types of recognizable perforated characters.

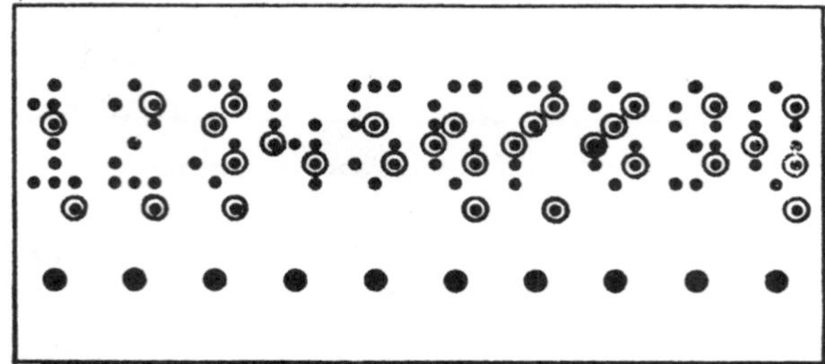

Fig. 11. Machine Recognizable Perforated Characters.

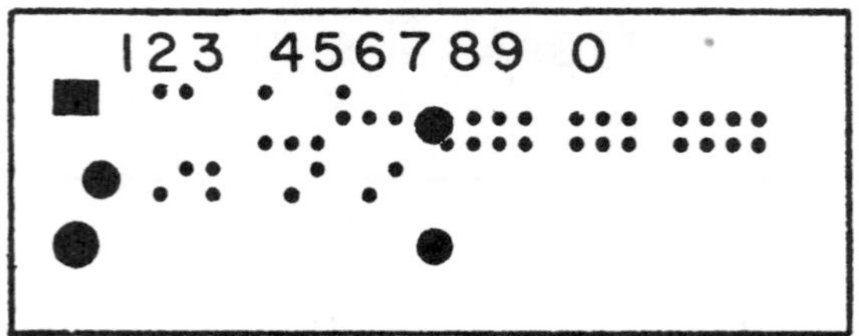

Fig. 12. Perforated Tag.

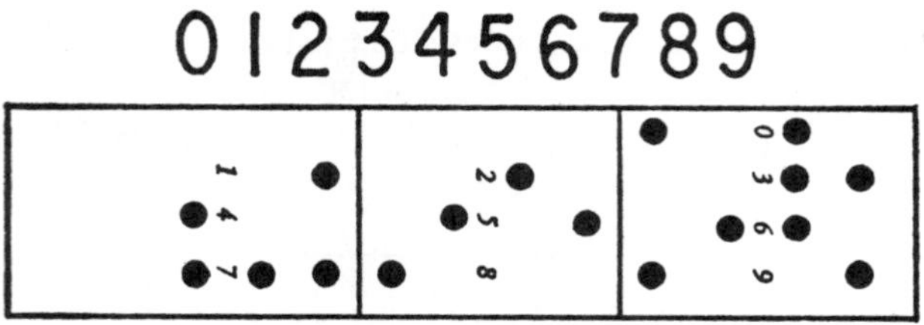

Fig. 13. Non-Standard Perforated Code.

Magnetic Disk. This medium has been expanded substantially in its use. The disk has become a major factor in computer and minicomputer operations, and data transmission.

Disks are divided into cylinders, tracks, and sectors (see figure 11).

The recordings on disks consist of densely packed combinations of magnetic spots representing numbers and letters.

One advantage of disk over tape is instantaneous access to a specific sector. Magnetic tape must be moved in sequential order.

Intercouplers. Though being obsolesced by the ever-increasing use of minicomputers, office equipment has been intercoupled with paper tape punches and card punches through use of electromechanical devices. Actuating the keyboard of such a machine results in punching (selectively) the same data onto paper tape or cards.

MACHINES USED IN INTEGRATED DATA PROCESSING (OTHER THAN EDP)

The preceding discussion covered the available means or tools of communication among machines. Those media are used to transmit data from one machine to another. The discussion that follows concerns the machines that do the communicating. For this purpose these machines have been classified as follows:

1. Equipment for recording data at source.
2. Equipment for producing by-product machine sensible media.
3. Other equipment for recording in machine sensible language.
4. Data-transmission equipment.
5. Conversion and reproduction equipment.
6. Sorting, selecting, and merging equipment.
7. Calculating equipment.
8. Printing equipment.
9. Supporting equipment.

Equipment for recording data at source. A basic concept of integrated data processing is the capture of data in machine sensible form as early in the processing as possible. The ultimate in achieving this objective is the recording of data at the source. Another basic concept is the maintenance of fixed data in a machine sensible form. These concepts are an integrated part of the source recording systems discussed in this chapter. Among the equipment for recording data at its source are transaction recorders, point-of-sale registers and recorders, imprinters, and perforators.

Transaction recorders. Of a number of types of transaction recorders available, all have two common characteristics:

1. The input of fixed data is by means of a medium that can be read by the recorder, and
2. The data is compiled in a machine sensible medium.

Most transaction recorders provide for manual input of variable data by means of keyboards, levers, or dials. Repetitive information, such as dates and department numbers, can be recorded automatically. The media used for the input of fixed data (employee clock number or social security number, job number, credit card number, etc.) include embossed plates or cards, standard punched cards, short cards, and edgepunched cards that print a machine-recognizable code.

The data that enters into the transaction recorders is compiled in one or more of the following:

1. A central computer connected to the recorder.
2. A tape within the machine.
3. A central compiler that is cable-connected with the transaction recorder.

Output from the compiler is generally in the form of punched paper tape or punched cards. However, output from the central computer can be on any of the above described media, usually magnetic tape or disk.

If printed codes are used for the recording, optical scanning and conversion to other media are required.

► TYPICAL APPLICATION: In a large job shop, transaction recorders are located in each major department. When a job in process is received in a department, it is recorded by inserting the identification card accompanying the material into the recorder and keying in the receiving code. The data (captured in punched-paper tape by the central compiler) is used to prepare reports showing the location of the order in the shop and (by comparison with the production schedule) orders that are behind schedule.

When a machine operator starts to work on a job, he inserts a plastic badge, perforated with his clock number and the job identification card, into the transaction recorder. Upon completion of the job, he reinserts his badge and the identification card and keys in the operation number and quantity produced. This data is used to produce daily production control reports and accumulated job costs.

When a customer makes a purchase in a store, he presents his embossed credit card to the sales clerk. The sales clerk inserts the card into a terminal connected to a central computer system and keys in the dollar amount of the sale. Within seconds the customer's number on the embossed card is read and transmitted to the computer which accesses the customer record corresponding to his number. The status of the customer record is evaluated and a signal is transmitted back to the terminal to accept or reject the credit of the customer for the particular sale.

Point-of-sale recorders. This is a specialized type of transaction recorder which has been developed for retail store operations. In its simplest form a cash register is intercoupled with a paper tape punch. Some systems provide for the use of a perforated tag reader.

The level and scope of capability has expanded into Electronic Point of Sale (E.P.O.S.) systems which can not only perform the above functions, but can also process customer credit cards for credit checks, record and classify sales, and check and update inventory levels.

► TYPICAL APPLICATION: In a retail store, the above functions are performed through control of a stored programmed minicomputer which is connected to a group of cash registers. The minicomputer reads the sales data entered at each connected register simultaneous with its recording, develops totals, and processes and analyzes reports such as inventory turnover.

Sales data is entered into this E.P.O.S. configuration in three ways:

1. The above described perforated ticket.
2. Key entries.
3. Optical reading of price imprints on the merchandise. This is accomplished through a "wand" which is connected to the register or terminal which is used to "fan" across the price on the particular item.

Imprinters and perforators. Two types of imprinters are available. One type imprints using machine-recognizable characters or codes. For further processing with this type of imprinter, the characters or code must be read by optical scanning equipment.

The second type duplicates perforations from the imprinting plate into a punched card. Some equipment of this type can enter variable data by means of levers.

► TYPICAL APPLICATION: In a gasoline service station application, a two-part sales ticket is imprinted using a standard imprinter. The duplicate (a card) is read by optical scanning equipment and the credit card number is punched into it. Cards are then sorted by credit card number for mailing to the customers along with their monthly statements.

Equipment for producing by-product machine sensible media. It is frequently possible to obtain machine sensible media such as punch cards, punched-paper tape, or optically readable printed data, as a by-product of a required operation. Some equipment of this type can also read the above described media. Examples of machines in this category are typewriters (flexowriters), adding machines, accounting machines, calculating machines, and cash registers.

Typewriters. There are several typewriters on the market that can produce punch cards, punched-card tape, or optically readable print as a by-product of the typing operation. The data generated may be selected by the operator, or, with some added equipment, by a machine program. Some equipment of this type can read paper tape, edge-punched cards, and/or punched cards. Typewriter-punches are useful when it is necessary to produce a document such as a purchase order, which includes data to be used in future processing.

► TYPICAL APPLICATION: A Company prepares its checks on a weekly cycle using punched-card equipment to produce the checks. Checks written outside of the cycle are prepared on a typewriter-card punch. The cards prepared in this operation are combined with those used in the regular processing for distribution of expenses and other analyses.

Adding machines. Adding machine-punches are frequently used for recording data to be processed by a service bureau. The wide use of this equipment is accounted for by its relatively low cost and the fact that the accuracy of the data recording can be visually checked. One of the most effective uses of adding machine-punches is to capture input data as a by-product of checking the accuracy of source documents.

► TYPICAL APPLICATION: In a retail store sales audit application, sales slip totals are checked using an adding machine-punch. In the operation, the department and sales clerk numbers are entered and punched using the nonadd key. Sales slip items are then totaled and the total is punched. The data captured during the operation are used in the preparation of departmental sales analyses and the computation of commissions.

Accounting machines. Most accounting machines can be intercoupled with a paper-tape punch or a card punch. The production of by-product tape or cards eliminates the need for recording individual transactions on ledger cards. Instead, summaries for each account classification are prepared from the by-product tape or cards.

► TYPICAL APPLICATION: In a remittance advice check writing application (see figure 14), the vendor's invoice data are entered on the remittance advice section of a voucher check. Distribution account numbers and amounts are punched into paper tape. When the check portion is completed, the check number and amount are punched. The paper tape is processed by a service bureau to prepare an expense distribution summary and, also, to create punched cards for use in reconciling bank accounts.

Calculating machines. Many electromechanical and externally-programmed electronic calculating machines can be intercoupled with paper tape or card punches. Also, some equipment of this type can read punched-paper tape or punched cards. Usually, this equipment operates most effectively in applications that make use of the reading ability.

► TYPICAL APPLICATION: In an invoice inventory control application, an invoice shipping documents form is prepared using a typewriter controlled calculator. The customer's name and address, shipping information, terms, etc., are entered automatically from data in punched cards. Likewise, for each item, the merchandise description and sale price are entered from data in cards; only the quantity shipped is entered manually. Each line item is extended automatically and the invoice is totaled.

The inventory cards used in this application contain inventory balances. As a by-product of the operation, new inventory cards containing adjusted balances are produced. Also, a paper tape is punched that contains standard costs of merchandise as well as selected data typed on the invoice. This type is used in sales and cost of goods sold analyses and in accounts receivable procedures.

Other equipment for recording in machine sensible language. Frequently, it is not feasible to record data at the source or to obtain it as a by-product of another operation. It becomes necessary then to enter the data from source documents using keypunches or other keydriven machines. The most common devices used for entering the data are card punches, paper-tape punches, magnetic ink character inscribers, and other perforators.

Card punches. A large percentage of the data that enters into a punched-card system are keypunched. Keypunching is still a method for preparing data for input into an EDP system. With the exception of some keypunches that print the characters punched in the card, no typed copy is produced. Neither is it possible, without auxiliary equipment to accumulate the amounts that are punched. Because of these factors, key-verification procedures are frequently used.

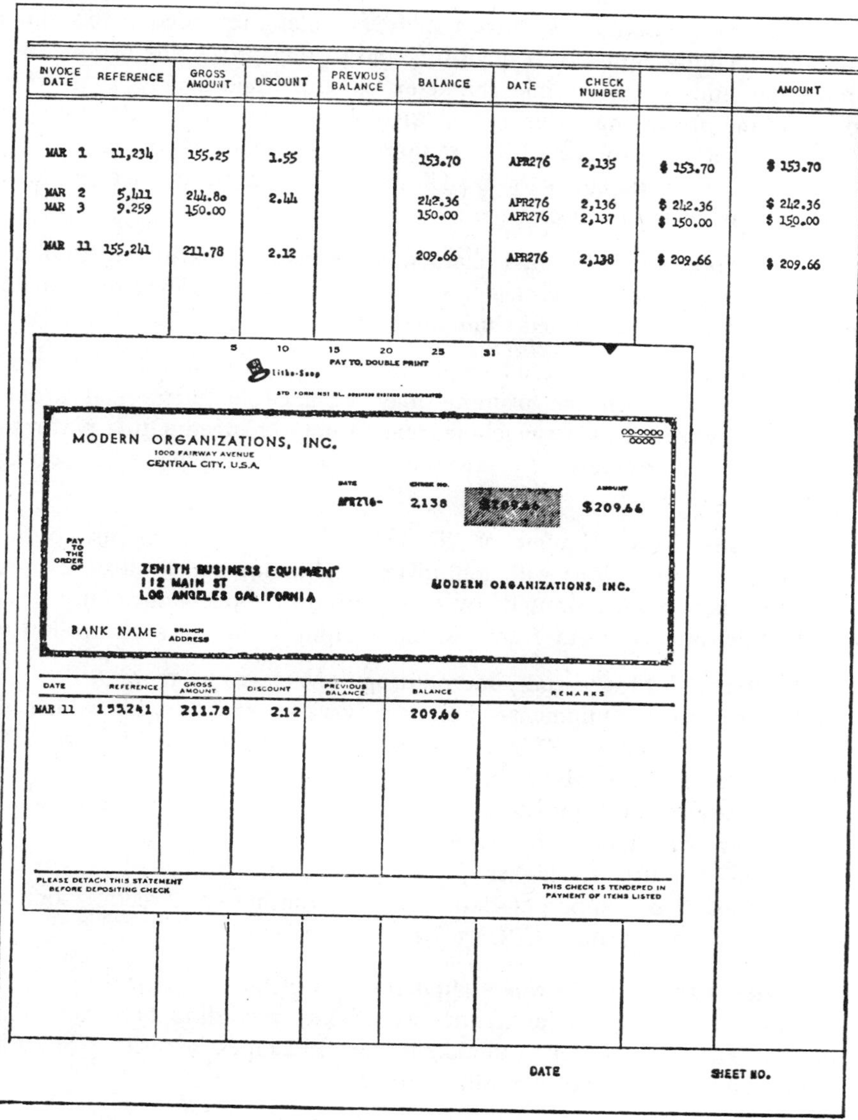

INVOICE DATE	REFERENCE	GROSS AMOUNT	DISCOUNT	PREVIOUS BALANCE	BALANCE	DATE	CHECK NUMBER		AMOUNT
MAR 1	11,234	155.25	1.55		153.70	APR276	2,135	$ 153.70	$ 153.70
MAR 2	5,411	244.80	2.44		242.36	APR276	2,136	$ 242.36	$ 242.36
MAR 3	9,259	150.00			150.00	APR276	2,137	$ 150.00	$ 150.00
MAR 11	155,241	211.78	2.12		209.66	APR276	2,138	$ 209.66	$ 209.66

5 10 15 20 25 31

PAY TO, DOUBLE PRINT

Litho-Snap

MODERN ORGANIZATIONS, INC.
1000 FAIRWAY AVENUE
CENTRAL CITY, U.S.A.

00-0000
0000

DATE	CHECK NO.	AMOUNT
APR276-	2138	$209.66

PAY TO THE ORDER OF

ZENITH BUSINESS EQUIPMENT
112 MAIN ST
LOS ANGELES CALIFORNIA

MODERN ORGANIZATIONS, INC.

BANK NAME BRANCH ADDRESS

DATE	REFERENCE	GROSS AMOUNT	DISCOUNT	PREVIOUS BALANCE	BALANCE	REMARKS
MAR 11	155,241	211.78	2.12		209.66	

PLEASE DETACH THIS STATEMENT BEFORE DEPOSITING CHECK

THIS CHECK IS TENDERED IN PAYMENT OF ITEMS LISTED

DATE SHEET NO.

Fig. 14. Accounting Machine Invoice Distribution Application.

Paper tape punches. Most punched-paper tape is produced as a result of other operations and is converted into cards for subsequent processing. However, some equipment uses punched-paper tape as input, particularly small electronic computers.

Adding-machine punches and typewriter-punches are used most frequently for punching paper tape. If five-channel teletype code is used in the system, a teletype machine may be used as a perforator.

Magnetic ink character inscribers. Generally, systems involving optically recognizable printed characters convert such characters, recorded at the source, into another medium. Additional recording and further processing is done using the new medium. Magnetic ink character systems (specifically as used by banks) continue processing by using the original medium and key-driven equipment that are required to record, for example, the amount of the check. Some equipment, especially designed for banks, performs as a proof machine at the same time it inscribes the checks.

Other perforators. Perforated characters are used primarily in installment coupon book applications. Characters are perforated using a lever set machine. Several books may be perforated simultaneously.

Perforated tags are prepared by equipment that prints and perforates at the same time, although the printing may include characters that are not punched. Data, once set in the machine, remain until changed. Other perforated media are generally prepared by machines controlled by punched-paper tape or punched cards.

Data Transmission Equipment. There has been increasing use of data transmission in organizations with multiplant, multioffice and multistore operations. Data may be transmitted over a variety of telephone lines, radio waves, or microwaves. Data transmission equipment includes the following:

1. Teletype—for low speeds, and utilizing punched-paper tape.
2. Punched-card equipment—there are various speeds with which this hardware functions. This equipment is frequently associated with Remote Job Entry (RJE) to computers.
3. Magnetic Tape Equipment—this hardware is used for both sending and receiving data at higher speeds.
4. Disks—also used for higher speed transmission.
5. Computer to computer—data may be transmitted directly from one computer mainframe (CPU) to another.

Conversion and reproduction equipment. Use of this equipment overall has *declined* as a result of the increasing use of key recording hardware which provides for data entry direct to minicomputers and tapes or disks. Conversion can be effected through use of the following:

1. Punched-paper tape—these media are used for low-volume processing.
2. Other perforated media examples are the perforated tags which are used in point-of-sale registers in retail stores. The data entered to computers or converted to other visible media such as punch cards, usually concurrent with data recording.
3. Optical character and magnetic ink recognition—these media are being used with increasing frequency to convert optically recognizable characters, bar codes, or specifically placed marks to computers, tapes or disks, or punch cards.

4. Punched cards—this medium has been used for all sorts of needed conversions. As with other media, computers are being used more frequently to effect these data conversions.
5. Magnetic Tape and Disk—using computers for converting data on these media is the fastest means of data conversion.

Sorting, selecting, and merging equipment. These functions are done primarily by computers today. However, some sorting, collating and selecting is done by the below described hardware as well:

1. *Punched card equipment.* Includes sorter and collator with pockets for appropriate selection.
2. *Optical character and magnetic ink recognition.* Sorting and selection is accomplished similarly on this equipment, utilizing selected "pockets" to facilitate the process.
3. *Paper tape equipment.* Limited selection can be accomplished through this hardware.

Calculating equipment. There has been increasing use of electronic "intelligent" terminals and computers and minicomputers as calculating equipment superseding punched card and punched-paper tape equipment. These terminals include the following:

1. Electronic Point of Sale (E.P.O.S.) Registers at retail stores.
2. Cathode Ray Tube (CRT) Video Terminals.
3. Typewriters.

All these terminals can perform calculations and can provide data conversion to computers (or minicomputers). They have been described above.

However, there are three types of electromechanical calculating equipment which, though obsolescent, are used for calculating:

1. Punched-card calculating printer. Controlled externally by control panel wiring.
2. Key-entry calculators (e.g., bookkeeping machines) with external control panel wiring.
3. Punched-paper tape equipment.

Printing Equipment. This equipment is also being operated under control of computer programs with increasing frequency. Printing from punched cards or punched-paper tape is an obsolescent function. However, there are some installations still in operation, and some have various calculate capabilities.

Also, there are magnetic tape to printer installations.

None of the above installations provide the calculating flexibility of the stored program computer or minicomputer.

Supporting equipment. To facilitate the handling of media used in integrated data processing and provide protection from loss, mutilation, or accidental destruction, there are many types of filing equipment and devices for these media. And there are paper printing, reproducing, collating, decollating, and microfilming devices to expedite handling and processing and provide security.

THE TOOLS OF INTEGRATED DATA PROCESSING—ELECTRONIC SYSTEMS

As has been described and referenced repeatedly in the preceding sections, internally programmed electronic computers are being used with rapidly increasing frequency for integrated data processing, and are superseding most of the electromechanical and externally wired and programmed devices.

Input integration is achieved through use of key-entry (CRT video terminals typewriters, teletypes,), optical character recognition (OCR, scanning) and magnetic ink character recognition (MICR) equipment, punched and perforated tape and tag equipment, and magnetic tapes, disks and drums.

Integrated data processing is further facilitated through data transmissions, which through moderns (data set) can transmit data from one of the above described devices to another, and from one computer to another. Outputs of integrated data processing are recorded on magnetic tapes and disks, printers, typewriters, CRT video terminals, card and paper tape punches, and microfilm and associated printers.

23

Data Processing Systems

CONTENTS

23

Data Processing Systems

Alvin M. Silver, Eng.Sc.D.

A relatively short time ago, in the early 1950s, computer data processing appeared on the business scene. The past 25 years has seen the ever increasing growth of electronic data processing with the computer now ubiquitous in business and in our society. Today, there are very few business situations in which the accountant does not find electronic data processing in one form or another.

The rapid growth of the field and its technical nature has given rise to many misconceptions about data processing systems, and these misconceptions have further complicated an already complicated subject. The apparent simplicity of the inexpensive hand held electronic calculator and the daily contact with computer billing systems, reservations systems, and point of sale equipment, make it appear as though the application of computer technology to business data processing is relatively simple. The abundance of horror stories about unsuccessful computer systems makes it clear that the utilization of computers in business is more complicated than it appears to be. The accountant's involvement with business data processing systems requires that he have a basic knowledge of management systems and computer data processing systems.

This chapter attempts to remove the veil of mystery and misconception from the subject, introducing the accountant to modern management information systems and computer data processing by presenting:

1. Basic data processing and systems concepts.
2. Data processing system objectives.
3. Management information systems.
4. The data processing system life cycle.
5. The task of determining the feasibility of a proposed computer system.
6. System design and the programming of computers.
7. The implementation process and its inherent problems.
8. Computer system concepts and the types of computers.
9. Alternatives for obtaining computer resources.
10. The nature of future developments in this field.

THE ACCOUNTANT'S VIEW OF EDP

This introductory section contains a discussion of the accountant's role in data processing systems: two extreme views of computer data processing, and a comparison of computer data processing and other mechanized forms of data processing.

The accountant's role in electronic data processing. Almost all accountants in the course of their professional careers, will have some contact with data processing systems. Many others, especially those connected with large public accounting firms, will find that the computer has drastically affected the work that they must perform for their clients. It may be well to distinguish between the two roles normally played by an accountant in relation to data processing systems. One of the roles is the accountant as a management consultant, and the other is the accountant as an auditor.

Role as management consultant. The role of the accountant in this area is difficult and has always been so. The accountant is often consulted about business problems which are far from his area of expertise and this is especially true in computer data processing systems. The design of information systems and the application of computers to those systems is a highly technical task which is complex in nature and requires specialized knowledge. The accountant can assist a client in making financial and managerial decisions relating to the feasibility of a data processing project just as he would provide guidance in decision making about other major financial undertakings. The decision to utilize computers is no different from a decision to launch a new product or build a new facility insofar as the accountant is concerned. Each of these undertakings involves significant client resources and the assumption of risk. The accountant has a very valuable service to perform for the client in the role of a prudent business manager who carefully reviews all the data to determine the potential costs and benefits from any proposed client undertaking.

The accountant who has specialized training and experience in the computer information system area can assist the client in many other ways. He can assist the client in the determination of the area(s) suitable for conversion to computer data processing and in the information system feasibility study, analysis of present systems and in the design of the proposed systems, selection of equipment, and in the selection and training of personnel. Finally, he can assist in the implementation of the information system.

Role as auditor. The role of an accountant as an auditor in the design and implementation of computer based management information systems is perhaps not so well publicized, but is even more important. It is more important because it is in this role that the accountant has special expertise to assist his client in controlling the implementation of any financial system and, in particular, a management information system. He has knowledge of the client's personnel, operations and control systems, and should assist the client in making sure that no aspect of existing control is lost in the conversion to a computer system.

The accountant should advise on the control aspects of the proposed system to ensure accuracy of input data, accuracy of machine processing, and accuracy of output. He should see that the responsibilities of methods and operating personnel are properly separated in accordance with good internal control techniques. He should ensure that changes of any sort to data files, in any form, from manual record to punch cards, to magnetic media, or to programs, are properly documented to leave an adequate audit trail. He must make sure that proper control and audit procedures are a part of the new system.

Once the system is installed and working satisfactorily, the auditor's work is *not* finished. He should not be content merely to audit around the computer based system. Instead, he should endeavor to utilize the computer system as far as possible in his audit by preparing his own programs or using packaged audit programs, but, in any case, he should carry his audit right into the computer system.

Finally the accountant should be prepared to comment on the efficiency and reliability of the system whenever he considers it to be necessary. (See Chapter 28 for the details of the mechanics of auditing electronic data processing systems.)

Two extreme views of electronic data processing. To some, at one extreme, electronic data processing is just another improvement in mechanization, having the same basic concepts as other forms of clerical mechanization. These people would use computers only for those applications that have been previously mechanized or that have been considered generally suitable for mechanization by more conventional methods.

This concept of electronic data processing as just another improvement in mechanization has persisted in many business organizations, even though these same organizations have moved from first generation computers to second generation computers to third generation computers and are now getting ready to move to the fourth generation of computer equipment. There has been some broadening of the areas being mechanized and some attempt at integration of functions and record keeping in most conversions to newer equipment. However, this has been of limited scope since it was often felt that there were sufficient difficulties in conversion from one generation of computer equipment to another without adding to them by attempting to redesign the information system. Computer vendors have encouraged the movement of the same information system from computer generation to computer generation by providing emulators (hardware or software that make the new computers perform as though they were the old computers) in an attempt to have their customers trade up to newer and more expensive equipment. Some organizations are still running punched card systems on third generation computer equipment.

At the other extreme, there are those people to whom the word "computer" conjures up a picture of the completely automatic office, instantaneously producing whatever is required at the mere push of a button. At the same time, these people look to the "computer" as a method of replacing most of their personnel and eliminating their "people" problems. The computer is viewed as a panacea for all business operating system ills as well as a solution to all personnel problems.

Both extreme views, like other extreme views in life, leave much to be desired. The mechanization approach is much simpler to visualize and easier to implement, but it does not fully utilize the flexibility, scope, and inherent potential of the newer computer systems. In many organizations utilizing this approach, the newer computer equipment cannot truly be economically justified because, by leaving many exceptions to be handled by manual methods, the mechanization approach ignores areas of operation in which clerical costs are high and operational problems great. The only organizations that are able to justify electronic data processing economically on this basis are those organizations whose products are mainly paper transactions, for example, banks, insurance companies, credit card companies, etc.

The second view, that of the computer doing everything and solving all problems, is equally economically unfeasible. Although our technology has made remarkable strides in improving the capabilities of large scale computers and in the development of small minicomputers or microcomputers (these are discussed later in this chapter), and greatly improved the price performance ratio of all computers, the power and low cost of any mechanized equipment cannot solve all operational and personnel problems within an organization. Many organizations have made progress in low level program decision making, but much theoretical and practical work needs to be done in order to understand the actual information flow and decision-making process in organizations. However, much is presently known and can be implemented in business data processing, and with proper system design and equipment selection there are many fruitful application areas for computers.

Comparison of EDP and other manual or mechanized processing. What are the major differences between processing data on computer equipment and processing by other manual or mechanized methods? What are the major advantages and disadvantages of computer data processing equipment?

Advantages of computer data processing equipment. The advantages are easy enough to state and are to a large extent known by actual or prospective users. They include:

1. *The speed of processing.* The speed of present computer equipment is measured in million instructions per second (mips). Modern computers can perform millions of calculations each second and masses of data can be processed or rearranged for various requirements or reports in a fraction of the time required by clerical or conventional mechanized methods.
2. *The accuracy of the equipment.* Modern computer equipment is extremely accurate and the probability of an undetected equipment error occurring is less than one per 10,000 hours of operation. Although the possibility of undetected equipment error occurring is very slight, computer systems are subject to many of the inherent input data problems

of other systems. Data processing by computer equipment also allows certain editing of input data and the detection of input errors that are not available in other systems.

3. *Elimination of repetitive data entry and greater processing control.* The storage of data in machine readable form eliminates the need to reenter data for each operation. This eliminates both the error that occurs when data is manually copied from one report to another, and the complete loss of a datum (e.g., an individual record may be lost when a clerk omits copying it from a list or if a punch card is lost). Greater processing control is possible since the high speed of computer equipment enables control totals to be recalculated often and compared to earlier totals at each step of the processing.
4. *Decision-making ability.* Most clerical operations involve several logical paths. If one number is greater than another, then one course of action must be taken; if smaller, another. These minor decisions must be made, often without realization, whenever clerical work is performed. The same logical clerical decision making occurs in punched card systems when a machine operator chooses the next processing operation based on the results of a prior operation. The computer processor has the ability to make decisions necessary to select one course of action or another based on a decision rule at any time in the program. The computer can choose one path if the check amount is over a given limit, or choose another path if the inventory quantity is less than a predetermined amount. The computer, if correctly programmed, can handle any and all variations and automatically perform all processing on heterogeneous data from the raw state to the finished product. Lower-level decision making can thus be automated with the assurance of consistent application of decision rules.
5. *Smaller physical storage requirements.* Data can be recorded with accuracy on magnetic media, generally the major medium for mass data storage today, and stored in much less space than punched cards or manual documents. A 2,400 foot reel of magnetic tape, 9 to 10 inches in diameter by one half inch wide, is able to hold more data than one million fully punched cards. Microfiche and computer output microfilm (COM) have also greatly reduced the physical requirement for data storage.
6. *Operating costs.* Electronic data processing operating costs are much less than the operating costs for manual or punched card systems when any sizeable amount of data require processing. There is great economy of scale in electronic data processing, as with other automated equipment, in that as the amount of data to be processed increases, the average cost per item processed decreases. Since electronic data processing equipment costs are fixed over a range of output volumes, as are punched card processing costs, decreases in the amount of data to be processed result in higher average cost per item processed.

Disadvantages of computer data processing. There are disadvantages of computer data processing and they also need to be understood by actual or potential users. Among these disadvantages are:

1. *Long planning and implementation period.* The decision to develop and implement a major new system in an organization is a commitment on the part of management to allocate significant organizational resources to the project. Building an electronic data processing system is similar to building a new manufacturing, warehousing, or office building for the organization. The organization must determine requirements, design one or more alternative systems that meet the requirements, select the best alternative system, select and order equipment, program the system, convert to the new system, run parallel, and debug the system. On large systems like large building, the lead time for materials (equipment) and labor (programming) is long, resulting in a long period between conception and implementation.
2. *High start-up costs.* During the planning and implementation period costs continue to accumulate and there are no benefits from the new system since it is not operational. Using the building construction and computer data processing systems analogy again, this system start-up time is akin to architectural design and building construction time during which the owner incurs cost, but receives no benefit from the uncompleted building. Large system implementation projects, with start-up periods of over a year, can easily incur start-up costs of $750,000.
3. *Greater need for controls.* Clerical and punched card systems depend on people for much of the data processing. While this is a weakness of systems, it is also a strength in that people possess judgment while machines do not. The high speed of computer data processing equipment allows much useful work to be performed in a short time, but it also permits much damage to occur in an equally short time. There is a greater need to establish controls after each job step in a system so that errors may immediately be recognized and corrected. Electronic data processing systems have some built-in controls to protect against machine malfunction. For example, most write operations (data transferred to machine readable media such as punch cards, magnetic tape or disk) are immediately followed by a read operation and the data read is compared against the original data to see that the write operation was correctly done.
4. *Centralization of processing.* In clerical systems, the work load is spread out over a number of people and, generally, if one person is not available, the remaining work can be transmitted to another person. This is also true in punched card systems where, with multiple machine work centers, a machine breakdown can be alleviated by transferring the work to another machine. Earlier developments in the computer industry were geared toward the building of larger and larger computer systems

with greater processing capabilities, resulting in larger machines but higher total costs. The higher the costs of the equipment, the less likely it is that companies are able to afford the luxury of backup or standby equipment. Thus, a major breakdown can assume the proportions of a major catastrophe. Fortunately, while the trend toward larger machines still continues for some applications with extremely high data processing volumes, the development of minicomputers and microcomputers has lead toward the decentralizing of data processing into many smaller machines. With many smaller computers it is possible to transfer the work from one computer to another in the case of machine breakdown, and it is also possible to afford a standby or spare computer. However, as with any other automated machine process, there is a certain amount of centralization of processing that makes electronic data processing systems more sensitive to machine failure than clerical systems.

5. *Organizational implementation problems.* Major undertakings in companies affect organization structure, responsibilities, and power. Information flows are the veins and arteries of the corporate body with the survival of the company depending on its information flow. New systems require changes in work patterns, responsibilities, and in many cases the power relationships among employees. Many people resist change, and organizational change is always a slow process. The implementation of major information systems involves considerable modification and decision-making flow of an organization, and requires a long and costly implementation period to change organizational relationships.
6. *Flexibility.* Computer data processing systems are more difficult to change than are manual or punched card systems. An advantage of computers is that they process data with great precision, but that great precision is at the cost of very detailed instructions. A system change may require a new set of detailed instructions (program) to be prepared which is much more difficult than an explanation to a clerk in a manual system.
7. *Fixed cost of operation.* Computer data processing equipment is relatively insensitive to processing volume changes in a predefined area. Clerical systems may be continually modified to reflect changes in processing volume and the cost of an operation varies directly with the transaction volume. As transaction volume decreases in an electronic data processing system, the average cost to process a transaction usually increases. A good example of this phenomenon is the brokerage industry in the latter 1960s and early 1970s. The industry's back office operation was mainly manual with some mechanized processing. As stock trading volume grew, the industry tried to respond by adding more people, but was unable even with the additional people to maintain functioning systems based on procedures that were designed for much smaller volumes. The brokerage industry then developed computer systems for back office operations and was successfully able to handle the

larger volumes. However, this period of rising stock trading volume was followed by a decline in stock trading volume and the brokerage industry found current unit transaction processing cost increasing. One of the reasons for the many brokerage house mergers was the desire to more fully utilize expensive computer data processing systems that had large idle capacity. On the other hand, when stock trading volume increased in the mid-1970s, the industry was able to handle the increased volume since the existing electronic data processing systems were relatively insensitive to changes in transaction volume.

A comparison of the relative strengths and weaknesses of manual, punched card, and computer systems is shown in Figure 1.

		*Comparative Ranking**		
Factor	*Explanation*	*Manual*	*Punch Card*	*Computer*
Planning and Implementation Period	Time required to install system Shorter periods are preferred	1	2	3
Processing Speed	Average processing time	3	2	1
Accuracy	Error rate	3	2	1
Workload Response	Impact on system due to workload changes	3	2	1
Information Retrieval	Ability to retrieve information	2	3	1
Processing Consistency	Follow instructions consistently	3	2	1
Control Requirements	Need for processing controls	3	1	2
Processing Complexity	Ability to handle complex logic	2	3	1
Learning Ability	Ability to learn by trial and error	1	2	3
Flexibility	Ease of making changes	1	3	2

*1 = Best

Fig. 1. Comparative Advantage of Manual, Punch Card and Computer Systems.

BASIC DATA PROCESSING SYSTEM CONCEPTS

This section will focus on basic data processing system concepts that are common to all data processing systems. The methods used to implement the system may vary greatly, from the use of clerical personnel in a manual system to a highly automated computer system, but the environment in which the system operates, system objectives, and the development process should be the same from the viewpoint of an accountant or manager.

Definition of some data processing terms. In any discussion of data processing systems, the words data, information, and system appear over and over again and should be defined:

Data. The term data means facts and usually refers to unstructured facts. Unstructured fact is the raw material for data processing since, in order for data to have any value, it must be structured and organized so that it is meaningful to the recipient.

Information. Information is a commodity that has value, which implies that the information is not known before it is received since the receipt of something which is known has no value. Information is selected data or data that have been arranged or manipulated in some fashion to be meaningful to the recipient. Information is a message that has surprise value to the recipient. Decision making uses information and information can also be defined as knowledge that allows the recipient to make or improve the making of a decision. The terms "information" and "data" are often used interchangeably since it is quite possible for one person's information to be another person's data if the required aggregation and data processing are different for the two individuals.

System. A system is a set of relationships among interrelated objects and is usually goal oriented. A system is not a random set of objects, but rather objects which can be identified as belonging together since they interact to produce a goal or objective. A system has a boundary which is delineated by those features which separate the objects and relationships from the outside environment. The interrelationships or interfaces between the system and its environment are called the inputs and outputs of the system. A data processing system is an organized set of methods and procedures designed to manipulate data in order to produce information for achieving one or more objectives. A generalized data processing system is depicted in Figure 2.

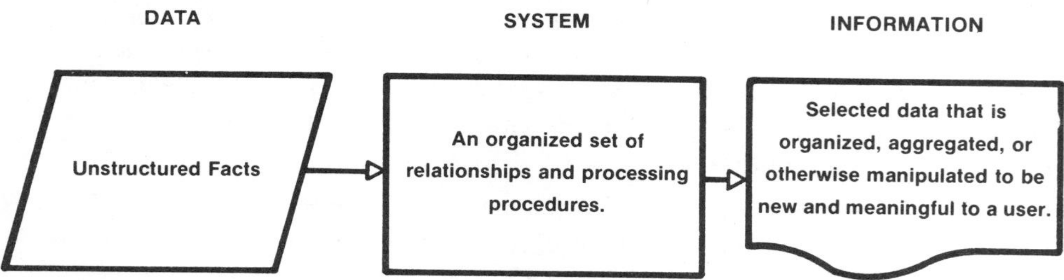

Fig. 2. Generalized Data Processing System.

Data processing system objectives. From an accountant's viewpoint the data processing system of an organization has two goals, namely, to facilitate the management of operations and to capture data to provide transactional financial information to the accountant for analysis, auditing, and statement purposes. Much of the data that must be collected to achieve either of the above goals is common to both and in fact, can be collected at the same time in the same area of company operations, so that processing for one objective can produce by-product information for the other objective. It is this commonality of data requirements that makes electronic data processing economically attractive.

Commonality of data can best be appreciated by considering the functional areas of the organization that generate data as a result of daily operations and interactions with other functions. Functional areas within a business interact with each other and also interact with external groups such as customers, vendors, banks, and agencies within the public sector. It is easy to visualize the common data for both goals by enumerating the functional areas and transactions of a typical manufacturing concern:

1. Marketing. (Bids, sales orders, back orders, customer contracts, advertising contracts, etc.)
2. Engineering. (Research and development commitments, bills of materials, development budget, quality and reliability reports, etc.)
3. Purchasing. (Quotations, purchase orders, etc.)
4. Receiving. (Receiving reports, inspection reports, etc.)
5. Inventory Control. (Inventory receipt, inventory requisitions, stock records, fiscal accounts, etc.)
6. Manufacturing. (Material requisitions, purchase requisitions, production orders, tool orders, material scrap reports, labor reports, production progress reports, etc.)
7. Shipping. (Shipping orders, bills of lading, etc.)
8. Accounting. (Customer invoices, vendor invoices, customer checks, company payments, time cards, payroll checks, budgets, statements, etc.)

Management Functions. A data processing system to facilitate the management of operations must recognize the management functions in a business enterprise. Although there are different views of the management processes, a widely accepted view holds that the management process can be subdivided into four functions or phases. The four management functions are: planning, organizing, directing and controlling.

1. *Planning.* Planning may be defined as the determination of objectives before action is taken, and the development of the series of steps necessary to achieve the objective. Objectives in the planning process are specified in terms of sales, profits, market share, product line, and output volumes. A plan considers the current status, future objectives, specific detailed steps, and the time frames for achieving the objective.

   In smaller organizations planning may be done informally and there may be no written overall plan. In medium and larger sized organizations the planning function is accomplished by a formal process with a written statement of the plan and detailed subplans. In both cases, current financial information is necessary for preparation of budgets for future time periods.
2. *Organizing.* Once the overall plan is determined, there must be a mechanism for converting the plan to action. An organizational structure must be developed and that structure must explicitly define the relationship of people and resources within the firm. The function

of each person within the organization in terms of duties and responsibilities must be clearly defined so that the organization moves together toward the common set of organizational objectives.

3. *Directing.* The directing phase is the execution or action phase where resources are manipulated according to the plan in order for the organization to achieve its objectives. This phase consists of the dissemination of information in the form of orders and the execution of the orders. This phase also involves the training and motivating of personnel so that they can perform their assigned functions in the plan.
4. *Controlling.* The controlling function monitors all activity to determine whether the activity and the result of the activity are according to plan. This phase compares the results of a planned activity with the planned results in order to detect any variances. This phase depends heavily on the flow of information for both reporting and evaluation. Controlling is the measurement and use of information to affect or regulate a future course of action.

   The controlling function provides the key feedback ingredient for successful closed look management systems. The entire management process is iterative as is shown in the management cycle depicted in Figure 3.

Imbedded within the entire management process are decision-making processes that require information and generate information. Thus an overall information flow system is often referred to as a Management Information System.

Management information system. An important concept in data processing systems is the "total system" concept that views the organization in terms of its management process, decision-making process, organizational structure, and information flow system. The "total system" concept is an approach to data processing that views the entire organization as a single unit composed of many interrelated subsystems that must function effectively together so that the objectives of the organization are achieved. A caveat is important at this point. The "total system" concept does not mandate that all elements of an organization be automated into one large all-encompassing data processing system. Rather, the concept suggests that a data processing system must relate to other elements of an organization and provide interfaces with those elements so that the organization can function effectively.

A data processing system that functions as an integrated part of an organization is often referred to as a Management Information System (MIS) or sometimes as a Management Information and Control System (MICS). A Management Information System is a set of subsystems that are interconnected to fulfill the information requirements necessary to plan, organize, direct, and control business operations. The system should produce and deliver timely and accurate information for management decision making, so that the organization may achieve its goals. It is important to note that what are being discussed are management information systems and not equipment and, in fact, the two should be considered separately. Many data processing systems contain the most modern computer equipment but are not effective management information

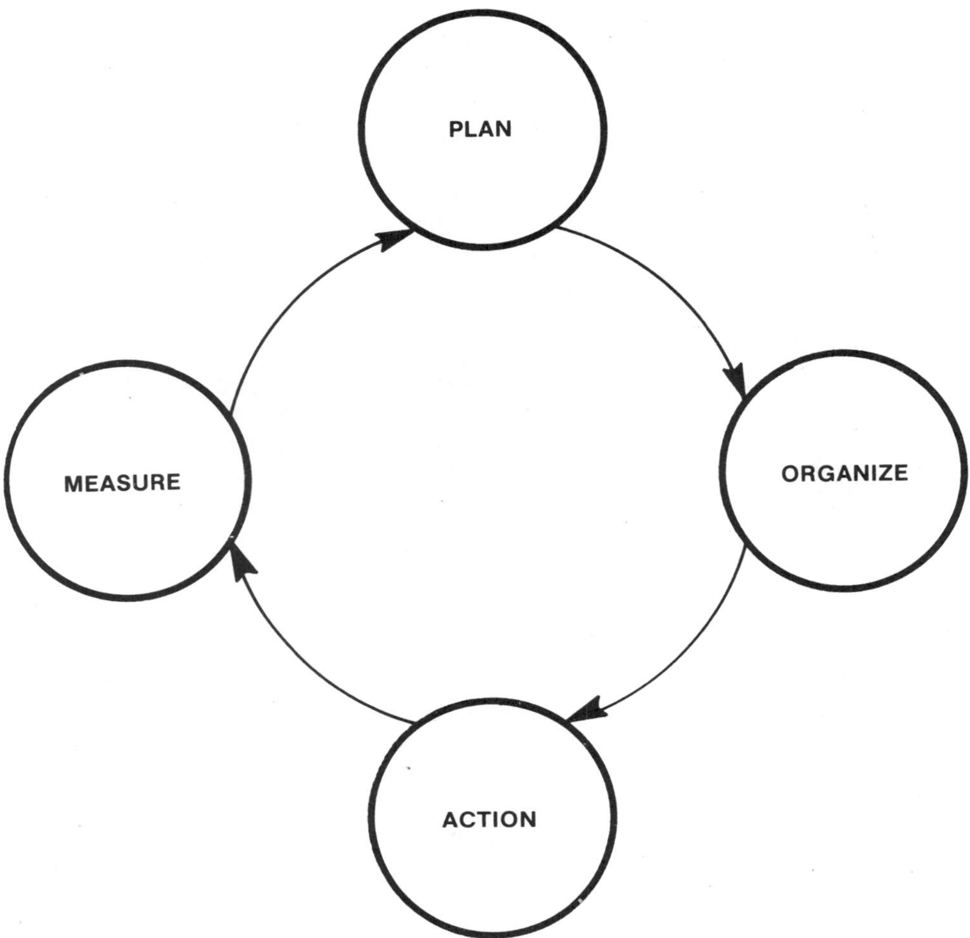

Fig. 3. The Management Cycle.

systems, while on the other hand, many effective management information systems are completely manual.

The following brief review of the history and evolution of management information systems is valuable in that it tends to explain the state of some current data processing systems. Many computer based data processing systems are merely automated copies of prior manual or punched card data processing systems and have their roots in earlier approaches to data processing.

Custodial accounting systems. The first data processing systems were concerned with historical accounting data and can be called custodial accounting systems. The emphasis was on what had occurred and not on information flow for management decision making. These systems were concerned with summarizing accounting transactions to reduce or eliminate clerical personnel.

Manual methods, bookkeeping equipment, punched card equipment, and, later, computers were utilized to process batches of data. Each application was treated as a separate system with very little effort devoted to integrating records and common data that might serve more than one function. Data processing systems were designed as cost-cutting (reduction of clerical effort) systems and not as profit-making systems, without the realization that information has value. There was a proliferation of records and it usually took a long time to produce historical information.

Responsibility reporting systems. The next step in the evolution of data processing systems was the classification of data according to activity and responsibility. These data processing systems were viewed as responsibility reporting systems and were an outgrowth to some extent of equipment developments. The basis for allocating costs and revenue was the firm's organization structure and chart of accounts. Responsibility reporting systems allocated both the controllable and noncontrollable expenses to specific departments or organizational units within the firm with unit managers being held responsible for unfavorable variances of controllable costs from the plan or budget. The information presented was usually in dollar terms concerning past events with little or no future projections. Although these systems were an improvement over the older custodial accounting systems, they also suffered in timeliness due to the limitations of manual methods, bookkeeping machines, and punched card equipment. The responsibility reporting systems were the beginning of data processing systems that recognized the commonality of data between accounting statements and management reports.

Utilization of computer data processing systems in the accounting area was considered as just another step in the further mechanization of the data processing function. Each individual application was treated as a separate system. This piecemeal approach toward data processing systems was the result of conforming to the organizational boundaries that have traditionally existed in organizations. These early installations were also justified on the basis of the computer's ability to perform accounting tasks more economically, rather than on the value of information. Early computer data processing systems concentrated on accounting applications and the data processing department became a part of the accounting department in an organization. The later development of manufacturing and marketing applications led to the realization that much of the data processed for marketing and manufacturing applications was useful to the accounting applications and vice versa because of the commonality of the data.

Integrated systems and the data base. The development of data processing applications in manufacturing, marketing, and other functional areas of the organization was geared to mesh with the management and decision-making processes within the organization. Computer based information systems were developed to provide planning and control information to support the management decision making process. The operational data being processed were no longer measured in dollars, but rather in quantitative units most closely related to the functional area of the organization (for example, finished product quantity on hand, and finished product quantity on order; raw material quantity; customer delivery requirement dates; vendor delivery performance in days late; personnel attributes such as skills, foreign languages, and educational background; etc.)

The computer information system became the formal mechanism of information flow within the organization instead of merely a system for processing historical data. An integrated management information system mirrors the network of interrelationships within an organization and most often is a network of interrelated subsystems for supporting the operational activities of the firm. Although the system provides for routine transaction processing, the system objective is to provide information for managing. Data is manipulated, aggregated, analyzed, and presented before management decision making. The data that is processed comes both from routine transaction processing and external sources and data obtained from routine transaction processing is used to automate low-level routine decision making in the organization. For example, the processing of inventory transactions and the calculation of inventory position enables the information system to evaluate the inventory status in light of preprogrammed decision rules and to automatically produce a purchase order or manufacturing work order document. Another example is the processing of accounts receivable transactions and the calculation of accounts receivable balances by time period with the data used to generate collection letters in accordance with programmed decision rules.

The management information system uses data from external sources (provided to the system as transactions) to assist management in measuring progress toward achieving goals or in formulating new policies and objectives. For example, data on competitors' sales and economic conditions are processed to present information on the firm's market share and to support management future planning.

It is in this area of future planning that management information systems are making valuable contributions to the organization. The management process involves planning, and planning, by definition, is the formulating of a course of action for the future. Management information systems, in a supportive role for management, project current data to provide information about probable future states of the organization. This occurs more often than most people realize in that data processing systems automatically implement inventory reordering decisions which imply future needs or a forecasted demand for the inventory. It is common for management information systems to project operating statements for future periods based on current data and an extrapolation of current variances and trends. Management information systems can also contain simulation capability which allows managers to use the current base of data within the system to project information about the future, based on one or more assumptions about events in the future.

The development of integrated management information systems involves the storage of large amounts of data. Much of the data is common to more than one functional area of the organization and need not be stored in separate records for applications in each functional area of the organization. This centralization of data is a feature of management information systems and particularly computer based management information systems. To some extent, the development of a centralized data base became technically and economically feasible with changes in computer technology (high-density, direct-access magnetic disk storage). The data base concept implies that a single item of data, a datum, is stored only in one place within the system, although it may be used in many applications. For example, a customer's name is maintained in one place, but it is required for addressing order confirmations, addressing invoices, addressing accounts receivable statements, identifying accounts receivable record, etc. Data base technology is concerned with the capture, storage, and retrieval of large amounts of data for subsequent data processing operations. Computer based management information systems often contain separate data base subsystems for this purpose, for example, IBM's IMS (Information Management System) and DL/I (Data Language 1); Univac's DMS (Data Management System), IDMS (Integrated Data Management Systems), and other proprietary packaged subsystems with names like ADABAS, and TOTAL. Data base systems maintain an organization and structure that makes it possible to store data in a prescribed manner, but to retrieve the data in many different sequences. Most management information systems in modestly sized organizations and larger are computer based, so that much of the discussion about data base technology relates to computers. However, manual management information systems can also have these characteristics. For example, the traveling requisition system for inventory control often contained purchasing data, inventory usage data, vendor delivery data, engineering data, and manufacturing data on a single piece of paper (or card) that traveled among the functional activity areas of an organization.

Data processing system life cycle. The idea of a life cycle is not limited to data processing systems, but a similar concept is applied, for example, to a new product. The basis of the life cycle concept is that every data processing system goes through similar processes as it is conceived, developed, implemented, modified, and eventually dies (discontinued). The life cycle concept is a generalization of past history and enables some measure of the future to be forecasted. Knowing something about the future allows for planning and the creation of a control mechanism. There are various definitions of the phases in the data processing system life cycle, but the differences are mainly semantic and in the method of assigning activities to the phases. Most views agree on the essential activities and flow of the life cycle, and the necessity for control during the entire process. The data processing system life cycle is defined here to contain the following seven phases:

1. Preliminary study and feasibility assessment.
2. System analysis and design.
3. Equipment procurement, procedure, and program development.
4. Implementation.

5. Post implementation evaluation.
6. System modification.
7. System discontinuation.

The accountant is likely to be most heavily involved during phases 1, 4, 5 and 7, namely preliminary study and feasibility assessment, implementation, post implementation evaluation, and system discontinuation.

Preliminary study and feasibility assessment. The data processing system life cycle starts with management's unhappiness with a given situation or a desire for additional information. This is the "problem" and should be clearly defined as the objective of the new data processing system. The desire for a new system may be motivated by cost-cutting objectives, profit-making objectives, or some combination of both. Cost-cutting objectives are characterized as an attempt to obtain essentially the same results (outputs) at a reduced cost. For example, a study may be initiated to reduce the cost of processing customer payment transactions. In this case there is satisfaction with the output of the system, but dissatisfaction with the process itself. On the other hand, a study may be initiated to increase profits by obtaining different results from the system. A study of the customer payment transaction process in an attempt to increase cash availability by reducing processing time, or a management's request for information on store merchandise inventory every morning so that depleted items might be replenished and available for sale are examples of profit-making objective studies. In each instance there is a belief that doing something in a different fashion will result in economic gain.

Information systems and other organizational changes are capital investments even though they frequently are not treated as such in accounting records. Any change requires that resources be spent in order to achieve benefits. Usually the resources are spent in the current period and the benefits are received over a longer period of time following the completion of the change. Therefore, data processing system feasibility studies concentrate on first determining whether the change is economically feasible. The result of the feasibility study provides sufficient detail for each alternative so that management can weigh the capital investment with other alternative capital investments to select the investment with the highest return. A feasibility report contains as a minimum the following sections:

A. *Objectives.* The feasibility studies contains a section on objectives which clearly defines the goals of the system, the reasons that motivated the study. Management objectives can take many directions, for example:

   1. Reduce equipment cost by changing computers.
   2. Reduce data processing personnel cost by substituting equipment for manual effort.
   3. Reduce time required to present information reports so that more timely management decisions can be made.
   4. Improve customer service and relations to increase sales.

5. Reduce costs by eliminating conflicting and overlapping activities within the organization.
6. Improve internal control.
7. Provide increased capacity for future growth.
8. Provide a facility for computer based models and operations research to improve overall operations.

B. *New System Description.* This section of the feasibility study contains a description of the existing system and the general specifications for the new system. The general specifications of the new system describe: what the new system will do, how it will do it, the resources required, and how the new system attains the objectives previously stated.

C. *Time and Resource Requirements.* The time frames for the next phases of the data processing system life cycle and the organization resources required during the life of the system are described in this section. Approximate start and completion dates for each phase, and the other company resources required during each phase are defined. The other organization resources include computer time on the existing system, a portion of the manufacturing capacity lost during the implementation phase, out-of-pocket expenditures in dollars, and other resources required.

D. *Cost and Benefits.* This section contains an economic analysis of the cost and benefits of the new system. The costs are presented by category and by time period for cash flow and return on investment analysis. The benefits are similarly stated and include the economic value of the tangible benefits, estimated value of the intangible benefits, and a statement of the benefits that cannot be quantified. This section includes an economic analysis of the feasible alternatives considered. Figure 4 is a typical economic analysis for a system alternative.

E. *Recommendations.* The purpose of the feasibility study is to assess the feasibility of a system to meet objectives. This section states the recommendation of the person or group that prepared the feasibility study. The recommendations logically flow from the data presented in the feasibility study and may or may not advocate the continuance of the project. Sometimes the most profitable portion and decision in a data processing life cycle is the recommendation in the feasibility study not to continue the project. It is here that the accountant's analytical ability can best serve the client. However, it should be remembered that the assumption of some small measure of risk is a part of business operation and is responsible for business success.

The recommendations in this section (if the recommendation is to go forward) contain a plan for action for the next phases of the data processing system life cycle. The plan for action lists the tasks required for subsequent phases through phase five, the post implementation evaluation. This high-level listing of tasks is accompanied by the scheduled time frame for the tasks and may also be accompanied by a Gnatt chart or PERT network presentation. The plan for action also includes the setting up of a group that will be responsible for monitoring the data processing system development progress through the implementation phase. A separate group is also created to do the post implementation evaluation which is similar to an audit of the preceding phases.

ECONOMIC ANALYSIS

ALTERNATIVE 3—REPLACE OLD EQUIPMENT

	YEAR					
ESTIMATED BENEFITS	1	2	3	4	5	Total
Equipment Rental Reduction	—	$ 80,000	$200,000	$220,000	$242,000	$ 742,000
Space Rental Reduction	($ 5,000)	10,000	40,000	44,000	48,400	137,400
Personnel Reduction (includes taxes and fringe benefits	—	150,000	300,000	330,000	363,400	1,143,000
Improved Inventory Control Value (including savings on reduced inventory value and inventory obsolescence)	—	300,000	250,000	275,000	302,500	1,127,500
Total Benefits (Cost)	($ 5,000)	$540,000	$790,000	$869,000	$956,300	$3,150,300

	YEAR					
ESTIMATED COSTS	1	2	3	4	5	Total
Initial Costs						
Feasibility Study*	$ 45,000					$ 45,000
System Design, Programming, and Testing	220,000	$ 50,000				270,000
Training		30,000				30,000
Computer Room Modification	15,000					15,000
File Conversion	12,000					12,000
Other Implementation Costs	3,000	15,000				18,000
Other Initial Costs	2,000	2,000				4,000
Total Initial Costs	$297,000	$ 97,000				$ 394,000
Operating Costs						
Data Processing Equipment Rental (including maintenance)	$ 75,000	$300,000	$330,000	$363,000	$399,300	$1,467,300
Additional Personnel (includes taxes and fringe benefits)	25,000	50,000	55,000	60,500	66,600	257,100
System and Program Maintenance	—	10,000	20,000	30,000	30,000	90,000
Forms and Supplies	5,000	20,000	22,000	24,200	26,600	97,800
Other Operating Costs	3,000	10,000	11,000	12,100	13,300	49,400
Total Operating Costs	$108,000	$390,000	$438,000	$489,800	$535,800	$1,961,600
Total Annual Costs	$405,000	$487,000	$438,000	$489,800	$535,800	$2,355,600
Net Benefit (Cost) Before Taxes	($410,000)	$ 53,000	$352,000	$379,200	$420,500	$ 794,700

Return on Investment (ROI) approximately 47% per year.

*Can be eliminated as sunk cost.

Fig. 4. Economic Analysis of Data Processing System Alternative.

Systems analysis and design. The general specifications from the feasibility study serve to define the overall requirements of the system. The system design proceeds within the constraint of the feasibility study, but should not view those constraints as absolutes. If an improvement on the original feasibility study specifications can be made, it should be made after appropriate approval. There is much need for creativity during this phase, but the system design should be closely monitored to ensure that the design reflects the system objectives.

The detail system analysis step, which precedes the system design, focuses on the details of the present system to determine the detail design requirements. The detail analysis step also seeks to determine the exceptions in the information flow since these too must be known for proper system design. A thorough review of the existing system and appropriate data results in parameters for the design effort and often some preliminary design decisions.

Some of the questions that must be answered during this phase are:

Output

1. What reports will be produced by the system?
2. What is the format of each report?
3. What is the distribution of each report?
4. What is the issue frequency of each report?
5. What controls are necessary to ensure that reports are complete, accurate, and on time?

Files

1. What data must be stored within the system?
2. How will the data be organized into files?
3. What manual files will be maintained?
4. What computer files will be maintained?
5. What will be the file size and file growth rate?
6. What type of storage media will be used for the file?
7. How is the file organized and accessed?
8. What is the layout of the file records?

Input

1. What is the source of the data?
2. What source documents are used or must be provided?
3. Who completes the source documents and how often?
4. How will the source document data be converted to machine readable form?
5. What controls are necessary for accuracy and completeness of input data?

Processing

1. What manual processing is required?
2. What machine processing is required?
3. What computer processing is required?
4. What is the transaction volume?

5. How frequently must processing be performed?
6. What type of equipment is required?
7. What computer language(s) will be used?
8. What type of personnel is required for processing?
9. What error control procedures are necessary?

Testing

1. How will the system be tested?
2. What test data will be used for the system test?
3. What acceptance criteria will be used for the system test?

Implementation

1. How will personnel be trained?
2. Who will do the training?
3. What written procedures are to be prepared?
4. How will data be converted for the new system?
5. How will error be controlled?
6. What is the acceptance criteria for user acceptance?

The systems analysis and design phase prepares the working drawings and detail specifications for the subsequent phases. At the end of the system analysis and design phase, the system has been subdivided into subsystems and program specifications prepared. File layouts, report and screen formats, input record layouts, run diagrams, and controls are also prepared.

At this point, the detail plans for the system have been developed and it is worthwhile to reexamine the economic analysis performed in the feasibility study. With more current and accurate data available, this step provides management with a more accurate appraisal of the outcome and an opportunity to rethink the options available. This step of reevaluation should be done periodically throughout all the phases as a means of avoiding any economic surprises.

Equipment procurement, procedure, and program development. Equipment procurement involves the determination of the specific type of equipment, the selection of a vendor, the placing of a purchase order, and the actual delivery of the equipment. Equipment procurement may not be a step in this phase if the equipment is in place and the data processing system is an additional application or a modification of an existing application. The first step in the equipment procurement process is the determination of the specific type of equipment and possible suppliers. The system description developed during the feasibility study phase, as well as the basic system design developed during the prior phase, are used as the basis of a bid invitation for suppliers. The number of suppliers solicited depends on the dollar value of the equipment to be procured and the type of equipment. The smaller the dollar amount or the more specialized the equipment, the fewer the manufacturers invited to bid. The list of potential suppliers should be reviewed very carefully so that bid invitations are sent only to the best three to five manufacturers. The cost of evaluating the bid proposals is directly proportional to the number of the vendors involved, and three to five judiciously selected vendors usually provides a sufficient range of technology, system options, and price. One or more members of the procurement team is designated as vendor liaison personnel to familiarize vendors with the organization and its particular data processing problems. The invitation to bid is a comprehensive document that provides required information to vendors and assures that the same information is used by all competing vendors. The effort expended in the preparation of the invitation to bid is worthwhile, since it informs the vendors about the requirements that they must meet, minimizes the number of questions, and assures uniformity in proposal format to provide a valid basis for comparing competing equipment. The contents of the invitation to bid include:

1. General information about the organization.
2. Present data processing systems.
3. Future data processing system plans.
4. The new information system specification.
5. Basic system design specifications and flow charts.
6. Required proposal format and data to be furnished by each vendor.

Items 4 and 5 can be obtained from the work done during the earlier phases. The information system specifications and basic design specifications contain a clear detailed definition of the new information system so that vendors' proposals can clearly show how the proposed equipment meets the organization's needs. The vendor's proposals will contain standard approaches that are applicable to any potential customer if the invitation to bid lacks a clear detailed definition of the information system design.

Vendor proposals are compared to each other and to the invitation to bid in order to select a vendor. The factors considered in evaluating vendor proposals are:

1. How well the vendor's equipment meets the system design specification requirements.
2. Flexibility of vendor's equipment and system (ease of configuration changes, modularity of equipment, upgrading flexibility for future growth, etc.).
3. Cost.
4. Availability of rental, purchase, or lease arrangements.
5. Equipment delivery schedule (meets equipment requirements timetable).
6. Availability of adequate equipment maintenance.
7. Local area equipment backup.
8. Installation requirements.
9. Adequate and dependable software (software is defined later in this chapter).
10. Vendor's assistance (installation, programming, and training).
11. Physical installation requirement and costs.
12. Projected life cycle costs.
13. Availability of equipment for program tests prior to delivery.
14. Compliance with terms of bid invitation and other considerations.

A timetable for the physical tasks of installation is prepared after the selection of a vendor. The physical installation tasks include selection of the area, environmental conditioning (air conditioning, heating, humidity), fire and security protection, and physical modifications to the area (raise floors, electrical connections, water connections, etc.). The vendor selection step often overlaps the earlier system design phase if a major new system is being developed or a major change in the data processing system is being made. This occurs if decisions on programming language, file organization, and operating systems are necessary for the development of the detail program specifications.

Procedure and program development. The detail procedures for system operation, both manual and computer, are now prepared. The procedure manuals are written in a form most easily understood by the personnel who will use them. The user procedure manuals contain a detailed description of all manual input and output from the system with an explanation of the source, responsibility, and control for input source data, and a description of the system output format, frequency, and distribution. The computer personnel procedures contain the detail operating instructions for all programs, runs, subsystems and the overall system. These procedures also contain a description of the test data and the results obtained with the test data.

Program development involves the translating of program specifications into detailed instructions for machine processing. A program is a set of instructions in a programming language (programs, programming languages, and flowcharts are discussed later in this chapter) that enables the computer to perform the required data processing. Each program is documented with a program description, program flowchart, program listing and compilation, a test plan for testing the program, test data, and the results of the test data. Much of this material is used in the documentation for computer operating personnel.

Implementation. The implementation phase is the most critical phase for system success. It is generally a major undertaking that cuts across functional area organization structure and involves the development of new communication lines and personal relationships within the organization. This phase is most critical since it is analogous to the action phase of the management process, while the prior life cycle phases are analogous to the planning phase. Nothing is accomplished unless the system is implemented.

Implementation is often considered a single phase within a systems life cycle. This phase is considered to occur after system design and construction and immediately prior to user operation of the system. To some, implementation is synonymous with operational training. The view taken by this author is that the implementation process spans the life cycle of the system and that certain activities enhance the probability of successful implementation.

Involving the user in the design process has many advantages. User involvement focuses the design effort on questions of operational significance rather than on the development of new and more sophisticated techniques that are not of particular interest or use to the user. This avoids the design in which the new sophisticated techniques are elegant solutions to problems which are irrelevant to the user.

Early and continual involvement in the design effort by the user has its psychological advantages. The user develops a sense of involvement in the system and identifies the system objectives with his own objective set. This personal involvement on the part of a user leads him to accept the system as a desirable means for obtaining one of his own ends or objectives. After a period of prolonged involvement, the user can visualize the operational environment being created by the system and it becomes familiar to him. The operating manager develops a better understanding of the system and this attenuates his reluctance to operate in the changed business environment created by the new system. Personal identification on the part of the operating manager gives him a stake in seeing that the system succeeds, as system success is equated to personal success. Common objectives shared by both the system designers and users, reduce problems during the transitional stage of the system life cycle (usually called the implementation phase).

There are many design alternatives available to the system designer during the detail design phase and programming of a system since there are very few things that need to be accomplished that cannot be done by two or more different means. The means chosen may make no difference in system function but contain a trade-off between design ease and ease in use. It is only natural that an individual choose an alternative which is more favorable to him. It is therefore not surprising that system designers tend to choose those alternatives that simplify their design effort rather than an alternative that will reduce the effort required on the part of the user. In general, where there is a design trade-off between system designer convenience and user convenience the decision should be made to favor the user. Very rarely can it be demonstrated that the solution with the greatest system designer convenience is the best solution for the organization.

System terminology is another area in which the alternative chosen usually favors the system designer at the expense of the user. It is natural for people to attempt to communicate in a language which is most familiar to them. As the technology in various fields has developed, the language has become specialized to describe the technology. System designers and computer specialists have developed their technical language to such a point that the operating manager may not understand it. On the other hand, operating managers develop specialized language to describe the particular business environment in which they operate. It is sometimes equally difficult for the system designers or computer specialists to understand the operating manager. Each group accuses the other of using jargon which simply stated means, "I don't understand your language." It is important that the required user interfaces be developed in a form and language that is clearly and readily understood by the various user groups.

User training spans a longer time period than it is usually acknowledged. User training cannot be confined to the time immediately prior to the transitional stage. The operating manager's involvement in system design is actually part of the training process. As the user participates in the development of design concepts and explores design alternatives, he achieves a greater understanding of the subtle relationships among design variables. In a large complex data processing system it is often difficult to understand the interaction of various elements and to predict their effect on the total data processing system operation. However, no matter how difficult it might be to predict the performance of the system under a wide variety of operating conditions, the operating managers and other users must achieve at least a basic understanding of variable interaction. There is a need for training user personnel at all levels. System training documentation tailored to the different levels within an organization must be developed. It is not unusual for many information system phases to exceed their budgetary allotment and scheduled time. As a result, a reduction of effort and a time compression are applied to this later implementation phase so that the completion date may be met. User training, as a later step in this phase, is reduced and problems encountered during the transitional phase can be attributed to inadequate user training.

The implementation of a new data processing system usually involves conversion of a great deal of data from one media to another. The data base needs to be built to start the system and this conversion step requires a one time processing of many more transactions than are normal for the system. For example, a computer based accounts receivable system that replaces a manual accounts receivable system, requires that all customer data on the accounts receivable records be keyed into the new system and then stored in the proper form in the files being maintained by the computer system.

The high workload of the conversion step usually occurs, unfortunately, during the period of parallel operation. The parallel operation step involves operating both the old system and the new system until all of the start-up problems of the new system have been solved and the new system has been proven. Adequate planning for sufficient resources must be provided during this period since this step, of the entire system life cycle, places the greatest strain on the organization. Consider what is occurring at this point. Personnel are operating a new system with which they are unfamiliar; a larger than normal volume of data must be handled (conversion data); and the data must be processed twice, once by the new system and once by the old system, requiring duplicate manual effort and greater equipment throughout. Careful detailed planning with sufficient allocation of resources is necessary for this critical step.

Post implementation evaluation. This phase of the data processing system life cycle is often omitted, but it is an important phase for the organization to measure what has been accomplished and to learn from the past in order to improve future planning ability. This phase is analogous to the measurement step in the management cycle and in many organizations it is a particularly painful step. The post implementation evaluation compares the projections of the feasibility study with the results obtained from the new system. This is an audit of the information system after the system has been in operation for a suitable period of time, say six months to a year, to see if the promised results have been achieved. The objectives of the feasibility study and the reasons advanced for developing the new information system are compared with the results obtained. In particular, the economic analysis is reviewed and the cost of developing the system is compared to the estimated cost; the benefits obtained from the new system are compared to the estimated benefits; and a new economic analysis is prepared. Users are interviewed to determine if the new information system is meeting their requirements. The fact that a post implementation evaluation will be held is an incentive to careful planning and control of the development process. In addition, this phase discloses weaknesses in the development process; provides data to improve future information systems development planning; and discovers features of the information system that should be modified in the next phase, or that the new system should be discontinued. This post implementation audit and evaluation is repeated at periodic intervals, perhaps every two years, during the remaining life of the system. Continued measurement of information system performance provides the basis for the modifications of the system that occur as organization requirements change. The audit also provides that data for determining the end of the useful life of the information system and the commencement of a new data processing system life cycle.

System modification. An organization is a dynamic entity that changes over time, and an information system that is to continue to serve the organization must also change over time. The basic system design completed in an earlier phase explicitly recognizes the need for later information system modification. The basic system design provides flexibility by modular subsystem and program design to ease the process of information system modification. The more flexible an information system, the more amenable the system is to modification, the longer the life of the information system.

Good documentation also aids the process of system modification. In many cases the cost expended during the information system modification phase in the life cycle is greater than the original development cost of the system. The realization of this fact encourages necessary planning for information system modification during the original information system design phase. The extra effort and expense to build flexibility within the information system and to provide good documentation pays good dividends in future years.

The process of system modification repeats the earlier phases in the data processing system life cycle to some extent, depending on the nature of the modification. Feasibility, systems analysis and design, procedure and program development, and implementation are all necessary for an information system modification. Post implementation evaluation is used to evaluate the effectiveness of the information system modification.

System discontinuation. An information system has a finite life. At some point in time, the technology changes or the changes in the nature and requirements of the organization are such that the existing information system is no longer the most effective means of providing information to the organization.

This point in the system life cycle is also reached when successive system modifications over a long period of time have made the system inefficient. An organization may continue to operate with an obsolete information system and only a post implementation and audit evaluation or a new feasibility study can bring this to light. The economic analysis to determine whether to replace the old information system should not consider prior information system development costs or unamortized values since these are sunk costs. The new feasibility study considers future costs of the old information system as opposed to alternate costs of a new information system and weighs the difference, along with the benefits, to determine if the information system should be discontinued or replaced.

COMPUTER SYSTEM CONCEPTS

The computer system within the information system can be categorized into general categories by computer system purpose and by type of equipment. A given computer system consists of major components that are classified as hardware, software, firmware, and telecommunications equipment. This section explores general computer categories, computer system components, types of data processing, computer system configurations (collection and arrangement of computer system components), and some alternatives for obtaining computer resources.

General computer system categories. Computer systems can be categorized by intended purpose into three major categories: process control, scientific, and business; and two other categories—analog or digital based on computer type. Although almost any computer system can be used for data processing in all three categories, there are particular requirements in each category that make a particular computer system most effective for a given category. There is a continuing trend to developed general purpose computers capable of performing well in all categories, but this involves some compromise of features and some price disadvantage.

Process control computer systems. A process control environment is one in which the computer system monitors and controls the process in real-time. The process could be a chemical manufacturing process where the computer system constantly obtains input data from devices that measure variables (temperature, pressure, weight, velocity, etc.), tests the data against predetermined control limits, makes computations to determine the steps necessary to obtain the desired process state, and provides output signals to cause a change in a variable. For example, the process control system may receive data on temperature at a particular point in the process, calculate the desired temperature, and provide an output signal to a valve that throttles the flow of fuel to the process. Process control computers in warehouses automatically store material and retrieve material for shipment or subsequent use within the manufacturing facility, or control the flow of baggage along conveyors to airplane loading areas in an air terminal. In many cases, process control computer systems also perform business data processing since they provide information on business operations. For example, a warehousing process control computer system maintains inventory and shipment records and provides current inventory and shipping order status information.

Process control computer systems usually accept data from many sources and service many controls so that the computer system is designed to operate on many concurrent or almost simultaneous inputs. The system is designed to service the inputs in real-time (at the time that the input actually occurs) and provide real-time output to control the process.

Scientific computer systems. A characteristic of scientific data processing systems is extensive computation, but very few data input or output operations. A scientific computer system requires very fast internal processing for computation, with the computation involving very large or very small numbers, with great precision. Scientific data processing usually involves a very short data input cycle, a relatively long processing or computation cycle, and a relatively short data output cycle so that the scientific computer systems can use slower input and output devices than can business computer systems.

Business computer systems. Business computer systems are characterized by large data input and output operations with minimal computation requirements for each record. There is a larger number of input transactions (invoices, payroll records, inventory receipts, sales orders, etc.), simple processing (addition, subtraction, etc.), and a large volume of output reports (order registers, sales journals, inventory transactions listings, etc.). Business computer systems are characterized by high speed input and output devices, instructions to facilitate data conversion and editing of data into report information, and relatively minimal arithmetic computational speed requirements and data precision.

Analog computer systems. Analog computer systems, an older category of computer systems, operate on problems that originate in the physical sciences. The models representing the physical reality are in mathematical form (algebraic equations, differential equations, magnitude and logical relationships) and the variables can be represented in physical quantities (voltage, resistance, distance). The analog computer system operates by measuring rather than counting, as is done in the digital computer, and the most common physical representations are voltage and impedance. The analogous physical variable is manipulated; for example, voltage is made higher or lower to correspond to larger or smaller values of the variable in the physical problem. Physical relationships are used to model the mathematical relationships, and the resultant output is read from a measuring device, a meter, cathode ray tube display, or physical positioning device. Analog computer systems are usually more expensive and less precise than corresponding digital computer systems today and have generally been supplanted by digital computer systems in scientific problem solving.

Digital computer systems. Digital computer systems represent numbers by discrete values of a physical condition and operate on the numbers by counting them instead of measuring them as is done in analog computer systems. The precision obtainable in a digital computer system is limited only to the number of digits used to represent the quantity and not to the precision inherent in the physical device—the size of the dial or the number of graduations on the dial in an analog computer system. Most digital computers use a binary system of discrete values for representing data. Most business data processing systems use digital computer systems.

Computer hardware. Any calculating equipment can logically be called a computer but in data processing systems the term refers to equipment with specific characteristics. It is generally agreed that in order for equipment to be designated as a computer it must have the following characteristics:

1. *Electronic Processing.* Electronic elements (transistors, dials, resistors, etc.) to control and process data.
2. *Internal Storage.* Internal storage (memory) for storing both data and the program that controls the processing of the data.
3. *Stored Program.* A set of instructions (program) that specify the detailed sequence of operations for processing stored in the memory. The storage of the program makes the equipment automatic in that all operations are predetermined and no human intervention is required during processing.
4. *Program Modification.* The ability to change the instructions stored in memory during processing. The data and the program instructions are in a common form and the equipment is usually able to modify instructions as well as data.

The hardware components of a computer system can be classified as input or output devices, central processing unit (processing, control and memory) and secondary online storage devices. Most modern business computer data processing systems have secondary online storage devices although there are many systems that do not. The generalized relationship among the devices is shown in Figure 5.

Input Devices. The purpose of an input device is to provide instructions or data to the central processing unit. The input device is online (attached) to the central processing unit and the operation of the input device is controlled by the central processing unit. In modern computers the data received from the input device are buffered—held or controlled without requiring central processing unit time—until the data are to be used. A typical cycle for an input device is as follows:

1. The central processing unit decodes an instruction to read one physical record (block) from a specific input device.
2. The central processing unit sends a signal to the control unit for the input device. The control unit starts operation of the input device. If the input device is inoperable or busy, the control unit sends a signal back to the central processing unit or waits, depending on program instructions.

COMPUTER SYSTEM HARDWARE

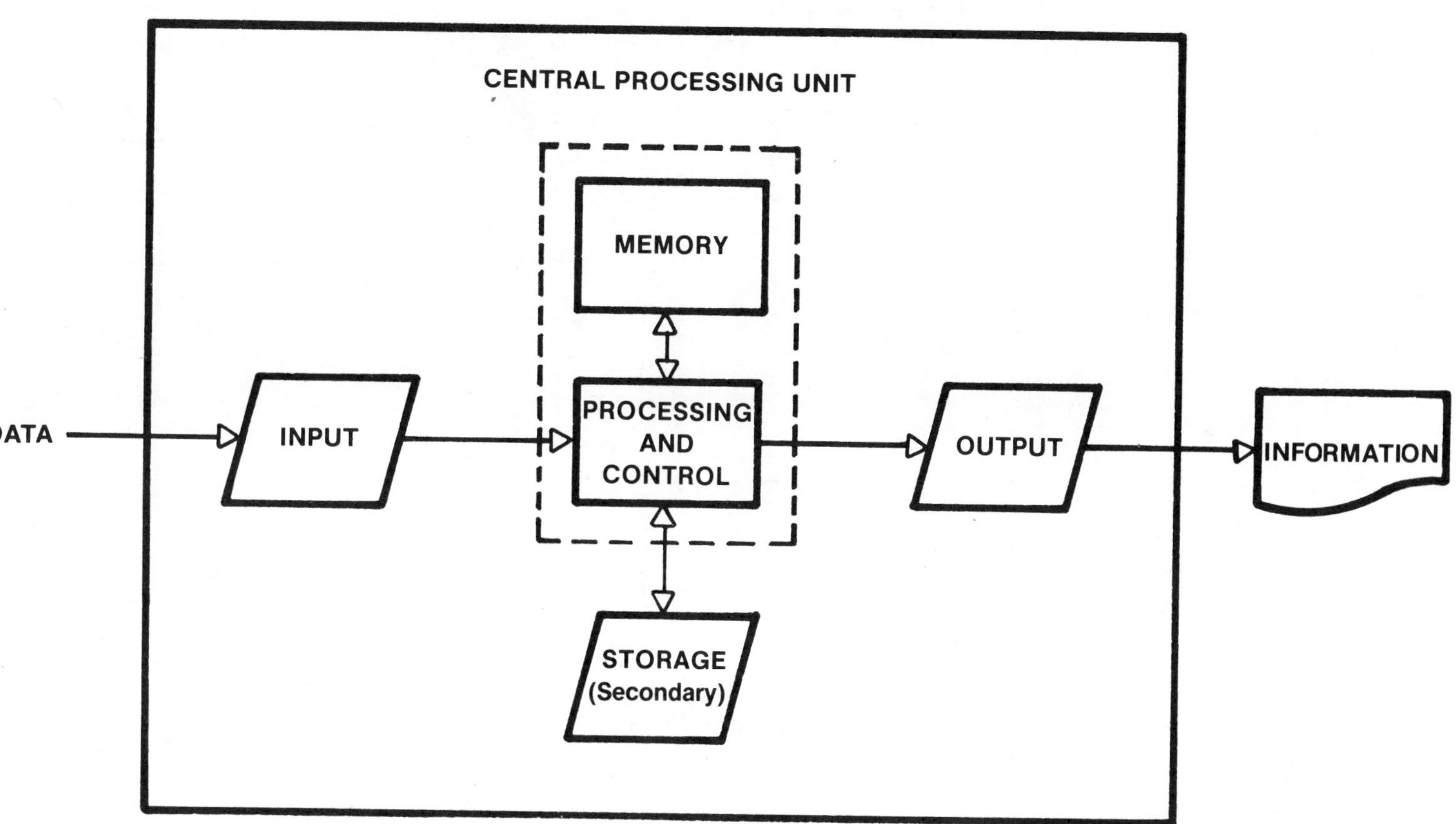

Fig. 5. Computer System Hardware Relationships.

3. The input device reads the data from the physical record media and transforms the data to electrical signals.
4. The control unit receives and checks the electrical signals from the input device.
5. The control unit transmits the data to a specified memory location of the central processing unit.
6. The control unit transmits a signal to the central processing unit indicating that the input operation is complete.

The central processing unit's internal speed is usually much greater than the data transfer rate of the input device, and the above buffered input cycle indicates that the central processing unit is free to perform other processing after step 2. The control unit for input devices may be a separate unit, or in the case of older computer systems and some current small computer systems, may be a part of the central processing unit. If the control unit's functions are part of the central processing unit's operation, (no control unit) then the input cycle is considered non-buffered since the processing unit is not free for other work during the input cycle. Most modern computers contain control units or microcomputers (very small computers) to control the input cycle. The connection between the central processing unit and the input device is called the interface. The term *channel* is used to indicate an interface with a control unit for managing the transfer of data between an input device and the central processing unit.

The variety of devices available as input units is large and growing every year. Many of the devices serve more than one purpose in that they are input/output devices or input/output storage devices and this section will focus on the input characteristics of such devices.

Input devices translate data contained on punched cards, punched paper tape, magnetic tape or cassettes, magnetic disc or diskettes, and other media as well as data from switch settings, key depressions and other physical conditions from light signals to electrical signals. There are input devices that read printed characters (optical character recognition—OCR), magnetic ink characters (magnetic ink character recognition—MICR), and even devices for voice input. No matter how exotic the input media, the purpose of the input device is to translate data from the media into a data form that can be processed by the central processing unit.

Central processing unit. The central processing unit contains the circuitry for processing and controlling the flow of data, and the main memory or primary storage of the computer system. Main memory or primary storage contains the program—the detailed instructions—and the data for processing. An arithmetic unit within the central processing unit does arithmetic operations, comparisons, indexing, etc., for the processing of data. A control unit within the central processing unit directs the arithmetic unit and the entire computer system in accordance with the instructions. The central processing unit is connected to the input, output, and secondary storage devices by interface data paths called channels.

The execution of an instruction in a typical central processing unit proceeds as follows:

1. The address of the next instruction is contained in an instruction counter that is part of the control unit. Control unit circuits decode the address of the instruction and send electrical signals to the main memory in order to read or get the next instruction.
2. The main memory provides the requested data which are moved to the control unit.
3. The instruction data are decoded into an operation code (indicating what operation is to be performed) and operands, which are codes for the data or devices that will be used (input device, output device, storage unit, data in memory, etc.).
4. The operation code signals are transmitted to activate the appropriate units. The operand address for data in main memory activates the circuits necessary to read the data from main memory and transmit the data to the arithmetic unit or activates an input device to read data and transmit the data to a predetermined address in main memory.
5. The operations are performed in registers—temporary storages in which operations take place.
6. The instruction counter is incremented (change the address of the next instruction) and the next instruction cycle is ready to commence.

This generalized instruction execution cycle is the same in most computers: there is an instruction cycle to fetch and decode an instruction and to set the next instruction address in the instruction counter; and there is an execution cycle to execute the desired operations. The entire process is controlled by timing pulses, measured in nanoseconds (one billionth of a second), that control the flow of signals in the form of electrical pulses.

Most computers represent data in media having only two recognizable states—on or off. This may be represented by electrical switches that are open or closed, magnetic elements with two directions of polarity, or electrical charges that are high or low. Electronic elements are used in computers because of their speed, but other elements with the same properties of two states could be used, such as a mechanical switch which is either on or off.

With data represented in two states, the two states can be designated as zero or one. This two state system is called a binary system. Each representation or digit is either a zero or a one and is called a bit which is an abbreviation of **bi**nary dig**it**. All arithmetic and logical operations within the central processing unit are based on the state of a bit or string of bits.

A single bit is only capable of representing two values, but a computer needs the capability of representing many more values. A computer needs the capability of storing at least 10 different numeric digits, 26 upper case alphabetical characters, 26 lower case alphabetical characters, and approximately 20 special characters, so that a group or string of bits is used to represent character. Commonly eight bits are grouped together to represent a character of computer data. The eight bits are called a byte and are capable of representing 256 (2^8) different characters. A computer is able to move a certain number of bits in parallel (at the same time), depending on the number of duplicate circuits provided in the data paths and registers. The number of bits that can be moved in parallel is often referred to as a computer word. The computer word length—string of bits that are handled in parallel—can be 8, 12, 16, 24, 32, 36, etc., depending on the computer equipment. The greater the number of parallel paths or duplicate circuits provided, the higher the cost of the computer equipment and the greater is its throughput capacity.

Storage devices. Storage devices can be classified into two classes: online storage, and offline storage or external storage. Online storage devices can be further divided into two types: primary storage and secondary storage. The memory, referred to above as part of the central processing unit, is a primary storage device.

Primary storage devices. Primary storage devices must be capable of moving data at extremely fast rates to support central processing unit operations. Since all instructions and data are stored in primary storage, the speed of primary storage is a limiting factor to central processing unit operating speed. Various physical devices are used for primary storage, each having different characteristics in terms of speed, cost, size, and permanency of data storage.

Early computers used magnetic drums that rotated at high speeds for primary storage. Data could be transferred to or from the magnetic drum in milliseconds (one thousandths of a second), which is considered too slow for modern computers. Magnetic drums are still used as secondary storage devices since their operating speeds are acceptable for secondary storage. Magnetic core, magnetic thin film, or semiconductor devices are used for primary storage today. A magnetic core is a donut shaped circle of molded ferrite powder about the size of a pinhead. The magnetic cores are strung on wires which are used to magnetize the cores and sense the presence of magnetism in the cores. A single bit of data can be stored in each magnetic core and a computer system with 128,000 characters of primary storage contains over 1,000,000 magnetic cores.

Thin film primary storage devices vary from manufacturer to manufacturer, but usually consist of very thin spots of metallic alloy on a metal, ceramic, or glass surface. The metallic spots are connected by very thin wires and operate in a similar fashion to magnetic core memory. Magnetic thin film memory is usually faster than core memory.

Semiconductor primary storage consists of circuits etched into very tiny silicon chips. Semiconductor memory makes use of the two states of the semiconductor—conducting, or not conducting a current. The advantages of semiconductor memory over magnetic core memory are increased speed and great reduction in size. However, semiconductor main memory is impermanent and dependent on an uninterrupted supply of power. Unlike core memory, the loss of power destroys the contents of semiconductor memory. The first major use of semiconductor main memory was the IBM System/370 Model 145 that was first installed in 1971.

Secondary storage devices. Secondary storage devices are slower than primary storage devices and are used to store large amounts of data that are not required as frequently by the central processing unit. The ratio of online secondary storage to primary storage may range from 500 to one to 5,000 to one. The principle method of storing data in secondary storage devices is to use a material capable of being magnetized, or a coating with such capability on a base material surface, although other types of secondary storage devices are in use. The presence or absence of magnetism or the state of magnetic polarity indicates the data state. Various forms of magnetic disk devices are the most popular devices for secondary storage.

The magnetic disk is similar in appearance to a phonograph record and is a plastic disk that is coated on both sides with a ferrous oxide recording material. Data are recorded as magnetized spots on each side of the disk. One or more magnetic disks are mounted concentrically around a central rod and are called disk packs. A disk pack may consist of one, six, or eleven magnetic disks and is capable of storing from one million to over two hundred million characters of data. A less expensive version of the magnetic disk consists of a single flexible disk, capable of storing approximately two hundred fifty thousand data characters, and is called a diskette.

Data is stored serially in circles on the surface of the disk somewhat like a phonograph record except that the data is magnetically encoded and in concentric circles rather than a large spiral. A complete circle of data on one surface of the disk is called a track as shown in Figure 6. A track is normally divided into smaller data groups called sectors. Concentric data tracks on each recording surface are called data cylinders and represent all storage area for data that can be accessed without movement of the read/write arm. The arms of a magnetic disk device contain read/write heads that read the polarity or change the polarity on the surface of the magnetic disk. Magnetic storage devices are considered direct access devices in that any item of data can be obtained as quickly as any other. (Magnetic tape storage is discussed in the next section as an external storage device because data is recorded sequentially on the magnetic tape and the device is not a direct access device.) Each sector of a magnetic disk pack is directly addressable by the central processing unit. A command to access data results in the movement of the arm to position the read head over the appropriate track and a delay until the particular sector is passing under the read head.

While the accessing of data from main memory is measured in nanoseconds (one billionth of a second), the accessing of data from magnetic disk secondary storage is measured in milliseconds (one thousandth of a second). The slower speed of the magnetic disk device is caused by the necessary mechanical motion, of both arm and disk, required to place the data sector into position for reading or writing. The time required for movement of the arm is referred to as access motion time and the wait time for the appropriate portion of the disk to pass under the read head is known as rotational delay time or latency time.

Magnetic disk packs are usually removable and can therefore be used for external storage, which is discussed later in this section. A magnetic disk drive

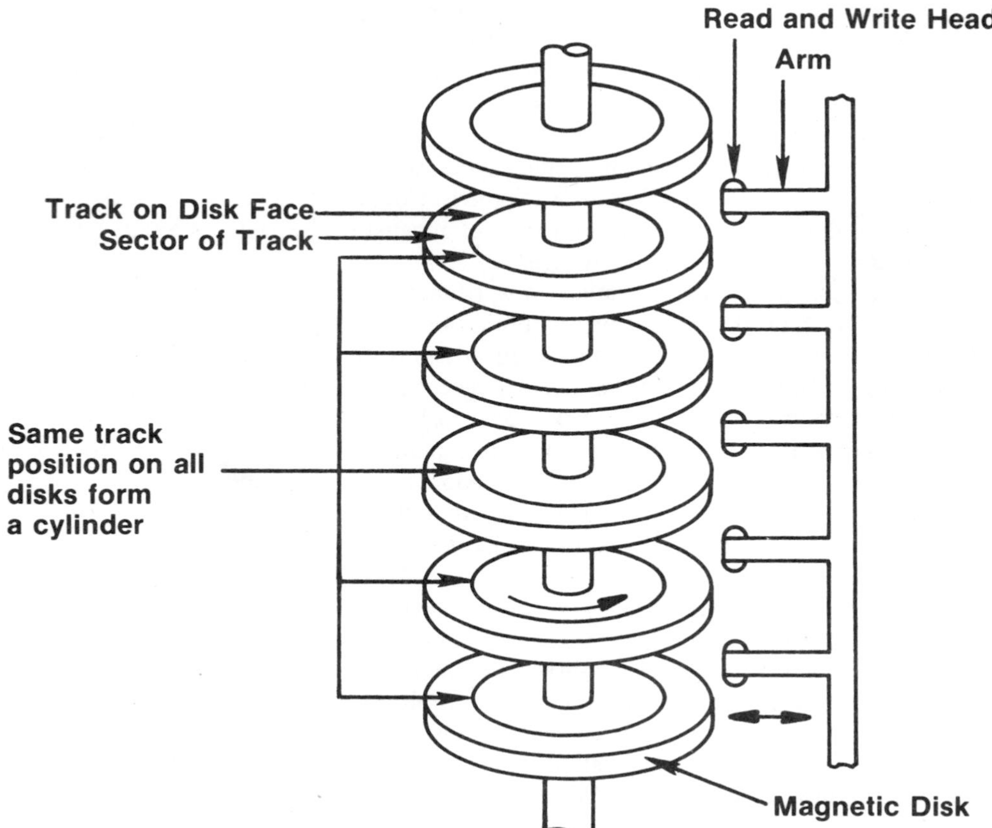

Fig. 6. Schematic Representation of Disk Storage.

with a magnetic disk pack mounted on the drive is considered an online device, since the magnetic disk pack on the drive is directly available to the central processing unit.

Magnetic drum and magnetic card devices are also used for secondary storage. The magnetic drum is a cylinder with an outer surface coating that can be magnetized. Drum size limits the quantity of data that can be stored, but some magnetic drums are capable of storing several million characters of data. The data storage capacity of a magnetic drum is usually smaller than a magnetic disk device, but the access time is usually less.

Magnetic card devices contain individual cards of a material capable of being magnetized and the central processing unit can address a particular record on any card within the device. National Cash Register (NCR) manufactures a magnetic card device with the trade name of CRAM (Card Random Access Memory). The IBM 2321 Data Cell device is similar in that it uses magnetic strips for data storage. Other secondary storage devices using directly accessible magnetized cylinders or lazer technology are also available.

External storage. External storage or offline storage consists of various media that contain data in a form suitable for direct entry into a computer system. Punched cards, punched paper tape, magnetic stripe cards, magnetic tape, magnetic disk packs, etc. are included in this category. External storage provides a means of retaining data that is not currently required but is needed for future operation. For example, employee data for payroll purposes may be required for a half an hour once a week for preparing the weekly payroll. In this case the data are much less expensively stored on a magnetic disk or a reel of magnetic tape and put onto an online device only when required.

Magnetic tape devices, although online to the central processing unit, are considered input or output devices since they use reels of magnetic tape that are considered as external storage media. Data is recorded sequentially on magnetic tape and may be feasibly accessed only in sequential fashion. In effect, to access the inventory record of a particular item requires that each record be read from the magnetic tape and skipped until the particular record of the inventory item is located. This characteristic of magnetic tape device makes it a poor secondary storage device, but the low cost of magnetic tape, and the reading and writing speed of the device make magnetic tape an excellent medium for external storage.

Storage data organization. Secondary storage and external storage devices or media contain data that must be organized in some fashion so that the data can be identified. The method of storage organization varies according to storage, retrieval, and processing requirements. A definition of commonly used terms to describe data organization follows:

1. *Field.* A field is a set of characters used together and indentified as a data item. For example, an inventory identification number of 6832 is a data item consisting of four numbers and is referred to as the inventory number field. An employee's name contains the characters of the name and is called the employee name field.
2. *Record.* A group of fields with a common relationship, treated as a single object for data processing purposes, is known as a record. For example, an inventory record might contain the inventory number, inventory description, quantity on hand, and cost fields for a specific inventory material. A payroll record for an employee might contain employee number, employee name, pay rate, and number of dependents' fields for a given employee.
3. *File.* A group of records of a given type is a file. For example, employee records taken as a group are the employee file. All inventory records taken together are called the inventory file.
4. *Data Base.* A group of files organized into a single unit with a logical relationship between the files, and the records and fields within the files, is called a data base. A characteristic of data base organization is that a data field is maintained in a single location and available for many different uses. For example, a single inventory description field is available for order processing, inventory transaction reporting, and inventory evaluation reports.

Data storage must be organized in some manner for data processing to be feasible and efficient. Each data storage character is the same as all others to the computer system and it is the predetermined data organization scheme that enables the computer system to locate and assign meaning to any data character.

Output devices. The purpose of output devices is to provide information to users of the data processing system or to provide data in machine readable form for later input to the computer system. Online output devices produce punched cards, punched paper tape, magnetic tape, printed reports, video displays, and bar codes or other characters for optical reading. The most common output device to provide information to the users of the data processing system is a printer. The printer produces reports, bills, and other documents that result from data processing. Other output devices can plot curves (graph or x-y plotter) or produce microfilm records for the user. Computer output microfilm (COM) devices are usually used offline with magnetic tape as input.

A wide variety of cathode ray terminals (CRT) are being used for both output devices and also input devices. The cathode ray tube is similar to a television picture tube and is widely used as an output device. A keyboard connected to the CRT or a light pen enables the device to be used as an input device as well.

Software. Software is the generic term for all computer system programmed instructions. The purpose of software is to instruct the computer hardware to perform the steps necessary for data processing. The term includes programs that are classified as: computer operating system utility programs, library programs, programming language assemblers, compilers, and interpreters; program generators, data base management systems applications programs, and a group of instructions known as firmware or microcode. All of the previous program groups consist of one or more programs.

A computer program is a set of detailed instructions to direct the step by step operation of the computer system in order to perform the desired data processing. As a set of instructions, it is similar to other instructions used in organizations such as operating procedures, procedure manuals, and equipment operating instructions. The major difference is the precision or extreme detail contained in the computer program. Procedure manuals or equipment operating instructions assume that the reader is a human being with background knowledge and intelligence. A computer program is designed to be read and executed by a computer system with no knowledge or intelligence and the instructions therefore are designed to govern each detailed step in the data processing procedure. A computer program is an algorithm which reflects the steps required to perform a procedure or solve a problem. The steps necessary to prepare a program are summarized as:

1. Program planning and algorithm definition.
2. Instruction coding.
3. Assembling, compiling, or interpreting—the translation of the written instruction into the machine language used by the computer system.
4. Debugging or testing the program.

5. Documenting—preparing written material that explains the logic of the algorithm and its implementation so that the writer or someone else can understand the objective of the program and the instruction coding. A widely used technique for program planning and documentation is the flowchart.

Flowchart. A flowchart is a graphic model of a system or a portion of a system. The technique of flowcharting predates the development of computers and was widely used as a systems analysis and documentation tool for manual systems. A variety of organizations have attempted to standardize flowcharting symbols so that it is possible for anyone to interpret the work of another person. Figure 7, Flowchart Symbols, contains widely used flowchart symbols and flowcharting conventions.

A flowchart can be prepared with various levels of detail. A system flowchart depicts the document flow and processing steps for a system. A macro program flowchart outlines the program sequence, calculations, and logic of a program; while a micro program flowchart expands on the outline and contains the more detailed steps and logic requirements. Figures 8, 9, and 10, system flowchart, macro program flowchart, and micro program flowchart respectively are portions of a payroll system.

Program coding translates the algorithm contained in the micro level program flowchart into detailed instructions for the computer system.

Programming language. Programming languages are used to produce coded statements that instruct the computer system to perform operations. A prior section indicated that all program instructions and data are contained in memory in the form of binary data, a zero or a one. Program coding can be performed at various levels ranging from machine (known as absolute) language to higher level procedure and problem oriented languages. All programming languages other than machine language must be translated into machine language since the computer system hardware is designed to recognize only instructions in a certain form. The group of instructions that the machine is designed to recognize is called the computer system instruction set. The process of converting the programming language statements into instructions within the computer system instruction set is known as assembly, compilation, or interpretation. Figure 11 depicts program statements at various levels of programming languages. Figure 11 illustrates the higher level languages are closer to mathematical and natural languages and are therefore easier for a programmer to use. During the early stage of computer development all program instructions were required to be written in either machine language or an assembly language. As the use of computers grew more widespread, and the number of programs being written increased, the higher level programming languages were developed to facilitate program coding. Today, few programs are written in machine language, although programming continues to be done in a symbolic assembly language. The more common programming languages are explored below.

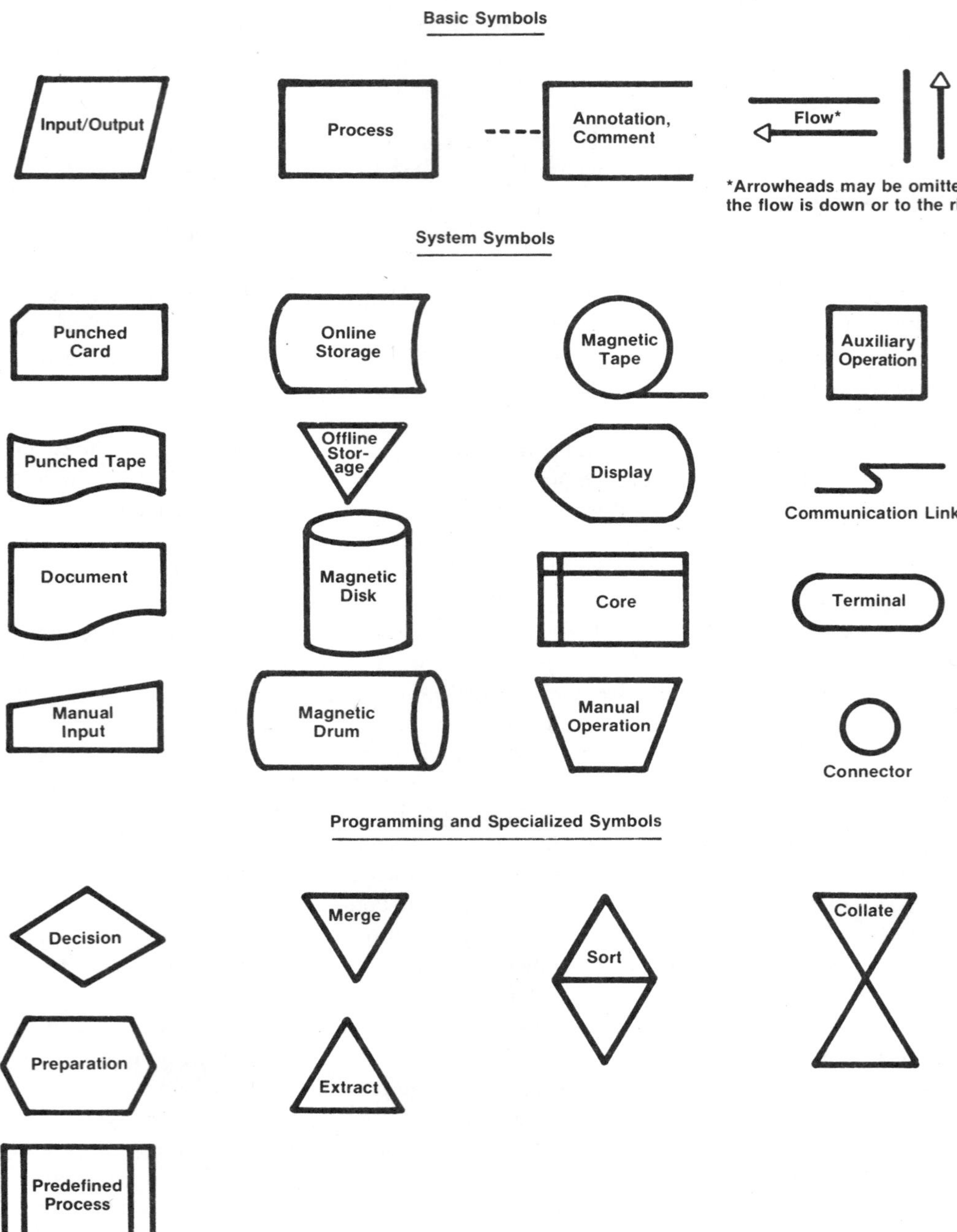

Fig. 7. Flowchart Symbols.

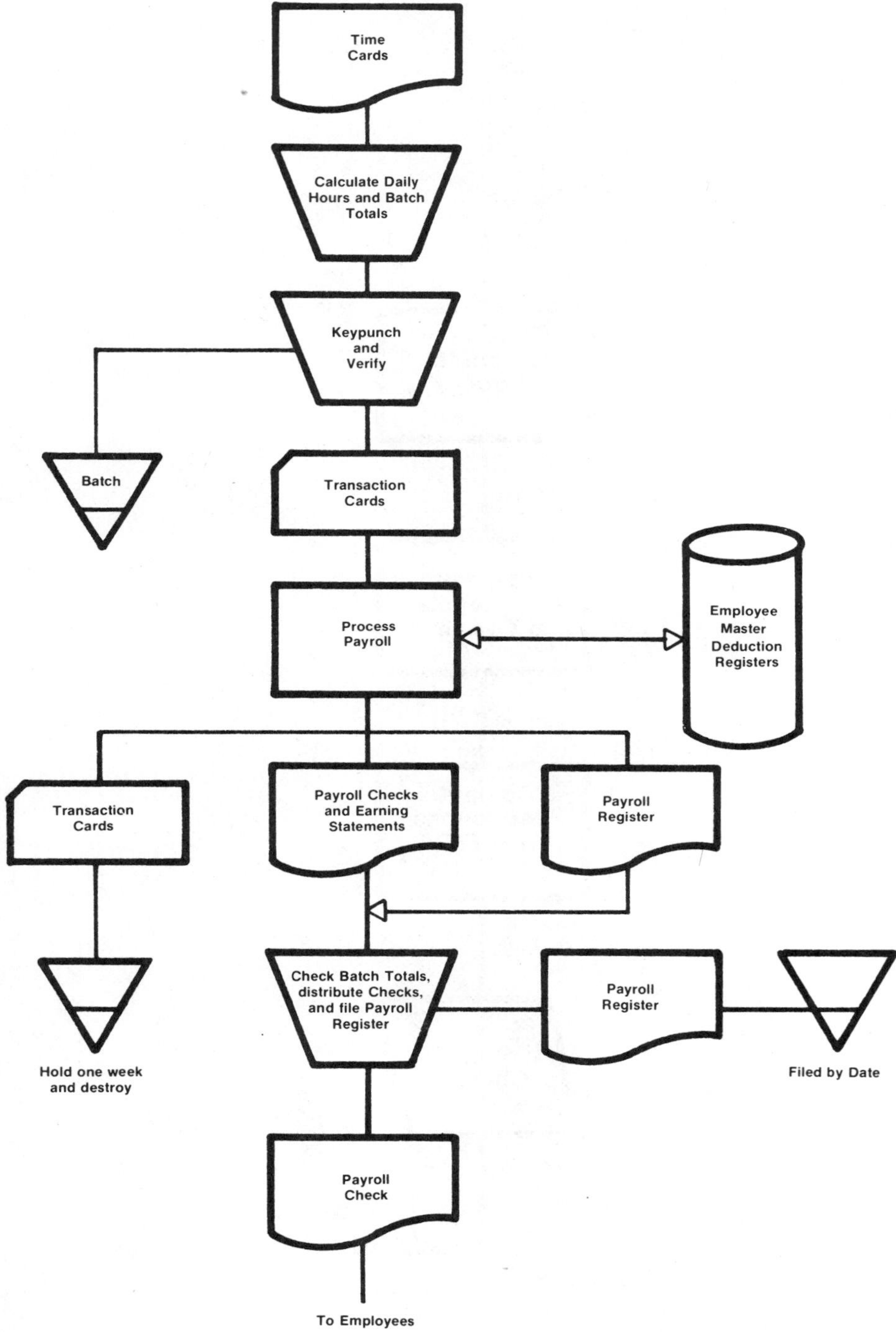

Fig. 8. Portion of a Payroll System Flowchart.

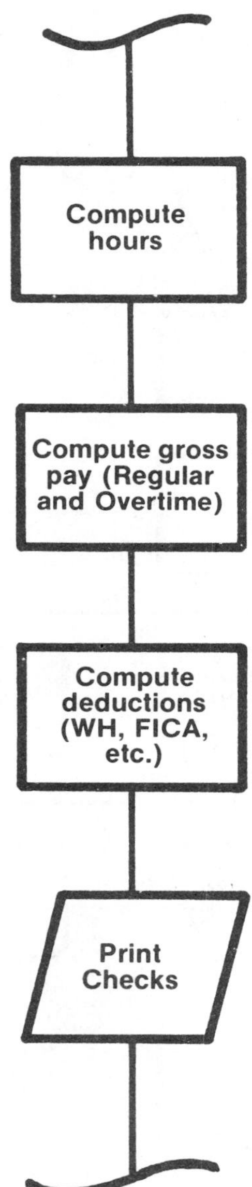

Fig. 9. Portion of Macro Level Program Flowchart.

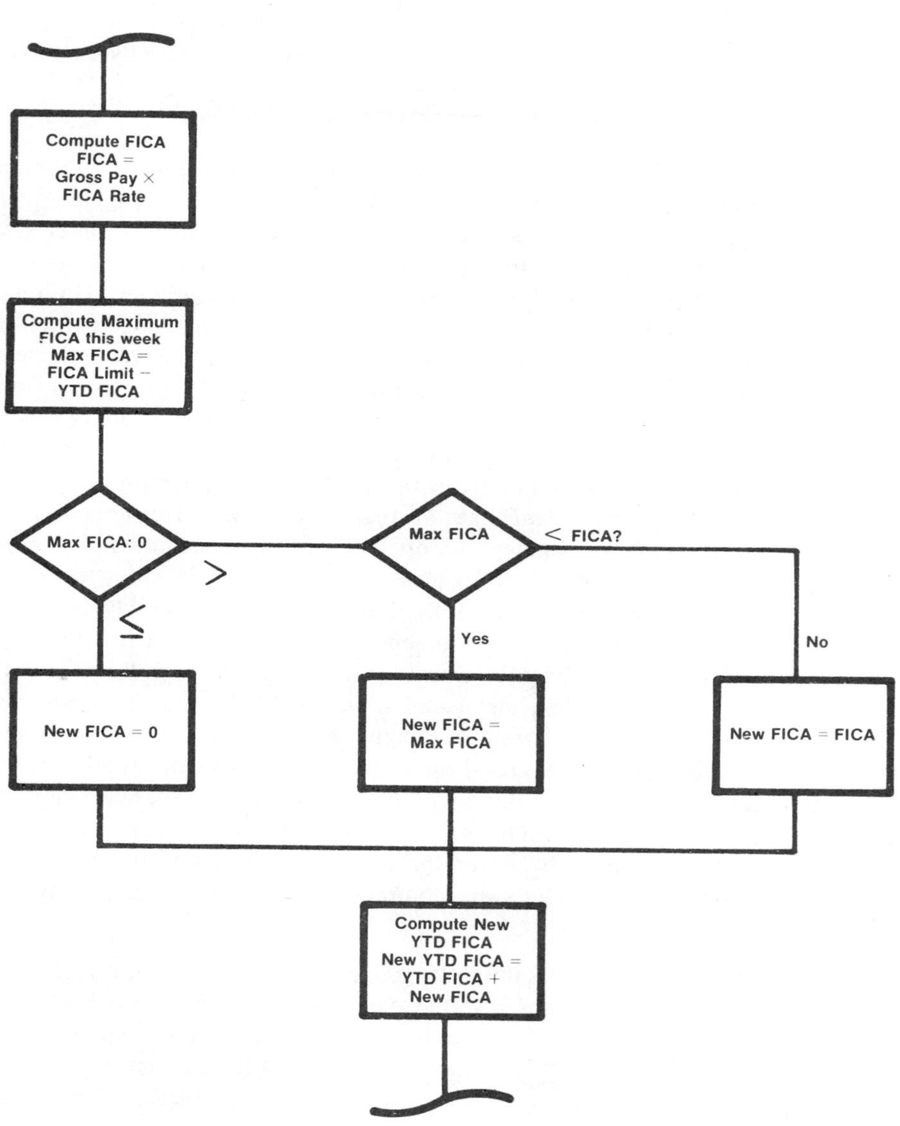

Fig. 10. Portion of Micro Level Program Flowchart.

Machine language in binary	01101011110011010101001111000110 10101111001010100001111010111001
Symbolic assembly Language	L 4, OLDB A 4, CASH ST 4, NEWB
Procedure Oriented Language	
BASIC	N1 = O1 + C2
FORTRAN	NEWB = OLDB + CASH
COBOL	ADD OLDB AND CASH GIVING NEWB

Fig. 11. Program Coding At Various Programming Language Levels.

Assembly Languages. Assembly languages are the lowest level of computer instruction coding currently in use. Assembly language coding provides the programmer with access to each instruction within the computer system instruction set. A computer instruction set usually contains instructions that allow byte and bit manipulation as well as character manipulation. The programmer has absolute control over each machine instruction executed and it is possible for the programmer to write very efficient code. (Efficient in this context means that the computer processing time can be minimized.) However, since assembly language is the furthest away from mathematical and natural languages, it is the most difficult language for programmers to use in coding. Most assembly languages are symbolic assembly languages so that they allow the programmer to code with symbolic names as opposed to absolute data locations or machine instructions. For example, the machine operation code for an addition operation might be 14, but a symbolic assembly language allows the programmer to use a mnemonic code such as A for the addition operation. Also, the programmer can specify a storage location with a symbol such as CASH, instead of a numerical data location address. Program statements in assembly language, known as source code, are translated by a program, called an assembler, into machine code known as object code. This translation process which translates one assembly language code statement into one machine language instruction is known as the assembly process. After the assembly process is complete, the object code is loaded into the computer system for execution by the computer system.

FORTRAN. This programming language is one of the earliest high level programming languages and the name is an acronym for *FOR*mula *TRAN*slation. The earliest users of computers were engineers and scientists. FORTRAN is a scientific problem solving language designed to allow programmers to easily translate scientific statements of the problem in terms of mathematical formulas and mathematical relationships into program code. FORTRAN statement source code is converted into object code by a FORTRAN language compiler. The compilation process may generate more than one machine instruction for each source code statement. In this language, as in other high level programming languages, there is a certain loss of absolute control over machine operation and in making full use of the computer instruction set, but the language is far easier for the programmer to use and is more efficient from a program coding standpoint.

Over the years the FORTRAN language has matured as has the use of computers. Various FORTRAN language extensions provide facilities for utilizing the newer storage devices and file access methods as well as providing facilities for real time applications. The FORTRAN language has been standardized and is widely used throughout the world. An advantage of using a high level language, such as FORTRAN or some other standard language, is that programs prepared in the language can be executed on almost any type of computer since a FORTRAN language compiler is available on most computing systems.

BASIC. The name BASIC is an acronym for *B*eginners *A*ll-Purpose *S*ymbolic *I*nstruction *C*ode. The language was designed to make computer use easier for simple problem solving by students. The language was developed at Dartmouth College for writing programs at typewriter type terminals in a time sharing environment. A time sharing environment means that the terminal is online to the computer and has direct and immediate access to computer resources. An advantage of the BASIC language is that it is extremely easy to learn—requires two to four hours to learn—and is easy to apply. The BASIC language has also matured over the years with many additional features added to enhance the language. The BASIC language is in widespread use on time sharing systems and is also widely used for implementing systems on business minicomputer systems. Most implementations of the BASIC language are interpreters. An interpreter is a program that executes the source program—in this case the BASIC language statements—directly and does not compile object code. Interpreters are more efficient for programs that are infrequently used and do not require a great amount of computer time since an interpreter avoids the computer time required for compilation. However, the interpreting process must be repeated each time the program is executed. Other computer languages—APL and GPSS discussed below—are also interpreter type languages.

COBOL. COBOL is an acronym for *CO*mmon *B*usiness *O*riented *L*anguage and is a language specifically designed for business data processing. Business data processing problems are characterized by a high volume of input and output data, a fair amount of data manipulation, and a relatively low level of computation. COBOL was designed with this in mind and designed to reduce the necessary skill level of programming personnel. COBOL language statements are written in sentences and paragraphs and with a grammar very close to the natural language. The language has been standardized and is widely used for commercial data processing. As a widely used standard language, COBOL programs also have the advantage of portability in that most major business data processing computer manufacturers provide COBOL compilers so that programs can be implemented on a wide variety of computer equipment. Because of the similarity to the natural language, COBOL programs have the advantage of being almost completely self documenting.

Other Programming Languages. There are many other programming languages available, some more popular than others. PL/1 is a language developed by IBM in an attempt to design a new programming language that would have the best facilities of FORTRAN and COBOL. PL/1 is frequently used on IBM computer systems, but the language has not gained widespread acceptance by other computer manufacturers. APL is another scientific language designed by Iverson, an IBM employee. APL is a powerful language for scientific problem solving and is becoming more popular among scientists and engineers. Another scientific language ALGOL, an acronym for *ALGO*rithmic *L*anguage, is very popular in Europe but not as popular in the United States. ALGOL is considered more elegant and precise than FORTRAN and the Association for Computing Machinery (ACM) uses ALGOL as the computer language for computer algorithms published in its journals.

There is also a wide variety of languages available for solving problems in particular areas. There are languages for simulation problem solving, GPSS, SIMSCRIPT, GASP, FINSIM, etc.; for text and string processing, SNOBOL; and APT for programming numerically controlled machine tools. Another popular business programming language, RPG (Report Program Generator), is discussed in the Programming Generator section since it is technically not a programming language.

Program generators. A program generator is a routine or program that is capable of producing other programs from specifications. The specification format is very rigidly defined and can be very extensive. The program generator may generate the program as either a set of program language source statements or a set of object code instructions. If the program is generated in source statement form, then it is compiled by the particular programming language compiler. The most widely used program generator is RPS (Report Program Generator) that is extensively used on the IBM System/3 and the System/32. RPG was designed originally as a simple specification form technique for producing reports from a description of the report. The facilities of the language have been considerably enhanced so that it is now possible to do many other things with RPG.

Computer operating systems are often customized by the use of program generators that generate an operating system for a particular computer configuration. Many small business minicomputer vendors have developed program generators that produce BASIC language programs for generating reports and displays, or interactive processing.

Operating systems. An operating system is a set of programs that acts as a supervisor to control the operation of a computer system. Routines within the operating system supervise the execution of programs; provide an interface to all input, output, and storage devices that are online to the system; schedule the resources of the computer; handle hardware and software errors; control restarts; coordinate teleprocessing communications; and control operations in a multi-programming, multiprocessing, or time sharing mode. In virtual memory systems, the operating system allocates memory to various tasks in progress, controls the swapping of memory between primary storage and secondary storage, provides address translation for executing programs, and provides memory protection to prevent inadvertent program interaction.

Utility programs. Utility programs are standardized routines for performing frequently required processes such as copying, sorting, merging, testing, etc. For example, most computer systems contain utility programs for loading a program into memory, printing a record or a file from magnetic disk or magnetic tape storage, copying a punched card file onto magnetic disk or magnetic tape, punching a card from magnetic tape or magnetic disk, copying the contents of a magnetic tape or magnetic disk file onto another magnetic tape or magnetic disk, dumping memory (printing the entire contents of memory), and providing facilities for testing and tracing the operations of a program.

Library programs. Library programs are similar to utility programs in that they are standardized routines for performing particular operations. Library programs are usually routines that perform particular mathematical or statistical operations and can be included into a program by a programmer. For example, a particular program may require the calculation of a square root, and a library routine in the program library has the capability of performing this operation. Therefore, the programmer need not write the code necessary to perform the operation but only the code necessary to call this routine from the library.

Application programs. Application programs are the programs that are written to perform the data processing necessary for the information system. In effect, these are the programs written for the application. Another use of the term application programs applies this name to complete program systems that solve particular problems common to many users. For example, a generalized payroll system may be capable of performing payroll data processing for many different organizations, or a billing program systems may be designed for specific industry applications (brokerage firms, electric utilities, paper distributors, etc.). Other examples are critical path analysis (PERT, CPM, etc.), linear programming or inventory simulations application packages that contain programs that are generalized and useful to a wide segment of industry. Application programs of this type are usually ready to be used, requiring only that the data be prepared in accordance with given specifications.

Data base management systems. The rapid rise of data base applications has led to the development of preprogrammed systems for performing common functions associated with data base processing. In effect, data base management systems are a specific type of application program. The organization of a data base and the maintenance of the data contained therein is extremely complex and requires extensive programming. Security and privacy requirements as well as the complexity of the programs made it desirable to create a system for all manipulation of data within the data base. From the programmers point of view, a data base management system simplifies programming of data storage and retrieval, since the programmer is only required to write simple macro coding for given processes. When the application program is executed, the macro instructions call prewritten data base management system routines that contain the necessary code for accessing the data base. Data base management systems have been developed by many different vendors and are extensively used in management information systems.

Firmware. Firmware or microcode is a particular approach to computer design. On one hand, the computer system can contain the necessary hardware to perform particular operations and interface with particular devices. This in effect requires that as computer requirements change or as technology changes, the computer hardware must be redesigned or a greater variety of computer hardware must be manufactured for each specialized application. Another approach is to design very generalized computer hardware and to depend on the software (programs) to provide the flexibility for each application. The disadvantage of the latter approach is that the software requires main memory and is slower in execution than is hardware circuitry, since the software instructions must be decoded by the computer system.

A third method is called microprogramming and had its first major use by IBM in the design of System/360. Using this method, the computer hardware is designed in a generalized fashion and the customizing is done by a particular type of program called a microprogram or microcode. Each instruction within a computer causes several sets of gates (switches) to be opened or closed in order to implement the logic circuitry to perform the operation. The microcode is contained in a special high speed read only memory (ROM) and is used to replace the "hardwired" circuitry that directs sets of micro instructions that perform the signal or impulse gating. The term Read Only Memory (ROM) indicates that the computer can read from the given section of memory, but not write into the section. This provides an unalterable section of memory that is protected against inadvertent change.

Firmware has been used for: emulation—the implementation of an instruction set of one computer on a different computer—; input and output control interfaces to permit the interfaces to be modified as technology changes without the need for hardware changes; and to provide specialized instructions or programs required for particular users.

Firmware is a technique that allows economies of scale in computer hardware manufacture and at the same time allows extreme customization or flexibility of the computer hardware. Although users do not normally write microcode, this facility is available in some computers and has found particular application in process control computer systems.

Telecommunications. In the past, data processing systems usually operated by having input data sent to the computer center by mail, teletype message, or telephone conversation; keying the data to transform it into machine readable media; computer systems processing of the data and the preparation of reports; and sending the reports to users by mail or messenger service. Today, data processing systems are characterized by having the ability to receive data from and transmit data to remote locations. This transmission of data is called telecommunications, teleprocessing or data communications. The data may be transmitted over regular telephone voice lines, specialized or conditioned telephone voice lines, radio or microwave bands, or earth satellites. This ability to transmit and receive data at remote locations has made it possible to link one or more remote locations to a central computer in order to provide online inquiry or transaction processing. Telecommunications are also used for linking computers together to improve data processing system reliability and to facilitate data processing load balancing. Current data processing applications in airline reservations, banking, stock market operation, credit checking, and in many other manufacturing and service organizations would not be possible without this telecommunications ability.

Telecommunications systems consist of three types of devices or facilities: input and output devices, interface devices (Modern or Data Set), and the communication facility. Figure 12(a) illustrates a typical telecommunication system. Figures 12(b) and (c) illustrate a telecommunication system with a computer receiving and transmitting data.

Communication facility. The link between two points that are in communication with each other is known as the communications facility. This communication facility may be wires, radio waves or some combination of both. A communication facility circuit or channel may be classified into one of three basic types known as simplex, half-duplex, or full-duplex. A simplex channel allows only one way transmission of data. A half-duplex channel allows transmission of data in both directions, but permits the transmission of data in only one direction at a time. A stock market ticker tape printer and news service printer are examples of receive only devices that can utilize a simplex channel. Teletype or Telex terminals and airline reservation keyboard video displays are examples of devices that require at least half-duplex communication channels. The other type of communication channel is the full-duplex channel which permits the transmission of data in both directions simultaneously.

Another characteristic of a communication channel is the speed at which data can be transmitted. Data is transmitted in bit (binary digit) form where the bit takes one of two states characterized as either zero or one. The two states may be represented by different frequencies, phase changes, or amplitude changes and all three techniques are in use. Communications channels are classified by their maximum data transmission speed usually measured in bits per second (bps). The service classification or band width of the channel determines the maximum data transmission speed because the width of the band determines the frequency range that can be accommodated, with high frequency

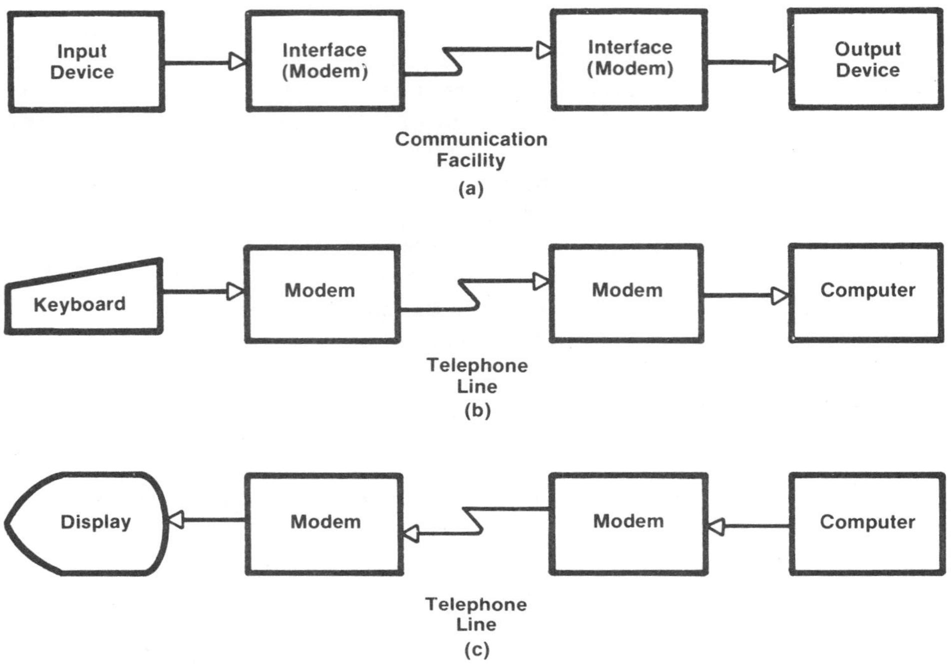

Fig. 12. Telecommunications System.

band width corresponding to higher permissible data transmission speeds. Narrow band service is capable of transmitting up to about 300 bits per second. Typical speeds are in the 45 to 150 bit per second range with teletype, Telex, and TWX services using this type of a narrow band channel. This class of transmission channel is sometimes referred to as sub-voice band.

Voice band channels are a second type of service or service class and are capable of transmitting a frequency range or bandwidth of approximately 3000 Hertz (cycles per second) for regular dial-up public lines and 4000 Hertz for leased lines. This service class is known as voice band because it was originally used for voice communication in normal telephone use. The maximum data speed for this type of service ranges up to 2400 bits per second, but it is possible to increase this maximum rate if the line is properly conditioned. Voice band service, because of its ready availability, is routinely used for time sharing service, and the transmission of data in the form of punched paper tape, punched cards, or even magnetic cassettes and tapes. In effect, this service band permits data transmission between any locations that are connected by ordinary telephone service. WATS (Wide Area Telephone Service) also provides voice band grade channels and can be substituted for long distance telephone service.

The third and last class of communication channels is called the broad band class and has a much higher band width than the voice band class. It may involve special radio or TV bands, or microwave and satellite communication systems that operate at very high frequencies measured in kiloHertz (thousandths of cycles per second). Telepak is a broad band private line service of American Telephone and Telegraph (ATT) that can be leased on a fixed cost per month based on mileage and independent of usage. Various other vendors (Datatran, Tymnet, etc.) offer similar service that use microwave or other transmission techniques, with some vendors providing packet transmission over their own communications system. It is possible to subdivide broad band service into a number of voice band or narrow band services.

Interface Devices. Various devices are used to interface the computer equipment, input and output devices with the communication facility. These devices convert the usual constant level direct current pulses of computer equipment and input and output devices into signals suitable for transmission over the communcation lines and also reverse the process for the receiving device. The conversion is called modulation and demodulation, and an interface device that performs this function is known as a Modem or Data Set.

A variety of codes can be used for data transmission with ASCII (American Standard Code for Information Interchange) being the most popular standard code. Adoption of this eight bit code—seven bit character code and an eighth bit for parity checking (verifying data transmission integrity)—facilitates the interchange of data among computers, input, and output devices supplied by a wide variety of vendors. The telephone companies supply Data-Phone Data Sets (Modem) to interface computer, input, and output devices to the communications lines.

Input and output devices. Practically any type of device is available as an input or output device for a telecommunications system. Input devices for reading punched cards, punched paper tape, magnetic cassettes, magnetic tape, etc. and converting the data into signals for telecommunications are available as are output devices that can be connected to the telecommunications system and produce punched card, punched tape, magnetic cassette, magnetic tape, etc. Portable printers and portable video display units, both with keyboards, are also available so that data processing systems can be designed to collect data from and transmit data to people not in a fixed location (salespersons, insurance agents, etc.) as long as they have access to a telephone. Many interesting applications have been developed that use a very common instrument as an input device, namely, the touch tone telephone, and provide output in the form of voice response. With a system of this type, a person does not need any special equipment other than a touch tone telephone to communicate with the data processing system. For example, a salesperson can inquire about material availability and take an order while sitting at a customer's office. The salesperson calls a special number, keys the product number using the touch tone telephone, and listens to a voice response giving information about inventory availability. The salesperson could also key the customer number and quantity to place an immediate order.

Data processing system mode of operation. There are basically two approaches to business data processing and these approaches are somewhat dependent on the data storage file organization. The two approaches are known as batch processing—periodic processing of accumulated batches of data—and online or immediate processing—the processing of transactions as they occur or very soon afterwards in the same sequence in which they are generated. Online processing is so named because the devices for recording transactions are directly connected or are online to the computer system.

A major factor influencing the mode of business data processing is the accessibility of the data in the secondary storage devices. Data records within a file in the secondary storage device may be available for accessing only sequentially or the records may be directly accessible. Older computer systems—in which the principle secondary storage device was magnetic tape—operated in a batch processing mode because magnetic tape storage devices permit only sequential access to records. Sequential access means that records are available only in a given sequence and in order to access the 226th record in a file requires that the system access and pass over 225 records before locating the desired records. For example, updating a customer accounts receivable record with new invoices may present a situation in which the 225 customers have no new invoices and the 226th customer has a new invoice for accounts receivable balance updating. Sequential accessing of records in the secondary storage device also implies that the transactions to be processed against the master file be in the same sequence as the records on the secondary storage device. This requires the transaction records be sorted into the desired sequence. Sequential secondary storage also implies economies of scale in processing larger batches of input transactions less frequently since this reduces the number of "passes"—updating of the master file—and the concomitant reading and writing operations associated with master file updating on sequential storage devices.

The development of secondary storage direct access devices, such as magnetic disk drive devices, radically altered the mode of data processing. With a direct access storage device it is possible to obtain any record in a time that is almost independent of the record's position in the file. In applications employing direct access secondary storage devices it is practical to process few transactions relative to the size of the master file or even one transaction against the master file as is required in online processing. An added advantage of using direct access secondary storage devices is that there is usually no need to sort the input transactions, thus eliminating this step because of the reduced amount of computer time required and the reduced elapsed time between the occurrence of the transaction and the updating of the file record. Direct access secondary storage devices and direct access processing are widely used in modern business data processing systems.

It is also possible to use a direct access storage device in a sequential mode to retrieve records in a given sequence or in different given sequences. For example, it is possible to produce employee listings in employee number sequence, alphabetic employee name sequence, and employee number within department number sequence, all from the same master file without sorting the master file into the desired sequence. This is a great advantage over sequential access secondary storage devices since, on a sequential access storage device, the records are maintained in only one given sequence and to produce an output report in a different sequence requires a sorting operation.

Economical storage of data in direct access secondary storage devices was probably the greatest factor that led to the widespread use of the online processing mode. Many current data processing system applications would not be possible without a direct access storage device to support the online system. For example, airline reservation systems and credit checking systems would not be possible unless the computer system was capable of providing immediate direct access to the required data. Although many data processing applications require direct access methods, there are others that more naturally lend themselves to sequential processing even if the secondary storage device is a direct access storage device. For example, payroll and accounts receivable statement preparation are data processing activities that occur periodically and are more naturally processed in the batch processing mode. The decision as to the data processing mode and the type of secondary storage device to be used requires careful consideration because the computer configuration and equipment requirements change with the processing mode and secondary storage scheme. The principal decision variables concern the amount of data required for the application, and the need for current information status to provide operational control in the management system of the organization.

Computer system configurations. A computer system consists of some combination of input, output, and storage devices, and central processing units. This is referred to as the computer system configuration. The development of a wide variety of devices manufactured by many different vendors specializing in particular types of devices, interfacing standards, and microprocessors that allow flexible interfacing among devices, makes it possible to consider all the devices as modules or building blocks and to provide an almost unlimited number of computer system configurations. Computer system configurations can range from a purchase price of $2,000 for a microcomputer system to over $3,000,000 for a large scale computer system.

Interestingly, in many cases, the cost of the peripheral (input, output and secondary storage) devices costs much more than the central processing unit. The wide range of costs and the wide variety of devices available for any system blur the precise definition and classification of computer system configurations into micro, mini, small, medium, or large scale systems. A brief description of several types of computer system configurations is presented in this section with the configurations classified as:

1. Microcomputers
2. Minicomputers
3. Small card oriented systems
4. Small magnetic disk systems
5. Medium scale systems
6. Large scale systems

Microcomputers. The newest development in data processing is the common availability of microcomputers or microprocessors which are sometimes called "systems-on-a-chip." A microprocessor is usually characterized by small word length (four bits), slower cycle time, and limited main memory (as low as 256 words), and a very low price ($300). Microprocessors have been used primarily to provide "intelligence" to some common input and output devices. This enables some data processing to be done directly in the input or output device to reduce the work required of the main data processing system and to provide some information reporting capability without reliance on the main data processing system. Although the main use of microcomputers has been in intelligent terminals, interface devices, and process control applications (controllers for process industry operations, electronic calculators, and in automobiles for braking and fuel systems), it is possible to obtain data processing systems built around microprocessors for limited data processing applications. For example, the Altair 8800 system with a teletypewriter for input and output, a magnetic type cassette or diskette for secondary storage, and a BASIC language interpreter is available at a purchase price of less than $4,000.

Minicomputers. The development of minicomputer systems for business data processing has had great impact on data processing activities in both large and small organizations. Originally, a minicomputer system was defined as a programmable general purpose computer system available in a minimum configuration with a purchase price of less than $20,000. These systems were characterized by a word length of eight, twelve, or sixteen bits, and a main memory of 2,048 or 4,096 words. The early minicomputers were quite slow compared to those available today and had only fairly limited memory expansion capabilities. Today minicomputers are available in word length of 32 bits (same as some large scale computers), main memory of 128,000 or 256,000 words, and cycle times equivalent to those found in large scale systems. It is possible to attach many high speed peripherals to a minicomputer and in this way provide the data processing capability needed for most business applications. Magnetic disk direct access storage devices as well as high speed printers and video display input and output devices are routinely combined with minicomputers to provide online data processing capability for large, and more importantly, small organizations. A minicomputer system with two video display terminals, 20 million bytes of secondary direct acess magnetic disk storage, and a medium speed printer can be purchased for under $40,000. This is equivalent to a rental price of under $1,000 per month (equivalent monthly rental provides basis of comparison with other data processing systems).

Many vendors (Digital Equipment Corporation, Data General, Microdata, Interdata, IBM, Honeywell, etc.) provide minicomputer configurations for business data processing. The IBM System/32, DEC 300 and 500 series data systems, Honeywell H316 system, NCR 399 system, etc. are typical of the small minicomputer systems configurations available for online business data processing.

Small card oriented computer system configurations. The small punched card oriented computer system was a powerful extension of punched card data processing systems that previously used electromechanical equipment. These computer systems were available as direct replacements for older punched card processing accounting machines at a comparable price. The monthly rental for these computer systems ranges from $1,000 to $2,500 per month and the most famous and widely used system of this genre was the IBM System/3. The Univac 1004, 1005 and 9200 series, and the Honeywell 58 system are also typical of this type of computer configuration. As newer technology developed, in the area of lower cost magnetic tape transport devices, magnetic disk and diskette storage devices, and video displays, these were incorporated into previously all punched card system configurations and small magnetic disk oriented systems were developed. Although many small punched card oriented systems are in use, more and more organizations are changing to small magnetic disk oriented configurations or minicomputer system configurations.

Small magnetic disk oriented computer system configurations. Small magnetic disk oriented system configurations contain many of the same devices found in the small punched card oriented systems with the addition of magnetic disk storage. The addition of direct access secondary devices radically alters the capability of the computer system since it makes possible transaction or online processing instead of sequential storage organization and processing. A simple application, such as preparation of invoices, requires extensive card manipulations in a small punched card oriented system configuration. The printing of an invoice requires at a minimum, the customer's name and address and the detail line items for the invoice. This means that this data must be available sequentially (one punched card after another) or simultaneously (two separate punched card readers) and requires offline card processing to obtain the required sequence of punched cards. The addition of direct access secondary storage allows the computer system to access the customer's name and address when required and eliminates much offline punched card processing.

Small magnetic disk oriented systems rent for approximately $1,500 to $5,500 per month. IBM System/3 models 6, 8, 12 and 15, Univac 9200 series, and the NCR Century 100 series are typical of this type of computer system configuration. Many data processing systems utilizing this computer system configuration are designed to operate in the batch processing mode, or single user transaction oriented mode where the transactions are usually batched for processing. This is true even though the computer system equipment has the capability to support online and even telecommunications applications—it is another case in which the application of the technology lags behind the development of the technology.

Medium scale computer system configurations. As an organization's data processing requirements expand, either in number of transactions to be processed or the size of the data base, the organization requires another computer system configuration or a different and larger computer system configuration. Medium scale computer system configurations generally range from $6,000 to $50,000 per month. This is a wider range of prices than the previous classes and illustrates the wide range of possible computer configuration in this classification.

Medium scale computer system configurations contain: 256,000 to 1,000,-000 bytes of main memory; 4 to 6 magnetic disk drives with 200 to 400 million bytes of online secondary storage; one or two printers at rates of 600 to 2,500 lines per minute; 4 to 6 magnetic tape drives; and can support online input/output hard copy and video display terminals, and a wide variety of telecommunications and special purpose devices. A medium scale computer configuration has a sophisticated operating system that allows: multiprogramming (more than one program operating at the same time), multiprocessing (more than one central processing unit operating simultaneously), and often uses a virtual memory technique that dynamically increases the number and size of programs running simultaneously on the computer. These systems have a wide range of utility, library, and language processor programs. IBM System/360 model 30 to model 50, System/370 model 135 to model 158; Univac 1100/10 and/20, series 90; and larger models of NCR Century 100 systems are typical of medium scale computer system configurations.

Large scale computer system configurations. Some organizations require extremely powerful data processing systems and computer system configurations. These requirements arise from very high transaction volume processing, online support many users simultaneously, or the high computational requirements of scientific data processing. The large scale computer system provides the necessary power at prices that range from $75,000 to $200,000 per month or more, with a large scale computer system configuration usually renting for more than $100,000 per month. Large scale computer systems have extremely fast central processing units; main memory of 1 to 3 megabytes (one million bytes), that may be segmented into two types of main memory, one possessing extemely high access speed; the ability to process instructions in parallel rather than serially and in many cases are multicomputer systems, or at least use minicomputer and microcomputer systems for specific data processing tasks. The IBM System/360 model 65 and larger, larger versions of the Univac 1100 system, Univac system 1108, IBM System/370 model 165 and larger, and various larger models manufactured by Control Data Corporation are typical of computer system configurations in this category. As can be imagined, these computer system configurations use extensive software operating systems that control the vast complex of computer system devices and provide a wide range of programming and operational support to users.

Alternatives for obtaining data processing resources. An organization's data processing requirements can be satisfied in a variety of ways. The firm may own or rent and operate its own computer facility; buy computer time from a time-share vendor or buy block time, or use a service bureau to provide the necessary data processing.

An organization that owns or rents its own computer equipment has basically two alternatives. The first is to manage the computer center as another department within the organization, and the second is to subcontract the management of the computer facility. This process of subcontracting the computer system management is called obtaining facility management, and there are specialized firms that provide this service. Facility management is usually defined as the use of an outside organization to manage the operation of computer data processing facility under a long term agreement. The contract may cover a period of from one to six years and include all activities or just a portion of the data processing operation. For example, a facility management contract can cover the day-to-day data processing operations, but not the system design or development activities, which may be handled on a project by project basis, or by another vendor, or by the organization itself.

The primary reason for an organization's use of a facility management firm is based on the belief that computer systems are too technical and complex to be managed by general line executives. This view has been fostered by some data processing professionals, but there is really no reason why a data processing facility should not be managed by the same type of management executive that manages research and development departments, engineering departments, and highly technical manufacturing facilities. Sometimes there are economies to be obtained from a facility management vendor when the vendor has particular expertise or concentration in a certain industry. For example, some facility management firms specialize in health care agencies such as Blue Cross and Blue Shield, while other vendors have particular expertise in stock brokerage activities. In this case the facility management firm can develop software and procedures that can be used for more than one organization and amortize the development cost over a greater number of organizations. The results from facility management are mixed at this date, but the concept appears to be becoming less popular.

The organization may rent the full time use of a computer system or buy block time. Block time refers to the purchase of a specified amount of computer time at a specified time of day. This, in effect, is renting a computer system by the hour and the vendor of block time usually provides no services or programming. The user organization provides its own programs and operations personnel. The user organization has the same responsibility as operating its own computer system resources except for the installation and maintenance of the computer equipment. This type of arrangement arises when organizations have excess computer system time. For example, an organization may rent a computer system and use it only during one shift and therefore have computer system time available on two other shifts. The organization might then look to the selling of block time as a means of increasing its revenues or partially offsetting its costs of computer system operation.

The second major alternative for obtaining data processing resources is time sharing. Time sharing refers to the concurrent utilization of a computer system by many independent users with each operating independently, that is without being able to detect the presence of other users on the system. In many cases, each user's requirement is small enough so that many users can simultaneously share the resources of a large computer system. Companies have developed to provide this type of computer resource to many users and have profited from the economies of scale available from combining small users. This type of computer resource varies greatly over time. Academic and teaching institutions, and certain types of scientific and engineering problem solving users have this characteristic and were the first users of time sharing.

The relationship between the organization and a time share vendor is analogous to the relationship between a telephone customer and the telephone company. The organization need not understand the operation of the telephone exchange, but only needs to know how to operate its telephone and expects that service will be available on demand. In the same fashion an organization using computer time sharing is primarily concerned with the operation of its input and output devices, but not with the operation of the computer system itself. The organization expects that the computer resources are available on demand and operate properly.

Many time sharing services have specialized in particular industries, as is true of facility management firms. These time share vendors have developed generalized programs for handling routine business tasks such as order entry, invoicing, maintaining inventory records, maintaining accounts receivable records, processing payroll, etc. An advantage to the user organization is that it need not pay the entire development cost of these systems since the time share vendor amortizes the cost over the many organizations using the system. This advantage to user organizations is also a disadvantage in that this requires that the user organization adopt the standardized data processing procedures rather than develop a data processing system and procedures that are more akin to the manner in which the organization operates.

There are two ways in which time share vendors charge for the use of computer system resources. The first method involves maintaining records of actual computer resources used and charging for the use of each resource. For example, an organization might use 500 seconds of CPU time, perform 2000 disk accesses, require 200,000 bytes of main memory for processing, and write 4,000 lines of output to a printer. The user organization would then be charged for each resource separately according to the amount used. In this case the user would also pay for the amount of online secondary storage used. On the other hand, many business oriented time share vendors charge for resource use on a transaction basis. That is, the user would be charged for each inquiry; each invoice printed, based on the number of lines on the invoice; and each other transaction processed or document produced. The user organization would also pay for online secondary storage based on the number of inventory item or accounts receivable records stored.

There are basically two approaches to using time share computer resources. The first is conversational processing and the second is remote batch processing or remote job entry (RJE). Conversational processing allows the user to be online to the computer system and to obtain service on demand. The user's hard copy or video display input/output device has immediate access to the computer and performs as though the user had his own online computer system.

Remote batch processing is, just as the name implies, the batch processing of data from a remote location. In this case, the input device is a device capable of reading machine readable media, such as punched cards, and the user is online to the system only during the time that the input device is reading the punched cards or an output device is printing a report. This is analogous to a conventional batch processing system where the user keys the transactions on an intermediate medium and accumulates the transactions into a batch. After transmission of the input data the user might be required to wait a few hours until his batch job is completed. At that time, the output from his batch job would be printed on an output device at his remote location. It is evident that the alternative data processing modes discussed in an earlier section are available independently of whether the user organization has its own computer system resources or uses a time share vendor.

The use of a service bureau is the third major alternative for obtaining data processing resources. This is another case in which it is difficult to draw a fine line to distinguish a service bureau from a time share vendor, and in fact, service bureaus (an older name) are increasingly referring to themselves as data centers, time share centers or service centers. The distinguishing feature of the service bureau is its willingness to assume all data processing tasks associated with an application. This usually includes picking up the input documents from a user, keying the documents into machine readable media, performing all data processing, and delivering the output reports back to the user. The service bureau performs these services for a fee usually dependent on transaction volume. In most cases, the service bureau will develop the system and write all the programs for the user organization. This assumption of overall responsibility usually differentiates the service bureau from a time share vendor. As might be expected, the direct cost of using a service bureau is higher than that of using a time share vendor because of the extra services involved.

The determination of the proper computer system configuration requires careful analysis of the organization's information system requirements and the synthesis of those requirements into an operational system for the organization. Much of the analysis requires detailed knowledge of the various types of computer equipment available and the viable methods of operation. In addition, highly technical knowledge is required to estimate storage requirements, transaction volumes, and processing and peripheral device speed requirements as well as the effort required for system design, programming, and implementation. In addition, there are many alternatives for obtaining data processing resources involving various combinations of data processing resources.

To some extent, the quality of management is dependent on the availability of information and the flow of information within the organization. The accountant, in both his roles as auditor and advisor to management, can attempt to ensure that the information system of the organization is functioning properly and in control. The accountant provides management assistance in his area of expertise and assists management in obtaining whatever specialized expertise is required for the development of effective management information systems.

A LOOK INTO THE FUTURE

It is always interesting, but sometimes very dangerous, to attempt to forecast the future. Past and current developments are known, and in some cases the future can be extrapolated from them. On the other hand, our society is a complex system in which it is sometimes difficult to know or understand the interrelationships among the component parts. One thing is clear, the past 25 years has seen the steady and sometimes astronomical growth of computer processing in business and in our society. The future will, no doubt, contain the development of even more powerful computer processors and peripheral devices, and an increasing number of computer systems in use. I believe, however, that the most dramatic growth will occur in the number of smaller computer systems in use.

Computer processing cycle time has been reduced by about two orders of magnitude in the past 25 years. Even the measurement unit, which used to be microseconds (one millionth of a second), has been changed to nanoseconds (one billionth of a second). Early computers in the 1950s had main memory cycle times of 10 to 15 microseconds or 10,000 to 15,000 nanoseconds while current memory cycles are less than 50 nanoseconds. The effect of this increased speed is sharply reduced costs of computation. The number of computer operations performed per dollar is increasing at an average annual rate of about 85%. This means that each year it is possible to obtain 185 computer operations for the same cost of performing 100 computer operations last year. There has been a concomitant dramatic improvement in the power and cost of peripheral devices as well. Nowhere has this been more dramatic than in online magnetic disk storage devices where the capacity of a disk pack has gone from under 3,000,000 bytes to approximately 100,000,000 bytes. The per byte cost of online secondary storage has decreased at almost the same rate that online secondary storage capacity has increased. Online input and output devices, from hard copy to video display, have increased in speed, decreased in cost, and have more "intelligence"—the ability to do some data processing within the device.

It has been postulated (Grosch's Law) that computer power increases as a function of the cost squared. That is, four times as much computing power can be obtained at twice the cost. This has been true and in some measure it provided the impetus for large scale computer systems in that there were economies of sale to be obtained from the larger systems. (Why buy four small computers to do data processing at four separate locations when a single computer can provide the necessary computer power at the cost of only two of the smaller computer systems?) However, the movement toward centralized computer facilities has attenuated and the trend is now toward decentralized or distributed computer power. A corollary to an increase in the number of computer operations per dollar is that it costs less to do a given number of computer operations. This has made it feasible to provide smaller units of computer power to the source of the data and at the location of the need for data processing. It is now possible to economically provide computer power to practically any size organization. Today minimal computer data processing systems are available for less than $500 per month. In the future the cost should fall to under $250 per month for a combination data processing and word processing computer system—which makes such a computer system feasible for an organization requiring any significant amount of record keeping, clerical work and typing.

The future should also contain some improvements in source data automation. OCR (Optical Character Recognition) equipment is capable of reading machine printed and some handwritten data. Improvements in OCR equipment will reduce the cost of data entry, now estimated to be at a rate of approximately $5,000,000,000 per year in the United States. Computer telecommunications will improve as more and more minicomputer and microprocessors are used in the communications network, so that the single largest source of data will be an input device that is capable of reading machine encoded media (credit card) and the touch tone key signals. It is estimated that more than 85% of current medium sized and larger computer systems have teleprocessing capability with the percentage expected to exceed 95% in the near future. Advanced computer based telecommunications systems, such as Telenet and Datran, will make large scale computer message handling economically feasible for both terminal to terminal and computer to computer dialogues. The future holds greater promise for organization to organization data processing communication than for the much heralded electronic funds transfer systems. It is now technically feasible for one firm to transmit an invoice to another firm automatically by computer through a telecommunication system. Although this is not current practice, precedent does exist in the government's acceptance of payroll data in machine readable form.

Computer software development has lagged behind computer hardware improvements. Computer software is as important as the computer hardware in developing an operational information system for an organization. There has been widespread standardization of a few programming languages with COBOL the most frequently used for business data processing. The newer minicomputer and microcomputer systems have tended to use languages such as FORTRAN and BASIC and only a few have COBOL compilers. Data base systems with their own languages have been developed and will continue to be developed as larger and larger data bases are created. There have been a number of attempts to develop a single language that would combine the advantages of the widely used COBOL and FORTRAN programming languages. PL/1 was heralded as this language, but only widely supported by IBM. PL/1 will probably not become more popular, but a newer language will be developed to combine the capabilities of COBOL, FORTRAN and a Data Base language.

Computer processor and peripheral equipment will continue to increase in power and decrease in cost. The development of less costly input devices and the resultant greater use of computer based data telecommunications data processing networks will increase the range and number of computer data processing applications. We can only speculate as to the rate of growth, but we can be certain that in the future computers will play an even larger and more important role in business organizations and in society.

24

Planning the Audit Program

CONTENTS

24

Planning the Audit Program

Robert E. Hammond, CPA and
John F. Wagner, CPA

The audit program is an important document that sets forth decisions covering what is to be done and how to do it. These decisions are based upon knowledge of the client, his business, method of operation, and the anticipated reliability of his records.

► BEAR IN MIND: An audit program is but a guide to the auditor in applying the necessary audit procedures that will provide sufficient competent evidential matter through inspection, observation, inquiry, computation, and confirmation to afford a reasonable basis for an expression of opinion on the financial statements being audited. The customary opinion states that the financial statements present fairly the financial position, results of operations and changes in financial position in conformity with generally accepted accounting principles, and that such principles have been consistently applied in the current period in relation to the preceding period. In addition, informative disclosures in the financial statements are regarded as reasonably adequate unless the auditor's report is qualified to indicate omissions. The auditor must be flexible in providing for modifications in the program that were not anticipated in its original preparation prior to audit. Also, the scope of the examination set forth in the audit program must be conditioned by the purpose and nature of the engagement, and by the degree and adequacy of internal control.

This chapter discusses the considerations involved in planning the audit program, listing key audit steps in such major areas as cash, accounts receivable, inventories, and trade accounts payable. Particular attention is given to internal control as it affects the planning of the audit. In this connection, representative sections of an internal control questionnaire are furnished in Appendix A following the chapter. Appendix B presents a plan of attack on the problem of auditing a client in an unfamiliar industry.

IMPORTANCE OF PLANNING THE AUDIT PROGRAM

Planning the program for audit is important in all types of examinations. The program itself and the planning are influenced by:

1. Size of the business being audited.
2. Whether this is a first engagement, or a subsequent audit.

Size of the business being audited. The complexity of the examination normally increases with the size of the organization being audited. A number of subsidiaries or branches, several products, or mere volume itself, add to the audit task. As the size increases, the degree of internal control usually increases also.

As the size of the company increases, the complexity of the data processing system generally increases. A data processing system may range from a manual system of bookkeeping in a small business, to a highly sophisticated computerized system in a large business. Changes from the manual system result in changes in the "audit trail," consisting of ledgers, journals, work sheets, and documentation that enable an auditor to trace an original transaction forward to the financial statements or from the financial statements back to the original transaction. Computerization has enabled companies to eliminate or reduce source documentation ordinarily used in manual or mechanized systems. As a result, processing controls shift from people to the computer. The data processing systems in use require different skills of the auditor and affect the design of the audit program. The more complex electronic data processing (EDP) will require the auditor to apply specialized expertise in EDP in designing the audit program and performing the necessary audit procedures.

► WARNING: Many small businesses have excellent controls and checks, while some large enterprises have been found deficient in their operating controls. Therefore, the audit program must be designed according to the auditor's findings on internal control, rather than according to the size of the client.

First engagements. The preparation of the audit program for a new client may logically develop in three stages:

1. The broad phases of the program can be outlined at the beginning of the engagement. Provision should be made for verification of opening balances; either by review of prior auditors' working papers (if the client has been previously examined) or by other means. The possible need for a qualification or denial of an opinion because of opening balances should be discussed with the client at this time.
2. After the review of internal control and accounting procedures has been made, the details of the program that are affected by elements of weakness or strength found in the system of internal control can be sketched in.
3. As the audit proceeds, specific procedures on detailed phases of the program can be further developed.

► NOTE: Every auditor at some time or other is called upon to audit a new client in an industry with which the auditor is unfamiliar. The audit of a new client who is in an unfamiliar industry entails additional complications beyond those normally associated with the first engagements. These problems are recognized and dealt with in Appendix B of this chapter.

Subsequent audits. In each subsequent engagement, the program is restudied and modified, if necessary, in the light of (1) the experience gained in past examinations, and (2) important changes in the business or the internal control or accounting methods of the client. As it is carried forward from year to year, the program may be changed by addenda sheets or completely revised and rewritten. When a program has been superseded, it should not be destroyed but should be filed with the working papers on the engagement to which it last applied. Even if there have not been any modifications in the program, the fact that it has been challenged and left as is should be annually noted therein.

WHAT THE AUDITOR MUST KNOW ABOUT THE CLIENT

To plan an auditing program intelligently, the auditor must be informed as to the affairs and activities of his client. Whether it is an auditor's first engagement with the client or a repeat (because the auditing personnel may change), the audit program should first outline the following important matters, the knowledge of which is essential to the program's preparation:

1. Client's history and business.
2. Purpose and nature of engagement.
3. Time schedule and staff requirements.

Client's history and business. Before accepting a new client, the auditor should satisfy himself as to the desirability of the engagement. If the concern is unknown to him, he should inquire into its standing, financial responsibility, background, nature of business, and similar pertinent matters. The auditor should also try to determine the reputation of the concern, and the honesty and integrity of its principal executives and major stockholders. These inquiries, together with subsequent studies, will develop the following matters of importance to him:

1. Date and state of incorporation or commencement of business.
2. Names and businesses of subsidiaries or affiliates. The auditor should be aware of all companies associated with the client through common ownership.
3. Summary of products or services, methods of distribution, status in the industry or within the geographical area.
4. Locations of plants and offices together with a description of activities at each location.

► NOTE: This can be of particular importance in connection with planning for assigning portions of the audit to branches of the auditing firm or in corresponding with the client's plants and offices.

5. Financial and advisory consultants. List banking connections (both commercial and underwriting), attorneys, insurance advisors, etc.

6. The names and titles of officers and key employees. The list should indicate the superior officer to whom each person reports and the functions of each person listed. If available, this information may be obtained from a chart of organization.

► SUGGESTION: As it may have some bearing on the adequacy of internal control, the auditor should ascertain if any of those listed are related and, if so, the relationship.

7. The names and affiliations of directors and major stockholders.

Purpose and nature of engagement. Although the auditor cannot ordinarily control the use of his audit report, he should know whether its primary use is for inclusion in the annual report, for release to equity owners and credit grantors, issuance to governmental bodies, or for some other purpose.

If the financial statements are to be included in filings (registration statements, annual reports, etc.) with the Securities and Exchange Commission, the working papers may require expansion in order to have available those details not otherwise required.

Although the auditor reviews the computations of taxes (including Federal and state income taxes) in the course of his examination, if his engagement includes the preparation of such returns, he must plan to have all the necessary detailed information in his working papers.

Time schedule and staff requirements. Tax returns, at least in a preliminary form, must be filed within their due dates, as must all other governmental reports, such as 10K's to the SEC. Substantially all corporations provide for release of their financial statements at the same time that notice is given for annual stockholders' meetings. Factors such as these establish deadlines for the completion of the auditor's report. Accordingly, the auditor must schedule his work and staff assignments to meet these deadlines, providing for some leeway in the event an unforeseen complication delays the anticipated completion of the audit.

Staff requirements as to time of partners, supervisors, senior accountants, and assistant accountants are carefully projected. These in turn must be coordinated with requirements of other client engagements in order to attain economical staff utilization.

THE CLIENT'S ACCOUNTING AND MANAGEMENT POLICIES

Review prior audited financial statements. In order for the auditor to be able to express an opinion as to consistency, his review of the statements for the preceding fiscal year must be sufficient to provide an adequate basis for such opinion. Applied to the balance sheet, this means a comparison of the bases of valuation used for the principal assets, as well as the policies with respect to establishing and using allowances or reserves, and reflecting liabilities. The accounting principles and practices followed in the preparation of the income statement are also reviewed and compared with those of the preceding year.

On first examinations, if financial statements have been examined by other independent accountants in prior years, such statements and the accountants' reports should be reviewed for a number of years with particular attention to the latest year. These reports of other independent accountants may reduce the amount of investigation into prior history ordinarily required. This, together with the auditor's own inquiry, furnishes the data regarding accounting and management policies to be outlined in the audit program.

On subsequent audits, the policies and practices outlined in the prior audit program are compared with those of the year under audit.

Summarize significant accounting and management policies. As a part of the audit program, it is desirable to outline the client's policies with respect to major accounting and management policies for reference by the auditors, and to check for consistency with prior years. Although the major policy areas vary according to the activities of the business, they generally include the following matters:

1. Inventories.
2. Depreciation.
3. Income taxes.
4. Other items.

Inventories. The basis of valuation such as "lower of cost or market," and further, the method of determining cost, that is, last-in, first-out cost, first-in, first-out cost, average cost, and the like, should be described. One portion of the inventory may sometimes be valued on one basis, and another on a different basis. The procedures for determining inventory quantities should also be described. Matters such as recognition of slow-moving and obsolete inventories are worth commenting upon.

Depreciation. As there are a number of acceptable methods of providing for the amortization of depreciable assets, the method or methods adopted should be explained. Whether or not fully depreciated assets are eliminated from the accounts should be stated. If the recorded depreciation is different from that claimed for income tax purposes, it should be noted in the comments. Similarly, a comment should be made concerning management policy as to the minimum dollar amount of items to be capitalized, as a company will often expense capital items of only nominal value.

Income taxes. The amount of taxable income is frequently different from the amount of income per books before taxes. This difference may be either a permanent or a timing difference, or a combination of both. In this section the auditor should account for management policies that cause the timing difference.

Other items. There are other accounting practices that can vary according to management policy. Examples of such items are pensions, profit-sharing plans, vacation accruals, reserves for advertising allowances, and the like. The program should set forth the bases for their determination.

► NOTE: The review as to consistency is needed to determine whether or not the financial statements are comparable with those of prior years. Accordingly, changes in policies that have little or no effect upon current or future operating results do not require disclosure.

INTERNAL ACCOUNTING CONTROL AND PROCEDURES

What is internal control? Internal control relates to all activities of the organization. Internal accounting control comprises the plan of organization and the records and procedures concerned with the safeguarding of assets and the reliability of financial records for preparing financial statements and accounting for assets. An adequate system of internal accounting control requires separation of functions and duties. At least the following functions should have separate personnel handling the records: general ledger accounting, billing and accounts receivable accounting, cashier's accounting, approval of data supporting disbursements, and check signing. More extensive systems of internal control expand the divisions of duties and usually provide some degree of internal audit, such as having a person or department whose duty it is to check the work of others, but who does not originate either transactions or accounting entries.

The importance of adequate controls. Adequate accounting controls are essential to insure a continuous check of the accuracy of the records being accumulated, and to avoid errors in interpretation and computation. They also provide the means of disclosing errors in judgment. Although it may be proper to assume that employees are honest, it is unfair to permit weaknesses in accounting controls to tempt them toward dishonesty. A good internal accounting control system is the best safeguard against both employee error and employee dishonesty. Furthermore, good internal accounting control has additional importance to both the client and the auditor.

The importance of internal controls for the client. An important tool for management is financial data furnished frequently and promptly. The data must be reliable for the client to act with confidence, and accurate to avoid harmful decisions. For example, an understatement of inventories could result in decisions to increase production beyond reasonable needs, and to decline sales orders for products actually available. Internal accounting controls help attain reliability and accuracy.

The importance of internal controls for the auditor. The degree of internal accounting control has a direct bearing on the extent of detailed checking required by the auditor to satisfy himself as to the reliability of the records. The auditor is normally able to perform his examination by means of test-checking the recording of the client's transactions. However, if there is no system of internal accounting control, or if it is inadequate, the auditor must make an extensive audit in order to be satisfied that the accounting records are reliable.

In such a situation, the auditor is checking transactions to determine the correctness of the figures themselves, rather than to evaluate the operation of the internal accounting control system. Even then he might not be sure that all of the transactions have been recorded. As the system of internal control becomes more extensive, the auditor usually can reduce the extent of the test checks, ultimately resulting in his test checking the application of the system itself.

When the client has internal auditors. As the size of the business increases, and as its operations expand into multiple areas, a greater need develops for an internal auditor or an internal auditing department. Although the activities of the internal auditor are not always confined to accounting matters, it is in that area that the outside auditor is concerned with his work. The internal auditor, in the performance of his duties to management, checks the work of others in much the same way as the outside auditor. Accordingly, the findings of the internal auditor can be utilized by the outside auditor, *providing that ability and freedom of opinion are present.* As a prerequisite to his acceptance of the findings of an internal audit, the outside auditor must satisfy himself as to the quality and independence of that audit.

► COMMENT: If the work of the internal auditor is to be effective, he must have a thorough knowledge of the techniques of auditing, and must be responsible to a person or persons other than those whose work he examines. The independent accountant can ascertain the ability of the internal auditor by evaluating his prior experience, and by reviewing and testing his working papers. The work of the internal auditor cannot be substituted for the work of the independent auditor; however, it can be considered by the latter in determining the nature, timing and extent of his work.

Review the system of internal control. In determining the audit procedures to be applied and the amount of detail to be checked, it is essential that the accounting system and methods of internal accounting control be thoroughly reviewed. The independent accountant's report on financial statements ordinarily contains a representation "our examination . . . included such tests of the accounting records and such other auditing procedures as we considered necessary in the circumstances." To make such a statement requires a review to disclose (1) the nature of the internal accounting controls established, (2) whether such internal controls were so designed as to reduce to the minimum the possibilities of material errors and defalcations, and (3) whether or not the prescribed internal accounting controls were effectively maintained. The findings developed by this review determine the details of the audit program.

► NOTE: In practice, there is usually no distinct line of demarcation between the review of internal accounting control and the audit procedure itself. Frequently they start together, with audit procedures being adapted to the accounting methods and internal control systems in use. On first engagements, however, it is essential that at least the major matters pertaining to systems of internal accounting control and methods be covered prior to the start of audit procedures.

The internal control memorandum. The auditor should prepare a written outline covering the accounting system in use, and the methods of internal accounting control in effect for the period covered by the examination. This outline sets forth the flow of transactions, the nature of the records kept, and the names and duties of employees involved and their functional relationship to each other. The outline should be typed, dated and signed by the preparing accountant. It is carried forward from year to year, reviewed on each engagement, and brought up to date as to any significant changes since the last examination.

Appendix A to this chapter is a sample of a questionnaire used in preparing the internal control memorandum. This questionnaire covers certain major accounting areas: cash; purchasing and receiving; inventories; sales, shipping and accounts receivable; securities; properties and patents; and payrolls.

Responsibility for internal control. It is management's primary responsibility to see that there exists an adequate system of internal accounting control. Independent auditors are often requested to design the system. In such event, the auditor's responsibility is extended. In the absence of such assignment, the auditor's responsibility is limited to advising management as to weaknesses disclosed during the course of audit and review. It is advisable that the auditor's report of deficiencies in internal accounting control be in writing (a letter or memorandum form is common), so that it can be referred to in conferences with the executives involved.

► WARNING: Be sure that the importance of the matter is understood. If corrective measures are not promptly taken, top management, Board of Directors, or audit committee of the Board of Directors, should be advised.

PREPARING THE AUDIT PROGRAM

In preparing the audit program, the auditor should give consideration to the basic audit techniques of computation, confirmation, observation, inquiry, etc. as they relate to the accounts under examination. (See Chapter 25, *Audit Tools and Techniques.*)

Form of audit program. The working papers that comprise a minimum audit program should include statements of:

1. The nature of the engagement.
2. The procedures to be followed on important phases of the examination.
3. The procedures that are special to the particular examination, including departures from normal procedures.
4. The extent of the detailed testing of transactions.
5. The program of examination of branches and subsidiaries, if any.
6. The timing of specific areas of audit work.

The program should contain a summary statement of the reasoning supporting decisions on the important or unusual phases of the engagement. This is particularly true when the program departs from what are considered normal procedures. Although the auditor's judgment may have dictated the departure from normal audit procedures, the auditor must be prepared, if the occasion arises, to justify the departure.

The audit program and internal control. As previously discussed, the extent of detailed checking of transactions is related to, and varies with, the degree of internal accounting control. An extensive accounting control system ordinarily reduces the amount of testing the auditor must do. The control and care used by the client in determining inventory quantities and the accuracy of perpetual inventory records reduce the required test counts by the auditor. Thus, a good system of internal control operates to reduce the cost of the audit to the client.

Specific areas of examination. A typical audit program provides the following key audit steps in such major areas as:

1. Cash on hand, and on deposit.
2. Accounts receivable.
3. Inventories.
4. Trade accounts payable.

Cash on Hand:

1. Count all cash on hand at the home office as near to the close of accounting period as practicable, maintaining control over the funds until count is completed. The count should be made in the presence of the fund custodian and ordinarily should be made concurrently with inspection of notes receivable and investments. Surprise counts and second counts are frequently advisable. Obtain reçeipts for return of cash and securities inspected.

2. Reconcile cash funds to date of balance sheet and check to ledger accounts.

3. List and obtain approval and support of items other than cash included in funds.

4. Cash funds should be cleared of amounts representing disbursements prior to date of balance sheet, unless minor in amount.

5. Cash for deposit should be traced into subsequent bank deposits, and checked to ledger accounts and cash records. If amounts are material, consideration should be given to accompanying the deposit to the bank depository or requesting confirmation of the receipt of the deposit from the depositary.

6. Secure a list of cash funds held in branches or at other offices. For those not counted, obtain from their custodians acknowledgments that include detailed lists of all items other than cash in such funds.

Cash on Deposit:

1. Obtain directly from all depositaries, certificates covering bank balances, loans, and other information as at the date of the balance sheet. Correspond with each depositary with which the company did business during the year.

2. Examine paid bank checks and compare with cash disbursement records for a reasonable period prior to balance sheet date.

3. Trace recorded cash receipts (usually for not less than one month) directly to individual deposits shown by the bank statements, with special attention to transactions at or near the end of the year.

4. Make a sufficient review of the data supporting disbursements to indicate that disbursements are supported as a matter of procedure. This procedure includes a review of basic payroll records.

5. Reconcile all bank balances reported by the depositaries with the amounts on deposit shown by the records of the company.

6. It is desirable to obtain directly statements of principal bank accounts for a subsequent month or to a cut-off date, and to trace out in-transit items and outstanding checks at the audit date. An alternate procedure would be to make a second bank reconciliation, independently confirming the balances.

7. Watch for unrecorded checks and, if practicable, account for outstanding checks by inspecting paid checks returned in succeeding months. Investigate large or old checks that remain outstanding at cut-off or subsequent date.

8. Trace amounts for deposits in transit to deposits shown by cut-off bank statement. Consider comparing individual items included in such deposits with the cash receipts record and with the detailed accounts receivable records on a test basis. Request confirmation of deposit in transit if material and the cut-off statements are not received directly from the banks.

9. Review supporting data for reconciling items other than deposits in transit and outstanding checks.

10. Watch for incorrect balances in cash accounts, resulting from including cash received after the close of the accounting period, or from holding open the cash disbursements record or not releasing checks.

11. Trace all bank transfers during period for which cash transactions were tested and all those during a reasonable period prior to and subsequent to the balance sheet date, noting particularly check payment data and "out" and "in" dates.

12. Segregate all bank overdrafts.

13. Segregate all cash funds that are subject to withdrawal restrictions. Segregate foreign funds, and check applicable exchange rates and restrictions.

14. Make a general review of cash transactions near the close of the period (before and after) to ascertain if there have been any large items of an unusual nature, such as payment of officers' accounts, temporary reduction of notes payable, temporary discounting of notes receivable, new financing, or other extraordinary receipts or disbursements. This review of cash transactions ordinarily should include the period from the balance sheet date to date of completion of filed work.

15. Test footings of cash receipts and cash disbursements for periods covered by the test of cash transactions, including transactions within one month prior to balance sheet date. Check postings of cash records to general ledger accounts for the same period.

16. Review statements from banks for all dormant or inactive bank accounts for the period under audit.

Accounts Receivable:

1. Prepare or check the trial balance of individual accounts, showing age, subsequent payments, future datings, and installment accounts. Determine amounts due beyond one year. In checking individual ledger accounts, watch for and investigate unusual items debited or credited to such accounts. If subsequent payments are relied on as evidence of validity, or in judging adequacy of allowance for losses, sufficient tests should be made to establish their authenticity.

2. Segregate credit balances, accounts of officers, directors, employees and principal shareholders, accounts with affiliates, deposits and advances, consignments, etc.

3. Request confirmation from debtors, usually on a test basis, unless the aggregate of the accounts receivable is relatively insignificant. In the selection of confirmation methods, the following should be considered:

   a. The positive type of confirmation request is preferable in situations where a limited number of individual balances are of relatively major importance, or where there is reason to believe that the possibility of disputes, inaccuracies, or irregularities in the accounts is greater than usual.
   b. The negative type of confirmation request may be acceptable in the majority of cases, but should not be used where there are clear indications that it is inadequate, such as with receivables from the United States Government, chain-store organizations, etc.
   c. Generally, ordinary requests for confirmation of either of the types referred to above will produce no response from the United States Government or from certain large concerns such as some chain-store organization. In many instances, however, a confirmation request can be tailored to fit the particular situation and responses can be obtained.
   d. The account selected should be a representative sample. In addition, it may be desirable to request confirmation of accounts with large balances, past-due accounts, and accounts of an unusual nature which do not fall within the selected sample. Consideration should be given to the use of statistical sampling in selecting accounts to be confirmed. However, in selecting the sample the auditor should be sure that the mass of accounts from which the sample is selected is whole (e.g., that he has access to all the accounts that might be selected).
   e. In using the positive type of confirmation request, make every practical effort to obtain a reply. Second requests should be mailed to customers from whom replies have not been received after a reasonable period of time.

4. Apply alternative procedures to substantiate accounts of debtors not replying to positive requests, or accounts from the United States Government or other debtors to which no requests for confirmation were sent because there

were clear indications that no responses would be obtained from such accounts. Such procedures may include the following:

a. Support collections subsequent to the confirmation date by inspection of incoming checks or remittance advices. Trace invoice numbers and amounts collected to the customer's account and trace collected amounts to the records of cash receipts and to the bank deposit.
b. Examine invoice copy, shipping record, and purchase order.
c. Establish the existence of the recorded debtor if there is any question as to that fact.

5. If accounts are confirmed at a date other than the balance sheet date, review control account entries made between the confirmation date and the balance sheet date. Consider requesting confirmation of any large accounts existing at the balance sheet date that were not confirmed at the prior date.

6. Ascertain the amounts, if any, of accounts discounted, sold or assigned, with or without recourse, and request confirmation from the purchaser or assignee where appropriate. It may also be necessary to request confirmation of these accounts from the customers.

7. Test the sales cut-off by examining invoices and shipping documents for several days prior to and subsequent to the balance sheet date. Trace the invoices to sale and receivable records for the purpose of determining that sales are recorded in the proper accounting period, the period in which the goods were shipped.

8. Determine collectibility of the accounts receivable:

a. Compare the current year's aging with that of prior years for an appraisal or evaluation of the accounts in the aggregate.
b. Obtain Dun & Bradstreet reports or other independent information from other sources on customers whose accounts are significant in relation to the financial statements.
c. Discuss the collectibility of the accounts with the credit manager or other responsible official of the company and summarize his comments for the working papers.
d. Investigate past due accounts by indicating collections since the balance sheet date and examining correspondence with the customers, collection agency reports, and other data in the credit file.
e. Prepare analysis of the allowance for doubtful accounts for the period, comparing the bad debt provisions and experience with the previous years.
f. Observe whether charge offs, either to the allowance or directly to expense, have been properly authorized. Consider sending requests for positive confirmation covering larger accounts charged off in the current period.
g. Determine that accounts considered uncollectible have been charged off and consider the adequacy of the allowance for doubtful accounts.

9. Investigate adequacy of allowances for cash discounts on unpaid balances originated within the discount period, for returns of merchandise after the balance sheet date, for charges in dispute, and for other losses. Review credit memorandums issued subsequent to the balance sheet date but not entered in the accounts as of that date, and determine whether additional credit memorandums which would affect the period under audit are to be issued.

10. Review collectibility of accounts discontinued or sold with recourse. Determine whether an allowance for losses on collection of these accounts is required.

11. Compare total sales and charges to the accounts receivable control for a reasonable period prior to the closing date, and for other periods during the year. Investigate abnormal increases and charges to receivables near year end.

12. Determine that goods consigned to agents or under order from customers for future delivery, title to which has not passed to customers, are properly carried in inventory, not in accounts receivable.

Inventories:

1. Investigate inventory practices of the concern:
   a. Ascertain the practice of the concern in establishing its physical inventories. This will include dates of inventory taking, the extent to which year-end inventory is based on perpetual inventory records, whether any inventory is in the possession of consignees, warehousemen, or other outside parties, and the approximate dollar amount of inventory at each location.
   b. Inquire into the procedure for taking physical inventory, and obtain copies of inventory instructions. (This ordinarily should be done in advance of the inventory date.) Determine the extent of the physical inventory. Which inventory classes and amounts are not physically determined? If the concern relies on periodic test checks of quantities, ascertain the frequency and extent of checks, and note the nature and extent of adjustments.
   c. Review the inventory instructions and obtain answers to the following questions:
      (1) Who drafted the inventory instructions?
      (2) What will be the form of instructions and how will they be issued?
      (3) Which persons will be responsible for supervising the physical inventory?
      (4) Will the stock be prearranged and are precautions being taken for clearing work in process to natural cut-off points?
      (5) Is the plant to be shut down during the inventory period?
      (6) Are employees who are responsible for goods also the ones who will count the inventory?
      (7) Will tag numbers or inventory sheets be accounted for before and after distribution and collection?

(8) Are precautions being taken to insure accurate description of units, determination of quantities by count, weight or other measurement, and what are the instructions for identifying obsolete and slow-moving items?

(9) Are there plans for proper receiving and shipping cut-offs?

(10) What are the methods to be followed in transcribing the original counts to sheets or summaries?

(11) Who will make the original extensions and footings, and will they be rechecked?

(12) Who will determine prices in the first instance, and will they be rechecked?

(13) Will inventories be reviewed and approved by department heads or other supervising persons?

(14) Are there plans for determining quantities at outside locations?

2. Procedures with respect to inventory quantities:

a. Inventories physically taken at balance sheet date—auditor present.

Wherever practicable and reasonable, the auditor should be present when physical inventories are taken to observe the methods of inventory taking, and to assure himself that adequate procedures have been adopted and are being followed. In addition to observing procedures, the auditor may expand his examination to include a test of quantities. Where the inventory taking is not adequately planned and controlled, the accountant *must* make extensive tests of quantities.

The auditor should be alert for possible double counts, empty containers, "hollow squares", or items or areas that may not have been counted. Visit all departments to observe procedures. Watch for and ask client personnel taking the inventory about unsalable, damaged, slow-moving, and obsolete items and note for further investigation.

Obtain cut-off information by visiting receiving and shipping areas and acquiring information about several shipments and receipts immediately prior to inventory date. Ascertain that in these areas a clear separation is made between items to be inventoried and those to be excluded from inventory.

b. Inventories physically taken within a reasonable time prior or subsequent to balance sheet date—auditor present.

Determine that the internal controls are adequate to permit satisfactory accounting for the changes in the inventory accounts during the interim period. The same procedure as outlined in paragraph (a) should be followed. In addition, because adequate records must exist to support interim changes, the auditor must make such auditing tests and checks of the inventory accounts and records as are necessary to corroborate the interim changes.

c. Inventories physically taken at or near year-end—auditor not present.

When it is not possible to be present at the time of inventory taking, if the inventory movement is not extensive, it may be possible at a date near year-end to make test counts of the larger items and reconcile the counts to the year-end inventory. Where well-kept and controlled perpetual inventory records are available, the auditor should make tests of inventory quantities at interim dates selected by him. In addition, inventory procedures followed by the concern must be investigated by inquiring of persons actually making the counts, by reviewing forms and records of the counts, and by conducting such further investigation as may be appropriate. Further, the auditor should make such auditing tests, and checks of the inventory accounts and records, as are necessary to satisfy himself as to the dependability of the perpetual inventory records.

d. Inventories physically taken, but not at or near the balance sheet date.

If complete physical inventory is taken at a date not coincident with the balance sheet date or near such date, the auditor should be present when physical inventories are taken to observe the methods of inventory taking, and to assure himself that adequate procedures have been adopted and followed as in (a). When it is not possible to be present at the time of inventory taking, the procedures in (c) should be followed. Further, the auditor should make such auditing tests and checks of the inventory accounts and records as are necessary to satisfy himself as to the dependability of the perpetual inventory records. Test the listing of the inventory from the perpetual records to the final inventory sheets. If it is found that the perpetual inventory records are not well kept, consideration should be given to the necessity of having a physical inventory taken at or close to the balance sheet date.

e. No complete physical inventories taken as of any date, but individual items are counted from time to time (at least once a year) to verify the book records.

The auditor shall make satisfactory test checks and examinations to assure himself that adequate procedures have been adopted and followed. When a portion of the test checks are made he shall be present to observe the methods of inventory taking and to assure himself that adequate procedures have been followed. When it is not possible to be present when physical tests are made by the concern, the accountant shall make tests of quantities at any selected date.

In addition to observing procedures, the auditor may expand his examination to include a test of quantities as of any selected date. The auditor shall test the listing of the inventory from the perpetual records to the final inventory sheets and review client counts in support of quantity adjustments and review large differences. Where the auditor finds that important differences exist or that satisfactory inventory checks have not been made during the period, consideration should be given to the necessity of a complete physical inventory.

f. If inventories are distributed in a number of locations, test observance of procedures (and counts, if made) should be made at representative locations, giving due consideration to the nature and size of the inventory at each location and its relative importance.

3. If any significant amount of inventory is in the possession of consignees, warehousemen or other outside parties, confirm by test communication. If material in relation to company's current assets or total assets, review the company's control procedures, determine reputation and financial standing of custodian and consider observation of physical counts.

► NOTE: Where the amount with any one party is significant, supplemental inquiry should be made as to the existence and financial responsibility of the holder through local banks, Dun & Bradstreet reports, etc.

4. Trace test counts made at inventory taking into final inventory. Review final inventory to identify items of significant value not counted, and consider the desirability of accounting for the existence of some of these items.

Test the transcribing of client's original counts to the inventory sheets or summarize and test conversions such as units into weights, weights into units, pounds into gallons, etc.

5. Check data obtained at the time of physical inventory relating to receiving and shipping cut-offs. Test purchase and receiving records and sales and shipping records to determine that (a) all materials received have been inventoried, (b) liabilities have been recorded for all materials and costs included in the inventories, (c) liabilities have not been recorded for items not inventoried, (d) accounts receivable have been charged for all products shipped and all products shipped have been excluded from inventory and (e) accounts receivable have not been charged for products included in inventory. Attention should be directed to inventory in transit to see that these items are properly recorded in the accounts.

6. Make tests of computations of inventory; e.g., extensions, footings, recapitulations, etc.

7. Inventory pricing basis:

a. Ascertain the method of pricing—lower of cost or market, retail method, etc. Where prices are based on cost, ascertain whether this is: average; first-in, first-out; last-in, first-out; standard; specific lot; or other basis of determination. Investigate the reliability of costs.

b. Make test checks of prices used by referring to cost records, purchase invoices, market quotations, commitments, and selling prices.

c. If average cost is used, ascertain what method was employed and over what period.
d. If standard costs are used, determine whether such costs differ materially from actual costs. Investigate variance accounts and include comments in working papers as to their effect on inventory prices. Ascertain policy and practice as to changes in standards. If changes occurred during period, investigate effect on inventory pricing.
e. Review overhead rates to determine whether they are reasonable. This would include method of computation, comparison with actual for current and prior years, and inquiry into nature of items included therein.
f. Ascertain whether or not all classes of inventory have been subjected to replacement market price tests.
g. See if inventory has been valued on basis consistent with that of preceding period. If not, get full data on nature and effect of inconsistency.
h. See if trade discounts, special rebates, and similar price reductions have been eliminated.
i. Investigate margin of selling prices over inventory prices.

8. Make an inquiry regarding existence of damaged, slow-moving, overstocked, out-of-style, and obsolete inventories and of commitments for additional quantities of similar merchandise. Determine to what extent prices used on these items allow for such factors. Where possible, make comparison with recent sales prices.

9. Prepare a summary of inventories by locations and compare with the preceding year's summary. Investigate any unusual variations. Show separately amounts for supplies and repair parts.

10. On first examinations, prepare summaries of inventories at beginning of period, investigate cut-off of purchases and sales to that date, and make tests of computations and basis of pricing.

11. If the company prepares dollar-valued inventories from perpetual records, compare these book inventories with physical inventories at closing date, and investigate substantial differences.

12. Prepare a schedule showing gross profit realized on sales in comparison with preceding year results. Where practical, prepare it by departments, products or other natural divisions. Also prepare schedules showing turn-over of inventory.

13. Determine how intercompany and interplant profits have been accounted for.

14. Summarize adjustments between book and physical inventories and obtain explanations of significant adjustments. Compare adjustments with those of the preceding year.

15. If it is customary to receive deliveries under purchase contracts not promptly billed, request confirmation of the quantities delivered by communication with the vendor, and see that the proper liability was recorded.

16. If there is contract work in progress, investigate to determine whether or not a loss on the completed contract is indicated.

17. See that no merchandise consigned to the company is included in inventory. Consider correspondence with vendors who customarily consign goods to the company, even though the books may show no balance.

18. Ascertain whether any part of the inventory has been pledged to secure indebtedness of the company.

19. Determine whether insurance is carried with respect to inventory wherever located.

20. If statistics are available, it is desirable to make a general reconciliation of quantities of principal products sold with goods produced and purchased during the period, or to make such other overall quantity comparisons as may be feasible.

Trade Accounts Payable:

1. Prepare trial balance or check the company's trial balance of accounts payable, separating trade accounts payable, accounts with affiliates, amounts due to officers, directors or stockholders, etc. Also observe if discounts are usually taken and if there are past due amounts of importance. Separate debit balances, investigating to determine their collectibility and whether they include temporary returns of goods over the year-end, and consider requesting confirmation.

2. Compare a sufficient number of available statements from creditors with accounts payable to indicate generally the correctness of such individual accounts. When statements from principal suppliers or creditors are not available, they should be requested.

3. Obtain confirmation from creditor if any important account appears to be improperly stated. Consider communication if account is in dispute. In some instances, the condition of the records or other reasons may make extensive communication with recorded or possible unrecorded creditors advisable.

4. Review receiving records, vouchers, journal entries, and cash records subsequent to date of balance sheet to determine whether or not all significant trade accounts payable (such as liabilities for materials in transit, uncompleted plant additions under contract, and various expense items, not definitely known until some time after the balance sheet date) have been included.

5. Review accrued or unpaid payrolls, officers' salaries, accrued taxes (Federal, state, and local), payroll taxes, insurance, commissions, interest, royalties, rentals, etc.

Appendix A

Internal Control Questionnaire

CASH

	Answer	
	Yes	*No*
CASH RECEIPTS		
1. Is all incoming mail that is addressed to the company opened and distributed by someone other than the cashier for independent verification of keeper?	___	___
2. a. Is a record of the money and checks received prepared by the person opening the mail?	___	___
b. If so, is this record given to someone other than the cashier for independent verification of the amount received?	___	___
c. Is this record compared with the cash receipts book regularly?	___	___
3. Are the duties of the person who keeps the cash receipts records limited to the keeping of such records?	___	___
4. Are cash receipts entered and deposited intact daily?	___	___
5. Are bank deposits prepared and made by someone other than the cash receipts or accounts receivable bookkeepers?	___	___
a. Who makes such deposits? (Position)		
6. Are duplicate receipted deposit slips received from the bank and checked by someone other than the employee making up the deposit?	___	___
7. Are receipts given for over-the-counter collections?	___	___
a. If such receipts are given, are they prenumbered and/or accounted for?	___	___
b. Are duplicates retained?	___	___
8. Do customers remit directly to the company rather than to salesmen, deliverymen, etc.?	___	___
9. Are cash receipts posted to accounts receivable records from collection advices or data other than the cash item itself?	___	___

	Answer Yes	Answer No
10. Are collections of branch and sales offices deposited in special bank accounts?	____	____
a. If so, are there restrictions on the withdrawal of such funds?	____	____
11. Does someone other than the cashier or cash receipts or accounts receivable bookkeepers review or approve entries for customers' discounts or allowances, so as to minimize the possibility of misappropriation of cash through recording of fictitious discounts or allowances?	____	____
12. Are the totals of daily cash receipts proved with account receivable controls?	____	____
a. If so, is the procedure done by someone not associated with the recording of cash receipts or accounts receivable records?	____	____
13. On a separate sheet describe the procedures and control of the receipts, if any, from the following sources:		
a. C.O.D. sales.		
b. Cash sales.		
c. Sales of scrap.		
d. Sales of equipment.		
e: Interest and dividends from securities.		
f. Rentals.		
g. Bad debt recoveries.		
h. Other sources.		
14. Is the cashier precluded from access to the general and subsidiary ledgers?	____	____

Cash Disbursements

	Yes	No
1. Is the person who keeps the voucher register or accounts payable records limited to such duties?	____	____
2. Are vendors' invoices audited in the accounting department?	____	____
3. Does the audit of vendors' invoices include check of:		
a. Quantities to purchase orders and receiving reports?	____	____
b. Terms and prices to purchase orders?	____	____
c. Extensions and footings?	____	____
d. Account distribution?	____	____

	Answer	
	Yes	*No*
4. Is there a procedure to insure prompt recording of invoices received? (Describe)	____	____
5. Are details of accounts payable or vouchers payable balanced monthly with general ledger controls?	____	____
6. Are debit balances reviewed periodically?	____	____
a. What disposition is usually made of such debit balances?		
b. Who authorizes adjustment of debit balances, or the writing-off of such balances?		
7. Are supporting data attached to and filed with vouchers?	____	____
8. Are vouchers approved for payment?	____	____
a. By whom? (Position)		
9. Are the monthly statements received from creditors independently checked to the accounts payable records?	____	____
a. By Whom? (Position)		
10. Is the person who keeps the cash disbursements records limited to that duty?	____	____
11. Are prenumbered checks used?	____	____
12. Do checks require more than one signature?	____	____
13. If single signature, is there a limitation on the amount for which a check may be drawn?	____	____
a. What is such amount?		
14. Are supporting invoices or other data presented to officials for inspection simultaneously with the checks for signature?	____	____
15. Do the client's procedures prohibit anyone connected with cash receipts or disbursements or accounts payable from having access to the checks after they are signed?	____	____
16. Are supporting data controlled and cancelled so as to minimize possibility of improper or duplicate payment?	____	____
17. Are there procedures that obviate the necessity of officials signing blank checks for use during their absence?	____	____
18. Is there proper approval of entries for disposition of N. S. F. checks or other bank charges?	____	____
19. Does the client policy prohibit disbursement directly from cash receipts?	____	____

	Answer	
	Yes	*No*
20. Is the use of "exchange checks" and/or accommodation checks prohibited?	____	____
21. Are check protectors used?	____	____
22. Are spoiled and voided checks mutilated so as to prevent reuse?	____	____
23. Is the supply of unused checks controlled? (Describe)	____	____
24. Is it the client's policy not to issue checks payable to bearer or cash?	____	____
25. Are check signing machines used?	____	____
26. If so, are the machine and signature plates kept under effective control? (Describe)	____	____
27. Are daily totals of disbursements to vendors proved with account payable controls? By whom? (Position)	____	____

Reconciliation of Bank Accounts

	Yes	No
1. Are bank accounts reconciled promptly upon receipt of bank statements?	____	____
2. Who opens bank statements? (Position)		
3. Are bank accounts reconciled by employees who do not prepare or approve checks, do not have access to ledgers, or do not originate cash entries?	____	____
4. Are reconciliations approved by an accounting official of the Company? By whom? (Position)	____	____
5. Does the reconciliation procedure include:		
a. Comparison of cancelled checks with cash disbursements records as to number, date, payee, and amount?	____	____
b. Examination of spoiled and voided checks?	____	____
c. Accounting for numerical sequence of checks?	____	____
d. Comparison with bank statements of dates and amounts of daily deposits as shown by the cash receipts records?	____	____
e. Tracing of transfers between banks, bank accounts, branches, etc.?	____	____

Petty Cash

	Yes	No
1. Is petty cash maintained on an imprest fund basis?	____	____

	Answer	
	Yes	*No*
2. Are payments evidenced by receipts prepared in ink?	____	____
3. Are such receipts cancelled upon reimbursement so as to minimize possibility of reuse?	____	____
4. Are disbursements approved?	____	____
5. If personal checks are cashed from the petty cash fund, is approval required?	____	____
6. Is each fund handled by only one person?	____	____
7. Is such person directly responsible for such fund?	____	____
8. Are the custodians of the petty cash funds divorced from other duties in connection with cash receipts or disbursements?	____	____
9. Are reimbursement checks made payable to the fund custodian?	____	____
10. Is a postage meter machine used?	____	____

PURCHASING AND RECEIVING

1. Is there a purchasing department, or is the purchasing function under the direction of one person?	____	____
2. If so, is it entirely independent of:		
a. The accounting department?	____	____
b. The receiving and shipping department?	____	____
3. Are purchase orders:		
a. Prepared for all purchases of materials, goods, and services not under contract?	____	____
b. Noted for receipt of materials, goods, or services?	____	____
c. Attached to or cross referenced to invoices?	____	____
4. Are purchase order forms prenumbered?	____	____
5. Do purchase orders show terms and prices?	____	____
6. Are vendors' invoices for materials or goods shipped directly to customers by suppliers matched with sales invoices to insure billing to customers?	____	____
7. Are there procedures in effect to assure proper credit for materials or goods returned to vendors?	____	____
8. If employee accommodation purchases are made, are the same procedures followed as for regular purchases?	____	____
9. Are receiving reports prepared by the receiving department?	____	____
a. Are such reports prenumbered?	____	____

	Answer	
	Yes	*No*
10. Are copies of receiving reports:		
a. Filed permanently in the receiving department?	____	____
b. Furnished to the accounting department?	____	____
c. Furnished to the purchasing department?	____	____
11. Does the receiving department deliver, or supervise the delivery of, each item received to the proper stores or department location?	____	____
12. Is the receiving department area physically located separately from the shipping department?	____	____
13. Are provisions made for inspection or test as to specifications and quality of goods received?	____	____
14. Are persons connected with receipt of materials and the keeping of receiving records denied authority to initiate purchases or to approve invoices?	____	____
15. Does the receiving department operate independently of the shipping department?	____	____
16. Is the accounting department notified promptly of purchased goods returned to the vendor?	____	____

INVENTORIES

1. On a separate sheet describe the following:
   a. Procedures for recording in subsidiary records (receiving, perpetual inventory, etc.) and general ledger materials received from suppliers, including the timely reporting thereof.
   b. Existing safeguards to prevent improper removal of materials and goods from storeroom.
   c. Cycle or other interim inventory programs in effect in storerooms, including procedures followed for the reporting and recording of differences in quantities disclosed thereby.
   d. Procedures followed in checking inventory for overstocked and slow moving items.
   e. Methods of handling and reporting scrap sales.
   f. Safeguards employed as to materials returned to suppliers, to insure proper credit from the vendor.
2. On a separate sheet describe the record-keeping for the following:
   a. Work in process.
   b. Movement of products from work in process to storerooms.

	Answer	
	Yes	*No*
c. Release of products for shipment to customers.		
d. Employees' time in manufacturing departments.		
e. Defective work.		
f. Scrap.		
g. Long standing uncompleted orders on file.		
3. State the method of costing used (e.g., standard costs, job order costs, process costs, etc.).		
4. If standard costs are used, how frequently are standards revised?		
5. Are significant variances from standards investigated as to cause?	____	____
6. What is the accounting disposition for variances?		
7. Are production reports reconciled with materials used?	____	____
8. Are production records kept on a departmental basis?	____	____
9. With respect to perpetual inventory records:		
a. Are they maintained for:		
(1) Raw materials?	____	____
(2) Supplies and repair parts?	____	____
(3) Work in process?	____	____
(4) Finished products?	____	____
b. Do they show prices as well as quantities?	____	____
c. Are they periodically balanced against accounting controls?	____	____
d. Are they adjusted to continuous or periodic physical counts?	____	____
e. If so, who authorizes such adjustments? (Position)		
10. What procedures and controls are there for items:		
a. Out on consignment to others?		
b. Stored in public warehouses?		
c. Held on consignment from others?		
d. Shipped directly to customers by vendors?		
e. Being fabricated by, or in custody of subcontractors?		
f. Written off (or down) as obsolete, defective, etc.?		
11. With respect to physical inventories:		
a. How frequently, and when, are complete physical counts made?		

	Answer	
	Yes	*No*
b. Are adequate written instructions issued therefor?	____	____
c. Are prenumbered inventory tickets used and accounted for?	____	____
d. Are recounts made, at least where variations from perpetual records are significant?	____	____
e. Are counts made by employees other than those responsible for the custody of the particular item?	____	____
f. Is provision made for proper cut-off on production, receipts, and shipments during the count?	____	____
g. Are significant overages and shortages carefully investigated?	____	____
h. Do the procedures for listing, pricing, and computing the detailed inventories provide for sufficient review and recheck to insure accuracy?	____	____

12. Planning and scheduling:
    Outline briefly the company's practices and their effectiveness in controlling inventories.
13. Commitments:
    Outline briefly the company's practices and their effectiveness in controlling inventory commitments.

SALES, SHIPPING, AND ACCOUNTS RECEIVABLE

Sales and Shipping

1. Are sales orders controlled numerically?	____	____
2. Are sales invoices prenumbered?	____	____
3. Are sales invoices checked:	____	____
a. As to quantities, prices, extensions and footings?	____	____
b. Against customers orders, shipping advices, etc?	____	____
c. As to credit terms?	____	____
4. Are records of sales, returns, and allowances summarized and reported to the accounting department daily?	____	____
5. Do credit memos for returned sales, price adjustments and other allowances require executive approval?	____	____

	Answer	
	Yes	*No*
6. Are storerooms non-accessible to employees of the shipping department?	____	____
7. Is there a double check on quantities shipped?	____	____
8. Is billing done by employees who have no connection with cash, shipping, or accounts receivable?	____	____
9. Are the following classes of sales accounted for in substantially the same manner as regular credit sales of merchandise:		
a. Sales to employees?	____	____
b. C.O.D. sales?	____	____
c. Sales of property and equipment?	____	____
d. Cash sales of merchandise?	____	____
e. Scrap and waste?	____	____

10. On a separate sheet describe the procedures followed from the receipt of the sales order to shipment and billing, including the following:
    a. How sales originate and how sales orders are controlled.
    b. How sales orders are checked or approved for prices and terms.
    c. When are orders approved for credit and by whom? Is this person independent of the sales department?
    d. Procedures as to the release for shipment of goods from storerooms, authorization, and timely reporting thereof. Are prenumbered shipping advices prepared?
    e. Procedures followed with respect to cash sales, miscellaneous sales, and sales to employees.
    f. Safeguards employed as to shipments to insure billing to customers.
    g. How shipping charges (e.g., freight, express, etc.) are handled and approved.

Accounts Receivable

	Yes	No
1. Are the duties of the employees who maintain the accounts receivable divorced from any other duties?	____	____
2. Are independent control accounts maintained outside of the accounts receivable section?	____	____

	Answer Yes	No
3. Are such control accounts based on control figures (billings, collections, etc.) obtained directly from original sources?	____	____
4. Are the accounts receivable details balanced regularly against the independent controls?	____	____
5. Are the detailed trial balances and agings checked periodically by someone other than the employees who maintain the ledgers?	____	____
6. Are monthly statements sent to all customers?	____	____
If not, to what extent are they mailed?		
7. Are statements prepared by someone other than the accounts receivable bookeeper?	____	____
8. Are statements mailed to customers by someone who has no access to cash and who is independent of the accounts receivable bookkeepers and the billing clerks?	____	____
9. Insert the position of the person who performs the following duties:		
a. Passes upon extension of credit and approves credit terms.		
b. Follows up the collection of receivables.		
c. Follows up exceptions reported by customers.		
d. Authorizes charge-off of uncollectible receivables.		
e. Maintains control over uncollectible receivables after they have been charged-off.		
10. Are credit memos for returns, allowances, etc. controlled by prenumbered forms and/or are they accounted for?	____	____
11. Are credit memos authorized or approved by employees or executives who have no access to cash?	____	____
12. Are credit memos supported, in the case of returned goods, by signed receiving tickets?	____	____

NOTES RECEIVABLE

	Yes	No
1. Are acceptances of notes and renewals properly approved or authorized by a responsible official?	____	____
By whom? (Position)		
2. Are notes on hand regularly balanced with controlling account?	____	____
3. Who has possession and control of negotiable paper and collateral? (Position)		

	Answer	
	Yes	*No*
4. Is there a procedure to ascertain that interest income is received when due?	____	____

SECURITY INVESTMENTS

	Yes	No
1. Are securities kept in a safe deposit box or with an outside custodian?	____	____
If not, describe.		
2. If securities are kept in a safe deposit box, is dual control maintained?	____	____
Is a record maintained of visits to the safe deposit vault?	____	____
3. Are securities in the name of the client?	____	____
4. Are purchases and sales of securities authorized or approved by the Board of Directors?	____	____
An officer?	____	____
5. Is a record of securities maintained that shows essential information such as title, principal amount or number of shares, certificate numbers, date acquired, cost, etc?	____	____
6. Is there a procedure to ascertain that all dividend and interest income is received when due?	____	____
7. Are security investments which have been written off or fully reserved against followed up as to possible realization?	____	____

PROPERTIES AND PATENTS

	Yes	No
1. Are major capital additions authorized by the Board of Directors?	____	____
2. Are actual expenditures checked against authorized expenditures?	____	____
3. Are retirements and sales authorized by a responsible official?	____	____
By whom? (Position)		
4. Describe the procedures followed to ascertain that all dispositions of property are properly recorded.		
5. Does the client follow the same accounting policy with respect to both major and minor capital expenditures?	____	____
Is there a sound policy in force for the differentiation between capital additions and maintenance and repairs? Explain.	____	____

	Answer	
	Yes	*No*
6. Are rates of depreciation and amortization approved by a responsible official?	____	____
By whom? (Position)		
7. Are detailed asset records maintained?	____	____
a. Are such records balanced periodically with general ledger control accounts?	____	____
8. Are major repairs approved by the Board of Directors or by a responsible official?	____	____
(If other than by the Board of Directors, indicate position.)		
9. Is the company assured that the patents arising from its research expenditures are issued in its name and not in the name of some individual?	____	____

PAYROLLS

	Yes	*No*
1. Who authorizes employment? (Position)		
2. Who authorizes initial rates of pay? (Position)		
3. Who authorizes subsequent changes in rates of pay? (Position)		
4. How are pay rates determined (e.g., by union contract, published company policy, merit of each individual case, etc)?		
5. Do personnel records show rates of pay?	____	____
6. Is a form of original time record maintained?	____	____
a. Indicate type used (clock cards, job cards, piecework tickets, time cards, attendance records, etc.).		
7. Who prepares such time records? (Position)		
8. Who prepares the payrolls? (Position)		
9. Does preparation of payroll include		
a. Check of original time records?	____	____
b. Check against employment and rate cards?	____	____
c. Check against production records, if pay is on a piecework basis?	____	____
10. Describe the methods of computing and recording overtime payments.		
11. Are the payroll totals checked against labor distribution totals independently compiled in other departments from the original time records?	____	____
12. Is an internal audit made of the payrolls?	____	____
(Describe)		
13. What approvals are required on the payrolls and		

	Answer Yes	No
supporting documents for drawing net amount of payroll on general cash funds?		
14. Is payment made by check?	____	____
15. Who prepares the checks? (Position)		
16. Who signs payroll checks? (Position)		
17. Is the person who signs the payroll checks divorced from other duties in connection with the preparation of payroll checks?	____	____
18. How are checks delivered to the employees?		
19. If payrolls are paid in cash, describe the procedures.		
20. Are the payroll bank accounts reconciled by employees who have no other functions with respect to the payrolls?	____	____
21. Is control maintained over unclaimed checks or pay envelopes? (Describe)	____	____
22. If pay advances are made to employees, are they properly approved and controlled? (Describe)	____	____
23. Are there safeguards against continuation on payrolls of names of individuals discharged or otherwise not entitled to pay?	____	____
24. Are commissions paid to salesmen controlled by tie-in with total unit or dollar sales?	____	____

RELATED PARTY TRANSACTIONS

	Yes	No
1. Does the company have procedures for identifying and properly accounting for related party transactions? Explain in a separate memorandum.	____	____
2. Does the company have procedures that prohibit directors or management from exercising significant influence over related party transactions? Explain in a separate memorandum.	____	____

Appendix B

Auditing a Client in an Unfamiliar Industry

An auditor should welcome the chance to venture into unfamiliar territory, since this step will no doubt help maintain his professional growth and expand his practice. At the same time, however, the auditor should recognize that in order to properly uphold his professional standards and be of maximum service to a new client in an industry that is unfamiliar to him, he must quickly become familiar with the special accounting, business, and tax problems of the industry. And he must do this before beginning the audit.

► EXAMPLE: An auditor beginning his first engagement in the field of security and commodity brokerage must be prepared to cope with many special problems and unfamiliar situations that will confront him during the audit. First of all, there are regulations and requirements of the Securities and Exchange Commission, the Commodity Futures Trading Commission, state regulatory bodies, and the particular exchange of which the broker may be a member. Then there are the special planning and administrative problems, arising from such factors as the liquid nature of brokers' assets, making it desirable to audit all assets at the same time so that there is no chance of substitution, and the fact that active securities must be counted on the opening day of the audit and checked out to the stock record so that the securities can be released for deliveries on the following business day. Additionally, for the first time, the auditor may be faced with such unfamiliar records as the Blotter, the Stock Record, and Margin Record, and such unfamiliar accounts as Fail to Receive, Fail to Deliver, Deposits with Clearing Corporations—Stock Borrowed, and Stock Loaned. In addition, these enterprises usually maintain a sophisticated EDP system, either in-house or through a service bureau, the programs of which are tailored to their needs and the nature of the business. Competence to evaluate the built-in controls over the vast number of transactions processed by the system is most important.

Many resources are available to help in meeting these problems. Through intelligent use of these resources, it is possible to become fairly well acquainted with the particular qualities and problems of an industry even before developing actual experience with clients in that industry.

► WARNING: Before embarking on a research program on behalf of a new client in a new industry, it is well to weigh carefully the time and energy that will be required. Unless there is a prospect of obtaining additional clients in the same industry, the additional fees from one engagement may not warrant the investment in learning time.

Accounting libraries. Since an accounting library is most likely to contain the information needed, the best and probably the easiest way to proceed is to obtain access to a good accounting library. Most of the professional accounting associations maintain excellent libraries for the use of their members and these offer probably the quickest way to obtain information about any accounting, auditing, or tax problems. Public libraries run a poor second in quantity and currency of books stocked in these areas.

Although the number of new pronouncements by the AICPA, SEC, CASB, and the FASB over the past few years has increased, much of the material issued in prior years remains useful. *The Accountants' Index,* compiled annually by the American Institute of Certified Public Accountants, is a useful time-saver to use in locating this material. It lists all of the books, articles and pamphlets published during the year that deal with accounting, auditing and tax matters, including publications from all English speaking countries. The index contains a listing by author, title, and subject matter.

Books available. The *Encyclopedia of Accounting Systems* (Revised and enlarged), Jerome K. Pescow, General Editor, is a three-volume set that describes and illustrates accounting systems for 72 diversified industries. This set contains an explanation of any special characteristics of the industry that affect the accounting system, as well as the usual information about charts of accounts, books of original entry, cost systems, payroll systems, reports to management, peculiarities of procedures, increased and more sophisticated use of data processing and computer systems, etc. *The Portfolio of Accounting Systems for Small and Medium-Sized Businesses,* Marjorie D. James, Editor, explains the unusual features of the businesses and procedures unique to them, and the resolution of problems inherent in them. The publication covers seventy businesses ranging from auction galleries and beauty shops to taxicab services and veterinarians. *The Handbook of Accounting Methods,* J. K. Lasser, Editor, also offers information about accounting practices in selected industries.

If the industry that an auditor wants to become familiar with is included in books such as these, he can take a long step towards learning about this industry by acquiring one of these books. Of course, more than a mere reading of the text is required. Close study is required to gain full insight into the accounting system and ramifications of industry practices that are offered in such books.

If the unfamiliar industry happens to be covered in one of the seventeen Industry Audit Guides published by the American Institute of CPA's, you are fortunate in that an entire audit in considerable detail is available for study.

The guides cover not only the basic auditing procedures that should be employed in examining the accounts of a business in that industry, but also provide considerable insight into the peculiarities and nuances of that industry; the following is a list of the guides:

1. Audits of Government Contractors
2. Audits of Voluntary Health & Welfare Organizations

3. Audits of State and Local Governmental Units, includes Statement of Position—Accrual of Revenues and Expenditures by State and Local Governmental Units.
4. Audits of Service-Center-Produced Records
5. Audits of Investment Companies
6. Audits of Finance Companies
7. Audits of Colleges and Universities
8. Audits of Stock Life Insurance Companies
9. Audits of Savings and Loan Associations
10. Hospital Audit Guide
11. Audits of Employee Health & Welfare Benefit Funds
12. Medicare Audit Guide
13. Audits of Banks
14. Audits of Personal Financial Statements
15. Audits of Brokers and Dealers in Securities
16. Audits of Fire & Casualty Insurance Companies, includes Statement of Position—Revision of Form of Auditor's Report (Audits of Fire and Casualty Insurance Companies)
17. Audits of Construction Contractors

While neither the accounting systems nor the auditing procedures depicted in these guides may be directly transferable to a new client's company, most of the practices, systems, and auditing procedures will be applicable.

Among other publications of the Institute are four Industry Accounting Guides. While auditing procedures are not covered, these guides deal with the accounting for franchise fee revenue, retail land sales, motion picture films, and profit recognition on sales of real estate.

The Institute periodically publishes a listing of all of its publications currently in use, and is an excellent place to start in finding information about a particular industry or problem.

Many books are available that describe accounting problems, systems, and other pertinent information of one particular industry. If any such books have been written about the new client's industry, a wealth of all kinds of pertinent information can be obtained from them. The following are examples of such accounting studies in depth:

AUTHOR	TITLE
National Health Council, Inc.	*Standards of Accounting and Financial Reporting for Voluntary Health and Welfare Organizations.* (Revised 1974)
Nelson & Turk	*Financial Management for the Arts: A Guidebook for Arts Organizations*
Scheps & Davidson	*Accounting for Colleges and Universities*
Gross	*Financial and Accounting Guide for Nonprofit Organizations*
Lynn and Freeman	*Fund Accounting Theory and Practice*

Professional magazines. If no book can be found that contains information about the new client's industry, another excellent source is still available—current or back issues of professional magazines. These magazines contain innumerable accounting and auditing studies of different industries, as well as many articles dealing with limited aspects of an accounting or auditing situation. The articles dealing with limited aspects generally offer a great deal of information in difficult areas, as it is the problem areas that tend to be selected as areas for study and writing.

The following professional magazines contain industry write-ups of the kind that is most apt to benefit an auditor in an industry that is new to him:

1. The Journal of Accountancy.
2. Management Accounting.
3. Publications of the various state C.P.A. societies.

Publications of the larger auditing firms, sometimes obtainable at accounting libraries, also may contain articles about specific industries. See Chapter 35, *Obtaining New Business,* for a more complete list of professional organizations and their publication.

Trade associations. Many trade associations are interested in the accounting, auditing, and tax problems of their members. Some associations have prepared manuals of recommended cost systems, charts of accounts, and the like for the use of their members. Some associations compile industry averages of costs, expenses, ratios, etc. Whether or not a new client is a member of such a trade association, contacting the association may prove valuable. Even if the particular association has no accounting material of any kind, it may know of a book relating to its industry. The names and addresses of all trade associations in the United States can be obtained from the *Encyclopedia of Associations,* published by the Gale Research Corp., Detroit, Michigan.

Government publications. Another source of information about the industry in which you will be a "new" auditor are the publications of the United States Government Printing Office, sold by the Superintendent of Documents, Washington, D. C. Among the publications that may be of interest to an auditor are bulletins describing the outlook for an entire industry; financial, accounting, or economic studies; and analyses of product standards and grading. If the new client is in a regulated industry, publications of prescribed charts of accounts and recommended accounting procedures will surely be available. If there is any degree of regulation in the industry, an auditor should prepare himself with a complete knowledge of the account classifications and other requirements in order to do a satisfactory auditing job. These regulatory requirements are usually obtained by writing directly to the regulating agency.

Equipment manufacturers. Major equipment manufacturers provide consultant liaison services to auditing firms which include distribution of equipment and software manuals, information releases on new products and services, and industry oriented announcements of software developed by the manufacturers' customers. In particular, IBM and Burroughs have a well developed, responsive liaison program, including periodicals aimed directly at the auditing community. IBM's numerous "Application Briefs" provide useful information about industry problems and techniques.

Other companies in the same industry. Unless the new client is alone in his field, and this would be quite rare, there are certain to be other companies with problems similar to his. Stockholder reports and the Annual Report on Form 10K filed with the Securities and Exchange Commission of such publicly-owned companies may well be worth studying. If an auditor is acquainted with an employee in one of these other companies, or has a professional colleague with a client in the same industry, such sources may prove invaluable. Personal contacts such as these may furnish more useful information in an hour or two of conversation than any other means in a much larger amount of time.

Personal sources. Frequently, when an auditor is obtaining a new client by the recommendation of a mutual friend, that person will be a prime source of information about the company and its accounting and auditing requirements. He may be in a position either to obtain previous financial statements, or to introduce the auditor to an accounting officer who can give him information. If the company uses any organizational charts, accounting manuals, or policy or procedural manuals of any type, such materials are required reading before starting the audit. In fact, almost any kind of company publication is bound to have useful information in it.

► NOTE: The practicing accountant is faced with the necessity of acquiring information about the company for his first meeting with his client-to-be as well as for the audit. The more information you have about a prospective client's business, the more intelligently you can speak with him Bear in mind that although we are discussing methods of acquiring knowledge about auditing an unfamiliar industry, these same methods can be used to obtain information for your first meeting with the prospective client.

More suggestions. If the new client is large enough to be listed on one of the stock exchanges, a great deal of information may be obtained from previous years' reports submitted to meet the exchange's listing requirements. As a further source, Dun & Bradstreet, Inc. offers its subscribers full analyses of any information about a business that affects its credit rating.

Further steps that an auditor might take preliminary to the audit itself include acquiring some knowledge of the overall field in which his client is operating. He may want to find out, for example, if his client's industry is dependent on the well-being of any other industry, what economic function is filled by the industry, and how vulnerable it is to the ups and downs of the economic cycle.

In researching the general economic setting of the industry, an indispensable tool is any trade journal or magazine for that industry. Even if a particular trade magazine is very limited in scope, it will at least enable an auditor to become familiar with any special terminology used in that field. Some trade magazines, of course, offer a great deal more than others and are, in fact, an education in themselves about such aspects of the industry as accounting, taxes, manufacturing processes, selling problems, and the like.

It is possible that the new client is in an industry where a large amount of specialized technical knowledge is required. The auditor may feel that he does not have all of the qualifications to meet the specialized requirements of the engagement, and the necessary research is too arduous for him to undertake. In this case, he should consider the possibility of engaging another accountant who is especially qualified in this field to act in an advisory capacity. With this type of assistant on the first audit, the auditor may be able to proceed with confidence and develop the specialized know-how to undertake subsequent audits on his own.

Tax research. Along about this time, it might very well be opportune to start research into tax problems or at least see if any is required. Not all industries have special tax situations but some do—and just as the new client's industry is unfamiliar, so may be these tax situations. In fact, just to mention the name of certain fields immediately brings to mind certain tax problem areas, such as:

Construction—Completed-contracts or percentage-of-completion basis for unfinished contracts.

Oil, gas and mining—Estimates of depletion.

Retailing—Inventory valuation and local taxes.

Tax problem areas in other fields may be less well known, but they nevertheless exist. Research into the general principles of the particular tax area prepares the auditor to evaluate the practical handling of tax situations that he will see in the course of his audit, and to spot any poor or overlooked elections or other errors in the tax returns of his client.

Summary. The auditor faced with the problem of a new client in an unfamiliar industry can use this appendix to best advantage by regarding it as a checklist of resources available to him.

This checklist has not included textbooks or tax services because these resources are familiar to auditors. They would undoubtedly be one of the first sources referred to if the kind of information sought could be obtained from them. None of the other information sources that have been mentioned is meant to be used exclusively or is to be preferred over another source. Obviously, a range of alternatives has been presented, and one takes from among them what can be most easily obtained and is most useful.

The Encyclopedia of Accounting Systems has been mentioned as containing write-ups of the accounting systems of 72 industries. The following is a list of the industries contained in each volume of this three-volume set:

VOLUME I

1. Advertising Agencies and Public Relations Firms.
2. Airports.
3. Architects and Engineers.
4. Automobile Repair Shops.
5. Bakeries.
6. Building Contractors.
7. Carbonated Beverage Producers.
8. Cement Producers.
9. Chemicals, Synthetics and Dyes Manufacturers.
10. Children's Dress Manufacturing.
11. Churches.
12. Clubs.
13. Commercial Banks.
14. Commercial Finance Companies.
15. Cotton Goods Converters.
16. Cotton and Synthetic Weaving Mills.
17. Dairy Plants.
18. Dentists.
19. Department Stores.
20. Drug Manufacturing.
21. Electric, Gas and Water Utilities.

VOLUME II

22. Electronic Appliance Manufacturers.
23. Estates and Trusts—Corporate Fiduciary.
24. Estates and Trusts—Individual Fiduciary.
25. Farms and Ranches.
26. Flour Milling.
27. Food Canning and Freezing.
28. Food Stores—Chain.
29. Funeral Directing.
30. Furniture Stores.
31. Health Associations.
32. Hosiery Manufacturing.
33. Hospitals.
34. Hotels.
35. Independent Retail Specialty Stores.
36. Insurance Brokers and Agents.
37. Investment Companies and Clubs.
38. Knitted Fabrics Manufacturing.
39. Labor Unions.
40. Laundries and Dry Cleaners.
41. Lawyers.
42. Limited-Price Variety Stores.
43. Logging and Lumber Manufacturing.
44. Lumber and Building Material Suppliers.
45. Machine Shops.
46. Magazine Publishing.
47. Manufacturer's Contracting Distributors.

VOLUME III

48. Meat Packing Plants.
49. Metal Mining Companies.
50. Newspaper and Magazine. Distributors.
51. Newspaper Publishing.
52. Paint, Varnish, and Lacquer Producers.
53. Paperboard Mills.
54. Petroleum Production.
55. Physicians.
56. Plumbing and Heating Contractors.
57. Printing.
58. Real Estate Brokers.
59. Restaurants.
60. Rubber Processing.
61. Sand and Gravel.
62. Savings and Loan Associations.
63. Security and Commodity Brokerage.
64. Shoe Manufacturing.
65. Structural Steel Fabricators.
66. Tanning and Processing Leather.
67. Television Broadcasting.
68. Theatres—Motion Picture.
69. Travel Agencies.
70. Wholesalers (Dry Goods).
71. Women's Apparel Chains.
72. Women's Coat and Suit Manufacturing.

One final note — the American Institute of CPA's has available its CPAudio Cassette Series' I and II. These cassettes cover a myriad of subjects too numerous to list here. However, for example, you can obtain cassettes which cover such subjects as observation of inventory in a jewelry store or meat packing company, improvement of staff motivation, specialization in the accounting profession, estate planning, EDP systems in internal control, computer security, retail audit training, and many more.